Blender 2.3 Guide

the official

Blender 2.3 Guide

free 3D creation suite for modeling, animation, and rendering

NO STARCH
PRESS

produced and edited by Ton Roosendaal and Stefano Selleri
printed and distributed by No Starch Press

THE OFFICIAL BLENDER 2.3 GUIDE © 2004 Stichting Blender Foundation

Editor: Stefano Selleri

Contributors:
Alejandro Conty Estevez, Alex Heizer, Bart Veldhuizen, Bastian Salmela, Carsten Wartmann, Chris Williamson, Christian Plessl, Claudio Andauer, Eric Oberlander, Florian Findeiss, Jason Oppel, Joeri Kassenaar, Johnny Matthews, Karsten Dambekalns, Kent Mein, Lyubomir Kovachev, Manuel Bastioni, Martin Kleppmann, Martin Middleton, Martin Poirier, Matt Ebb, Reevan McKay, Stefano Selleri, Tim Howe, Ton Roosendaal, William Pollock, Willian Padovani Germano, Xavier Ligey

Design and DTP: Samo Korosec and Stefan Rasberger, froodee design bureau, www.froodee.com

Production: Ton Roosendaal, Blender Foundation, Entrepotdok 42 t/o, 1018 AD Amsterdam, the Netherlands; www.blender.org; info@blender.org

Printed and distributed by: No Starch Press, Inc., 555 De Haro Street, Suite 250, San Francisco, CA 94107, United States of America; www.nostarch.com. Printed in Hong Kong.

2 3 4 5 6 7 8 9 10 - 07 06 05 04

Library of Congress Cataloging-in-Publication Data
The Official Blender 2.3 guide : free 3D creation suite for modeling, animation, and rendering / edited by Ton Roosendaal and Stefano Selleri.
    p. cm.
  ISBN 1-59327-041-0
  1. Computer graphics. 2. Computer animation. 3. Three-dimensional display systems. 4. Blender (Computer file)
I. Roosendaal, Ton. II. Selleri, Stefano.

T385 .026 2004
006.6'96--dc22

                                          2003023350

Table Of Contents

Table Of Contents

Table Of Contents

Table Of Contents

ABOUT THIS BOOK

When I first stumbled across Blender in 2001, while reading a leading Italian Linux Magazine, I would never have thought writing this foreword now. Although I already had interest in 3D, and played with 3D software for a little while, it was thanks to Blender and its community I got completely hooked to 3D art creation.

Blender was born Closed Source, as you can read more about in the following section. In October 2002 Blender's main author, Ton Roosendaal, supported by an awesome user community effort, managed to collect funds sufficient to open Blender's sources, to establish the Blender Foundation and a brand new Open Source project.

Among the tasks of the Blender Foundation is of course keeping an up-to date Open Content documentation available. To this aim the Blender Documentation Board was appointed, and this Book originates from the Board efforts during 2003. Based on raw material from the old 2.0 guide, written by Carsten Wartmann, the Documentation Board, led by Bart Veldhuizen and myself, coordinated the community efforts.

Notwithstanding our intention to keep the documentation as consistent as possible, we preferred to leave each contributor the freedom to express their individual writing styles. This book is the result of a true community effort, with many authors not being professional writers, nor having English as their mother language. This might lead to style differences from chapter to chapter, but understanding the text should always be clear.

The full text for this book is available on www.blender.org, where we keep updating and improving it every day. There you can also find the Erratum and Addendum for this guide, which you as reader are cordially invited for to contribute to.

The very first steps of the Open Content documentation were the setting up of the XML DocBook system by Felix Rabe and Bart Veldhuizen which, together with the CVS system set-up by Stefan Arentz, allowed for efficient, distributed team work.

ACKNOWLEDGMENTS.ABOUT THIS BOOK

An enthusiastic support came from Claudio Andauer, Manuel Bastioni, Karsten Dambekalns, Alejandro Conty Estevez, Florian Findeiss, Wouter van Heyst, Tim Howe, Joeri Kassenaar, Martin Kleppman, Lyubomir Kovachev, Johnny Matthews, Kent Mein, Martin Middleton, Jason Oppel, Willem-Paul van Overbruggen, Bastian Salamela, Bart Veldhuizen and Chris Williamson. All of them contributed with brand new material. Those who authored a full chapter or large section of this Book have their name on them too, all the others made as precious contributions but too scattered all over the text to allow for spotting each of them. The Python Team (Stephen Swaney, Willian Padovani Germano, Joseph Gilbert, Michel Selten, Jacques Guignot, Alex Molem), on their side, contributed with such a sheer amount of data for the Blender Python API that it was not possible to include it in the book without making page numbers use 4 digits; hence it is included only in the accompanying CD.

Many other people contributed not by writing but rather by carefully re-reading and checking what was written, contributing valuable tips to enhance clarity and, being so many of the author non-native English speakers, to enhance English. Among these are Matt Ebb, William Padovani Germano, Kent Mein, Christian Plessl, Martin Poirier each checked some part of this Book, but a very special thank goes to Eric Oberlander, who actually checked almost the entire book material, and is the only one, besides Bart and myself, with writing access to the CVS. Last but not least of these precious reviewers was William Pollock, of NoStarch Press.

A very special thank is lastly deserved to Samo Korosec and Stefan Rasberger (of froodee design bureau), for having given all the messy DocBook XML gathered the amazing graphical outlook and concept you have now in your hands, and again to Matt Ebb for having contributed the HTML page.

I would lastly wish to express my gratitude to my wife Chiara, who not only withstanded my many evenings at the keyboard, but even joined with me the 2003 Blender Conference to see what it's all about.

Stefano Selleri
Florence, February 2004

BLENDER FOUNDATION FOREWORD

Whilst this is the second book as being published by the Blender Foundation, it is actually the first book that's based on a true community effort, an achievement I am extremely proud of.

This book has been made possible by a lot of software development work behind the scenes, barely visible for most users, nor in this book. So I would like to devote this book and this foreword to everyone who has contributed to one Blender's releases since it became open source:

Alejandro Conty Estevez, Alex Molem, Alexander Ewering, Alfredo Greef, Chris Want, Daniel Dunbar, Daniel Fairhead, Douglas Bischoff, Florian Eggenberger, Hans Lambert-mont, Jacques Guignot, Jiri Hnidek, John Walton, Johnny Matthews, Joseph Gilbert, Kent Mein, Laurence Bourn, Maarten Gribnau, Martin Poirier, Matt Ebb, Michel Selten, Nathan Letwory, Nathan Vegdahl, Rob Haarsma, Robert Wenzlaff, Roel Spruit, Simon Clitherow, Stefan Gartner, Stephen Swaney, Willian Padovani Germano, Wouter van Heyst, and the person I forgot...

THANKS EVERYONE!!!

ACKNOWLEDGMENTS.BLENDER FOUNDATION FOREWORD

And here's a special big hug for the support to keep our websites and shop alive:

Bart Veldhuizen, Douglas Tolzman, Matt Ebb, Stefan Arentz, Timothy Kanters, Anja Vugts-Verstappen, Wouter van Heyst.

Although you find my name on the cover, most of the editing work for this book has been done by Stefano Selleri, whom I think deserves all the credits. Thanks a lot Stefano, you've done a great job!

And lastly I want to give a special thanks to Samo Korosec and Stefan Rasberger (froodee design bureau) for the great design work that has been done. The unexpected and unwanted long production time of the book was certainly worth waiting for!

Ton Roosendaal
Chairman Blender Foundation
Amsterdam, February 2004

HOW TO USE THIS BOOK

This book has been written to give a full overview of all possibilities the current 2.3x releases of Blender offer. It effectively replaces the previous 2.0 Guide, and will please new users as well as experienced 3d artists. All screenshots and texts in this book have been updated and checked for the 2.31 release of Blender, but the exciting 2.32 release (february 2004) just made it in the book as an extra chapter.

Since the interactive 3d part of Blender hasn't been revived yet in the blender.org open source projects, we didn't include chapters on game creation though. For people interested in that, the *Blender Gamekit* book still serves as perfect companion to this manual, although that's only valid with older (2.25) releases of Blender.

For artists new to Blender, the first thing you could do is to check out the color section. Look what Blender can do, it is worth reading this huge book! Then insert the CD in your drive and open `index.html` with your preferred browser. Look at the bottom of the page and play the demo animations (DivX required). Now, if you haven't done so already, install Blender from the CD. Chapter 2 will help you with that.

Whichever graphical production are you interested in you should start by reading Part I. Also interesting for experienced Blender users since several novelties were introduced in the 2.3x interface. New users are advised to read Chapter 4 following the example there contained since it accurately describes the creation of an animation from scratch.

Once you grasped Blender Basics, the whole Part II will lead you through learning the basics of Blender world, Objects, Materials, Lights and Environment. This is what you need to know to build nice still scenes. If you are focused on these, then jump to Part IV, where Blender Rendering engine is described to let you get the most from it.

PREFACE.HOW TO USE THIS BOOK

If, on the other hand you are interested in digital animations, Part III is a must. Its three Chapters describe in detail how to move Objects in time, how to deform them and how to animate characters.

Part V holds chapters where modeling and animation mix together. You will learn to use animation as a modeling tool, the Particle System, and how to use Blender as a Video Editor.

Parts I to V cover everything to make you a CG artist, but Blender provides you with more than this. Blender is extensible via a scripting language and a plugin system, as you will learn in Part VI.

It is also possible to render the scenes you created in Blender with an external renderer. Among the many, YafRay has become the preferred external rendering engine for photorealistic results. Blender and YafRay are getting more and more integrated. Part VII is dedicated to this.

Part VIII provides a full reference to Blender, all Windows, Buttons and HotKeys are described here.

Part IX contains the latest news. All novelties of Blender 2.32 – and they are a lot – are described here, new lamps, new modeling tools, new rendering options!

Finally Part X prides few appendices, a comprehensive HotKeys list, a Graphic Card compatibility list, technical information on coding Blender and contributing to its documentation, as well as the licenses.

CHAPTERS 1 2 3 4

PART I

INTRODUCTION TO BLENDER

This first part of the Documentation will guide you through Blender downloading, installing and, if you elect to download the sources, building.

Blender exhibits a very peculiar interface, higly optimized for 3D graphics production. this might look hard to the new user, at the beginning, but will prove its strength in the long run. You are highly recommended to read *Understanding the Interface* carefully both to get familiar with the interface and with the conventions used in the Book.

The last chapter of this part, *Your First Animation in 30 + 30 Minutes*, will also let you have a glimpse of Blender capabilities. Of course Blender can do much more than that, but that is just a quick start.

CH. 1 INTRODUCTION

WHAT IS BLENDER?, BLENDER'S HISTORY, FREE SOFTWARE AND THE GPL, GETTING SUPPORT - BLENDER'S COMMUNITY

What is Blender?

Blender is an integrated suite of tools enabling the creation of a broad range of 3D content. It offers full functionality for modeling, rendering, animation, post-production, creation and playback of interactive 3D content with the singular benefits of cross-platform operability and a download file size of less than 2.5MB.

Aimed at media professionals and artists, Blender can be used to create 3D visualizations, stills as well as broadcast quality video, while the incorporation of a real-time 3D engine allows for the creation of 3D interactive content for stand-alone playback.

Originally developed by the company 'Not a Number' (NaN), Blender now is continued as 'Free Software', with the sources available under GNU GPL.

Key Features:

- Fully integrated creation suite, offering a broad range of essential tools for the creation of 3D content, including modeling, animation, rendering, video post production and game creation;
- Small executable size, for easy distribution;
- Cross platform, with OpenGL based GUI, ready to use for all flavours of Windows, Linux, OSX, FreeBSD, Irix and Sun;
- High quality 3D architecture enabling fast and efficient creation work-flow;
- Free support channels via www.blender3d.org;
- More than 250.000 people worldwide user community;

INTRODUCTION.BLENDER'S HISTORY

You can download the latest version of Blender at download.blender.org.

Blender's History

In 1988 Ton Roosendaal co-founded the Dutch animation studio *NeoGeo*. NeoGeo quickly became the largest 3D animation studio in the Netherlands and one of the leading animation houses in Europe. NeoGeo created award-winning productions (European Corporate Video Awards 1993 and 1995) for large corporate clients such as multi-national electronics company Philips. Within NeoGeo Ton was responsible for both art direction and internal software development. After careful deliberation Ton decided that the current in-house 3D tool set for NeoGeo was too old and cumbersome to maintain and upgrade and needed to be rewritten from scratch. In 1995 this rewrite began and was destined to become the 3D software creation suite we all now know as *Blender*. As NeoGeo continued to refine and improve Blender it became apparent to Ton that Blender could be used as a tool for other artists outside of NeoGeo.

In 1998, Ton decided to found a new company called Not a Number (NaN) as a spin-off of NeoGeo to further market and develop Blender. At the core of NaN was a desire to create and distribute a compact, cross platform 3D creation suite for free. At the time this was a revolutionary concept as most commercial modelers cost several thousands of (US) dollars. NaN hoped to bring professional level 3D modeling and animation tools within the reach of the general computing public. NaN's business model involved providing commercial products and services around Blender. In 1999 NaN attended its first Siggraph conference in an effort to more widely promote Blender. Blender's first 1999 Siggraph convention was a huge success and gathered a tremendous amount of interest from both the press and attendees. Blender was a hit and its huge potential confirmed!

On the wings of a successful Siggraph in early 2000, NaN secured financing of 4.5 million EUR from venture capitalists. This large inflow of cash enabled NaN to rapidly expand its operations. Soon NaN boasted as many as fifty employees working around the world trying to improve and promote Blender. In the summer of 2000, Blender v2.0 was released. This version of Blender added the integration of a game engine to the 3D suite. By the end of 2000, the number of users registered on the NaN website surpassed 250,000.

Unfortunately, NaN's ambitions and opportunities didn't match the company's capabilities and the market realities of the time. This overextension resulted in restarting NaN with new investor funding and a smaller company in April 2001. Six months later NaN's first commercial software product, *Blender Publisher* was launched. This product was targeted at the emerging market of interactive web-based 3D media. Due to disappointing sales and the ongoing difficult economic climate, the new investors decided to shut down all NaN operations. The shutdown also included discontinuing the development of Blender. Although there were clearly shortcomings in the current version of Blender, with a complex internal software architecture, unfinished features and a non-standard way of providing the GUI, enthusiastic support from the user community and customers who had purchased Blender Publisher in the past, Ton couldn't justify leaving Blender to disappear into oblivion. Since restarting a company with a sufficiently large team of developers wasn't feasible, in March 2002 Ton Roosendaal founded the non-profit organization *Blender Foundation*.

The Blender Foundation's primary goal was to find a way to continue developing and promoting Blender as a community-based Open Source[1] project. In July 2002, Ton managed to get the NaN investors to agree to a unique Blender Foundation plan to attempt to Blender as open source. The "Free Blender" campaign sought to raise 100,000 EUR so that the Foundation could buy the rights to the Blender source code and intellectual property rights from the NaN investors and subsequently release Blender to the open source community. With an enthusiastic group of volunteers, among them several ex-NaN employees, a fund raising campaign was launched to "Free Blender." To everyone's surprise and delight the campaign reached the 100,000 EUR goal in only seven short weeks. On Sunday October 13, 2002, Blender was released to the world under the terms of the GNU General Public License (GPL). Blender development continues to this day driven by a team of far-flung, dedicated volunteers from around the world led by Blender's original creator, Ton Roosendaal.

Blender's history and road-map

- 1.00 Jan 1995 Blender in development at animation studio NeoGeo
- 1.23 Jan 1998 SGI version published on the web, IrisGL
- 1.30 April 1998 Linux and FreeBSD version, port to OpenGL and X
- 1.3x June 1998 NaN founded
- 1.4x Sept 1998 Sun and Linux Alpha version released
- 1.50 Nov 1998 First Manual published
- 1.60 April 1999 C-key (new features behind a lock, $95), Windows version released
- 1.6x June 1999 BeOS and PPC version released
- 1.80 June 2000 End of C-key, Blender full freeware again
- 2.00 Aug 2000 Interactive 3D and real-time engine
- 2.10 Dec 2000 New engine, physics and Python
- 2.20 Aug 2001 Character animation system
- 2.21 Oct 2001 Blender Publisher launch
- 2.2x Dec 2001 Mac OS X version

---

[1] http://www.opensource.org

- *13 October 2002 Blender goes Open Source, 1st Blender Conference*
- 2.25 Oct 2002 Blender Publisher becomes freely available
- Tuhopuu1 Oct 2002 The experimental tree of Blender is created, a coder's playground.
- 2.26 Feb 2003 The first true Open Source Blender
- 2.27 May 2003 The second Open Source Blender
- 2.28x July 2003 First of the 2.28x series.
- 2.30 October 2003 At the 2nd Blender Conference the 2.3x UI makeover is presented.
- 2.31 December 2003 Upgrade to stablize 2.3x UI project.
- 2.32 January 2004 Major overhaul of internal rendering capabilities.

About Free Software and the GPL

When one hears about "free software", the first thing that comes to mind might be "no cost". While this is true in most cases, the term "free software" as used by the Free Software Foundation (originators of the GNU Project and creators of the GNU General Public License) is intended to mean "free as in freedom" rather than the "no cost" sense (which is usually referred to as "free as in free beer"). Free software in this sense is software which you are free to use, copy, modify, redistribute, with no limit. Contrast this with the licensing of most commercial software packages, where you are allowed to load the software on a single computer, are allowed to make no copies, and never see the source code. Free software allows incredible freedom to the end user; in addition, since the source code is available universally, there are many more chances for bugs to be caught and fixed.

When a program is licensed under the GNU General Public License (the GPL):

- you have the right to use the program for any purpose;
- you have the right to modify the program, and have access to the source codes;
- you have the right to copy and distribute the program;
- you have the right to improve the program, and release your own versions.

In return for these rights, you have some responsibilities if you distribute a GPL'd program, responsibilities that are designed to protect your freedoms and the freedoms of others:

- You must provide a copy of the GPL with the program, so that the recipient is aware of his rights under the license.
- You must include the source code or make the source code freely available.
- If you modify the code and distribute the modified version, you must license your modifications under the GPL and make the source code of your changes available. (You may not use GPL'd code as part of a proprietary program.)
- You may not restrict the licensing of the program beyond the terms of the GPL. (You may not turn a GPL'd program into a proprietary product.)

For more on the GPL, check the GNU Project Web site[2]. For reference, a copy of the GNU General Public License is included in Appendix F.

Getting support - the Blender community

Being freely available from start, even while closed source, helped a lot in Blender's diffusion. A large, stable and active community of users has gathered around Blender since 1998.

The community showed its best in the crucial moment of freeing Blender itself, going Open Source under GNU GPL in late summer 2002.

The community itself is now subdivided into two, widely overlapping sites:

The Development Community, centered around the Blender Foundation site[3]. Here is the home of the development projects, the Functionality and Documentation Boards, the CVS repository with Blender sources, all documentation sources, and related public discussion forums. Developers coding on Blender itself, Python scripters, documentation writers, and anyone working for Blender development in general can be found here.

The User Community, centered around the independent site www.elysiun.com. Here Blender artists, Blender gamemakers and any Blender fan gathers to show their creations, get feedback on it, and ask help to get better insight in Blender functionality. Blender Tutorials and the Knowledge Base can be found here as well.

These two websites are not the only Blender resources. The Worldwide community exhibits a lot of independent sites, in local languages or devoted to specialized topics. A constantly updated listing of Blender resources can be found at the abovementioned sites.

---

[2] http://www.gnu.org
[3] http://www.blender.org

INTRODUCTION.THE BLENDER COMMUNITY

For immediate online feedback there are three chat boxes permanently opened on irc.freenode.net. You can join these with your favorite IRC client.

Chatboxes are #blenderchat, #blenderqa and #gameblender. The first of these is accessible even without a IRC client but with a plain Java enabled Web Browser through the elYsiun site[4]).

---

[4] http://www.elysiun.com

CH. 2 INSTALLATION

INSTALLATION, BUILDING BLENDER FROM THE SOURCES

Blender is available both as binary executables and as source code on the Foundation site (http://www.blender.org/). From the main page look for the 'Downloads' section.

However, for correct usage of this book, using the version as provided on the included 2.3 Guide CDROM is highly recommended. Where in the text below "download" is mentioned, we also assume retrieving it from the CDROM.

Downloading and installing the binary distribution

The Binary distributions comes in 6 basic flavors:

- Windows
- Linux
- MacOSX
- FreeBSD
- Irix
- Solaris

The Linux flavor comes actually in 4 different sub-flavors, for Intel and PowerPC architectures, with statically linked libraries or for dynamic loading libraries.

The difference between the dynamic and the static flavor is important. The static build has the OpenGL libraries compiled in. This makes Blender running at your system without using hardware accelerated graphics. Use the static version to check if Blender runs fine when the dynamic version fails! OpenGL is used in Blender for all drawing, including menus and buttons. This dependency makes a proper and compliant OpenGL installation at your system a requirement. Not all 3D card manufacturers provide such compliancy, especially cheaper cards aimed at the gaming market.

Of course since renderings are made by Blender rendering engine in core memory and by the main CPU of your machine, a graphic card with hardware acceleration makes no difference at rendering time.

INSTALLATION.INSTALLATION

Windows

Quick Install
Download the file `blender-2.3#-windows.exe`, being `2.3#` the version number, from the downloads section of the Blender Website. Start the installation by double-clicking the file. This presents you with some questions, for which the defaults should be ok. After setup is complete, you can start Blender right away, or use the entry in the Start menu.

In-depth Instruction
Download the file `blender-2.3#-windows.exe` from the downloads section of the Blender Website. Choose to download it (if prompted), select a location and click "Save". Then navigate with explorer to the location you saved the file in and double-click it to start the installation.

The first dialog presents you the license. You are expected to accept it if you want the installation to go any further. After accepting the license, select the components you wish to install (there is just one, Blender) and the additional actions you want to take. There are three: Add a shortcut to the Stat menu, Add Blender's icon to desktop, associate .blend files with Blender. By default they are all checked. If you don't want some action to be taken simply uncheck it. When done, click on `Next`.

Select a place to install the files to (the default should do well), and click `Next` to install Blender. Press `Close` when installation is over.

Afterwards you will be asked whether you want to start Blender immediately. Blender is now installed and can be started by means of the Start menu (an entry named "Blender Foundation" has been created by the setup routine) or by double-clicking a Blender file (`*.blend`).

MacOS X

Install
Download the file `blender-2.3#-darwin-6.6-powerpc.dmg` from the downloads section of the Blender Website. Extract it by double-clicking the file. This will open a directory with several files.

Since Blender uses OpenGL for the entire GUI, and Mac OSX draws the entire Desktop with OpenGL as well, you will need to verify first you have sufficient VRAM in your system. Below 8 MB VRAM Blender will not run at all. Up to 16 MB VRAM you will need to set your system at "1000s of colors" (System Preferences -> Displays).

You now can use Blender by double clicking the Blender icon. Or drag the `Blender` icon to the Dock to make an alias there. Blender starts by default in a smaller window. Use the "+" button in the window header to maximize. More hints and tips about the OSX version can be found in the file `OSX tips.rtf` in the installation directory.

Linux

Quick Install

Download the file `blender-2.3#-linux-glibc#.#.#-ARCH.tar.gz` from the downloads section of the Blender Website. Here `2.3#` is Blender version, `#.#.#` is glibc version and `ARCH` is the machine architecture, either `i386` or `powerpc`. You should get the one matching your system, remember the choice between static and dynamic builds.

Unpack the archive to a location of your choice. This will create a directory named `blender-2.3#-linux-glibc#.#.#-ARCH`, in which you will find the `blender` binary.

To start blender just open a shell and execute `./blender`, of course when running X.

In-depth Instructions

Download the file `blender-2.3#-linux-glibc#.#.#-ARCH.tar.gz` from the downloads section of the Blender Website. Choose to download it (if prompted), select a location and click "Save". Then navigate to the location you wish blender to install to (e.g. `/usr/local/`) and unpack the archive (with `tar xzf /path/to/blender-2.3#-linux-glibc#.#.#-ARCH.tar.gz`). If you like, you can rename the resulting directory from `blender-2.3#-linux-glibc#.#.#-ARCH` to something shorter, e.g. just blender.

Blender is now installed and can be started on the command line by entering `cd /path/to/blender` followed by pressing the enter key in a shell. If you are using KDE or Gnome you can start Blender using your file manager of choice by navigating to the Blender executable and (double-) clicking on it.

If you are using the Sawfish window manager, you might want to add a line like `("Blender" (system "blender &"))` to your `.sawfish/rc` file.

To add program icons for Blender in KDE

1. Select the "Menu Editor" from the System submenu of the K menu.

2. Select the submenu labeled "Graphics" in the menu list.

3. Click the "New Item" button. A dialog box will appear that prompts you to create a name. Create and type in a suitable name and click "OK". "Blender" or "Blender 2.3#" would be logical choices, but this does not affect the functionality of the program.

4. You will be returned to the menu list, and the Graphics submenu will expand, with your new entry highlighted. In the right section, make surethe following fields are filled in: "Name", "Comment", "Command", "Type" and "Work Path".

- The "Name" field should already be filled in, but you can change it here at any time.
- Fill the "Comment" field. This is where you define the tag that appears when you roll over the icon.
- Click the folder icon at the end of the "Command" field to browse to the blender publisher program icon. Select the program icon and click "OK" to return to the Menu Editor.
- The "Type" should be "Application".
- The "Work Path" should be the same as the "Command", with the program name left off. For example, if the "Command" field reads /home/user/blender-publisher-#.##-linux-glibc#.#.#-ARCH/blender, the "Work Path" would be /home/user/blender-publisher-#.##-linux-glibc#.#.#-ARCH/.

5. Click "Apply" and close out of the Menu Editor.

To add a link to Blender on the KPanel, right-click on a blank spot on the KPanel, then hover over "Add", then "Button", then "Graphics", and select "Blender" (or wha-tever you named the menu item in step 3). Alternately, you can navigate through the "Configure Panel" submenu from the K menu, to "Add", "Button", "Graphics", "Blen-der".

To add a Desktop icon for Blender, open Konquerer (found on the Panel by default, or in the "System" submenu of the K menu) and navigate to the blenderpublisher program icon where you first unzipped it. Click and hold the program icon, and drag it from Konquerer to a blank spot on our Desktop. You will be prompted to Copy Here, Move Here or Link Here, choose Link Here.

To add program icons for Blender in GNOME

1. Select "Edit menus" from the Panel submenu of the GNOME menu.

2. Select the "Graphics" submenu, and click the "New Item" button.

3. In the right pane, fill in the "Name:", "Comment:" and "Command:" fields. Fill the "Name:" field with the program name, for example "Blender". You can name this whatever you'd like, this is what appears in the menu, but does not affect the functionality of the program. Fill the "Comment:" field with a descriptive comment. This is what is shown on the tooltips popups. Fill the "Command:" field with the full path of the blenderpublisher program item, for example, `/home/user/blender-publisher-#.##-linux-glibc#.#.#-ARCH/blender`

4. Click the "No Icon" button to choose an icon. There may or may not be an icon for Blender in your default location. You can make one, or look for the icon that goes with KDE. This should be `/opt/kde/share/icons/hicolor/48x48/apps/blender.png`. If your installation directory is different, you can search for it using this command in a Terminal or Console: `find / -name "blender.png" -print`

5. Click the "Save" button and close the Menu Editor.

To add a Panel icon, right-click a blank area of the Panel, then select "Programs", then "Graphics", then "Blender". Alternatively, you could click the GNOME menu, then select "Panel", then "Add to panel", then "Launcher from menu", then "Graphics", and "Blender".

To add a Desktop icon for Blender, open Nautilus (double-click the Home icon in the upper-left corner of your Desktop, or click the GNOME menu, then "Programs", then "Applications", and "Nautilus"). Navigate to the folder which contains the blenderpublisher program icon. Right-click the icon, and drag it to the Desktop. A menu will appear asking to Copy Here, Move Here, Link Here or Cancel. Select Link Here.

FreeBSD

Install
Download the file blender-2.3#-freebsd-#.#-i386.tar.gz from the downloads section of the Blender Website. Here `2.3#` is Blender version, `#.#` is FreeBSD version and `i386` is the machine architecture.

To start blender just open a shell and execute `./blender`, of course when running X.

Irix

Install
Download the file `blender-2.3#-irix-6.5-mips.tar.gz` from the downloads section of the Blender Website. Here `2.3#` is Blender version, `6.5` is Irix version and `mips` is the machine architecture.

INSTALLATION.BUILDING BLENDER FROM SOURCE

To start Blender just open a shell and execute `./blender`, of course when running X. Blender was originally developed for the IRIX platform, but is currently not actively being maintained for all IRIX workstation versions. For some workstations performance troubles have been reported.

Solaris

Install
Download the file `blender-2.3#-solaris-2.8-sparc.tar.gz` from the downloads section of the Blender Website. Here `2.3#` is Blender version, `2.8` is Solaris version and `sparc` is the machine architecture.

Currently no further instructions for Sun Solaris are available. Please use the Blender website forums for support.

Building Blender from source

This document describes the tools necessary to build Blender from source, either from CVS or from a source package. Building from CVS requires the use of more tools. While this may be a bit more troublesome than building from a source package, this may be necessary for some people. For example, when you want to build Blender for an unsupported platform or when you want to implement some new features.

This is a very early version of this document. This means that it is incomplete and that some procedures or concepts might be incorrect for your system. Please keep this in mind when reading this. Also keep in mind Blender is a complex product which will require you to create the right environment for.

Getting the sources

The following paragraphs will describe how and where to get the sources needed for building Blender.

Get the latest stable source package
The sources are available on CDROM accompanying this book. You can also download it from the website, `http://www.blender3d.org/Download/?sub=Source`

Get the latest sources from CVS
CVS stands for Concurrent Versioning System. It is a software configuration tool that keeps the various source files in a central repository. CVS enables developers to quickly update to the latest state of the repository and commit changes. The tool

keeps track of the changes between each version of a file. To get the current state of the repository, you don't need to have a username for accessing the sources. This feature is optional, but in an opensource development, it's almost a requirement. To commit changes to the repository, however, you need to have developer access. Since this document only describes how to get the latest state of the sources, the commit procedures are not described here.

To get the latest state of the sources use:

```
export CVSROOT=:pserver:anonymous@cvs.blender.org:/cvs01
```

```
cvs login
```

password: **Enter**

```
cvs -z3 co blender
```

Please do not use a higher level of compression for accessing the Blender server.

If you already have a working set of files obtained from the server, you can use the `update` command to update the sources to the current state of the repository. `cd` to the blender source tree on your system and type in the following command:

```
cvs -z3 update .
```

External libraries needed

Blender is a package that uses a lot of external packages for expanding its functionality. Each of these packages have, just as Blender, a history of changes. Newer versions of such a package will probably have more features and less known problems. As a developer it is exciting to work with the latest features available to get the most out of the tool. However, the number of developers out there is much lower than the number of end-users who are not interested in the latest feature, these users want an application that works. Since Blender has to run on multiple platforms, all those platforms have to have the same minimum functionality available in the external packages.

The table below displays the packages needed and the minimum version of those packages. Over time it is possible that those minimum versions are increased as the demand for the newer features is high.

INSTALLATION.BUILDING BLENDER FROM SOURCE

Library	Version
glibc	2.2.4
libjpeg	6b
libpng	1.0.14
libsdl	1.0
libz	1.1.4
mesa	3.4.2
openAL	N/A
openGL	1.1 (1.2 for engine)
python	2.2

Not all libraries apply to all platforms. The following table gives an overview of the currently supported platforms and the required libraries. An 'X' means that it is needed, a '-' means that it is not needed and an 'O' means that it is optional.

Library	Linux	Windows	FreeBSD	IRIX	MacOS X
glibc	x	-	x	x	x
libjpeg	x	x	x	x	x
libpng	x	x	x	x	x
libsdl	o	o	o	o	o
libz	x	x	x	x	x
mesa	x	x	x	-	-
openAL	x	x	x	x	x
openGL	-	-	-	x	x
python	x	x	x	x	x

Tools needed

Having the necessary libraries installed and the Blender sources downloaded to your system means that you're now able to build Blender. The entire build process requires some tools to be available on your system. In the table below, the list of tools along with the minimum version is shown. The third column shows if the tool is required for CVS only ('X'). If the tool is not required for a source package build, a '-' is shown.

Tool	Version	CVS	Note
autoconf	2.53	x	
automake	1.6.2	x	
cvs	1.11.1p1	x	
docbook	3.1	o	
doxygen	N/A	o	
gawk	3.1.0	x	
gcc	2.96	-	
gettext	0.11	-	
gmake	3.79.1	-	
m4	1.4	x	
sed	3.02	x	
sh	2.05.1	-	
Visual C++	6.0 SP5	-	Windows only

Python

Python is not included in this table although it is used to build Blender. The reason that it is not included is because Python is also needed as an external library and thus has to be installed already as has been written in the previous section.

Building Blender

There are two build systems for using gcc or cc compilers; regular Makefiles, which stem from the period Blender was developed in the company NaN, and the automake/autoconf "configure" style one. Using "configure" can write over the NaN Makefiles, so you have to choose either one.

For Windows MSVC, Blender supports usage of project files and workspaces.

The files describing detailed build information are located in the blender root directory:

- `INSTALL`: general information, download links for libraries
- `INSTALL.AUTO`: using autoconf and configure scripts
- `INSTALL.MAKE`: using regular makefiles
- `INSTALL.MSVC`: using Microsoft Visual C project files

Technical Support

- portal: `http://www.blender.org`
- overview: `http://www.blender.org/docs/get_involved.html`
- mailinglist: `http://www.blender.org/mailman/listinfo/bf-committers/`
- bug tracker: `http://projects.blender.org/tracker/?group_id=9`
- IRC: `irc.freenode.net, #blendercoders`

CH. 3   UNDERSTANDING THE INTERFACE

CONCEPT, NAVIGATION, FUNCTIONS

by Martin Kleppmann

If you are new to Blender, you should get a good grip on how to work with the user interface before modelling. The concepts behind Blender's interface are non-standard, and different from other 3D software packages. Windows users especially will need to get used to the different way that Blender handles controls, such as button choices and mouse movements. But this difference is in fact one of Blender's great strengths: once you understand how to work the Blender way, you will find that you can work exceedingly quickly and productively.

Furthermore, Blender's interface greatly changed in the transition from version 2.28 to version 2.3, so even experienced users might profit from this chapter.

Blender's Interface Concept

The user interface is the vehicle for two way interaction between the user and the program. The user communicates with the program via the keyboard and the mouse, the program gives feedback via the screen and its windowing system.

Keyboard and mouse

Blender's interface makes use of three mouse buttons and a wide range of hotkeys (for a complete in-depth discussion refer to Part VIII). If your mouse has only two buttons, you can emulate the middle mouse button (the Section called *User preferences and Themes* describes how). A mouse wheel can be used, but it is not necessary as there are also appropriate keyboard shortcuts.

This book uses the following conventions to describe user input:

* The mouse buttons are called **LMB** (left mouse button), **MMB** (middle mouse button) and **RMB** (right mouse button).

UNDERSTANDING THE INTERFACE.CONCEPT

- If your mouse has a wheel, **MMB** refers to clicking the wheel as if it were a button, while **MW** means rolling the wheel.
- Hotkey letters are named by appending **KEY** to the letter, i.e. **GKEY** refers to the letter g on the keyboard. Keys may be combined with the modifiers **SHIFT**, **CTRL** and/or **ALT**. For modified keys the **KEY** suffix is generally dropped, for example **CTRL-W** or **SHIFT-ALT-A**.
- **NUM0** to **NUM9**, **NUM+** and so on refer to the keys on the separate numeric keypad. NumLock should generally be switched on.
- Other keys are referred to by their names, such as **ESC**, **TAB**, **F1** to **F12**.
- Other special keys of note are the arrow keys, **UPARROW**, **DOWNARROW** and so on. Because Blender makes such extensive use of both mouse and keyboard, a "golden rule" has evolved among Blender users: keep one hand on the mouse and the other on the keyboard! If you normally use a keyboard that is significantly different from the English keyboard layout, you may want to think about changing to the English or American layout for your work with Blender. The most frequently used keys are grouped so that they can be reached by the left hand in standard position (index finger on **FKEY**) on the English keyboard layout. This assumes that you use the mouse with your right hand.

The window system

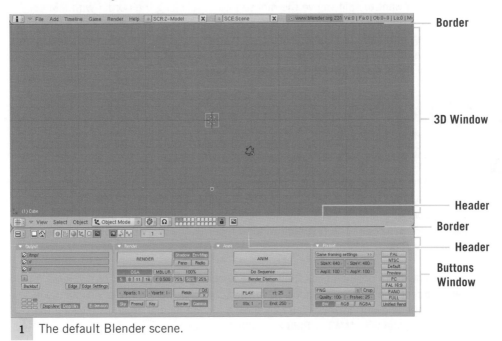

1 The default Blender scene.

2 The Split menu for creating new windows.

Figure 1 shows the screen you should get after starting Blender (except for the added text and lines). At default it is separated into three windows: The main menu at the top, the large 3D Window and the Buttons Window at the bottom. Most windows have a header (the strip with a lighter grey background containing icon buttons - for this reason we will also refer to the header as the window *ToolBar*); if present, the header may be at the top (as with the Buttons window) or the bottom (as with the 3D Window) of a window's area.

If you move the mouse over a window, note that its header changes to a lighter shade of grey. This means that it is *focused*; all hotkeys you press will now affect the contents of this window.

You can easily customize Blender's window system to suit your needs and wishes. You can create a new window by splitting an existing one in half. Do so by focusing the window you want to split (move the mouse into it), clicking the border with **MMB** or **RMB**, and selecting Split Area (fig. 2). You can now set the new border's position by clicking with **LMB**, or cancel your action by pressing **ESC**. The new window will start as a clone of the window you split, but can then be set to a different window type, or to display the scene from a different point of view.

Interface Items: Labels in the interface buttons, menu entries and, in general, all text shown on the screen is highlighted in this book like this.

Create a new vertical border by choosing Split Area from a horizontal border, and vice versa. You can resize each window by dragging a border with **LMB**. To reduce the number of windows, click a border between two windows with **MMB** or **RMB** and choose Join Areas. The resulting window receives the properties of the previously focused window.

To set a header's position click **RMB** on the header and choose Top or Bottom. You can also hide the header by choosing No Header, but this is only advisable if you know all the relevant hotkeys. You can show a hidden header again by clicking the window's border with **MMB** or **RMB** and selecting Add Header.

Window types

Each window frame may contain different types and sets of information, depending upon what you are working on. These may include 3D models, animation, surface materials, Python scripts, and so on. You can select the type for each window by clicking its header's leftmost button with **LMB** (fig. 3).

We'll explain the functions and usage of the respective window types later in this book. For now we only need to concern ourselves with the three window types that are already provided in Blender's default scene:

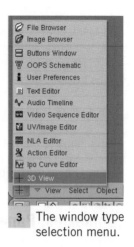

3 The window type selection menu.

3D Viewport

Provides a graphical view into the scene you are working on. You can view your scene from any angle with a variety of options; see the Section called *Navigating in 3D Space* for details. Having several 3D Viewports on the same screen can be useful if you want to watch your changes from different perspectives at the same time.

Buttons Window

Contains most tools for editing objects, surfaces, textures, Lights, and much more. You will need this window constantly if you don't know all hotkeys by heart. You might indeed want more than one of these windows, each with a different set of tools.

User preferences (Main menu)

This window is usually hidden, so that only the menu part is visible - see the Section called *User preferences and Themes* for details. It's rarely used though, since it contains global configuration settings.

There are several novelties in Blender 2.30. First of all window headers tends to be much cleaner, less cluttered by buttons, and menus are now present in many headers.

Most window headers, immediately next to this first "Window Type" Menu button exhibit a set of menus; this is one of the main new features of the 2.30 interface. Menu now allows to directly access many of the features and commands which previously were only accessible via hot keys or arcane buttons. Menus can be hidden and showed via the triangular button next to them.

Menus are not only window-sensitive (they change with window type) but also context sensitive (they change with selected object) so they are always very compact, showing only actions which can actually be performed.

All Menu entries shows the relevant hotkey shortcut, if any. Blender Workflow is at his best when hotkeys are used. So the rest of this Book will mostly present you hot-keys, rather than Menu entries. Menus are anyway precious since they give a comple-te as possible overview of all tools and commands Blender offers.

One feature of windows that sometimes comes in handy for precise editing is that of maximizing to full screen. If you use the appropriate `View>>Maximize Window` Menu entry or the hotkey **CTRL-DOWNARROW**, the focused window will extend to fill the whole screen. To return to normal size, use `View>>Tile Window` the button again or **CTRL-UPARROW**.

Contextes, Panels and Buttons

Blender's buttons are more exciting than those in most other user interfaces, and they become ever more nice in 2.30. This is largely due to the fact that they are vector-based and drawn in OpenGL, which makes them elegant and zoomable.

Buttons are mostly grouped in the Button Window. As for Blender 2.3 The Button Window shows six main contextes, which can be chosen via the first icon row in the header (fig. 4), each of which might be subdivided into a variable number of sub-contexts, which can be chosen via the second icon row in the header (fig. 4):

- Logic — shortcut **F4**
- Script — no shortcut
- Shading — shortcut **F5**
  - Lamp — no shortcut
  - Material — no shortcut
  - Texture — shortcut **F6**
  - Radio — no shortcut
  - World — shortcut **F8**
- Object — shortcut **F7**
- Editing — shortcut **F9**
- Scene — shortcut **F10**
  - Rendering — no shortcut
  - Anim/Playback — no shortcut
  - Sound — no shortcut

Once the Context is selected by the user, the sub-context is usually determined by Blender on the basis of the active Object. For example for the "Shading" context if a Lamp Object is selected then sub-context shows Lamp Buttons, if a Mesh or other renderable Object is selected then Material Buttons is the active sub-context, and if a Camera is selected the active sub-context is World.

UNDERSTANDING THE INTERFACE.CONCEPT

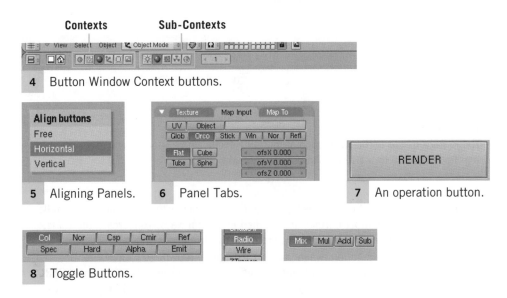

4 Button Window Context buttons.

5 Aligning Panels. **6** Panel Tabs. **7** An operation button.

8 Toggle Buttons.

The most notable novelty in the interface is probably the presence of Panels to logically group buttons. Each panel is the same dimension. They can be moved around the Button Window by **LMB** click and drag on their header. Panels can be aligned by **RMB** on the Buttons Window and chosing the desired layout from the Menu which appears (fig. 5).

MW scrolls Panels in their align direction, **CTRL-MW** and **CTRL-MMB** zoomspanels in and out. Single panels can be collapsed/expanded by **LMB** on the triangle left on their header. Particularly complex Panels areorganized in Tabs. Clicking **LMB** on a Tab in the Panel header changes the shown buttons (fig. 6). Tabs can be "taken out" of a panel to form independent panels by clicking **LMB** on their header and dragging them out. In a similar way separate Panels can be turned to a single panel with Tabs by dropping one Panel's header into another.

As a last interface item in the chain there are several kind of buttons which are disposed in the Panel:

Operation Button
These are buttons that perform an operation when they are clicked (with **LMB**, as all buttons). They can be identified by their brownish color in the default Blender scheme (fig. 7).

Toggle Button
Toggle buttons come in various sizes and colors (fig. 8). The colors green, violet, and grey do not change functionality, they just help the eye to group the buttons and recognize the contents of the interface more quickly. Clicking this type of button does not perform any operation, but only toggles a state as "on" or "off."

Some buttons also have a third state that is identified by the text turning yellow (the Ref button in figure 8). Usually the third state means "negative," and the normal "on" state means "positive."

9 Number Buttons.

10 Datablock link Buttons.

Radio Buttons

Radio Buttons are particular groups of mutually exclusive Toggle Buttons. No more than one Radio Button in a given group can be "on" at one time.

Num Buttons

Number buttons (fig. 9) can be identified by their captions, which contain a colon followed by a number. Number buttons are handled in several ways: To increase the value, click **LMB** on the right of the button, where the small triangle is shown; to decrease it, click on the left of the button, where another triangle is shown. To change the value in a wider range, hold down **LMB** and drag the mouse to the left or right. If you hold **CTRL** while doing this, the value is changed in discrete steps; if you hold **SHIFT**, you'll have finer control over the values. **ENTER** can be used in place of **LMB** here.

You can enter a value from the keyboard by holding **SHIFT** and clicking **LMB**. Press **SHIFT-BACKSPACE** to clear the value; **SHIFT-LEFTARROW** to move the cursor to the beginning; and **SHIFT-RIGHTARROW** to move the cursor to the end. Press **ESC** to restore the original value.

Some number buttons contain a slider rather than just a number with side triangles. The same method of operations applies, except that single **LMB** clicks must be performed on the left or on the right of the slider, while clicking on the label or the number automatically enters keyboard input mode.

Menu Buttons

Use the Menu buttons to choose from dynamically created lists. Menu buttons are principally used to link DataBlocks to each other. (DataBlocks are structures like Meshes, Objects, Materials, Textures, and so on; by linking a Material to an Object, you assign it.) You'll see an example for such a block of buttons in figure 10. The first button (with the tiny up and down pointing triangles) opens a menu that lets you select the DataBlock to link to by holding down **LMB** and releasing it over the requested item. The second button displays the type and name of the linked DataBlock and lets you edit its name after clicking **LMB**. The "X" button clears the link, the "car" button generates an automatic name for the DataBlock, and the "F" button specifies whether the DataBlock should be saved in the file even if it is unused (unlinked).

Unlinked objects: Unlinked data is not lost until you quit Blender. This is a powerful Undo feature. if you delete an object the material assigned to it becomes unlinked, but is still there! You just have to re-link it to another object or press the "F" button.

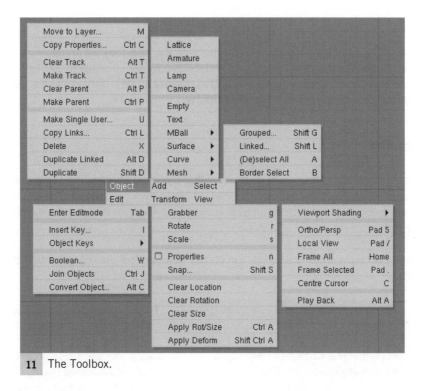

Move to Layer...	M					
Copy Properties...	Ctrl C	Lattice				
Clear Track	Alt T	Armature				
Make Track	Ctrl T	Lamp				
Clear Parent	Alt P	Camera				
Make Parent	Ctrl P	Empty				
Make Single User...	U	Text				
Copy Links...	Ctrl L	MBall ▸	Grouped...	Shift G		
Delete	X	Surface ▸	Linked...	Shift L		
Duplicate Linked	Alt D	Curve ▸	(De)select All	A		
Duplicate	Shift D	Mesh ▸	Border Select	B		

Object   Add   Select
Edit   Transform   View

Enter Editmode	Tab	Grabber	g	Viewport Shading	▸	
Insert Key...	I	Rotate	r	Ortho/Persp	Pad 5	
Object Keys	▸	Scale	s	Local View	Pad /	
Boolean...	W	☐ Properties	n	Frame All	Home	
Join Objects	Ctrl J	Snap...	Shift S	Frame Selected	Pad .	
Convert Object...	Alt C	Clear Location		Centre Cursor	C	
		Clear Rotation		Play Back	Alt A	
		Clear Size				
		Apply Rot/Size	Ctrl A			
		Apply Deform	Shift Ctrl A			

11   The Toolbox.

Toolbox

By pressing **SPACE** in the 3D Viewport, or by holding **LMB** or **RMB** with a still mouse for more than half a second opens the Toolbox. This contains 6 main contextes, arranged on two lines, each of which opens menus and submenus.

Three of these contextes opens the same three menus present in the 3D Viewport header, of other three `Add` allows adding new Objects to the scene while `Edit` and `Transform` shows all possible operations on selected Object(s) (fig. 11).

Screens

Blender's flexibility with windows lets you create customized working environments for different tasks, such as modeling, animating, and scripting. It is often useful to quickly switch between different environments within the same file. This is made possible by creating several screens: All changes to windows as described in the Section called *The window system* and the Section called *Window types* are saved within one screen, so if you change your windows in one screen, other screens won't be affected. But the scene you are working on stays the same in all screens.

Three different default screens are provided with Blender; they are available via the SCR Menu Buttons in the User Preferences Window header shown in figure 12. To change to the next screen alphabetically, press **CTRL-RIGHTARROW**; to change to the previous screen alphabetically, press **CTRL-LEFTARROW**.

Scenes

It is also possible to have several scenes within the same Blender file. The scenes may use one another's objects or be completely separate from one another. You can select and create scenes with the SCE Menu Button buttons in the User Preferences Window header (fig. 12).

When you create a new scene, you can choose between four options to control its contents:

- Empty creates an empty scene.
- Link Objects creates the new scene with the same contents as the currently selected scene. Changes in one scene will also modify the other.
- Link ObData creates the new scene based on the currently selected scene, with links to the same meshes, materials, and so on. This means that you can change objects' positions and related properties, but modifications to the meshes, materials, and so on will also affect other scenes unless you manually make single-user copies.
- Full Copy creates a fully independent scene with copies of the currently selected scene's contents.

Navigating in 3D Space

Blender lets you work in three-dimensional space, but our monitor screens are only two-dimensional. To be able to work in three dimensions, you must be able to change your viewpoint as well as the viewing direction of the scene. This is possible in all of the 3D Viewports.

Even if we will describe the 3D Viewport Window, most non-3D windows use an equivalent series of functions, for example it is even possible to translate and zoom a Buttons Window and its Panels.

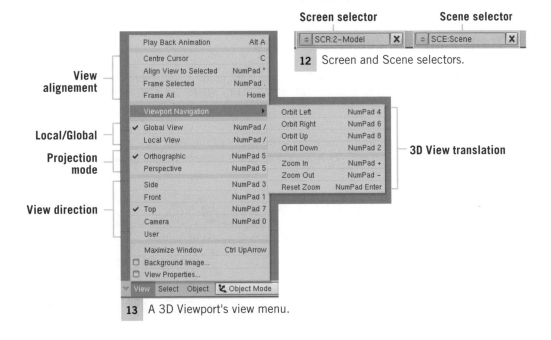

Screen selector **Scene selector**

12 Screen and Scene selectors.

13 A 3D Viewport's view menu.

The viewing direction (rotating)

Blender provides three default viewing directions: Side, Front, and Top. As Blender uses a right-hand coordinate system with the Z axis pointing upwards, "side" corresponds to looking along the X axis, in the negative direction; "front" along the Y axis; and "top" along the Z axis. You can select the viewing direction for a 3D Viewport with the View Menu entries (fig. 13) or by pressing the hotkeys **NUM3** for "side", **NUM1** for "front", and **NUM7** for "top".

Remember that most hotkeys affect the window that has focus, so check that the mouse cursor is in the area you want to work in before your use the hotkeys!

Apart from these three default directions, the view can be rotated to any angle you wish. Click and drag **MMB** on the Viewport's area: If you start in the middle of the window and move up and down or left and right, the view is rotated around the middle of the window. If you start at the edge and don't move towards the middle, you can rotate around your viewing axis. Play around with this function until you get the feeling for it.

To change the viewing angle in discrete steps, use **NUM8** and **NUM2**, which correspond to vertical **MMB** dragging. Or use **NUM4** and **NUM6**, which correspond to horizontal **MMB** dragging.

Translating and Zooming the View

To translate the view, hold down **SHIFT** and drag **MMB** in the 3D Viewport. For discrete steps, use the hotkeys **CTRL-NUM8**, **CTRL-NUM2**, **CTRL-NUM4** and **CTRL-NUM6** as with rotating.

You can zoom in and out by holding down **CTRL** and dragging **MMB**. The hotkeys are **NUM+** and **NUM-**. The View>>Viewport Navigation sub-menu holds these functions too (fig. 13).

Wheel Mouse

If you have a wheel mouse, you can perform all of the actions that you would do with **NUM+** and **NUM-** by rotating the wheel (**MW**). The direction of rotation selects the action.

If You Get Lost

If you get lost in 3D space, which is not uncommon, two hotkeys will help you: **HOME** changes the view so that you can see all objects (View>>Frame All Menu entry,) while **NUM.** zooms the view to the currently selected objects (View>>Frame Selected Menu entry.)

Perspective and Orthographic Projection

Each 3D Viewport supports two different types of projection. These are demonstrated in figure 14: orthographic (left) and perspective (right).

Our eye is used to perspective viewing because distant objects appear smaller. Orthographic projection often seems a bit odd at first, because objects stay the same size independent of their distance: It is like viewing the scene from an infinitely distant point. Nevertheless, orthographic viewing is very useful (it is the default in Blender and most other 3D applications), because it provides a more "technical" insight into the scene, making it easier to draw and judge proportions.

Perspective and Orthographic

Perspective view is geometrically constructed this way: you have a scene in 3D and you are an observer palced in a point O. The 2D perspective scene is built by placing a plane, a sheet of paper where the 2D scene is to be drawn in front of point O, perpendicular to the viewing direction. For each point P in the 3D scene a line is drawn, passing from O and P. The intersection point S between this line and the plane is the perspective projection of that point. By projecting all points P of the scene you get a perspective view.

In an orthographic projection, also called "orthonormal", on the other hand, you have a viewing direction but not a viewing point O. The line is then drawn through point P so

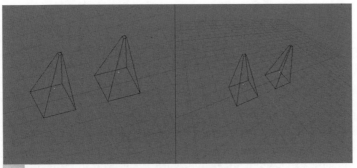

14 Orthographic and perspective projection modes.

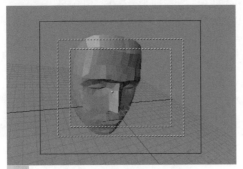

15 Demonstration of camera view.

16 A 3D Viewport's draw mode menu.

that it is parallel to the viewing direction. The intersections S between the line and the plane is the orthographic projection. And by projecting all point P of the scene you get the orthographic view.

To change the projection for a 3D Viewport, choose View>>Orthographic or View>>Perspective Menu entries (fig. 13). The hotkey **NUM5** toggles between the two modes.

Note that changing the projection for a 3D Viewport does not affect the way the scene will be rendered. Rendering is in perspective by default. If you need to create an Orthographic rendering, select the camera and press Ortho in the EditButtons (**F9**) Camera Panel.

The View>>Camera Menu entry sets the 3D Viewport to camera mode (Hotkey: **NUM0**). The scene is then displayed as it will be rendered later (see figure 15): the rendered image will contain everything within the outer dotted line. Zooming in and out is possible in this view, but to change the viewpoint, you have to move or rotate the camera.

Camera Projections

Draw mode

Depending on the speed of your computer, the complexity of your Scene, and the type of work you are currently doing, you can switch between several drawing modes:

- Textured: Attempts to draw everything as completely as possible, though it is still no alternative to rendering. Note that if you have no lighting in your scene, everything will remain black.
- Shaded: Draws solid surfaces including the lighting calculation. As with textured drawing, you won't see anything without lights.
- Solid: Surfaces are drawn as solids, but the display also works without lights.
- Wireframe: Objects only consist of lines that make their shapes recognizable. This is the default drawing mode.
- Bounding box: Objects aren't drawn at all; instead this mode shows only the rectangular boxes that correspond to each object's size and shape. The drawing mode can be selected with the appropriate Menu Button in the header (Figure 3-15) or with hotkeys: **ZKEY** toggles between wireframe and solid display, **SHIFT-Z** toggles between wireframe and shaded display.

Local view

When in local view, only the selected objects are displayed, which can make editing easier in complex scenes. To enter local view, first select the objects you want (see the Section called Selecting objects in Chapter 5) and then use the View>>Local View Menu entry; use the View>>Global View Menu entry to go back to Global View. (fig. 13). The hotkey is **NUM/**, which toggles Local/Global View.

The layer system

3D scenes often become exponentially more confusing with growing complexity. To get this under control, objects can be grouped into "layers," so that only the layers you select are displayed at any one time. 3D layers differ from the layers you may know from 2D graphics applications: they have no influence on the drawing order and are there (except for some special functions) solely to provide the modeler with a better overview.

Blender provides 20 layers; you can choose which are to be displayed with the small unlabeled buttons in the header (fig. 17). To select only one layer, click the appropriate button with **LMB** to select more than one, hold **SHIFT** while clicking.

UNDERSTANDING THE INTERFACE.**FUNCTIONS**

17 A 3D Viewport's layer buttons.

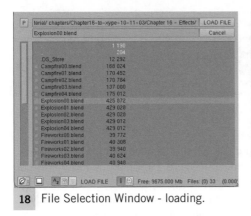

18 File Selection Window - loading.

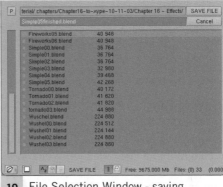

19 File Selection Window - saving.

To select layers via the keyboard, press **1KEY** to **OKEY** (on the main area of the keyboard) for layers 1 through 10 (the top row of buttons), and **ALT-1** to **ALT-O** for layers 11 through 20 (the bottom row). The **SHIFT** key for multiple selection works for these hotkeys too.

By default, the lock button directly to the right of the layer buttons is pressed; this means that changes to the viewed layers affect all 3D Viewports. To select only certain layers in one window, deselect locking first.

To move selected objects to a different layer, press **MKEY**, select the layer you want from the pop-up dialog, then press the Ok button.

The vital functions

Loading files

Blender uses the .blend file format to save nearly everything: Objects, scenes, textures, and even all your user interface window settings.

To load a Blender file from disk, press **F1**. The focused window then temporarily transforms into the File Selection Window as shown in figure 18. The bar on the left can be dragged with **LMB** for scrolling. To load a file, select it with **LMB** and press **ENTER**, or simply click it with **MMB**.

The upper text box displays the current directory path, and the lower one contains the selected filename. The P button (**PKEY**) moves you up to the parent directory and the button with the dash maintains a list of recently used paths. On Windows operating systems, the latter also contains a list of all drives (C:, D:, etc).

Blender expects that you know what you are doing! When you load a file, you are not asked to save unsaved changes to the scene you were previously working on: completing the file load dialog is regarded as being enough confirmation that you didn't do this by accident. Make sure that you save your files.

Saving files

Saving files is like loading files: When you press **F2**, the focused window temporarily changes into a File Selection Window, as shown in figure 19. Click the lower edit box to enter a filename. If it doesn't end with ".blend," the extension is automatically appended. Then press **ENTER** to write the file. If a file with the same name already exists, you will have to confirm that you want to save the file at the overwrite prompt.

The save dialog contains a little feature to help you to create multiple versions of your work: Pressing **NUM+** or **NUM-** increments or decrements a number contained in the filename. To simply save over the currently loaded file and skip the save dialog, press **CTRL-W** instead of **F2** and just confirm at the prompt.

Rendering

This section will give you only a quick overview of what you'll need in order to render your scene. You'll find a detailed description of all options in Chapter 14.

The render settings are in the Scene Context and Rendering Buttons sub-context (Figure 3-20) which is reached by clicking the , or by pressing **F10**.

For now we are only interested in the Format Panel. here the size (number of pixels horizontally and vertically) and file format of the image to be created are handled. You can set the size using the SizeX and SizeY buttons. Clicking the selection box below (in Figure 3-20, "Targa" is chosen) opens a menu with all available output formats for images and animations. For still images we might choose Jpeg, for example.

Now that the settings are complete, the scene may be rendered by hitting the RENDER button in the Render Panel or by pressing **F12**. Depending on the complexity of the scene, this usually takes between a few seconds and several minutes, and the progress is displayed in a separate window. If the scene contains an animation, only the current frame is rendered. (To render the whole animation, see the Section called *Rendering Animations* in Chapter 14.)

20 Rendering options in the Rendering Buttons.

21 User preferences window.

If you don't see anything in the rendered view, make sure your scene is constructed properly. Does it have lighting? Is the camera positioned correctly, and does it point in the right direction? Are all the layers you want to render visible?

A rendered image is not automatically saved to disk. If you are satisfied with the rendering, you may save it by pressing **F3** and using the save dialog as described in the Section called Saving files. The image is saved in the format you selected previously in the DisplayButtons.

Blender does not add the type extension automatically to image files! You should type the extension explicitly, if you need it.

File Extensions

User preferences and Themes

Blender has a few options that are not saved with each file, but which apply to all of a user's files instead. These preferences primarily concern user interface handling details, and system properties like mouse, fonts, and languages.

As the user preferences are rarely needed, they are neatly hidden behind the main menu. To make them visible, pull down the window border of the menu (usually the topmost border in the screen). The settings are grouped into seven categories which can be selected with the violet buttons shown in Figure 3-21.

Because most buttons are self-explanatory or display a helpful tool-tip if you hold the mouse still over them, we won't describe them in detail here. Instead, we will just give you an overview of the preference categories:

View & Controls
Settings concerning how the user interface should react to user input, such as which method of rotation should be used in 3D views. Here you can also activate 3-button mouse emulation if you have a two-button mouse. **MMB** can then be input as **ALT-LMB**.

Edit Methods
Lets you specify the details for the workings of certain editing commands like duplicate.

Language & Fonts
Select an alternative TrueType font for display in the interface, and choose from available interface languages.

Themes
Since version 2.30 Blender allows the utilization of Themes to define custom interface colors. You can create and manage themes from here.

Auto Save
Auto saves can be set so that you will have an emergency backup in case something goes wrong. These files are named Filename.blend1, Filename.blend2, etc.

System & OpenGL
You should consult this section if you experience problems with graphics or sound output, or if you don't have a numerical keypad and want to emulate it (for laptops). Furthermore here you can set the light scheme for Solid and shaded draw modes.

File Paths
Choose the default paths for various file load dialogs.

Setting the default scene
You don't like Blender's default window set-up, or want specific render settings for each project you start, or you want to save your Theme? No problem. You can use any scene file as a default when Blender starts up. Make the scene you are currently working on the default by pressing **CTRL-U**. The scene will then be copied into a file called `.B.blend` in your home directory.

You can clear the working project and revert to the default scene anytime by pressing **CTRL-X**. But remember to save your changes to the previous scene first!

CH. 4 QUICKSTART

MODELLING, STILL RENDERING, LIGHTING, MATERIALS AND TEXTURES, RIGGING, SKINNING, POSING, ANIMATION RENDERING

Your first animation in 30 + 30 minutes

This chapter will guide you step-by-step through the animation of a small „Ginger-bread Man" character. We'll describe all actions completely, but we'll assume that you have read the entire Chapter 3, and that you understand the conventions used throughout this book.

In the first 30 minutes of this tutorial we'll build a *still* gingerbread man. Then, in the next 30 minutes, we'll give him a skeleton and animate a walk cycle.

Warming up

Fire up Blender by double clicking its icon or running it from the command line. Blender will open showing you, from top view, the default set-up: a camera, a cube and a lamp. The cube is pink, meaning it is selected (fig. 1). Select the lamp with **RMB** and delete it by pressing the **XKEY** and confirm by clicking the Erase Selected entry in the dialog which appears.

Now select the camera with **RMB** and press **MKEY**. A small toolbox, like the one in figure 2, will appear beneath your mouse, with the first button checked. Check the rightmost button on the top row and then the OK button. This will move your camera to layer 10.

Blender provides you with 20 layers to help you organize your work. You can see which layers are currently visible from the group of twenty buttons in the 3D window toolbar (fig. 3). You can change the visible layer with **LMB** and toggle visibility with **SHIFT-LMB**.

Building the body

Change to the front view with **NUM1** and select the cube (**RMB**). Press TAB to switch the cube from *Object Mode* to *Edit Mode*, a mode in which you can move the single

QUICKSTART.MODELLING

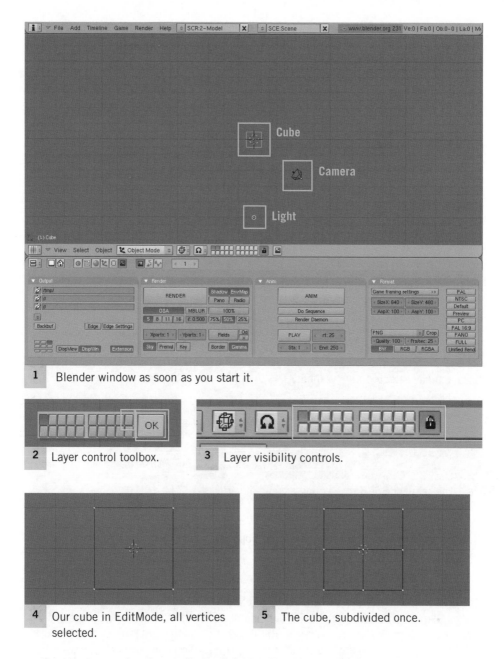

1 Blender window as soon as you start it.

2 Layer control toolbox.

3 Layer visibility controls.

4 Our cube in EditMode, all vertices selected.

5 The cube, subdivided once.

vertices that comprise the mesh. By default, all vertices are selected (yellow - unselected vertices are pink).

We will call our Gingerbread man "Gus". Our first task is to build Gus's body by working on our cube in Edit Mode. To see the Blender tools that we'll use for this purpose, press the button showing a square with yellow vertices in the Button window header (fig. 7), or press **F9**.

Now locate the `Subdivide` button in the `Mesh Tools` panel and press it once (fig. 8). This will split each side of the cube in two, creating new vertices and faces (fig. 5).

With your cursor hovering in the 3D window press **AKEY** to deselect all elements. Vertices will turn pink. Now press **BKEY**; the cursor will change to a couple of orthogonal grey lines. Move your mouse above to the top left of the cube, press and hold **LMB**, then drag the mouse down and to the right so that the grey box encompasses all the leftmost vertices. Now release the **LMB**. This sequence, which let you select a group of vertices in a box, is summarized in figure 6.

Box Select

On many occasions you may have vertices hidden behind other vertices, as is the case here. Our subdivided cube has 26 vertices, yet you can only see nine because the others are hidden.

A normal **RMB** click selects only one of these stacked vertices, whereas a box select selects all. Thus, in this case, even if you see only three vertices turning yellow you have actually selected nine vertices.

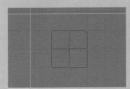  

6   The sequence of Box selecting a group of vertices.

Now press **XKEY** and, from the menu that pops up, select `Vertices` to erase the selected vertices (fig. 9).

Undo

Since version 2.3 blender has a Mesh Undo feature. pressing **UKEY** in Edit Mode makes Blender Undo last Mesh edit, keeping pressing **UKEY** rolls back changes as long as the Undo buffer allows, while **SHIFT-U** re-do changes. **ALT-U** opens a menu with a list of possible undos so at you can easily find the point to which you want to roll back.

Mesh Undo works only in Edit Mode and only for one mesh at a time. Undo data is not lost when you swich out of Edit Mode until you start editing a *different* mesh. Another way to revert to the previously saved state is to press **ESC** in the middle of an action. This cancels the action, reverting to the previous state.

QUICKSTART.MODELLING

7 The Editing Context.

8 The Edit Buttons window for a Mesh.

Now, using the sequence you just learned, Box Select the two top-rightmost vertices (fig. 10, left). Press **EKEY** and click on the `Extrude` menu entry to extrude them. This will create new vertices and faces which you can move and which will follow the mouse. Move them to the right.

To constrain the movement horizontally or vertically, click **MMB** while moving. You can switch back to unconstrained movement by clicking **MMB** again.
Alternatively you can use **XKEY** to constrain movement to x axis, **YKEY** for y axis and so on.

9 The pop-up menu of the Delete (XKEY) action.

Let's create Gus's arms and legs. Move these new vertices one and a half squares to the right, then click **LMB** to fix their position.

Extrude again with **EKEY** then move the new vertices another half square to the right. Figure 10 show this sequence.

Gus should now have a left arm (he's facing us). We will build the left leg the same way by extruding the lower vertices. Try to produce something like that shown in figure 11.

We use the Extrude tool three times to produce the leg. We don't care about elbows, but we will need a knee later on!

The CD contains a .blend file with this example, saved at various modelling phases. The first file, *Quickstart00.blend* contains what you should have obtained up to now.

Subsequent steps are numbered progressivley, *Quickstart01.blend*, *Quickstart02.blend* and so on, while *Quickstart.blend* contains the final result. This standard applies to all other examples in the Book.

10 Extruding the arm in two steps.

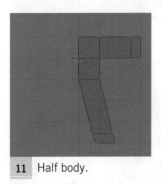

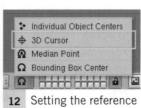

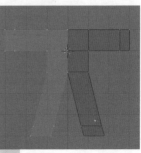

11 Half body.

12 Setting the reference center to the cursor.

13 Flip the copy of the half body to obtain a full body.

Now we'll create the other half of Gus:

1. Select all vertices (**AKEY**) and choose the 3D Cursor entry in the Rotation/ Scaling Pivot Menu of the 3D Window header (fig. 12).

2. Press **SHIFT-D** to duplicate all selected vertices, edges, and faces. These new are in Grab mode, press **ESC** to exit from this mode without moing the vertices.

3. Press **MKEY** to open the Mirror Axis Menu. Choose Global X. The result is shown in figure 13.

4. Deselect all then reselect all by pressing **AKEY** twice, then eliminate the coincident vertices by pressing the Remove doubles button (fig. 14). A box will appear, notifying you that eight vertices have been removed.

Pivot Point

In Blender, scaling, rotating and other mesh modifications occur either with respect to the cursor position, the object center, or the barycenter of the selected items, depending upon which entry of the Rotation/Scaling Pivot Menu (fig. 12) is active. The crosshair button selects the cursor as reference.

14 The Editbuttons window.

If you extrude and, in the process of moving you change your mind and press **ESC** to recover, the extruded vertices will still be there, in their original location! While you can move, scale, or rotate them by pressing **GKEY**, you probably don't want to extrude them again. To fully undo the extrusion, look for the `Remove Doubles` button, highlighted in Figure 14. This will eliminate coincident vertices.

To place the cursor at a specific grid point, position it next to where you want it and press **SHIFT-S** to bring up the Snap Menu. The entry `Curs->Grid` places the cursor exactly on a grid point. The `Curs->Sel` places it exactly on the selected object. The other entries move objects other than the cursor.

15 The sequence of adding a head.

Gus Needs a head:

1. Move the cursor so that it is exactly one grid square above Gus' body (fig. 15, left). Add a new cube here by pressing **SPACE** or holding the LMB in the 3D Window, with the mouse still, for more than half a second. From the toolbox which appears select menu `Add`. Since you are in Edit Mode only meshes can be added. Select `Cube`. In the following we will use the notation (**SPACE**>>Add>>Cube) to quickly describe toolbox operation.

2. Press **GKEY** to switch to Grab Mode and move the newly created vertices down, constraining the movement with **MMB**, for about one third of a grid unit (fig. 15, right).

3. This produces a rough figure at best. To make it smoother, locate the `SubSurf` Toggle Button (fig. 16) in the `Mesh` panel and switch it on. Be sure to set both the two Num-Buttons below to 2.

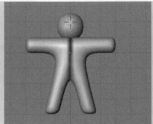

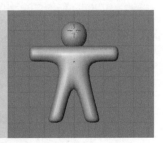

16 The Editing Context Panels.

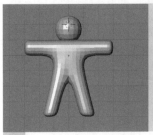

17 Setting Gus to smooth.

SubSurfacing is an advanced modeling tool, it dynamically refines a given coarse mesh creating a much denser mesh and locating the vertices of the finer mesh so that they smoothly follow the original coarse mesh. The shape of the Object is still controlled by the location of the coarse mesh vertices, but the rendered shape is the smooth, fine mesh one.

4. Switch out of Edit Mode (**TAB**) and switch from the current default Wireframe mode to Solid mode with **ZKEY** to have a look at Gus. He should look like figure 17 left.

5. To make Gus look smooth, press the SetSmooth button in figure 16. Gus will now appear smooth but with funny black lines in his middle (figure 17, middle). These lines appear because the SubSurfed finer mesh is computed using information about the coarse mesh normal directions, which may not be self consistent, that is, some face normals might point outward, some inward, if extrusions and flippings have been made. To reset the normals, switch back to Edit Mode (**TAB**), select all vertices (**AKEY**), and press **CTRL-N**. Click with **LMB** on the Recalc normals outside box which appears. Now Gus should be nice and smooth, as shown in figure 17, right. Press **MMB** and drag the mouse around to view Gus from all angles. Oops, he is too thick! To fix that, switch to side view **NUM3**. Now, switch to Edit Mode (if you are not there already), then back to Wireframe mode (**ZKEY**), and select all vertices with **AKEY** (figure 18, left).

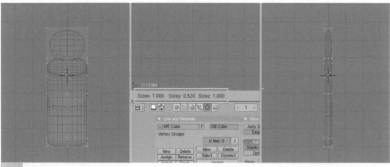

18 Slimming Gus using constrained scaling.

Let's make Gus thinner:

1. Press **SKEY** and start to move the mouse horizontally. (Click **MMB** to constrain scaling to just one axis or press **YKEY** to obtain the same result.) If you now move the mouse toward Gus he should become thinner but remain the same height.

2. The three numbers on the 3DWindow toolbar show the scaling factor. Once you constrained scaling, only one of these numbers will vary. Press and hold **CTRL**. The scale factor will now vary in discrete steps of value 0.1. Scale Gus down so that the factor is 0.2, then set this dimension by clicking **LMB**.

3. Return to Front view and to Solid mode (**ZKEY**), then rotate your view via **MMB**. Gus is much better now!

Let's see what Gus looks like

We're just about ready to see our first rendering, but first, we we've got some work to do.

1. **SHIFT-LMB** on the top right small button of the layer visibility buttons in the 3D Window toolbar (fig. 19) to make both Layer 1 (Gus's layer) and Layer 10 (the layer with the camera) visible.

19 Making both layer 1 and 10 visible.

Remember that the *last* layer selected is the active layer, so all subsequent additions will automatically be on layer 10.

2. Select the camera (**RMB**) and move it to a location like (x=7, y=-10, z=7). Do this by pressing **GKEY** and dragging the camera while keeping **CTRL** pressed to move it in steps of 1 grid unit.

Entering precise locations and rotations

If you prefer to enter numerical values for an object's location you can do so by pressing **NKEY** and modifying the NumButtons in the Panel that appears (fig. 20).

20   The Panel for numerical input of object position/ rotation etc.

To make the camera point at Gus, keep your camera selected then select Gus via **SHIFT-RMB**. The camera should be magenta and Gus light pink. Now press **CTRL-T** and select the Old Track entry in the pop up. This will force the camera to track Gus and always point at him. This means that you can move the camera wherever you want and be sure that Gus will always be in the center of the camera's view.

Tracking

If the tracking object already has a rotation of its own, as is often the case, the result of the **CTRL-T** sequence might not be as expected. If it is not, select the tracking object (in our example the camera), and press **ALT-R** to remove any object rotation. Once you do this the camera will really track Gus.

Figure 21 shows top, front, side and camera view of Gus. To obtain a camera view press **NUMO**.

Now we need to create the ground for Gus to stand on.

1. In top view (**NUM7**), and *out* of Edit Mode, add a plane (**SPACE**>>Add>>Mesh>>Plane).

It is important to be out of Edit Mode, otherwise the newly added object would be part of the object currently in Edit Mode, as it was for Gus' head when we added it. If the cursor is where figure 21 shows, such a plane would be in the middle of Gus's body.

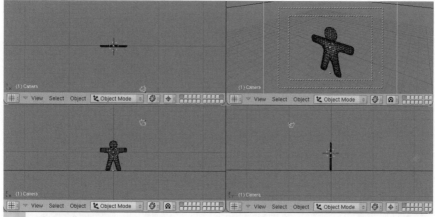

21 Camera position with respect to Gus.

22 Set the reference to Object center.

2. Switch to Object Mode and Front view (**NUM1**) and move (**GKEY**) the plane down to Gus's feet, using **CTRL** to keep it aligned with Gus.

3. Switch the reference center from cursor (where we set it at the beginning) to object by pressing the highlighted menu entry in figure 22.

4. Go to Camera view (**NUM0**) and, with the plane still selected, press **SKEY** to start scaling.

5. Enlarge the plane so that its edges extend beyond the camera viewing area, as indicated by the outer white dashed rectangle in Camera view.

Now, some light!

1. In Top view (**NUM7**), add a Lamp light (**SPACE**>>ADD>>Lamp) in front of Gus, but on the other side of the camera; for example in (x=-9, y=-10, z=7) (fig. 23).

2. Switch to the Lamp Buttons in the Shading context via the button with a lamp in the Button Window toolbar (fig. 24) or **F5**.

3. In the Buttons Window, Preview Panel, press the Spot toggle button to make the lamp a Spotlight (fig. 25) of pale yellow (R=1, G=1, B=0.9). Adjust ClipSta: Num Button to 5, Samples: to 4, and Soft: to 8.

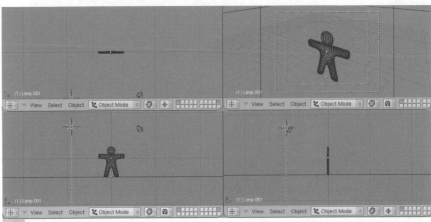

23 Inserting a Lamp.

24 The Lamp Buttons window button.

25 Spot light settings.

4. Make this spotlight track Gus just as you did for the camera by selecting Spot, **SHIFT**-selecting Gus, and by pressing **Ctrl-T**. If you added the spot in Top View you should not need to clear its rotation via **Alt-R**.

5. Add a second lamp in the same location as the spot, and again in Top View, with (**SPACE**>>Add>>Lamp). Make this lamp a **Hemi** lamp with energy of 0.6 (fig. 26).

Use two or more lamps to help produce soft, realistic lighting, because in reality natural light never comes from a single point. You will learn more about this in Chapter 9.

Two lamps?

We're almost ready to render. As a first step, go to the Scene context and Render buttons by pressing the image-like icon in the Button window toolbar (fig. 27) or **F10**.

26 The Hemi lamp settings.

27 The Rendering Buttons window buttons.

28 The Rendering Buttons window.

In the Render Buttons, `Format` Panel, set the image size to 640x480 with the Num buttons at the top. In the `Render` Panel set the `Shadows` Toggle Button top center to On, and the `OSA` Toggle Button left to On as well (fig. 28). These latter controls will enable shadows and oversampling (OSA) which will prevent jagged edges.

Now press the `RENDER` button or **F12**. The result, shown in figure 29, is actually quite poor. We still need materials, and lots of details, such as eyes, and so on.

29 Your first rendering. Congratulations!

Saving

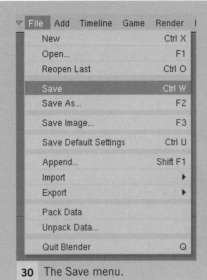

If you have not done so already, now would be a good time to save your work, via the `File>>Save` menu shown in figure 30, or **CTRL-W**. Blender will warn you if you try to over-write an existing file.

Blender does automatic saves into your system's temporary directory. By default, this happens every four minutes and the file name is a number. Loading these saves is another way to undo unwanted changes.

30 The Save menu.

Materials and Textures

It's time to give Gus some nice cookie-like material:

1. Select Gus. Then, in the Button Window header, select the Shading Context by pressing the red dot button (fig. 31) or using the **F5** key.

2. The Button window will be almost empty because Gus has no materials yet. To add a material, click on the Menu Button in the `Material` Panel (the one with two triangles, pointing up and down) and select `ADD NEW` (fig. 32).

3. The Buttons window will be populated by Panels and Buttons and a string holding the Material name, "Material" by default, will appear next to the Menu Button. Change this to something meaningful, like GingerBread.

4. Modify the default values as per figure 33 to obtain a first rough material.

5. Press the Menu Button in the Textures Panel area (fig. 34) and select `Add new`. We're adding a texture in the first channel. Call it "GingerTex".

6. Select the Texture Buttons by clicking the button in figure 35 or by pressing **F6**.

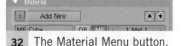

31 The Material Buttons window Button.

32 The Material Menu button.

33 The Material Buttons window and a first gingerbread material.

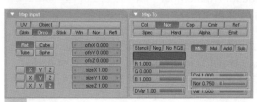

34 The Textures menu button in the Material Buttons.

35 The Texture Buttons window Button.

36 The Textures Buttons window with a stucci texture.

37 Settings for the Stucci texture in the Material Buttons window.

7. From the columns of ToggleButtons which appear in the `Texture` Panel select `Stucci` and set all parameters as in figure 36.

8. Return to the Material buttons (**F5**) and set the `Map Input` and `Map To` tabs of the `Texture` Panel as in figure 37. Release the `Col` Toggle Button and set the `Nor` Toggle Button, then raise the `Nor` slider to 0.75. These changes will make our Stucci texture act as a „bumpmap" and make Gus look more biscuit-like.

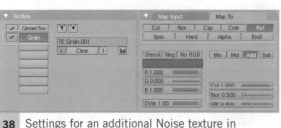

38 Settings for an additional Noise texture in channel 2.

39 A very simple material for the ground.

40 Layer visibility buttons on the toolbar.

9. Now add a second texture, name it "Grain", and make it affect only the `Ref` property with a 0.4 `Var` (fig. 38). The texture itself is a plain `Noise` texture.

10. Give the ground an appropriate material, such as the dark blue one shown in figure 39.

To give some finishing touches we'll add eyes and some other details.

1. First make Layer 1 the only one visible by clicking with **LMB** on the layer 1 button (fig. 40). This will hide the lamps, camera, and ground.

2. Place the cursor at the center of Gus's head. (Remember that you are in 3D so be sure to check at least two views to be sure!)

3. Add a sphere (**SPACE**>>Add>>Mesh>>UVsphere). You will be asked for the number of `Segments:` (meridians) and `Rings:` (parallels) into which to divide the sphere. The default of 32 is more than we need here, so use a value of 16 for both. The sphere is in the first image at the top left of the sequence in figure 41.

4. Scale the sphere down (**SKEY**) to a factor 0.1 in all dimensions, then switch to side view (**NUM3**) and scale it only in the horizontal direction (**YKEY**) a further 0.5 (see the second two images in figure 41).

5. Zoom a little if necessary via **NUM+**, **MW**, or **CTRL-MMB**, and drag the sphere (**GKEY**) to the left so that it is halfway into the head (as shown in the first image in the second row of figure 41).

6. Return to front view (**NUM1**) and move the sphere sideways, to the right. Place it where Gus should have an eye.

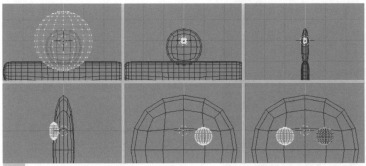

41 Sequence for creation of the eyes.

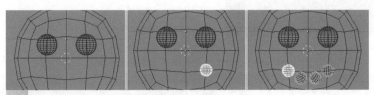

42 Creating a mouth with Spinning tools.

7. Flip a duplicate around the cursor by following the sequence you learned when flipping Gus's body. (Select the crosshair toolbar button, in Edit Mode **AKEY** to select all, **SHIFT-D**, **ESC MKEY**, Global X Menu entry.) Now Gus has two eyes.

8. Exit Edit Mode (**TAB**), and place the cursor as close as you can to the center of Gus's face. Add a new sphere and scale and move it exactly as before, but make it smaller and place it lower than and to the right of the cursor, centerd on the SubSurfed mesh vertex (fig. 42).

9. Now, in the Edit Buttons (**F9**), locate the group of buttons at bottom in the Mesh Tools Panel (fig. 43). Set Degr: to 90, Steps: to 3, and verify that the Clockwise: TogButton is on. Then, with all vertices still selected, press SpinDup. This will create three duplicates of the selected vertices on an arc of 90 degrees, centered around the cursor. The result should be Gus's mouth, like the last image of the sequence shown in figure 42.

43 The Spin Tools buttons in the Edit Buttons window.

Now that you have learned the trick, add three more of these ellipsoids to form Gus's buttons. Once you have made one button, you can simply exit Edit Mode, press **SHIFT-D** to create a duplicate, and move the duplicat into place, as shown in figure 44.

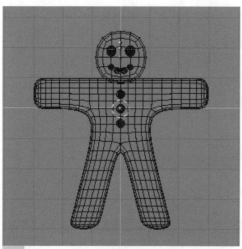

44 The complete Gus.

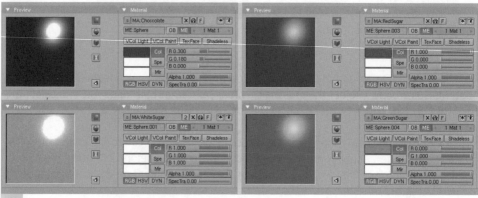

45 Some other candy materials.

Give the eyes a chocolate-like material, like the one shown at the top-left in figure 45. Give the mouth a white sugar like material, like the bottom-left shown in figure 45, and give the buttons a red, white, and green sugar like material, which you can also see in figure 45.

Objects sharing a material

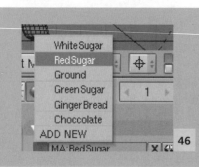

To give one object the same material as another object, select that material in the Menu list which appears when you press the Menu Button Button-Window Material Panel.

46 Selecting an existing material from the Material Menu.

47 The complete Gus still rendering.

Once you have finished assigning materials, make layer 10 visible again (you should know how), so that lights and the camera also appear, and do a new rendering (**F12**). The result should look more or less like figure 47.

Save your image, if you so wish, by pressing **F3**. Enter the name of your image in the file window and save.

You must choose the image format (JPEG, PNG, and so on) by setting it in the Rendering buttons before pressing **F3** (fig. 27) and using the Menu (fig. 48) in the Format Panel. Blender does *not* add an extension to the file name; you must enter one if you wish.

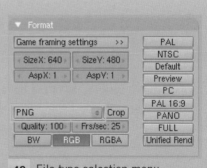

48 File type selection menu in the Rendering Buttons

Image types and extension

Rigging

If we were going for a still picture, our work up to this point would be enough, but we want Gus to move! The next step is to give him a skeleton, or Armature, which will move him. This is called the fine art of rigging. Gus will have a very simple rigging: four limbs (two arms and two legs) and a few joints (no elbows, only knees), but no feet or hands. To add the rigging:

1. Set the cursor where the shoulder will be, press **SPACE**>>Add>>Armature. A rhomboidal object will appear, a bone of the armature system, stretching from cursor to mouse pointer. Place the other end of the armature in Gus's hand (fig. 49) with **LMB**. This will fix the bone and create a new one from the end point of the previous one, producing a bone chain. We don't need any other bones right now, so press **ESC** to exit.

2. Stay in Edit Mode, then move the cursor to where the hip joint will be and add a new bone (**SPACE**>>Add>>Armature) down to the knee. Press **LMB** and a new bone should automatically appear there. Stretch this bone down to the foot (fig. 50).

3. Now place the cursor in the center and select all bones with **AKEY**. Duplicate them with **Shift-D** and exit grab mode with **ESC** then flip them with **SKEY** with Cursor Pivot point and by numerically entering a -1 scaling factor along the x direction (fig. 51).

Bone Position

The bones we are adding will deform Gus's body mesh. To produce a neat result, try to place the bone joints as shown in the illustrations.

Once you've selected all of the bones (**AKEY**), the Edit Buttons window should show an `Armature Bones` Panel which should show the Armature buttons (fig. 52).

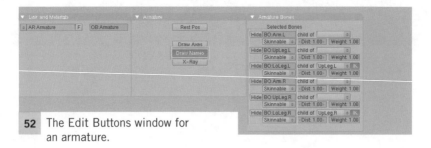

52 The Edit Buttons window for an armature.

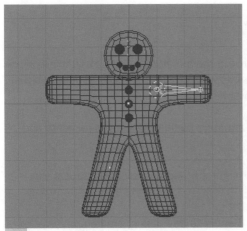

49 Adding the first bone, an elbowless arm.

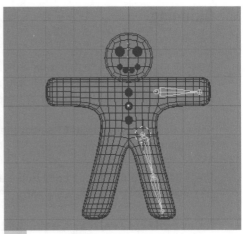

50 Adding the second and third bones, a leg bone chain.

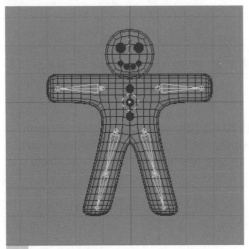

51 The complete armature after duplicating and flipping.

Press the Draw Names button to see the names of the bones, then **SHIFT-LMB** on the names in the Armature Bones Panel (fig. 52) to change them to something appropriate like Arm.R, Arm.L, UpLeg.R, LoLeg.R, UpLeg.L, and LoLeg.L. Exit Edit Mode with (**TAB**).

It is very important to name your bones with a trailing „.L' or „.R' to distinguish between left and right ones, so that the Action editor will be able to automatically flip your poses.

Naming Bones

Skinning

Now we must make it so that a deformation in the armature causes a matching deformation in the body. We do this with Skinning, which assigns vertices to bones so that the formers are subject to the latters' movements.

1. Select Gus's body, then **SHIFT** select the armature so that the body is magenta and the armature is light pink.

2. Press **CTRL-P** to parent the body to the armature. A pop up dialog will appear (fig. 53). Select the Use Armature entry.

3. A new menu appears, asking if you want Blender to do nothing, create empty vertex groups, or create and populate vertex groups (fig. 54).

4. We'll use the automatic skinning option. Go ahead and select Create From Closest Bones.

    Now select only Gus's body and go to Edit Mode (**TAB**). You will notice in the Edit Buttons (**F9**) Window and Link and Materials Panel, the presence of a Vertex Group menu and buttons (fig. 55).

    By pressing the Menu Button a menu with all available vertex group pops up (six in our case, but a truly complex character, with hands and feet completely rigged, can have tens of them (fig. 56)! The buttons Select and Deselect show you which vertices belong to which group.

    Select the Right arm (Arm.R) group and, with all vertices de-selected (**AKEY**, if needed) press Select. You should see something like fig. 57.

    The vertices marked with yellow squares in figure 57 belong to the deformation group, but they should not. The autoskinning process found that they were very close to the bone so it added them to the deformation group. We don't want them in this group because, since some are in the head and some are in the chest, adding them to the deformation group would deform those body parts. To remove them from the group, deselect all the other vertices, those which should *remain* in the group using Box selection (**BKEY**), but use **MMB**, not **LMB**, to define the box, so that all vertices within the box become deselected.

    Once only the ,undesired' vertices are selected, press the Remove button (fig. 55) to eliminate them from group Arm.R.

    Deselect all (**AKEY**) then check another group. Check them all and be sure that they look like those in figure 58.

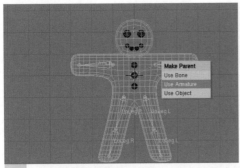

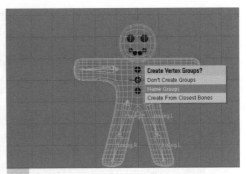

53 The pop-up menu which appears when parenting an Object to an Armature.

54 Automatic Skinning options.

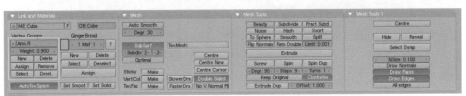

55 The vertex groups buttons in the Edit Buttons window of a mesh.

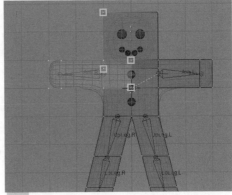

56 The menu with the vertex groups automatically created in the skinning process.

57 Gus in Edit Mode with all the vertices of group Arm.R selected.

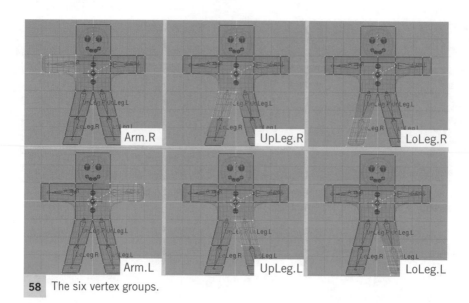

58 The six vertex groups.

Vertex groups

Be very careful when assigning or removing vertices from vertex groups. If later on you see unexpected deformations, you might have forgotten some vertices, or placed too many in the group. You can modify your vertex groups at any time.

Other details

Our deformations will affect only Gus's body, not his eyes, mouth, or buttons, which are separate objects. While this is not an issue to consider in this simple animation, it's one that must be taken into account for more complex projects, for example by parenting or otherwise joining the various parts to the body to make a single mesh. (We'll describe all of these options in detail in later Chapters.)

Posing

Once you have a rigged and skinned Gus you can start playing with him as if he were a doll, moving his bones and viewing the results.

1. Select the armature only, then select Pose Mode from the „Mode" Menu (fig. 59). This option only appears if an armature is selected (or use **CTRL-TAB**).

QUICKSTART.POSING

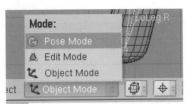

59 The toggle button to switch to pose mode in the 3D Window toolbar.

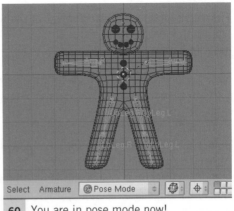

60 You are in pose mode now!

2. The armature will turn blue. You are in Pose Mode. If you now select a bone it will turn cyan, not pink, and if you move it (**GKEY**), or rotate it (**RKEY**), the body will deform!

Blender remembers the original position of the bones. You can set your armature back by pressing the `RestPos` button in the Armature Edit Buttons (fig. 52).

While handling bones in pose mode you will notice that they act as rigid, unextensible bodies with spherical joints at the end. You can actually grab only the first bone of a chain and all the other will follow it. All subsequent bones in the chain cannot be grabbed and moved, you can only rotate them, so that the selected bone rotates with respect to the previous bone in the chain while all the subsequent bones of the chain follow its rotation.

This procedure, called `Forward Kinematics` (FK) is easy to follow, but it makes precise location of the last bone of the chain difficult. We can use another method, `Inverse Kinematics` (IK) where you actually define the position of the *last* bone in the chain, and all the other assume a position, automatically computed by Blender, to keep the chain without gaps. Hence precise positioning of hands and feet is much easier.

We'll make Gus walk by defining four different poses relative to four different stages of a stride. Blender will do the work of creating a fluid animation.

Original position

Forward and Inverse Kinematics

1. First, verify that you are at frame 1 of the timeline. The frame number appears in a NumButton on the right of the Buttons Window Toolbar (fig. 61). If it is not set to 1, set it to 1 now.

2. Now, by rotating only one bone at a time (**RKEY**), we'll raise UpLeg.L and bend LoLeg.L backwards while raising Arm.R a little and lowering Arm.L a little, as shown in figure 62.

3. Select all bones with **AKEY**. With the mouse pointer on the 3D Window, press **IKEY**. A menu pops up figure 63. Select LocRot from this menu. This will get the position and orientation of all bones and store it in a pose at frame 1. This pose represents Gus in the middle of his stride, while moving his left leg forward and above the ground.

4. Now move to frame 11 either by entering the number in the NumButton or by pressing **UPARROW**. Then move Gus to a different position, like figure 64, with his left leg forward and right leg backward, both slightly bent. Gus is walking in place!

5. Select all bones again and press **IKEY** to store this pose at frame 11.

6. We now need a third pose at frame 21, with the right leg up, because we are in the middle of the other half of the stride. This pose is the mirror of the one we defined at frame 1. Therefore, return to frame 1 and, in the Armature Menu in the 3D Window header select the Copy Pose entry. (fig. 65). You have copied the current pose to the buffer.

7. Go to frame 21 and paste the pose with the Paste Flipped Pose option in the Armature Menu(fig. 66). This button will paste the cut pose, exchanging the positions of bones with suffix .L with those of bones with suffix .R, effectively flipping it!

    The pose is there but it has not been stored yet! You must press **IKEY** with all bones selected.

8. Now apply the same procedure to copy the pose at frame 11 to frame 31, also flipping it.

9. To complete the cycle, we need to copy the pose at frame 1 without flipping to frame 41. Do so by copying it as usual, and by using Paste Pose entry. End the sequence by storing the pose with **IKEY**.

Checking the animation

To preview your Animation, set the current frame to 1 and press **Alt-A** in the 3D window.

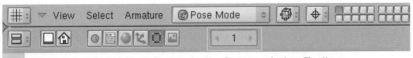

61 The current frame Num Button in the Button window Toolbar.

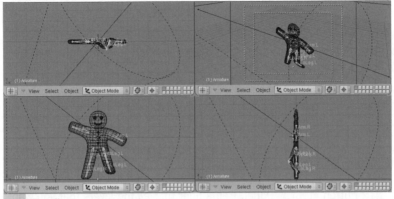

62 Our first pose.

63 Storing the pose to the frame.

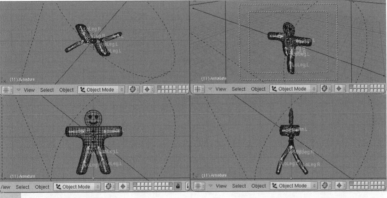

64 Our second pose.

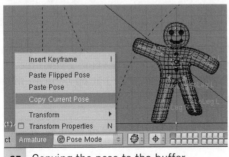

65 Copying the pose to the buffer.

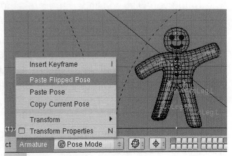

66 Pasting the copy as a new, flipped, pose.

Gus walks!

The single step in-place is the core of a walk, and once you have defined one there are techniques to make a character walk along a complex path. But, for the purpose of our Quick Start, this single step in-place is enough.

1. Change to the Rendering Buttons (**F10**) and set the animation start and end to 1 and 40 respectively (fig. 67). Because frame 41 is identical to frame 1, we only need to render frames from 1 to 40 to produce the full cycle.

2. Select AVI Raw as the file type in `Format` Panel (fig. 67). While this is generally not the best choice, mainly for file size issues (as will be explained later on), it is fast and it will run on any machine, so it suits our needs. (You can also select AVI Jpeg to produce a more compact file, but using lossy Jpeg compression and obtaining a movie that some external render might not be able to play.)

3. Finally, press `ANIM` button in `Anim` Panel. Remember that *all* the layers that you want to use in the animation must be shown! In our case, these are layers 1 and 10.

Stopping a Rendering

If you make a mistake, like forgetting to set layer 10 to on, you can stop the rendering process with the **ESC** key.

Our scene is pretty simple, and Blender will probably render each of the 40 images in few seconds. Watch them as they appear.

Stills

Of course you can always render each of your animation frames as a still by selecting the frame you wish to render and pressing the `RENDER` button.

Once the rendering is complete you should have a file named `0001_0040.avi` in a `render` subdirectory of your current directory - the one containing your `.blend` file. You can play this file directly within Blender by pressing the `Play` button beneath the `ANIM` button (fig. 67). The animation will automatically cycle. To stop it press **ESC**.

We have produced only a very basic walk cycle. There is much more in Blender, as you'll soon discover!

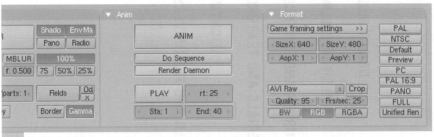

67 Setting the Rendering Buttons for an animation.

PART II

MODELLING, MATERIALS AND LIGHTS

As you have seen in the quick start chapter in *Part I* the creation of a 3D scene needs at least three key point: Models, Materials, Lights. In this part we will go deep into each of these.

Once you are done with this part you can either go to the *Part IV* if you want to get the most of Blender rendering engines on still images, or either read *Part III* to learn all Blender's animation capabilities. *Part V* on the other hand gives you even more modelling tools.

CH. 5 OBJECT MODE

CONCEPT, BOOLEAN OPERATIONS

by Martin Kleppmann

The geometry of a Blender scene is constructed from one or more Objects: Lamps, Curves, Surfaces, Cameras, Meshes, and the basic objects described in the Section called *Basic Objects* in Chapter 6. Each object can be moved, rotated and scaled in *ObjectMode*. For more detailed changes to the geometry, you can work on the mesh of an Object in *EditMode* (see the Section called *EditMode* in Chapter 6).

Once you've added a basic object via **SPACE**>>Add **menu, Blender ch**anges into EditMode by default if the Object is a Mesh, a Curve or a Surface. You can change to ObjectMode by pressing **TAB**. The object's wireframe, if any, should now appear pink, meaning that the object is now selected and active.

Selecting objects

To select an object, click it with the **RMB**. To select multiple objects, hold down **SHIFT** and click with the **RMB**. Generally, the last object to be selected becomes the *active* one: It appears in light pink, whereas the non-active selected objects appear purple. The definition of the active object is important for various reasons, including parenting.

To deselect the active object, click it again with **RMB**, if multiple Objects are selected hold **SHIFT** to maintain the other selected. Press **AKEY** to select all objects in the scene (if none are currently selected) or to deselect all (if one or more is selected). **BKEY** activates *Border select*. Use Border select to select a group of objects by drawing a rectangle while holding down **LMB**. You will select all objects that lie within or touch this rectangle.

Border select adds to the previous selection, so to select only the contents of the rectangle, deselect all with **AKEY** first. Use **MMB** while you draw the border to deselect all objects within the rectangle.

OBJECT MODE.CONCEPT

Moving (translating) objects

To move groups of objects, press **GKEY** to activate *Grab mode* for all selected objects. The selected objects will be displayed as white wireframes and can be moved with the mouse (without pressing any mouse button). To confirm the new position, click **LMB** or press **ENTER**; to cancel Grab mode, click **RMB** or press **ESC**. The header of the 3D Window displays the distance you are moving.

To lock movement to an axis of the global coordinate system, enter Grab mode, move the object roughly along the desired axis, then press **MMB**. To deactivate locking press **MMB** again. As a new 2.3 feature you can constrain movement to a given axis by pressing **XKEY**, **YKEY** or **ZKEY**. A single key constrains movement to the corresponding global axis, as **MMB** does. a second keypress of the same key constrains movement to the corresponding Object local axis. A third keypress of the same key removes constrains. Lines are drawn to let you better visualize the constraint.

Once grabbing is activated you can enter the Object translation numerically by simply typing in a number. This will let you enter the first co-ordinate shown in the 3D Window header. You can change co-ordinate with **TAB** use **NKEY** to exit/re-start numeric input mode, **ENTER** to finalize and **ESC** to exit. **BACKSPACE** will return to original values. Please note that you must use the keyboard **.KEY** not the **NUM.** for decimals.

If you keep **CTRL** pressed while moving the object you will activate snap mode, and the object will move by a whole number of Blender units (grid squares). Snap mode ends when you release **CTRL** so be sure to confirm the position before releasing it.

The location of selected objects can be reset to the default value by pressing **ALT-G**.

If you are striving for very fine and precise positioning, keep **SHIFT** pressed as you move. This way a large mouse movement will translate to a small object movement, which allows for fine tuning.

You can also enter Grab mode by drawing a straight line while holding down **LMB**.

Rotating objects

To rotate objects, activate Rotate mode by pressing **RKEY**. As in Grab mode, you can change the rotation by moving the mouse, confirm with **LMB**, or **ENTER** cancel with **RMB** or **ESC**.

Rotation in 3D space occurs around an axis, and there are various ways to define this axis. Blender defines an axis by direction and a point that it passes through. For example, by default, the direction of the axis is orthogonal to your screen. If you are viewing the scene from the front, side, or top, the rotation axis will be parallel to one of the global coordinate system axes. If you are viewing the scene from an angle, the rotation axis is angled too, which can easily lead to a very odd rotation of your object. In this case, you may want to keep the rotation axis parallel to the coordinate system axes. Toggle this behaviour by pressing **MMB** during Rotate mode and watch the angle display in the window header.

Alternatively, once you are in rotate mode, you can press **XKEY**, **YKEY** or **ZKEY** to constrain rotation along that axis of the *global reference*. By pressing **XKEY-XKEY** (**XKEY** twice) you constrain rotation around the x axis of the Object *local reference*. The same is true for double **YKEY** and **ZKEY**. As for Grab, a third keypress removes constraints.

It is possible to have a numerical imput for rotation exactly as it was for translations. Select the point for the rotation axis to pass through with the pertinent menu in the header of the 3D window, as discussed below (fig. 1).

- *Bounding Box Center* - the axis passes through the center of the selection's bounding box. (If only one object is selected, the point used is the center point of the object, which might not necessarily be in the geometric center. In figure 1 it is on the middle of the rightmost edge, marked by a purple dot. For more on this point, see the Section called EditMode in Chapter 6.)
- *Median Point* - the axis passes through the median point of the selection. This difference is only relevant in *EditMode*, and the 'Median' point is the barycentrum of all vertices.
- *3D Cursor* - the axis passes through the 3D cursor. The cursor can be placed anywhere you wish before rotating. You can use this option to easily perform translations the at the same time that you rotate an object.
- *Individual Object Centers* - each selected object receives its own rotation axis, all mutually parallel and passing through the center point of each object, respectively. If you select only one object, you will get the same effect as with the first button. If you're just getting started with rotation, don't worry too much about the foregoing details. Just play around with Blender's tools and you'll get a feeling for how to work with them.

Keeping **CTRL** pressed switches to snap mode. In snap mode rotations are constrained to 5° steps. Keeping **SHIFT** pressed allows fine tuning here too. The rotation of selected objects can be reset to the default value by pressing **ALT-R**.

 Blender Gesture System: You can also enter Rotate mode by drawing a circular line while holding down **LMB**.

OBJECT MODE.CONCEPT

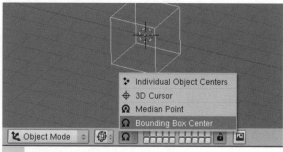

| 1 | The Pivot Point selection menu. |

Scaling/mirroring objects

To change the size of objects, press **SKEY**. As in grab mode and rotate mode, scale the objects by moving the mouse, confirm with **LMB** or **ENTER**, and cancel with **RMB** or **ESC**.

Scaling in 3D space requires a center point. This point is defined with the same buttons as the axis' pivot point for rotation (fig. 1). If you increase the size of the object, all points are moved away from the selected center point; if you decrease it, all points move towards this point.

By default, the selected objects are scaled uniformly in all directions. To change the proportions (make the object longer, broader, and so on), you can lock the scaling process to one of the global coordinate axes, just as you would when moving objects. To do so, enter scale mode, move the mouse a bit in the direction of the axis you want to scale, then press **MMB**. To return to uniform scaling, press **MMB** again. You will see the scaling factors in the header of the 3D window.

Again all considerations on constraining to given axis made for Grabbing still holds, as well as those on numerical input.

Here again **CTRL** switches to snap mode, with discrete scaling at 0.1 steps. Press **SHIFT** for fine tuning. The scaling of selected objects can be reset to the default value by pressing **ALT-S**.

Mirroring objects is a different application of the scale tool. Mirroring is effectively nothing but scaling with a negative factor in one direction. To mirror in the direction of the X or Y axes, press **SKEY** to go to scaling mode, then switch to numeric input. Select the desired coordinates and enter '-1' as scaling factor.

Blender Gesture System: You can also enter scale mode by drawing a V-shaped line while holding down **LMB**.

| 2 | The Transform Properties Panel in the 3D View. |

Transform Properties Panel

Say you want to display the position/rotation/scaling of your object in numbers. Or, you want to enter the location, rotation, and scaling values for an object directly at once. To do so, select the object you want to edit and press **NKEY**. The Transform Properties Panel (fig. 2) is displayed. **SHIFT**-**LMB**-click a number to enter a value, then press OK to confirm the changes or move the mouse outside the window to cancel.

The panel also displays the Object name in the OB: Button. You can edit it from here.

Duplicate

To duplicate an object, press **SHIFT-D** to create an identical copy of the selected objects. The copy is created at the same position, in Grab mode.

This is a new object except that it shares any Material, Texture, and IPO with the original. These attributes are linked to both copies and changing the material of one object also changes the material of the other. (You can make separate materials for each, as described in the Materials Chapter.)

You can create a *Linked Duplicate* rather than a real duplicate by pressing **ALT-D**. This will create a new object with *all* of its data linked to the original object. If you modify one of the linked objects in EditMode, all linked copies are also modified.

Parenting (Grouping)

To create a group of objects, you must first make one of them the parent of the others. To do so, select at least two objects, press **CTRL-P**, and confirm on the dialog Make Parent?. The *active* object will be made the parent of all the others. The center of all children is now linked to the center of the parent by a dashed line. At this point, grabbing, rotating, and scaling the parent will do the same to the children being grabbed, rotated and scaled likewise.

OBJECT MODE.CONCEPT

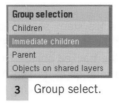

3 Group select.

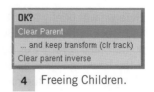

4 Freeing Children.

Parenting is a very important tool with many advanced applications, as we'll see in later chapters.

Press **SHIFT-G** with an active object to see the Group Selection menu (fig. 3). This Contains:

- `Children` - Selects all the active objects' children, and the children's children, up to the last generation.
- `Immediate Children` - Selects all the active objects' children but not these latter's children.
- `Parent` - Selects the parent of the active object.
- `Objects on shared layers` - This actually has nothing to do with parents. It selects all objects on the same layer(s) of the active object.

Move the child to the parent by clearing its origin (select it and press **ALT-O**) Remove a parent relation via **ALT-P**. You can (fig. 4):

- `Clear parent` - Frees the children, which return to their original location, rotation, and size.
- `Clear parent...and keep transform` - Frees the children, and keeps the location, rotation, and size given to them by the parent.
- `Clear parent inverse` - Places the children with respect to the parent as if they were placed in the Global reference. This effectively clears the parent's trans formation from the children.

Tracking

To make an object rotate so that it faces another object, and keep this facing even if either object is moved, select at least two objects and press **CTRL-T**. A dialog appears asking if you want to use a Track *constraint* or the old (Pre-2.30) track system. The Track constraint will be analyzed in the Section called *Constraints* in Chapter 13 and is the preferred method.

Here we will briefly treat the old track system, so, let's assume you have selected Old Track in the dialog. By default the inactive object(s) now track the active object so that their local y axis points to the tracked object. However, this may not happen if the tracking object already has a rotation of its own. You can produce correct tracking by canceling the rotation (**ALT-R**) of the tracking object.

The orientation of the tracking object is also set so that the z axis is upward. To change this, select the tracking object, change the Button Window to Object Context (🔧 , or **F7**) and select the track axis from the first row of six radio buttons and the upward-pointing axis from the second in the Anim Settings Panel (fig. 5).

To clear a track constraint, select the tracking object and press **ALT-T**. As with clearing a parent constraint, you must choose whether to lose or save the rotation imposed by the tracking.

Other Actions

Erase
Press **XKEY** or **DEL** to erase the selected objects. Using **XKEY** is more practical for most people, because it can easily be reached with the left hand on the keyboard.

Join
Press **CTRL-J** to join all selected objects to one single object. (The objects must be of the same type.) The center point of the resulting object is obtained from the previously active object.

Select Links
Press **SHIFT-L** to select all objects sharing a link with the active one. You can select objects sharing an IPO, data, material, or texture link (fig. 6).

Boolean operations

Boolean operations are particular actions which can be taken only on mesh type objects. While they will work for all Mesh objects, they are really intended for use with solid, closed objects with a well defined interior and exterior region. Thus, it is very important to define the normals in each object consistently, that is all each normal of each face should point outward. See Chapter 6 for further info on normals and on why you can end up with normals pointing partually outward and partially inward.

In the case of open objects, the interior is defined mathematically by extending the boundary faces of the object to infinity. As such, you may find that you get unexpected results for these objects.

OBJECT MODE.BOOLEAN OPERATIONS

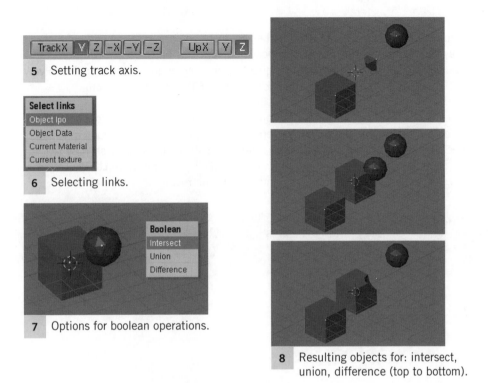

5   Setting track axis.

6   Selecting links.

7   Options for boolean operations.

8   Resulting objects for: intersect, union, difference (top to bottom).

A boolean operation never affects the original operands, the result is always a new Blender object.

Boolean operations are invoked by selecting exactly two meshes and pressing **WKEY**. There are three types of boolean operations to choose from in the popup menu, Intersect, Union and Difference.

The boolean operations also take materials and UV-Textures into account, producing objects with material indices or multi UV-mapped objects.

Consider the objects in figure 7.

- The Intersect operation creates a new object whose surface encloses the volume common to *both* original objects.
- The Union operation creates a new object whose surface encloses the volume of *both* original objects.
- The Difference operation is the only one in which the order of selection is important. The active object (light purple in wireframe view) is subtracted from the selected object. That is, the resulting object surface encloses a volume which is the volume belonging to the selected *and inactive* object, but *not* to the selected *and active* one.

Figure 8 shows the results of the three operations.

The number of polygons generated can be very large compared to the original meshes, especially when using complex concave objects. Furthermore, the polygons that are generated can be of generally poor quality: very long and thin and sometimes very small. Try using the Mesh Decimator (*EditButtons* - **F9**) to fix this problem.

Vertices in the resulting mesh that fall on the boundary of the two original objects often do not match up, and boundary vertices are duplicated. This is good in some respects because it means that you can select parts of the original meshes by selecting one vertex in the result and pressing the select linked button (**LKEY**). This is handy if you want to assign materials and such to the result.

Sometimes the boolean operation can fail with a message saying ("An internal error occurred -- sorry"). If this occurs, try to move or rotate the objects just a very small amount.

CH. 6 MESH MODELING

CONCEPT, BASIC EDITING, TOOLS, SUBDIVISION SURFACES, META OBJECTS

The principal Object of a 3D scene is usually a *Mesh*. In this chapter we will first enumerate the basic mesh objects, or *primitives*, then follow with a long series of sections describing in detail the action which can be taken on Mesh Objects.

Basic Objects

To create a basic Object press **SPACE** and select "Add>>Mesh", or, access the 'add'-menu by pressing **SHIFT-A** or simply hold **LMB** on 3D Window, for more than half a second. Select the basic object you'd like to create from the menu. We describe every basic object or *primitive* you can create within Blender below. Figure 1 also shows the variety of basic objects that can be created.

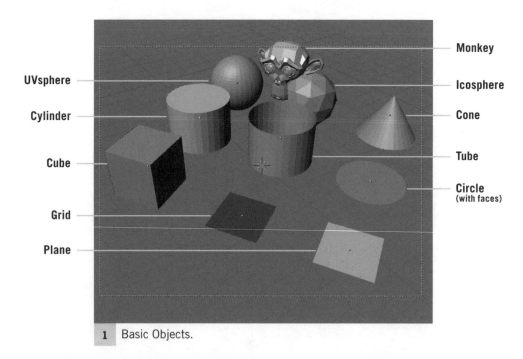

1 Basic Objects.

MESH MODELLING.CONCEPT

Plane
A standard plane contains four vertices, four edges, and one face. It is like a piece of paper lying on a table; it is not a real three-dimensional object because it is flat and has no thickness. Objects that can be created with planes include floors, tabletops, or mirrors.

Cube
A standard cube contains eight vertices, 12 edges, and six faces, and is a real three-dimensional object. Objects that can be created out of cubes include dice, boxes, or crates.

Circle
A standard circle is comprised of n vertices. The number of vertices can be specified in the popup window which appears when the circle is created. The more vertices the circle contains, the smoother its contour will be. Examples of circle objects are disks, plates, or any kind of flat and round object.

UVSphere
A standard UVsphere is made out of n segments and m rings. The level of detail can be specified in the popup window which appears when the UVsphere is created. Increasing the number of segments and rings makes the surface of the UVsphere smoother. Segments are like Earth meridians, going pole to pole, rings are like Earth parallels. Example objects that can be created out of UVspheres are balls, beads or pearls for a necklace.

If you specify a six segment, six ring UVsphere you'll get something which, in top view, is a hexagon (six segments), with five rings plus two points at the poles. Thus, one ring fewer than expected, or two more, if you count the poles as rings of radius 0.

Icosphere
An Icosphere is made up of triangles. The number of subdivisions can be specified in the window that pops up when the Icosphere is created; increasing the number of subdivisions makes the surface of the Icosphere smoother. At level 1 the Icosphere is an icosahedron, a solid with 20 equilateral triangular faces. Any increasing level of subdivision splits each triangular face into four triangles, resulting in a more spherical appearance. Icosphere's are normally used to achieve a more isotropical and economical layout of vertices than a UVsphere.

Cylinder
A standard cylinder is made out of n vertices. The number of vertices in the circular cross-section can be specified in the popup window that appears when the object is created; the higher the number of vertices, the smoother the circular cross-section becomes. Objects that can be created out of cylinders include handles or rods.

Tube

A standard tube is made out of *n* vertices. The number of vertices in the hollow circular cross-section can be specified in the popup window that appears when the object is created; the higher the number of vertices, the smoother the hollow circular cross-section becomes. Objects that can be created out of tubes include pipes or drinking glasses. (The basic difference between a cylinder and a tube is that the former has closed ends.)

Cone

A standard cone is made out of *n* vertices. The number of vertices in the circular base can be specified in the popup window that appears when the object is created; the higher the number of vertices, the smoother the circular base becomes. Objects that can be created out of cones include spikes or pointed hats.

Grid

A standard grid is made out of *n* by *m* vertices. The resolution of the x-axis and y-axis can be specified in the popup window which appears when the object is created; the higher the resolution, the more vertices are created. Example objects that can be created out of grids include landscapes (with the proportional editing tool) and other organic surfaces.

Monkey

This is a gift from old NaN to the community and is seen as a programmer's joke or "Easter Egg". It creates a monkey's head once you press the Oooh Oooh Oooh button. The Monkey's name is *Suzanne* and is Blender's mascotte.

EditMode

When working with geometric objects in Blender, you can work in two modes: ObjectMode and EditMode. Basically, as seen in the previous section, operations in ObjectMode affect whole objects, and operations in EditMode affect only the geometry of an object, but not its global properties such as the location or rotation.

In Blender you switch between these two modes with the **TAB** key. EditMode only works on one object at a time: the active object. An object outside EditMode is drawn in purple in the 3D Windows (in wireframe mode) when selected; it is black otherwise. The active object is drawn black in EditMode, but each vertex is highlighted in purple (fig. 2). Selected vertices are drawn in yellow (fig. 3) and, if appropriate buttons in the Editing (**F9**) Context Mesh Tools 1 Panel are pressed (Draw Faces and Draw Edges) also selected edges and faces are highlighted.

MESH MODELLING.CONCEPT

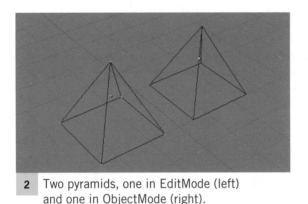

2 Two pyramids, one in EditMode (left) and one in ObjectMode (right).

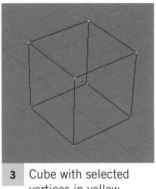

3 Cube with selected vertices in yellow.

Structures: Vertices, Edges and Faces

In basic meshes, everything is built from three basic structures: *Vertices*, *Edges* and *Faces*. (We're not talking about Curves, NURBS, and so forth here.) But there is no need to be disappointed: This simplicity still provides us with a wealth of possibilities that will be the foundation for all our models.

Vertices
A vertex is primarily a single point or position in 3D space. It is usually invisible in rendering and in ObjectMode. (Don't mistake the center point of an object for a vertex. It looks similar, but its bigger and you can't select it.)

To create a new vertex, change to EditMode, hold do **CTRL**, and click with the **LMB**. Of course, as a computer screen is two-dimensional, Blender can't determine all three vertex coordinates from one mouse click, so the new vertex is placed at the depth of the 3D cursor 'into' the screen. Any vertices selected previously are automatically connected to the new one with an edge.

Edges
An edge always connects two vertices with a straight line. The edges are the 'wires' you see when you look at a mesh in wireframe view. They are usually invisible on the rendered image. They are used to construct faces. Create an edge by selecting two vertices and pressing **FKEY**.

Faces
A Face is the most high level structure in a mesh. Faces are used to build the actual surface of the object. They are what you see when you render the mesh. A Face is defined as the area between either three or four vertices, with an Edge on every side. Triangles always work well, because they are always flat and easy to calculate.

Take care when using four-sided faces, because internally they are simply divided into two triangles each. Four-sided faces only work well if the Face is pretty much flat (all points lie within one imaginary plane) and convex (the angle at no corner is greater than or equal to 180 degrees). This is the case with the faces of a cube, for example. (That's why you can't see any diagonals in its wireframe model, because they would divide each square face into two triangles. While you could build a cube with triangular faces, it would just look more confusing in EditMode.)

An area between three or four vertices, outlined by Edges, doesn't have to be a face. If this area does not contain a face, it will simply be transparent or non-existent in the rendered image. To create a face, select three or four suitable vertices and press **FKEY**.

Basic Editing

Most simple operations from ObjectMode (like selecting, moving, rotating, and scaling) work identically on vertices as they do on objects. Thus, you can learn how to handle basic EditMode operations very quickly. The only notable difference is a new scaling opti-on, **ALT-S** which scales the selected vertices along the direction of the normals (shrinks-fattens). The truncated pyramid in figure 4, for example, was created with the following steps:

1. Add a cube to an empty scene. Enter EditMode.

2. Make sure all vertices are deselected (purple). Use border select (**BKEY**) to select the upper four vertices.

3. Check that the scaling center is set to *anything but* the 3D cursor (see fig. 1 in Chapter 5), then switch to scale mode (**SKEY**), reduce the size, and confirm with **LMB**.

4. Exit EditMode by pressing **TAB**.

One Extra feature for Edit Mode is the Mirroring tool. If you have some vertices selected and you press **MKEY** you will be presented with a Menu containing nine options. You can select from these to mirror the selected vertice with respect to any of the X,Y or Z axis of the Global, Local, or Viewing reference.

One additional feature of EditMode is the CircleSelect mode. It is invoked by pres-sing **BKEY** twice instead of only once, as you would for BorderSelect. A light grey circle is drawn around the cursor and any **LMB** click selects all vertices within. **NUM+** and **NUM-** or the **MW**, if any, enlarge or shrink the circle.

MESH MODELLING.BASIC EDITING

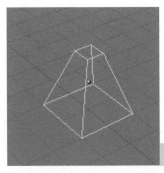

4 Chopped-off pyramid.

5 Edit Context.

All operations in Edit Mode are ultimately performed on the vertices; the connected edges and faces automatically adapt, as they depend on the vertices' positions. To select an edge, you must select the two endpoints or either place the mouse on the edge and press **CTRL-ALT-RMB**. To select a face, each corner must be selected.

Edit Mode operations are many, and most are summarized in the Editing Context Buttons window, accessed via the (🔲) button of header or via **F9** (fig 5). Note the group of buttons in the Mesh Tools 1 Panel.

- NSize - Determines the length, in Blender Units, of the normals to the faces, if they are drawn.
- Draw Normals - Toggle Normals drawing. If this is ON, face normals are drawn as cyan segments.
- Draw Faces - If this is ON, faces are drawn as semi-transparent blue, or as semi-transparent purple if they are selected. If this is OFF, faces are invisible.
- Draw Edges - Edges are always drawn black, but if this button is ON, selected edges are drawn in yellow. Edges joining a selected node and an un-selected one have a yellow-black gradient.
- All Edges - Only those edges strictly necessary to show the object shape are shown in Object mode. You can force Blender to draw all edges with this button.

Of course all these colors are customizable in the Theme editor.

With **WKEY** you can call up the "Specials" menu in EditMode (fig. 6). With this menu you can quickly access functions which are frequently required for polygon-model-ling.

You can access the entries in a PopupMenu by using the corresponding numberkey. For example, pressing **WKEY** and then **1KEY** you will subdivide the selected vertices without having to touch the mouse at all.

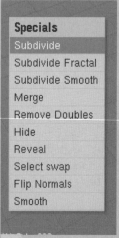

Specials

Subdivide
Subdivide Fractal
Subdivide Smooth
Merge
Remove Doubles
Hide
Reveal
Select swap
Flip Normals
Smooth

6 Specials Menu.

- Subdivide - Each selected edge is split in two, new vertices are created at middle points, and faces are split too, if necessary.
- Subdivide Fractal - As above, but new vertices are randomly displaced within a user-defined range.
- Subdivide Smooth - As above, but new vertices are displaced towards the baricentrum of the connected vertices.
- Merge - Merges selected vertices into a single one, at the baricentrum position or at the cursor position.
- Remove Doubles - Merges all of the selected vertices whose relative distance is below a given threshold (0.001 by default).
- Hide - Hides selected vertices.
- Reveal - Shows hidden vertices.
- Select Swap - All selected vertices become unselected and vice-versa.
- Flip Normals - Change the Normals directions in the selected faces.
- Smooth - Smooths out a mesh by moving each vertex towards the baricentrum of the linked vertices.
- Mirror - Same as **MKEY** described above.

Many of these actions have a button of their own in the Mesh Tools Panel of the Edit Buttons Window (fig. 5). The Remove doubles threshold can be adjusted here, too.

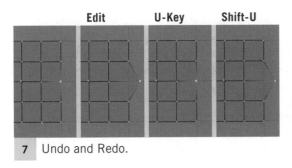

| Edit | U-Key | Shift-U |

7 Undo and Redo.

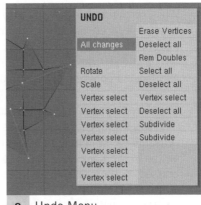

8 Undo Menu.

Mesh Undo

As for Blender 2.3 we finally have a true Undo. It works only for Meshes and only in Edit Mode.

Mesh undo works in the background saving copies of your mesh in memory as you make changes. Pressing the **UKEY** in mesh EditMode reverts to previously saved mesh, undoing the freshly performes edit operation (fig. 7).

Undo operations are only stored for one mesh at a time. You can leave and re-enter EditMode for the same mesh without losing any undo information, but once another mesh is edited, the undo information for the first is gone.

Pressing **SHIFT-U** re-does the last undo operation (fig. 7). Pressing **ALT-U** brings up the undo menu (fig. 8). This lists all the undo steps by name so you can quickly find your way back to a known good point in your work. The **ALT-U** menu also contains the option All Changes. This option is more powerfull than merely pressing **UKEY** repeadetly, and will reload the mesh data as it was at the beginning of your edit session even if you have used up all your undo steps.

Edit undo can be memory intensive. A mesh of 64,000 faces and verts can use over 3Mb of RAM per undo step. In case you are on a machine that is strapped for RAM, there is in the User Preference Window, under Edit Methods, a NumButton for determining the maximum number of undo steps saved. The allowed range is 1-64. The default is 32.

Smoothing

As seen in the previous sections, polygons are central to Blender. Most objects in Blender are represented by polygons and truly curved objects are often approximated by polygon meshes.

When rendering images, you may notice that these polygons appear as a series of small, flat faces (fig. 9). Sometimes this is a desirable effect, but usually we want our objects to look nice and smooth. This section shows you how to smooth an object, and how to apply the AutoSmooth filter to quickly and easily combine smooth and faceted polygons in the same object.

There are two ways to activate Blender's face smoothing features. The easiest way is to set an entire object as smooth or faceted by selecting a mesh object, in ObjectMode, switching to the Editing Context (**F9**), and clicking the Set Smooth button in the Link and Materials Panel (fig. 10). The button does not stay pressed, but forces Blender to assign the "smoothing" attribute to each face in the mesh. Now, rendering the image with **F12** should produce the image shown in figure 11. Notice that the outline of the object is still strongly faceted. Activating the smoothing features doesn't actually modify the object's geometry; it changes the way the shading is calculated across the surfaces, giving the illusion of a smooth surface.

Click the Set Solid button in the same Panel to revert the shading to that shown in figure 9.

Alternatively, you can choose which faces to smooth by entering EditMode for the object with **TAB**, then selecting the faces and clicking the Set Smooth button (fig. 12). When the mesh is in editmode, only the selected faces will receive the "smoothing" attribute. You can set solid faces (removing the "smoothing" attribute) in the same way: by selecting faces and clicking the Set Solid button.

It can be difficult to create certain combinations of smooth and solid faces using the above techniques alone. Though there are workarounds (such as splitting off sets of faces by selecting them and pressing **YKEY**), there is an easier way to combine smooth and solid faces, by using AutoSmooth.

Press the AutoSmooth button in the Mesh Panel of the Edit Buttons (fig. 13) to tell Blender to decide which faces should be smoothed on the basys of the angle between faces (fig. 14). Angles on the model that are sharper than the angle specified in the Degr NumBut will not be smoothed. Higher values will produce more smoothed faces, while the lowest setting will look identical to a mesh that has been set completely solid.

Only faces that have been set as smooth will be affected by the AutoSmooth feature. A mesh, or any faces that have been set as solid will not change their shading when AutoSmooth is activated. This allows you extra control over which faces will be smoothed and which ones won't by overriding the decisions made by the AutoSmooth algorithm.

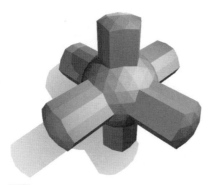

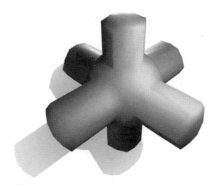

9   Simple un-smoothed test object.

11   Same object as in fig. 9, this time completely smoothed by 'Set Smooth'.

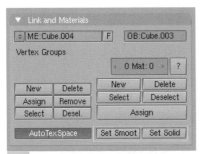

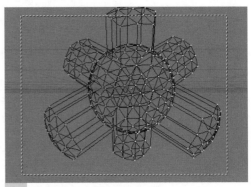

10   Set Smooth and Set Solid buttons of EditButtons context.

12   Object in editmode with some faces selected.

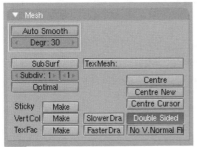

13   AutoSmooth button group in the EditButtons context.

14   Same test object with AutoSmooth enabled.

Proportional Editing Tool

When working with dense meshes, it can become difficult to make subtle adjustments to the vertices without causing nasty lumps and creases in the model's surface. When you face situations like these, use the proportional editing tool. It acts like a magnet to smoothly deform the surface of the model, without creating lumps and creases.

In a top-down view, add a plane mesh to the scene with **SPACE**>>Add>>Mesh>>
Plane. Subdivide it a few times with **WKEY**>>Subdivide (or by clicking on the Sub-
divide button in the Editing Context Mesh Tools Panel) to get a relatively dense mesh (fig. 15). Or, add a grid directly via **SPACE**>>Add>>Mesh>>Grid, specifying the number of vertices in each direction. When you are finished, deselect all vertices with **AKEY**.

 Vertex limit: A single mesh can have no more than 65,000 vertices.

Select a single vertex in the mesh by clicking it with **RMB** (fig. 16).

While still in EditMode, activate the proportional editing tool by pressing **OKEY** or by using the Mesh>>Proportional Editing Menu entry (fig. 17).

Switch to a front view (**NUM 1**) and activate the grab tool with **GKEY**. As you drag the point upwards, notice how nearby vertices are dragged along with it (fig. 18).

Change the curve profile used by either using the Mesh>>Proportional Fa-
loff submenu or by pressing **SHIFT-O** to toggle between the two options Sharp and Smooth. Note that you cannot do this while you are in the middle of a proportional editing operation; you will have to press **ESC** to cancel the editing operation before you can change the curve.

When you are satisfied with the placement of the vertex, press **LMB** to fix its position. If you are not satisfied, nullify the operation and revert your mesh to the way it looked before you started dragging the point with **ESC** key.

While you are editing you can increase or decrease the radius of influence (shown by the dotted circle in figure 18) by pressing **NUM+** and **NUM-** respectively. As you change the radius, the points surrounding your selection will adjust their positions accordingly.You can also use **MW** to enlarge and shrink the circle.

You can use the proportional editing tool to produce great effects with the scaling (**SKEY**) and rotation (**RKEY**) tools, as figure 19 shows.

Combine these techniques with vertex painting to create fantastic landscapes. Figure 20 shows the results of proportional editing after the application of textures and lighting.

MESH MODELLING.PROPORTIONAL EDITING TOOL

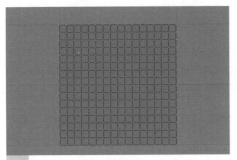

15 A planar dense mesh.

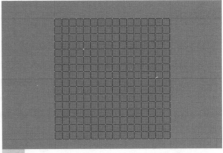

16 A planar dense mesh with just one selected vertex.

17 Proportional Editing icon (**OKEY**) and schemes.

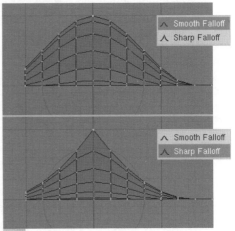

18 Different 'Magnets' for proportional Editing.

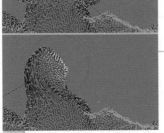

— **Scaling**

— **Rotation**

19 A landscape obtained via Proportional Editing.

20 Final rendered landscape

Extrude

One tool of paramount importance for working with Meshes is the "Extrude" command (**EKEY**). This command allows you to create cubes from rectangles and cylinders from circles, as well as to very easily create such things as tree limbs.

Although the process is quite intuitive, the principles behind Extrude are fairly elaborate as discussed below.

- First, the algorithm determines the outside edge-loop of the Extrude; that is, which among the selected edges will be changed into faces. By default, the algorithm considers edges belonging to two or more selected faces as internal, and hence not part of the loop.
- The edges in the edge-loop are then changed into faces.
- If the edges in the edge-loop belong to only one face in the complete mesh, then all of the selected faces are duplicated and linked to the newly created faces. For example, rectangles will result in cubes during this stage.
- In other cases, the selected faces are linked to the newly created faces but not duplicated. This prevents undesired faces from being retained 'inside' the resulting mesh. This distinction is extremely important since it ensures the construction of consistently coherent, closed volumes at all times when using Extrude.
- Edges not belonging to selected faces, which form an 'open' edge-loop, are duplicated and a new face is created between the new edge and the original one.
- Single selected vertices which do not belong to selected edges are duplicated and a new edge is created between the two.

Grab mode is automatically started when the Extrude algorithm terminates, so newly created faces, edges, and vertices can be moved around with the mouse.

Extrude is one of the most frequently used modelling tools in Blender. It's simple, straightforward, and easy to use, yet very powerful. The following short lesson describes how to build a sword using Extrude.

The Blade

1. Start Blender and delete the default plane. In top view add a mesh circle with eight vertices. Move the vertices so they match the configuration shown in figure 21.

2. Select all the vertices and scale them down with the **SKEY** so the shape fits in two grid units. Switch to front view with **NUM1**.

MESH MODELLING.CREATING A BLADE

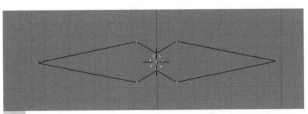

21 Deformed circle, to become the blade cross section.

22 Extrude button in EditButtons context.

23 Extrude confirmation box.

24 The Blade.

3. The shape we've created is the base of the blade. Using Extrude we'll create the blade in a few simple steps. With all vertices selected press **EKEY**, or click the `Extrude` button in the `Mesh Tools` Panel of the Editing Context (**F9** - fig. 22). A box will pop up asking `Ok? Extrude` (fig. 23).

Click this text or press **ENTER** to confirm, otherwise move the mouse outside or press **ESC** to exit. If you now move the mouse you'll see that Blender has duplicated the vertices, connected them to the original ones with edges and faces, and has entered grab mode.

4. Move the new vertices up 30 units, constraining the movement with **CTRL**, then click **LMB** to confirm their new position and scale them down a little bit with the **SKEY** (fig. 24).

5. Press **EKEY** again to extrude the tip of the blade, then move the vertices five units up. To make the blade end in one vertex, scale the top vertices down to 0.000 (hold **CTRL** for this) and press **WKEY**>`Remove Doubles` (fig. 25) or click the `Rem Doubles` button in the EditButtons (**F9**). Blender will inform you that it has removed seven of the eight vertices and only one vertex remains. The blade is complete! (fig. 26)

25 Mesh Edit Menu.

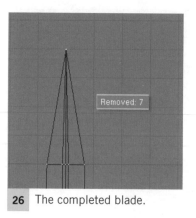

26 The completed blade.

The Handle

6. Leave Edit Mode and move the blade to the side. Add a UVsphere with 16 segments and rings and deselect all the vertices with the **AKEY**.

7. Borderselect the top three rings of vertices with **BKEY** and delete them with **XKEY**>>Vertices (fig. 27).

8. Select the top ring of vertices and extrude them. Move the ring up four units and scale them up a bit (fig. 28), then extrude and move four units again twice and scale the last ring down a bit (fig. 29).

9. Leave EditMode and scale the entire handle down so that it's in proportion with the blade. Place it just under the blade.

The Hilt

By now you should be used to the 'extrude>move>scale' sequence, so try to model a nice hilt with it. Start out with a cube and extrude different sides a few times, scaling them where needed. You should be able to get something like that shown in figure 30.

After texturing, the sword looks like figure 31.

As you can see, extrude is a very powerful tool that allows you to model relatively complex objects very quickly (the entire sword was created in less than one half hour). Getting the hang of extrude>move>scale will make your life as a Blender modeler a lot easier.

MESH MODELLING.CREATING A BLADE

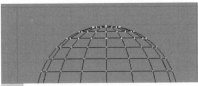

27 UV sphere for the handle: vertices to be removed.

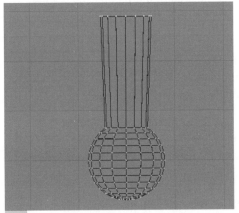

28 First extrusion for the handle.

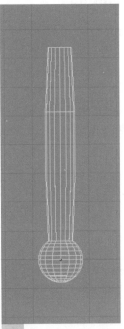

29 Complete handle.

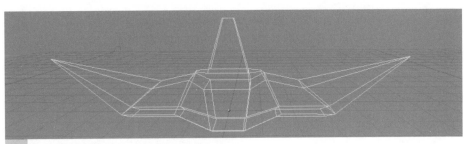

30 Complete Hilt.

31 Finished sword, with textures and materials.

Spin and SpinDup

Spin and spin dup are two other very powerful modelling tools allowing you to easily create bodies of revolution or axially periodic structures.

Spin

Use the Spin tool to create the sort of objects that you would produce on a lathe. (This tool is often called a "lathe"-tool or a "sweep"-tool in the literature, for this reason.)

First, create a mesh representing the profile of your object. If you are modeling a hollow object, it is a good idea to thicken the outline. Figure 32 shows the profile for a wine glass we will model as a demonstration.

In EditMode, with all the vertices selected, access the Editing Context (**F9**). The Degr button in the Mesh Tools Panel indicates the number of degrees to spin the object (in this case we want a full 360° sweep). The Steps button specifies how many profiles there will be in the sweep (fig. 33).

Like Spin Duplicate (discussed in the next section), the effects of Spin depend on the placement of the cursor and which window (view) is active. We will be rotating the object around the cursor in the top view. Switch to the top view with **NUM7**.

1. Place the cursor along the center of the profile by selecting one of the vertices along the center, and snapping the cursor to that location with **SHIFT-S**>>Curs->Sel. Figure 34 shows the wine glass profile from top view, with the cursor correctly positioned.

    Before continuing, note the number of vertices in the profile. You'll find this information in the Info bar at the top of the Blender interface (fig. 35).

2. Click the "Spin" button. If you have more than one window open, the cursor will change to an arrow with a question mark and you will have to click in the window containing the top view before continuing. If you have only one window open, the spin will happen immediately. Figure 36 shows the result of a successful spin.

3. The spin operation leaves duplicate vertices along the profile. You can select all vertices at the seam with Box select (**BKEY**) (fig. 37) and do a Remove Doubles operation.

    Notice the selected vertex count before and after the Remove Doubles operation (fig. 38).

    If all goes well, the final vertex count (38 in this example) should match the number of the original profile noted in figure 35 If not, some vertices were missed and you will need to weld them manually. Or, worse, too many vertices have been merged.

MESH MODELLING.SPIN AND SPINDUP

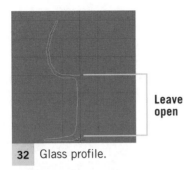

Leave open

32 Glass profile.

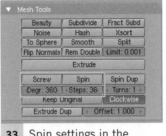

33 Spin settings in the EditButtons context.

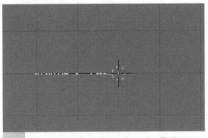

34 Glass profile, top view in Edit Mode, just before spinning.

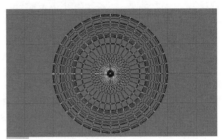

36 Spinned profile.

35 Number of vertices in the profile.

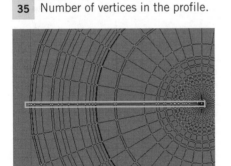

37 Seam vertex selection.

40 Final render of the glasses.

Before

After

38 Number of selected vertices before and after removing doubles.

Specials
Subdivide
Subdivide Fractal
Subdivide Smooth
Merge
Remove Doubles
Hide
Reveal
Select swap
Flip Normals
Smooth

39 Merge menu.

Merging two vertices in one

To merge (weld) two vertices together, select both of them by holding **SHIFT** and **RMB** on them. Press **SKEY** to start scaling and hold down **CONTROL** while scaling to scale the points down to 0 units in the X,Y and Z axis. **LMB** to complete the scaling operation and click the Remove Doubles button in the EditButtons window.

Alternatively, you can press **WKEY** and select Merge from the appearing Menu (fig. 39). Then, in a new menu, whoose whether the merged node will have to be at the center of the selected nodes or at the cursor. The first choice is better in our case.

All that remains now is to recalculate the normals by selecting all vertices and pressing **CTRL-N**>>Recalc Normals Outside. At this point you can leave EditMode and apply materials or smoothing, set up some lights, a camera and make a rendering. Figure 40 shows our wine glass in a finished state.

SpinDup

The Spin Dup tool is a great way to quickly make a series of copies of an object along a circle. For example, if you have modeled a clock, and you now want to add hour marks.

Model just one mark, in the 12 o'clock position (fig. 41). Select the mark and switch to the Editing Context with **F9**. Set the number of degrees in the Degr: Num Button in the Mesh Tools Panel to 360. We want to make 12 copies of our object, so set the Steps to 12 (fig. 42).

- Switch the view to the one in which you wish to rotate the object by using the key pad. Note that the result of the Spin Dupe command depends on the view you are using when you press the button.
- Position the cursor at the center of rotation. The objects will be rotated around this point.
- Select the object you wish to duplicate and enter EditMode with **TAB**.
- In EditMode, select the vertices you want to duplicate (note that you can select all vertices with **AKEY** or all of the vertices linked to the point under the cursor with **LKEY**) See figure 43.

To place the cursor at the precise location of an existing object or vertex, select the object or vertex, and press **SHIFT-S**>>CURS>>SEL.

MESH MODELLING.SPIN AND SPINDUP

41 Hour mark indicated by the rectangle.

42 Spin Dup buttons.

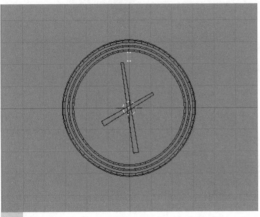

43 Mesh selected and ready to be SpinDuped.

- Press the Spin Dup button. If you have more than one 3DWindow open, you will notice the mouse cursor change to an arrow with a question mark. Click in the window in which you want to do your rotation. In this case, we want to use the front window (fig. 44).

If the view you want is not visible, you can dismiss the arrow/question mark with **ESC** until you can switch a window to the appropriate view with the keypad

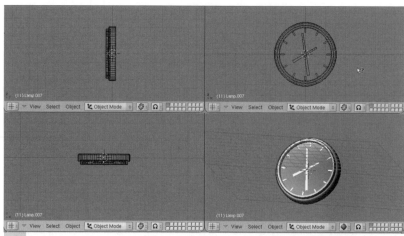

44 View Selection for SpinDup.

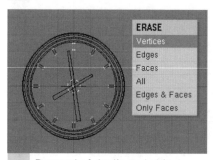

45 Removal of duplicated object.

46 Final Clock Render.

When spin-duplicating an object 360 degrees, a duplicate object is placed at the same location of the first object, producing duplicate geometry. You will notice that after clicking the Spin Dup button, the original geometry remains selected. To delete it, simply press **XKEY**>>VERTICES. The source object is deleted, but the duplicated version beneath it remains (fig. 45).

Avoiding Dublicates

If you like a little math you needn't bother with duplicates because you can avoid them at the start. Just make 11 duplicates, not 12, and not around the whole 360°, but just through 330° (that is 360*11/12). This way no duplicate is placed over the original object.

In general, to make *n* duplicates over 360 degrees without overlapping, just spin one less object over 360*(*n*-1)/*n* degrees.

Figure 46 shows the final rendering of the clock.

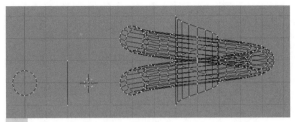

47 How to make a spring: before (left) and after (right) the Screwl tool.

Screw

The "Screw" tool combines a repetitive "Spin" with a translation, to generate a screw-like, or spiral-shaped,object. Use this tool to create screws, springs, or shell-shaped structures.

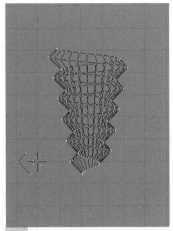

48 Enlarging screw (right) obtained with the profile on the left.

The method for using the "Screw" function is strict:

- Set the 3DWindow to *front view* (**NUM1**).
- Place the 3DCursor at the position through which the rotation axis must pass. Such an axis will be vertical.
- Ensure that an *open poly line* is available. This can be a single edge, as shown in the figure, or a half circle, or whatever. You need only to ensure that there are two 'free' ends; two vertices belonging to a single edge linking then to another vertex. The "Screw" function localizes these two points and uses them to calculate the translation vector that is added to the "Spin" per each full rotation (fig. 47). If these two vertices are at the same location, this creates a normal "Spin". Otherwise, interesting things happen!
- Select all vertices that will participate in the "Screw".
- Assign the Num Buttons Steps: and Turns: in the Mesh Tools Panel the desired values. Steps: determines how many times the profile is repeated within each 360° rotation, while Turns: sets the number of complete 360° rotations to be performed.
- Press Screw!

If there are multiple 3D Windows, the mouse cursor changes to a question mark. Click on the 3D Window in which the "Screw" is to be executed.

If the two "free" ends are aligned vertically the result is the one seen above. If they are not, the translation vector remains vertical, equal to the vertical component of the vector joining the two 'free' vertices, while the horizontal component generates an enlargement (or reduction) of the screw as shown in figure 48.

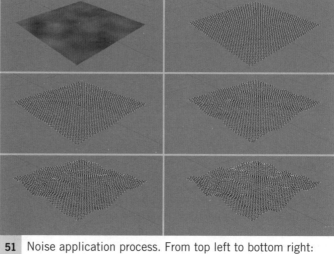

Specials
Subdivide
Subdivide Fractal
Subdivide Smooth
Merge
Remove Doubles
Hide
Reveal
Select swap
Flip Normals
Smooth

49 Subdivide tool.

51 Noise application process. From top left to bottom right: Plane with texture, subdivided plane, "Noise" button hit 2, 4, 6 and 8 times.

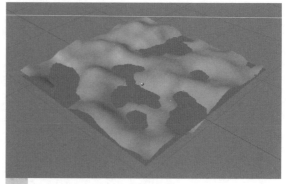

50 Noise Button in Edit Buttons.

52 Noise generated landscape.

Noise

The noise function allows you to displace vertices in meshes based on the grey-values of a texture applied to it. That way you can generate great landscapes or carve text into meshes.

Add a plane and subdivide it at least five times with the special menu **WKEY**>>Subdivide (fig. 49). Now add a material and assign a Clouds texture to it. Adjust the NoiseSize: to 0.500. Choose white as the color for the material and black as the texture color, to give us good contrast for the noise operation.

Ensure that you are in EditMode and that all vertices are selected, then switch to the Editing Context **F9**. Press the `Noise` button in the `Mesh Tools` Panel (fig. 50) several times until the landscape looks nice. Figure 51 shows the original - textured - plane as well as what happens as you press `Noise`. Remove the texture from the landscape now because it will disturb the look. Then add some lights, some water, set smooth and SubSurf the terrain, and so on (fig. 52).

> The noise displacement always occurs along the mesh's *z* coordinate, which is along the direction of the *z* axis of the Object local reference.

Warp Tool

The warp tool is a little-known tool in Blender, partly because it is not found in the EditButtons window, and partly because it is only useful in very specific cases. At any rate, it is not something that the average Blender-user needs to use every day.

A piece of text wrapped into a ring shape is useful when creating flying logos, but it would be difficult to model without the use of the warp tool. For our example, we'll warp the phrase "Amazingly Warped Text" around a sphere.

1. First add the sphere.

2. Then add the text in front view, in the Editing Context and `Curve and Surface` Panel set `Ext1` to 0.1 - making the text 3D, and set `Ext2` to 0.01, adding a nice bevel to the edge. Make the `BevResol` 1 or 2 to have a smooth bevel and lower the resolution so that the vertex count will not be too high when you subdivide the object later on (fig. 53 - and see the Section called *Text* in Chapter 7). Convert the object to curves, then to a mesh, (**ALT-C** twice) because the warp tool does not work on text or on curves. Subdivide the mesh twice, so that the geometry will change shape cleanly, without artifacts.

Switch to top view and move the mesh away from the 3D cursor. This distance defines the radius of the warp (see fig. 54.)

Place the mesh in Edit Mode (**TAB**) and press **AKEY** to select all vertices. Press **SHIFT-W** to activate the warp tool. Move the mouse up or down to interactively define the amount of warp (fig. 55). Holding down **CTRL** makes warp change in steps of five degrees.

Now you can switch to camera view, add materials, lights and render (fig. 56).

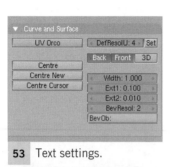

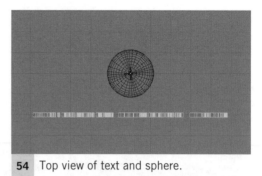

53 Text settings.

54 Top view of text and sphere.

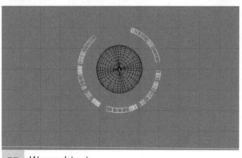

55 Warped text.

56 Final rendering.

Catmull-Clark Subdivision Surfaces

With any regular Mesh as a starting point, Blender can calculate a smooth subdivision on the fly, while modeling or while rendering, using Catmull-Clark Subdivision Surfaces or, in short *SubSurf*. SubSurf is a mathematical algorithm to compute a "smooth" subdivision of a mesh. This allows high resolution Mesh modelling without the need to save and maintain huge amounts of data. This also allows for a smooth 'organic' look to the models.

Actually a SubSurfed Mesh and a NURBS surface have many points in common inasmuch as both rely on a "coarse" low-poly "mesh" to define a smooth "high definition" surface. But there are also notable differences:

- NURBS allow for finer control on the surface, since you can set "weights" independently on each control point of the control mesh. On a SubSurfed mesh you cannot act on weights.

- SubSurfs have a more flexible modeling approach. Since a SubSurf is a mathematical operation occurring on a mesh, you can use all the modeling techniques described in this chapter on the mesh. These techniques are more numerous, and far more flexible, than those available for NURBS control polygons.

MESH MODELLING.SUBDIVISION SURFACES

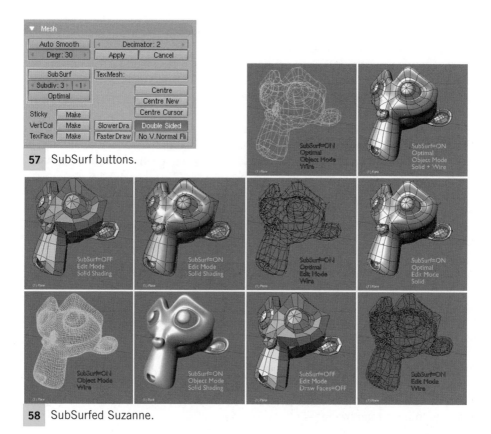

57 SubSurf buttons.

58 SubSurfed Suzanne.

SubSurf is a Mesh option, activated in the Editing Context Mesh Panel (**F9** - fig. 57). The Num Buttons immediately below it define, on the left, the resolution (or level) of subdivision for 3D visualization purposes; the one on the right the resolution for rendering purposes. You can also use **SHIFT-O** if you are in ObjectMode. This switches SubSurf On/Off. The SubSurf level is controlled via **CTRL-1** to **CTRL-4**, but only for the visualization.

Since SubSurf computations are performed both real-time, while you model, and at render time, and they are CPU intensive, it is usually good practice to keep the SubSurf level low (but non-zero) while modeling; higher while rendering.

As for version 2.3 Blender has a new SubSurfed-related button: Optimal This changes the way SubSurf mesh are drawn and can be of great help in modelling.

Figure 58 shows a series of pictures showing various different combinations on Suzanne Mesh.

Figure 59 shows a 0,1,2,3 level of SubSurf on a single square face or on a single triangular face. Such a subdivision is performed, on a generic mesh, for *each* square or rectangular face.

It is evident how each single quadrilateral face produces 4^n faces in the SubSurfed mesh. n is the SubSurf level, or resolution, while each triangular face produces $3*4^{(n-1)}$ new faces (fig. 59). This dramatic increase of face (and vertex) number results in a slow-down of all editing, and rendering, actions and calls for lower SubSurf level in the editing process than in the rendering one.

Blender's subdivision system is based on the Catmull-Clark algorithm. This produces nice smooth SubSurf meshes but any 'SubSurfed' face, that is, any small face created by the algorithm from a single face of the original mesh, shares the normal orientation of that original face.

This is not an issue for the shape itself, as figure 60 shows, but it is an issue in the rendering phase, and in solid mode, where abrupt normal changes can produce ugly black lines (fig. 61).

Use the **CTRL+N** command in EditMode, with all vertices selected, to make Blender recalculate the normals.

In these images the face normals are drawn cyan. You can enable drawing normals in the EditButtons (**F9**) menu.

Note that Blender cannot recalculate normals correcty if the mesh is not "Manifold". A "Non-Manifold" mesh is a mesh for which an 'out' cannot unequivocally be computed. Basically, from the Blender point of view, it is a mesh where there are edges belonging to *more* than two faces.

Figure 62 shows a very simple example of a "Non-Manifold" mesh. In general a "Non-Manifold" mesh occurs when you have internal faces and the like.

A "Non-Manifold" mesh is not a problem for conventional meshes, but can give rise to ugly artifacts in SubSurfed meshes. Also, it does not allow decimation, so it is better to avoid them as much as possible.

Use these two hints to tell whether a mesh is "Non Manifold":

* The Recalculation of normals leaves black lines somewhere.
* The "Decimator" tool in the Mesh Panel refuses to work stating that the mesh is "No Manifold".

The SubSurf tool allows for very good "organic" models, but remember that a regular Mesh with square faces, rather than triangular, gives the best result.

Figure 63 and 64 show an example of what can be done with Blender SubSurfs.

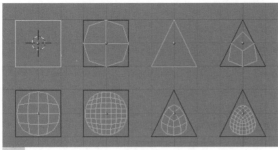

59 Different stages of SubDivision for a plane and a triangle.

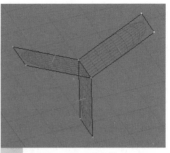

62 A "Non-Manifold" mesh.

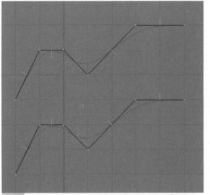

60 Side view of subsurfed meshes. With random normals (top) and with coherent normals (bottom).

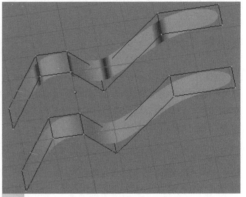

61 Solid view of SubSurfed meshes with inconsistent normals (top) and consistent normals (bottom).

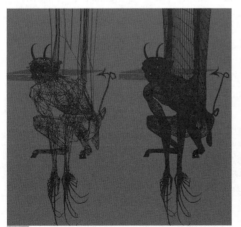

63 A Gargoyle base mesh (left) and pertinent level 2 SubSurfed Mesh (right).

64 Solid view (left) and final rendering (right) of the Gargoyle.

Edge Tools

Starting with Blender 2.30 some brand new modeling tools are being added. These are focused on Edge, as opposed to vertex, modeling.

A key issue in Modelling is often the necessity to add vertices in certain zones of the mesh, and this is often regarded as splitting, or adding, edges in a given region. Blender now presents two tools for this, a *Knife Tool* able to split edges in desired locations and a *face loop* tool, able to select face paths and split them consistently.

The Edge Tools are grouped in a menu which is linked to **KKEY** Hotkey, but each single tool has its own hotkey as well.

Knife Tool

The Knife Tool works by subdividing edges if both their verts are selected and the edge is intersected by a user-drawn "knife" line. For example, if you wish to cut a hole only in the front of a sphere, you can select only the front vertices, and then draw the line with the mouse.

To test the tool add a Grid Mesh. You will be in Edit Mode and all vertices are selected. Press **SHIFT-K** to go activate the Knife Tool. You are prompted to choose the type of cut: Exact will divide the edges exactly where the knife line crosses them, Centers divides an intersected edge at its midpoint. For this cut, we chose Centers.

Now you can click **LMB** and start drawing. If you move and click **LMB** you draw straight segments from clicked point to clicked point; if you hold **LMB** pressed while dragging you draw freehand lines. The polylines can be drawn with an arbitrary number of segments, but the intersection routines only detect one crossing per edge. Crossing back over an edge mulitple times does not perform additional cuts on it. **MMB** constrains drawing to an axis as expected. Snap to grid is not currently implimented, but is being looked at for future releases. When you are done drawing your line, hit **ENTER** to confirm the cut. **ESC** at any time cancels the operation. Figure 65 shows some examples.

With a large mesh, it will be quicker to select a smaller number of vertices, those defining only the edges you plan to split since the Knife will save time in testing selected vertices for knife trail crossings.

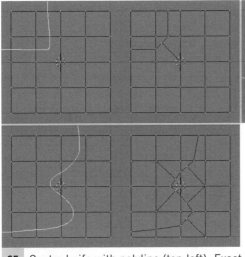

65 Center knife with polyline (top left); Exact Knife with single segment (top right) and Exact freehand knife (bottom left).

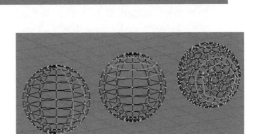

66 One opened (Left) and two closed (center and right) Faceloops.

Face Loop

The face loop tool allows to select and, eventually, split, a *loop* of faces. This loop is defined starting from an edge, below the mouse pointer, and the two faces sharing that edge.

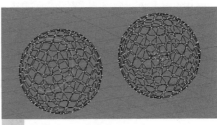

67 Splitting a faceloop.

The two faces belongs to the loop, every further face opposed to these is also part of the loop. The loop ends when a triangular face is reached or the loop closes on itself. Loop selection is activated with **SHIFT-R** (fig. 66).

By moving the mouse different face loops are highlighted. Press **LMB** or **ENTER** to select the desired one, **ESC** to exit.

If the face loop selection is enetered via **CTRL-R** rather than **SHIFT-R** then the action performed is not a mere selection, but the face loop is splitted in two along its median line. This is really precious to refine a mesh in a SubSurface-Friendly way (fig. 67).

Both Face Loop tools are present in the **KKEY** menu too.

Meta Objects

Meta Objects consist of spherical or tubular, cubical and so on elements that can affect each other's shape. You can only create rounded and fluid, 'mercurial,' or 'clay-like' forms that exist *procedurally*, that is are computed dynamically. Use Meta Objects for special effects or as a basis for modelling.

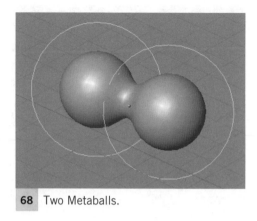

68 Two Metaballs.

Meta Objects are also called *implicit surfaces*, again to point out that are not *explicitely* defined by vertices (as mesh are) or control points (as surfaces are).

Meta Objects are defined by a *directing structure* which can be seen as the source of a static field. The field can be either positive or negative and hence the field generated by neighbouring directing structures can add or subtract.

The implicit surface is defined as the surface where the 3D field generated by all the directing structures assumes a given value. For example a Meta Ball, whose directing structure is a point, generate an isotropic field around it and the surfaces at constant field value are spheres centered at the directing point. Two neighbouring Metaballs interact and, if they are close enough, the two implicit surfaces merge in a single one (fig. 68).

In fact, Meta Objects are nothing more than mathematical formulas that perform logical operations on one another (AND, OR), and that can be added and subtracted from each other. This method is also called CSG, Constructive Solid Geometry. Because of its mathematical nature, CSG uses few memory, but requires lots of CPU to compute. To optimize this the implicit surfaces are *polygonized*. The complete CSG area is divided into a 3D grid, and for each *edge* in the grid a calculation is made, and if (and more importantly where) the formula has a turning point, a 'vertex' for the *polygonize* is created.

To create a Meta Object press **SPACE** and select Add>>MBall. You can select the base shapes: Ball, Tube, Plane, Ellipsoid, Cube.

MetaBalls have a point directing structure, MetaTubes have a segment as a directing structure, MetaPlanes a plane and MetaCubes a cube. The underlying structure becomes more evident as you lower the Wiresize and rise the Threshold values in the Meta Ball Panel.

MESH MODELLING.METABALLS

When in EditMode, you can move and scale the Meta Objects as you wish. This is the best way to construct static - opposed to animated - forms. Meta Objects can also influence each other *outside* EditMode. When outside EditMode you have much more freedom; the balls can rotate or move and they get every *transformation* of the Parents' Objects. This method requires more calculation time and is thus somewhat slow.

The following rules describe the relation between Meta Objects:

• All Meta Objects with the same 'family' name (the name without the number) influence each other. For example "MBall", "MBall.001", "MBall.002", "MBall.135". Note here that we are not talking about the name of the MetaBall ObData block.

• The Object with the family name *without* a number determines the basis, the resolution, *and* the transformation of the polygonize. It also has the Material and texture area and will be referred to as *base* Meta Object.

Only one Material can be used for a Meta Object set. In addition, Meta Objects saves a separate texture area; this normalises the coordinates of the vertices. Normally the texture area is identical to the *boundbox* of all vertices. The user can force a texture area with the **TKEY** command (outside of Edit Mode).

The fact that the base Object dictates the polygonalization implies that, if we have two Meta Objects and we move one of them we will see the poligonalization of the *non-base* Object change during motion, regardless of which of the two object is actually moving.

The Meta Ball Panel in Editing context presents few settings. If in Object Mode only this Panel is present. You can define here the polygonalization average dimension both in the 3D Viewport, via the Wiresize Num Button, and at rendering time, via tha Rendersize Num Button. THe lower these are the smoother the Meta Object is, and theslower its computation.

The Threshold Num Button is an important setting for MetaObject. It controls the 'field level' at which the surface is computed. To have a finer control, when in Edit Mode, the Stiffness Num Button of the Meta Ball Tools Panel allows to enlarge or restrict the MetaObject field of influence.

In this latter Panel you can also change the Meta Object type and set it negative, that is subtractive rather than addictive with other Meta Objects of the same set.

CH. 7 CURVES AND SURFACES

CURVES, SURFACES, EXRUDE ALONG PATH, SKINNING

Curves and surfaces are objects like meshes, but differ in that they are expressed in terms of mathematical functions, rather than as a series of points.

Blender implements Bézier and Non Uniform Rational B-Splines (NURBS) curves and surfaces. Both, though following different mathematical laws, are defined in terms of a set of "control vertices" which define a "control polygon." The way the curve and the surface are interpolated (Bézier) or attracted (NURBS) by these might seem similar, at first glance, to Catmull-Clark subdivision surfaces.

When compared to meshes, curves and surfaces have both advantages and disadvantages. Because curves are defined by less data, they produce nice results using less memory at modelling time, whereas the demands increase at rendering time.

Some modelling techniques, such as extruding a profile along a path, are only possible with curves. But the very fine control available on a per-vertex basis on a mesh, is not possible with curves.

There are times when curves and surfaces are more advantageous than meshes, and times when meshes are more useful. If you have read the previous Chapter, and if you read this you will be able to choose whether to use meshes or curves.

Curves

This section describes both Bézier and NURBS curves, and shows a working example of the former.

Béziers

Bézier curves are the most commonly used type for designing letters or logos. They are also widely used in animation, both as paths for objects to move along and as IPO curves to change the properties of objects as a function of time.

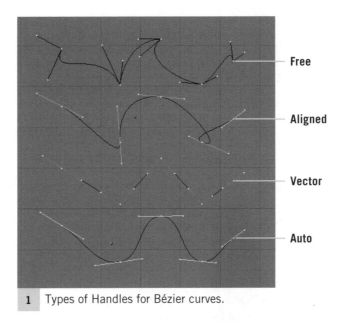

1 Types of Handles for Bézier curves.

A control point (vertex) of a Bézier curve consists of a point and two handles. The point, in the middle, is used to move the entire control point; selecting it also selects the other two handles, and allows you to move the complete vertex. Selecting one or two of the other handles allows you to change the shape of the curve by dragging the handles.

A Bézier curve is tangent to the line segment which goes from the point to the handle. The 'steepness' of the curve is controlled by the handle's length.

There are four types of handles (fig. 1):

- Free Handle (black). This can be used in any way you wish. Hotkey: **HKEY** (toggles between Free and Aligned);
- Aligned Handle (purple). These handles always lie in a straight line. Hotkey: **HKEY** (toggles between Free and Aligned);
- Vector Handle (green). Both parts of a handle always point to the previous handle or the next handle. Hotkey: **VKEY**;
- Auto Handle (yellow). This handle has a completely automatic length and direction, set by Blender to ensure the smoothest result. Hotkey: **SHIFT-H**.

Handles can be *grabbed*, *rotated* and *scaled* exactly as ordinary vertices in a mesh would.

As soon as the handles are moved, the type is modified automatically:

* Auto Handle becomes Aligned;
* Vector Handle becomes Free.

Although the Bézier curve is a continuous mathematical object it must nevertheless be represented in discerete form from a rendering point of view.

This is done by setting a *resolution* property, which defines the number of points which are computed between every pair of control points. A separate *resolution* can be set for each Bézier curve (fig. 2).

NURBS

NURBS curves are defined as rational polynomials, and are more general, strictly speaking, than conventional B-Splines and Bézier curves inasmuch they are able to exactly follow any contour. For example a Bézier circle is a polynomial *approximation* of a circle, and this approximation is noticeable, whereas a NURBS circle is *exactly* a circle. NURBS curves have a large set of variables, which allow you to create mathematically pure forms (fig. 3). However, working with them requires a little more theory:

* *Knots.* NURBS curves have a *knot* vector, a row of numbers that specifies the parametric definition of the curve. Two pre-sets are important for this. Uniform produces a uniform division for closed curves, but when used with open ones you will get "free" ends, which are difficult to locate precisely. Endpoint sets the knots in such a way that the first and last vertices are always part of the curve, which makes them much easier to place;

* *Order.* The *order* is the 'depth' of the curve calculation. Order '1' is a point, order '2' is linear, order '3' is quadratic, and so on. Always use order '5' for Curve paths because it behaves fluidly under all circumstances, without producing irritating discontinuities in the movement. Mathematically speaking this is the order of both the Numerator and the Denominator of the rational polynomial defining the NURBS;

* *Weight.* NURBS curves have a 'weight' per vertex - the extent to which a vertex participates in the "pulling" of the curve.

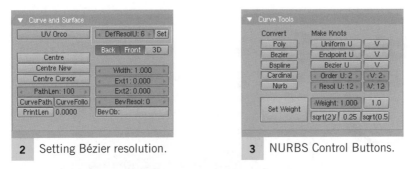

2   Setting Bézier resolution.

3   NURBS Control Buttons.

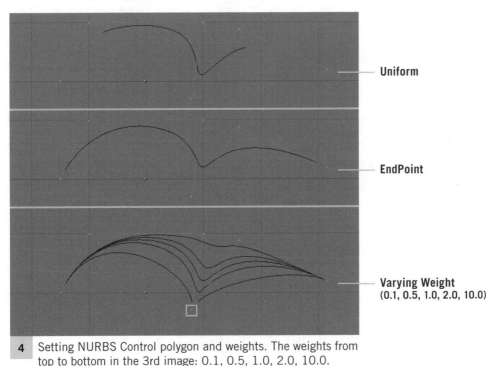

— Uniform

— EndPoint

— Varying Weight
(0.1, 0.5, 1.0, 2.0, 10.0)

4   Setting NURBS Control polygon and weights. The weights from
top to bottom in the 3rd image: 0.1, 0.5, 1.0, 2.0, 10.0.

Figure 4 shows the control polygon as well as the effect of varying a single knot
weight. As with Béziers, the resolution can be set on a per curve basis.

Working example

Blender's curve tools provide a quick and easy way to build great looking extruded text
and logos. We will use these tools to turn a rough sketch of a logo into a finished 3D
object.

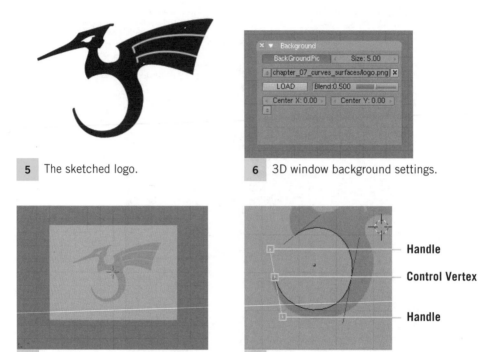

5 The sketched logo.

6 3D window background settings.

7 Logo sketch loaded as background.

8 Bézier handles.

Handle

Control Vertex

Handle

Figure 5 shows the design of the logo we will be building.

First, we will import our original sketch so that we can use it as a template. Blender supports TGA, PNG, and JPG format images. To load the image, select the `View>>Background Image...` menu entry of the 3D Window you are using. A transparent panel will appear, allowing you to select a picture to use as a background. Activate the `BackGroundPic` button and use the `LOAD` button to locate the image you want to use as a template (fig. 6). You can set the "strength" of the background pic with the `Blend` slider.

Get rid of the Panel with ESC or by pressing the x button in the panel header (fig. 7). You can hide the background image when you are finished using it by returning to the Panel and deselecting the `BackGroundPic` button.

Add a new curve by pressing **SPACE**`>>Curve>>Bézier Curve`. A curved segment will appear and Blender will enter EditMode. We will move and add points to make a closed shape that describes the logo you are trying to trace.

You can add points to the curve by selecting one of the two endpoints, then holding

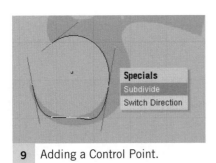

9 Adding a Control Point.

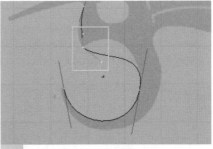

10 Vector (green) handles.

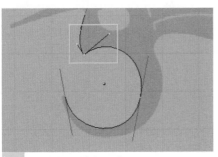

11 Free (black) handles.

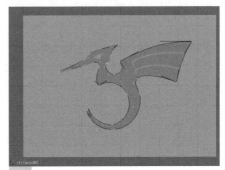

12 The finished outline.

CTRL and clicking **LMB**. Note that the new point will be connected to the previously selected point. Once a point has been added, it can be moved by selecting the control vertex and pressing **GKEY**. You can change the angle of the curve by grabbing and moving the handles associated with each vertex (fig. 8).

You can add a new point between two existing points by selecting the two points and pressing **WKEY**>>Subdivide (fig. 9).

Points can be removed by selecting them and pressing **XKEY**>>Selected. To cut a curve in two, select two adjacent control vertices and press **XKEY**>>Segment.

To make sharp corners, select a control vertex and press **VKEY**. You will notice that the color of the handles changes from purple to green (fig. 10). At this point, you can move the handles to adjust the way the curve enters and leaves the control vertex (fig. 11).

To close the curve and turn it into a single continuous loop, select at least one of the control vertices on the curve and press **CKEY**. This will connect the last point in the curve with the first one (fig. 12). You may need to manipulate additional handles to get the shape you want.

Leaving EditMode with **TAB** and entering shaded mode with **ZKEY** should reveal that the curve renders as a solid shape (fig. 13). We want to cut some holes into this shape to represent the eyes and wing details of the dragon.

Surfaces and Holes

When working with curves, Blender automatically detects holes in the surface and handles them accordingly to the following rules. A closed curve is always considered the boundary of a surface and hence rendered as a flat surface. If a closed curve is completely included within another one, the former is subtracted from the latter, effectively defining a hole.

Return to wireframe mode with **ZKEY** and enter EditMode again with **TAB**. While still in EditMode, add a circle curve with **SPACE**>>Curve>>Bézier Circle (fig. 14). Scale the circle down to an appropriate size with **SKEY** and move it with **GKEY**.

Shape the circle using the techniques we have learned (fig. 15). Remember to add vertices to the circle with **WKEY**>>Subdivide.

Create a wing cutout by adding a Bézier circle, converting all of the points to sharp corners, and then adjusting as necessary. You can duplicate this outline to save time when creating the second wing cutout. To do so, make sure no points are selected, then move the cursor over one of the vertices in the first wing cutout and select all linked points with **LKEY** (fig. 16). Duplicate the selection with **SHIFT-D** and move the new points into position.

To add more geometry that is not connected to the main body (placing an orb in the dragon's curved tail for example), use the **SHIFT-A** menu to add more curves as shown in figure 17.

Now that we have the curve, we need to set its thickness and beveling options. With the curve selected, go to the EditButtons (**F9**) and locate the Curves and Surface panel. The Ext1 parameter sets the thickness of the extrusion while Ext2 sets the size of the bevel. BevResol sets how sharp or curved the bevel will be.

Figure 18 shows the settings used to extrude this curve.

From Curves to Meshes

To perform more complex modeling operations, convert the curve to a mesh with **ALT-C**>>Mesh. Note that this is a one-way operation: you cannot convert a mesh back into a curve.

When your logo model is complete, you can add materials and lights and make a nice rendering (fig. 19).

13 Shaded Logo.

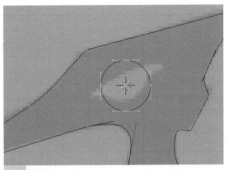

14 Adding a cricle.

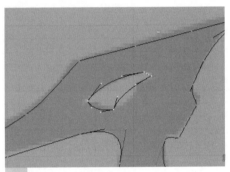

15 Defining the eye.

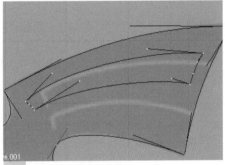

16 Defining the wings.

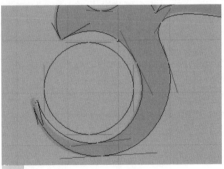

17 Orb placement within the tail.

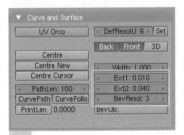

18 Bevel settings.

19 Final rendering.

Surfaces

Surfaces are actually an extension of NURBS curves. In Blender they are a separate ObData type.

Whereas a curve produces only one-dimensional interpolation, Surfaces have a second extra dimension. The first dimension is U, as for curves, and the second is V. A two-dimensional grid of control points defines the form for these NURBS surfaces.

Use Surfaces to create and revise fluid curved surfaces. Surfaces can be cyclical in both directions, allowing you to easily create a 'donut' shape, and they can be drawn as 'solids' in EditMode (zbuffered, with OpenGL lighting). This makes working with surfaces quite easy.

 Currently Blender has a basic tool set for Surfaces, with limited Ability to create holes and melt surfaces. Future versions will contain increased functionality in these areas.

You can take one of the various surface 'primitives' from the Add menu as a starting point (fig. 20). Note that you can choose 'Curve' and 'Circle' from the 'surface' menu! This is possible because NURBS curves are intrinsically NURBS Surfaces, simply having one dimension neglected.

 A NURBS 'true' curve and a NURBS 'surface' curve are not interchangeable, as you'll see as you follow the extruding process below and the skinning section further on.

When you add a 'surface' curve you can create a true surface simply by extruding the entire curve (**EKEY**). Each edge of a surface can then be extruded as you wish to form the model. Use **CKEY** to make the U or V direction cyclic. Be sure to set the 'knots' to Uniform or Endpoint with one of the pre-sets from the EditButtons Curve Tools panel.

When working with surfaces, it is handy to always work on a complete column or row of vertices. Blender provides a selection tool for this: **SHIFT-R**, "Select Row". Starting from the last selected vertex, a complete row of vertices is *extend* selected in the 'U' or 'V' direction. Choose Select Row again with the same vertex to toggle between the 'U' of 'V' selection.

NURBS can create pure shapes such as circles, cylinders, and spheres (remember that a Bézier circle is not a pure circle.) To create pure circles, globes, or cylinders, you must set the weights of the vertices. This is not intuitive, and you should read more on NURBS before trying this.

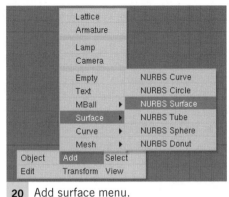

20 Add surface menu.

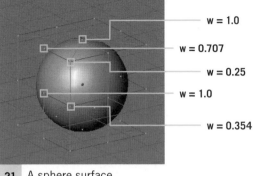

w = 1.0
w = 0.707
w = 0.25
w = 1.0
w = 0.354

21 A sphere surface.

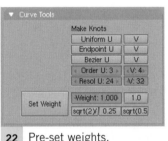

22 Pre-set weights.

23 Text examples.

Basically, to produce a circular arc from a curve with three control points, the end points must have a unitary weight, while the weight of the central control point must be equal to one-half the cosine of half the angle between the segments joining the points. Figure 21 shows this for a globe. Three standard numbers are included as presets in the EditButtons Curve Tools panel (fig. 22).

To read the weight of a selected vertex, press the **NKEY**.

Text

Text is a special curve type for Blender. Blender has its own built-in font but can use external fonts too, including both PostScript Type 1 fonts and TrueType fonts (fig. 23).

Open Blender or revert to a fresh scene by pressing **CTRL-X**. Add a TextObject with the Toolbox (SPACE>>Add>>Text). You can edit the text with the keyboard In Edit-Mode; a text cursor shows your position in the text. When you leave EditMode with

TAB, Blender fills the text-curve, producing a flat filled object that is renderable at once.

Now go to the EditButtons **F9** (fig. 24).

As you can see in the `Font` panel MenuButton, Blender uses its own `<builtin>` font by default when creating a new TextObject. Now click `Load Font`. Browse in the File-Window to a directory containing PostScript Type 1 or True Type fonts and load a new font. (You can download several free PostScript fonts from the web, and Microsoft Windows includes many TrueType fonts of its own - though in the latter case be aware that some of them are copyrighted!).

Try out some fonts. Once you've loaded a font, you can use the MenuButton to switch the font for a TextObject.

For now we have only a flat object. To add some depth, we can use the `Ext1:` and `Ext2:` buttons in the `Curve and Surface` panel just as we did with curves.

Use the `TextOnCurve:` option to make the text follow a 2D-curve. Use the alignment buttons above the `TextOnCurve:` text field in the `Font` panel to align the text on the curve.

One particularly powerful Blender function is that a TextObject can be converted with **ALT-C** to a Bézier curve, which allows you to edit the shape of every single character on the curve. This is especially handy for creating logos or when producing custom lettering. The transformation from text to curve is irreversible and, of course, a further transformation from curve to mesh is possible too.

Special Characters

Normally, a Font Object begins with the word "Text", which can be deleted simply with **SHIFT-BACKSPACE**. In EditMode, the Text Object only reacts to text input. Nearly all of the hotkeys are disabled. The cursor can be moved with the arrow keys. Use **SHIFT-ARROWLEFT** and **SHIFT-ARROWRIGHT** to move the cursor to the end of the lines or to the beginning or end of the text.

Nearly all 'special' characters are available. A summary of these characters follows:

- **ALT-c**: copyright
- **ALT-f**: Dutch Florin
- **ALT-g**: degrees
- **ALT-l**: British Pound
- **ALT-r**: Registered trademark

CURVES AND SURFACES.TEXT

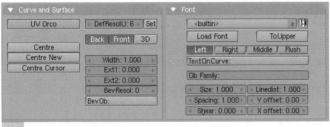

24 Text edit buttons.

- **ALT-s**: German S
- **ALT-x**: Multiply symbol
- **ALT-y**: Japanese Yen
- **ALT-1**: a small 1
- **ALT-2**: a small 2
- **ALT-3**: a small 3
- **ALT-?**: Spanish question mark
- **ALT-!**: Spanish exclamation mark
- **ALT->**: a double >>
- **ALT-<**: a double <<

All the characters on your keyboard should work, including stressed vowels and so on. If you need special characters (such as accented letters, which are not there on a US keyboard) you can produce many of them using a combination of two other characters. To do so press **ALT-BACKSPACE** within the desired combination to produce the special character. Some examples are given below.

You can also add complete ASCII files to a Text Object. Save the file as **/tmp/.cutbuffer** and press **ALT+V**.

- **AKEY, ALT-BACKSPACE, TILDE**: ã
- **AKEY, ALT-BACKSPACE, COMMA**: à
- **AKEY, ALT-BACKSPACE, ACCENT**: á
- **AKEY, ALT-BACKSPACE, OKEY**: å
- **EKEY, ALT-BACKSPACE, QUOTE**: ë
- **OKEY, ALT-BACKSPACE, SLASH**: ø

Otherwise you can write your text in a Blender Text Window, load text into such a window, or paste it into the window from the clipboard and press **ALT-M**. This creates a new Text Object from the content of the text buffer (Up to 1000 characters).

Extrude Along a Path

The "Extrude along path" technique is a very powerful modelling tool. It consists of creating a surface by sweeping a given profile along a given path.

Both the profile and the path can be a Bézier or a NURBS curve.

Let's assume you have added a Bézier curve and a Bézier circle as separate objects to your scene (fig. 25).

Play a bit with both to obtain a nice 'wing-like' profile and a fancy path (fig. 26). By default, Béziers exist only on a plane, and are 2D objects. To make the path span in all three directions of space, as in the example shown above, press the 3D button in the Curve EditButtons (**F9**) Curve and Surface panel (fig. 27).

Now look at the name of the profile object. By default it is "CurveCircle" and it is shown on the **NKEY** panel when it is selected. You can change it by **SHIFT-LMB** on the name, if you like (fig. 28).

Now select the path. In its EditButtons locate the BevOb: Text Button in the Curve and Surface panel and write in there the name of the profile object. In our case "CurveCircle" (fig. 29).

The result is a surface defined by the Profile, sweeping along the path (fig. 30).

To understand the results, and hence obtain the desired effects it is important to understand the following points:

- The profile is oriented so that its z-axis is tangent (*i.e.* directed along) the path and that its x-axis is on the plane of the path; consequently the y-axis is orthogonal to the plane of the path;

- If the path is 3D the "plane of the path" is defined locally rather than globally and is visually rendered, in EditMode, by several short segments perpendicular to the path (fig. 31);

- The y-axis of the profile always points upwards. This is often a source of unexpected results and problems, as we'll explain later on.

Tilting

To modify the orientation of the local path plane select a control point and press **TKEY**. Then move the mouse to change the orientation of the short segments smoothly in the neighborhood of the control point. **LMB** fixes the position, and **ESC** reverts to previous state.

CURVES AND SURFACES.EXTRUDE ALONG A PATH

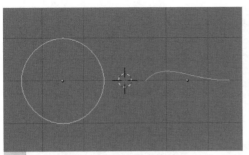

25 Profile (left) and path (right).

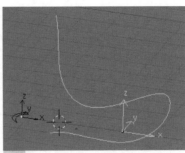

26 Modified profile (left) and path (right).

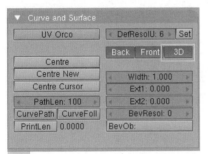

27 3D Curve button.

28 Profile name.

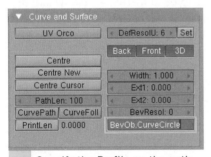

29 Specify the Profile on the path.

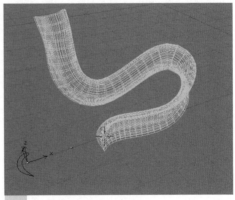

30 Extrusion result.

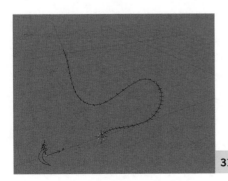

31 Path local plane.

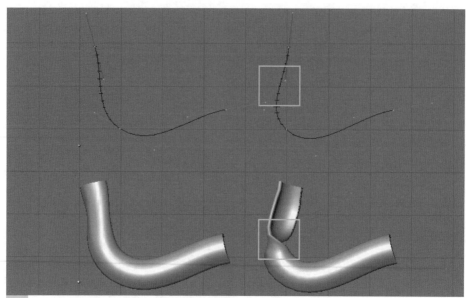

32 Extrusion problems due to y-axis constraint.

With the y-axis constrained upwards, unexpected results can occur when the path is 3D and the profile being extruded comes to a point where the path is exactly vertical. Indeed if the path goes vertical and then continues to bend there is a point where the y-axis of the profile should begin to point downwards. If this occurs, since the y-axis is constrained to point upwards there is an abrupt 180° rotation of the profile, so that the y-axis points upwards again.

Figure 32 shows the problem. On the left there is a path whose steepness is such that the normal to the local path plane is always upward. On the right we see a path where, at the point circled in yellow, such a normal begins to point down. The result of the extrusion presents an abrupt turn there.

The only solutions to this problems are: To use multiple - matching - paths, or to carefully tilt the path to ensure that a normal always points upwards.

If the orientation of the profile along the curve is not as you expected, and you want to rotate it for the entire path length, there is a better way to do so than tilting all path control points.

You can simply rotate the profile in EditMode on its plane. This way the profile will change but its local reference will not.

Changing profile orientation

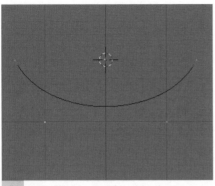

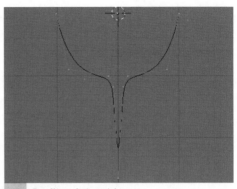

33 A Surface curve for skinning.

34 Profile of the ship.

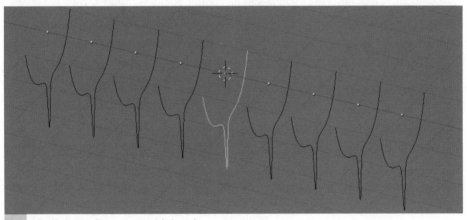

35 Multiple profiles along ship's axis.

Skinning

Skinning is the fine art of defining a surface using two or more profiles. In Blender you do so by preparing as many curves of the the desired shape and then converting them to a single NURBS surface.

As an example we will create a sailboat. The first thing to do, in side view (**NUM3**), is to add a Surface Curve. (Be sure to add a *Surface* curve and not a curve of Bézier or NURBS flavour, or the trick won't work (fig. 33).

Give the curve the shape of the middle cross section of the boat, by adding vertices as needed with the Split button and, possibly, by setting the NURBS to 'Endpoint' both on 'U' and 'V' (fig. 34) as needed.

Now duplicate (**SHIFT-D**) the curve as many times as necessary, to the left and to the right (fig. 35). Adjust the curves to match the various sections of the ship at different points along its length. To this end, blueprints help a lot. You can load a blueprint on the background (as we did for the logo design in this chapter) to prepare all the cross section profiles (fig. 36).

Note that the surface we'll produce will transition smoothly from one profile to the next. To create abrupt changes you would need to place profiles quite close to each other, as is the case for the profile selected in figure 36.

Now select all curves (with A or B) and join them (by pressing **CTRL-J** and by answering Yes to the question 'Join selected NURBS?'). This will lead to the configuration of figure 37.

Now switch to EditMode (**TAB**) and select all control points with **AKEY**; then press **FKEY**. The profiles should be 'skinned' and converted to a surface (fig. 38).

As should be evident from the first and last profiles in this example, the cross-sections need not be defined on a family of mutually orthogonal planes.

Tweak the surface, if necessary, by moving the control points. Figure 39 shows a shaded view. You will most probavly need to rise ResolU and RelolV to attain a better shape.

The only limitation to this otherwise very powerful technique is that all profiles must exhibit the same number of control points. This is why it is a good idea to model the most complex cross section first and then duplicate it, moving control points as needed, without adding or removing them, as we've shown in this example.

Profile setup

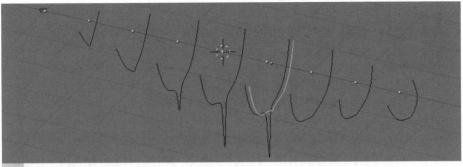

36 Multiple profiles of the correct shapes.

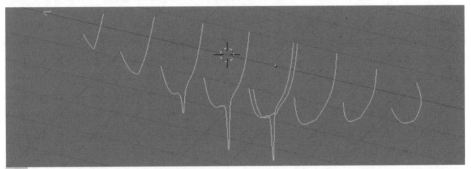

37 Joined profile.

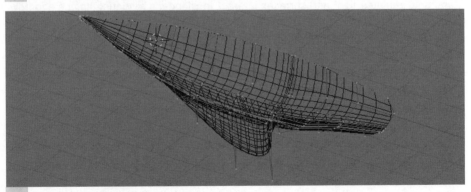

38 Skinned surface in edit mode.

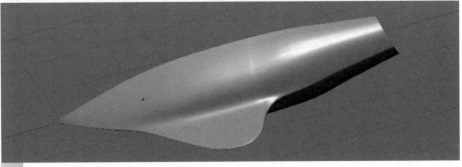

39 Final hull.

CH. 8 MATERIALS AND TEXTURES

DIFFUSION, SPECULAR REFLECTION, MATERIALS IN PRACTICE, TEXTURES, MULTIPLE MATERIALS, SPECIAL MATERIALS, ENVIRONMENT MAPS, SOLID AND HOLLOW GLAS, UV EDITOR AND FACE SELECT, TEXTURE PLUGINS

Before you can understand how to design effectively with materials, you must understand how imulated light and surfaces interact in Blender's rendering engine and how material settings control those interactions. A deep understanding of the engine will help you to get the most from it.

The rendered image you create with Blender is a projection of the scene onto an imaginary surface called the *viewing plane*.

The viewing plane is analogous to the film in a traditional camera, or the rods and cones in the human eye, except that it receives simulated light, not real light.

To render an image of a scene we must first determine what light from the scene is arriving at each point on the viewing plane. The best way to answer this question is to follow a straight line (the simulated light ray) backwards through that point on the viewing plane and the focal point (the location of the camera) until it hits a renderable surface in the scene, at which point we can determine what light would strike that int. The surface properties and incident light angle tell us how much of that light would be reflected back along the incident viewing angle (fig. 1).

Two basic types of phenomena take place at any point on a surface when a light ray strikes it: diffusion and specular reflection. Diffusion and specular reflection are distinguished from each other mainly by the relationship between the incident light angle and the reflected light angle.

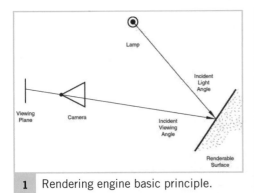

1   Rendering engine basic principle.

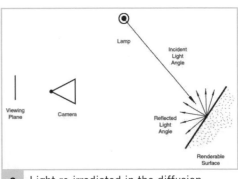

2   Light re-irradiated in the diffusion phenomenon.

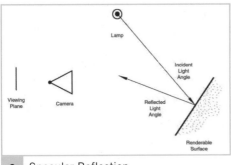

3   Specular Reflection

Diffusion

Light striking a surface and then re-irradiated via a Diffusion phenomenon will be scattered, i.e., re-irradiated in all directions isotropically. This means that the camera will see the same amount of light from that surface point no matter what the *incident viewing angle* is.

It is this quality that makes diffuse light *viewpoint independent*. Of course the amount of light that strikes the surface depends on the incident light angle. If most of the light striking a surface is reflected diffusely, the surface will have a matte appearance (fig. 2).

Since version 2.28, Blender has implemented three different mathematical formulae to compute diffusion. And, even more notably, the diffusion and specular phenomena, which are usually bound in a single type of material, have been separated so that it is possible to select diffusion and specular reflection implementation separately.

The three Diffusion implementations, or *shaders*, use two or more parameters each. The first two parameters are shared by all Diffuse Shaders and are the *Diffuse color*, or simply *color*, of the material, and the amount of incident light energy that is actually diffused. This latter quantity, given in a [0,1] range, is actually called `Refl` in the interface.

The implemented shaders are:

- *Lambert* -- This was Blender's default diffuse shader up to version 2.27. As such, all old tutorials refer to this, and all pre-2.28 images were created with this. This shader has only the default parameters.
- *Oren-Nayar* -- This shader was first introduced in Blender 2.28. It takes a some what more 'physical' approach to the diffusion phenomena because, besides the two default parameters, it has a third one which is used to determine the amount of microscopical roughness of the surface.
- *Toon* -- This shader was first introduced in Blender 2.28. It is a very 'un-physical' shader in that it is not meant to fake reality but to produce 'toonish' rendering, with clear light-shadow boundaries and uniformly lit/shadowed regions. Even though it is relatively simple, it still requires two more parameters which define the size of the lit area and the sharpness of the shadow boundaries.

A subsequent section, devoted to the actual implementation of the material, will analyze all these and their relative settings.

Specular Reflection

Unlike Diffusion, Specular reflection is *viewpoint dependent*. According to Snell's Law, light striking a specular surface will be reflected at an angle which mirrors the incident light angle, which makes the viewing angle very important. Specular reflection forms tight, bright highlights, making the surface appear glossy (fig. 3).

In reality, Diffusion and Specular reflection are generated by exactly the same process of light scattering. Diffusion is dominant from a surface which has so much small-scale roughness in the surface, with respect to wavelength, that light is reflected in many different directions from each tiny bit of the surface, with tiny changes in surface angle.

Specular reflection, on the other hand, dominates on a surface which is smooth, with respect to wavelength. This implies that the scattered rays from each point of the surface are directed almost in the same direction, rather than being diffusely scattered. It's just a matter of the scale of the detail. If the surface roughness is much smaller than the wavelength of the incident light it appears flat and acts as a mirror.

MATERIALS AND TEXTURES.SPECULAR REFLECTION

It is important to stress that the Specular reflection phenomenon discussed here is not the reflection we would see in a mirror, but rather the light highlights we would see on a glossy surface. To obtain true mirror-like reflections you would need to use a raytracer. Blender is not a raytracer as such, but it can produce convincing mirror-like surfaces via careful application of textures, as will be shown later on.

Like Diffusion, Specular reflection has a number of different implementations, or *specular shaders*. Again, each of these implementations shares two common parameters: the *Specular colour* and the energy of the specularity, in the [0-2] range. This effectively allows more energy to be shed as specular reflection as there is incident energy. As a result, a material has at least two different colors, a diffuse, and a specular one. The specular color is normally set to pure white, but it can be set to different values to obtain interesting effects.

The four specular shaders are:

- *CookTorr* -- This was Blender's only Specular Shader up to version 2.27. Indeed, up to that version it was not possible to separately set diffuse and specular shaders and there was just one plain material implementation. Besides the two standard parameters this shader uses a third, *hardness*, which regulates the width of the specular highlights. The lower the hardness, the wider the highlights.
- *Phong* -- This is a different mathematical algorithm, used to compute specular hlights. It is not very different from CookTor, and it is governed by the same three parameters.
- *Blinn* -- This is a more 'physical' specular shader, thought to match the Oren-Nayar diffuse one. It is more physical because it adds a fourth parameter, an *index of refraction (IOR)*, to the aforementioned three. This parameter is not actually used to compute refraction of rays (a ray-tracer is needed for that), but to correctly compute specular reflection intensity and extension via Snell's Law. Hardness and Specular parameters give additional degrees of freedom.
- *Toon* -- This specular shader matches the Toon diffuse one. It is designed to pro duce the sharp, uniform highlights of toons. It has no hardness but rather a Size and Smooth pair of parameters which dictate the extension and sharpness of the specular highlights.

Thanks to this flexible implementation, which keeps separate the diffuse and specular reflection phenomena, Blender allows us to easily control how much of the incident light striking a point on a surface is diffusely scattered, how much is reflected as specularity, and how much is absorbed. This, in turn, determines in what directions (and in what amounts) the light is reflected from a given light source; that is, from what sources (and in what amounts) the light is reflected toward a given point on the viewing plane.It is very important to remember that the material color is just one element in the rendering process. The color is actually the product of the light color and the material color.

Materials in practice

In this section we look at how to set up the various material parameters in Blender, and what you should expect as a result.

Once an Object is selected, by pressing the **F5** key or ⬤ you swithc to Shading context nd the material buttons window appears. This window will appear terribly empty, unless the Object already has a material linked to it. If there is no linked material, add a new one with the menu button (fig. 4).

Once you have added a material the buttons will appear as shown in figure 5.Four panels are present, left to right: a `Preview` panel, a `Material` panel, a `Shader` panel and a `Texture` panel (fig. 6) We will concentrate on the first three, for now.

The `Preview` panel shows the material preview. By default shows a plane seen from the top, but it can be set to a sphere or to a cube with the buttons on the right in the panel (fig. 7).

Material Colors

The panel, `Material` (fig. 8) allows, among others, the setting the material colors.

Each material can exhibit up to three colors:

- *The basic material color,* or the Diffuse color, or, briefly the *Color* tout court (`Col` button in the interface) which is the color used by the diffuse shader.
- *The Specular color,* indicated by the `Spe` button in the interface, is the color used by the specular shader.
- *The Mirror color,* indicated by the `Mir` button in the interface, is the color used by special textures to fake mirror reflections. (You'll find more information on this in the Environment Mapping section.)

The aforementioned buttons select the pertinent color, which is shown in preview immediately left to the button. The three sliders at the right allow you to change the values for the *actice* color in both a RGB scheme and in a HSV scheme. You can select these schemes via the `RGB` and `HSV` buttons at the bottom.

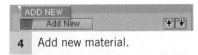

4 Add new material.

5 Material buttons.

6 Material Buttons Panels pertaining only to material shaders.

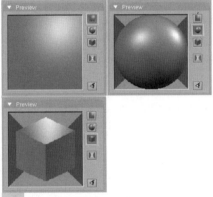

7 Material Preview, plane, sphere and cube.

8 Material colors buttons.

The DYN button is used to set the Dynamic properties of the Object in the RealTime engine (which is outside the scope of this book), while the four buttons above relate to advanced *Vertex Paint* and *UV Texture*.

The Shaders

The Shader panel (fig. 9). exhibits two MenuButtons allowing you to select one diffuse shader (on the right, fig. 10) and one specular shader (on the left, fig. 11).

The two sliders on the side, valid for all shaders, determine the intensity of the Diffusion and Specular phenomena. The Ref slider has a 0 to 1 range whereas the Spec has a 0 to 2 range. Speaking in strictly physical terms, if A is the light energy impinging on the object. *Ref* times A is the energy diffused and *Spec* times A is the energy specularly reflected. To be physically correct this must be *Ref* + *Spec* < 1 or the object would radiate more energy that it receives. But this is CG, so don't be too strict on physics.

9 Material shader buttons.

11 Material Specular shaders.

10 Material Diffuse shaders.

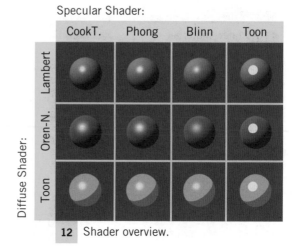

Specular Shader:

12 Shader overview.

Depending on the chosen shader other sliders may be present, allowing to set the various parameters discussed in the introduction.

For the sake of completness, figure 12 shows all possible combinations. Of course, since there are so many parameters, these are just a small sample.

Tweaking Materials

The remaining material buttons both in the `Material` and `Shaders` panels perform some interesting effects.

Figure 13 shows some interesting sliders. `Alpha`, governs the opacity of the material; 1 is fully opaque and 0 is fully transparent. `SpecTra` forces specularity highlights on transparent bodies to be opaque. `Shadeless` makes the material insensitive to its shading, giving it a uniformly diffuse color.

In the `Shaders` panel, the `Emit` slider gives, if non zero, an emitting property to the material. This property makes material visible even without lights and can be itself a source of light if the Radiosity engine is used (fig. 14).

The remaining column of buttons (fig. 15) activates some special features. Top `Halo` Button makes the material an 'Halo' material, which will be described later on. By default the `Traceable`, `Shadows` and `Radio` are activated. The first allows the material to *cast* shadows, while the second allows the material to *receive* shadows; the third allows the material to be taken into account if a Radiosity rendering is performed.

13 Additional material sliders.

14 Regular material (left), material with Alpha < 1 (center) and material with Emit > 0 (right)

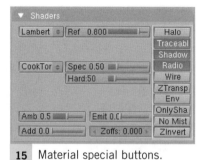

15 Material special buttons.

Wire renders the Object as a wireframe. ZTransp is necessary to activate the Alpha transparency effect.

The other buttons are not that used that often and are described In the reference at the end of the book.

Textures

The material settings that we've seen up to now produce nice, smooth, *uniform* objects. Of course, such objects are never true to reality, where disuniformities are most common.

Blender accounts for these disuniformities, whether in color, reflective or specular power, roughness, and so on, via *textures*.

Textures from the Material Point of View

In Blender, the Materials and Textures form separate blocks in order to keep the interface simple and to allow universal integration between Textures, Lamps, and World blocks.

The relationship between a Material and a Texture, called the 'mapping,' is two-sided. First, the information that is passed on to the Texture must be specified. Then the effect of the Texture on the Material is specified. The Texture panel on the right-

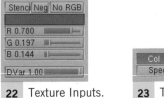

16 Texture Channels.

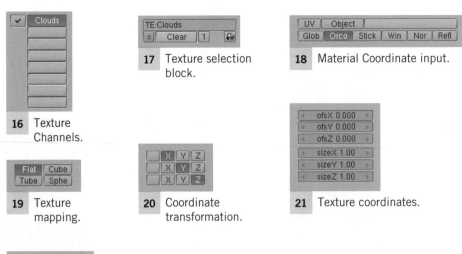

17 Texture selection block.

18 Material Coordinate input.

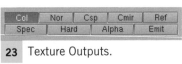

19 Texture mapping.

20 Coordinate transformation.

21 Texture coordinates.

22 Texture Inputs.

23 Texture Outputs.

hand side (and similar panes exists for the the Lamp and World buttons) defines all these calculations.

For an untextured material the panel shows a column of eight empty texture *channels* (fig. 16), by selecting one and pressing Add New or by selecting an existing texture with the MenuButton right below (fig. 17) you add a texture and the Panel shows two more tabs: Map Input and Map To The Tabs buttons are organized in the sequence in which the 'texture pipeline' is performed.

Each channel has its own individual mapping. By default, textures are executed one after another and then superimposed. As a result, an added second Texture channel can completely replace the first one! Next to each non-empty texture channel a check button allows to select or de-select a given channel. de-selected channels are simply removed from the pipeline.

The Texture itself is designated by its name, which you can edit in the Text Button above the Texture selection MenuButton.

Figure 18 shows the Map Input panel. Each Texture has a 3D coordinate (the texture coordinate) as input. The values passed to the texture as coordinates for each pixel of the rendered image belonging to a given material is computed according to these buttons:

MATERIALS AND TEXTURES.TEXTURES

- UV Uses a special kind of mapping called 'UV' mapping. This is especially useful when using images as textures, as we'll see in the Section *UV editor and FaceSelect*.
- Object Uses an Object as source of coordinates; usually an Empty. The Object name must be specified in the text button on the right. This is the preferred way to place a small image as a logo or whatever at a given point of the object.
- Glob Uses Blender Global 3D coordinates.
- Orco Uses the Object local, original, coordinates.
- Stick Uses the Object local, sticky, coordinates.
- Win Uses the rendered image window coordinates.
- Nor Uses the direction of the normal vector as coordinate.
- Refl Uses the direction of the reflection vector as coordinate.

If the texture is an image it is 2D, and we must map the 3D space onto it. The most flexible way to do so is with UV mapping, otherwise four possible pre-set mappings are provided (fig. 19).

The X,Y, and Z coordinates passed to the texture can be shuffled to obtain special effects. The buttons in figure 20 allow you to switch X into Y or Z and so on, or to turn them off.

Coordinates can be scaled and translated by assigning an offset (fig. 21).

Passing to the Map To tab, figure 22 shows the texture input settings. The three buttons determine whether the texture should be used as a Stencil (a Mask for subsequent texture channels); a Negative texture (assigning negative, rather than positive, values); or as a black and white (No RGB), intensity only, texture. The three sliders below these buttons define the texture base color, which can be overridden by color specifications inside the texture definition. Finally the last slider defines the intensity of the texture effect.

Figure 23 shows the toggle buttons which determine which characteristic of the material will be affected by the texture. Some of these button are three state buttons, meaning that the texture can be applied as positive or negative. All of these buttons are independent.

- Col (on/off) Uses the texture to alter the Material color.
- Nor (off/positive/negative) Uses the texture to alter the direction of the local normal. This is used to fake surface imperfections or unevenness via bump mapping.
- Csp (on/off) Uses the texture to alter the Specular color.
- Cmir (on/off) Uses the texture to alter the Mirror color.
- Ref, Spec, Hard, Alpha, Emit (off/positive/negative) Uses the texture to alter the Corresponding Material value.

The output settings (fig. 24) determine the strength of the effect of the Texture output. Mixing is possible with a standard value, including addition, subtraction, or multiplication. Textures give three types of output:

- RGB textures: return three values, which always affect color.
- Bump textures: return three values, which always affect the normal vector. Only the "Stucci" and "Image" texture can give normals.
- Intensity textures: return a single value. This intensity can control "Alpha," for example, or determine the strength of a color specified using the *mapping* buttons.

You can adjust the intensity of these settings separately using the pertinent sliders (fig. 24)

Textures themselves

Once a new texture has been added to a material, it can be defined by switching to the Texture Buttons (**F6**) or ▣ sub-context of the Shading context to obtain figure 25.

A new, empty texture Button Window presents two panels: a Texture `Preview` and a `Texture` panel, the latter with two tabs.

In the `Preview` panel toggle buttons define if this is a Material, Lamp or World texture, and a button `Default Var` allows to return texture parameters to default values.

The `Texture` tab replicates the texture channels and the Texture Menu Button of the linked Material. The two columns of Toggle Buttons selects the Texture type. The button `Image` allows an image to be loaded and used as a texture (the first button simply is "no texture"). The third button allows for the use of a very special kind of texture, the Environment Map (`EnvMap`). The last button (`Plugin`) allows for loading an external piece of code to define the texture. (These three buttons are rather unique and will be treated separately later on.) As soon as a texture type is chosen a new Panel appears, with a name matching the texture type, where texture parameters can be set.

The remaining buttons define 3D *procedural* textures, which are textures that are defined mathematically. They are generally simpler to use, and will give outstanding results once mastered. We will describe just one of these, the `Wood` button, leaving you to investigate further. (The reference chapter in this book contains a full details on each.)

`Wood` is a *procedural*, which means that each 3D coordinate can be translated directly into a color or a value. These types of textures are 'real' 3D. By that we mean that they fit together perfectly at the edges and continue to look like what they are meant to look like even when they are cut; as if a block of wood had really been cut in two.

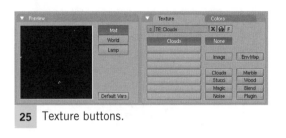

25 Texture buttons.

27 Copying and Pasting Textures.

26 Texture Colorband.

Procedural textures are *not* filtered or anti-aliased. This is hardly ever a problem: the user can easily keep the specified frequencies within acceptable limits.

Procedural texture can either produce colored textures or intensity only textures. If intensity only ones are used the result is a black and white texture, which can be greatly enhanced by the use of colorbands. The colorband is an often-neglected tool in the `Colors` tab in the `Texture` Panel that gives you an impressive level of control over how procedural textures are rendered. Instead of simply rendering each texture as a linear progression from 0.0 to 1.0, you can use the colorband to create a gradient which progresses through as many variations of color and transparency (alpha) as you like (fig. 26).

Skilled use of colorbands leads to really cool marble and cloud textures. To use it, select a procedural texture, such as `Wood`. Click the `Colorband` button.

The `Colorband` is Blender's gradient editor. Each point on the band can be placed at any location and can be assigned any color and transparency. Blender will interpolate the values from one point to the next. To use it, select the point you want to edit with the `Cur:` number button, then add and delete points with the `Add` and `Del` buttons. The RGB and Alpha values of the current point are displayed, along with the point's location on the band. Drag with the left mouse to change the location of the current point.

We can use two `Wood` textures to make ring patterns in two different scales, each of which will have different effects on the appearance of the wood. The `Wood` textures are identical except for the way in which they are mapped in the material buttons window, and in the different color bands used.

We will also also use a `Clouds` texture to make a grain pattern. To see the result of just one texture, isolated from the others, remember the Check buttons in the `Textu-re` Panel in Material Buttons.

28 First Wood ring texture.

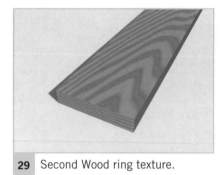

29 Second Wood ring texture.

30 Clouds texture.

31 Final result.

Copying texture settings

By adding an existing texture you link that texture, but all the Material mapping parameters remains as they are. To copy all texture settings, inclusive of mappings, you must copy a given texture channel and paste it into another by using the two arrow buttons in figure 27.

Figure 28 to 30 shows the three individual textures which, when combined in a single material and mapped to various material parameters, create a nice wood texture (fig. 31).

ImageTexture

The Image texture is the only true 2D texture, and is the most frequently used and most advanced of Blender's textures. The standard, built-in bump mapping and perspective-corrected mip-mapping, filtering, and anti-aliasing guarantee outstanding images (set DisplayButtons OSA to ON for this). Because pictures are two-dimensional, the way in which the 3D texture coordinate is translated to 2D must be specified in the *mapping* buttons (fig. 19).

32 Flat Mapping.

33 Cube Mapping.

34 Tube Mapping.

35 Sphere Mapping.

The four standard mappings are: Flat, Cube, Tube and Sphere. Depending on the overall shape of the object, one of these types is more useful.

The Flat mapping (fig. 32) gives the best results on single planar faces. It does produce interesting effects on the sphere, but compared to a sphere-mapped sphere the result looks flat. On faces not in the mapping plane the last pixel of the texture is repeated, which produces stripes on the cube and cylinder.

The cube-mapping (fig. 33) often gives the most useful results when the objects are not too curvy and organic (notice the seams on the sphere).

The tube-mapping (fig. 34) maps the texture around an object like a label on a bottle. The texture is therefore more stretched on the cylinder. This mapping is of course very good for making the label on a bottle or assigning stickers to rounded objects. However, this is not a cylindrical mapping so the ends of the cylinder are undefined.

The sphere-mapping (fig. 35) is the best type for mapping a sphere, and it is perfect for making a planet and similar stuff. It is often very useful for creating organic objects. It too produces interesting effects on a cylinder.

Moving a texture

As described in the previous section you can manipulate the texture in the texture part of the MaterialButtons. There is one more important feature to manipulate the textures.

When you select an object and press **TKEY**, you get the option to visually scale and move the texture space, but not to rotate the texture. The `Object` coordinate mapping is anyway much more flexible.

Multiple Materials

Most objects are assembled so that they can be modeled in parts, with each part composed of a different material. But on some occasions it may be useful to have an object modeled as a single Mesh, yet exhibiting different materials.

Consider the mushroom image shown in figure 36. This object is a single mesh to which we need to assign two materials: one for the stem and one for the cap. Here's how to do it.

1. Create a creamy stem material of your choice, and assign it to the entire mushroom. (fig. 37).

2. In a 3DWindow enter EditMode for the mushroom and select all the vertices belonging to the cap (fig. 38).

3. Go to the `Link and Material` Panel in the Mesh Edit Buttons (**F9**) and press `New` (fig. 39).

4. The mesh should now have two materials. The label should now read `2 Mat: 2` meaning that material number 2 out of 2 is active. The selected faces are assigned to this new material once you press the `Assign` button; the unselected faces keep any previous material assignment.

   To see which faces belong to which material use the `Select` and `Deselect` buttons. Switch among materials with the `Mat:` NumButton. You can have up to 16 materials per mesh.

5. At any rate, both mesh materials are instances of the same material! So, keeping the material you want to change active, switch to the Material Buttons (**F5**) where you will find a similar "2 Mat 2" button. The material now has two users, as indicated by the blue color in the name of the material, and the number button showing "2" (fig. 40).

36 Mushroom Mesh.

37 Mushroom with one mate-

38 Mushroom with cap vertices
        selected.

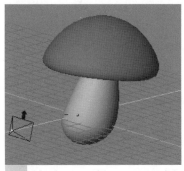

41 Mushroom with two materials.

39 Adding a new material
        to the mesh.

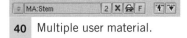

40 Multiple user material.

Click on the "2" and confirm the OK? Single user question. You have now duplicated the material. The original material is still called "Stem" and the duplicate is
"Stem.001". Rename the duplicate to "Cap". You can now edit the material as needed
to obtain a nice looking cap (fig. 41).

Textures

If your material uses textures they remain linked even after you make the material single-user. To unlink textures, so that you can edit the two materials textures separately, go to the TextureButtons for that material, and make the texture single-user as well.

Special Materials

Blender provides a set of materials which does not obey the shader paradigm and which are applied on a per-vertex rather than on a per-face basis.

Halo Materials

Press the Halo button in the materials (**F5**) buttons and the Material Buttons Shaders panel. Panels change as shown in figure 42.

As you can see, the Mesh faces are no longer rendered; instead a 'halo' is rendered at each vertex. This is most useful for particle systems because they generate free vertices, but it can also come in very handy when creating certain special effects, when making an object glow, or when creating a viewable light source.

As you can see in the three colors which, in standard material were Diffuse, Specular and Mirror colors are now relative to three different characteristics: the color of the halo itself, the color of any possible ring and the color of any possible line you might want to add with the relevant toggle buttons in figure 42.

Figure 43 shows the result of applying to a single vertex mesh a halo material. The halo size, alpha, and hardness can be adjusted with the pertinent sliders in figure 42. The Add sliders determine how much the halo colors are 'added to', rather than mixed with, the colors of the objects behind and together with other halos.

To set the number of rings, lines, and star points independently, once they are enabled with the relative Toggle Button, use the Num Buttons Rings:,Lines: and Star: . Rings and lines are randomly placed and oriented, to change their pattern you can change the Seed: Num Button which sets the random numbers generator seed.

Let's use a halomaterial to create a dotmatrix display.

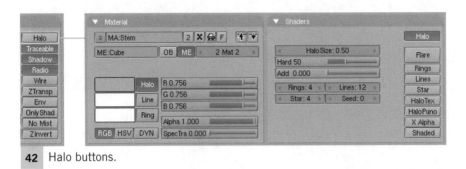

42 Halo buttons.

1. To begin, add a grid with the dimensions 32x16. Then add a camera and adjust your scene so that you have a nice view of the billboard.

2. Use a 2D image program to create some red text on a black background, using a simple and bold font. Figure 44 shows an image 512 pixels wide by 64 pixels high, with some black space at both sides.

3. Add a material for the billboard, and set it to the type `Halo`. Set the `HaloSize` to 0.06 and when you render the scene you should see a grid of white spots.

4. Add a Texture, then change to the Texture Buttons and make it an image texture. When you load your picture and render again you should see some red tinted dots in the grid.

5. Return to the Material Buttons and adjust the `sizeX` parameter to about 0.5 then render again; the text should now be centered on the Billboard.

6. To remove the white dots, adjust the material color to a dark red and render. You should now have only red dots, but the billboard is still too dark. To fix this enter Edit-Mode for the board and copy all vertices using the **SHIFT-D** shortcut. Then adjust the brightness with the `Add` value in the MaterialButtons.

You can now animate the texture to move over the billboard, using the `ofsX` value in the `Texture` panel of the MaterialButtons. (You could use a higher resolution for the grid, but if you do you will have to adjust the size of the halos by shrinking them, or they will overlap (fig. 45).

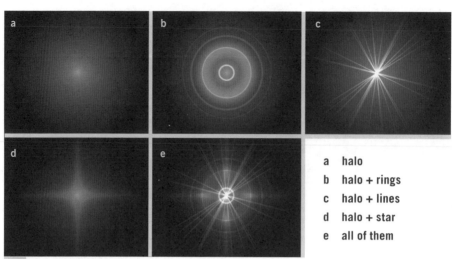

a   halo

b   halo + rings

c   halo + lines

d   halo + star

e   all of them

43   Halo results.

44   Dot matrix image texture.

45   Dot Matrix display

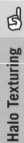

Halo Texturing

By default, textures are applied to objects with Object coordinates and reflects on the halos by affecting their color, as a whole, on the basis of the color of the vertex originating the halo.

To have the texture take effect *within* the halo, and hence to have it with varying colors or transparencies press the HaloTex button; this will map the whole texture to *every* halo. This technique proves very useful when you want to create a realistic rain effect using particle systems, or similar.

46 Lens Flare settings.

47 Lens Flare.

Lens Flares

Our eyes have been trained to believe that an image is real if it shows artifacts that result from the mechanical process of photography. *Motion blur, Depth of Field*, and *lens flares* are just three examples of these artifacts. The first two are discussed in the Chapter 14; the latter can be produced with special halos.

A simulated lens flare tells the viewer that the image was created with a camera, which makes the viewer think that it is authentic. We create lens flares in Blender from a mesh object using first the `Halo` button and then the `Flare` options in the `Shaders` Panel of the material settings. Try turning on `Rings` and `Lines`, but keep the colors for these settings fairly subtle. Play with the `Flares:` number and `Fl.seed:` settings until you arrive at something that is pleasing to the eye. You might need to play with `FlareBoost:` for a stronger effect (fig. 46). (This tool does not simulate the physics of photons traveling through a glass lens; it's just a eye candy.)

Blender's lens flare looks nice in motion, and disappears when another object occludes the flare mesh (fig. 47).

Environment Maps

The shiny surfaces that Blender generates show specular highlights. The ironic thing about these specular shaders, though, is that they are sensitive only to lamps. Specifically, specular shaders surfaces show you a bright spot as a mirror-like reflection of a lamp.

This all makes sense except that if you turn the camera directly toward the lamp you won't see it! The camera sees this light only if it is being reflected by a specular shader, not directly. On the other hand, objects that appear very bright in your scene (that reflect a lot of light to the camera) but are not lamps don't show up in these highlights.

It is easy enough to make a lamp which is directly visible to the camera by placing some renderable object in the scene which looks like some appropriate sort of lamp fixture, flame, sun, and so on. However, there is no immediate fix for the fact that surrounding objects do not show up on specular highlights.

In a word, we lack *reflections*. This is the sort of problem we will address using the technique of environment mapping.

Just as we render the light that reaches the viewing plane using the camera to define a viewpoint, we can render the light that reaches the surface of an object (and hence, the light that might ultimately be reflected to the camera).

Blender's environment mapping renders a cubic image map of the scene in the six cardinal directions from any point. When the six tiles of the image are mapped onto an object using the `Refl` input coordinates, they create the visual complexity that the eye expects to see from shiny reflections.

It's useful to remember here that the true goal of this technique is *believability*, not *accuracy*. The eye doesn't need a physically accurate simulation of the light's travel; it just needs to be lulled into believing that the scene is real by seeing the complexity it expects. The most unbelievable thing about most rendered images is the sterility, not the inaccuracy.

The first step to follow when creating an environment map is to define the viewpoint for the map. To begin, add an empty to the scene and place it *in the specular position of the camera with respect to the reflecting surface*. (This is possible, strictly speaking, only for planar reflecting surfaces.)

Ideally, the location of the empty would mirror the location of the camera across the plane of the polygon onto which it is being mapped. It would be ridiculously difficult to create a separate environment map for every polygon of a detailed mesh, so we take advantage of the fact that the human eye is very gullible.

In particular, for relatively small and complex objects, we can get away with simply placing the empty near the center. We name the empty `env` so that we can refer to it by name in the environment map settings.

We will create a reflective sphere over a reflective plane, using the set up depicted in figure 48.

Note the 'env' Empty is placed exactly below the camera, at a distance from the reflecting plane equal to 3 blender units, which is equal to the height of the camera over the same plane.

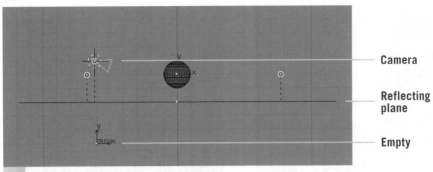

48 Environment Map utilization example.

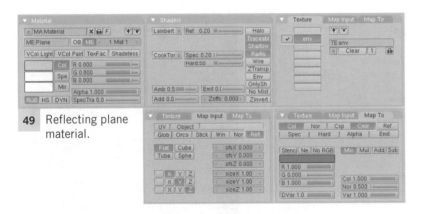

49 Reflecting plane material.

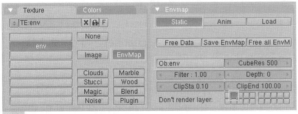

50 Reflecting plane EnvMap settings.

Now, let's place some lights, leave the sphere without a given material, and move the plane to a *different layer*. For example, say that everything is on layer 1, except for the plane which is in layer 2.

Give the plane a low `Ref` and `Spec` material and add a texture on channel two with the parameters in figure 49.

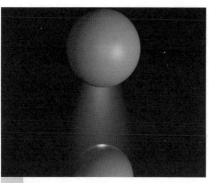

51 Sphere on a reflecting surface.

52 Reflecting sphere on a reflecting surface.

53 Reflecting sphere on a reflecting surface with multiple reflections.

55 Reflecting sphere on a reflecting water with multiple reflections.

Note both the Refl mapping and the Cmir effect. We use channel 2 and not 1 because we will need channel 1 later on in this example.

Now define the newly assigned texture as an EnvMap in the Texture Buttons (**F6**), as in (fig. 50). In the Envmap Panel, note the Ob: field containing the name of the Empty with respect to which we compute the EnvMap. Note also the resolution of the cube on which the EnvMap will be computed and, most important, the Don't render layer: buttons.

Because the EnvMap is computed from the Empty location it must have an unobstructed view of the scene. Since the reflecting plane would completely hide the sphere, it must be on its own layer which must be marked as 'Not renderable' for the EnvMap calculation.

Pressing **F12** starts the rendering process. First, six different square images comprising the EnvMap are computed, after which the final image is produced, of the sphere reflected over the plane (fig. 51).

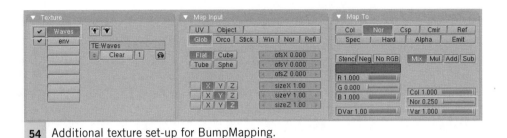

54 Additional texture set-up for BumpMapping.

To add more visual appeal to the scene, add a big sphere encompassing the whole scene and map a sky image onto it to fake a real, cloudy world. Then add a new Empty in the center of the Sphere and move the Sphere to Layer 3. Next, give the sphere an EnvMap exactly as you did for the plane (but this time layer 3 must not be rendered!)

Now add some cylinders, to make the environment even more interesting, and, before pressing **F12** return to the plane's texture and press the Free Data button. This will force Blender to recalculate the EnvMap for the new, different, environment.

This time in the rendering process twelve images, six for each EnvMap, will be computed. The result is in figure 52. The sphere is shiner than the plane due to slightly different settings in the materials.

But wait, there is a problem! The Sphere reflects the Plane, but the Plane reflects a dull grey Sphere! This is because the Plane EnvMap is computed *before* the sphere EnvMap. As such, when it is computed the sphere is still dull grey, while when the Sphere EnvMap is computed the plane already has its Reflection.

To fix this locate the `Depth` Num Button in the `Envmap` panel of the Texture buttons and set it to 1 both for the plane and the sphere EnvMap texture. This force recursive computation of EnvMaps. Each EnvMap is computed, then they are recomputed as many times as 'Depth' is set to, always one after the other. The result is visible in figure 53 .

Now, if you are still wondering why the first texture channel of the Plane material was kept empty... Add a new texture to the first channel of the plane material. Make it `Glob`, affecting the `Nor` with a 0.25 intensity (fig. 54).

This new texture should be of `Stucci` type; tune the `Noise Size` down to 0.15 or so.If you now render the image the plane will look like rippled water (fig. 55).

You must have the BumpMap on a channel preceding the EnvMap because textures are applied in sequence. If you were to do this the other way around the reflection would appear to be broken by waves.

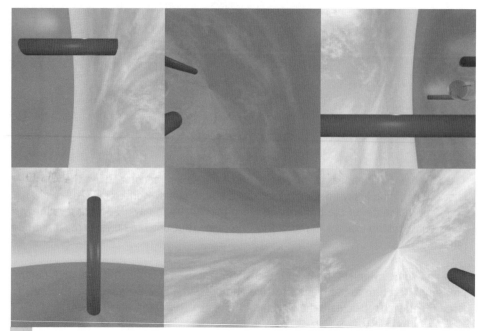

56 The EnvMap as it is stored.

You can save EnvMaps for later use and load them with the pertinent buttons in the Texture Buttons. You can also build your own envmap. The standard is to place the six images mapped on the cube on two rows of three images each, as in figure 56.

Blender allows three types of environment maps, as you can see in figure 50:

- `Static` - The map is only calculated once during an animation or after loading a file.
- `Anim` - The map is calculated each time a rendering takes place. This means moving Objects are displayed correctly in mirroring surfaces.
- `Load` - When saved as an image file, environment maps can be loaded from disk. This option allows the fastest rendering with environment maps.

You can animate the water of the previous example by setting an IPO for the `ofsX` and `ofsY` values of the texture placement in the Material Buttons. Rendering the animation would then show moving ripples on the surface, with reflections changing accordingly!

The EnvMap of the Plane needs to be computed only once at the beginning if nothing else moves! Hence it can be `static`. The Envmap on the sphere is another matter, since it won't reflect the changes in the reflections in the water unless it is computed at each frame of the animation. Hence it should be of type `Anim`

If the camera is the only moving object and you have a reflecting plane, the Empty must move too and you must use `Anim` EnvMaps. If the object is small and the Empty is in its center, the EnvMap can be `Static`, even if the object itself rotates since the Empty does not move. If, on the other hand, the Object translates the Empty should follow it and the EnvMap be of `Anim` type.

Other settings are:

- `Filter:` - With this value you can adjust the sharpness or blurriness of the reflection.
- `Clipsta, ClipEnd` - These values define the clipping boundaries when rendering the environment map images.

EnvMap calculation can be disabled at a global level by the `EnvMap` Tog Button in the `Render` Panel of the Rendering Buttons.

Solid and Hollow Glass

Glass and tranparent materials are generally tricky to render because they exhibit *refraction*; that is, the bending of light rays due to the different *optical density*, or *index of refraction* of the various materials. Unfortunately, to fully account for refraction a ray tracer is mandatory. Still, we can produce convincing results in Blender using EnvMaps and advanced Texturing techniqus.

Consider a scene with some basic geometries, including a cube, a cone, a sphere, and a torus. As a first example we will make the sphere look like a solid ball of glass and, as a second example, that same sphere will become a glass bubble.

To create this effect, we need to make the light appear to bend as it passes through the sphere, since we would expect objects behind the solid glass sphere to appear heavily warped, as if through a very thick lens. On the other hand, the hollow glass sphere center should be almost transparent while the sides should deflect light.

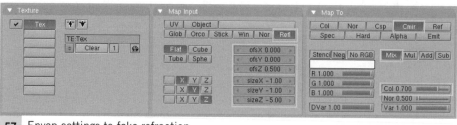

57 Envap settings to fake refraction.

Solid Glass

1. To begin, we set up an environment map for the sphere's material just as we did for the ball in the previous section, with an empty which locates the EnvMap's perspective at the center of the sphere.

2. To fake Refraction we'll tweak the output mapping with the ofsZ, sizeX, sizeY, sizeZ and Col sliders to warp the map in a way that creates the effect of refraction. To do so, use the settings in figure 57.

3. Select the Mir RGB material sliders and lower the R and G a bit to give the texture a blue tint. (Our experience with the idiosyncrasies of Blender's handling of mirror colors dictates this unintuitive approach when combining environment-mapped reflections and refractions in a single material.)

4. Turn the Ref slider all the way down (fig. 58). You should now have produced a blue-tinted refraction of the environment.

5. Shiny glass also needs a reflection map, so we'll place the same texture into another texture channel. Press the Add, Col, and Emit buttons, and use the Refl button for the coordinates. Make the material Color black and turn Emit all the way up (fig. 59).

6. This changes our first texture considerably. In order to return the refraction texture to a nice blue tint, we have to add a new texture, leaving the texture type set to None. Select the Mix and Cmir buttons, and set the Col slider about halfway up. Click the Neg button and set the texture input RGB sliders to a dark blue (fig. 60).

7. The final result should look like figure 61. The refraction effect is most noticeable when the scene is animated.

MATERIALS AND TEXTURES.**SOLID AND HOLLOW GLASS**

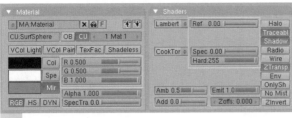

58 Material settings.

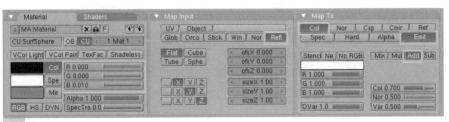

59 Reflection Map.

60 Final touches.

61 Rendering.

62 Setting transparency.

63 Setting reflections.

Hollow Glass

The procedure we've described above works fine for a solid lump of glass, but how do we produce the appearance of hollow glass, like a vase?

Thin glass has strong refraction only where it slopes away from the eye at a steep angle. We can easily mimic this effect by using Blender's `Blend` texture to control the object's transparency, as well as another transparency texture to keep the bright highlights visible.

1. Add a new texture to the material. Select `Blend` as the type and select the `Sphere` option.

2. Return to the material buttons. Select `Nor` as the mapping type, and disable the X and Y axes in the input coordinates.

3. `Mix` the texture with `Alpha`, then move the `Alpha` material slider to 0.0 and set the `ZTransp` option (fig. 62).

This produces the effect of nice transparency as the surface angles toward the eye, but we want the bright environment-mapped reflections to show up on those otherwise-transparent areas. For example, if you look at glass windows, you will see that bright light reflecting from the surface is visible, preventing you from seeing through a pane that would otherwise be transparent. We can produce this effect easily by selecting the environment-mapped reflection texture in the material window and enabling the `Alpha` option (fig. 63).

That's all there is to it. The result should look like figure 64.

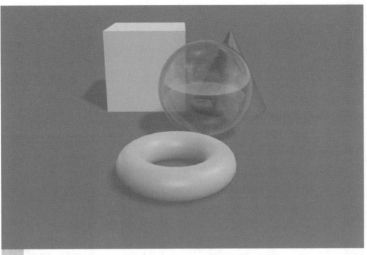

64 Hollow glass.

UV editor and FaceSelect

Introduction

The UV-Editor allows you to map textures directly onto the faces of meshes. Each face can have individual texture coordinates and an individual image assigned to it, and can be combined with vertex colors to make the texture brighter or darker or to give it a color.

By using the UV-Editor each face of the Mesh is assigned two extra features:

- *four UV coordinates* - These coordinates define the way an image or a texture is mapped onto the face. These are 2D coordinates, which is why they're called UV, to distinguish them from XYZ coordinates. These coordinates can be used for rendering or for realtime OpenGL display.
- *a link to an Image* - Every face in Blender can have a link to a different image. The UV coordinates define how this image is mapped onto the face. This image then can be rendered or displayed in realtime.

A 3D window has to be in "Face Select" mode to be able to assign Images or change UV coordinates of the active Mesh Object.

65 Faceselect mode in the 3D Window header Mode menu.

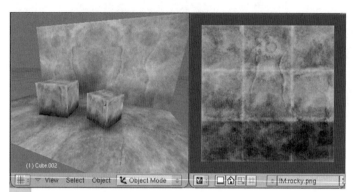

66 3Dwindow and ImageWindow.

67 UV pre-sets.

Assigning Images to faces

First add a Mesh Object to your Scene, then enter the FaceSelect Mode with **FKEY** or by choosing the UV face select entry in the Mode menu (Fig. 65).

Your Mesh will now be drawn Z-buffered. If you enter the Textured draw mode (**ALT-Z**, also called "potato mode") you will see your Mesh drawn in white, which indicates that there is currently no Image assigned to these faces.

Press **AKEY** and all of the faces of the Mesh will be selected and highlighted by dotted lines.

Change one window into the Image Window with **SHIFT-F10**. Here you an load or browse an image with the Load button. Images have to be multiples of 64 pixels (64x64, 128x64 etc.) to be able to drawn in realtime (note: most 3D cards don't support images larger than 256x256 pixels). However, Blender can render all assigned images regardless of size when creating stills or animations.

Loading or browsing an image in FaceSelect automatically assigns the image to the selected faces. You can immediately see this in the 3D window (when in Textured view mode - fig. 66).

MATERIALS AND TEXTURES.UV EDITOR AND FACE SELECT

Selecting faces

You can select faces with RightMouse or with BorderSelect (**BKEY**) in the 3D window. If you have problems with selecting the desired faces, you can also enter EditMode and select the vertices you want. After leaving EditMode the faces defined by the selected vertices should be selected as well.

Only one face is active. Or in other words: the Image Window only displays the image of the active face. As usual within Blender, only the last selected face is active and selection is done with **RMB**.

Editing UV coordinates

In the ImageWindow you will see a representation of your selected faces as yellow or purple vertices connected with dotted lines. You can use the same techniques here as in the Mesh EditMode to select, move, rotate, scale, and so on. With the Lock button pressed you will also see realtime feedback in 3D of what you are doing.

In the 3D window, you can press **UKEY** in FaceSelect mode to get a menu to calculate UV coordinates for the selected faces (fig. 67).

- *Cube* - This determines cubical mapping. A number requester asks for a scaling property.
- *Cylinder, Sphere* - Cylindrical/spherical mapping, calculated from the center of the selected faces.
- *Bounds to 1/8, 1/4, 1/2, 1/1* - UV Coordinates are calculated using the projection as displayed in the 3D window, then scaled to the given fraction of the image texture.
- *Standard 1/8, 1/4, 1/2, 1/1* - Each face gets a set of default square UV coordinates which are then scaled to the requested fraction of the image texture.
- *From Window* - UV coordinates are calculated using the projection as displayed in the 3D window.

68 The ImageWindow Toolbar.

69 Vertex colors modulate texture.

UV editing tools.

In the ImageWindow Toolbar (fig. 68) the third button keeps your UV polygons square while editing them, while the fourth clips them to the size of the image.

Some tips:

- Press **RKEY** in the 3D window to get a menu that allows rotation of the UV coordinates.
- It is sometimes necessary to move image files to a new location on your hard disk. To do so, press the Replace button in the Image Window header to get a Replace Image name window. You can fill in the old directory name, and the new one. Pressing OK changes the paths of all images used in Blender using the old directory. (Note: use as new directory the code "//" to indicate the directory where the Blender file is).
- You can also use FaceSelect and VertexPaint (**VKEY**) simultaneously. Vertex painting then only works on the selected faces. This feature is especially useful to paint faces as if they don't share vertices. Note that the vertex colors are used to modulate the brightness or color of the applied image texture (fig. 69).

MATERIALS AND TEXTURES.TEXTURE PLUGINS

Rendering and UV coordinates

Even without an image assigned to faces, you can render textures utilizing the UV coordinates using the green "UV" button in the MaterialButtons (**F5**) menu.

To render the assigned Image texture as well, press the "TexFace" button in the MaterialButtons. Combine this with the "VertexCol" option to use vertex colors too.

Texture Plugins

As a final note on texture, let's look at the fourth texture type button, Plugin.

Blender allows the dynamic linking at run time of shared objects, both texture and sequence plugins. In both cases these objects are pieces of C code written according to a given standard (see Chapter 21). In the case of texture plugins, these chunk of code defines function accepting coordinates as input and providing a Color, Normal and Intensity output, exactly as the procedural Textures do.

To use a Texture plugin, select this option, and then click the Load Plugin button which appears in the Texture Buttons. A neighboring window will turn to a File Select window in which you can select a plugin. These plugins are .dll files on Windows and .so files on various Unix flavors.

Once a plugin is loaded it turns the Texture Buttons window into its own set of buttons, as described in the individual plugin references.

CH. 9 LIGHTING

INTRODUCTION, LAMP TYPES, SHADOWS, VOLUMETRIC LIGHT, TWEAKING LIGHT

Introduction[1]

Lighting is a very important topic in rendering, standing equal to modelling, materials and textures.

The most accurately modelled and textured scene will yield poor results without a proper lighting scheme, while a simple model can become very realistic if skilfully lit.

Lighting, sadly, is often overlooked by the inexperienced artist who commonly believes that, since real world scenes are often lit by a single light (a lamp, the sun, etc.) a single light would also do in computer graphics.

This is false because in the real world even if a single light source is present, the light shed by such a source bounces off objects and is re-irradiated all over the scene making shadows soft and shadowed regions not pitch black, but partially lit.

The physics of light bouncing is simulated by Ray Tracing renderers and can be simulated within Blender by resorting to the Radiosity (Chapter 15) engine.

Ray tracing and radiosity are slow processes. Blender can perform much faster rendering with its internal scanline renderer. A very good scanline renderer indeed. This kind of rendering engine is much faster since it does not try to simulate the real behaviour of light, assuming many simplifying hypothesis.

In this chapter we will analyse the different type of lights in Blender and their behaviour, we will analyse their strong and weak points, ending with describinga basic 'realistic' lighting scheme, known as the three point light method, as well as more advanced, realistic but, of course, CPU intensive, lighting schemes.

---

[1] This chapter was written before Blender 2.32 was made, which has a lot of improvements for the rendering system. See chapter 29.

LIGHTING.LAMP TYPES

1 Lamp Buttons.

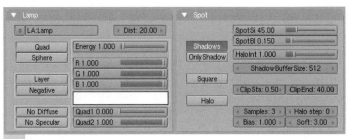

2 Lamp General Buttons.

Lamp Types

Blender provides four Lamp types:

- Sun Light
- Hemi Light
- Lamp Light
- Spot Light

Any of these lamps can be added to the scene by pressing **SPACE** and by selecting the Lamp menu entry. This action adds a *Lamp Light* lamp type. To select a different lamp type, or to tune the parameters, you need to switch to the Shading Context window(**F5**) and Lamp sub-context (✳).

A column of toggle buttons, in the Preview Panel, allows you to choose the lamp type.

The lamp buttons can be divided into two categories: Those directly affecting light, which are clustered in the Lamp and Spot Panels, and those defining textures for the light, which are on the right Texture Panel, exhibiting two Tabs. These latter and are very similar to those relative to materials. In the following subsections we will focus on the first two Panels (fig. 2), leaving a brief discussion on texture to the *Tweaking Light* section.

The Lamp Panel contains buttons which are mostly general to all lamp types, hence deserve to be explained beforehand.

Negative - makes the light cast 'negative' light, that is, the light shed by the lamp is subtracted, rather than added, to that shed by any other light in the scene.

Layer - makes the light shed by the lamp affect only the objects which are on the same layer as the lamp itself.

No Diffuse - makes the light cast a light which does not affect the 'Diffuse' material shader, hence giving only 'Specular' highlights.

No Specular - makes the light cast a light which does not affect the 'Specular' material shader, hence giving only 'Diffuse' shading.

Energy - the energy radiated by the lamp.

R, G, B sliders - the red, green and blue components of the light shed by the lamp.

Sun Light

The simplest light type is probably the Sun Light (fig. 3). A Sun Light is a light of constant intensity coming from a given direction. In the 3D view the sun light is represented by an encircled yellow dot, which of course turns to purple when selected, plus a dashed line.

This line indicates the direction of the sun's rays. It is by default normal to the view in which the sun lamp was added to the scene and can be rotated by selecting the sun and by pressing **RKEY**.

The lamp buttons which are of use with the sun are plainly those described in the 'general' section. An example of sun light illumination is reported in figure 4. As is evident, the light comes from a constant direction, has an uniform intensity and *does not cast shadows*.

This latter is a very important point to understand in Blender: no lamp, except for the "Spot" type, casts shadows. The reason for this lies in the light implementation in a scanline renderer and will be briefly discussed in the 'Spot' and 'Shadows' subsections.

Lastly, it is important to note that since the Sun light is defined by its energy, colour and *direction*, the actual *location* of the Sun light itself is not important.

LIGHTING.LAMP TYPES

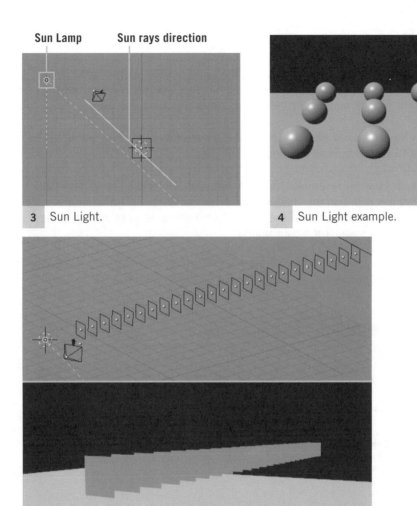

3 Sun Light.

4 Sun Light example.

5 Sun Light example.

Figure 5 shows a second set-up, made by a series of planes 1 blender unit distant one from the other, lit with a Sun light. The uniformity of lighting is even more evident. This picture will be used as a reference to compare with other lamp types.

A Sun light can be very handy for a uniform clear day-light open-space illumination. The fact that it casts no shadows can be circumvented by adding some 'shadow only' spot lights. See the Tweaking Light section!

Sun Tips

Hemi Light

The Hemi light is a very peculiar kind of light designed to simulate the light coming from a heavily clouded or otherwise uniform sky. In other words it is a light which is shed, uniformly, by a glowing hemisphere surrounding the scene (fig. 6).

It is probably the least used Blender light, but it deserves to be treated before the two main Blender Lights because of its simplicity.

This light set-up basically resembles that of a Sun light. Its location is unimportant, while its orientation is important. Its dashed line represents the direction in which the maximum energy is radiated, that is the normal to the plane defining the cut of the hemisphere, pointing towards the dark side.

The results of an Hemi Light for the 9 sphere set up are shown in figure 7 the superior softness of the Hemi light in comparison to the sun light is evident.

Hemi Light Tip

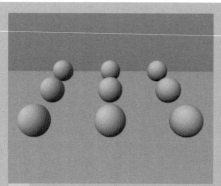

To achieve quite realistic, were it not for the absence of shadows, outdoor lighting you can use both a Sun light, say of Energy 1.0 and warm yellow/orange tint, and a weaker bluish Hemi light faking the light coming from every point of a clear blue sky. Figure 8 shows an example with relative parameters. The figure also uses a World. See the pertinent chapter.

8 Outdoor Light example. Sun Light Energy = 1 RGB = (1.,0.95,0.8) Sun direction in a polar reference is (135°, 135°). Hemi Light Energy=0.5 RGB=(0.64,0.78,1.) pointing down.

Lamp Light

The Lamp light is an omni-directional point light, that is a dimensionless point radiating the same amount of light in all directions. In blender it is represented by a plain, circled, yellow dot.

6 Hemi Light conceptual scheme.

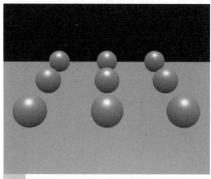

7 Hemi Light example.

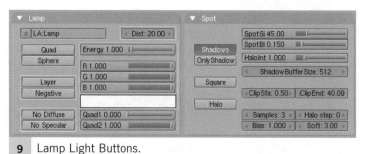

9 Lamp Light Buttons.

Being a point light source the light rays direction on an object surface is given by the line joining the point light source and the point on the surface of the object itself. Furthermore, light intensity decays accordingly to a given ratio of the distance from the lamp.

Besides the above-mentioned buttons three more buttons and two sliders in the Lamp Panel are of use in a Lamp light (fig. 9):

Distance - this gives, indicatively, the distance at which the light intensity is half the Energy. Objects closer than that receive more light, object further than that receive less light.

Quad - If this button is off, a linear - rather unphysical - decay ratio with distance is used. If it is on, a more complex decay is used, which can be tuned by the user from a fully linear, as for Blender default, to a fully - physically correct - quadratic decay ratio with the distance. This latter is a little more difficult to master, it is governed by the two Quad1 and Quad2 Num Buttons and will be explained later on.

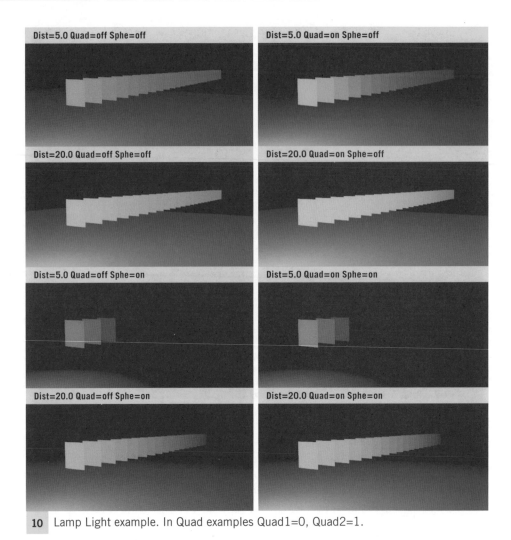

10   Lamp Light example. In Quad examples Quad1=0, Quad2=1.

Sphere - If this button is pressed the light shed by the source is confined in the Sphere of radius Distance rather than going to infinity with its decay ratio.

Following figure 10 shows the same set-up as in the latter Sun light example, but with a Lamp light of different Distance values and with Quadratic decay on and off.

The effect of the Distance parameter is very evident, while the effect of the Quad-button is more subtle. In any case the absence of shadows is still a major issue. As a matter of fact only the first plane should be lit, because all the others should fall in the shadow of the first.

LIGHTING.LAMP TYPES

For the Math enthusiasts, and for those desiring deeper insight, the laws governing the decay are the following.

Let D be the value of the Distance Numeric Button, E the value of the Energy slider and r the distance from the Lamp to the point where rhe light intensity I is to be computed.

If the Quad and the Sphere buttons are off:

$$I = E * \frac{D}{D+r}$$

It is evident what affirmed before: That the light intensity equals half the energy for $r = D$.

If the Quad Button is on:

$$I = E * \frac{D}{D + Q_1 * r} * \frac{D^2}{D^2 + Q_2 * r^2}$$

This is a little more complex and depends from the Quad1 (Q_1) and Quad2 (Q_2) slider values. Nevertheless it is apparent how the decay is fully linear for $Q_1 = 1$, $Q_2 = 0$ and fully quadratic for $Q_1 = 0$, $Q_2 = 1$, this latter being the default. Interestingly enough if $Q_1 = Q_2 = 0$ then light intensity does not decay at all.

If the Sphere button is on the above computed light intensity I is further modified by multiplication by the term which has a linear progression in r from 0 to D and is identically 0 otherwise.

If the Quad button is off and the Sphere button is on:

$$I = E * \frac{D}{D+r} * \begin{cases} \dfrac{D-r}{D} & \text{if } r < D \\ 0 & \text{otherwise} \end{cases} =$$

$$= \begin{cases} E * \dfrac{D-r}{D+r} & \text{if } r < D \\ 0 & \text{otherwise} \end{cases}$$

If both the Quad and the Sphe buttons are on:

$$I = E * \frac{D}{D + Q_1 r} * \frac{D^2}{D^2 + Q_1 r^2} * \begin{cases} \frac{D-r}{D} & \text{if } r < D \\ & \text{otherwise} \\ 0 \end{cases} =$$

$$= \begin{cases} E * \frac{D-r}{D + Q_1 r} * \frac{D^2}{D^2 + Q_2 r^2} & \text{if } r < D \\ & \text{otherwise} \\ 0 \end{cases}$$

Figure 11 might be helpful in understanding these behaviours graphically.

Lamp Light Tip

Since the Lamp light does not cast shadows it shines happily through walls and the like. If you want to achieve some nice effects like a fire, or a candle-lit room interior seen from outside a window, the Sphere option is a must. By carefully working on the Distance value you can make your warm firelight shed only within the room, while illuminating outside with a cool moonlight, the latter achieved with a Sun or Hemi light or both.

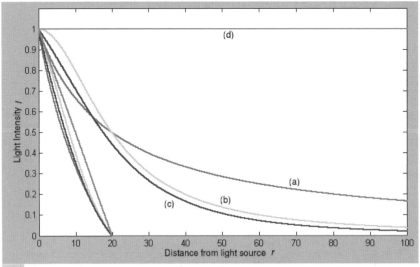

11 Light decays: a) Blender default linear; b) Blender default quadratic with Quad1=0, Quad2=1; c) Blender quadratic with Quad1=Quad2=0.5; d) Blender quadratic with Quad1=Quad2=0. Also shown in the graph the same curves, in the same colours, but with the Sphere button turned on.

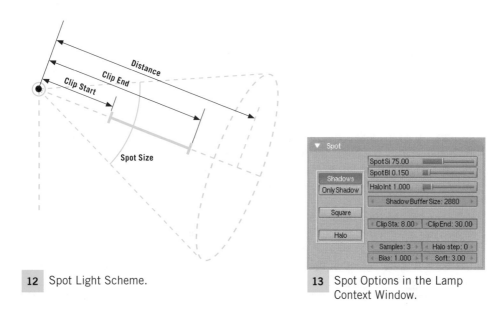

12 Spot Light Scheme.

13 Spot Options in the Lamp Context Window.

Spot Light

The Spot light is the most complex of Blender lights and indeed among the most used thanks to the fact that it is the only one able to cast shadows.

A Spot light is a cone shaped beam generated from the light source location, which is the tip of the cone, in a given direction. Figure 12 should clarify this.

The Spot light uses all buttons of a Lamp Light, and with the same meaning, but it is so more complex that it needs a second Panel of buttons (fig. 13): Spot.

Spot Options

Shadows - toggles shadow casting on and off for this spot.

Only Shadow - let the spot cast only the shadow and no light. This option will be analysed later on it the 'Tweaking Light' section.

Square - Spot lights usually by default cast a cone of light of circular cross-section. There are cases where a square cross section would be helpful, and indeed have a pyramid of light rather than a cone. This button toggles this option.

Halo - let the spot cast a halo as if the light rays were passing through a hazy medium. This option is explained later on in the 'Volumetric Light' section.

Spot Buttons

The rightmost column of buttons in the Spot Panel handles Spot geometry and shadows (fig. 14):

SpotSi - the angle at the tip of the cone, or the Spot aperture.

SpotBl - the blending between the light cone and the surrounding unlit area. The lower the sharper the edge, the higher the softer. Please note that this applies only to the spot edges, not to the softness of the edges of the shadows cast by the spot,these latter are governed by another set of buttons described in the 'Shadows' subsection.

HaloInt - If the Halo button is On this slider defines the intensityof the spot halo. Again, you are referred to the 'Volumetric Light' section.

The bottom button group of the Spot light governs shadows and it is such an ample topic that it deserves a subsection by its own. Before switching to Shadows, figure 15 shows some results for a Spot light illuminating our first test case for differentconfigu-rations.

In figure 15 shadows are turned off! Shadows are treated in next section.

Shadows

The lighting schemes analysed up to now produce on the objects only areas which are more or less lit, but no cast- or self-shadowing, and a scene without proper shado-wing looses depth and realism.

On the other hand, proper shadow calculation requires a full - and slow - ray tracer. For a scan liner, as Blender is, shadows can be computed using a *shadowbuffer* for shadow casting lights. This implies that an 'image', as seen from the Spot Light itself, is 'rendered' and that the distance for each point from the spotlight saved. Any point of the rendered image further than any of those points is then considered to be in shadow.

The shadow buffer stores this data. To keep the algorithm compact, efficient and fast this shadow buffer has a size which is fixed from the beginning and which in Blender can be from 512x512 to 5120x5120. The higher value is the most accurate.

The user can control the algorithm via the bottom buttons in the Spot Panel (fig. 16).

LIGHTING.SHADOWS

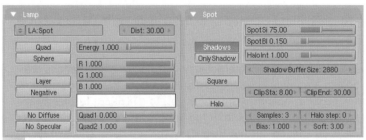

14 Spot Buttons in the Lamp Context Window.

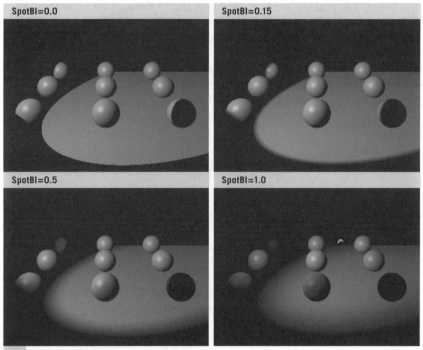

15 Spot Light Examples for SpotSi=45°

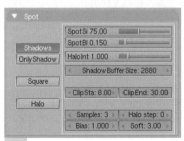

16 Spot Light shadow buttons.

`ShadowBuffSize` - Numeric Button, from 512 to 5120, defining the shadow buffer size.

`ClipSta, ClipEnd` - To further enhance efficiency the shadow computations are actually performed only in a predefined range of distances from the spot position. This range goes from `ClipSta`, nearer to the Spot light, to `ClipEnd`, further away (fig. 17). All objects nearer than `ClipSta` from the Spot light are never checked for shadows, and are always lit. Objects further than `ClipEnd` are never checked for light and are always in shadow. To have a realistic shadow `ClipSta` must be less than the smallest distance between any relevant object of the scene and the spot, and `ClipEnd` larger than the largest distance. For the best use of the allocated memory and better shadow quality, ClipSta must be as large as possible and `ClipEnd` as small as possible. This minimizes the volume where shadows will be computed.

`Samples` - To obtain soft shadows the shadow buffer, once computed, is rendered via its own anti-aliasing algorithm which works by averaging the shadow value over a square of a side of a given number of pixels. Samples is the number of pixels. Its default is 3, that is a 3x3 square. Higher values give better anti-aliasing, and a slower computation time.

`Bias` - Is the bias used in computing the shadows, again the higher the better, and the slower.

`Soft` - Controls the softness of the shadow boundary. The higher the value, the softer and more extended the shadow boundaries will be. Commonly it should be assigned a value which ranges from the same value of the `Sample` NumButton to double that value.

`Halo step` - The stepping of the halo sampling for volumetric shadows when volumetric light is on. This will be explained in the 'Volumetric light' section.

For Shadows to be rendered, they must be enabled at a *global* level. This means that he `Shadow` Button of the `Render` Panel in the Scene Context and Render Buttons must be on!

Volumetric Light

Volumetric light is the effect you see in a hazy air, when the light rays become visible because of light scattering which occurs due to mist, fog, dust etc. If used carefully it can add much realism to a scene... or kill it.

The volumetric light in Blender can only be generated for Spot Lights, once the `Halo` button in the `Spot` Panel is pressed (fig. 18) is pressed.

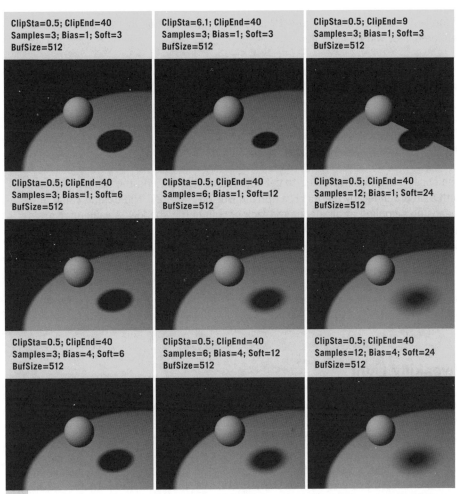

ClipSta=0.5; ClipEnd=40
Samples=3; Bias=1; Soft=3
BufSize=512

ClipSta=6.1; ClipEnd=40
Samples=3; Bias=1; Soft=3
BufSize=512

ClipSta=0.5; ClipEnd=9
Samples=3; Bias=1; Soft=3
BufSize=512

ClipSta=0.5; ClipEnd=40
Samples=3; Bias=1; Soft=6
BufSize=512

ClipSta=0.5; ClipEnd=40
Samples=6; Bias=1; Soft=12
BufSize=512

ClipSta=0.5; ClipEnd=40
Samples=12; Bias=1; Soft=24
BufSize=512

ClipSta=0.5; ClipEnd=40
Samples=3; Bias=4; Soft=6
BufSize=512

ClipSta=0.5; ClipEnd=40
Samples=6; Bias=4; Soft=12
BufSize=512

ClipSta=0.5; ClipEnd=40
Samples=12; Bias=4; Soft=24
BufSize=512

17 Spot Light shadow examples. Top middle picture: only the back part of the Sphere is in the buffer, thus the smaller shadow. Top right picture: all objects beyond ClipEnd are in the shadow.

18 Spot Light halo button.

If the test set up shown in figure 19 is created, and the Halo button pressed, the rendered view will be like figure 20.

The volumetric light effect is rather strong. The intensity of the Halo can be regulated with the HaloInt slider (fig. 21). Lower values corresponding to weaker halos.

The result is interesting. We have volumetric light, but we lack volumetric shadow! The halo passes through the sphere, yet a shadow is cast. This is due to the fact that the Halo occurs in the whole Spot Light cone unless we tell Blender to do otherwise.

The cone needs to be sampled to get volumetric shadow, and the sampling occurs with a step defined by the HaloStep NumButton (fig. 22). The default value of 0 means no sampling at all, hence the lack of volumetric shadow. A value of 1 gives finer stepping, and hence better results, but with a slower rendering time (fig. 23), while a higher value gives worse results with faster rendering (fig. 24).

A value of 8 is usually a good compromise between speed and accuracy.

HaloStep values

Tweaking Light

Ok, now you've got the basics. Now we can really talk of light. We will work on a single example, more complex than a plain 'sphere over a plane' setup, to see what we can achieve in realistic lighting with Blender.

We will resort to the setup in figure 25. The simian figure is Cornelius[2], Suzanne's baby brother. He has a somewhat shiny light brown material ($R = 0.8$, $G = 0.704$, $B = 0.584$, Ref = 0.7, Spec = 0.444, Hard = 10 - Yes, not very monkey-like, but we are talking of lights, not of materials!) and stands on a blue plane ($R=0.275$, $G=0.5$, $B=1.0$, Ref=0.8, Spec=0.5, Hard=50). For now he's lit by a single spot (Energy=1.0, $R=G=B=1.0$, SpotSi=45.0, SpotBl=0.15, ClipSta=0.1, ClipEnd=100, Samples=3, Soft=3, Bias=1.0, BufSize=512).

A rendering of Cornelius in this setup, with OSA=8 and Shadows enabled gives the result in figure 26. The result is ugly. You have very black, unrealistic shadows on Cornelius, and the shadow cast by Cornelius himself is unacceptable.

The first tweak is on ClipSta and ClipEnd, if they are adjusted so as to encompass the scene as tightly as possible (ClipSta=5, ClipEnd=21) the results get definitely better, at least for projected shadow. Cornelius's own shadow is still too dark (fig. 27).

---

[2] Cornelius the monkey was modelled by Willem-Paul van Overbruggen.

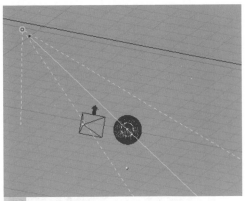

19 Spot Light setup.

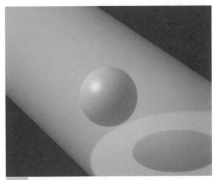

20 Halo rendering.

21 Halo Intensity Slider.

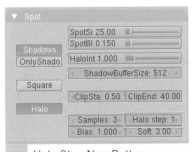

22 Halo Step NumButton.

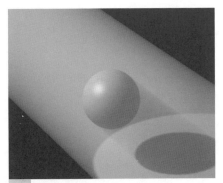

23 Halo with volumetric shadow,
Halo Step = 1

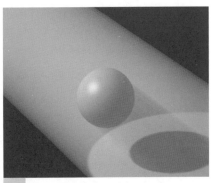

24 Halo with volumetric shadow,
Halo Step = 12

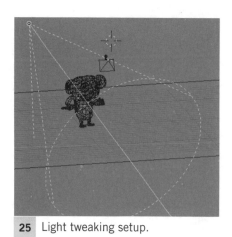

25 Light tweaking setup.

26 Simple Light Spot set up.

To set good values for the Clipping data here is a useful trick: Any object in Blender can act as a Camera in the 3D view. Hence you can select the Spot Light and switch to a view from it by pressing **CTRL-NUM0**. What you would see, in shaded mode, is shown in figure 28.

All stuff nearer to the Spot than ClipSta and further from the spot than ClipEnd is not shown at all. Hence you can fine tune these values by verifying that all shadow casting objects are visible.

What is still really lacking is the physical phenomenon of diffusion. A lit body sheds light from itself, hence shadows are not completely black because some light leaks in from neighbouring lit regions.

This light diffusion is correctly accounted for in a Ray Tracer, and in Blender too, via the Radiosity Engine. But there are set-ups which can fake this phenomenon in an acceptable fashion.

We will analyse these, from simplest to more complex.

Three point light

The three point light set-up is a classical, very simple, scheme to achieve a scene with softer lighting. Our Spot Light is the main, or *Key*, Light of the scene, the one casting shadow. We will add two more lights to fake diffusion.

The next light needed is called the *Back Light*. It is placed behind Cornelius (fig. 29).

27 Single Spot Light set up with appropriate Clipping.

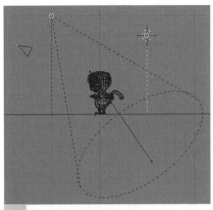

29 Back Light set up.

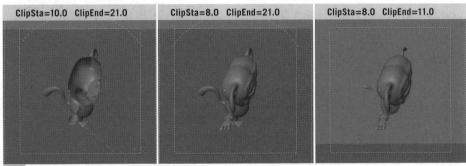

ClipSta=10.0 ClipEnd=21.0   ClipSta=8.0 ClipEnd=21.0   ClipSta=8.0 ClipEnd=11.0

28 Spot Light Clipping tweak. Left: ClipSta too high; Centre: Good; Right: ClipEnd too low.

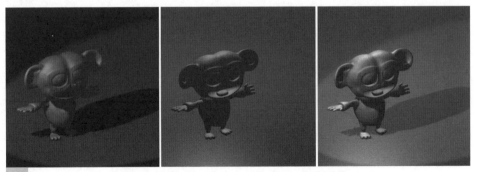

30 Key Light only (left), Back Light only (centre) and both (right).

This illuminates the hidden side of our character, and allows us to separate the foreground of our picture from the background, adding an overall sense of depth. Usually the Back Light is as strong as the Key Light, if not stronger. Here we used an Energy 1 Lamp Light (fig. 30).

The result is already far better. Finally, the third light is the *Fill* Light. The Fill light's aim is to light up the shadows on the front of Cornelius. We will place the Fill Light exactly at the location of the camera, with an Energy lower than the lower of Key and Back Lights (fig. 31). For this example an Energy = 0.75 has been chosen (fig. 32).

The Fill light makes visible parts of the model which are completely in darkness with the Key and Back light only.

The three-point set up can be further enhanced with the addition of a fourth light, especially when a bright coloured floor is present, like in this case.

If there is a bright coloured floor our eye expects the floor to diffuse part of the light all around, and that some of this light impinges on the model.

To fake this effect we place a second spot exactly specular to the Key Light with respect to the floor. This means that - if the floor is horizontal and a z=0, as it is in our example, and the Key light is in point (x=-5, y=-5, z=10), then the floor diffuse light is to be placed in (x=-5,y=-5,z=-10), pointing upward (fig. 33).

The energy for this light should be lower than that of the Key Light (here it is 0.8) and its colour should match the colour of the floor (here R = 0.25, G = 0.5, B = 1.0). The result is shown in figure 34.

Please note that we used a Spot light and not a lamp, so it would be completely blocked by the floor (shadowed) unless we set this spot shadeless by pressing the appropriate button.

Indeed we could have used a Lamp but if the floor is shiny the light it sheds is more reflected than diffused. Reflected light, physically is itself a cone coming from the specular source.

You can further enhance the effect by making the Spot cast shadows and by setting its ClipStart value high enough so that the plane cast no shadow, or by making it affecting only its layer and placing the floor on another layer.

Three point light - Outdoor

By using a Spot light as a key light the previous method is sadly bound to indoor settings or, at maximum, outdoor settings at night time. This is because the Key light is at a finite distance, its rays spread and the floor is not evenly illuminated.

If we were outdoor on a clear sunny day all the floor would be evenly lit, and shadows would be cast.

LIGHTING.TWEAKING LIGHT

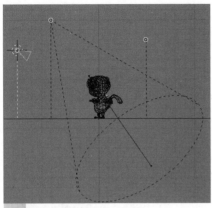

31 Fill Light set up.

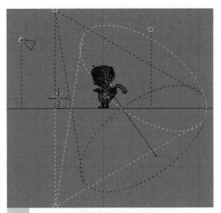

33 Floor Diffuse Light set up.

32 Key and Back Light only (left) Fill Light only (centre) and all three (right).

34 Four Light set up.

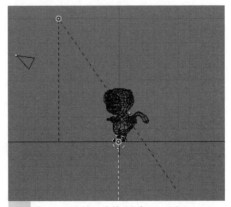

35 Sun and Hemi light for outdoor set up.

To have a uniform illumination all over the floor a Sun light is good. And if we add a Hemi light for faking the light coming from all points of the sky (as in figure 8) we can achieve a nice outdoor light... but we have no shadows!

The setup of the Key light (the sun, R = 1.0, G = 0.95, B = 0.9, Energy = 1.0) and the Fill/Back Light (both represented by the Hemi, R = 0.8, G = 0.9, B = 1.0, Energy = 0.4) is shown in figure 35 and the relevant rendering in figure 36.

The lack of shadow makes Cornelius appear as if he were floating in space. To have a shadow let's place a Spot coincident with the sun and with the same direction. Let's make this spot a Shadow Only Spot (with the appropriate button). If Energy is lowered to 0.9 and all other settings are kept at the values used in the previous example (BufSize = 512, Samples = 3, Soft = 3, Bias = 1, ClipSta = 5, ClipEnd = 21) the result is the one of figure 37 (center).

The shadow is a bit blocky because Cornelius has many fine details and the BufSize is too small, and the Sample value is to low to correctly take them into account. If BufSize is raised to 2560, Samples to 6 and Bias to 3.0 the result is the one in figure 37 (right). Much smoother.

Area Light[3]

The concept of Light coming from a point is an approximation. No real world light source is dimensionless. All light is shed by surfaces, not by points.

This has a couple of interesting implications, mainly on shadows:

- Sharp shadows does not exist: shadows have blurry edges
- Shadow edge blurriness depends on the relative positions and sizes of the light, the shadow casting object and the object receiving the shadow.

The first of this issues is approximated with the 'Soft' setting of the Spot light, but the second is not. To have a clearer understanding of this point imagine a tall thin pole in the middle of a flat plain illuminated by the Sun.

The Sun is not a point, it has a dimension and, for us earthlings, it is half of a degree wide. If you look at the shadow you will notice that it is very sharp at the base of the pole and that it grows blurrier as you go toward the shadow of the tip. If the pole is tall and thin enough its shadow will vanish.

To better grasp this concept have a look at figure 38. The sun shed light, the middle object obstruct sun rays completely only in the gray region. For a point in the yellow region the Sun is partially visible, hence each of those point is partially lit.

---

[3] Since Blender 2.32 Blender has a built-in Area lamp type. See also chapter 29.

| Sun + Hemi Light | Sun + Hemi Light + Shadow Only Spot | Sun + Hemi Light + Shadow Only Spot with turned parameters |

37 Outdoor rendering.

36 Sun and Hemi light for outdoor rendering.

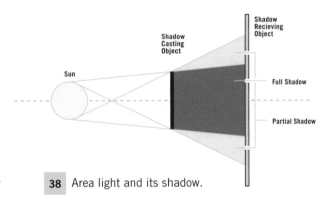

38 Area light and its shadow.

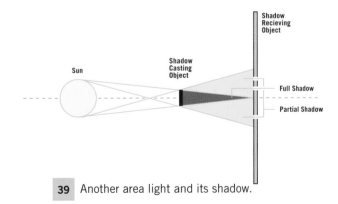

39 Another area light and its shadow.

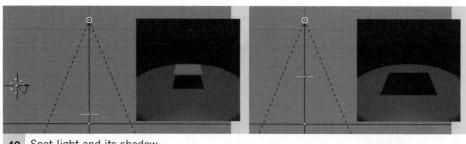

40 Spot light and its shadow.

The yellow region is a partial shadow region where illumination drops smoothly from full light to full shadow. It is also evident, that this transition region is smaller next to the shadow casting object and grow larger far away from it. Furthermore, if the shadow casting object is smaller than the light casting object (and if the light casting object is the sun this is often the case) there is a distance beyond which only partial shadow remains (fig. 39).

In Blender, if we place a single Spot at a fixed distance from a first plane and look at the shadow cast at a second plane as this second plane gets further away we notice that the shadow gets larger but not softer (fig. 40).

To fake an area light with Blender we can use several Spots, as if we were sampling the area casting light with a discrete number of point lights.

This can either be achieved by placing several Spots by hand, or by using Blender's DupliVert feature (the Section called *DupliVerts* in Chapter 17), which is more efficient.

Add a Mesh Grid 4x4. Where the spot is, be sure normals are pointing down, by letting Blender show the Normals and eventually flipping them, as explained in the Section called *Basic Editing* in Chapter 6 (fig. 41). Parent the Spot to the Grid, select the Grid and in the Object Context Anim Settings Panel (**F7**) press DupliVert and Rot. Rot is not strictly necessary but will help you in positioning the Area Light later on. You will have a set of Spots as in figure 42.

Then decrease the Energy of the Spot. If for a single Spot you used a certain energy, now you must subdivide that energy among all the duplicates. Here we have 16 spots, so each should be allotted 1/16 of Energy (that is Energy=0.0625).

The same two renderings of above, with this new hacked area light will yield to the results in figure 43. The result is far from the expected, because the Spot light sampling of the Area light is too coarse. On the other hand a finer sampling would yield to higher number of duplicated Spots and to unacceptable rendering times.

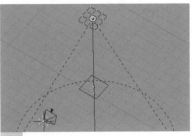

41 Grid setup.

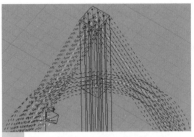

42 Spot light and its dupliverts.

43 Fake area light with multiple spots.

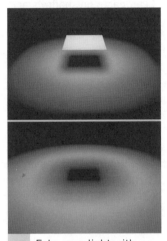

44 Fake area light with multiple soft spots.

A much better result can be attained by softening the spots, that is setting `SpotBl`=0.45, `Sample`=12, `Soft`=24 and `Bias`=1.5 (fig. 44).

Finally,shows what happens to Cornelius once the Key Light is substituted with 65 duplicated Spots of Energy=0.0154 in a circular pattern. Please note how the shadow softly goes from sharp next to the feet to softer and softer as it gets further away from him. This is the correct physical behavior.

45 Cornelius under Area Light.

Global Illumination (and Global Shadowing)

The above techniques work well when there is a single, or anyway finite number of lights, casting distinct shadows.

The only exceptions are the outdoor setting, where the Hemi Light fakes the light cast by the sky, and the Area Light, where multiple spots fakes a light source of finite extension.

The first of these two is very close to nice outdoor lighting, were it not for the fact that the Hemi Light casts no shadows and hence you don't have realistic results.

To obtain a really nice outdoor setting, especially for cloudy daylight, you need light coming from all directions of the sky, yet casting shadows!

This can be obtained by applying a technique very similar to the one used for the Area Light setup, but using half a sphere as a parent mesh. This is usually referred to as "Global Illumination".

You can either use a UVsphere or an IcoSphere, the latter has vertices evenly distributed whereas the former has a great concentration of vertices at poles. Using an IcoSphere hence yields a more 'uniform' illumination, all the points of the sky radiating an equal intensity; a UVsphere casts much more light from the pole(s). Personally I recommend the IcoSphere.

Let's prepare a setup, comprising a plane and some solids, as in figure 46. We will use simple shapes to better appreciate the results.

Switch to top view and add an IcoSphere, a subdivision level 2 IcoSphere is usually enough, a level 3 one yields even smoother results. Scale the IcoSphere so that it completely, and loosely, contains the whole scene. Switch to front view and, in Edit-Mode, delete the lower half of the IcoSphere (fig. 47). This will be our "Sky Dome" where the spots will be parented and dupliverted.

Again in Top View add a Spot Light, parent it to the half IcoSphere (**CTRL-P**) and press the DupliVert and Rot buttons exactly as in the previous example. The result, in FrontView, is the one in figure 48.

This is not what we want, since all spots point outwards and the scene is not lit. This is due to the fact that the IcoSphere normals point outward. It is possible to invert their directions by selecting all vertices in Edit Mode and by pressing the Flip Normals button in the Mesh Tools Panel of the Editing (**F9**) Context (fig. 49).

LIGHTING.GLOBAL ILLUMINATION

46 Global Illumination scene.

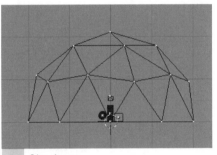

47 Sky dome.

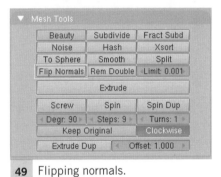

49 Flipping normals.

48 Sky dome with duplicated spots.

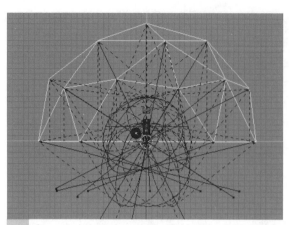

50 Correct sky dome and dupliverted Spot Lights.

This leads to the new configuration in figure 50.

To obtain good results select the original Spot Light and change its parameters to a wide angle with soft boundaries (SpotSi=70.0; SpotBl=0.5); with suitable ClipSta and ClipEnd values; in this case 5 and 30, respectively, in any case appropriate values to encompass the whole scene; increase samples to 6 and softness to 12. Decrease energy to 0.1; remember you are using many spots, so each must be weak (fig. 51).

Now you can make the rendering. If some materials are given and a world set, the result should be that of figure 52. Note the soft shadows and the 'omnidirectional' lighting. Even better results can be achieved with a level 3 IcoSphere.

This Global Illumination technique effectively substitutes, at a very high computational cost, the Hemi for the above outdoor setting.

It is possible to add a directional light component by faking the Sun either via a single spot or with an Area Light.

An alternative possibility is to make the IcoSphere 'less uniform' by subdividing one of its faces a number of times, as is done for one of the rear faces in figure 53. This is done by selecting one face and pressing the Subdivide button, again in the Mesh Tools Panel of the Editing (**F9**) Context. Then de-select all, re-select the single inner small face and subdivide it again, and so on.

The result is a very soft directional light together with a global illumination sky dome or, briefly, an anisotropic sky dome (fig. 54). This is quite good for cloudy conditions, but not so good for clear sunny days. For really clear days, it is better to keep the sky dome separate from the Sun light, so as to be able to use different colours for each.

LIGHTING.GLOBAL ILLUMINATION

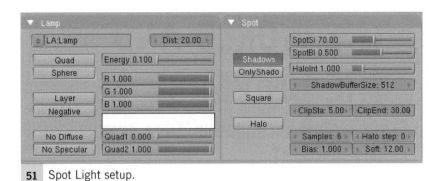

51 Spot Light setup.

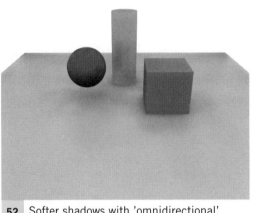

52 Softer shadows with 'omnidirectional' lightning.

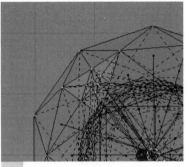

53 Making spots denser in an area.

54 Anisotropic skydome render.

CH. 10 THE WORLD AND THE UNIVERSE

THE WORLD BACKGROUND, MIST, STARS, AMBIENT LIGHT

Blender provides a number of very interesting settings to complete your renderings by adding a nice background, and some interesting 'depth' effects. These are accessible via the Shading Context (**F5**) and World Buttons sub-context (🌐) shown in figure 1. By default a very plain uniform world is present. You can edit it or add a new world.

The World Background

The simplest way to use the World Buttons is to provide a nice gradient background for images. The buttons in the World Panel (fig. 2) allow you to define the color at the horizon (HoR, HoG, HoB buttons) and at the zenith (ZeR, ZeG, ZeB buttons).

These colors are interpreted differently, according to the Buttons in the Preview Panel (fig. 2):

- Blend - The background color is blended from horizon to zenith. If only this button is pressed, the gradient runs from the bottom to the top of the rendered image regardless of the camera orientation.

- Real - If this button is also pressed the blending is dependent on the camera orientation. The horizon color is exactly at the horizon (on the x-y plane), and the zenith color is used for points vertically above and below the camera.

- Paper - If this button is pressed the gradient occurs on the zenith-horizon-zenith colors. Thus, there are two transitions on the image, which reflect the camera rotation but which keep the horizon color to the center and the zenith color to the extremes.

1   World Buttons.

2   Background colors.

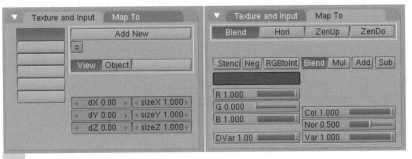

3   Texture buttons.

The World Buttons also provide a `Texture` Panel with two Tabs. They are used much like the Materials textures, except for a couple of differences (fig. 3):

- There are only six texture channels.

- `Texture mapping` - Has only the `Object` and `View` options, with View being the default orientation.

- `Affect` - Texture affects color only, but in four different ways: It can affect the `Blend` channel, making the Horizon color appear where the texture is non-zero; the color of the `Horizon`; and the color of the Zenith, up or down (`Zen Up`, `Zen Down`)

Mist

Mist can greatly enhance the illusion of depth in your rendering. To create mist, Blender basically mixes the background color with the object color and enhances the strength of the former, the further the object is away from the camera. The Mist settings are in the Mist Stars Physics Panel and are shown in figure 4.

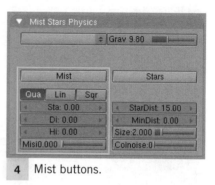

4 Mist buttons.

The Mist Button toggles mist on and off. The row of three Toggle Buttons below this button set the decay rate of the mist as Quadratic, linear, and Square Root. These settings control the law which governs the strength of the mist as you move further away from the camera.

The mist begins at a distance from the camera as defined by the Sta: button, and is computed over a length defined by the Di: button. Objects further from the camera than Sta+Di are completely hidden by the mist.

By default, the mist covers all of the image uniformly. To produce a more realistic effect you might want to have the mist decrease with height (altitude, or z) using the Hi: NumButton. If the value of this button is non-zero it sets, in Blender units, an interval, around z=0 in which the mist goes from maximum intensity (below) to zero (above).

Finally, the Misi: NumButton defines the intensity, or strength, of the mist.

Figure 5 shows a possible test setup.

Figure 6 shows the results with and without mist. The settings are shown in figure 7; the texture is a plain procedural cloud texture with Hard noise set.

Mist distances

To see what the mist will actually affect, select your camera, go to Editing Context (**F9**) and press the Show Mist TogButton in the Camera Panel. The camera will show mist limits as a segment projecting from the camera starting from Sta and of distance Di.

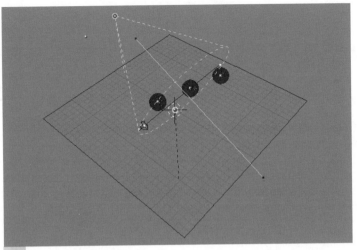

5 | Mist test setup.

6 | Rendering without mist (left) and with mist (right).

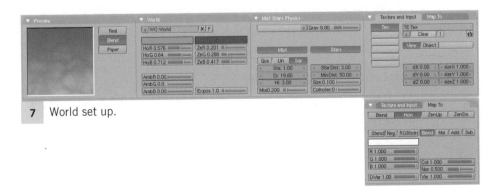

7 | World set up.

Stars

Stars are randomly placed halo-like objects which appear in the background. The star settings are again in the `Mist Stars Physics` Panel (fig. 8).

When creating stars, you must first understand a few important concepts:

`StarDist`: is the *average* distance between stars. Stars are intrinsically 3D feature that are placed in space, not on the image!

`Min Dist`: Is the *minimum* distance from the camera at which stars are placed. This should be greater than the distance from the camera to the *furthest* object in your scene, unless you want to risk having stars appear *in front* of your objects.

The `Size:` NumButton defines the actual size of the star halo. Keep this much smaller than the proposed default, to keep the material smaller than pixel-size and create pin-point stars which are much more realistic.

The `ColNoise:` NumButton adds a random hue to the otherwise plain white stars. It is usually a good idea to add a little `ColNoise`.

Figure 9 shows the same misty image of figure 7 but with stars added. The stars settings are shown in figure 10.

Ambient Light

The `World` Panel also contain the sliders to define the Ambient light. The effect of Ambient light is to provide a very simple alternative to Global Illumination, inasmuch as it lights up shadows.

Using Ambient light together with other light sources can give convincing results in a fraction of the time required by true GI techniques, ut of course quality cannot compare.

The Ambient light sliders are shown in figure 11.

9 Star rendering.

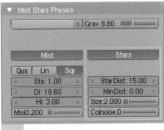

8 Star buttons.

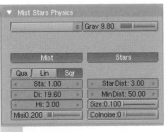

10 Star settings.

11 Ambient light settings.

PART III

ANIMATION

If you are ready to go into Computer Graphics animation then this is your part. Here we will analyze Blender's feature for what concerns moving Objects in 3D space and deforming Objects in time.

The most relevant chapter is the one dedicated to Character Animation, where the incredible Blender's capabilities are unveiled.

CH. 11 ANIMATION OF UNDEFORMED OBJECTS

KEYFRAMES, IPO CURVES AND IPO KEYS, OTHER APPLICATIONS OF IPO CURVES, PATH ANIMATION

Objects can be animated in many ways. They can be animated as Objects, changing their position, orientation or size in time; they can be animated by deforming them; that is animating their vertices or control points; or they can be animated via very complex and flexible interaction with a special kind of object: the Armature.

In this chapter we will cover the first case, but the basics given here are actually vital for understanding the following chapters as well.

Three methods are normally used in animation software to make a 3D object move:

- *Key frames*
  Complete positions are saved for units of time (frames). An animation is created by interpolating an object fluidly through the frames. The advantage of this method is that it allows you to work with clearly visualized units. The animator can work from one position to the next and can change previously created positions, or move them in time.

- *Motion Curves*
  Curves can be drawn for each XYZ component for location, rotation, and size. These form the graphs for the movement, with time set out horizontally and the value set out vertically. The advantage of this method is that it gives you precise control over the results of the movement.

- *Path*
  A curve is drawn in 3D space, and the Object is constrained to follow it according to a given time function of the position along the path.

The first two systems in Blender are completely integrated in a single one, the IPO (InterPOlation) system. Fundamentally, the IPO system consists of standard motion curves. A simple press of a button changes the IPO to a key system, without conversion, and with no change to the results. The user can work any way he chooses to with the keys, switching to motion curves and back again, in whatever way produces the best result or satisfies the user's preferences.

The IPO system also has relevant implication in Path animations.

IPO Block

The IPO block in Blender is universal. It makes no difference whether an object's movement is controlled or the material settings. Once you have learned to work with object IPOs, how you work with other IPOs will become obvious. Anyway Blender does distinguish between different *types* of IPOs and the interface keeps track of it automatically.

Every type of IPO block has a fixed number of available *channels*. These each have a name (LocX, SizeZ, etc.) that indicates how they are applied. When you add an IPO Curve to a channel, animation begins immediately. At your discretion (and there are separate channels for this), a curve can be linked directly to a value (LocX...), or it can affect a variance of it (dLocX...). The latter enables you to move an object as you would usually do, with the Grabber, without disrupting the IPO. The actual location is then determined by IPO Curves *relative* to that location.

The Blender interface offers many options for copying IPOs, linking IPOs to more than one object (one IPO can animate multiple objects.), or deleting IPO links. The IPO Window Reference section gives a detailed description of this. This chapter is restricted to the main options for application.

Key Frames

The simplest method for creating an object IPO is with the "Insert key" (**IKEY**) command in the 3DWindow, with an Object selected. A Pop-up menu provides a wide selection of options (fig. 1). We will select the topmost option: Loc. Now the current location X-Y-Z, is saved and everything takes place automatically:

- If there is no IPO block, a new one is created and linked to the object.
- If there are no IPOCurves in the channels LocX, LocY and LocZ, these are created.
- Vertices are then added in the IPOCurves with the exact values of the object location.

We go 30 frames further on (3 x **UPARROW**) and move the object. Again we use **IKEY** Now we can immediately press **ENTER** since Blender remembers our last choiche and will highlight it. The new position is inserted in the IPO Curves. We can see this by slowly paging back through the frames (**LEFTARROW**). The object moves between the two positions.

In this way, you can create the animation by paging through the frames, position by position. Note that the location of the object is *directly* linked to the curves. When you change frames, the IPOs are always re-evaluated and re-applied. You can freely move the object within the same frame, but as soon as you change frame, the object 'jumps' to the position determined by the IPO.

The rotation and size of the object are completely free in this example. They can be changed or animated with the Insert key procedure by selecting from the **IKEY** menu the other options such as Rotation, Size and any combination of these.

The IPO Curves

Now we want to see exactly what happened. The first Screen initialised in the standard Blender start-up file is excellent for this. Activate it with **CTRL-LEFTARROW**. At the right we see the IPO Window displayed (fig. 2). You can of course turn any window into an IPO Window with the pertinent Window Type menu entry, but it is more handy to have both a 3D Window and an IPO Window at the same time. This shows all the IPO Curves, the channels used and those available. You can zoom in and out the IPO Window and translate it just as every other Blender Window.

In addition to the standard channels, which can be set via **IKEY**, you have the *delta* options, such as dLocX. These channels allow you to assign a *relative* change. This option is primarily used to control multiple objects with the same IPO. In addition, it is possible to work in animation 'layers'. You can achieve subtle effects this way without having to draw complicated curves.

Each curve can be selected individually with the **RMB**. In addition, the Grabber and Size modes operate here just as in the 3DWindow. You can select IPOs also by clicking the color button in the right channel names column. By clicking the IPO channel name you effectively hide/show the relative curve. Selecting all curves (**AKEY**) and moving them to the right (**GKEY**), you can move the complete animation in time. Each curve can be placed in EditMode individually, or it can be done collectively. Select the curves and press **TAB**. Now the individual vertices and *handles* of the curve are displayed. The Bézier handles are coded, like it is in the the Curve Object:

- Free Handle (black). This can be used any way you wish. Hotkey: **HKEY** (switches between Free and Aligned).
- Aligned Handle (pink). This arranges all the handles in a straight line. Hotkey: **HKEY** (toggles between Free and Aligned).
- Vector Handle (green). Both parts of a handle always point to the previous or next handle. Hotkey: **VKEY**.
- Auto Handle (yellow). This handle has a completely automatic length and direction. Hotkey: **SHIFT-HKEY**.

1 | Insert Key Menu.

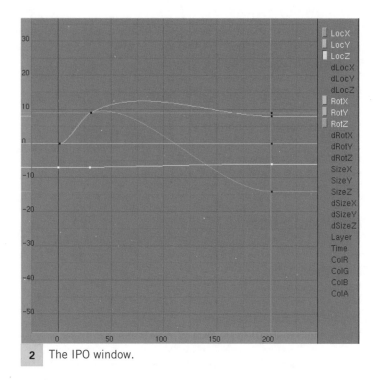

2 | The IPO window.

Handles can be moved by first selecting the middle vertex with **RMB**. This selects the other two vertices as well. Then immediately start the Grab mode with **RMB**-hold and move. Handles can be *rotated* by first selecting the end of one of the vertices and then use the Grabber by means of the **RMB**-hold and move action.

As soon as handles are rotated, the type is changed automatically:

• Auto Handle becomes Aligned.
• Vector Handle becomes Free.

"Auto" handles are placed in a curve by default. The first and last Auto handles always move horizontally, which creates a fluid interpolation.

The IPOCurves have an important feature that distinguishes them from normal curves: it is impossible to place more than one curve segment horizontally. Loops and circles in an IPO are senseless and ambiguous. An IPO can only have 1 value at a time. This is automatically detected in the IPOWindow. By moving part of the IPOCurve horizontally, you see that the selected vertices move 'through' the curve. This allows you to duplicate parts of a curve (**SHIFT-D**) and to move them to another time frame.

It is also important to specify how an IPOCurve must be read *outside* of the curve itself. There are four options for this in the `Curve>>Extend Mode` Submenu in the IPO Window header (fig. 3).

Thre effect of each of these can be appreciated in figure 4.

The options from top to bottom:

Extend Mode Constant:
The ends of selected IPOCurves are continuously (horizontally) extrapolated. It is the default behaviour.

Extend Mode Extrapolation:
The ends of the selected IPOCurves continue in the direction in which they ended.

Extend Mode Cyclic:
The complete width of the IPOCurve is repeated cyclically.

Extend Mode Cyclic Extrapolation:
The complete width of the IPOCurve is extrapolated cyclic.

In addition to Béziers, there are two other possible types for IPOCurves. Use the **TKEY** command, and the dialog which then pops-up, or the `Curve>>Interpolation Mode` submenu entry to select them. The interpolation of the selected IPOCurves can be set to:

- `Constant` - after each vertex of the curve, this value remains constant. No interpolation takes place.
- `Linear` - linear interpolation occurs between the vertices.
- `Bezier` - the standard fluid interpolation.

The IPO curves need not be set only by Key Framing. They can also be drawn 'by hand'. Use the **CTRL-LMB** command. Here are the rules:

There is no IPO block yet (in this window) *and* one *channel* is selected:
a new IPOBlock is created along with the first IPOCurve with one vertex placed where the mouse was clicked.

There is already an IPO block, and a *channel* is selected without an IPOCurve:
a new IPOCurve with one vertex is added.

There is already an IPO block, and a *channel* is selected withh an existing IPOCurve:
A new point is added to the selected IPOCurve.

ANIMATION OF UNDEFORMED OBJECTS.THE IPO CURVES

3   IPO extension options menu.

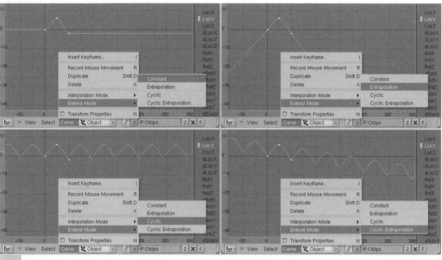

4   Extended IPOs.

This is *not* possible if multiple IPOCurves are selected or in EditMode.

This is the best method for specifying axis rotations quickly: Select the object; in the IPOWindow, press one of the "Rot" channels and use **CTRL-LMB** to insert two points. If the axis rotation must be continuous, you must use the `Curve>>Extend Mode>>Extrapolation` Menu entry.

Make an object rotate

One disadvantage of working with motion curves is that the *freedom* of transformations is limited. You can work quite intuitively with motion curves, but only if this can be processed on an XYZ basis. For a location, this is outstanding, but for a size and rotation there are better mathematical descriptions available: matrices (3x3 numbers) for size and quaternions (4 numbers) for rotation. These could also have been processed in the channels, but this can quite easily lead to confusing and mathematically complicated situations.

Limiting the *size* to the three numbers XYZ is obvious, but this limits it to a rectangular distortion. A diagonal scaling such as 'shearing' is impossible. Simply working in hierarchies can solve this. A *non*-uniform scaled Parent will influence the rotation of a Child as a 'shear'.

The limitation of the three number XYZ rotations is less intuitive. This so-called Euler rotation is not uniform - the same rotation can be expressed with different numbers - and has the bothersome effect that it is *not* possible to rotate from any position to another, the infamous *gimbal lock*. While working with different rotation keys, the user may suddenly be confronted with quite unexpected interpolations, or it may turn out to be impossible to force a particular axis rotation when making manual changes. Here, also, a better solution is to work with a hierarchy. A Parent will *always* assign the specified axis rotation to the Child. (It is handy to know that the X, Y and Z rotations are calculated one *after* the other. The curve that affects the RotX channel, *always* determines the X axis rotation).

Luckily, Blender calculates everything internally with matrices and quaternions. Hierarchies thus work normally, and the Rotate mode does what you would expect it to. Only the IPOs are a limitation here, but in this case the ease of use prevails above a not very intuitive mathematical purity.

IPO Curves and IPO Keys

The easiest way to work with motion curves is to convert them to IPO Keys. We return to the situation in the previous example: we have specified two positions in an object IPO in frame 1 and frame 31 with **IKEY**. At the right of the screen, you can see an IPO Window. We set the current frame to 21 (fig. 5).

Press **KKEY** while the mouse cursor is in the 3D Window. Two things will happen now:

- The IPO Window switches to IPO Key mode.
- The selected object is assigned the "DrawKey" option.

The two actions each have separate meanings.

- The IPO Window now draws vertical lines through all the vertices of all the visible IPO Curves (IPOs are now black). Vertices with the same 'frame' value are linked to the vertical lines. The vertical lines (the "IPOKeys") can be selected, moved or duplicated, just like the vertices in EditMode. You can translate the IPOKeys only horizontally.
- The object is not only shown in its current position but 'ghost' objects are also shown at all the Key positions. In addition to now being able to visualize the key positions of the object, you can also modify them *in* the 3D Window. In this example, use the Grab mode on the object to change the *selected* IPOKeys.

ANIMATION OF UNDEFORMED OBJECTS.IPO CURVES

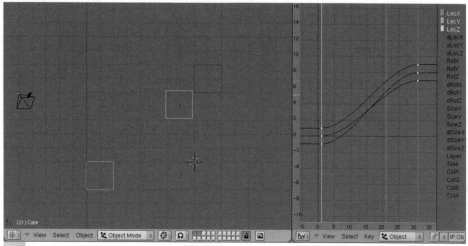

5 The IPOKey mode.

Below are a number of instructions for utilizing the power of the system:

- You can only use the **RMB** to select IPOKeys in the IPOWindow. Border select, and *extend* select, are also enabled here. Select all IPOKeys to transform the complete animation system in the 3DWindow.
- The "Insert Key" always affects *all* selected objects. The IPOKeys for multiple objects can also be transformed simultaneously in the 3DWindow. Use the **SHIFT-K** command: Show and select all keys to transform complete animations of a group of objects all at once.
- Use the **PAGEUP** and **PAGEDOWN** commands to select subsequent keys in the 3DWindow.
- You can create IPOKeys with each arrangement of channels. By consciously *excluding* certain channels, you can force a situation in which changes to key positions in the 3DWindow can only be made to the values specified by the visible channels. For example, with only the channel LocX selected, the keys can only be moved in the X direction.
- Each IPOKey consists of the vertices that have *exactly* the same frame value. If vertices are moved manually, this can result in large numbers of keys, each having only one curve. In this case, use the **JKEY** ("Join") command to combine selected IPOKeys. It is also possible to assign selected IPOKeys vertices for *all* the visible curves: use **IKEY** in the IPOWindow and choose "Selected keys".
- The DrawKey option and the IPOKey mode can be switched on and off independently. Use the button EditButtons->DrawKey to switch off this option or object. You can switch IPOKey mode on and off yourself with **KKEY** in the IPOWindow. Only **KKEY** in the 3DWindow turns on/off both the DrawKey and IPOKey mode.

Other applications of IPO Curves

There are several other application for IPOs other than just animating an Object movement.

The IPO Type Menu Buttons in the header (fig. 6) allow IPO Block type selection, the active one there is the Object IPO described up to now, but there are Material IPO, World IPO, Vertex Keys IPO, Constraints IPO and Sequence IPO. Not every entry is always present, depending on context. Curve IPO block appears if the selected object is a Curve and not a Mesh, the Lamp IPO, appears only if the selected object is a Lamp.

Material IPO is a way of animating a Material. Just as with objects, IPO Curves can be used to specify 'key positions' for Materials. With the mouse in the ButtonsWindow, the command **IKEY** calls up a pop-up menu with options for the various Material variables. If you are in a Material, Lamp or World IPO Block then a small Num Button appears next to the IPO type Menu in the IPO Window toolbar. This indicates which texture channel is active. The mapping for all 8 channels can be controlled with IPO-Curves!

Strictly speaking, with textures two other animations are possible. Since Objects can give texture coordinates on other objects (Each object in Blender can be used as a source for texture coordinates. To do this, the option "Object" must be selected in the green "Coordinates input" buttons and the name of the object must be filled in. An inverse transformation is now performed on the global render coordinate to obtain the *local* object coordinate) it is possible to animate the texture simply by animating the location, size, and rotation of the object.

Furthermore, at each frame, Blender can be made to load another (numbered) Image as a texture map instead of having a fixed one. It is also possible to use SGI movie files or AVI files for this.

The Time IPO

With the Time IPO curve you can manipulate the animation time of objects without changing the animation or the other IPOs. In fact, it changes the mapping of animation time to global animation time (fig. 7).

To grasp this concept, make a simple keyframe-animation of a moving object, from a position to another in, say, 50 frames. Then select the Time channel and create a Time IPO in the IPO Window going from point (1,1) to point (50,50). It is easy to set the start and end point of an IPO by using **NKEY** and entering the values numerically.

ANIMATION OF UNDEFORMED OBJECTS.IPO CURVES

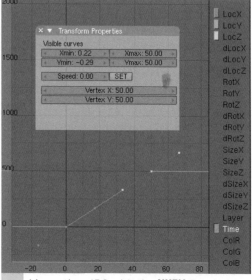

6 The IPO Type Menu.

7 Linear time IPO with the **NKEY** Panel open.

In frames where the slope of the Time IPO is positive, your object will advance in its animation. The speed depends on the value of the slope. A slope bigger than 1 will animate faster than the base animation. A slope smaller than 1 will animate slower. A slope of 1 means no change in the animation, negative power slopes allow you to reverse the animation.

The Time IPO is especially interesting for particle systems, allowing you to "freeze" the particles or to animate particles absorbed by an object instead of emitted. Other possibilities are to make a time lapse or slow motion animation.

You need to copy the Time IPO for every animation system to get a full slow motion. But by stopping only some animations, and continue to animate, for example, the camera you can achieve some very nice effects (like those used to stunning effect in the movie "The Matrix")

Multiple Time IPOs

Path Animation

A different way to have Objects move in the space is to constrain them to follow a given path.

When objects need to follow a path, or it is too hard to animate a special kind of movement with the keyframe method (Think of a planet following its way around the Sun. Animating that with keyframes is virtually impossible) curve objects can be used for the 3D display of an animation path.

If the Curve object contains more than a single continuous curve only the first curve in the object is then used.

As for tracking there are two Path animation methods, the old, pre 2.30 method described here and the new method, which actually defines a constraint, which will be described in the Section called *Constraints* in Chapter 13. When parenting an Object to a Curve you will be asked to choose a `Normal Parent` or a `Follow Path` option. The Former is what you need for conventional Path animation, but other actions needs to be taken later. The second option creates a "Follow Path" Constraint, and it is all you need to do.

Any kind of curve can become a path by setting the option `CurvePath` Toggle Button in the Editing Context window (**F9**) to ON (fig. 8).

When a Curve has childs it can be turned to a Path by selecting it, going int the Editing Context (**F9**) and activating the `CurvePath` Toggle button in the Curve and Surface Panel. Child objects of the Curve will now move along the specified path. It is a good idea to set the Curve to 3D via the 3D Toggle Button of the Curve Edit Buttons so that the paths can be freely modelled.

Otherwise, in the Add menu under Curve->Path, there is a primitive with the correct settings already there. This is a 5th order NURBS spline, which can be used to create very fluid, continuous movements.

Normally a Path is 100 frames long and it is followed in 100 frames by children. You can make it longer or shorter by varying the `PathLength:` Num Button.

The *speed* along a path is determined with an appropriate curve in the IPO Window. To see it, in the IPO Window Header button you must select the `Curve` type for the IPO block. A single channel, `Speed` is there. The complete path runs in the IPO Window between the vertical values 0.0 and 1.0. Drawing a curve between these values links the time to the position on the path. Backward and pulsing movements are possible with this. For most paths, an IPO Curve must run *exactly* between the Y-values

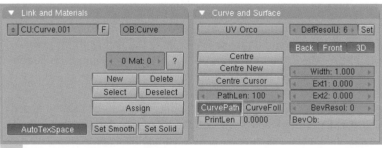

8 The Editing Context and `Curve and Surface` Panel.

9 Tracking Buttons.

0.0 and 1.0. To achieve this, use the Number menu (**NKEY**) in the IPO Window. If the IPO Curve is deleted, the value of `PathLen` determines the duration of the path. A linear movement is defined in this case. The Speed IPO is a finer way of controlling Path length. The path is long 1 for time IPO, and if the time IPO goes from 0 to 1 in 200 frames then the path is 200 frames long.

Using the option `CurveFollow`, in the `Curve and Surface` Panel, a rotation is also given to the Child objects of the path, so that they permanently point in the direction of the path. Use the "tracking" buttons in the `Anim settings` Panel of the Object (**F7**) context to specify the effect of the rotation (fig. 9) as you would do for Tracking:

`TrackX, Y, Z, -X, -Y, -Z` This specifies the direction axis, i.e. the axis that is placed on the path.

`UpX, UpY, UpZ` Specifies which axis must point 'upwards', in the direction of the (local) positive Z axis. If the `Track` and the `Up` axis coincides, it is deactivated.

Curve paths have the same problem of Bevelled curves for what concern the definition of the "Up" direction.

To visualize these rotations precisely, we must make it possible for a Child to have its own rotations. Erase the Child's rotation with **ALT-R**. Also erase the "Parent Inverse": **ALT-P.** The best method is to 'parent' an *unrotated* Child to the path with the command **SHIFT-CTRL-PKEY**: "Make parent without inverse". Now the Child jumps directly to the path and the Child points in the right direction.

3D paths also get an extra value for each vertex: the 'tilt'. This can be used to specify an axis rotation. Use **TKEY** in EditMode to change the tilt of selected vertices in Edit-Mode, e.g. to have a Child move around as if it were on a roller coaster.

Figure 10 shows a complex application. We want to make a fighter dive into a canyon, fly next to the water and then rise again, all this by following it with our camera and, possibly, having reflection in the water!

To do this we will need three paths. Path 1 has a fighter parented to it, the fighter will fly following it.

The fighter has an Empty named 'Track' Parented to it in a strategic position. A camera is then parented to another curve, Path 2, and follows it, tracking the 'Track' Empty. The Fighter has a constant Speed IPO, the camera has not. It goes faster, then slower, always tracking the Empty, and hence the fighter, so we will have very fluid movements of the camera from Fighter side, to Fighter front, other side, back, etc. (fig. 11).

Since we want our fighter to fly over a river, we need to set up an Env Map for the water surface to obtain reflections. But the Empty used for the calculations must be always in specular position with respect to the camera... and the camera is moving along a path!

Path 3 is hence created by mirroring path 2 with respect to the water plane, by duplicating it, and using **SKEY, YKEY** – and by entering -1 as a factor with the keyboard – in Edit Mode with respect to the cursor, once the cursor is on the plane.

The Empty for the Env Map calculation is then parented to this new path, and the Time IPO of Path 2 is copied to Path 3. Figure 12 shows a rendered frame. Some particle systems were used for trails.

The scene presents many subtle tricks, as fog, a sky sphere encircling the scene and so on.

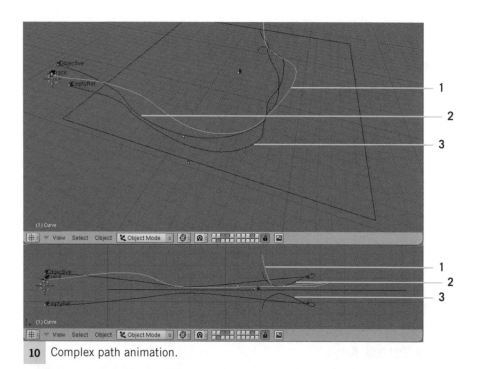

10 Complex path animation.

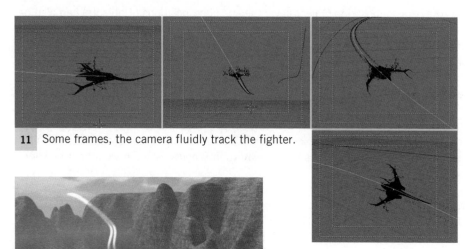

11 Some frames, the camera fluidly track the fighter.

12 A frame of the final animation.

CH. 12 ANIMATION OF DEFORMATIONS

ABSOLUTE VERTEX KEYS, RELATIVE VERTEX KEYS, LATTICE ANIMATION

Animating an Object/Material, is not the only thing you can do in Blender. You can change, reshape, deform your objects in time!

There are many ways of achieving this actually, and one technique is so powerful and general there is a full chapter for it: Character animation. The other techniques will be handled here.

Absolute Vertex Keys

VertexKeys (as opposed to Object keys, the specified positions of objects) can also be created in Blender; VertexKeys are the specified positions of vertices *within* an Object. Since this can involve thousands of vertices, separate motion curves are not created for each vertex, the traditional Key position system is used instead. A single IPOCurve is used to determine how interpolation is performed and the times at which a Vertex-Key can be seen.

VertexKeys are part of the Object Data, not of the Object. When duplicating the Object Data, the associated VertexKey block is also copied. It is not possible to permit multiple Objects to share the same VertexKeys in Blender, since it would not be very practical.

The Vertex Key block is universal and understands the distinction between a Mesh, a Curve, a Surface or a Lattice. The interface and use is therefore unified. Working with Mesh VertexKeys is explained in detail in this section, which also contains a number of brief comments on the other Object Data.

The first VertexKey position that is created is always the *reference* Key. This key defines the texture coordinates. Only if this Key is *active* can the faces and curves, or the *number* of vertices, be changed. It is allowed to assign other Keys a different number of vertices. The Key system automatically interpolates this.

ANIMATION OF DEFORMATIONS.ABSOLUTE VERTEX KEYS

Insert Vertex Keys
Relative keys
Absolute keys

1 Insert Key Menu.

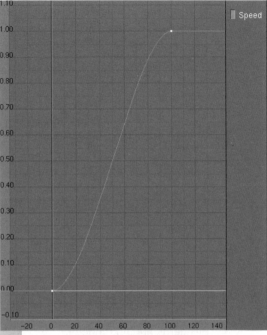

2 Reference Key and Speed IPO.

A practical example is given below. When working with VertexKeys, it is very handy to have an IPO Window open. Use the first Screen from the standard Blender file, for example. In the IPO Window, we must then specify that we want to see the VertexKeys. To do this use the IPO type Menu Button and select `Vertex`. Go to the 3DWindow with the mouse cursor and press **IKEY**. With a Mesh object selected and active. The "Insert Key" menu has several options, the latter being `Mesh`. As soon as this has been selected, a new dialog appears (fig. 1) asking for Relative or absolute Vertex Key.

We will choose `Absolute Keys`; a yellow horizontal line is drawn in the IPO Window. This is the first key and thus the *reference* Key. An IPO Curve is also created for "Speed" (fig. 2).

Creating VertexKeys in Blender is very simple, but the fact that the system is very sensitive in terms of its configuration can cause a number of 'invisible' things to happen. The following rule must therefore be taken into consideration.

As soon as a VertexKey position is inserted it is *immediately active*. All subsequent changes in the Mesh are linked to *this* Key position. It is therefore important that the Key position be added *before* editing begins.

Vertex Key creation

Go a few frames further and again select: **IKEY**, `Mesh` (in the 3D Window). The second Key is drawn as a light blue line. This is a normal Key; this key and all subsequent Keys affect only the vertex information. Press **TAB** for EditMode and translate one of the vertices in the Mesh. Then browse a few frames back: nothing happens! As long as we are in EditMode, other VertexKeys are *not* applied. What you see in EditMode is *always* the *active* VertexKey.

Leave EditMode and browse through the frames again. We now see the effect of the VertexKey system. VertexKeys can only be selected in the IPO Window. We always do this *out* of Edit Mode: the 'contents' of the VertexKey are now temporarily displayed in the Mesh. We can edit the specified Key by starting Editmode.

There are three methods for working with Vertex Keys:

The 'performance animation' method. This method works entirely in EditMode, chronologically from position to position:

- Insert Key. The reference is specified.
- A few frames further: Insert Key. Edit the Mesh for the second position.
- A few frames further: Insert Key. Edit the Mesh for the third position.
- Continue the above process...

The 'editing' method.

- We first insert all of the required Keys, unless we have already created the Keys using the method described above.
- Blender is *not* in EditMode.
- Select a Key. Now start EditMode, change the Mesh and leave EditMode.
- Select a Key. Start EditMode, change the Mesh and leave EditMode.
- Continue the above process....

The 'insert' method

- Whether or not there are already Keys and whether or not we are in EditMode does not matter in this method.
- Go to the frame in which the new Key must be inserted.
- Insert Key.
- Go to a new frame, Insert Key.
- Continue the above process...

While in EditMode, the Keys cannot be switched. If the user attempts to do so, a warning appears.

Each Key is represented by a line which is drawn at a given height. Height is chosen so that the key intersects the "Speed" IPO at the frame at which the Key is taken.

Both the IPO Curve and the VertexKey can be separately selected with **RMB**. Since it would otherwise be too difficult working with them, selection of the Key lines is swit-

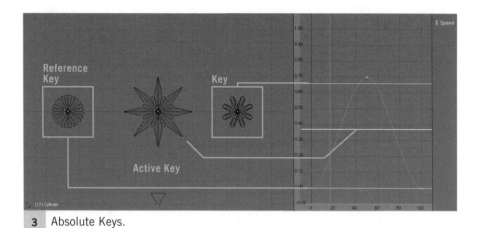

3 Absolute Keys.

ched off when the curve is in Edit Mode. The *channel* button can be used to temporarily hide the curve (**SHIFT-LMB** on "Speed") to make it easier to select Keys.

The Key lines in the IPO Window, once taken, can be placed at any vertical position. Select the line and use Grab mode to do this. The IPO Curve can also be processed here in the same way as described in the previous chapter. Instead of a 'value', however, the curve determines the interpolation between the Keys, e.g. a sine curve can be used to create a cyclical animation.

During the animation the frame count gives a certain value of the speed IPO, which is used to chose the Key(s) which is/are to be used, possibly with interpolation, to produce the deformed mesh.

The Speed IPO has the standard behaviour of an IPO, also for interpolation. The Key line has three different interpolation types. Press **TKEY** with a Key line selected to to open a menu with the options:

- `Linear`: interpolation between the Keys is linear. The Key line is displayed as a dotted line
- `Cardinal`: interpolation between the Keys is fluid, the standard setting.
- `BSpline`: interpolation between the Keys is extra fluid and includes four Keys in the interpolation calculation. The positions are no longer displayed precisely, however. The Key line is drawn as a dashed line.

Figure 3 shows a simple Vertex Key animation of a cylinder. When run the cylinder deforms to a big star, then deforms to a small star, then, since the Speed IPO goes back to 0 the deformation is repeated in reverse order.

Some useful tips:

* Key positions are *always* added with IKEY, even if they are located at the same position. Use this to copy positions when inserting. Two key lines at the same position can also be used to change the effect of the interpolation.
* If *no* Keys are selected, EditMode can be invoked as usual. However, when you leave EditMode, all changes are undone. Insert the Key *in* EditMode in this case.
* For Keys, there is *no* difference between selected and *active*. It is therefore not possible to select multiple Keys.
* When working with Keys with differing numbers of vertices, the faces can become disordered. There are no tools that can be used to specify *precise* sequence of vertices. This option is actually suitable only for Meshes that have only vertices such as Halos. ·

Curve and Surface Keys

As mentioned earlier, Curve and Surface Keys work exactly the same way as Mesh Keys. For Curves, it is particularly interesting to place Curve Keys in the bevel object. Although this animation is *not* displayed real-time in the 3DWindow, it will be rendered.

Lattice Keys

As soon as one Key is present in a Lattice, the buttons that are used to determine the resolution are blocked.

Relative VertexKeys

Relative Vertex Keys (RVK) works differently inasmuch only the difference between the reference mesh and the deformed mesh is stored. This allows for blending several keys together to achieve complex animations.

We will walk through RVK via an example.

We will create a facial animation via RVK. While Absolute Vertex Keys are controlled with only *one* IPO curve, Relative Vertex Keys are controlled by one interpolation curve for every key position, which states 'how much' of that relative deformation is used to produce the deformed mesh. This is why relative keys can be mixed (added, subtracted, etc.).

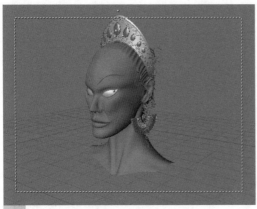

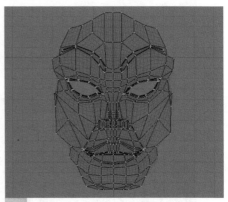

| 4 | The female head we want to animate. | | 5 | All but the face vertices hidden. |

For facial animation, the base position might be a relaxed position with a slightly open mouth and eyelids half open. Then keys would be defined for left/right eye-blink, happy, sad, smiling, frowning, etc.

The trick with relative vertex keys is that only the vertices that are changed between the base and the key affect the final output during blending. This means it is possible to have several keys affecting the object in different places all at the same time.

For example, a face with three keys: smile, and left/right eye-blink could be animated to smile, then blink left eye, then blink right eye, then open both eyes and finally stop smiling - all by blending 3 keys. Without relative vertex keys 6 vertex keys would have needed to be generated, one for each target position.

Consider the female head in figure 4.

To add a RVK just press **IKEY** and select Mesh as for AVK, but, from the pop up menu select Relative Keys This stores the reference Key which will appear as an yellow horizontal line in the IPO window.

Relative keys are defined by inserting further vertex keys. Each time the **IKEY** is pressed and Mesh selected a new horizontal line appears in the IPO window. If frame number is augmented each time the horizontal line are placed one above the other. For an easier modelling let's hide all vertices except those of the face (fig. 5).

Now move to another frame, say number 5, and add a new Key. A cyan line will appear above the yellow, which now turns orange. Switch to Edit mode and close left eye lid.

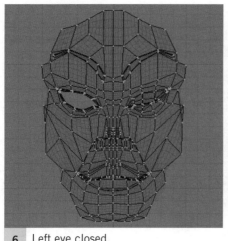

6 Left eye closed.

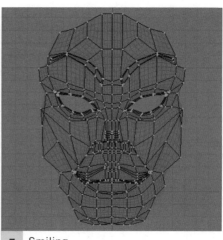

7 Smiling.

When you are done exit from Edit Mode. If you select the reference key you will see the original mesh. If you select your first RVK you will se the deformed one (fig. 6).

Repeat the step for the right eye. Beware that the newly inserted key is based on the mesh of the currently *active* key, so it is generally a good idea to select the reference key before pressing **IKEY**

Then add a smile (fig. 7).

Your IPO Window will look like figure 8.

The vertical order of the Vertex Keys (the blue lines) from bottom to top determines its corresponding IPO Curve, i.e. the lowest blue key line will be controlled by the Key1 curve, the second lowest will be controlled by the Key2 curve, and so on.

No IPO is present for the reference mesh since that is the mesh which is used if all other Keys have an IPO of value 0 at the given frame.

Select Key1 and add an IPO with your favourite method. Make it look like figure 9.

This will make our mesh undeformed up to frame 10, then from frame 10 to frame 20 Key 1 will begin to affect the deformation. From frame 20 to frame 40 Key 1 will completely overcame the reference mesh (IPO value is 1), and the eye will be completely closed. The effect will fade out from frame 40 to frame 50.

You can check with **ALT-A**, or by setting the frame numbers by hand. The second option is better, unless your computer is really powerful!

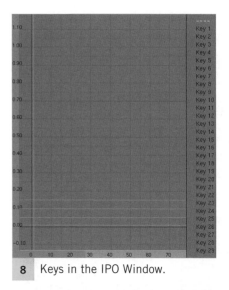

8   Keys in the IPO Window.

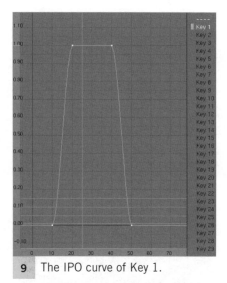

9   The IPO curve of Key 1.

10   Clipboard buttons.

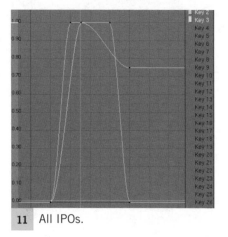

11   All IPOs.

Copy this IPO by using the down pointing arrow button in the IPO Window toolbar (fig. 10). Select the Key 2 and paste the curve with the up pointing arrow. Now both keys will have the same influence on the face and both eyeds will close at a time.

It may happen that the toolbar is longer than the window and some buttons are not shown. You can pan horizontally all toolbars by clicking **MMB** on them and dragging the mouse.

Add also an IPO for Key 3 Let's make this different (fig. 11).

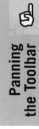

Panning the Toolbar

12 Sequence.

13 RVK in Action Window.

This way the eyes closes and she begins to smile, smile is at maximum with closed eyes, then she smile 'less' while eyes re-open and keeps smiling (fig. 12).

The IPO Curve for each key controls the blending between relative keys. These curves should be created in the typical fashion. The final position is determined by adding all of the effects of each individual IPO Curve.

Action Window

You can operate with RVK also in the Action (**SHIFT-F12**), not IPO, Window (fig. 13). The influence of any Key is given via a slider. Marks are present at Key points (i.e. where the IPO would have a control point).

Values out of [0,1] range

An important part of Relative Keys is the use of additive or extrapolated positions. For example, if the base position for a face is with a straight mouth, and a key is defined for a smile, then it is possible that the negative application of that key will result in a frown. Likewise, extending the IPO Curve above 1.0 will "extrapolate" that key, making an extreme smile.

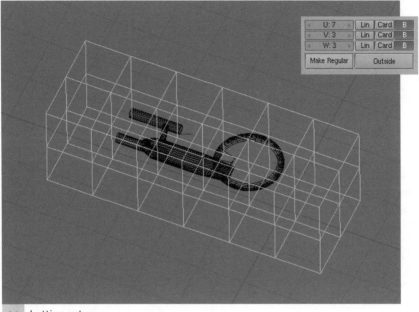

14 Lattice setup.

Lattice Animation

Parenting a mesh to a lattice is a nice way to apply deformations to the former while modelling, but it is also a way to make deformations in time!

You can use Lattices in animations in two ways:

- Animate the vertices with Vertex Keys (or Relative Vertex Keys);
- Move the Lattice or the child object of the Lattice

The first technique is basically nothing new than what contained in the previous two sections but applied to a lattice which has an object parented to it.

With the second kind you can create animations that squish things between rollers, or achieve the effect of a well-known space ship accelerating to warp-speed.

Make a space ship and add a lattice around the ship. Set the lattice parameters (**F9**, Editing context) identical to the ones seen in figure 14.

Select the ship, extend the selection to the lattice (holding **SHIFT** while selecting), and press **CTRL-P** to make the lattice the parent of the ship. You should not see any deformation of the ship because the lattice is still regular.

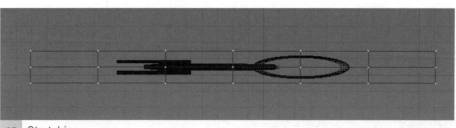

15 Stretching.

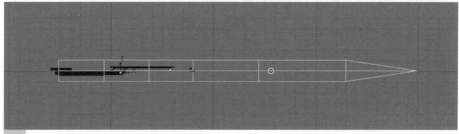

16 Final lattice deformation.

For the next few steps it is important to do them in EditMode. So now select the lattice, enter EditMode, select all vertices (**AKEY**), and scale the lattice along its x-axis (press **MMB** while initiating the scale) to get the stretch you want. The ship's mesh shows immediately the deformation caused by the lattice (fig.15).

Now edit the lattice in EditMode so that the right vertices have an increasing distance from each other. This will increase the stretch as the ship goes into the lattice. The right ends vertices I have scaled down so that they are nearly at one point; this will cause the vanishing of the ship at the end (fig. 16).

Select the ship again and move it through the lattice to get a preview of the animation. Now you can do a normal keyframe animation to let the ship fly through the lattice.

Camera Tracking

With this lattice animation, you can´t use the pivot point of the object for tracking or parenting. It will move outside the object. You will need to vertex-parent an Empty to the mesh for that. To do so, select the Empty, then the mesh, enter EditMode and select one vertex, then press **CTRL-P.**

17 Some frames of the resulting animation.

CH. 13 CHARACTER ANIMATION

GENERAL TOOLS, THE ARMATURE OBJECT, SKINNING, POSEMODE, NON LINEAR ANIMATION, CONSTRAINTS, RIGGING A HAND AND A FOOT, RIGGING MECHANICS, HOW TO SETUP A WALKCYCLE USING NLA

Introduction: Light, Camera and... ACTION !

As we have seen in the the Section called *Rigging* in Chapter 4 Blender uses *Armatures* for character animation. An armature is just like a skeleton which, once parented to our character mesh, will let us define a number of *poses* for our character along the timeline of our animation.

An armature is made up of an arbitrary number of *bones*. The size, position and orientation of every bone in your armature is up to you, and you will find thru this chapter that different situations will require a particular arrangement of bones for your character to work properly.

As you animate your armature you will find that is better to organize several related poses in something called an *action*, which is more or less the same as in real world. When we walk, we can imagine ourselves passing through several instantaneous poses as if we were in the frames of a moving picture, the whole process of the walk is an action in the end. But there are actions and actions. As an animator you will need to acquire the capability of knowing how to split any natural movement or action into several more simple actions that will be easier to dealing with. Working with simpler actions commonly saves time and work (and why not: money!) since these actions are usually reusable.

Once you have set-up your first actions you will be able to combine them using the powerful Blender's *Non Linear Animation* (or *NLA*) editor giving to your character a living mood and natural manners.

In this chapter we will cover every single detail of Blender functionalities related to Armatures, Actions and NLA Editor. Furthermore we will see several armature set-ups that will give you a starting point for your own creations and ideas. Relax and enjoy.

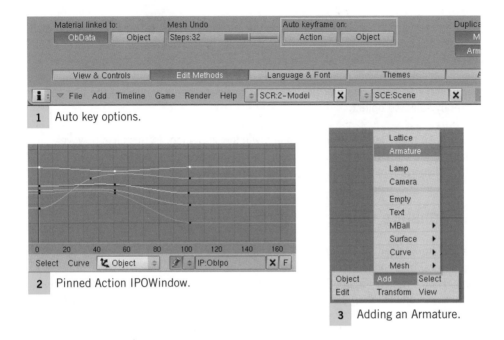

1   Auto key options.

2   Pinned Action IPOWindow.

3   Adding an Armature.

General Tools

There are few Blender features which can make your life easier while animating a character. Let's see them, before going deep into details.

The auto-key feature can be found in the InfoWindow. When it is enabled, Blender will automatically set KeyFrames when you move Objects. This is helpful for people who are not used to explicitly inserting KeyFrames with **IKEY**. There are two separate toggles for auto-keying: one for Object Mode and one for Pose Mode. These two options can be set independently of one another from the `Edit Method` group of buttons in the User Preferences Window (fig. 1).

Auto Keyframe on `Object` will set KeyFrames for Objects that are moved in Object Mode. Users who are familiar with the Blender interface will likely want to leave this option disabled.

Auto Keyframe on `Action` sets KeyFrames for transformations done in Pose Mode. This ensures that you will not lose a pose by forgetting to insert KeyFrames. Even users who are familiar with the Blender interface may find this to be a useful feature.

It is possible to display different IPOs in different windows. This is especially valuable while editing Actions, which have a different IPO for each bone.

You can "pin" an IPO or Action (lock it to the current window) by pressing the pin icon in the header of the window (fig. 2). The contents of the window will stay there, even when the object is deselected, or another object is selected. Note that the color of the IPO block menu will change, along with the background color of the IPO Window. These serve as reminders that the window is not necessarily displaying the IPO of the currently selected object.

The browse menu is still available while a window is pinned. In this case however, changing the current data will not affect the current object; it merely changes which data is displayed.

The Armature Object

The armature Object is the key Object of character animation. It is an object comprising several interconnected or not interconnected "bones". A series of interconnected bones is an "Inverse Kinematics (IK) Chain" or simply "Chain" of bones. An is something more complex than a standard Parent relation inasmuch not only the movements of the "Parent" bone are transmitted to the children, but also the movements of the last child of the chain can transmit up in the chain to the parent bone if an Inverse Kinematics solution is asked for. Bones can be moved as if they were a set of rigid, undeformable Object with perfect joints. Consider an armature to be like a skeleton for a living creature. The arms, legs, spine and head are all part of the same skeleton object.

To create a new armature, select **SPACE**>>Add>>Armature from the Toolbox (fig. 3). A new bone will appear with its root at the location of the 3D cursor. As you move the mouse, the bone will resize accordingly. **LMB** will finalize the bone and start a new one that is the child of the previous one. In this way you can make a complete chain. Pressing **ESC** will cancel the addition of the bone.

You can add another bone to an armature while it is in Edit Mode with **SPACE**>>Add>>Armature from the toolbox again. This will start the bone-adding mode again, and the new bones you create will be a part of the current armature but will form a separate chain.

You can also extrude bones from existing bones by selecting a bone joint and pressing **EKEY**. The newly created bone will be a child of the bone it is extruded from, but *not* of its IK chain.

While in Edit Mode, you can perform the following operations to the bones in an armature.

- *Adjusting*
  Select one or more bone joints and use any of the standard transformation operations to adjust the position or orientation of any bones in the armature. Note that IK chains cannot have any gaps between their bones and as such moving the end point of a bone will move the start point, or *root* of its child.

  You can select an entire IK chain at once by moving the mouse cursor over a joint in the chain and pressing **LKEY**. You can also use the boundary select tool (**BKEY**).

- *Deleting*
  You can delete one or more bones by selecting its start and end points. When you do this you will notice the bone itself will be drawn in a highlighted color. Pressing **XKEY** will remove the highlighted bones. Note that selecting a single point is not enough to delete a bone.

- *Point Snapping*
  It is possible to snap bone joints to the grid or to the cursor by using the snap menu accessible with **SHIFT-S**.

- *Numeric Mode*
  For more precise editing, pressing **NKEY** will bring up the numeric entry box. Here you can adjust the position of the start and end points as well as the bone's roll around its own axis.

  An easy way to automatically orient the z-axis handles of all selected bones (necessary for proper use of the pose-flipped option) is to press **CTRL-N**. Remember to do this before starting to create any animation for the armature.

- *Undo*
  While in Edit Mode, you can cancel the changes you have made in the current editing session by pressing **UKEY**. The armature will revert to the state it was in before editing began.

It is also possible to join two Armatures together into a single Object. To do this, ensure you are in Object Mode, select both armatures and press **CTRL-J**.

Bones Naming

Assigning meaningful names the bones in your armatures is important for several reasons. First it will make your life easier when editing Actions in the Action Window. Second, the bone names are used to associate Action channels with bones when you are attempting to re-use Actions, and third the names are used when taking advantage of the automatic pose-flipping feature.

Note that bone names need only be unique within a given armature. You can have several bones called "Head" so long as they are all in different armatures.

To change the names of one or more bones, select the bones in Edit Mode and switch to the Editing Context Buttons with **F9**. A list of all the selected bones should appear in the `Armature Bones` Panel (fig. 4). Change a bone's name by **SHIFT-LMB** in the bone's name box and typing a new name.

It is easier to name the bones by either only editing one bone at a time, or by making sure the `DrawNames` option is enabled in the EditButtons **F9** (fig. 5).

Pose Flipping Conventions

Character armatures are typically axially symmetrical. This means that many elements are found in pairs, one on the left and one on the right. If you name them correctly, Blender can flip a given pose around the axis of symmetry, making animation of walk-cycles much easier.

For every bone that is paired, suffix the names for the left and right with either ".L" and ".R" or ".Left" and ".Right". Bones that lie along the axis of symmetry or that have no twin need no suffix. Note that the part of the name preceding the suffix should be identical for both sides. So if there are two hands, they should be named "Hand.R" and "Hand.L".

Parenting and IK chain

To change parenting relationships within the armature, select the bone that should be the *child* and switch to the `Armature Bones` Panel of the Edit Buttons Window. Next to the bone there should be a menu button labelled `Child Of`. To make the bone become the child of another bone, pick the appropriate parent from the list. Note that this is much easier if the bones have been correctly named. To dissolve a parenting relationship, choose the blank entry in the list.

Note that the parenting menu only contains the names of valid parents. Bones that cannot be parents (such as children of the current bone) will not be displayed.

The IK toggle next to each bone with a parent is used to determine if the IK solver should propagate its effects across this joint. If the IK button is active, the parent's end point will be moved to match its child's start point. This is to satisfy the requirement that there are no gaps in an IK chain. Deactivating the IK button will not restore the child's start point to its previous location, but moving the point will no longer affect the parent's end point.

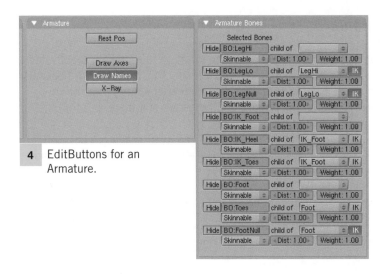

4 EditButtons for an Armature.

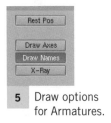

5 Draw options for Armatures.

There can be only one IK relation between a Bone and it's child so only one of the IK Tog Buttons of the children of a given bone can be set at a time.

To get the best results while animating, it is necessary to ensure that the local axes of each bone are consistent throughout the armature. This should be done before any animation takes place.

It is also necessary that when the armature object is in its untransformed orientation in object Mode, the front of the armature is visible in the front view, the left side is visible in the left view and so on. You can ensure this by orienting the armature so that the appropriate views are aligned and pressing **CTRL-A** to apply size and rotation. Again, this should be done before any animation takes place.

Setting Local Axes

The orientation of the bones' *roll handles* is important to getting good results from the animation system. You can adjust the roll angle of a bone by selecting it and pressing **NKEY**. The exact number that must be entered here depends on the orientation of the bone.

The z-axis of each bone should point in a consistent direction for paired bones. A good solution is to have the z-axes point upwards (or forwards, when the bone is vertically oriented). This task is much easier if the "Draw Axes" option is enabled in the Armature Panel in the Edit Buttons Window.

The Armature Panel

This panel just contains few toggle buttons. When the Rest Pos toggle is activated (fig. 5), the armature will be displayed in its rest position. This is useful if it becomes necessary to edit the mesh associated with an armature after some posing or animation has been done. Note that the Actions and poses are still there, but they are temporarily disabled while this button is pressed.

Draw Axes and Draw Names toggles allow the local axes of each bone and its name to be displayed in the 3D Viewport.

The X-Ray toggle prevents the armature bones to be hidden by your model when in solid/shaded mode.

Skinning

Once the Armature - the 'character skeleton' - is ready it is necessary to parent the character 'skin' to it. Skinning is a technique for creating smooth mesh deformations with an armature. Essentially the skinning is the relationship between the vertices in a mesh and the bones of an armature, and how the transformations of each bone will affect the position of the mesh vertices.

When making a child of an armature, several options are presented:

Parent to Bone

In this case, a popup menu appears allowing you to choose which bone should be the parent of the child(ren) objects. This is great for robots, whose body parts are *separate* meshes which are not expected to bend and deform when moving.

Parent to Armature

Choosing this option will deform the child(ren) mesh(es) according to their vertex groups. If the child meshes don't have any vertex groups, they will be subject to automatic skinning. Indeed a second menu appears, asking:

- Don't create groups - does nothing else, automatic skinning is used;
- Name Groups - creates empty vertex groups whose names matches the bone names, but no vertices are assigned to them;
- Create from closest bone - you want to create and populate automatically vertex groups.

CHARACTER ANIMATION.SKINNING

Parent to Armature Object

Choosing this option will cause the child(ren) to consider the armature to be an Empty for all intents and purposes.

If you are going for character animation then most of the times you will parent your character to the Armature using the "Armature" Option. You are strongly advised to use the `Name Groups` option. This will provide you with the groups already created, saving the tedious operations of creating an naming them, and possibly avoiding typing errors.

The `Create from closest bone` feature is currently under heavy development. It will use the "Bone types" which can be defined via the menu right of the `IK Tog` Buttons (fig. 4) for optimal result.

Currently only the `Skinnable` and `Unskinnable` options are working. The first option makes Vertex Group be created (and populated, if this is asked for) for the given bone, the second option causes that bone to be ignored in the skinning process.

The current vertex assignment algorithm creates non-optimal vertex groups, hence it is highly recommended to check each group, one by one.

If a mesh does not have any vertex groups, and it is made the armature-child of an armature, Blender will attempt to calculate deformation information on the fly. This is very slow and is not recommended. It is advisable to create and use vertex groups instead.

The `Weight` and `Dist` settings next to the `IK` are only used by the automatic skinning which is a deprecated feature because it requires lot of CPU, produces slow downs and worse result than other methods.

Weight and Dist

Vertex Groups

Vertex groups are necessary to define which bones deform which vertices. A vertex can be a member of several groups, in which case its deformation will be a weighted average of the deformations of the bones it is assigned to. In this way it is possible to create smooth joints.

To add a new vertex group to a mesh, you must be in Edit Mode. Create a new vertex group by clicking on the `New` button in the mesh's Edit Buttons `Mesh Tools 1` Panel (fig. 6).

A vertex group can be subsequently deleted by clicking on the `Delete` button.

Change the active group by choosing one from the pull-down group menu.

Vertex groups must have the *same* names as the bones that will manipulate them. Both spelling and capitalization matter. This is why automatic name creation is so useful! Rename a vertex group by **SHIFT-LMB** on the name button and typing a new name. Note that vertex group names must be unique within a given mesh.

Vertices can be assigned to the active group by selecting them and clicking the `Assign` button. Depending on the setting of the `Weight` button, the vertices will receive more or less influence from the bone. This weighting is only important for vertices that are members of more than one bone. The weight setting is not an absolute value; rather it is a relative one. For each vertex, the system calculates the sum of the weights of all of the bones that affect the vertex. The transformations of each bone are then divided by this amount meaning that each vertex always receives exactly 100% deformation.

Assigning 0 weight to a vertex will effectively remove it from the active group.

To remove vertices from the current group select them and click the `Remove` button.

Pressing the `Select` button will add the vertices assigned to the current group to the selection set. Pressing the `Deselect` button will remove the vertices assigned to the current group from the selection set. This is handy to check which vertices are in which group.

Weight Painting

Weight painting is an alternate technique for assigning weights to vertices in vertex groups. The user can "paint" weights onto the model and see the results in real-time. This makes smooth joints easier to achieve.

To activate weight-painting mode, select a mesh with vertex groups and click on the weight paint icon (fig. 7).

The active mesh will be displayed in Weight-Color mode. In this mode dark blue represents areas with no weight from the current group and red represent areas with full weight. Only one group can be visualized at a time. Changing the active vertex group in the Edit Buttons will change the weight painting display.

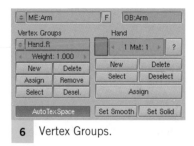

6 Vertex Groups.

7 Weight Paint Button.

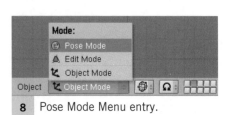

8 Pose Mode Menu entry.

Weights are painted onto the mesh using techniques similar to those used for vertex painting, with a few exceptions. The "color" is the weight value specified in the mesh's Edit Buttons. The `opacity` slider in the vertex paint Buttons is used to modulate the weight. To erase weight from vertices, set the weight to "0" and start painting.

It is quite easy to change the weigth since **TAB** will take you out of Weight Paint Mode into Edit Mode and Panels will automatically match the Context.

Posemode

To manipulate the bones in an armature, you must enter Pose Mode. In Pose Mode you can only select and manipulate the bones of the active armature. Unlike Edit Mode, you cannot add or delete bones in Pose Mode.

Enter Pose Mode by selecting an armature and pressing **CTRL-TAB**. Alternatively you can activate Pose Mode by selecting an armature and clicking on the `Pose Mode` menu entry in the `Mode` Menu of the 3D Window header (fig. 8). You can leave Pose Mode by the same method, or by entering Edit Mode.

In Pose Mode, you can manipulate the bones in the armature by selecting them with **RMB** and using the standard transformation keys: **RKEY**, **SKEY** and **GKEY**. You cannot "grab" (translate) bones that are IK children of another bone, since the IK chain must stay continuous.

Press **IKEY** to insert KeyFrames for selected bones.

If you want to clear the posing for one or more bones, select the bones and press **ALT-R** to clear rotations, **ALT-S** to clear scaling and **ALT-G** to clear translations. Issuing these three commands with all bones selected will return the armature to its rest position.

It is frequently convenient to copy poses from one armature to another, or from one Action to a different point in the same Action. This is where the pose copying tools in the `Armature` Menu come into play.

For best results, be sure to select all bones in Edit Mode and press **CTRL-N** to auto-orient the bone handles before starting any animation.

To copy a pose, select one or more bones in Pose Mode, select the `Armature>>Copy Current Pose` Menu entry in the 3D Window header (fig. 9). The transformations of the selected bones are stored in the copy buffer until needed or until another copy operation is performed.

To paste a Pose, simply chose the `Armature>>Paste Pose` Menu entry (fig. 9). If `Action` auto key framing is active, KeyFrames will be inserted automatically.

To paste a mirrored version of the Pose (if the character was leaning left in the copied Pose, the mirrored Pose would have the character leaning right), use the `Armature>>Paste Flipped Pose` Menu entry (fig. 9). Note that if the armature was not set up correctly, the paste flipped technique may not work as expected.

Action Window

An Action is made of one or more Action channels. Each channel corresponds to one of the bones in the armature, and each channel has an Action IPO associated with it. The Action Window provides a means to visualize and Edit all of the IPOs associated with the Action together.

 You can activate the Action Window with **SHIFT-F12** (fig. 10).

For every key set in a given Action IPO, a marker will be displayed at the appropriate frame in the Action Window. This is similar to the "Key" mode in the IPO Window. For Action channels with constraint IPOs, there will be one or more additional constraint channels beneath each Action channel. These channels can be selected independently of their owner channels (fig. 11).

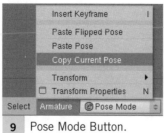

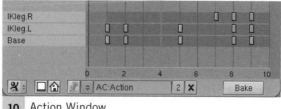

9 Pose Mode Button.

10 Action Window.

11 Action Window with a Constraint.

A block of Action keys can be selected by either **RMB** on them or by using the boundary select tool (**BKEY**). Selected keys are highlighted in yellow. Once selected, the keys can be moved by pressing **GKEY** and moving the mouse. Holding **CTRL** will lock the movement to whole-frame intervals. **LMB** will finalize the new location of the keys, while **ESC** cancels the Action and returns to previous state.

A block of Action keys can also be scaled horizontally (effectively speeding-up or slowing-down the Action) by selecting number of keys and pressing **SKEY**. Moving the mouse horizontally will scale the block. **LMB** will finalize the operation.

Delete one or more selected Action keys by pressing **XKEY** when the mouse cursor is over the KeyFrame area of the Action Window.

A block of Action keys can be duplicated and moved within the same Action by selecting the desired keys and pressing **SHIFT-D**. This will immediately enter grab mode so that the new block of keys can be moved. Subsequently **LMB** will finalize the location of the new keys. **ESC** will exit grab, but won't remove duplicates.

You can also delete one or more entire Action or constraint channels (and all associated keys) by selecting the channels in the left-most portion of the Action Window (the selected channels will be highlighted in blue). With the mouse still over the left-hand portion of the window, press **XKEY** and confirm the deletion. Note that there is no undo so perform this operation with care. Also note that deleting an Action channel that contains constraint channels will delete those constraint channels as well.

Baking Actions

If you have an animation that involves constraints and you would like to use it in the game engine (which does not evaluate constraints, and is not covered in this Book), you can bake the Action by pressing the BAKE button in the Action Window ToolBar. This will create a new Action in which every frame is a KeyFrame. This Action can be played in the game engine and should display correctly with all constraints removed. For best results, make sure that all constraint targets are located within the same armature.

You can actually see the Action IPO associated to a bone in the IPO Window instead than in the Action Window if you switch to IPO Window (fig. 12). The Action IPO is a special IPO type that is only applicable to bones. Instead of using Euler angles to encode rotation, Action IPOs use quaternions, which provide better interpolation between Poses.

Quaternions use a four-component vector. It is generally difficult and unintuitive to describe the relationships of these quaternion channels to the resulting orientation, but it is often not necessary. It is best to generate quaternion KeyFrames by manipulating the bones directly, only editing the specific curves to adjust lead-in and lead-out transitions.

Non Linear Animation

Non Linear Animation is a technique somewhat akin to RVK used to merge different, simple, Actions in complex, fluid Actions. The NLA Window gives an overview of all of the animation in your scene. From here you can edit the timing of *all* IPOs, as if they were in the Action Window. Much of the editing functionality is the same as the Action Window.

You can display the NLAWindow with **CTRL-SHIFT-F12** (fig. 13).

You can also use this window to perform Action blending and other Non-Linear Animation tasks. You add and move Action Strips in a fashion similar to the Sequence Editor, and generate blending transitions for them.

In the NLA Window Actions are displayed as a single strip below the object's strip; all of the KeyFrames of the Action (constraint channel KeyFrames included) are displayed on one line (fig. 14). To see an expanded view of the Action, use the Action Window.

Objects with constraint channels will display one or more additional constraint strips below the object strip. The constraint strip can be selected independently of its owner object (fig. 15).

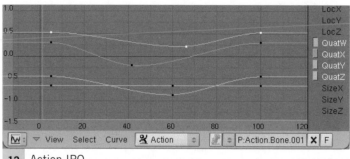

12   Action IPO.

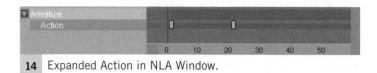

13   NLA Window.

14   Expanded Action in NLA Window.

15   Expanded Constraint in NLA Window.

RMB clicking on object names in the NLA Window will select the appropriate objects in the 3D Window. Selected object strips are drawn in blue, while unselected ones are red.

You can remove constraint channels from objects by clicking **RMB** on the constraint channel name and pressing **XKEY**.

Note that only armatures, or objects with IPOs will appear in the NLA Window.

Working with Action Strips

Action strips can only be added to Armature objects. The object does not necessarily need to have an Action associated with it first.

Add an Action strip to an object by moving the mouse cursor over the object name in the NLA Window and pressing **SHIFT-A** and choosing the appropriate Action to add from the popup menu. Note that you can only have one Action strip per line.

You can select, move and delete Action strips along with other KeyFrames in the NLA Window.

The strips are evaluated top to bottom. Channels specified in strips later in the list override channels specified in earlier strips.

You can still create animation on the armature itself. Channels in the local Action on the armature override channels in the strips. Note that once you have created a channel in the local Action, it will always override all Actions. If you want to create an override for only part of the timeline, you can convert the local Action to an Action strip by pressing **CKEY** with your mouse over the armature's name in the NLA Window. This removes the Action from the armature and puts it at the end of the Action strip list.

Each strip has several options which can be accessed by selecting the strip and pressing **NKEY** (fig. 16). The options available are as follows:

- StripStart/StripEnd - The first and last fame of the Action strip in the timeline

- ActionStart/ActionEnd - The range of keys to read from the Action. The end may be less than the start which will cause the Action to play backwards.

- Blendin/Blendout - The number of frames of transition to generate between this Action and the one before it in the Action strip list.

- Repeat - The number of times the Action range should repeat. Not compatible with Use Path setting.

- Stride - The distance (in Blender units) that the character moves in a single cycle of the Action (usually a walk cycle Action). This field is only needed if Use Path is specified.

- Use Path - If an armature is the child of a path or curve and has a Stride value, this button will choose the frame of animation to display based on the object's position along the path. Great for walkcycles.

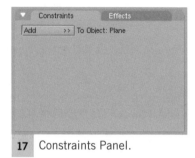

16	NLA Action Strip Options.

17	Constraints Panel.

- `Hold` - If this is enabled, the last frame of the Action will be displayed forever, unless it is overridden by another Action. Otherwise the armature will revert to its rest position.

- `Add` - Specifies that the transformations in this strip should *add* to any existing animation data, instead of overwriting it.

Constraints

Constraints are filters that are applied to the transformations of bones and objects. This section is actually quite general and does not apply only to character animation since many other animations can benefit from constrains.

Blender Constraints can provide a variety of services including tracking and IK solving.

To add a constraint to an object, ensure you are in object Mode and in Object Context (**F7**) and that an Object is selected. If you are adding a Constraint to a Bone be sure to be in Pose Mode rather than Object Mode and select a Bone. The Object Context Buttons Window will present a `Constraints` Panel (fig. 17). Click on the `Add` button. A menu of possible constraints will appear.

Once you selected the desired constraint its buttons will appear. A constraint can be deleted by clicking on the "X" icon next to it. A constraint can be collapsed by clicking on its orange triangle icon. When collapsed, a constraint can be moved up or down in the constraint list by clicking on it at choosing `Move Up` or `Move Down` from the popup menu.

For most constraints, a target must be specified in the appropriate field. In this field you must type in the name of the desired target object. If the desired target is a bone, first type in the name of the bone's armature. Another text box will appear allowing you to specify the name of the bone.

Constraint Types

Several Constrains are possible. All applies to Bones, some applies also to other Objects:

- `Copy Location` - The constraint forces the Object to have an one or more co-ordinates (chosen via the three Toggle Buttons) of its location equal to those of the target (fig. 18).

- `Copy Rotation` - This constraint copies the global rotation of the target and applies it to the constraint owner (fig. 19).

- `Track To` - This constraint causes the constraint owner to point one of its axes (by default the Y-axis) to point towards the target either in its positive or negative direction, depending on the selected Radio Button. The Object rotation will be computed so that another one of its axis (by default the Z-axis) will point up, again this can be changed via the pertinent Radio Buttons (fig. 20).

- `Locked Track` - This constraint causes the constraint owner to point one of its axes (by default the Y-axis) to point towards the target either in its positive or negative direction, depending on the selected Radio Buttons. The Object rotation will be computed so that another one of its axis (by default the Z-axis) direction is *fixed*, again this can be changed via the pertinent Radio Buttons.
  Actually this means that the Object is rotated around it fixed axis so that the Target lyes on the plane defined by the locked axis and the pointing axis (fig. 21).

- `Follow Path` - This constraint needs the Target to be a Curve or Path. It causes the constraint owner to follow the path in time.
  By default the Object translates along the curve in 100 frames. You can make the Object orientation follow the curve with the `CurveFollow` Toggle Button and by setting the Radio Buttons below to define which axis should be tangent to the curve and which should point up. To change the number of frames in which the Path is followed you need to edit the Curve's Speed IPO (fig. 22).

- `IK Solver` (Bone Only) - To simplify animation of multi-segmented limbs (such as arms and legs) you can add an IK solver constraint. IK constraints can only be added to bones. Once a target is specified, the solver will attempt to move the *root* of the constraint-owning bone to the target, by re-orienting the bone's parents

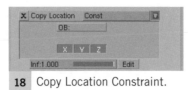

18 Copy Location Constraint.

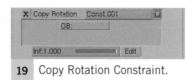

19 Copy Rotation Constraint.

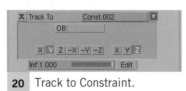

20 Track to Constraint.

21 Lock Track.

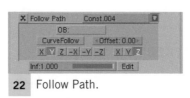

22 Follow Path.

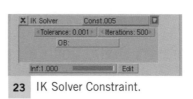

23 IK Solver Constraint.

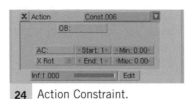

24 Action Constraint.

(but it will not move the root of the chain). If a solution is not possible, the solver will attempt to get as close as possible. Note that this constraint will override the orientations on any of the IK bone's parents (fig. 23).

If the Target of the IK Constraint is another bone of the *same* Armature, as it is warmly recomended, you must make sure that this bone, usually denominated IK_Tool, is *not* the child of any other bone of the IK chain, or weird results will happen.

- `Action` (Bone Only) - An Action constraint can be used to apply an Action channel from a different Action to a bone, based on the rotation of another bone or object. The typical way to use this is to make a muscle bone bulge as a joint is rotated. This constraint should be applied to the bone that will actually do the bulging; the target should point to the joint that is being rotated (fig. 24).

The AC field contains the name of the Action that contains the flexing animation. The only channel that is required in this Action is the one that contains the bulge animation for the bone that owns this constraint.

The Start and End fields specify the range of motion from the Action.

The Min and Max fields specify the range of rotation from the target bone. The Action between the start and end fields is mapped to this rotation (so if the bone rotation is at the Min point, the Pose specified at Start will be applied to the bone). Note that the Min field may be higher than the Max.

The pulldown menu specifies which component of the rotation is to be considered.

* `Null` - This is a constraint that does nothing at all; it doesn't affect the object's transformation directly. The purpose of a null constraint is to use it as a separator, and why this might be necessary will be clarified in the following section (fig. 25).

Constraints Evaluation Rules and Precedence

Constraints can be applied to objects or bones. In the case of constraints applied to bones, any constraints on the armature *object* will be evaluated before the constraints on the bones are considered.

When a specific constraint is evaluated, all of its dependencies will have already been evaluated and will be in their final orientation/positions. Examples of dependencies are the object's parent, its parent's parents (if any) and the hierarchies of any targets specified in the constraint.

Within a given object, constraints are executed from top to bottom. Constraints that occur lower in the list may override the effects of constraints higher in the list. Each constraint receives as input the results of the previous constraint. The input to the first constraint in the list is the output of the IPOs associated with the object.

If several constraints of the same type are specified in a contiguous block, the constraint will be evaluated *once* for the entire block, using an average of all the targets. In this way you can constrain an object to track to the point between two other objects, for example. You can use a `Null` constraint to insert a break in a constraint block if you would prefer each constraint to be evaluated individually.

Looping constraints are not allowed. If a loop is detected, all of the constraints involved will be temporarily disabled (and highlighted in red). Once the conflict has been resolved, the constraints will automatically re-activate.

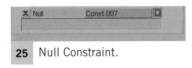

25 Null Constraint.

Influence

The influence slider next to each constraint is used to determine how much effect the constraint has on the transformation of the object.

If there is only a single constraint in a block (a block is a series of constraints of the same type which directly follow one another), an influence value of 0.0 means the constraint has no effect on the object. An influence of 1.0 means the constraint has full effect.

If there are several constraints in a block, the influence values are used as ratios. So in this case if there are two constraints, A and B, each with an influence of 0.1, the resulting target will be in the centre of the two target objects (a ratio of 0.1:0.1 or 1:1 or 50% for each target).

Influence can be controlled with an IPO. To add a constraint IPO for a constraint, open an IPO Window and change its type to constraint by clicking on the chain icon. Next click on the Edit IPO Button next to the constraint you wish to work with. If there is no constraint IPO associated with the constraint yet, one will be created. Otherwise the previously assigned IPO will be displayed. At the moment, KeyFrames for constraint IPOs can only be created and edited in the IPO Window, by selecting the INF channel and **CTRL-LMB** in the IPO space.

When blending Actions with constraint IPOs, note that only the IPOs on the armature's local Action IPOs are considered. Constraint IPOs on the Actions in the motion strips are ignored.

In the case of armatures, the constraints IPOs are stored in the current Action. This means that changing the Action will change the constraint IPOs as well.

Rigging a Hand and a Foot

The Hand

by Lyubomir Kovachev

Setting up a hand for animation is a tricky thing. The gestures, the movements of wrists and fingers are very important, they express emotional states of the character and interact with other characters and objects. That's why it's very important to have an efficient hand set-up, capable of doing all the wrist and fingers motions easily.

We'll use a simple cartoony arm mesh in this tutorial (fig. 26).

The following set-up uses one IK solver for the movement of the whole arm and four other IK solvers, one for each finger. The rotation of the wrist is achieved by a simple FK bone.

OK. Take a look at the arm mesh and let's start making the armature.

Position the 3D cursor in the shoulder, go to front view and add an armature. Make a chain of three bones - one in the upper arm, the second one in the lower arm and the third one should fit the palm, ending at the beginning of the middle finger. This is called a chain of bones (fig. 27).

Now change the view to side view and displace the bones so that they fit in the arm and palm properly (fig. 28, 29).

Zoom in the hand and position the cursor at the root of the bone positioned in the palm. Add a new bone, pointing right, with the same length as the palm bone. This will be the IK solver for the arm (fig. 30).

Position the 3D cursor at the beginning of the middle finger and in front view start building a new chain, consisting of four bones (fig. 31). Three of them will be the actual bones in the finger, and the fourth bone will be a null bone - this is a small bone, pointing to the palm, that will help turning the whole chain to an IK chain later.

Again, change to side view and reshape the bones so that they fit the finger well. It could be a tricky part and you may also view the scene using the trackball while reshaping the bones (fig. 32).

Now add the IK solver for this finger chain. Position the 3D cursor at the root of the null bone and add bone with the length of the other three bones in the finger (fig. 33).

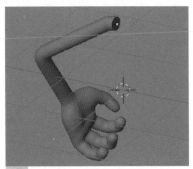

26   The Arm model.

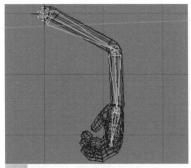

27   Drawing the armature.

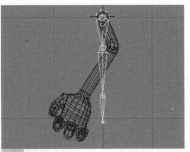

28   The armature in side view.

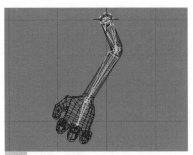

29   Placing the armature in side view.

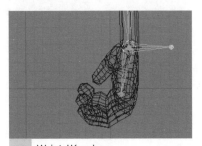

30   Wrist IK solver.

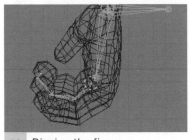

31   Rigging the finger.

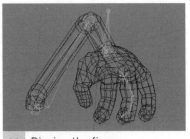

32   Rigging the finger.

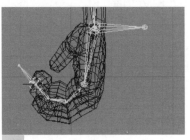

33   Adding the finger IK solver.

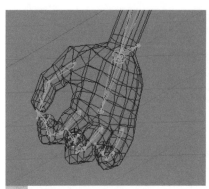

34 Rigging the other fingers.

Repeat the same for the creation of the IK chains for the other three fingers. The only difference with the thumb is that it has two actual bones, instead of three. You can just copy and paste the chain and just reshape, reshape, reshape... (fig. 34).

The time has come for the boring part - naming of the bones. You cannot skip this, because you'll need the bone names in the skinning part later. Bones are named as in figure 35.

The names of the bones of finger 1 and finger 2 are not shown here. They are identical to the names of the bones of finger 3, only the number changes.

Now let's do some parenting.

Select the root thumb bone "ThumbA.R" (fig. 36) and in the edit menu click in the "child of" field and choose "Hand.R". You've just parented the thumb bone chain to the hand bone.

By repeating the same process parent the following bones (fig. 37):

- "Fing1A.R" to "Hand.R"
- "Fing2A.R" to "Hand.R"
- "Fing3A.R" to "Hand.R"
- "IK_thumb.R" to "Hand.R"
- "IK_fing1.R" to "Hand.R"
- "IK_fing2.R" to "Hand.R"
- "IK_fing3.R" to "Hand.R"

CHARACTER ANIMATION.THE HAND

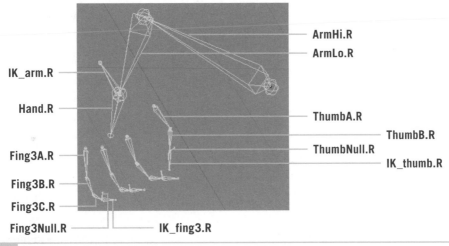

35 Naming overview.

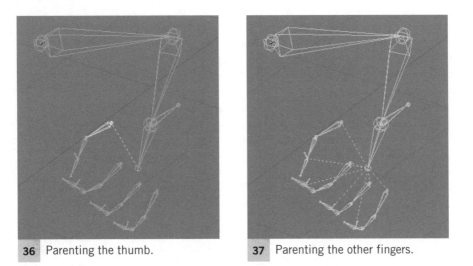

36 Parenting the thumb. **37** Parenting the other fingers.

Why did we do all this? Why did we parent so much bones to "Hand.R"? Because when you rotate the hand (i.e. "Hand.R") all the fingers will follow the hand. Otherwise the fingers will stay still and only the palm will move and you'll get very weird result.

No IK tool bone is child of any bone of the chain it controls. All of them are children of "Hand.R".

Time to add constraints. Enter pose mode (fig. 38) and go in Object Context (**F7**). Choose "Hand.R" and add an IK solver constraint to it in the `Constraints` Panel. In the OB field type the object name: "Armature". The bone goes to the centre of the armature, but we'll fix this now. In the new BO field, that appeared in the constraint window, type the bone name "IK_arm.R". This will be the IK solver bone controlling the arm motion (fig. 39).

Now by repeating the same procedure:

- select "ThumbNull.R" and add IK solver "IK_thumb.R",
- select "Fing1null.R" and add IK solver "IK_fing1.R",
- select "Fing2null.R" and add IK solver "IK_fing2.R",
- select "Fing3null.R" and add IK solver "IK_fing3.R".

You're finished with the bone part. In pose mode select different IK solvers and move them to test the IK chains. Now you can move the fingers, the thumb, the whole arm and by rotating the "Hand.R" bone you can rotate the whole hand.

So let's do the skinning now. It's the part when you tell the mesh how to deform. You'll add vertex groups to the mesh. Each vertex group should be named after the bone that will deform it. If you don't assign vertex groups, the deformation process will need much more CPU power, the animation process will be dramatically slowed down and you'll get weird results. It's highly recommended (almost mandatory) that you use subdivision surfaces meshes for your characters with low vertex count. Otherwise if you use meshes with lots of vertices, the skinning will be much more difficult. Don't sacrifice detail, but model economically, use as less vertices as possible and always use SubSurf.

Parent the Mesh to the Armature, int the Pop-Up select `Armature` and in the following select `Name Groups`. Your Mesh will be enriched by empty Vertex Groups.

Select the arm mesh, enter Edit Mode and switch to Editing (**F9**) Context. In the `Mesh Tools 1` of the Edit Buttons Window notice the small group of buttons with the word `Group` on top. Thanks to the automatic naming feature you have already all the groups you needed created (fig. 40).

Actually the automatic Grouping scheme has created vertex groups also for the "IK" and "null" bones *unless* you have set them `Unskinnable` before. These are useless and you can safely delete.

Now let's do the tricky part: Select the vertex group "ArmHi.R" from the edit buttons by clicking on the small button with the white minus sign. Now look at the 3D window. Select all the vertices that you want to be deformed by the "ArmHi.R" bone (fig. 41).

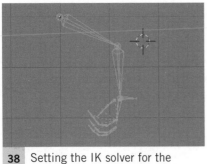

38 Setting the IK solver for the wrist. Selecting the bone.

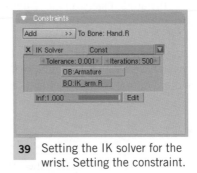

39 Setting the IK solver for the wrist. Setting the constraint.

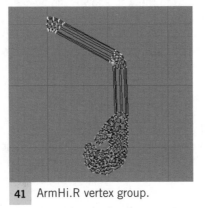

40 Vertex group names.

41 ArmHi.R vertex group.

42 Assigning vertices to a group.

Now press the `Assign` button in the edit buttons window (fig. 42). You've just added the selected vertices to the "ArmHi.R" vertex group. These vertices will be deformed by the "ArmHi.R" bone.

Repeat the same steps for the other vertex groups: select vertices and assign them to the corresponding group. This is a tricky process. Do it carefully. If you've assigned some vertices to a certain group by mistake, don't worry. Just select the unneeded vertices and press the `Remove` button. You can add a vertex to more than one vertex group. For example the vertices that build joints (of fingers, wrist, elbow, etc.) could be assigned to the two vertex groups that are situated close to it. You can also assign vertices to deform with different strength. The default strength is 1.000, but you can add vertices with strength 0.500 or less. The lower the strength value, the less deformation for that vertex. You can make a vertex deform 75% by one bone and 25% by another, or 50% by one and 50% by another. It's all a matter of testing the deformation until you achieve the result you want. In general if your arm model has half-flexed joints (as the model in this tutorial you will get good results without using strength values different than 1.000. My own rule of thumb when modelling a character is:

always model the arms fingers and legs half-flexed, not straight. This is a guarantee for good deformation.

When you're finished adding vertices to vertex groups, if you haven't made any Mistakes, you'll have a well set up arm with a hand. Select the armature, enter pose mode, select the different IK solvers and test the arm and fingers (fig. 43).

The Foot

The set-up of legs and feet is maybe the most important thing in the whole rigging process. Bad foot set-up may lead to the well known "sliding-feet" effect, which is very annoying and usually ruins the whole animation. A well made complex foot set-up must be capable of standing still on the ground while moving the body, and doing other tricky stuff like standing on tiptoe, moving the toes, etc. Now we're going to discuss several different foot set-ups that can be used for different purposes.

First let's see how a bad foot set-up looks like (fig. 44).

Start building a bone chain of three bones - one for the upper leg, the second one for the lower leg and the third one for foot. Now move the 3D cursor at the heel joint and add another bone - this will be the IK solver. Now add that bone as an IK solver constraint to the foot bone (fig. 45).

Test the armature: in pose mode grab the IK solver and move it - it's moving OK. Now grab the first bone in the chain (the upper leg) and move it. The foot is moving too and we don't want this to happen! (fig. 46)

Usually in an animation you'll move the body a lot. The upper leg bone is parented to the body and it will be affected by it. So every time you make your character move or rotate his body, the feet will slide over the ground and go under it and over it. Especially in a walkcycle, this would lead to an awful result.

Now maybe you think this could be avoid by adding a second IK solver at the toes (fig. 47). Let's do it. Start a new armature. Add a chain of four bones: upper leg, lower leg, foot and toes. Add two IK solvers - one for the foot and one for the toes. Parent the toe IK solver bone to the foot IK solver bone.

The toe IK solver is parented to the Foot IK solver. This latter must *not* be children of any other bone in the armature. Be sure of this and, to delete a parent relationship, remember that you can do so by selecting the empty entry in the `Child of:` menu. Remember to check this for all subsequent examples.

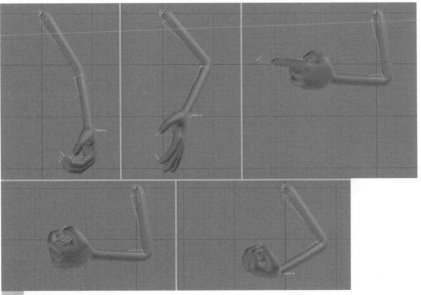

43 Different Poses.

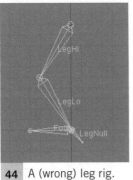

44 A (wrong) leg rig.

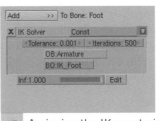

45 Assigning the IK constraint.

46 The rig in pose mode.

47 Adding a toe and some more IKA.

48 Moving the leg.

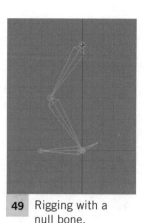

49 Rigging with a null bone.

50 Rigging with a null bone.

Test this setup - grab the upper leg bome and move it (fig. 48). Well, now the sliding isn't so much as in the previous setup, but it's enough to ruin the animation.

Start a new armature. Make a chain if three bones - upper leg, lower leg and a null bone. The null bone is a small bone, that we'll add the IK solver to. Now position the 3D cursor at the heel and add the foot bone. Now add the foot bone as an IK solver constraint to the null bone (fig. 49). (You can also add another bone as an IK solver and add a "copy location" constraint to the foot bone, with the IK solver as target bone.)

Test this - now it works. When you move the upper leg the foot stands still (fig. 50). That's good. But still not enough. Move the upper leg up a bit more. The leg chain goes up, but the foot stays on the ground. Well, that's a shortcoming of this set-up, but you're not supposed the raise the body so much and not move the IK solver up too during animation...

Again, build a chain of three bones - upper leg, lower leg and null bone. Position the 3D cursor at the heel and add a chain of two bones - the foot bone and the toes bone. Now add an IK solver to the foot bone (fig. 51).

Test it. This is a good set-up with stable, isolated foot and moving toes. But you still cannot make standing on tiptoe with this set-up.

Build a chain of three bones - upper leg, lower leg and null bone (name it LegNull) (fig. 52). Starting at the heel point, make a second chain of two bones only - foot bone (Foot) and a small null bone (FootNull). Position the 3D cursor at the end of the foot bone and add the toes bone (Toes). From the same point create an IK solver bone (IK_toes). Now position the 3D cursor at the heel and add another IK solver there (IK_heel). Finally, starting somewhere near the heel, add a bigger IK solver (IK_foot) (fig. 53).

CHARACTER ANIMATION.THE FOOT

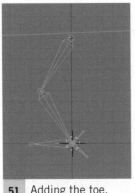

51 Adding the toe.

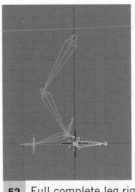

52 Full complete leg rig.

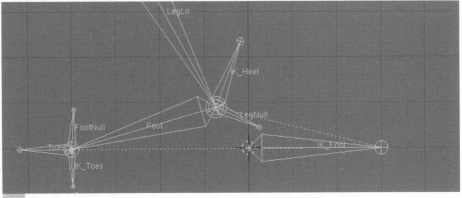

53 Zoom on the foot rig.

Now let's add the constraints. Do the following:

- To the bone "Toes" add a copy location contraint with target bone "IK_toes".

- To "FootNull" - an IK solver constraint (target - "IK_toes")

- To "Foot" - copy location (target - "LegNull").

- To "LegNull" - IK solver (target - "IK_heel")

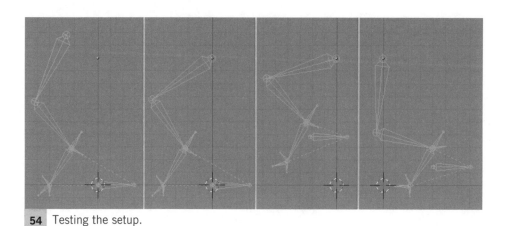

54 Testing the setup.

Well, that's it. Now test the armature (fig. 54). Grab "IK_foot" and move it up. Now grab "IK_toes" and move it down. The foot changes it's rotation, but it looks like the toes are disconnected from it. But if you animate carefully you'll always manage to keep the toes from going away from the foot. Now return the armature to it's initial pose. grab "IK_heel" and "LegHi" and move them up. Now the character is standing on his tiptoes. The foot may appear disconnected from the toes again, but you can fix the pose by selecting "IK_heel" only and moving it a bit forward or backwards. This setup may not be the most easy one for animation, but gives you more possibilities that the previous set-ups. Usually when you don't need to make your character stand on tiptoe, you've better stick to some of the easier set-ups. You'll never make a perfect set-up. You can just improve, but there will always be shortcomings.

Rigging Mechanics

Armatures are great also for rigging mechanical stuff, like robots, WarriorMechs etc (fig. 55).

First step is to create the mesh for the arms. We are not here for organic, we are here for mechanics. So no single mesh thing. The arm/leg/whatever is made of rigid parts, each part is a single mesh, parts moves/rotates one with respect to the other.

Although figure 55 has four spider-like legs arms, each of which have 5 sections, it is clearer to explain the tricks with just a single joint arm.

My suggestion is this: make the arm with two equal sections, and the forearm, on the right, made by just one section. Note the cylinders which represents the shoulder (left) the elbow (centre) and the wrist (right) (fig. 56).

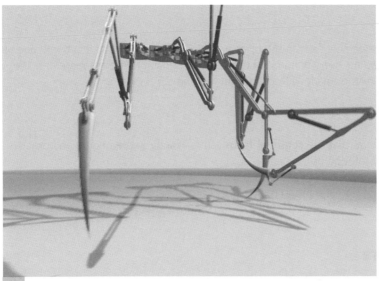

55 Four spider-mech legs.

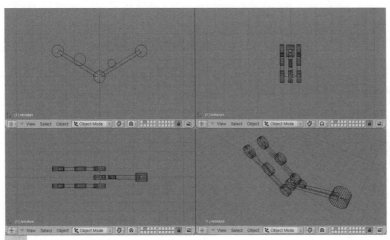

56 The Arm model.

The other cylinders in the middle of the arm and forearm are the places where the piston will be linked to.

Note that it is much easier if the axis of mutual rotation (shoulder, elbow, etc.) are exactly on grid points. This is not necessary though, if you master well Blender Snap menu.

Pivot axis

Then add the mechanical axes in the pivot points. Theoretically you should add one at each joint and two for every piston. For the sake of simplicity here there are only the two axes for the piston, made with plain cylinders (fig. 57).

Note two things:

- It is fundamental that the centre of the mesh is exactly in the middle and exactly on the axis of rotation of the piston.

- Each axis must be parented to the pertinent arm mesh.

The Armature

Now it is time to set up the armature. Just two bones are enough (fig. 58).

To have an accurate movement, the joints must be precisely set on the pivoting axis (this is why I told you to place such axes on grid points before, so that you can use the Move Selected To Grid feature).

Name the bones smartly (Arm and Forearm, for example). Parent the Arm Mesh to the armature, selecting the *Bone* option and the Arm bone. Do the same with the forearm mesh and forearm bone.

Parent to Bone

Parent to bone effectvely makes the Object follow the bone without any deformation. This is what should happen for a robot which is made by undeformable pieces of steel!

If you switch to pose mode you can move your arm by rotating the bones (fig. 59). You can add an IK solver as we did in the previous section if you like.

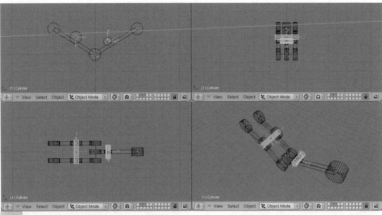

57 The Arm model with pivot axis.

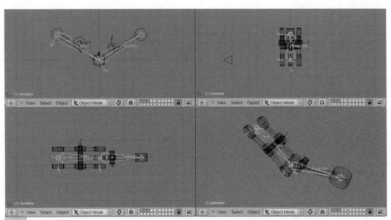

58 The Arm model and its armature.

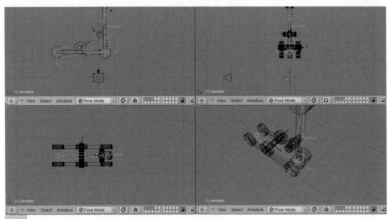

59 The Arm model in Pose Mode

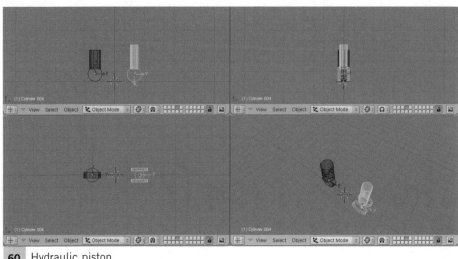

60 Hydraulic piston.

Hydraulics

Make a piston with two cylinders, a larger one and a thinner one, with some sort of a nice head for linking to the pivoting points (fig. 60).

It is *mandatory* for the two pieces to have the mesh centre exactly on the respective pivoting axis.

Place them in the correct position and parent each piston piece to the pertinent mesh representing the axis (fig. 61).

If you now rotate the two pieces in the position they should have to form a correct *still* image you get a nice piston (fig. 62, left).

But if you switch to pose mode and start moving the Arm/Forearm the piston gets screwed up... (fig. 62, right).

To make a working piston you must make each half piston track *the other half piston's pivot axis* cylinder mesh (not the other half piston! This would create a constraint loop). This is why the position of all the mesh centres is so critical (fig. 63).

Select half a piston, select the other half piston's axis mesh, and, in Object Context (**F7**) and `Constraints` panel add a Track To Constraint. The buttons below X, Y... must be appropriately set (fig. 64).

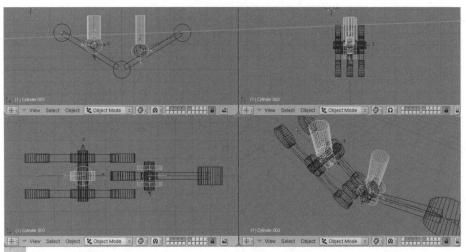

61 Hydraulic piston on the arm.

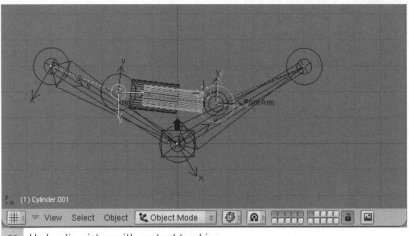

62 Hydraulic piston in pose mode.

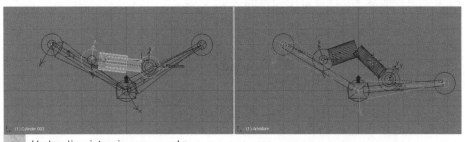

63 Hydraulic piston with mutual tracking.

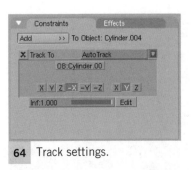

64 Track settings.

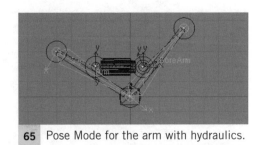

65 Pose Mode for the arm with hydraulics.

If you prefear Old Track, remember also to press the `PowerTrack` button in the `Anim Setting` Panel for a nicer result.

Now, if you switch to pose mode and rotate your bones the piston will extend and contract nicely, as it should in reality (fig. 65).

Next issue now is, since pistons work with pressurized oil which is sent into them, for a really accurate model we should add some tubes. But how to place a nicely deforming tube going from arm to piston? The two ends should stick to two rigid bodies reciprocally rotating. This requires IK!

First add a mesh in the shape of the tube you want to model (fig. 66).

Personally I prefer to draw the tube in its bent position as a bevelled curve. This is done by adding a Bézier curve, adding a Bézier circle, and using the Bézier circle as BevOb of the Bezier curve. Then convert that to a mesh **ALT-C** to be able to deform it with an armature.

Then add an armature. A couple of bones are enough. This armature should go from the tube 'fixed' end to the tube 'mobile' end. Add a third bone which will be used for the Inverse Kinematics solution (fig. 67).

Be sure that the armature is parented to the object where the 'fixed' part of the tube is, well, fixed. In this case the robot arm. Add also an Empty at the 'mobile' end of the tube (fig. 68).

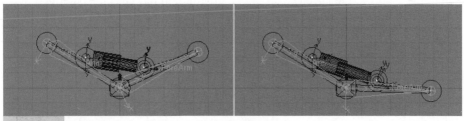

65 continued   Pose Mode for the arm with hydraulics.

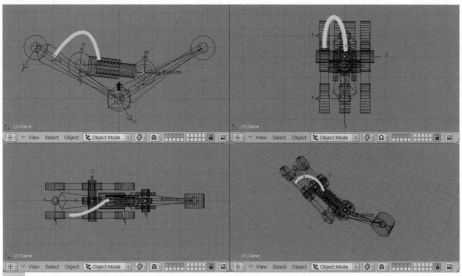

66   Adding a flexible tube.

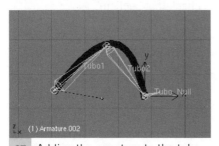

67   Adding the armature to the tube.

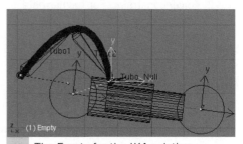

68   The Empty for the IKA solution.

Parent the Empty to the 'mobile' part of the structure. In this case the outer part of the piston to which the tube is linked. In pose mode go to the Object Context and Constraints Panel. Select the last bone, the one which starts from where the tube ends, and Add a constrain. Select the IK solver type of constrains and Select the newly created Empty as target Object OB: (fig. 69). You can play with Tolerance and Iterations if you like.

Lastly, parent the tube to the Armature via the 'Armature' option. Create Vertex groups if you like. Now if, in pose mode, you move the arm, the two parts of the piston keeps moving appropriately, and the Empty follows. This obliges the IK Armature of the tube to move, to follow the Empty, and, consequently, the Tube to deform (fig. 69).

 You can use a bone of the Armature, instead than an empty, as an IK solver, but in this case you cannot parent the bone to the moving object. You can on the other hand, use a Copy Location constraint, but this is not as easy since the copy location would move the end of the Armature to the center of the moving object, which is not the right place.

How to setup a walkcycle using NLA

In this tutorial we will set up a walkcycle and use it with the Path option in the Blender NLA Editor. Before starting let me tell you that you will need to have a basic knowledge of the animation tools, (armature set up), in order to follow the text, and have a lot of patience. It is highly recommendable to have read all the precedent NLA related part of the Book.

We are going to use a character set up like the one explained in *Hand and Foot tutorial*, that is with feet bone split up from the leg and using an extra null bone to store the IK solver constraint. For further details please check that section!

Having a rigged charcter, the first thing we need to do is to define actions: "WALKCYCLE", "WAVE_HAND" and "STAND_STILL". In WALKCYCLE and STAND_STILL there will be KeyFrames set for almost all control bones while in "WAVE_HAND" there are KeyFrames only for the arm and hand. This will allow our character to simultaneously wave its hand while walking.

The main idea behind this is to work on each single movement and later on combining everything in the NLA window.

The path to success

There are two main ways to animate a walkcycle, first one is to make the character actually advance through the poses of the cycle and the second one is to make the character walk *in place* thus without real displacement.

by Claudio 'Malefico' Andaur

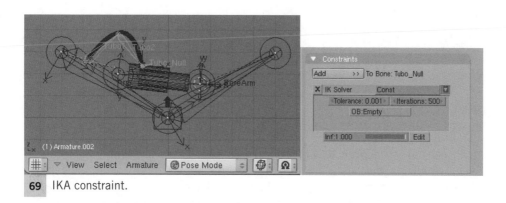

69 IKA constraint.

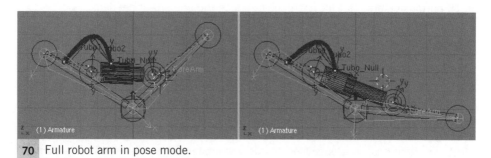

70 Full robot arm in pose mode.

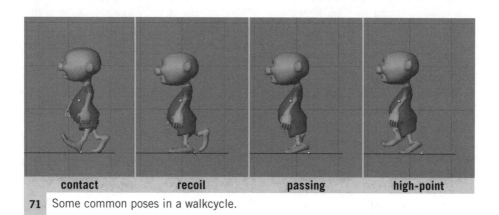

| contact | recoil | passing | high-point |

71 Some common poses in a walkcycle.

The later option though is more difficult to set up, is the best choice for digital animation and it is our choice for this tutorial.

The whole walkcycle will be an "action" for our armature, so let's go an create a new action and switch to "pose mode" to get something like Pose 1 (the so called *contact pose* in figure 71.

There are some details to bear in mind at the time of setting up an armature for walk-cycle. If we attend to Blender's naming convention introduced in the Section called *The Armature Object* you will be able to paste flipped poses. Also, before parenting your armature to your model, be sure their local axis are aligned to the global axis by selecting them and pressing **CTRL-SHIFT-A**

To animate our walking model we will restrict us to animate a few control bones. In the case of the legs we are going to animate its feet since the IKA solvers will adjust the leg bones better than us. To ensure that feet will move in fixed distances, please activate the `Grab Grid` option in the User Preferences Window `View and Controls` buttons before start moving bones, reduce the grid size if needed.

A nice method is to hide, with the relative toggle button, all the bones we are not going to set KeyFrames for. This way is easier to see the model during animation and keeps our task simple.

Normally a walkcycle involves four poses, which are commonly known as *contact, recoil, passing*, and *high-point*. Take a look at figure 71.

Most important pose is "Contact pose". Most animators agree every walkcycle should start by setting up this pose correctly. Here the character cover the wider distance it's capable to do in one step. In "Recoil pose", the character is in its lower position, with all its weight over one leg. In "High-point pose", the character is in its higher position, almost falling forwards. "Passing pose" is more like an automatic pose in-between recoil and high-point.

The work routine is as follows:

1. Pose the model in contact pose in frame 1

2. Insert KeyFrames for the control bones of your armature (those you use for grabbing, mainly IK solvers).

3. Without deselecting them press the "Copy Pose" button. Now the bone's location and rotations have been stored in memory.

4. Go a few frames forward and press "Paste Flip Pose". The flip pose will be pasted in this frame, so if in the previous frame the left leg was forwards now it will be backwards, and viceversa.

5. Now once again select your control bones and insert KeyFrames for them.

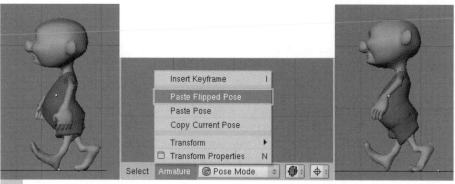

72 Use copy, paste and paste-flip pose menu entries to be happy!

6. Go a few frames forward again (it is recommendable that you use the same number of frames than before, an easy choice is to go just 10 frames every ahead time) and press "Paste Pose", this will paste the initial pose ending the cycle. This way we have achieved a "Michael Jackson" style walkcycle since our character never lift its feet up from the ground.

7. To fix it, go to some intermediate position between the first two poses and move the feet to get something like the Recoil Pose in figure 71, where the waist reaches its lower position.

8. Insert KeyFrames and copy the pose.

9. Now go to a frame between the last two poses (inverse contact and contact) and insert the flip pose . Insert the required KeyFrames and we are done.

If at the contrary you see that the mesh is weirdly deformed, don't panic! Go into EditMode for the armature, select all bones and press CTRL+N. This will recalculate the direction of bones rolls which is what makes the twisting effect.

Recalculating bone rolls

You should follow the same routine for all the poses you want to include in your walk-cycle. I normally use the contact, recoil, and a high point poses and let Blender to make the passing pose.

Now if you do **ALT-A** you will see our character walking almost naturally.

It will be very useful to count how many Blender Units (B.U.) are covered with each step, which can be done counting the grid squares between both feet in Pose 1. This number is the STRIDE parameter that we are going to use later on in the NLA window.

Now we will focus on make the character actually advance through the scene.

First of all deselect the walkcycle action for our armature so it stops moving when pressing **ALT-A**. To do this, press the little X button besides the action name in the action window.

Then we will create a PATH object for our hero in the ground plane, trying not to make it too curve for now (the more straight the better), once done let's parent the character's Armature to the path (a *normal* parent, not a Follow Path!). If everything went OK, we will see our character moving stiff along the path when pressing **ALT-A**.

Now go to the NLA window and add the walkcycle action in a channel as a NLA strip. With the strip selected press **NKEY** and then push the Use Path button.

It is convenient that at the moment of adding actions in the NLA window, that no action is selected for the current armature. Why? Because instead of a NLA strip, we'll see the individual KeyFrames of the action being inserted in the armature channel and this KeyFrames will override any prior animation strips we could have added so far. Anyway, if you do insert an action in this way, you can always convert the KeyFrames into a NLA strip by pressing **CKEY**.

Now if you start the animation again some funny things might happen. This is due to we haven't set the Stride parameter.

This value is the number of Blender Units that should be covered by a single walkcycle and is very important that we estimate it with accuracy. Once calculated we should enter it in the Stride Num Button which appears if once you have selected the strip you press the **NKEY**.

If we adjust it well and if the walkcycle was correctly set up, our character should not "slide" across the path.

One way to estimate the Stride value accurately is to count how many grid squares there are between the toes of the feet in Pose 1. This value multiplied by 2 and by the grid scale (normally 1 grid square = 1 B.U. but this could not be the case, for instance in the example 2 grid squares = 1 B.U.) will render the searched STRIDE value.

In the example there are 7.5 squares with GRID=1.0, since the Grid scale is 1.0 we have: STRIDE = 7.5 x 1.0 x 2 = 15

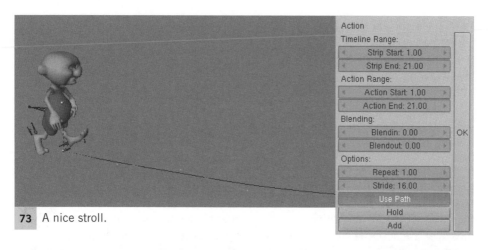

73 A nice stroll.

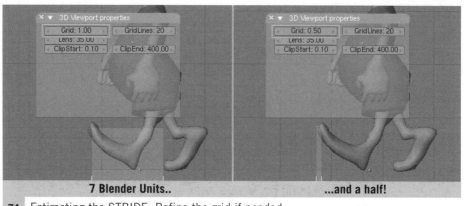

74 Estimating the STRIDE. Refine the grid if needed.

It's likely that we want our character to walk faster or slower or even stop for a while. We can do all this by editing the path's Speed curve.

Select the path and open an IPO window. There we will see a Speed curve normalized between 0 and 1 in ordinates (Y axis) and going from frame 1 to the last one in the X axis. The Y coordinate represents the relative position in the path and the curve's slope is the speed of the parented objects. In Edit Mode we will add two points with the same Y coordinate. This flat part represents a pause in the movement and it goes from frame 40 to frame 60 in the figure.

The problem here is that when our character stops because of the pause in the curve, we will see him in a "frozen" pose with a foot on the ground and the other in the air.

To fix this little problem we will use the NLA window. What we have to do is to insert the STAND_STILL action, this is a pose where our character is at rest. I have defined this action as only one frame by erasing all displacements and rotations of the bones. (See Clearing Transformations), and then moving a couple of bones to get a resting attitude.

Since the pause is from frame=78 to frame=112 we should insert this "still" action exactly there for it to perfectly fit the pause. For the animation doesn't start nor end briskly we can use the BlendIn and BlendOut options, where we can set the number of frames used to blend actions and in this way doing a more natural transition between them. In this way the character will smoothly change its pose and everything will look fine. If we do use a BlendIn or BlendOut value, to be set in the **NKEY** dialog, then we should start the action BlendIn frames earlier and finish it BlendOut frames later, because the character should be still moving while changing poses.

We can of course combine different walkcycles in the same path as for instance change from walking to running in the higher speed zone.

In all these situations we will have to bear in mind that the different efects will be added from one NLA strip to the precedent strips. So, the best option is to insert the walkcycle and still strips before any other.

Moving hands while walking

To add actions in the NLA window we have to locate the mouse pointer over the armature's channel and press **SHIFT-A**. A menu with all available actions will pop up. If we don't locate the pointer over an armature channel an error message ERROR: Not an armature" will pop up instead.

So, place the pointer over the armature strip and press **SHIFT-A** and add the "WAVE_HAND" action.

As this particular action is just the waving of the left arm to say "hello" during some point in the walkcycle, we will not use the "Use Path" option but move it in time so it overlaps the arms KeyFrames from the walkcycle action. Move the pointer over the strip and press **NKEY** or just drag it and scale it to your satisfaction.

Since this action is the last to be calculated (remember Blender evaluates actions from Top to Bottom in the NLA Editor), it will override any KeyFrames defined for the bones involved in the precedent actions.

Well, there is no much left to say about NLA and armatures. Now it is time for you to experiment and to show the results of your work to the world. One last recommen-

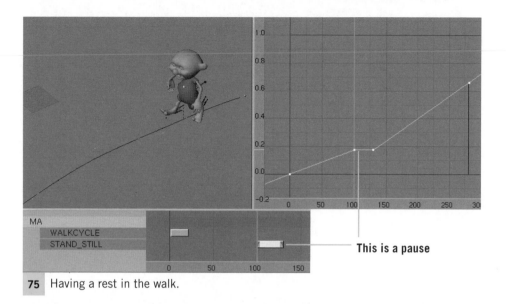

This is a pause

75 Having a rest in the walk.

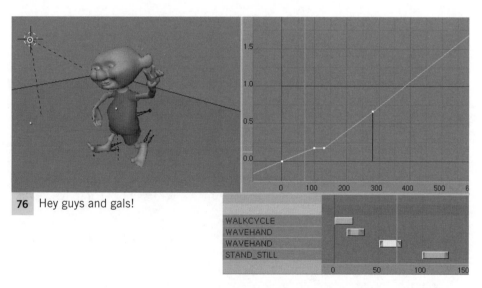

76 Hey guys and gals!

dation though: it is possible to edit KeyFrames in the NLA window. We can duplicate frames (**SHIFT-D**), grab KeyFrames (**GKEY**) and also erase KeyFrames (**XKEY**), but if you do erase KeyFrames be careful because they will be lost forever from the currently selected action. So be careful and always convert to NLA strip before erasing anything.

Bye and good luck blenderheads !!

Gallery

This color insert presents, due to space limitations, only a selection of the renderings presented at the 2003 Blender conference.

These images are also present on the CD, which also contains several animations, in DivX format, presented at the same conference.

The latter two images show Blender at work with two different set-ups for the interface and two different themes.

There are hundreds and thousands of Blender artwork of matching quality. Each Blender community site exhibits at least a forum were user post artwork and some have full fledged galleries.

You can visit www.blender.org, www.elysiun.com and the emerging independent gallery http://centralsource.com/blenderart/.

DRAGON SNAKE, NICO HAGEN
Modelled and rendered in Blender, some post processing.

MINI, XAVIER <richie> LIGEY
Modelled in Blender, rendered in YafRay.

JUNIOR, <H@dj>

Modelled and rendered in Blender.

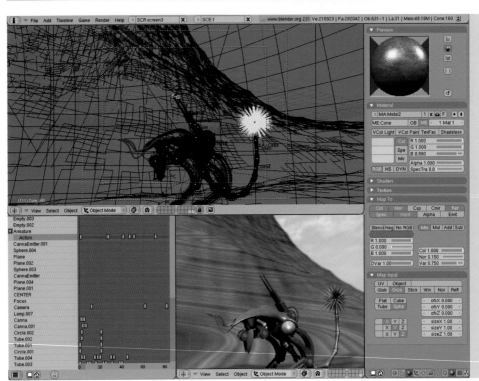

BLENDER 2.3x, INTERFACE

Rounded Theme on a complex Robot Animation.

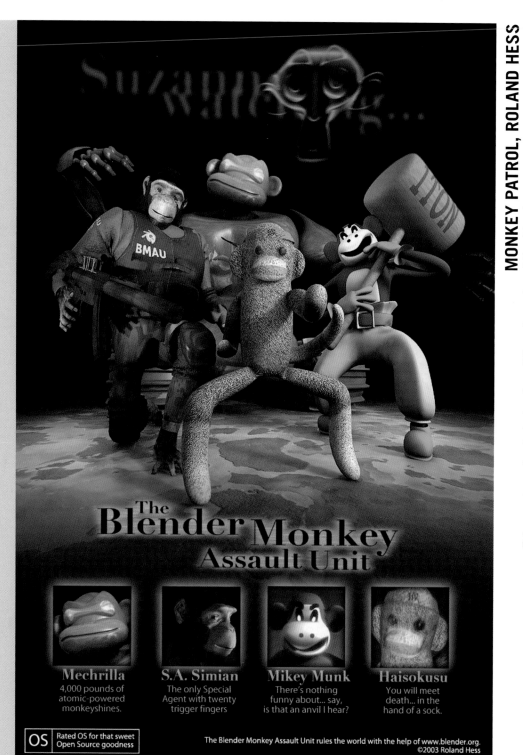

LEGO CAR, HANS PACKET
Modelled in Blender, rendered in YafRay.

CONCEPT CAR, DOMINIC AGORO-OMBAKA
Modelled and rendered in Blender.

Burt.S.

TROPHY 0, BURT S.
Modelled and rendered in Blender.

BIZZARRINI, SPEEDTITI
Modelled in Blender, rendered in YafRay.

FISHERMAN PIER, KEVIN GIBSON

Modelled and rendered in Blender, a little postpro.

DUTCH SHEEP BARN, ROLAND HESS

Modelled and rendered in Blender.

RUSTY CITY, ENDRE <endi> BARATH
Modelled and rendered in Blender, a little postpro.

MONUMENT, ENDRE <endi> BARATH
Modelled and rendered in Blender, a little postpro.

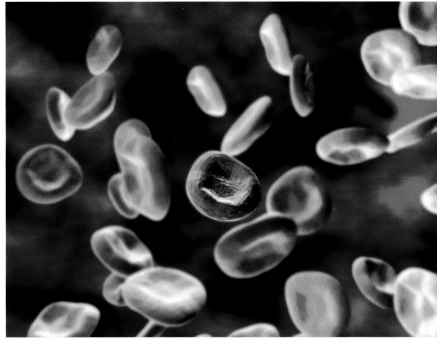

(inspired by a scene by Adrian Thompson)

BLOODCELLS, STEN <ztonzy> SJÖBERG

Modelled and rendered in Blender, a little postpro.

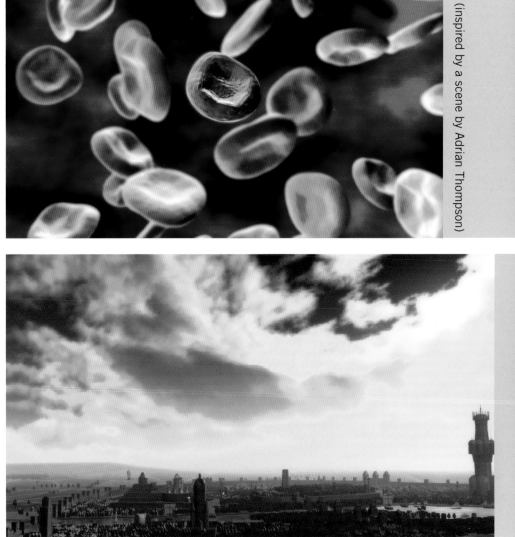

CITY OF BOREN, PAVEL CERNOHOUS

Modelled and rendered in Blender.

KNOT, HANS PACKET Modelled in Blender, rendered in YafRay.

PENCIL, HANS PACKET Modelled in Blender, rendered in YafRay.

EMPTY CITY, ENDRE <endi> BARATH

Modelled and rendered in Blender, a little postpro.

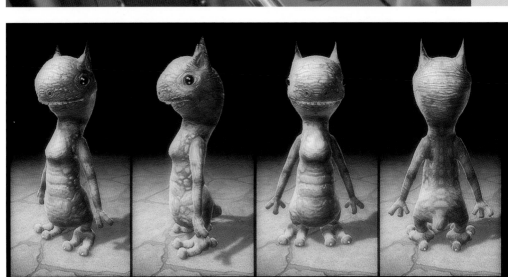

CHUMPY EEF, ENDRE <endi> BARATH

Modelled and rendered in Blender, a little postpro.

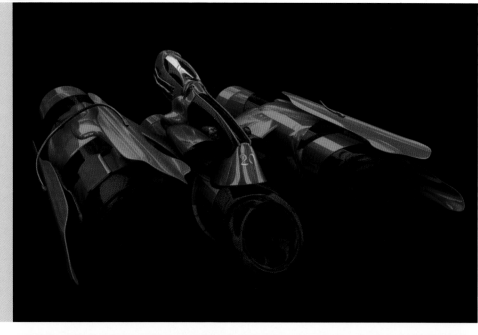

SUPERNOVA, JEAN-SÉBASTIEN GUILLEMETTE
Modelled and rendered in Blender, a little postpro.

F1 2003, DEREK <BgDM> MARSH
Modelled and rendered in Blender.

AT THE GATES OF DREAMS, <S68>

Modelled in Blender, rendereed in YafRay.

(inspired by an original work of M.C. Escher)

RELATIVITY, STEFANO <S68> SELLERI

Modelled in Blender, rendered in YafRay.

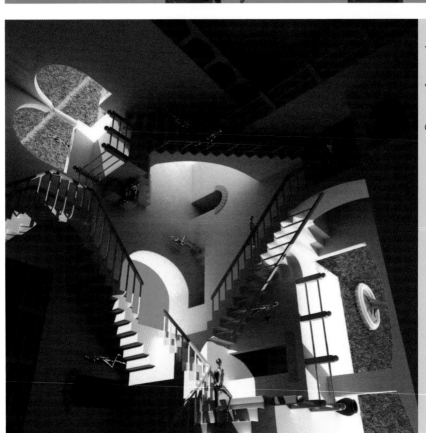

CIRO, STEFANO <S68> SELLERI
Modelled and rendered in Blender.

THE CATHEDRAL, STEFANO <S68> SELLERI
Modeled in Blender, rendered in YafRay.

AIRMAN, LANDIS R. FIELDS IV

Modelled and rendered in Blender.

AIRMAN CHARACTER SHEET, LANDIS R. FIELDS IV

Modelled and rendered in Blender.

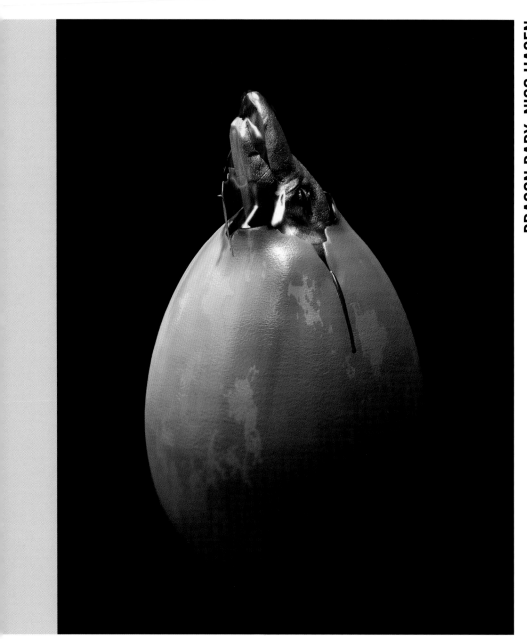

DRAGON BABY, NICO HAGEN
Modelled and rednered in Blender.

BLENDER 2.3x, INTERFACE

Default theme on an architectural scene.

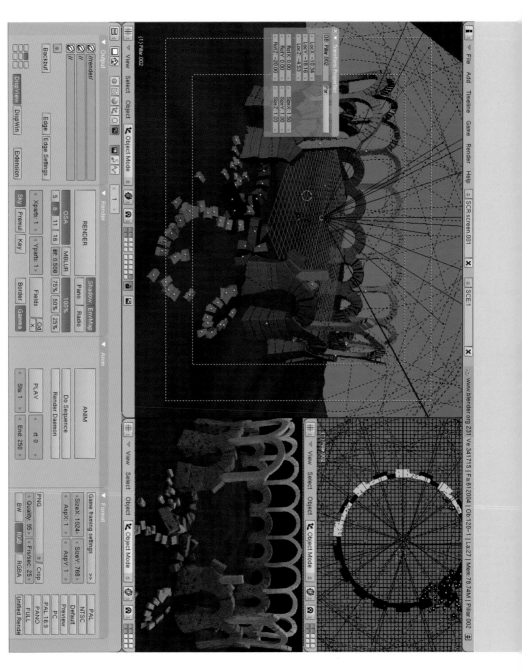

PART IV

RENDERING

There is more to the Blender rendering engine than what you see when you hit **F12**.

This part will guide you through all Blender's rendering features, from Motion Blur to Cartoon-like edges. And there is a full chapter dedicated to Blender's built in Radiosity engine, which allows for very realistic illuminations without using any lamp.

CH. 14 RENDERING

RENDERING BY PARTS, PANORAMIC RENDERINGS, ANTIALIASING, OUTPUT FORMATS, RENDERING ANIMATIONS, MOTION BLUR, DEPTH OF FIELD, CARTOON EDGES, THE UNIFIED RENDERER, PREPARING YOUR WORK FOR VIDEO

Rendering is the final process of CG (short of postprocessing, of course) and is the phase in which the image corresponding to your 3D scene is finally created.

The rendering buttons window is accessed via the Scene Context and Render Sub-context (**F10** or the 🔳 button). The rendering Panels and Buttons are shown in figure 1.

The rendering of the current scene is performed by pressing the big RENDER button in the Render panel, or by pressing **F12**. The result of the rendering is kept in a buffer and shown in its own window. It can be saved by pressing **F3** or via the File>>Save Image menu.

The image is rendered according to the dimensions defined in the Format Panel (fig. 2).

By default the dimensions SizeX and SizeY are 320x256 and can be changed as for any Num Button. The two buttons below define the aspect ratio of the pixels. This is the ratio between the X and Y dimensions of the pixel of the image. By default it is 1:1 since computer screen pixels are square, but can be varied if television shorts are being made since TV pixels are not square. To make life easier the rightmost block of buttons (fig. 3) provides some common presets:

- PAL 720x576 pixels at 54:51 aspect ratio.
- NTSC 720x480 pixels at 10:11 aspect ratio.
- Default Same as PAL, but with full TV options, as explained in the following sections.
- Preview 640x512 at 1:1 aspect ratio. This setting automatically scales down the image by 50%, to effectively produce a 320x256 image.
- PC 640x480 at 1:1 aspect ratio.
- PAL 16:9 720x576 at 64:45 aspect ratio, for 16:9 widescreen TV renderings.
- PANO Standard panoramic settings 576x176 at 115:100 aspect ratio. More about 'panoramic' renderings in the pertinent section.
- FULL 1280x1024 at 1:1 aspect ratio.

1 Rendering Buttons.

2 Image types and dimensions.

3 Image preset dimensions.

4 Rendering by parts buttons.

5 Panorama button.

Rendering by Parts

It is possible to render an image in pieces, one after the other, rather than all at one time. This can be useful for very complex scenes, where rendering small sections one after the other only requires computation of a small part of the scene, which uses less memory.

By setting values different from 1 in the Xpart and Ypart in the Render Panel (fig. 4) you force Blender to divide your image into a grid of Xpart times Ypart sub-images which are then rendered one after the other and finally assembled together.

Blender cannot handle more than 64 parts.

Panoramic renderings

To obtain nice panoramic renderings, up to a full 360° view of the horizon, Blender provides an automatic procedure.

If the Xparts is greater than 1 and the Pano button of the Render Panel is pressed (fig. 5), then the rendered image is created to be Xparts times SizeX wide and SizeY high, rendering each part by rotating the camera as far as necessary to obtain seamless images.

Figure 6 shows a test set up with 12 spheres surrounding a camera. By leaving the camera as it is, you obtain the rendering shown in figure 7. By setting Xparts to 3 and selecting Panorama the result is an image three times wider showing one more full camera shot to the right and one full to the left (fig. 8).

To obtain something similar without the Panorama option, the only way is to decrease the camera focal length. For example figure 9 shows a comparable view, obtained with a 7.0 focal length, equivalent to a very wide angle, or fish-eye, lens. Distortion is very evident.

To obtain a full 360° view some tweaking is necessary. It is known that a focal length of 16.0 corresponds to a viewing angle of 90°. Hence a panoramic render with 4 Xparts and a camera with a 16.0 lens yields a full 360° view, as that shown in figure 10. This is grossly distorted, since a 16.0 lens is a wide angle lens, and distorts at the edges.

To have undistorted views the focal length should be around 35.0. Figure 11 shows the result for a panorama with 8 Xparts and a camera with a 38.5 lens, corresponding to a 45° viewing angle.

The image is much less distorted, but special attention must be given to proportion. The original image was 320x256 pixels. The panorama in figure 10 is 4 x 320 wide. To keep this new panorama the same width, the SizeX of the image must be set to 160 so that 8 x 160 = 4 x 320. But the camera viewing angle width occurs for the largest dimension, so that, if SizeX is kept to 256 the image spans 45° vertically but less than that horizontally, so that the final result is not a 360° panorama unless SizeX ≥ SizeY or you are willing to make some tests.

Antialiasing

A computer generated image is made up of pixels, these pixels can of course only be a single colour. In the rendering process the rendering engine must therefore assign a single colour to each pixel on the basis of what object is shown in that pixel.

This often leads to poor results, especially at sharp boundaries, or where thin lines are present, and it is particularly evident for oblique lines.

To overcome this problem, which is known as *Aliasing*, it is possible to resort to an Anti-Aliasing technique. Basically, each pixel is 'oversampled', by rendering it as if it were 5 pixels or more, and assigning an 'average' colour to the rendered pixel.

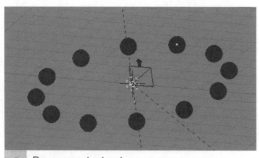

6   Panorama test set up.

7   Non-panoramic rendering.

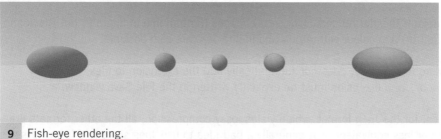

8   Panoramic rendering.

9   Fish-eye rendering.

10   Full 360° panorama with 16.0 lenses.

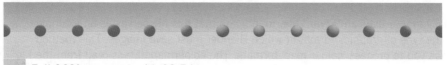

11   Full 360° panorama with 38.5 lenses.

The buttons to control Anti-Aliasing, or OverSAmple (OSA), are below the rendering button in the `Render` panel (fig. 12). By pressing the OSA button antialiasing is activated, by selecting one of the four numeric buttons below it, the level of oversampling (from 5 to 16) is chosen.

Blender uses a Delta Accumulation rendering system with jittered sampling. The values of OSA (5, 8, 11, 16) are pre-set numbers that specify the number of samples; a higher value produces better edges, but slows down the rendering.

Figure 13 shows a rendering with OSA turned off and with 5 or 8 OSA samples.

Output formats

The file is saved in whichever format has been selected in the pertinent Menu button in the `Format` Panel (fig. 2). From here you can select many image or animation formats (fig. 14).

The default image type is JPEG, but, since the image is stored in a buffer and then saved, it is possible to change the image file type after the rendering and before saving using this menu.

By default Blender renders color (RGB) images (bottom line in figure 2) but Black and White (BW) and colour with Alpha Channel (RGBA) are also possible.

Beware that Blender does *not* automatically add the extension to files, hence any `.tga` or `.png` extension must be explicitly written in the File Save window.

Except for the Jpeg format, which yields lossy compression, all the other formats are more or less equivalent. It is generally a bad idea to use Jpeg since it is lossy. It is better to use Targa and then convert it to Jpeg for web publishing purposes, keeping the original Targa.

Anyhow, for what concerns the other formats: TARGA raw is uncompressed Targa, uses a lot of disk space. PNG is Portable Network Graphics, a standard meant to replace old GIF inasmuch as it is lossless, but supports full true colour images. HamX is a self-developed 8 bits RLE format; it creates extremely compact files that can be displayed quickly. To be used only for the "Play" option. Iris is the standard SGI format, and Iris + Zbuffer is the same with added Zbuffer info.

Finally Ftype uses an "Ftype" file, to indicate that this file serves as an example for the type of graphics format in which Blender must save images. This method allows you to process 'colour map' formats. The colourmap data is read from the file and used to convert the available 24 or 32 bit graphics. If the option "RGBA" is speci-

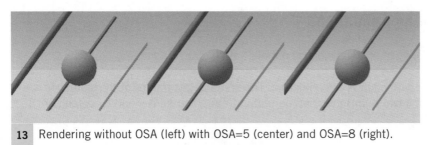

13 Rendering without OSA (left) with OSA=5 (center) and OSA=8 (right).

12 OSA buttons.

14 Image and animations formats.

15 Animation Codec settings.

fied, standard colour number '0' is used as the transparent colour. Blender reads and writes (Amiga) IFF, Targa, (SGI) Iris formats.

For what concerns animations:

- AVI Raw - saves an AVI as uncompressed frames. Non-lossy, but huge files.
- AVI Jpeg - saves an AVI as a series of Jpeg images. Lossy, smaller files but not as small as you can get with a better compression algorithm. Furthermore the AVI Jpeg format is not read by default by some players.
- AVI Codec - saves an AVI compressing it with a codec. Blender automatically gets the list of your available codecs from the operating system and allows you to set its parameters. It is also possible to change it or change its settings, once selected, via the Set Codec button which appears (fig. 15).

For an AVI animation it is also possible to set the frame rate (fig. 15) which, by default, is 25 frames per second.

Rendering Animations

The rendering of an animation is controlled via the `Anim` Panel (fig. 16).

The `ANIM` button starts the rendering. The first and last frames of the animation are given by the two NumButtons at the bottom (`Sta:` and `End:`), and by default are 1 and 250.

By default the 3D scene animation is rendered, to make use of the sequence editor the `Do Sequence` Tog Button must be selected.

By default the animation is rendered in the directory specified in the `Output` Panel (fig. 17). If an AVI format has been selected, then the name will be `####_####.avi` where the '####' indicates the start and end frame of the animation, as 4 digit integers padded with zeros as necessary.

If an image format is chosen, on the other hand, a series of images named ####, ('####' being the pertinent frame number) is created in the directory. If the file name extension is needed, this is obtained by pressing the `Extensions` Tog Button (fig. 17).

Complex Animations

Unless your animation is really simple, and you expect it to render in half an hour or less, it is always a good idea to render the animation as separate Targa frames rather than as an AVI file from the beginning.

This allows you an easy recovery if the power fails and you have to re-start the rendering, since the frames you have already rendered will still be there.

It is also a good idea since, if an error is present in a few frames, you can make corrections and re-render just the affected frames.

You can then make the AVI out of the separate frames with Blender's sequence editor or with an external program.

Motion Blur

Blender's animations are by default rendered as a sequence of *perfectly still* images.

This is unrealistic, since fast moving objects do appear to be 'moving', that is, blurred by their own motion, both in a movie frame and in a photograph from a 'real world camera'.

RENDERING.MOTIONS BLUR

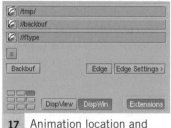

16 Animation rendering buttons.

17 Animation location and extensions.

18 Motion Blur buttons.

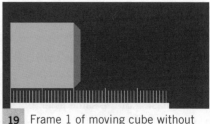

19 Frame 1 of moving cube without motion blur

20 Frame 2 of moving cube without motion blur

To obtain such a Motion Blur effect, Blender can be made to render the current frame and some more frames, in between the real frames, and merge them all together to obtain an image where fast moving details are 'blurred'.

To access this option select the MBLUR button next to the OSA button in the Render Panel (fig. 18). This makes Blender render as many 'intermediate' frames as the oversampling number is set to (5, 8, 11 or 16) and accumulate them, one over the other, on a single frame. The number-button Bf: or Blur Factor defines the length of the shutter time as will be shown in the example below. Setting the OSA Button is unnecessary since the Motion Blur process adds some antialiasing anyway, but to have a really smooth image OSA can be activated too. This makes each accumulated image have anti-aliasing.

To better grasp the concept let's assume that we have a cube, uniformly moving 1 Blender unit to the right at each frame. This is indeed fast, especially since the cube itself has a side of only 2 Blender units.

Figure 19 shows a render of frame 1 without Motion Blur, figure 20 shows a render of frame 2. The scale beneath the cube helps in appreciating the movement of 1 Blender unit.

Figure 21 on the other hand shows the rendering of frame 1 when Motion Blur is set and 8 'intermediate' frames are computed. Bf is set to 0.5; this means that the 8 'intermediate' frames are computed on a 0.5 frame period starting from frame 1. This is very evident since the whole 'blurriness' of the cube occurs on half a unit before and half a unit after the main cube body.

Figure 22 and 23 show the effect of increasing Bf values. A value greater than 1 implies a very 'slow' camera shutter.

Better results than those shown can be obtained by setting 11 or 16 samples rather than 8, but, of course, since as many *separate* renders as samples are needed a Motion Blur render takes that many times more than a non-motion blur one.

If Motion Blur is active, even if nothing is moving on the scene, Blender actually 'jitters' the camera a little between an 'intermediate' frame and the next. This implies that, even if OSA is off, the resulting images have nice Anti-Aliasing. An MBLUR obtained Anti-Aliasing is comparable to an OSA Anti-Aliasing of the same level, but generally slower.

This is interesting since, for very complex scenes where a level 16 OSA does not give satisfactory results, better results can be obtained using *both* OSA and MBlur. This way you have as many samples per frame as you have 'intermediate' frames, effectively giving oversampling at levels 25,64,121,256 if 5,8,11,16 samples are chosen, respectively.

Depth of Field

Depth of Field (DoF) is an interesting effect in real world photography which adds a lot to CG generated images. It is also known as Focal Blur.

The phenomenon is linked to the fact that a real world camera can focus on a subject at a given distance, so objects closer to the camera and objects further away will be out of the focal plane, and will therefore be slightly blurred in the resulting photograph.

The amount of blurring of the nearest and furthest objects varies a lot with the focal length and aperture size of the lens and, if skilfully used, can give very pleasing effects.

Blender's renderer does not provide an automatic mechanism or obtaining DoF, but there are two alternative way to achieve it. One relies solely on Blender's internals,

RENDERING.DEPTH OF FIELD

21 Frame 1 of moving cube with motion blur, 8 samples, Bf=0.5.

22 Frame 1 of moving cube with motion blur, 8 samples, Bf=1.0.

23 Frame 1 of moving cube with motion blur, 8 samples, Bf=3.0.

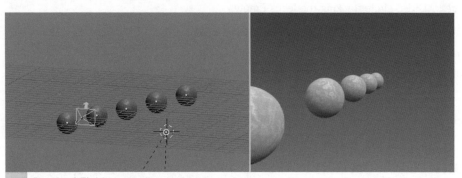

24 Depth of Field test scene.

and will be described here. The other requires an external sequence plugin and will be outlined in the Sequence Editor Chapter.

The hack to obtain DoF in Blender relies on skilful use of the Motion Blur effect described before, making the Camera move circularly around what would be the aperture of the 'real world camera' lens, constantly pointing at a point where 'perfect' focus is desired.

Assume that you have a scene of aligned spheres, as shown on the the left of figure 24. A standard Blender rendering will result in the image on the right of figure 24, with all spheres perfectly sharp and in focus.

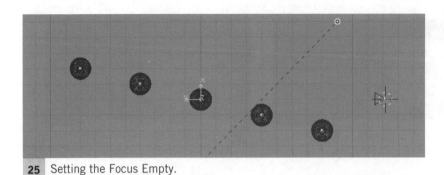

25 Setting the Focus Empty.

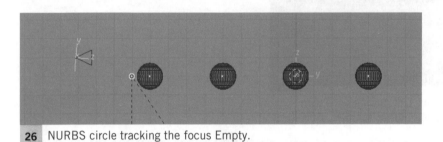

26 NURBS circle tracking the focus Empty.

The first step is to place an Empty (**SPACE**>>Add>>Empty) where the focus will be. In our case at the center of the middle sphere (fig. 25).

Then, assuming that your Camera is already placed in the correct position, place the cursor on the Camera (Select the Camera, **SHIFT-S**>>Curs>>Sel) and add a NURBS circle (**SPACE**>>ADD>>Curve>>NURBS Circle).

Out of EditMode (**TAB**) scale the circle. This is very arbitrary, and you might want to re-scale it later on to achieve better results. Basically, the circle size is linked to the physical aperture size, or diaphragm, of your 'real world camera'. The larger the circle the narrower the region with perfect focus will be, and the more blurred near and far objects will be. The smaller the circle the less evident the DoF blurring will be.

Now make the circle track the Empty whith a constraint or the old Tracking as in figure 26. Since the normal to the plane containing the circle is the local z-axis, you will have to set up tracking correctly so that the local z-axis of the circle points to the Empty and the circle is orthogonal to the line connecting its centre to the Empty.

Select the Camera and then the circle and parent the Camera to the circle (**CTRL+P**) The circle will be the Path of the camera so you can either use a normal parent relationship and then set the circle CurvePath Toggle Button on or use a Follow Path Parent relationship.

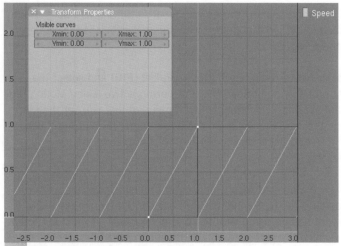

27 Speed IPO for the NURBS circle path.

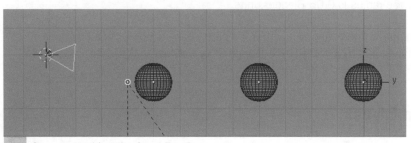

28 Camera tracking the focal Empty.

With the circle still selected, open an IPO window select the Curve IPO type. The only available IPO is 'Speed'. **CTRL+LMB** twice at random in the IPO window to add an IPO with two random points. Then set these points numerically by using **NKEY** to Xmin and Ymin to 0, Xmax and Ymax to 1. To complete the IPO editing make it cyclic via the Curve>>Extend Mode>>Cyclic Menu entry. The final result should be as shown in figure 27.

With these settings we have effectively made the Camera circle around its former position along the NURBS circle path in exactly 1 frame. This makes the Motion Blur option take slightly different views of the scene and create the Focal Blur effect in the end.

There is still one more setting to perform. First select the Camera and then the focal Empty, and make the Camera track the Empty the way you prefear. The Camera should now track the Empty, as in figure 28.

If you press **ALT-A** now you won't see any movement because the Camera does exactly one full circle path in each frame, so it appears to be still, nevertheless the Motion Blur engine will detect these moves.

The last touch is then to go to the rendering buttons window (**F10**) and select the MBLUR button. You most probably don't need the OSA button active, since Motion Blur will implicitly do some antialiasing. It is strongly recommended that you set the Motion Blur Factor to 1, since this way you will span the entire frame for blurring, taking the whole circle length. It is also necessary to set the oversamples to the maximum level (16) for best results (fig. 29).

A rendering (**F12**) will yield the desired result. This can be much slower than a non-DoF rendering since Blender effectively renders 16 images and then merges them. Figure 31 shows the result, to be compared with the one in figure 24. It must be noted that the circle has been scaled much less to obtain this picture than has been shown in the example screenshots. These latter were made with a large radius (equal to 0.5 Blender units) to demonstrate the technique better. On the other hand, figure 30 has a circle whose radius is 0.06 Blender units.

This technique is interesting and with it it's pretty easy to obtain small degrees of Depth of Field. For big Focal Blurs it is limited by the fact that it is not possible to have more than 16 oversamples.

Cartoon Edges

Blender's new material shaders, as per version 2.28, include nice toon diffuse and specular shaders.

By using these shaders you can give your rendering a comic-book-like or manga-like appearance, affecting the shades of colours, as you may be able to appreciate in figure 31. The effect is not perfect since real comics and manga also usually have china ink outlines. Blender can add this feature as a post-processing operation.

To access this option select the Edge button in the Output Panel of the Rendering (**F10**) Buttons (fig. 32). This makes Blender search for edges in your rendering and add an 'outline' to them.

Before repeating the rendering it is necessary to set some parameters. The Edge Settings opens a window to set these (fig. 33).

In this window it is possible to set the edge colour, which is black by default, and its intensity, Eint which is an integer ranging from 0 (faintest) to 255 (strongest). The other buttons are useful if the Unified render is used (see next section).

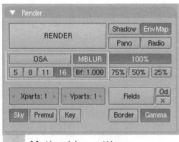

29 Motion blur settings.

30 Motion blur final rendering.

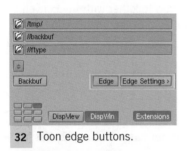

32 Toon edge buttons.

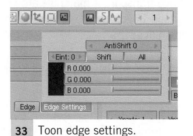

33 Toon edge settings.

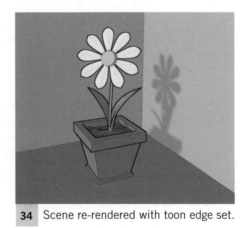

31 A scene with Toon materials.

34 Scene re-rendered with toon edge set.

Figure 34 shows the same image as figure 31 but with toon edges enabled, of black colour and maximum intensity (Eint=255).

The Unified Renderer

A less well known feature of Blender is the Unified Renderer button in the bottom right corner of the Rendering Buttons Format Panel (fig. 35).

Blender's *default* renderer is highly optimized for speed. This has been achieved by subdividing the rendering process into several passes. First the 'normal' materials are handled. Then Materials with transparency (Alpha) are taken into account. Finally Halos and flares are added.

This is fast, but can lead to less than optimum results, especially with Halos. The Unified Renderer, on the other hand, renders the image in a single pass. This is slower, but gives better results, especially for Halos.

Furthermore, since transparent materials are now rendered together with the conventional ones, Cartoon Edges can be applied to them too, by pressing the All button in the Edge Setting dialog.

If the Unified Renderer is selected an additional group of buttons appears in the Output Panel (fig. 36).

The Gamma slider is related to the OSA procedure. Pixel oversamples are blended to generate the final rendered pixel. The conventional renderer has a Gamma=1, but in the Unified Renderer you can vary this number.

The Post process button makes a dialog box appear (fig. 37). From this you can control three kinds of post processing: the Add slider defines a constant quantity to be added to the RGB colour value of each pixel. Positive values make the image uniformly brighter, negative uniformly darker.

The Mul slider defines a value by which all RGB values of all pixels are multiplied. Values greater than 1 make the image brighter, smaller than 1 make the image darker.

The Gamma slider does the standard gamma contrast correction of any paint program

Preparing your work for video

Once you mastered the animations trick you will surely start to produce wonderfull animations, encoded with your favourite codecs, and possibly you'll share it on the internet with all the community.

But, sooner or later, you will be struck by the desire of building an animation for Television, maybe burning you own DVDs.

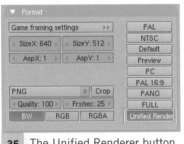

35 The Unified Renderer button.

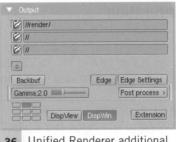

36 Unified Renderer additional buttons.

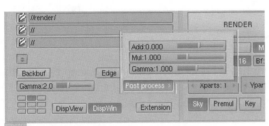

37 Unified Renderer postprocess submenu.

To spare you some disappointments here are some tips specifically targeted at Video preparation. The first and principal is to remember the double dashed white line in camera view!

If you render for PC then the whole rendered image, which lies within the *outer* dashed rectangle will be shown. For Television some lines and some part of the lines will be lost due to the mechanics of the electron beam scanning in your TV cathodic ray tube. You are guaranteed that what is within the *inner* dashed rectangle in camera view will be visible on the screen. Everything within the two rectangles may and may not be visible, depending on the given TV set you will see the video on.

Furthermore the rendering size is strictly dictated by the TV standard. Blender has three pre-set settings for your convenience:

PAL	720x576 pixels at 54:51 aspect ratio.
NTSC	720x480 pixels at 10:11 aspect ratio.
PAL 16:9	720x576 at 64:45 aspect ratio, for 16:9 widescreen TV renderings.

Please note the "Aspect Ratio" stuff. TV does *not* have square pixels as Computer monitors have, their pixel is somewhat rectangular, so it is necessary to generate *pre-distorted* images which will look crap on the computer but which will be shown nicely on a TV set.

Color Saturation

Most video tapes and video signals are not based at RGB model but on YUV, or YCrCb, model in Europe and YIQ in US, this latter being quite similar to the former. Hence some knowledge of this is necessary too.

YUV model sends info as 'Luminance', or intensity (Y) and two 'Crominance' signals, red and blue. Actually a Black and White TV set shows only luminance, while color TV sets reconstructs color from Crominances. It is:

$Y = 0.299R + 0.587G + 0.114B$
$U = Cr = R-Y$
$V = Cb = B-Y$

Whereas a standard 24 bit RGB picture has 8 bit for each channel, to keep bandwidth down, and considering that the Human eye is more sensitive to luminance that to crominance the former is sent with more bits than the two latter.

This results in a smaller dynamics of colors, in Video, than that you are used to on Monitors. You hence have to keep in mind not all colors can be correctly displayed. Rule of thumb is to keep the colors as 'greyish' or 'unsaturated' as possible, this can be roughtly converted in keeping the dynamics of your colors within 0.8.

In other words the difference between the highest RGB value and the lowest RGB value should not exceed 0.8 ([0-1] range) or 200 ([0-255] range).

This is not strict, something more than 0.8 is acceptable, but a RGB=(1.0,0,0) material will be very ugly.

Rendering to fields

The TV standard prescribes that there should be 25 frames per second (PAL) or 30 frames per second (NTSC). Since the phosphorous of the screen do not maintain luminosity too long this could produce a noticeable flickering. To minimize this TV do not represent frames as Computer does but rather represent half-frames, or *fields* at a double refresh rate, hence 50 half frames per second on PAL and 60 half frames per second on NTSC. This was originally bound to the frequency of power lines in Europe (50Hz) and US (60Hz).

In particular fields are "interlaced" in the sense that one field presents all the even lines of the complete frame and the subsequent field the odd ones.

RENDERING.FIELD RENDERING

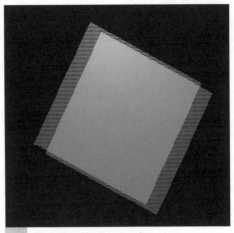

38 Field Rendering setup.

39 Field Rendering result.

Since there is a non-negligible time difference between each field (1/50 or 1/60 of a second) merely rendering a frame the usual way and split it into two half frames does not work. A noticeable jitter of the edges of moving objects would be present.

To optimally handle this issue Blender allows for field rendering. When the `Fields` button in the `Render` Panel is pressed (fig. 38). Blender prepares each frame in two passes, on the first it renders only the even lines, the it *advances in time by half time step* and renders all the odd lines.

This produces odd results on a PC screen (fig. 39) but will show correctly on a TV set.

The two buttons next to the `Fields` button forces the rendering of Odd fields first (`Odd`) and disable the half-frame time step between fields (`x`).

Setting up the correct field order Blender default setting is to produce Even field Before Odd field, this comply to European PAL standards. Odd field is to be scanned first on NTSC.

Of course if you make the wrong selection things go even worse that if no Field rendering at all was used.

Setting up the correct field order

CH. 15 RADIOSITY

THE BLENDER RADIOSITY METHOD, RADIOSITY RENDERING, RADIOSITY AS A MODELLING TOOL, RADIOSITY JUICY EXAMPLE

Most rendering models, including ray-tracing, assume a simplified spatial model, highly optimised for the light that enters our 'eye' in order to draw the image. You can add reflection and shadows to this model to achieve a more realistic result. Still, there's an important aspect missing! When a surface has a reflective light component, it not only shows up in our image, it also shines light at surfaces in its neighbourhood. And vice-versa. In fact, light bounces around in an environment until all light energy is absorbed (or has escaped!).

Re-irradiated light carries information about the object which has re-irradiated it, notably colour. Hence not only the shadows are 'less black' because of re-irradiated light, but also they tend to show the colour of the nearest, brightly illuminated, object. A phenomenon often referred to as 'colour leaking' (fig. 1).

In closed environments, light energy is generated by 'emitters' and is accounted for by reflection or absorption of the surfaces in the environment. The rate at which energy leaves a surface is called the 'radiosity' of a surface. Unlike conventional rendering methods, Radiosity methods first calculate all light interactions in an environment in a view-independent way. Then, different views can be rendered in real-time.

In Blender, since version 2.28 Radiosity is both a rendering and a modelling tool. This means that you can enable Radiosity within a rendering or rather use Radiosity to paint vertex colours and vertex lights of your meshes, for later use.

The Blender Radiosity method

First, some theory! You can skip to next section if you like, and get back here if questions arise.

During the late eighties and early nineties Radiosity was a hot topic in 3D computer graphics. Many different methods were developed, the most successful of these solutions were based on the "progressive refinement" method with an "adaptive subdivision" scheme. And this is what Blender uses.

RADIOSITY.THE BLENDER RADIOSITY METHOD

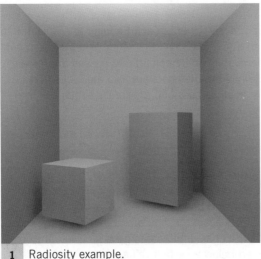

1 Radiosity example.

To be able to get the most out of the Blender Radiosity method, it is important to understand the following principles:

Finite Element Method

Many computer graphics or simulation methods assume a simplification of reality with 'finite elements'. For a visually attractive (and even scientifically proven) solution, it is not always necessary to dive into a molecular level of detail. Instead, you can reduce your problem to a finite number of representative and well-described elements. It is a common fact that such systems quickly converge into a stable and reliable solution.

The Radiosity method is a typical example of a finite element method inasmuch as every face is considered a 'finite element' and its light emission considered as a whole.

Patches and Elements

In the Radiosity universe, we distinguish between two types of 3D faces:

Patches
These are triangles or squares which are able to *send energy*. For a fast solution it is important to have as few of these patches as possible. But, to speed things up the energy is modelled as if it were radiated by the Patch's centre; the size of the patches should then be small enough to make this a realistic energy distribution. (For example, when a small object is located above the Patch centre, all energy the Patch sends is obscured by this object, even if the patch is larger! This patch should be subdivided in smaller patches).

Elements

These are the triangles or squares which *receive energy*. Each Element is associated to a Patch. In fact, Patches are subdivided into many small Elements. When an element receives energy it absorbs part of it (depending on its colour) and passes the remainder to the Patch, for further radiation. Since the Elements are also the faces that we display, it is important to have them as small as possible, to express subtle shadow boundaries and light gradients.

Progressive Refinement

This method starts with examining all available Patches. The Patch with the most 'unshot' energy is selected to shoot all its energy to the environment. The Elements in the environment receive this energy, and add this to the 'unshot' energy of their associated Patches. Then the process starts again for the Patch *now* having the most unshot energy. This continues for all the Patches until no energy is received anymore, or until the 'unshot' energy has converged below a certain value.

The hemicube method

The calculation of how much energy each Patch gives to an Element is done through the use of 'hemicubes'. Exactly located at the Patch's center, a hemicube (literally 'half a cube') consist of 5 small images of the environment. For each pixel in these images, a certain visible Element is color-coded, and the transmitted amount of energy can be calculated. Especially with the use of specialized hardware the hemicube method can be accelerated significantly. In Blender, however, hemicube calculations are done "in software".

This method is in fact a simplification and optimisation of the 'real' Radiosity formula (form factor differentiation). For this reason the resolution of the hemicube (the number of pixels of its images) is approximate and its careful setting is important to prevent aliasing artefacts.

Adaptive subdivision

Since the size of the patches and elements in a Mesh defines the quality of the Radiosity solution, automatic subdivision schemes have been developed to define the optimal size of Patches and Elements. Blender has two automatic subdivision methods:

1. Subdivide-shoot Patches

By shooting energy to the environment, and comparing the hemicube values with the actual mathematical 'form factor' value, errors can be detected that indicate a need for further subdivision of the Patch. The results are smaller Patches and a longer solving time, but a higher realism of the solution.

RADIOSITY.THE BLENDER RADIOSITY METHOD

2. Subdivide-shoot Elements

By shooting energy to the environment, and detecting high energy changes (gradients) inside a Patch, the Elements of this Patch are subdivided one extra level. The results are smaller Elements and a longer solving time and maybe more aliasing, but a higher level of detail.

Display and Post Processing

Subdividing Elements in Blender is 'balanced', that means each Element differs a maximum of '1' subdivide level with its neighbours. This is important for a pleasant and correct display of the Radiosity solution with Gouraud shaded faces. Usually after solving, the solution consists of thousands of small Elements. By filtering these and removing 'doubles', the number of Elements can be reduced significantly without destroying the quality of the Radiosity solution. Blender stores the energy values in 'floating point' values. This makes settings for dramatic lighting situations possible, by changing the standard multiplying and gamma values.

Radiosity for Modelling

The final step can be replacing the input Meshes with the Radiosity solution (button `Replace Meshes`). At that moment the vertex colours are converted from a 'floating point' value to a 24 bits RGB value. The old Mesh Objects are deleted and replaced with one or more new Mesh Objects. You can then delete the Radiosity data with `Free Data`. The new Objects get a default Material that allows immediate rendering. Two settings in a Material are important for working with vertex colours:

VColPaint
This option treats vertex colours as a replacement for the normal RGB value in the Material. You have to add Lamps in order to see the Radiosity colours. In fact, you can use Blender lighting and shadowing as usual, and still have a neat Radiosity 'look' in the rendering.

VColLight
The vertexcolors are added to the light when rendering. Even without Lamps, you can see the result. With this option, the vertex colours are pre-multiplied by the Material RGB colour. This allows fine-tuning of the amount of 'Radiosity light' in the final rendering.

As with everything in Blender, Radiosity settings are stored in a datablock. It is attached to a Scene, and each Scene in Blender can have a different Radiosity 'block'. Use this facility to divide complex environments into Scenes with independent Radiosity solvers.

Radiosity Rendering

Let's assume you have a scene ready, and that you want to render it with the Radiosity Rendering. The first thing to grasp when doing Radiosity is that no Lamps are necessary, but some meshes with Emit material property greater than zero are, since these will be the light sources.

You can build the test scene shown in figure 1, it is rather easy, just make a big cube, the room, give different materials to the side walls, add a cube and a stretched cube within and add a plane with an non-zero Emit value next to the roof, to simulate the area light (fig. 2).

You assign Materials as usual to the input models. The RGB value of the Material defines the Patch colour. The 'Emit' value of a Material defines if a Patch is loaded with energy at the start of the Radiosity simulation. The "Emit" value is multiplied with the area of a Patch to calculate the initial amount of unshot energy.

Check the number of "emittors" on Blender console! If this is zero nothing interesting can happen. You need at least 1 emitting patch to have light and hence a solution.

Emitting faces

When assigning materials be sure that all of them have the Radio toggle on to enable the Shader Panel of the Material subcontext buttons (fig. 3).

Please note that the light emission is governed by the direction of the normals of a mesh, so the light emitting plane should have a downward pointing normal and the outer cube (the room) should have the normals pointing inside, (flip them!)

Switch to the Radiosity ( ) sub-context of the Shading Context. The Panels, shown in figure 4, are two: Radio Rendering which governs Radiosity when used as a rendering tool (present case) and Radio Tool, which governs Radiosity as a modelling tool (next section).

The buttons define:

- Hemires: - the hemicube resolution; the color-coded images used to find the Elements that are visible from a 'shoot Patch', and thus receive energy. hemicubes are not stored, but are recalculated each time for every Patch that shoots energy. The "Hemires" value determines the Radiosity quality and adds significantly to the solving time.

RADIOSITY.RADIOSITY RENDERING

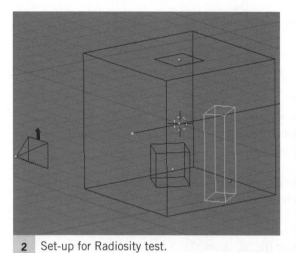

2 Set-up for Radiosity test.

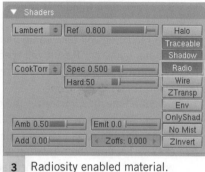

3 Radiosity enabled material.

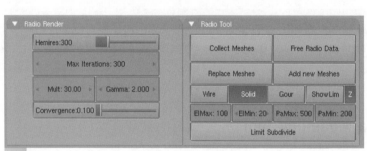

4 Radiosity buttons for radiosity rendering.

- `Max Iterations:` - the maximum number of Radiosity iterations. If set to zero Radiosity will go on until the convergence criterion is met. You are strongly adviced to set this to some non-zero number, usually greater than 100.

- `Mult:`, `Gamma:` - The colourspace of the Radiosity solution is far more detailed than can be expressed with simple 24 bit RGB values. When Elements are converted to faces, their energy values are converted to an RGB colour using the `Mult` and `Gamma` values. With the `Mult` value you can multiply the energy value, with `Gamma` you can change the contrast of the energy values.

- `Convergence:` - When the amount of unshot energy in an environment is lower than this value, the Radiosity solving stops. The initial unshot energy in an environment is multiplied by the area of the Patches. During each iteration, some of the energy is absorbed, or disappears when the environment is not a closed volume. In Blender's standard coordinate system a typical emitter (as in the example files) has a relatively small area. The convergence value in is divided by a factor of 1000 before testing for that reason.

Set the `Max Iterations:` to 100 and turn to the Scene Context and Render Sub-context (**F10**).

Locate the `Radio` Tog Button (fig. 5) in the `Render` panel and set it on to enable Radiosity, then Render (**F12**)!

The rendering will take some more time than usual, in the console you will notice a counter going on. Result will be quite poor (fig. 6, top) because the automatic radiosity render does not do adaptive refinement!

Select all meshes, one after the other, and, in EditMode subdivide it at least three times. The room, which is much bigger than the others, you can even subdivide four times. Set the `Max Iterations` a bit higher, 300 or more. Try again the Rendering (**F12**). This time the rendering will take even longer but the results will be much nicer, with soft shadows and colour leaking (fig. 6, bottom).

In the Radiosity Rendering Blender acts as for a normal rendering, this means that textures, Curves, Surfaces and even Dupliframed Objects are handled correctly.

Radiosity as a Modelling Tool

Radiosity can be used also as a Modelling tool for defining Vertices colours and lights. This can be very useful if you want to make further tweaks to your models, or you want to use them in the Game Engine. Furthermore the Radiosity Modelling allows for Adaptive refinement, whereas the Radiosity Rendering does not!

There are few important points to grasp for practical Radiosity Modelling:

Only Meshes in Blender are allowed as input for Radiosity Modelling. This because the process generates Vertex colours... and so there must be vertices. It is also important to realize that *each* face in a Mesh becomes a Patch, and thus a potential energy emitter and reflector. Typically, large Patches send and receive more energy than small ones. It is therefore important to have a well-balanced input model with Patches large enough to make a difference! When you add extremely small faces, these will (almost) never receive enough energy to be noticed by the "progressive refinement" method, which only selects Patches with large amounts of unshot energy.

RADIOSITY.RADIOSITY AS A MODELLING TOOL

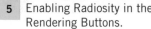

5 Enabling Radiosity in the Rendering Buttons.

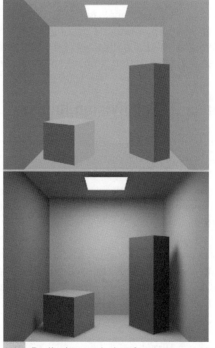

6 Radiosity rendering for coarse meshes (top) and fine meshes (bottom).

Only Meshes means that you have to convert Curves and Surfaces to Meshes (**CTRL+C**) before starting the Radiosity solution!

Non-mesh Objects

Phase 1: Collect Meshes

All selected and visible Meshes in the current Scene are converted to Patches as soon as the `Collect Meshes` button of the `Radio Tool` Panel is pressed (fig. 4). As a result a new Panel, `Calculation` appears. Blender now has entered the Radiosity Modelling mode, and other editing functions are blocked until the newly created button `Free Data` has been pressed. The `Phase` text above the buttons now says `Init` and shows the number of Patches and Elements.

After the Meshes are collected, they are drawn in a pseudo lighting mode that clearly differs from the normal drawing.

The `Radio Tool` Panel (fig. 7) shows three Radio Buttons: `Wire`, `Solid`, `Gour` these are three drawmode options independent of the indicated drawmode of a 3DWindow. Gouraud display is only performed after the Radiosity process has started. Press the `Gour` button, to have smoother results on curved surfaces.

Phase 2: Subdivision limits.

Blender offers a few settings to define the minimum and maximum sizes of Patches and Elements in the `Radio Tools` and `Calculation` Panels (fig. 8).

`Limit Subdivide` With respect to the values "PaMax" and "PaMin", the Patches are subdivided. This subdivision is also automatically performed when a "GO" action has started.

`PaMax, PaMin, ElMax, ElMin` The maximum and minimum size of a Patch or Element. These limits are used during all Radiosity phases. The unit is expressed in 0.0001 of the boundbox size of the entire environment. Hence, with default 500 and 200 settings maximum and minimum Patch size 0.05 of the entire model (1/20) and 0.02 of the entire model (1/50).

`ShowLim, z` This option visualizes the Patch and Element limits. By pressing the z option, the limits are drawn rotated differently. The white lines show the Patch limits, cyan lines show the Element limits.

Phase 3: Adaptive Subdividing

Last settings before starting the analysis (fig. 9).

`MaxEl` The maximum allowed number of Elements. Since Elements are subdivided automatically in Blender, the amount of used memory and the duration of the solving time can be controlled with this button. As a rule of thumb 20,000 elements take up 10 Mb memory.

`Max Subdiv Shoot` The maximum number of shoot Patches that are evaluated for the "adaptive subdivision" (described below) . If zero, all Patches with 'Emit' value are evaluated.

`Subdiv Shoot Patch` By shooting energy to the environment, errors can be detected that indicate a need for further subdivision of Patches. The subdivision is performed only once each time you call this function. The results are smaller Patches and a longer solving time, but a higher realism of the solution. This option can also be automatically performed when the GO action has started.

RADIOSITY.RADIOSITY AS A MODELLING TOOL

7 Gourad button.

8 Radiosity Buttons for Subdivision.

9 Radiosity Buttons.

`Subdiv Shoot Element` By shooting energy to the environment, and detecting high energy changes (frequencies) inside a Patch, the Elements of this Patch are selected to be subdivided one extra level. The subdivision is performed only once each time you call this function. The results are smaller Elements and a longer solving time and probably more aliasing, but a higher level of detail. This option can also be automatically performed when the `GO` action has started.

`SubSh P` The number of times the environment is tested to detect Patches that need subdivision.

`SubSh E` The number of times the environment is tested to detect Elements that need subdivision.

`Hemires`, `Convergence` and `Max iterations` in the `Radio Render` Panel are still active and have the same meaning as in Radiosity Rendering.

GO With this button you start the Radiosity simulation. The phases are:

1. *Limit Subdivide* - When Patches are too large, they are subdivided.

2. *Subdiv Shoot Patch* - The value of SubSh P defines the number of times the Subdiv Shoot Patch function is called. As a result, Patches are subdivided.

3. *Subdiv Shoot Elem* - The value of SubSh E defines the number of times the Subdiv Shoot Element function is called. As a result, Elements are subdivided.

4. *Subdivide Elements* - When Elements are still larger than the minimum size, they are subdivided. Now, the maximum amount of memory is usually allocated.

5. *Solve* - This is the actual 'progressive refinement' method. The mouse pointer displays the iteration step, the current total of Patches that shot their energy in the environment. This process continues until the unshot energy in the environment is lower than the Convergence value or when the maximum number of iterations has been reached.

6. *Convert to faces* - The elements are converted to triangles or squares with 'anchored' edges, to make sure a pleasant not-discontinue Gouraud display is possible.

This process can be terminated with **ESC** during any phase.

Phase 4: Editing the solution

Once the Radiosity solution has been computed there are still some actions to take (fig. 10).

Element Filter - This option filters Elements to remove aliasing artifacts, to smooth shadow boundaries, or to force equalized colours for the RemoveDoubles option.

RemoveDoubles - When two neighbouring Elements have a displayed colour that differs less than Lim, the Elements are joined. Lim value is used by the previous is expressed in a standard 8 bits resolution; a color range from 0 - 255.

FaceFilter - Elements are converted to faces for display. A FaceFilter forces an extra smoothing in the displayed result, without changing the Element values themselves.

Mult, Gamma (NumBut) - have the same meaning than in Radiosity Rendering.

10 Radiosity post process.

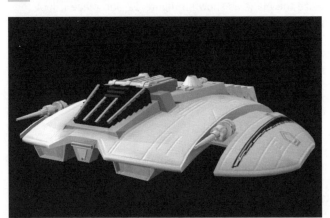

11 Radiosity rendered Cylon Raider.

`Add New Meshes` - The faces of the current displayed Radiosity solution are converted to Mesh Objects with vertex colours. A new Material is added that allows immediate rendering. *The input-Meshes remain unchanged.*

`Replace Meshes (But)` - As previous, but the input-Meshes are removed.

`Free Radio Data (But)` - All Patches, Elements and Faces are freed in Memory. You always must perform this action after using Radiosity to be able to return to normal editing.

Radiosity Juicy example

To get definitely away from dry theory and show what Radiosity Modelling can really achieve let's look at an example.

This will actually show you a true Global Illumination scene, with smoother results than the 'Dupliverted Spot Lights' technique shown in the Lighting Chapter to attain something like fig. 11.

Setting up

We have only two elements in the scene at start up: a Raider (if you remember some Sci-Fi Movie...) and a camera. The Raider has the default grey material, except for the main cockpit windows which are black. For this technique, we will not need any lamps.

The first thing that we will want to add to the scene is a plane. This plane will be used as the floor in our scene. Resize the plane as shown in figure 12 and place it just under the Raider. Leave a little space between the plane and the Raider bottom. This will give us a nice "floating" look.

Next, you will want to give the plane a material and select a colour for it. We will try to use a nice blue. You can use the setting in figure 13 for it.

The Sky Dome

We want to make a GI rendering, so the next thing that we are going to add is an icosphere. This sphere is going to be our light source instead of the typical lamps. What we are going to do is use its faces as *emitters* that will project light for us in multiple directions instead of in one direction as with a typical, single, lamp. This will give us the desired effect.

To set this up, add an icosphere with a subdivision of 3. While still in EditMode, use the **BKEY** select mode to select the lower portion of the sphere and delete it. This will leave us with our dome. Resize the dome to better fit the scene and match it up with your plane. It should resemble figure 14.

Next, we want to make sure that we have all the vertices of the dome selected and then click on the EditButtons (**F9**) and select Draw Normals. This allows us to see in which direction the vertices are "emitting". By default it will be outside, so hit the Flip Normals button, which will change the vertex emitter from projecting outward to projecting inward in our dome (fig. 15).

Now that we have created our dome, we need a new material. When you create the material for the dome change the following settings in the MaterialButtons (**F5**):

- Add = 0.000
- Ref = 1.000
- Alpha = 1.000
- Emit = 0.020

The Emit slider here is the key. This setting controls the amount of light "emitted" from our dome. 0.020 is a good default. Remember that the dome is the bigger part

RADIOSITY.THE JUICY EXAMPLE

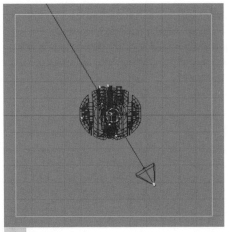

12 Add a plane.

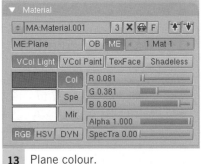

13 Plane colour.

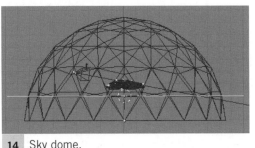

14 Sky dome.

16 Sky dome material.

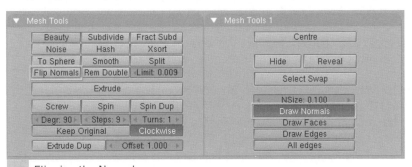

15 Flipping the Normals.

of the scene! you don't want too much light! But you can experiment with this setting to get different results. The lower the setting here though the longer the "solve" time later (fig. 16).

At this point we have created everything that we need for our scene. The next step will be to alter the dome and the plane from "double-sided" to "single-sided". To achieve this, we will select the dome mesh and then go back to the EditButtons (**F9**). Click the Double Sided button and turn it off (fig. 17). Repeat this process for the Plane.

The Radiosity solution

Now the next few steps are the heart and soul of Global Illumination. Go to side view with **NUM3** and use **AKEY** to select all of the meshes in our scene. Next hold **SHIFT** and double click on your camera. We do not want this selected. It should look similar to figure 18.

After selecting the meshes, go to camera view with **NUM0** and then turn on shaded mode with **ZKEY** so we can see inside our dome.

Now select the Shading context (**F5**) and the Radiosity Buttons Sub-context (🔲) in the Radio Tool Panel, click the Collect Meshes button. You should notice a change in your view in the colours. It should look similar to figure 19.

Next, to keep the Raider smooth like our original mesh, we will want to change from Solid to Gour. This will give our Raider its nice curves back, in the same way Set Smooth would in the EditButtons. You'll also need to change the Max Subdiv Shoot to 1 (fig. 20). Do not forget this step!

After you have set Gour and Max Subdiv Shoot, click Go and wait. Blender will then begin calculating the emit part of the dome, going face by face, thus "solving" the render. As it does this, you will see the scene change as more and more light is added to the scene and the meshes are changed. You will also notice that the cursor in Blender changes to a counter much like if it were an animation. Let Blender run, solving the Radiosity problem.

Letting Blender go to somewhere between 50-500 depending on the scene can do, for most cases. The solving time depends on you and how long you decide to let it run... remember you can hit **ESC** at any time to stop the process. This is an area that can be experimented with for different results. This can take from 1 to 5 minutes and your system speed will also greatly determine how long this process takes. Figure 21 is our Raider after 100 iterations.

After hitting the **ESC** key and stopping the solution, click Replace Meshes (or Add New Meshes) and then Free Radio Data. This finalizes our solve and replaces our previous scene with the new solved Radiosity scene.

RADIOSITY.THE JUICY EXAMPLE

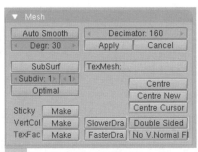

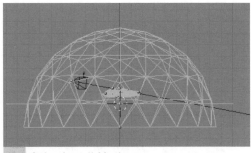

17 Setting Dome and plane to being 'single sided'.

18 Selecting all Meshes.

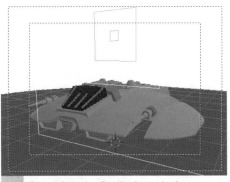

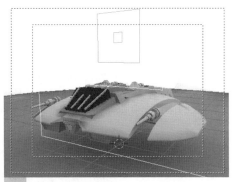

19 Preparing the Radiosity solution.

21 Radiosity solution.

20 Radiosity settings.

Adding rather than Replacing meshes is a form of Undo. You still have old meshes and you can re-run radiosity again! But you must move these new meshes to a new layer and hide the old layers before rendering!

Now we are ready for **F12** and render (fig. 22).

22 Rendering of the radiosity solution.

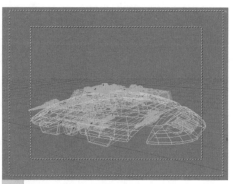

23 The Rider's mesh.

Texturing

There you go folks! You now have a very clean looking render with soft 360 degree lighting using Radiosity. Very nice... But the next thing we want to do is add textures to the mesh. So go back to our main screen area.

Now try selecting your mesh and you will notice that it selects not only the Raider but the plane and dome as well. That is because Radiosity created a new *single* mesh through the solution process. To add a texture though, we only want the Raider.

So, select the mesh and then go into EditMode. In EditMode we can delete the dome and plane since they are no longer needed. You can use the **LKEY** to select the proper vertices and press **XKEY** to delete them. Keep selecting and deleting until you are left with only the Raider. It should look like in figure 23. If we were to render it now with **F12**, we would get just a black background and our Raider. This is nice... but again, we want textures!

To add textures to mesh, we must separate out the areas that we are going to apply materials and textures to. For the Raider, We want to add textures to the wings and mid-section. To do this select the Raider mesh, and go back into EditMode. Select a vertex near the edge of the wing and then hit the **LKEY** to select linked vertices. Do the same on the other side. Next, click on the mid section of the ship and do the same thing. Select the areas shown in figure 24. When you have those, hit the **PKEY** to separate the vertices selected.

We now have our wing section separate and are ready to add the materials and textures. We want to create a new material for this mesh. To get a nice metallic look, we can use the settings in figure 25.

Time to add the textures. We want to achieve some pretty elaborate results. We will need two bump-maps to create grooves and two mask for painting and 'decals'. There are hence four textures for the Raider wings to be created, as shown in figure 26.

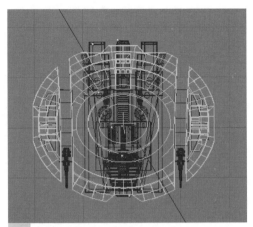

24 Seperating the Rider parts to be textured.

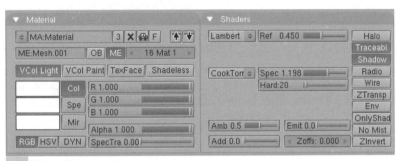

25 "Metallic" material.

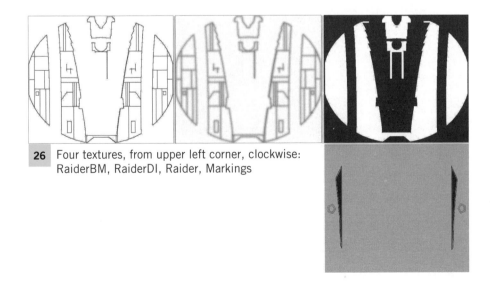

26 Four textures, from upper left corner, clockwise: RaiderBM, RaiderDI, Raider, Markings

The textures should be placed in four material channels in the rider top mesh. 'RaiderBM' and 'RaiderDI' should be set to a negative NOR (fig. 27a -click NOR twice, it will turn yellow). 'Raider' should be set up as negative REF (fig. 27b).

Which material?

A Mesh coming from a Radiosity solution typically has more than one material on it. It is important to operate on the right "original" material.

The result is the desired metallic plating for the hull of the Raider. Finally the fourth texture, 'Markings', is set to COL in the MaterialButtons (fig. 27c). This will give the Raider its proper striping and insignia. Our rider is quite flat, so the Flat projection is adequate. Were it a more complex shape some UV mapping would have been required to attain good results. The material preview for the mesh should look like figure 28.

Our textures *won't* show up in the rendering right now (except markings) because Nor and Ref type texture reacts to lighting, and there is no light source in the scene! Hence will now need to add a lamp or two, keeping in mind that our ship is still lit pretty well from the Radiosity solve, so lamps energy should be quite weak. Once you have your lamps, you try a test render. Experiment with the lamps until you get the results you like.

The final rendering (fig. 29) shows a nice well lit Raider with soft texturing.

RADIOSITY.THE JUICY EXAMPLE

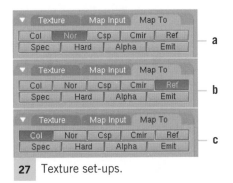

a

b

c

27 Texture set-ups.

28 Complete material preview.

29 Final rendering of the Raider.

PART V

ADVANCED TOOLS

There are tools and techniques wich cannot be clearly categorized in the Modelling or in the Animation parts because they use a mixture of the two.

This part is hence devoted to the use of Animation as a Modelling tool and to the Special Effects provided by blender.

In the Advanced Tools category falls also a very important tool, the Sequence Editor, a full fledged video editor able to give any of your animations a professional finishing.

CH. 16 SPECIAL MODELING TECHNIQUES

INTRODUCTION, DUPLIVERTS, DUPLIFRAMES, MODELLING WITH LATTICES

by Claudio "Malefico" Andaur

Introduction

Once we have overcome the "extrusion modelling fever" and started to look at more challenging modelling targets, we might start the quest for alternative methods to do the job. There are a group of modelling techniques in Blender which not only make our modelling job easier but sometimes make it *possible*.

These so called "special" modelling techniques involve not only some vertex manipulation but the use of non-intuitive procedures which require a deeper knowledge or experience from the user than the average beginner.

In this chapter we will describe these techniques in detail and explain their utility in several modelling applications which could not have been solved any other way.

DupliVerts

DupliVerts are not a rock band nor a dutch word for something illegal (well maybe it is) but is a contraction for "DUPLIcation at VERTiceS", meaning the duplication of a base Object at the location of the Vertices of a Mesh (or even a Particle system). In other words, when using DupliVerts on a mesh, on every vertex of it an instance of the base object is placed.

There are actually two approaches to modelling using DupliVerts. They can be used as an arranging tool, allowing us to model geometrical arrangement of objects (eg: the columns of a Greek temple, the trees in a garden, an army of robot soldiers, the desks in a classroom). The object can be of any object type which Blender supports.

The second approach is to use them to model an Object starting from a single part of it (i.e.: the spikes in a club, the thorns of a sea-urchin, the tiles in a wall, the petals in a flower).

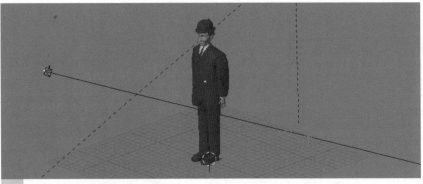

1 A simple scene to play with.

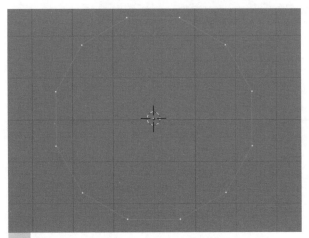

2 The parent mesh can be any primitive.

DupliVerts as an Arranging Tool

All you need is a base object (eg: the "tree" or the "column") and a mesh with its vertices following the pattern you have in mind.

I will use a simple scene for the following part. It consists of a camera, the lamps, a plane (for the floor) and a strange man I modelled after a famous Magritte's character (fig. 1). If you don't like surrealism you will find this part extremely boring.

Anyway, the man will be my "base Object". It is a good idea that he will be at the centre of the co-ordinate system, and with all rotations cleared. Move the cursor to the base object's centre, and From Top View add a mesh circle, with 12 vertices or so (fig. 2).

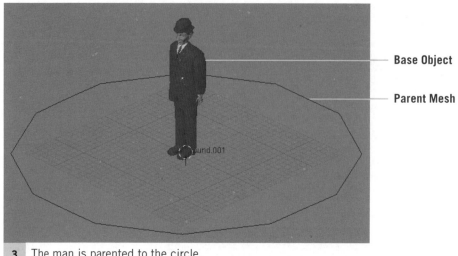

Base Object

Parent Mesh

3 The man is parented to the circle.

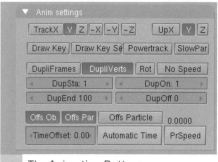

4 The Animation Buttons.

Out of Edit Mode, select the base Object and add the circle to the selection (order is very important here). Parent the base object to the circle by pressing **CTRL-P**. Now, the circle is the parent of the character (fig. 3). We are almost done.

Now select only the circle, switch the Buttons Window to the Object Context (via 🔧 or **F7**) and select the DupliVerts Button in the Anim Settings Panel (fig. 4).

Wow, isn't it great? Don't worry about the object at the centre (fig. 5). It is still shown in the 3D-views, but it will *not* be rendered. You can now select the base object and change it (rotate, scale) in EditMode and Dupliverted Objects will follow unchanged. If on the other hand you change it in Object Mode Dupliverted Objects will be affected as well.

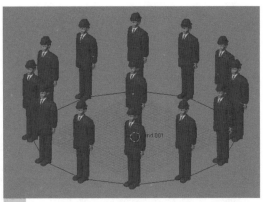

| 5 | In every vertex of the circle a man is placed. | 6 | Changing the size of the circle in EditMode. |

| 7 | A second row of Magritte's men. |

The base Object is not rendered if DupliVerted on a Mesh but it *is* rendered if Dupli-Verted on a Particle System!

Select the circle and scale it. You can see that the mysterious men are uniformly sca-led with it. Now enter the Edit Mode for the circle, select all vertices **AKEY** and scale it up about three times. Leave Edit Mode and the DupliVerted objects will update (fig. 6). This time they will still have their original size but the distance between them will have changed. Not only we can scale in Edit Mode, but we can also delete or add vertices to change the arrangement of men.

Select all vertices in Edit Mode and duplicate them (**SHIFT-D**). Now scale the new vertices outwards to get a second circle around the original. Leave Edit Mode, and a second circle of men will appear (fig. 7).

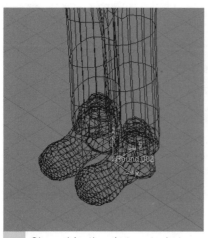

8 Show object's axis to get what you want.

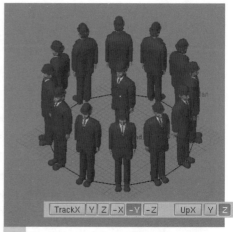

9 Negative Y Axis is aligned to vertex normal (pointing to the circle's center).

Until now all Magritte's men were facing the camera, ignoring each other. We can get more interesting results using the `Rot` Button next to the `DupliVerts` button in the `Anim Settings` Panel. With this Tog Button active, we can rotate the DupliVerted objects according to the normals of the parent Object. More precisely, the DupliVerted Objects axis are aligned with the normal at the vertex location.

Which axis is aligned (X, Y or Z) with the parent mesh normal depends on what is indicated in the `TrackX, Y, Z` buttons and the `UpX, Y, Z` buttons top in the `Anim Settings` Panel. Trying this with our surrealist buddies, will lead to weird results depending on these settings.

The best way to figure out what will happen is first of all aligning the "base" and "parent" objects' axis with the World axis. This is done selecting both objects and pressing **CTRL-A**, and click the `Apply Size/Rot?` menu.

Then make the axis of the base object and the axis and normals in the parent object visible (figure 8 - in this case, being a circle with no faces, a face must be defined first for the normal to be visible (actually to exist at all)).

Now select the base object (our Magritte's man) and play a little with the Tracking buttons. Note the different alignment of the axis with the different combinations of `UpX, Y, Z` and `TrackX, Y, Z` (fig. 9, 10, 11 and 12).

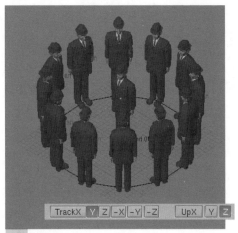

10 Positive Y axis is aligned to normal.

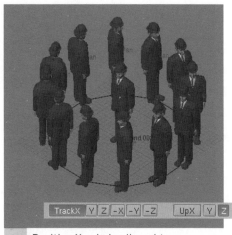

11 Positive X axis is aligned to normal.

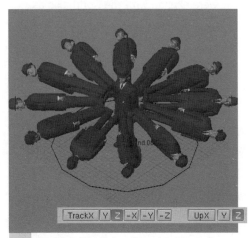

12 Positive Z axis is aligned to normal (weird, huh?).

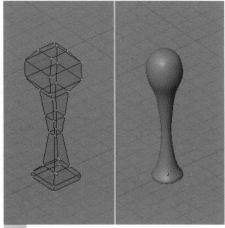

13 Strange tentacle and SubSurfed version.

DupliVerts to Model a Single Object

Very interesting models can be done using DupliVerts and a standard primitive.

Starting from a cube in Front View, and extruding a couple of times I have modelled something which looks like a tentacle when SubSurfs are activated (fig. 13). Then I added an Icosphere with 2 subdivisions.

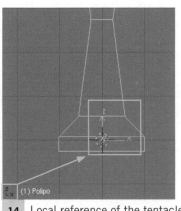

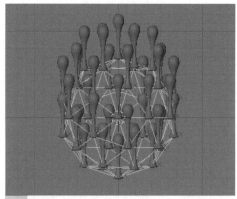

14 Local reference of the tentacle.

15 DupliVerts not rotated.

I had special care to be sure that the tentacle was located at the sphere centre, and that both the tentacle axis and the sphere axis were aligned with the world axis as above (fig. 14).

Now, I simply make the icosphere the parent of the tentacle. Select the icosphere alone and made it DupliVert in the Anim Settings Panel (fig. 15).

Press the Rot button to rotate the tentacles (fig. 16).

Once again to make the tentacle point outwards we have to take a closer look to its axis. When applying Rot, Blender will try to align one of the tentacle axis with the normal vector at the parent mesh vertex.

We didn't cared for the Parent circle for Magritte's men, but here we should care of the Sphere, and you will soon notice that it is *not* rendered. You probably would like to add an extra renderable sphere to complete the model.

You can experiment in Edit Mode with the tentacle, moving its vertices off the centre of the sphere, but the object's centre should always be at the sphere's centre in order to get a symmetrical figure. However take care not to scale up or down in one axis in Object Mode since it would lead to unpredictable results in the DupliVerted objects when applying the Rot button.

Once you're done with the model and you are happy with the results, you can select the tentacle and press **SHIFT-CTRL-A** and click on the Make duplis real ? menu to turn your virtual copies into real meshes (fig. 17).

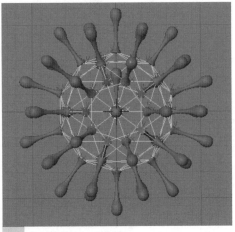

16 DupliVerts rotated.

17 Our model complete.

DupliFrames

You can consider DupliFrames in two different ways: an arranging or a modelling tool. In a way, DupliFrames are quite similar to DupliVerts. The only difference is that with DupliFrames we arrange our objects by making them to move rather than using the vertex of a mesh.

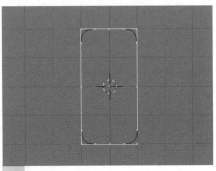

18 Link's outline.

DupliFrames stands for DUPLIcation at FRAMES and is a very useful modelling technique for objects which are repeated along a path, such as the wooden sleepers in a railroad, the boards in a fence or the links in a chain, but also for modelling complex curve objects like corkscrews, seashells and spirals.

Modelling using DupliFrames

We are going to model a chain with its links using DupliFrames.

First things come first. To explain the use of DupliFrames as a modelling technique, we will start by modelling a single link. To do this, add in front view a Curve Circle (Bézier or NURBS, whatever). In Edit Mode, subdivide it once and move the vertices a little to fit the link's outline (fig. 18).

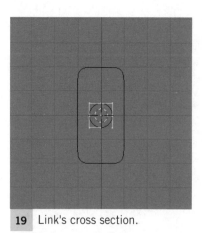

19 Link's cross section.

20 Curve's settings: Curve Path and Curve Follow.

Leave Edit Mode and add a Surface Circle object (fig. 19). NURBS-surfaces are ideal for this purpose, because we can change the resolution easily after creation, and if we need to, we can convert them to a mesh object. It is very important that you do not confuse Curve Circle and Surface Circle. The first one will act as the shape of the link but it will not let us do the skinning step later on. The second one will act as a cross section of our skinning.

Now parent the circle surface to the circle curve (the link's outline) as a Normal parent (Not a Curve Follow constraint). Select the curve and in the Object Context and Anim Settings Panel press CurvePath and CurveFollow (fig. 20).

It probably happens that the circle surface will appear dislocated. Just select it and press **ALT-O** to clear the origin (fig. 21).

If you hit **ALT-A** the circle will follow the curve. Now you probably will have to adjust the TrackX,Y,Z and UpX,Y,Z animation buttons, to make the circle go perpendicular to the curve path (fig. 22).

Now select the Surface Circle and go to Anim Settings Panel and press DupliFrames. A number of instances of the circular cross section will appear along the curve path (fig. 23).

You can adjust the number of circles you want to have with the DupSta, DupEnd, DupOn and DupOff buttons. These buttons control the Start and End of the duplication, the numebr of duplicates each time and also the Offset between duplications. If you want the link to be opened, you can try a different setting for DupEnd (fig. 24).

To turn the structure into a real NURBS-object, select the Surface Circle and press **CTRL-SHIFT-A**. A pop-up menu will appear prompting OK? Make Dupli's Real (fig. 25).

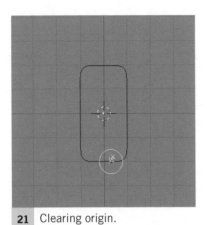

21 Clearing origin.

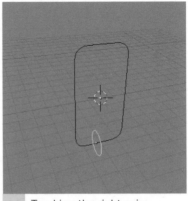

22 Tracking the right axis.

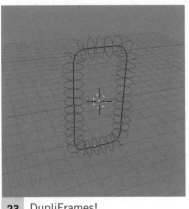

23 DupliFrames!

24 Values for DupliFrames. Note "DupEnd: 35" will end link before curve's end.

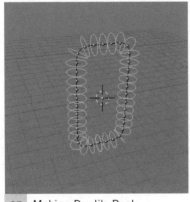

25 Making Dupli's Real.

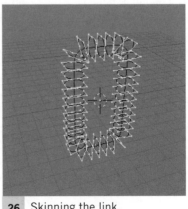

26 Skinning the link.

Do not deselect anything. We now have a collection of NURBS forming the outline of our object, but so far they are not skinned, so we cannot see them in a shaded preview or in a rendering. To achieve this, we need to join all the rings to one object. Withhout deselecting any rings, press **CTRL-J** and confirm the pop-up menu request. Now, enter EditMode for the newly created object and press **AKEY** to select all vertices (fig. 26). Now we are ready to skin our object. Press **FKEY** and Blender will automatically generate the solid object. This operation is called "Skinning" and is fully described in the Section called *Skinning* in Chapter 7.

When you leave Edit Mode, you can now see the object in a shaded view. But it is very dark. To correct this, enter Edit Mode and select all vertices, then press **WKEY**. Choose Switch Direction from the menu and leave Edit Mode. The object will now be drawn correctly (fig. 27).

The object we have created is a NURBS object. This means that you can still edit it. Even more interestingly, you can also control the resolution of the NURBS object via the Edit Buttons.

Here you can set the resolution of the object using ResolU and ResolV, so you can adjust it for working with the object in a low resolution, and then set it to a high resolution for your final render. NURBS objects are also very small in file size for saved scenes. Compare the size of a NURBS scene with the same scene in which all NURBS are converted (**ALT-C**) to meshes.

Finally you can delete the curve we used to give the shape of the link, since we will not use it anymore.

Arranging objects with DupliFrames

Now we will continue modelling the chain itself. For this, just add a Curve Path (we could use a different curve but this one gives better results). In Edit Mode, move its vertices until get the desired shape of the chain (fig. 28). If not using a Curve Path, you should check the button 3D in the Edit Buttons to let the chain be real 3D.

Select the object "Link" we modelled in the previous step and parent it to the chain curve, again as a normalpaernt. Since we are using a Curve Path the option CurvePath in the AnimButtons will be automatically activated, however the CurveFollow option will not, so you will have to activate it (fig. 29).

If the link is dislocated, select it and press **ALT-O** to clear the origin. Until now we have done little more than animate the link along the curve. This can be verified by playing the animation with **ALT-A**.

SPECIAL MODELING TECHNIQUES.DUPLIFRAMES

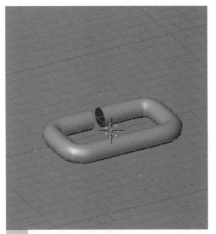

27 Skinning the link.

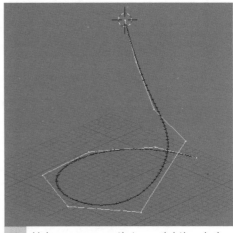

28 Using a curve path to model the chain.

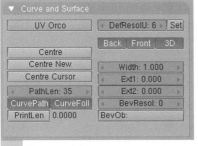

29 Curve settings.

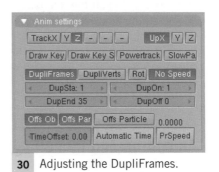

30 Adjusting the DupliFrames.

Now, with the link selected once again go to the Object Context and `Anim settings` Panel. Here, activate the option `DupliFrames` as before. Play With the `DupSta:`, `DupEnd:` and `DupOf:` NumButtons. Normally we are going to use `DupOf: 0` but for a chain, if using `DupOf: 0` the links are too close from each other you should change the value PathLen for the path curve to a lesser value, in the Editing Context and `Curve and Surface` Panel and then correspondingly change the `DupEnd:` value for the link to that number (fig. 30).

We need that the link rotates along the curve animation, so we have each link rotated 90 degrees respect the preceding one in the chain. For this, select the link and press Axis in the Edit Buttons to reveal the object's axis. Insert a rotation keyframe in the axis which was parallel to the curve. Move 3 or 4 frames ahead and rotate along that axis pressing **RKEY** followed by **XKEY-XKEY** (**XKEY** twice),**YKEY-YKEY**, or **ZKEY-ZKEY** to rotate it in the *local* X,Y or Z axis (fig. 31).

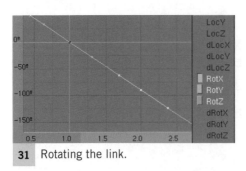

31 Rotating the link.

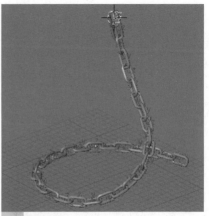

32 Dupliframed chain.

Open an IPO window to edit the rotation of the link along the path. Press the "Extrapolation Mode" so the link will continually rotate until the end of the path. You can edit the IPO rotation curve to make the link rotate exactly 90 degrees every one, two or three links (each link is a frame). Use **NKEY** to locate a node exactly at X=2.0 and Y=9.0, which correspond to 90 degrees in 1 frame (from frame 1 to 2).

Now we got a nice chain (fig. 32)!

More Animation and Modelling

You are not limited to use Curve Paths to model your stuff. These were used just for our own convenience, however in some cases there are no need of them.

In Front View add a surface circle (you should know why by now, fig. 33). Subdivide once, to make it look more like a square. Move and scale some vertices a little to give it a trapezoid shape (fig. 34).

Then rotate all vertices a few degrees. Grab all vertices and displace them some units right or left in X (but at the same Z location). You can use **CTRL** to achieve this precisely. Leave Edit Mode (fig. 35).

From now on, the only thing we are going to do is editing IPO animation curves. So you can call this "Modelling with Animation" if you like. We will not enter Edit Mode for the surface any more.

Switch to Top View. Insert a KeyFrame for rotation at frame 1, go ahead 10 frames and rotate the surface 90 degrees over its new origin. Insert one more KeyFrame. Open an IPO window, and set the rotation IPO to Extrapolation Mode (fig. 36).

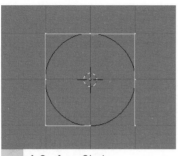

33 A Surface Circle.

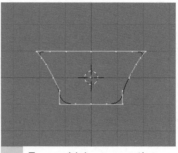

34 Trapezoidal cross-section.

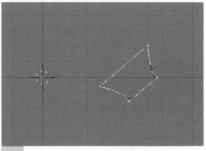

35 Trapezoidal cross-section.

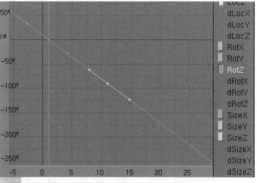

36 Rotation IPO for the cross-section.

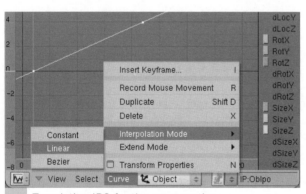

37 Translation IPO for the cross section.

Go back to frame 1 and insert a keyframe for Location. Switch to Front View. Go to frame 11 (just press **UPARROW**) and move the surface in Z a few grid units. Insert a new keyframe for Location. In the IPO window set the LocZ to Extrapolation Mode (fig. 37).

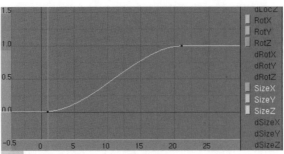

38 Size IPO for the cross section.

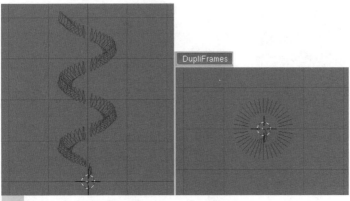

39 Corkscrew with DupliFrames activated.

Now, of course, go to the Animation buttons and press DupliFrames. You can see how our surface is ascending in a spiral thru the 3D space forming something like a spring. This is nice, however we want more. Deactivate DupliFrames to continue.

In frame 1 scale the surface to nearly zero and insert a keyframe for Size. Go ahead to frame 41, and clear the size with **ALT-S**. Insert a new keyframe for size. This IPO will not be in extrapolation mode since we don't want it scales up at infinitum, right (fig. 38)?

If you now activate DupliFrames you will see a beautiful outline of a corkscrew (fig. 39). Once again the last steps are: Make Duplis Real, Joining the surfaces, Select all vertices and skinning, Switch direction of normal if needed and leave Edit Mode (fig. 40).

You can see this was a rather simple example. With more IPO curve editing you can achieve very interesting and complex models. Just use your imagination.

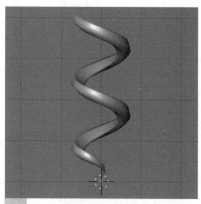

40 Corkscrew with Duplis made real.

Modelling with lattices

A Lattice consists of a non-renderable three-dimensional grid of vertices. Their main use is to give extra deformation to any child object they might have. These child objects can be Meshes, Surfaces and even Particles.

Why would you use a Lattice to deform a mesh instead of deforming the mesh itself in Edit Mode ?

There are some reasons for that:

1. First of all: It's easier. Since your mesh could have a zillion vertices, scaling, grabbing and moving them could be a hard task. Instead, if you use a nice simple lattice your job is simplified to move a couple of vertices.

2. It's nicer. The deformation you get looks a lot better!

3. It's fast! You can put all or several of your child objects in a hidden layer and deform them all at once.

4. It's a good practice. A lattice can be used to get different versions of a mesh with minimal extra work and consumption of resources. This leads to an optimal scene design, minimizing the amount of modelling job. A Lattice does not affect the texture coordinates of a Mesh Surface. Subtle changes to mesh objects are easily facilitated in this way, and do not change the mesh itself.

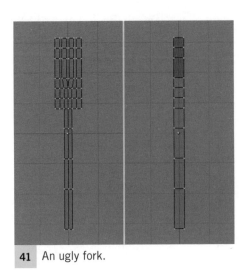

41 An ugly fork.

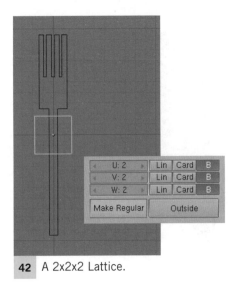

42 A 2x2x2 Lattice.

How does it work?

A Lattice always begins as a 2 x 2 x 2 grid of vertices (which looks like a simple cube). You can scale it up and down in Object Mode and change its resolution through the `Lattice` Panel in the Editing Context Buttons U,V,W.

After this initial step you can deform the Lattice in Edit Mode. If there is a Child Object, the deformation is continually displayed and modified. Changing the U,V,W values of a Lattice returns it to a uniform starting position.

Now we are going to see a very simple case in which having a lattice will simplify and speed up our modelling job.

I have modelled a very simple fork using a plane subdivided couple of times. It looks really ugly but it's all I need. Of course it is completely flat from a Side View. Wow, it is *really* ugly (fig. 41). The only important detail is that it has been subdivided enough to ensure a nice deformation in the Lattice step. You cannot bend a two vertices segment!

In Top View, now add a Lattice. Before changing its resolution, scale it up so it completely envelopes the fork's width (fig. 42). This is very important. Since I want to keep the lattice vertices count low (it doesn't make sense it has the same number of vertices than the mesh, right ?) I need to keep resolution low but still set the lattice to convenient size.

Adjust the Lattice resolution to complete the fork's length (fig. 43).

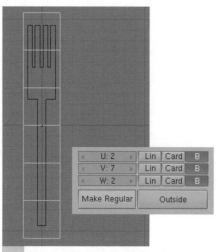

43 Use a suitable resolution, but don't exaggerate.

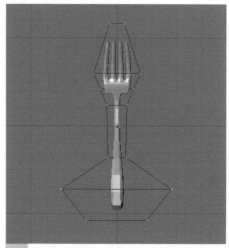

44 Deforming the lattice is a pleasure.

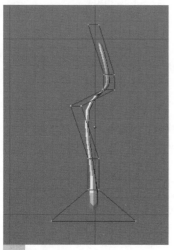

45 Bending things.

46 A nice fork.

Now, we are ready for the fun part. Parent the fork to the lattice, by selecting the fork and the lattice and pressing **CTRL-P**. Enter Edit Mode for the lattice and start selecting and scaling vertices (fig. 44). You might want to scale in X or Y axis separately to have more control over the lattice depth (to avoid making the fork thicker or thinner).

Note that if you move the fork up ad down inside the lattice, the deformation will apply in different parts of the mesh. Once you're done in Front View, switch to Side View. Select and move different vertices sections to give the fork the suitable bends (fig. 45).

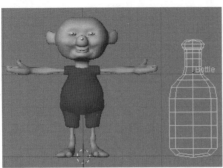

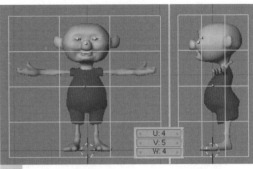

47 Poor guy...

48 Bending things.

You can get rid of the lattice now if you're not adding any other child object. But before doing it, you might want to keep your deformations! Just select the fork and press **CTRL-SHIFT-A** and click on the `Apply Lattice Deform?` menu entry.

On rare occasions, for fairly complex meshes, application of **CTRL-SHIFT-A** will *look like* it have screwed your mesh completely. This is false. Just step in and out of Edit Mode (**TAB**) and the mesh will be back nicely deformed as you expected.

You can use a lattice to model an object following another object's shape. For instance take a look at the following scene. I have modelled a bottle, and now I would like to confine a character inside it. He deserves it (fig. 47).

Add a lattice around the character. I didn't use a too high resolution for the lattice. I scaled it in X and Y to fit the lattice to the character (fig. 48).

Parent the character to the lattice, and then scale the lattice again to fit the dimensions of the bottle (fig. 49).

Now enter Edit Mode for the lattice. Press the `Outside` button in the `Lattice` Panel in the Editing Context to switch off the inner vertices of the lattice. We will switch them on later. Move and scale the vertices in front and side views until the character perfectly fits the bottle's shape (fig. 50).

You can select the lattice and do the modelling in one 3D window using Local View and see the results in another window using Global View to make your modelling comfortable (fig. 51).

Mad vertices

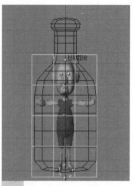

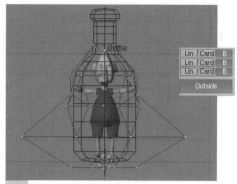

49 Scale the lattice to fit the bottle.

50 Edit Lattice so that the poor guy is comfortable in his bottle.

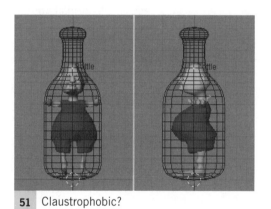

51 Claustrophobic?

52 Final Render. Believe me, he deserved it!

Hadn't we used a lattice it would have taken a lot more of vertex picking-and-moving work to deform the character (fig. 52).

Since lattices also supports RVK for vertex animation, quite interesting effects can be achieved with this tool.

Lattices can be used in many applications which require a "liquid-like" deformation of a mesh. Think of a genie coming out of his lamp, or a cartoon character with its eyes popping out exaggeratedly. And have fun!

CH. 17 EFFECTS

INTRODUCTION, BUILD EFFECT, PARTICLE EFFECTS, WAVE EFFECT

Introduction

There are three kind of effects which can be linked to an Object, ideally working during animations but in practice precious even for Stills.

Effects are added to an Object by selecting it, switching to the Object Context and locating the Effects Tab in the Constraints Panel (**F7** or ![icon]). By pressing the New Effect button of figure 1 an Effect is added.

The Delete button removes an effect, if one is there, while the drop down list which appears on the right once an effect is added (fig. 2) selects the type of effect.

More than one effect can be linked to a single Object. A row of small buttons, one for each effect, is created beneath the New Effect button, allowing you to switch from one to another to change settings.

The three effects are Build, Particles and Wave, the second being the most versatile. The following sections will describe each of them in detail.

Build Effect

The Build effect works on Meshes and causes the faces of the Object to appear, one after the other, over time. If the Material of the Mesh is a Halo Material, rather than a standard one, then the vertices of the Mesh, not the faces, appear one after another.

Faces, or vertices, appear in the order in which they are stored in memory. This order can be altered by selecting the Object and pressing **CTRL-F** out of EditMode. This causes faces to be re-sorted as a function of their value (Z co-ordinate) in the local reference of the Mesh.

EFFECTS.BUILD EFFECTS

1 Animation Buttons Window.

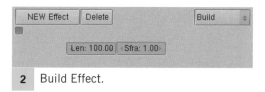

2 Build Effect.

Reordering

If you create a plane and add the Build effect to see how it works you won't be happy. First, you must subdivide it so that it is made up of many faces, not just one. Then, pressing **CTRL-F** won't do much because the Z-axis is orthogonal to the plane. You must rotate it in EditMode to have some numerical difference between the co-ordinates of the faces, in order to be able to reorder them.

The Build effect only has two NumBut controls (fig. 2):

> Len - Defines how many frames the build will take.
> Sfra - Defines the start frame of the building process.

Particle Effects

The particle system of Blender is fast, flexible, and powerful. Every Mesh-object can serve as an emitter for particles. Halos can be used as particles and with the DupliVert option, so can objects. These dupliverted objects can be any type of Blender object, for example Mesh-objects, Curves, Metaballs, and even Lamps. Particles can be influenced by a global force to simulate physical effects, like gravity or wind.

With these possibilities you can generate smoke, fire, explosions, Fireworks or even flocks of birds. With static particles you can generate fur, grass, and even plants.

A first Particle System

Reset Blender to the default scene, or make a scene with a single plane added from the top view. This plane will be our particle emitter. Rotate the view so that you get a good view of the plane and the space above it (fig. 3).

Switch to the Effects Tab in the Object Context (**F7** or 🗷) and click the button NEW Effect in the middle part of the Panel. Change the dropdown MenuButton from Build to Particles. The Particle Buttons are now shown (fig. 4).

Set the Norm: NumButton to 0.100 with a click on the right part of the button or use **SHIFT-LMB** to enter the value from the keyboard.

Play the animation by pressing **ALT-A** with the mouse over the 3DWindow. You will see a stream of particles ascending vertically from the four vertices.

Congratulations - you have just generated your first particle-system in a few easy steps!

To make the system a little bit more interesting, it is necessary to get deeper insight on the system and its buttons (fig. 5):

- The parameter Tot: controls the overall count of particles. On modern speedy CPUs you can increase the particle count without noticing a major slowdown. The total number of particles specified in the Tot: button are uniformly created along a time interval. Such a time interval is defined by the Sta: and End: NumButtons, which control the time interval (in frames) in which particles are generated.
- Particles have a lifetime, they last a given number of frames, from the one they are produced in onwards, then disappear. You can change the lifetime of the particles with the Life: NumButton.
- The Norm: NumButton used before made the particles having a starting speed of constant value (0.1) directed along the vertex normals. To make things more "random" you can set the Rand: NumButton to 0.1 too. This also makes the particles start with random variation to the speed.
- Use the Force: group of NumButtons to simulate a constant force, like wind or gravity. A Force: z: value of -0.1 will make the particles fall to the ground, for example.

This should be enough to get you started, but don't be afraid to touch some of the other parameters while you're experimenting. We will cover them in detail in the following sections.

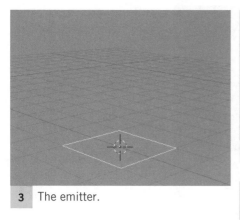

3 The emitter.

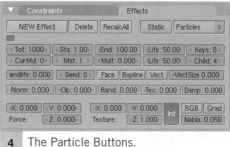

4 The Particle Buttons.

5 Particle settings.

6 Halo settings.

Rendering a particle system

Maybe you've tried to render a picture from our example above. If the camera was aligned correctly, you will have seen a black picture with greyish blobby spots on it. This is the standard Halo-material that Blender assigns a newly generated particle system.

Position the camera so that you get a good view of the particle system. If you want to add a simple environment, remember to add some lights. The Halos are rendered without light, unless otherwise stated, but other objects need lights to be visible.

Go to the Material Buttons (**F5**) and add a new material for the emitter if none have been added so far. Click the Button "Halo" from the middle palette (fig. 6).

7 Shooting stars.

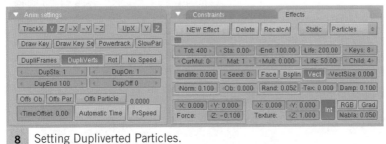

8 Setting Dupliverted Particles.

The Material Buttons change to the Halo Buttons. Choose `Line`, and adjust `Lines:` to a value of your choosing (you can see the effect directly in the Material-Preview). Decrease `HaloSize:` to 0.30, and choose a color for the Halo and for the lines (fig. 6).

You can now render a picture with **F12**, or a complete animation and see thousands of stars flying around (fig. 7).

Objects as particles

It is very easy to use real objects as particles, it is exactly like the technique described in Section called *DupliVerts* in Chapter17.

Start by creating a cube, or any other object you like, in your scene. It's worth thinking about how powerful your computer is, as we are going to have as many objects, as `Tot:` indicates in the scene. This means having as many vertices as the number of vertices of the chosen object times the value of `Tot:`!

9 | Dupliverted particles rendering.

Scale the newly created object down so that it matches the general scene scale.

Now select the object, then **SHIFT-RMB** the emitter and make it the parent of the cube using **CTRL-P.** Select the emitter alone and check the option DupliVerts in the Anim Settings Panel of the Object Context (**F7**). The dupliverted cubes will appear immediately in the 3DWindow.

You might want to bring down the particle number before pressing **ALT-A** (fig. 8).

Setting Dupliverted Particles.

In the animation you will notice that all cubes share the same orientation. This can be interesting, but it can also be interesting to have the cubes randomly oriented.

This can be done by checking the option Vect in the particle-parameters, which causes the dupli-objects to follow the rotation of the particles, resulting in a more natural motion (fig. 8). One frame of the animation is shown in fig. 9.

Take care to move the original object out of the camera view, because, differently than in regular Mesh Dupliverts, in Dupliverted particles it will also be rendered!

Original Object

Making fire with particles

The Blender particle system is very useful for making realistic fire and smoke. This could be a candle, a campfire, or a burning house. It's useful to consider how the fire is driven by physics. The flames of a fire are hot gases. They will rise because of their lower density when compared to the surrounding cooler air. Flames are hot and bright in the middle, and they fade and become darker towards their perimeter.

Prepare a simple set-up for our fire, with some pieces of wood, and some rocks (fig. 10).

The particle system

Add a plane into the middle of the stone-circle. This plane will be our particle-emitter. Subdivide the plane once. You now can move the vertices to a position on the wood where the flames (particles) should originate.

Now go to the Object Context **F7** and add a new particle effect to the plane. The numbers given here (fig. 11) should make for a realistic fire, but some modification may be necessary, depending on the actual emitter's size.

Some notes:

- To have the fire burning from the start of the animation make Sta: negative. For example, try -50. The value of End: should reflect the desired animation length.
- The Life: of the particles is 30. Actually it can stay at 50 for now. We will use this parameter later to adjust the height of the flames.
- Make the Norm: parameter a bit negative (-0.008) as this will result in a fire that has a bigger volume at its basis.
- Use a Force: Z: of about 0.200. If your fire looks too slow, this is the parameter to adjust.
- Change Damp: to 0.100 to slow down the flames after a while.
- Activate the Bspline Button. This will use an interpolation method which gives a much more fluid movement.
- To add some randomness to our particles, adjust the Rand: parameter to about 0.014. Use the Randlife: parameter to add randomness in the lifetime of the particles; a really high value here gives a lively flame.
- Use about 600-1000 particles in total for the animation (Tot:).

In the 3DWindow, you will now get a first impression of how realistically the flames move. But the most important thing for our fire will be the material.

EFFECTS.FIRE EXAMPLE

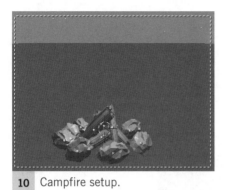

Campfire setup.

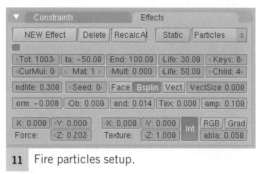

11 Fire particles setup.

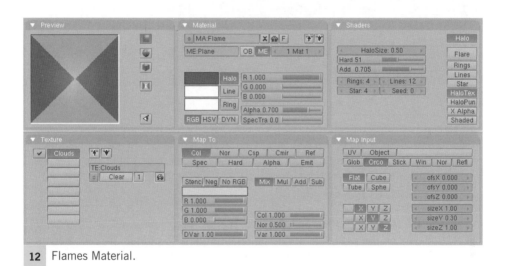

12 Flames Material.

The fire-material

With the particle emitter selected, go to the Shading Context **F5** and add a new
Material. Make the new material a halo-material by activating the Halo button. Also,
activate HaloTex, located below this button. This allows us to use a texture later.

Give the material a fully saturated red colour with the RGB-sliders. Decrease the Alpha value to 0.700; this will make the flames a little bit transparent. Increase the Add
slider up to 0.700, so the Halos will boost each other, giving us a bright interior to the
flames, and a darker exterior (fig. 12).

13 Flames Texture.

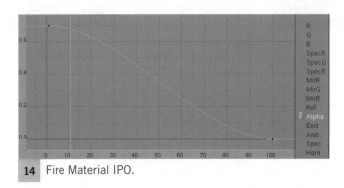

14 Fire Material IPO.

If you now do a test render, you will only see a bright red flame. To add a touch more realism, we need a texture. While the emitter is still selected, go to the Texture Panel and add a new Texture select the Cloud-type for it in the Texture (**F6**) Buttons. Adjust the NoiseSize: to 0.600 (fig. 13).

Go back to the Material Buttons **F5** and make the texture colour a yellow colour with the RGB sliders on the right side of the material buttons. To stretch the yellow spots from the cloud texture decrease the SizeY value down to 0.30.

A test rendering will now display a nice fire. But we still need to make the particles fade out at the top of the fire. We can achieve this with a material animation of the Alpha and the Halo Size.

Be sure that your animation is at frame 1 (**SHIFT-LEFTARROW**) and move the mouse over the Material Window. Now press **IKEY** and choose Alpha from the appearing menu. Advance the frame-slider to frame 100, set the Alpha to 0.0 and insert another key for the Alpha with **IKEY**. Switch one Window to an IPO Window. Activate the Material IPO Type by clicking the pertinent Menu Entry in the IPO Window header. You will see one curve for the Alpha-channel of the Material (fig. 14).

An animation for a particle material is always mapped from the first 100 frames of the animation to the lifetime of a particle. This means that when we fade out a material in frame 1 to 100, a particle with a lifetime of 50 will fade out in that time.

EFFECTS.FIRE EXAMPLE

15 Final rendering.

Now you can render an animation. Maybe you will have to fine-tune some parameters like the life-time of the particles. You can add a great deal of realism to the scene by animating the lights (or use shadow-spotlights) and adding a sparks particle-system to the fire. Also recommended is to animate the emitter in order to get more lively flames, or use more than one emitter (fig. 15).

A simple explosion

This explosion is designed to be used as an animated texture, for composing it with the actual scene or for using it as animated texture. For a still rendering, or a slow motion of an explosion, we may need to do a little more work in order to make it look really good. But bear in mind, that our explosion will only be seen for half a second (fig. 16).

As emitter for the explosion I have chosen an IcoSphere. To make the explosion slightly irregular, I deleted patterns of vertices with the circle select function in Edit Mode. For a specific scene it might be better to use an object as the emitter, which is shaped differently, for example like the actual object you want to blow up.

My explosion is composed from two particle systems, one for the cloud of hot gases and one for the sparks. I took a rotated version of the emitter for generating the sparks. Additionally, I animated the rotation of the emitters while the particles were being generated.

16 The explosion.

17 Material for the explosion cloud.

18 Material for the sparks.

19 Texture for both.

The materials

The particles for the explosion are very straightforward halo materials, with a cloud texture applied to add randomness, the sparks too have a very similar material, see figure 17 to figure 19.

Animate the Alpha-value of the Halo particles from 1.0 to 0.0 at the first 100 frames. This will be mapped to the life-time of the particles, as is usual. Notice the setting of Star in the sparks material (fig. 18). This shapes the sparks a little bit. We could have also used a special texture to achieve this, however, in this case using the Star setting is the easiest option.

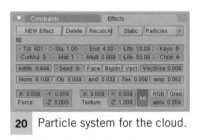

20 Particle system for the cloud.

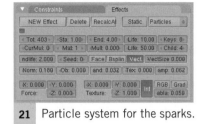

21 Particle system for the sparks.

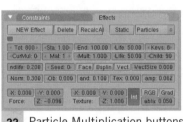

22 Particle Multiplication buttons.

The particle-systems

As you can see in figure 20 and figure 21, the parameters are basically the same. The difference is the `Vect` setting for the sparks, and the higher setting of `Norm:` which causes a higher speed for the sparks. I also set the `Randlife:` for the sparks to 2.000 resulting in an irregular shape.

I suggest that you start experimenting, using these parameters to begin with. The actual settings are dependent on what you want to achieve. Try adding more emitters for debris, smoke, etc.

Fireworks

A button we have not used so far is the `Mult:` button. The whole third line of buttons in the Panel is related to this. Prepare a plane and add a particle system to the plane.

Adjust the parameters so that you get some particles flying into the sky, then increase the value of `Mult:` to 1.0. This will cause 100% of the particles to generate child particles when their life ends. Right now, every particle will generate four children. So we'll need to increase the `Child:` value to about 90 (fig. 22). You should now see a convincing firework made from particles, when you preview the animation with **ALT-A**.

When you render the firework it will not look very impressive. This is because of the standard halo material that Blender assigns. Consequently, the next step is to assign a better material.

Ensure that you have the emitter selected and go to the Shading Context and Material Buttons (**F5**). Add a new material with the Menu Button, and set the type to `Halo`.

I have used a pretty straightforward halo material; you can see the parameters in figure 23. The rendered animation will now look much better, yet there is still something we can do.

While the emitter is selected go to the Editing Context **F9** and add a new material index by clicking on the `New` button in the `Link and Materials` Panel (fig. 24).

Now switch back to the Shading Context. You will see that the material data browse has changed colour to blue. The button labelled `2` indicates that this material is used by two users. Now click on the `2` button and confirm the popup. Rename the Material to "Material 2" and change the colour of the halo and the lines (fig. 25).

Switch to the particle parameters and change the `Mat:` button to "2". Render again and you see that the first generation of particles is now using the first material and the second generation the second material! This way you can have up to 16 (that's the maximum number of material indices) materials for particles.

Beside changing materials you also can use the material IPOs to animate material settings of each different material.

Further enhancements

Controlling Particles via a Lattice

Blender's particle system is extremely powerful, and the course of particles can not only be determined via forces but channelled by a lattice.

Prepare a single square mesh and add a particle system to it with a negative z-force and the general parameters in figure 26.

This could be good for the smoke of four small fires fire in a windless day, but we want to twist it! Add a lattice and deform it as in as in figure 27.

Parent the particle emitter to the lattice (**CTRL-P**). If you now select the particle emitter, switch to Animation buttons (**F7**) and press `RecalcAll` you will notice that the particles follows, more or less, the lattice (figure 28 on the left).

23 Fireworks Material 1.

24 Adding a second material to the emitter.

25 Fireworks Material 2.

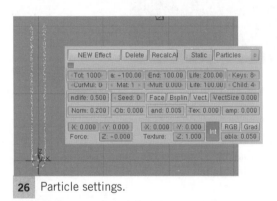

26 Particle settings.

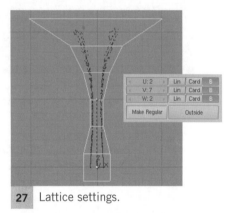

27 Lattice settings.

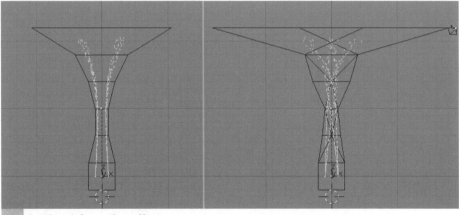

28 Lattice deformation effects.

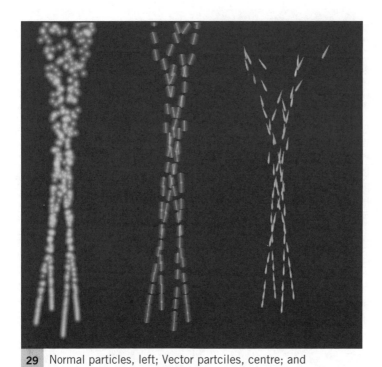

29 Normal particles, left; Vector partciles, centre; and
DupliVerted objects following the particles, right.

As a further tweak, rotate each horizontal section of the lattice 60 degrees clockwise
in top view, incrementally, as if you were making a screw. After this, recalculate again
the particles. The result is in figure 28 on the right.

The twist is evident, and of course you can achieve even stronger effects by rotating
the lattice more or by using a lattice with more subdivisions. If you give the emitter a
halo material and you render you will see something like figure 29 on the left.

If you select the emitter, turn to animation buttons and press the vect Particle
Button the particles will turn from points to segments, with a length and a direction
proportional to the particle velocity. A rendering now will give the result of figure 29 in
the middle.

It you now Duplivert an object to the emitter, by parenting it and by pressing the Duplivert button, the DupliVerted objects will have the same orientation of the original
object if the particles are normal particles, but will be rotated and aligned to the
particle direction if the Particles are set to vert. By selecting the Original Object and
by playing with the Track buttons you can change orientation (figure 29 on the right).

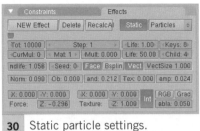

30 Static particle settings.

31 Material settings.

Static Particles

Static particles are useful when making objects like fibres, grass, fur and plants.

Try making a little character, or just a ball, to test the static particles. Try for example a small 'ball of fur' guy. An emitter is not rendered, so duplicate the mesh (or whatever object type you used and convert (**ALT-C**) it into a mesh). A fractal subdivide to the mesh to get some randomness into it, is usually a good idea. If you end up with mesh that is too dense, use "Remove Doubles" with an increased limit. Cut out parts with the circle select where you do not want to have fur.

Now, assign the particle system and, switch on the Static option.

Use these parameters in figure 30. With the combination of Life and Norm you can control the length of the hair. Use a force in a negative z-direction to let the hair bend. Check Face to generate the particles, not only on the vertices but also distributed on the faces. Also check Vect; this will generate fibre like particles. The step value defines how many particles per lifetime are generated. Set this to a lower value to get smoother curves for the particles, and be sure not to overlook setting the Rand value.

When you now render, you will get very blurred particles. The material used for static particles is very important, so add a material for the emitter in the Shading Context (**F5**).

32 Texture Colorband settings.   **33** Texture settings in the Material buttons.

34 Final result.

I use a very small Halosize (0.001). In the Number Button you can't see that, so to adjust click the button with the **LMB** while holding **SHIFT**. Enable the Shaded option to have the particles influenced by the lights in the scene, and then activate Halo-Tex. We are going to use a texture to shape the hairs (fig. 31).

Switch to the Texture sub-context (**F6**) and add a new Blend type texture. Choose Lin as sub-type. Activate the colorband option and adjust the colors as in figure 32. You will get a nice blend, from transparent through to purple and back again to transparent.

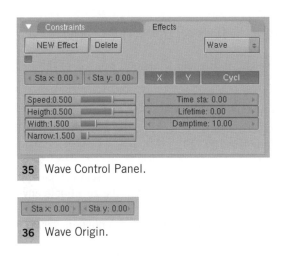

35 Wave Control Panel.

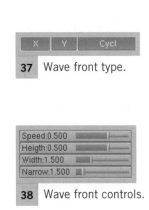

37 Wave front type.

38 Wave front controls.

Sta x: 0.00   Sta y: 0.00

36 Wave Origin.

Go back to the Material Buttons sub-context and make sure that Alpha is activated in the texture mapping output on the right of the Material Buttons. Then use sizeX and sizeY to shape the halo in the material preview to a small fiber (fig. 33).

If your fur is not dense enough, then increase the particle count with Tot or add more emitters. Also, change the particle parameters for these additional emitters a little so that you get some variation in the hairs (fig. 34).

Wave Effect

The Wave effect adds a motion to the Z co-ordinate of the Object Mesh.

The wave effect influence is generated from a given starting point defined by the Sta X and Sta Y Num Buttons. These co-ordinates are in the Mesh local reference (fig. 36).

The Wave effect deformation originates from the given starting point and propagates along the Mesh with circular wave fronts, or with rectilinear wave fronts, parallel to the X or Y axis. This is controlled by the two X and Y toggle buttons. If just one button is pressed fronts are linear, if both are pressed fronts are circular (fig. 37).

The wave itself is a gaussian-like ripple which can be either a single pulse or a series of ripples, if the Cycl button is pressed.

The Wave is governed by two series of controls, the first defining the Wave form, the second the effect duration.

For what concerns Wave Form, controls are Speed, Height, Width and Narrow (fig. 38).

The `Speed` Num Button controls the speed, in Units per Frame, of the ripple.

The `Height` Num Button controls the height, in Blender Units and along Z, of the ripple (fig.39).

If the `Cycl` button is pressed, the `Width` Num Button states the distance, in Blender Units, between the topmost part of two subsequent ripples, and the total Wave effect is given by the envelope of all the single pulses (fig. 39).

This has an indirect effect on the ripple amplitude. Being ripples Gaussian in shape, if the pulses are too next to each other the envelope could not reach the z=0 quote any more. If this is the case Blender actually lowers the whole wave so that the minimum is zero and, consequently, the maximum is lower than the expected amplitude value, as shown in figure 39 at the bottom.

The actual width of each Gaussian-like pulse is controlled by the `Narrow` Num Button, the higher the value the narrower the pulse. The actual width of the area in which the single pulse is significantly non-zero in Blender Units is given by 4 over the `Narrow` Value. That is, if `Narrow` is 1 the pulse is 4 Units wide, and if `Narrow` is 4 the pulse is 1 Unit Wide.

To obtain a Sinusoidal-like wave

To obtain a nice Wave effect similar to sea waves and close to a sinusoidal wave it is necessary that the distance between following ripples and the ripple width are equal, that is the `Width` Num Button value must be equal to 4 over the `Narrow` value.

The last Wave controls are the time controls (fig. 40). The three NumButs define:

`Time sta` the Frame at which the Wave begins;

`Lifetime` the number of frames in which the effect lasts;

`Damptime` is an additional number of frames in which the wave slowly dampens from the Amplitude value to zero. The Dampening occurs for all the ripples and begins in the first frame after the `Lifetime` is over. Ripples disappear over `Damptime` frames.

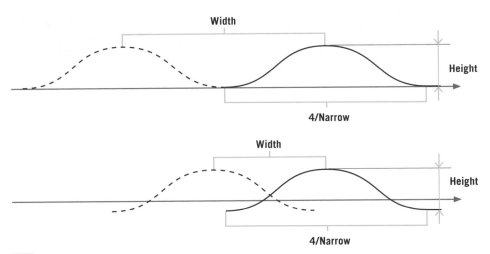

39 Wave front characteristics.

40 Wave time controls.

CH. 18 VOLUMETRIC EFFECTS

BASICS

Although Blender exhibits a very nice Mist option in the World Settings to give your images some nice depth, you might want to create true volumetric effects; mists and clouds and smoke which really looks like they occupy some space.

Figure 1 shows a set-up with some columns in a circular pattern, with some nice material of your choice for columns and soil and a World defining sky color.

Figure 2 shows, the relative rendering, whereas Figure 3 shows a rendering with Blender's built-in Mist. Mist setting in this particular case are: Linear Mist, Sta=1, Di=20, Hig=5.

But we want to create some truly cool, swirling, and, most important non-uniform mist. Blender built-in procedural textures, clouds for example, are intrinsically 3D, but are rendered only when mapped onto a 2D surface. We will achieve a 'volumetric' like rendering by 'sampling' the texture on a series of mutually parallel planes. Each of our planes will hence exhibits a standard Blender texture on its 2D surface, but the global effect will be of a 3D object. This concept will be clearer as the example proceeds.

With the camera at z=0 looking forward, turn to front view, and add a plane in front of the camera, with its centre aligned with the camera viewing direction. In side view move the plane where you want your volumetric effect to terminate. In our case somewhere beyond the furthest column. Scale the plane so that it encompasses all camera's viewing angle (Fig. 4). It is important to have a camera pointing along the y axis since we need the planes to be orthogonal to the direction of sight. We will anyway be able to move it later on.

After having checked that we're at frame 1, let's place a Loc KeyFrame (**IKEY**). We should now move to frame 100, move the plane much nearer to the camera, and set another Loc KeyFrame. Now, in the Object COntext Anim Settings Panel (**F7**) Press the DupliFrame button.

VOLUMETRIC EFFECTS.BASICS

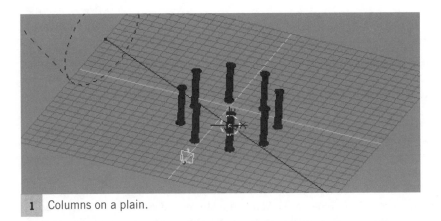

1 Columns on a plain.

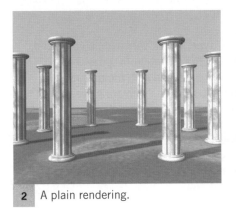

2 A plain rendering.

3 A rendering with builin Blender Mist

The 3D Window, in side view, will show something like figure 5. This is not good because planes are denser at the begin and at the end of the sweep. With the plane still selected change a window to an IPO window (**SHIFT-F6**). There will be three Loc IPOs, only one of which non-constant. Select it, switch to Edit Mode (**TAB**) and select both control points. Now turn them from smooth to sharp with (**VKEY**) figure 6.

The planes will now look as in figure 7. Parent the DupliFramed planes to the camera (select the plane, **SHIFT** select the camera, **CTRL-P.** You have now a series of planes automatically following the camera, always oriented perpendicularly to it. From now on you could move the camera if you so wish.

Now we must add the Mist material itself. The material should be Shadeless and cast no shadows to avoid undesired effects. It should have an small Alpha value (fig. 8). A material like this would basically act like Blender's built in mist, hence we would have no advantage in the resulting image. The drawback is that computing 100 transparent layer is very CPU intensive, especially if one desires the better results of the Unified Renderer.

You can use the `DupOff`: Num Button in the `Anim Settings` Panel to turn off some of the planes and hence have a faster, lower quality preview of what you are doing. For the final rendering you will then turn `DupOff` back to 0.

Pay attention to the Alpha value! the lesser planes you use the thinner will be the mist, so your final rendering will be much more 'Misty' than your previews!

The true interesting stuff comes when you add textures. We will need at least two: One to limit the Mist in the vertical dimension and keep it on the ground; The second to make it non uniform and with some varying hue.

As a first texture Add a Blend texture of "linear" type, with a very simple colorband, going from pure white, `Alpha=1` at a position 0.1 to pure white, `Alpha=0` at a position 0.9 (fig. 9). Add this only to the Alpha channel and as a multiplying (`Mul` Button) texture (fig. 10). To make our mist consistent as the Camera moves, and the planes follows, we have to set it `Global`. This will be true also for all other textures and will make the planes sample a fixed 3D volumetric texture. If you are planning an animation you will see a static mist, with respect to the scene, while the camera moves. Whichever other texture setting would show a Mist which is static with respect to the camera, hence being always the same while the camera moves, which is highly unrealistic.

If you want to anyway have a moving, swirling changing mist you can do so by animating the texture, as will be explained later on.

The Blend texture operates on X and Y directions, so if you want it to span vertically in the Global coordinates you will have to remap it (fig. 10). Please note that the blending from `Alpha=1` to the `Alpha=0` will occur from global z=0 to global z=1 unless additional offsets and scalings are added. For our aim the standard settings are OK.

If you now do a rendering, it doesn't matter where your camera, and planes, are. The mist will be thick below z=0, non-existent above z=1 and fading in between. If you're puzzled by this apparent complexity, think of what you would have got with a regular `Orco` texture and non-parented planes. If you had to move the camera, especially in animations, the results would become very poor as soon as the planes are not perpendicular to the camera any more. To end up with no mist at all if the camera were to become parallel to the planes!

VOLUMETRIC EFFECTS.BASICS

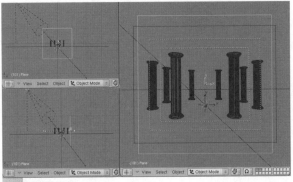

4 The plane set-up.

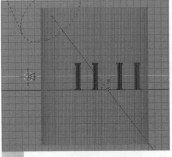

5 The Dupliframed plane.

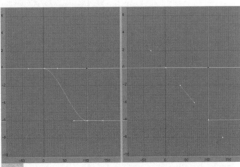

6 Reshaping the DupliFramed Plane IPO.

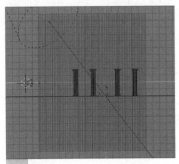

7 Reshaping the DupliFramed Plane IPO.

8 Basic Material settings.

The second texture is the one giving the true edge on the built in mist. Add a Cloud texture, make its Noise Size=2, Noise Depth=6 and Hard Noise on (fig. 11). Add colorband to this too, going from pure white with Alpha=1 at Position 0 to a pale bluish grey with Alpha=0.8 at a position of about 0.15, to a pinkish hue with Alpha=0.5 around position 0.2, ending to a pure white, Alpha=0 colour at position 0.3. Of course you might want to go to greenish-yellow for swamp mists etc.

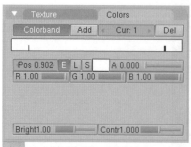

9 Height limiting texture.

10 Basic Material settings for cloud texture.

11 Cloud texture settings.

Use this texture on both Col and Alpha as a Mul texture, keeping al other settings to default. If you now render the scene the bases of your columns will be now masked by a cool mist (fig. 12). Please note that the Unified renderer gives much better results here.

If you are planning an animation and want your Mist to be animated like if it were moved by a wind it is this latter texture you must work on. Add a Material texture IPO, be sure to select the correct texture channel and add some IPO to the OfsX, OfsY and OfsZ properties.

12 Final rendering.

CH. 19 SEQUENCE EDITOR

LEARNING THE SEQUENCE EDITOR, SEQUENCE EDITOR PLUGINS

An often underestimated function of Blender is the Sequence Editor. It is a complete video editing system that allows you to combine multiple video channels and add effects to them. Even though it has a limited number of operations, you can use these to create powerful video edits (especially when you combine it with the animation power of Blender!) and, furthermore, it is extensible via a Plugin system quite alike the Texture plugins.

Learning the Sequence Editor

This section shows you a practical video editing example exhibiting most of the Sequence Editor built in features. We will put together several Blender made animations to obtain some stunning effects. One frame of the resulting edited animation is in figure 1.

First animation: two cubes

Let's start with something simple and see where it leads. Start a clean Blender and move the default plane. Split the 3D window and switch one of the views to the camera view with **NUM 0**. In the top-view, add a cube and move it just outside of the dotted square that indicates the camera view (fig. 2).

We want to create a simple animation of the cube moveing into view, rotating once, and then disappearing. Set the animation end to 61 (set the End: value in the Anim Panel of the Scene Context, Render Buttons **F10**) and insert a LocRot KeyFrame on frame 1 with **IKEY** and selecting LocRot from the menu which appears. This will store both the location and the rotation of the cube on this frame.

Go to frame 21 (press **UPARROW** twice) and move the cube closer to the camera. Insert another KeyFrame. On Frame 41, keep the cube on the same location but rotate it 180 degrees and insert another KeyFrame.

Finally on frame 61 move the cube out of view, to the right and insert the last KeyFrame.

1 Final result.

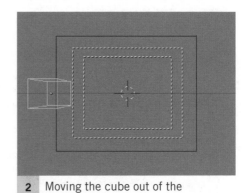

2 Moving the cube out of the camera view.

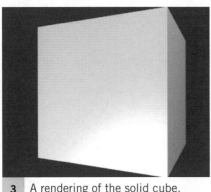

3 A rendering of the solid cube.

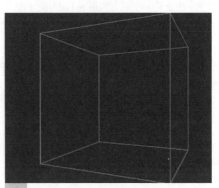

4 And a rendering of the Wire-Frame cube.

We will need two versions of the animation: one with a solid material and one with a WireFrame. For the material, we can use a plain white lit by two bright lamps - a white one and a blue one with an energy value of two (fig. 3).

For the WireFrame cube, set the material type to 'Wire' and change the color to green (fig. 4).

Enter an appropriate filename (for example 'cube_solid.avi') in the `Pics` field (first text button on top) of the Scene Context Render sub-context `Output` Panel (**F10**) (fig. 5).

Render the animation with the white solid cube. This will save it to your disk. Save it as an AVI file. Use AVI Raw if possible, because it yelds an higher quality - compression should be the last thing in the editing process - otherwise, if short of disk space use AVI Jpeg or AVI Codec, the first being less compressed and hence often of higher quality.

Now change the material to the green wire frame, render the animation again, saving the result as 'cube_wire.avi'.

You now have a 'cube_solid.avi' and 'cube_wire.avi' on your hard disk. This is enought for our first sequence editing.

First Sequence: delayed wireframe animation

The first sequence will use only the wireframe animation - twice - to create an interesting effect. We will create multiple layers of video, give them a small time offset and add them together. This will simulate the 'glowing trail' effect that you see on radar screens.

Start a clean Blender file and change the 3D window to a Sequence Editor window by pressing **SHIFT F8** or by selecting the Sequence Editor icon (▨) from the window header Window Type Menu.

Add a movie to the window by pressing **SHIFT-A** and selecting Movie (fig. 6) or by using the Add>>Movie Menu entry. From the File Select Window wich appears select the wireframe cube animation that you made before.

After you have selected and loaded the movie file, you will see a blue strip that represents it. After adding a strip, you are automatically in grab mode and the strip follows the mouse. he start and end frame are now displayed in the bar.

Take a closer look at the Sequence Editor screen now. Horizontally you see the time value. Vertically, you see the video 'channels'. Each channel can contain an image, a movie or an effect. By layering different channels on top of each other and applying effects, you can mix different sources together. If you select a video strip, its type, length and filename will be printed at the bottom of the window.

Move your video strip and let it start at frame 1. Place it in channel 1, that is on the bottom row and press **LMB** to finalize (fig. 7).

You can add *lead-in* and *lead-out* frames by selecting the triangles at the start and end of the strip (they will turn purple) and dragging them out. In the same way, you can define the 'length' in frames of a still image.

Duplicate the movie strip with **SHIFT-D**, place the duplicate in channel 2 and shift it one frame to the right. We now have two layers of video on top of each other, but only one will display. To mix the two layers you need to apply an effect to them.

Lead-in, Lead-out and stills

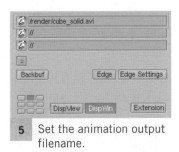

5 Set the animation output filename.

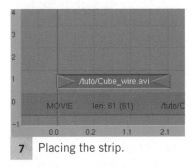

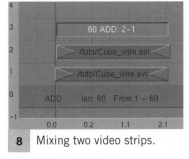

6 Adding a video strip.

7 Placing the strip.

8 Mixing two video strips.

9 Sequence Editor preview button.

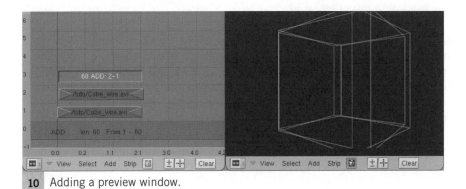

10 Adding a preview window.

Select both strips and press **SHIFT-A**. Select ADD from the menu that pops up. Otherwise use the Add>>Effect>>Add (fig. 8).

To see what's happening split the sequence editor window and select the image button in the header (fig. 9). This will activate the automatic preview (fig. 10). If you select a frame in the sequence editor window with the strips, the preview will be automatically updated (with all the effects applied!).

If you press **ALT-A** in the preview window, Blender will play back the animation. (Rendering of effects for the first time takes a lot of processing time, so don't expect a real-time preview!).

Windowless Preview

If you do not like the separate render window, switch to the Render Buttons (**F10**) and select DispView in the bottom left.

Now its time to add some more mayhem to this animation. Duplicate another movie layer and place it on channel 4. Add it to the existing ADD effect in video channel 3 with a new ADD effect. Repeat this once and you will have four WireFrame cubes in the preview window (fig. 11).

All the cubes have the same brightness now, but I would like to have a falloff in brightness. This is easily arranged: open an IPO window somewhere (**F6**) and select the sequence icon in its IPO Type Menu (fig. 12).

Select the first add strip (the one in channel 3), hold down **CTRL** and click **LMB** in the IPO window on a value of 1. This sets the brightness of this add operation to maximum. Repeat this for the other two add strips, but decrease the value a bit for each of them, say to around 0.6 and 0.3 (fig. 13).

Depending on the ADD values that you have just set, your result should look something like what is shown in figure 14.

Now we already have 7 strips and we have only just begun with our sequencing! You can imagine that the screen can quickly become very crowded indeed. To make your project more manageable, select all strips (**AKEY** and **BKEY** work here, too!), press **MKEY** and press **ENTER** or click on the Make Meta pop up. Otherwise you can use the Strip>>Make Meta Strip Menu entry. The strips will now be combined into a meta-strip, and can be copied or moved as a whole.

With the meta strip selected, press **NKEY** and enter a name, for example 'Wire/Delay', to better remember what it is (fig. 15).

Second animation: A delayed solid cube

Now it is time to use some masks. We want to create two areas in which the animation plays back with 1 frame time difference. This creates a very interesting glass-like visual effect.

Start by creating a black and white image like the one in figure 16. You can use a paint program or do it in Blender. The easiest way to do this in Blender is to create a

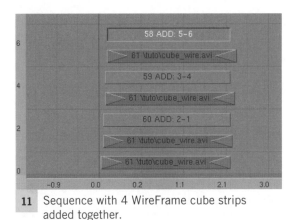

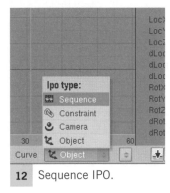

11 Sequence with 4 WireFrame cube strips added together.

12 Sequence IPO.

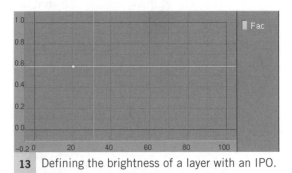

13 Defining the brightness of a layer with an IPO.

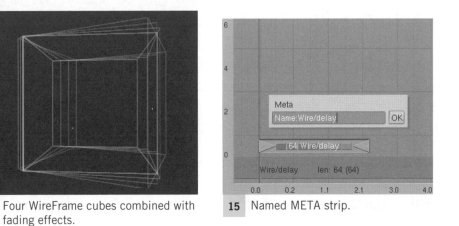

14 Four WireFrame cubes combined with fading effects.

15 Named META strip.

white material with an emit value of 1 or a shadeless white material on some bevelled Curve Circles. In this way, you do not need to set up any lamps. Save the image as mask.tga.

Switch to the sequence editor and move the meta strip that we made before out of the way (we will reposition it later). Add the animation of the solid cube (**SHIFT-A**>>Movie). Next, add the mask image. By default a still image will get a length of 50 frames in the sequence editor. Change it to match the length of the cube animation by **RMB** and **GKEY** to dragging out the arrows on the side of the image strip with the right mouse button.

Now select both strips (hold down **SHIFT**), press **SHIFT-A** and add a SUB (subtract) effect (fig. 17).

In the preview window you will now see the effect; the areas where the mask is white have been removed from the picture (fig. 18).

This effect is ready now; select all three strips and convert them into a META strip by pressing **MKEY**.

Now repeat the previous steps, except that you don't use the SUB effect but the MUL (multiply) effect (fig. 19). This time you will only see the original image where the mask image is white. Turn the three strips of this effect into a meta strip again.

For the final step I have to combine the two effects together. Move one of the meta strips above the other one and give it a time offset of one frame. Select both strips and add an ADD effect (fig. 20).

In the preview window you can now see the result of the combination of the animation and the mask (fig. 21).

When you are ready, select the two meta strips and the ADD effect and convert them into a new meta strip. (That's right! You can have meta strips in meta strips!)

To edit the contents of a meta strip, select it and press **TAB**. The meta strip will 'explode' to show its components and background will turn yellow/greenish to indicate that you are working inside a meta strip. Press **TAB** again to return to normal editing.

Getting into a Meta Strip

Third animation: a tunnel

We want a third 'effect' to further enrich our animation; a 3D 'tunnel' to be used as a background effect. This is really simple to create. First save your current work - you will need it later!

16 Animation mask.

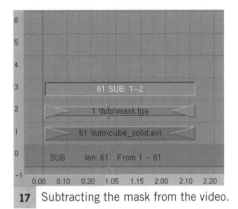

17 Subtracting the mask from the video.

18 Mask subtracted.

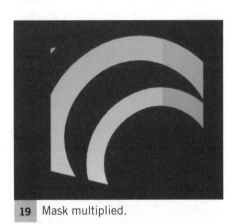

19 Mask multiplied.

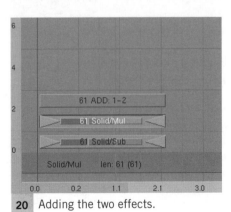

20 Adding the two effects.

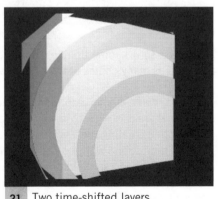

21 Two time-shifted layers

Start a new scene (**CTRL-X**) and delete the default plane. Switch to front view (**NUM 1**). Add a 20-vertex circle about 10 units under the z=0 line (the pink line in your screen) (fig. 22).

While still in Edit Mode, switch to side view (**NUM 3**) and snap the cursor to the origin by locating it roughly at the x,y,z=0 point and pressing **SHIFT-S**. Select Curs>>Grid.

We want to turn the circle into a circular tube, or torus. For this, we will use the Spin function. Go to the Editing Context (**F9**) and enter a value of 180 in the Degr Num-Button and enter '10' in the Steps NumButton in the Mesh Tools Panel. Pressing Spin will now rotate the selected vertices around the cursor at 180 degrees and in 10 steps (fig. 23).

Leave Edit Mode (**TAB**). With the default settings, Blender will always rotate and scale around the object's center which is displayed as a tiny dot. This dot is yellow when the object is unselected and pink when it is selected. With the cursor still in the origin, press the Center Cursor button in the Edit Buttons window to move the object center to the current cursor location. Now press **RKEY** and rotate the tube 180 degrees around the cursor.

Now it's time to move the camera into the tunnel. Open another 3D window and switch it to the camera view (**NUM0**). Position the camera in the side view window to match figure 24, the camera view should now match figure 25.

If not all of the edges of the tunnel are showing, you can force Blender to draw them by selecting All Edges Tog Button in the Mesh Tools 1 Panel of the Editing Context (**F9**).

Missing edges

To save ourselves some trouble, I want to render this as a looping animation. I can then add as many copies of it as I like to the final video compilation.

There are two things to keep in mind when creating looping animations. First, make sure that there is no 'jump' in your animation when it loops. For this, you have to be careful when creating the KeyFrames and when setting the animation length. Create two KeyFrames: one with the current rotation of the tube on frame 1, and one with a rotation of 90 degrees (hold down **CTRL** while rotating) on frame 51. In your animation frame 51 is now the same as frame 1, so when rendering you will need to leave out frame 51 and render from 1 to 50.

Please note that the number 90 degrees is not chosen carelessly, but because the tunnel is periodic with period 18°, hence you must rotate it by a multiple of 18°, and 90° is it, to guarantee that frame 51 is exactly the same than frame 1.

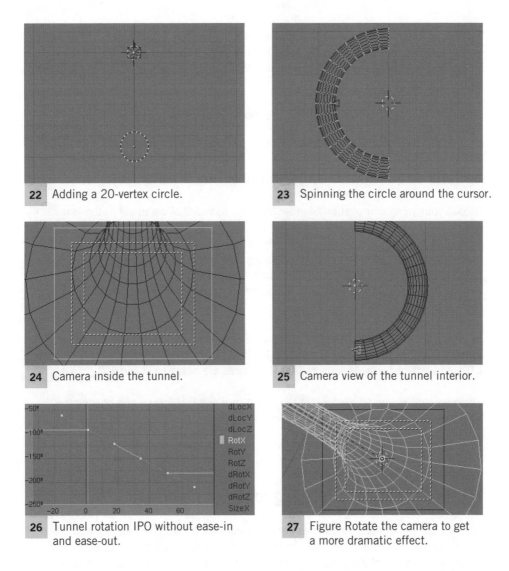

22 Adding a 20-vertex circle.

23 Spinning the circle around the cursor.

24 Camera inside the tunnel.

25 Camera view of the tunnel interior.

26 Tunnel rotation IPO without ease-in and ease-out.

27 Figure Rotate the camera to get a more dramatic effect.

Second, to get a *linear* motion you need to remove the ease-in and ease-out of the rotation. These can be seen in the IPO Window of the tube after inserting the rotation KeyFrames. The IPO smoothly starts and end, much like a cosine function. We want it to be straight. To do so select the rotation curve, enter editmode (**TAB**) and select all vertices (**AKEY**) and press **VKEY** ('Vector') to change the curve into a linear one (fig. 26).

To create a more dramatic effect, select the camera while in camera view mode (fig. 27). The camera itself is displayed as the solid square. Press **RKEY** and rotate it a bit. If you now play back your animation it should loop seamlessly.

For the final touch, add a blue WireFrame material to the tube and add a small lamp on the location of the camera. By tweaking the lamp's `Dist` value (attenuation distance) you can make the end of the tube disappear in the dark without having to work with mist (fig. 28).

When you are satisfied with the result, render your animation and save it as 'tunnel.avi'.

Second sequence: Using the tunnel as a backdrop

Reload your video compilation Blender file. The tunnel that we made in the last step will be used as a backdrop for the entire animation. To make it more interesting I will modify an `ADD` effect to change the tunnel into a pulsating backdrop. Prepare a completely black picture and call it 'black.tga' (try pressing **F12** in an empty Blender file. Save with **F3**, but make sure that you have selected the TGA file format in the Render Buttons window). Add both black.tga and the tunnel animation and combine them with an ADD effect (fig. 29).

Now with the `ADD` effect selected, open an IPO window and select the Sequence Editor button in its header. From frame 1-50, draw an irregular line by holding down **CTRL** and left-clicking. Make sure that the values are between 0 and 1 (fig. 30).

When you are ready, take a look at the result in a preview screen and change the animation into a meta strip.

Save your work!

Fourth Animation: a jumping logo

Let's create some more randomness and chaos! Take a logo (We can just add a text object) and make it jump through the screen. Again, the easiest way to do this is to add vertices directly into the IPO window (select a `LocX`, `LocY` or `LocZ` channel first), but this time you may need to be a bit more careful with the minimum and maximum values for each channel. Don't worry about the looks of this one too much - the next step will make is hardly recognizable anyway (fig. 31).

Save the animation as 'jumpylogo.avi'.

Fifth Animation: particle bars

Our last effect will use an animated mask. By combining this with the logo of the previous step, I will achieve a streaking effect that introduces the logo to our animation.

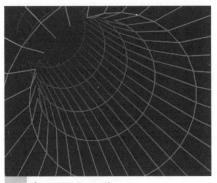

28 A groovy tunnel.

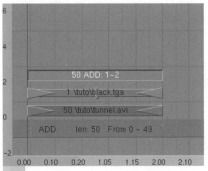

29 Setting up the backdrop effect.

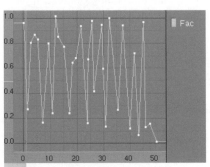

30 Adding randomnes with an irregular IPO.

31 Jumping logo.

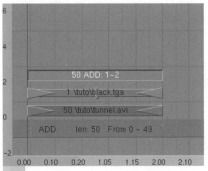

32 Particle system settings.

This mask is made by using a particle system. To set one up switch to side view, add a plane to your scene and while it is still selected switch to the Object Context(**F7**). In the `Effects` Tab of the `Constraints` Panel. Select `New effect` and then change the default effect `build` to `Particles`. Change the system's settings as indicated in figure 32.

Press **TAB** to enter Edit Mode, select all vertices and subdivide the plane twice by pressing **WKEY** and selecting Subdivide from the pop-up menu.

Next switch to front view and add another plane. Scale it along the X-axis to turn it into a rectangle (press **SKEY** and move your mouse horizontally. Then click **XKEY** or **MMB** to scale along the indicated axis only). Give the rectangle a white material with an emit value of one.

Now you need to change the particles into rectangles by using the dupliverts function. Select rectangle, then particle emitter and parent them. Select only the plane and in the Object Context and Anim Settings Panel, select the DupliVerts Button. Each particle is now replaced by a rectangle (fig. 33).

Let's now add some mist as a quick hack to give the rectangles each a different shade of grey. Go to the World Buttons window with **F5** to change to Shading Context, then click on the ▣ button and select Add New in the World Panel. The world settings will now appear.

By default, the sky will now be rendered as a gradient between blue and black. Change the horizon colors (HoR, HoG, HoB) to pure black (fig. 34).

To activate rendering of mist activate the Mist button in the middle of the screen. When using mist, you have to indicate on which distance from the camera it works. Select the camera, switch to the Editing Context enable ShowMist in the Camera Panel. Now switch to top view and return to the Shading Context (**F5**) and World Buttons. Tweak the Sta: and Di: (Start, Distance, respectively) parameters so that the mist covers the complete width of the particle stream (fig. 34 and 35).

Set the animation length to 100 frames and render the animation to disk. Call the file 'particles.avi' (fig. 36).

Third sequence: Combining the logo and the particle bars

By now you know the drill: reload your compilation project file, switch to the Sequence Editor window and add both 'particles.avi' and 'logo.avi' to your project. Combine them together with a MUL effect. Since the logo animation is 50 frames and the particles animation is 100 frames, you'll need to duplicate the logo animation once and apply a second MUL effect to it (fig. 37 and 38).

Combine these three strips into one meta strip. If you're feeling brave you can make a few copies and give them a small time offset just like with the WireFrame cube.

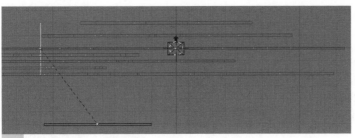

33 DupliVerted rectangles.

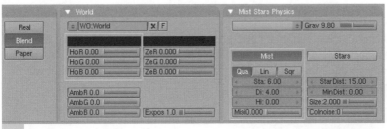

34 Setting up mist.

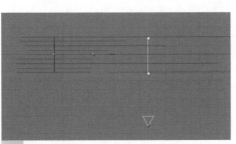

35 Setting the mist parameters.

36 Rendered particle rectangles.

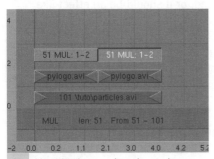

37 Use the logo animation twice.

38 The particles animation combined with the logo animation.

Sixth Animation: zooming logo

If you would combine all your animations so far you would get a really wild video compilation, but if this was your company's presentation you would want to present the logo in a more recognizable way. The final part of our compilation will therefore be an animation of the logo that zooms in very slowly. Prepare this one and save it as 'zoomlogo.avi'. Also prepare a white picture and save it as 'white.tga'.

We will now use the CROSS effect to first make a rapid transition from black to white, then from white to our logo animation. Finally, a transition to black will conclude the compilation.

Start off by placing black.tga in channel 1 and white.tga in channel 2. Make them both 20 frames long. Select them both and apply a cross effect. The cross will gradually change the resulting image from layer 1 to layer 2. In this case, the result will be a transition from black to white (fig. 39).

Next, add a duplicate of white.tga to layer 1 and place it directly to the right of black.tga. Make it about half as long as the original. Place the logo zoom animation in layer 2 and add a cross effect between the two. At this point, the animation looks like a white flash followed by the logo zoom animation (fig. 40).

The last thing that you need to do is to make sure that the animation will have a nice transition to black at the very end. Add a duplicate of black.tga and apply another cross effect. When you are ready, transform everything into a meta strip (fig. 41).

Assembling everything so far

We're at the end of our work! It's time add some of the compilations that we have made so far and see how our work looks. The most important thing to remember while creating your final compilation is that when rendering your animation, the sequence editor only 'sees' the top layer of video. This means that you have to make sure that it is either a strip that is ready to be used, or it should be an effect like ADD that combines several underlying strips.

The foundation of the compilation will be the fluctuating tunnel. Add a some duplicates of the tunnel meta strip and place them in channel one. Combine them into one meta strip. Do not worry about the exact length of the animation yet; you can always duplicate more tunnel strips.

On top of that, place the delayed wireframe cube in channel 2. Add channel 1 to channel two and place the add effect in channel 3 (fig. 42).

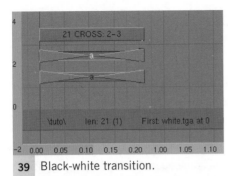

39 Black-white transition.

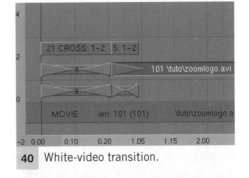

40 White-video transition.

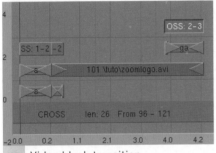

41 Video-black transition.

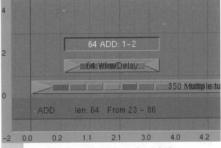

42 Combining the tunnel and the WireFrame cube.

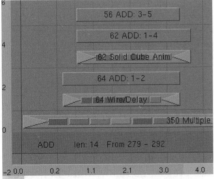

43 Combining the tunnel, WireFrame and solid cube.

Now we also want to add the solid cube animation. Place it in channel 4, overlapping with the WireFrame animation in channel 2. Add it to the tunnel animation in layer one. This is where things are starting to get a little tricky; if you would leave it like this, the animation in channel 5 (the solid cube together with the tube) would override the animation in channel 2 (the wireframe cube) and the wireframe cube would become invisible as soon as the solid cube shows up. To solve this, add channel 3 to channel 5 (fig. 43).

You will often need to apply some extra add operations to fix missing parts of video. This will most likely become apparent after you have rendered the final sequence.

Slide the Sequence Editor window a bit to the left and add the meta strip with the particle/logo animation in it. Place this strip in layer 2 and place an add effect in layer 3. For some variation, duplicate the WireFrame animation and combine it with the add in layer 3 (fig. 44).

Now go to the end of the tunnel animation strip. There should be enough place to put the logo zoom animation at the end and still have some space left before it (fig. 45). If not, select the tunnel strip, press **TAB** and add a duplicate of the animation to the end. Press **TAB** again to leave meta edit mode.

If there is still some space left, we can add a copy of the solid cube animation. To get it to display correctly, you will have to apply two add channels to it: one to combine it with the particle logo animation and one to combine it with the logo zoom animation (fig. 46).

Figure 47 shows the complete sequence.

Conclusion

We are now ready to render our final video composition! To tell Blender to use the Sequence Editor information while rendering, select the Do Sequence button in the Render Buttons window. After that, rendering and saving your animation works like before (be sure not to overwrite any of your AVI of the sequence!).

Sound Sequence Editor

Since Blender 2.28 there is a (still limited) Audio sequencing toolbox. You can Add WAV files via the **SHIFT-A** menu and selecting the Sound entry. A green audio strip will be created. No "high level" mixing features are present currently. You can have as many Audio strips as you wish and the result will be the mixing of all them. You can give each strip its own name and Gain (in dB) via the **NKEY** menu. This also let you set a strip to mute or "Pan" it; -1 is hard left, +1 is hard right. A "Volume" IPO can be added to the strip in the IPO Window as it is done for effect strips. The Fac channel is the volume here. IPO frames 1-100 correspond to the whole sample length, 1.0 is full volume, 0.0 is completely silent.

Blender cannot yet mix the sound in the final product of the sequence editor. The result of the sequence editor is hence a video file, if the ANIM button in the Anim Panel of the Scene Context, Render Sub-context is used as described before, or a *separate*

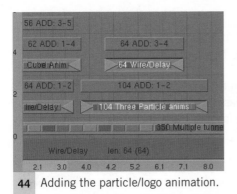

44 Adding the particle/logo animation.

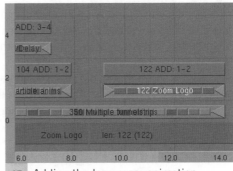

45 Adding the logo zoom animation.

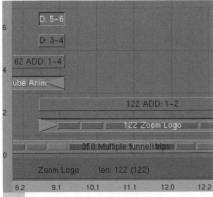

46 Adding one last detail.

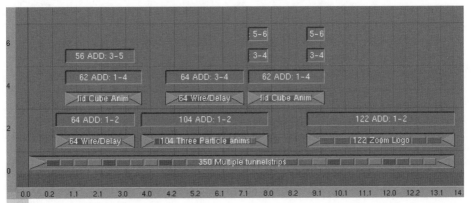

47 The complete sequence.

WAV file, containing the full audio sequence, in the same directory of the video file and with the *same name* but WAV extension. This audio file is created via the MIX-DOWN button in the `Sequencer` button of the Scene Context, Sound Sub-context.

You can mix Video and Audio later on with an external program. The advantage of using Blender's sequence editor lies in the easier synchronization attainable by sequencing frames and sound in the same application.

Sequence Editor Plugins

As said before Blender is extensible via a plugin system, and two kind of plugins may be found: Texture and Sequence plugins.

Sequence plugins works on strips in a way similar to that of conventional ADD, CROSS etc. operation. You must have at least a strip selected and press **SHIFT-A**>>Plugin or `Add`>>`Effect`>>`Plugin` Menu entry. This opens a File Selection Window in which you can select the desired plugin.

Plugin functionalities varies so much that it is not possible to describe them here. Differently than Texture Plugins Sequence Plugins do not have a Buttons in any Button Window, but their parameters are usually accessed via **NKEY**.

PYTHON SCRIPTING

PLUGINS

PART VI

EXTENDING BLENDER

Unlike many programs you might be familiar with, Blender is not monolithic and static. You can extend its functionalities even without having to modify the sources and recompile.

There are two ways of extensions: Python scripting and Binary Plugins, the former being the preferred and most used. This Part will describe both.

CH. 20 PYTHON SCRIPTING

THE TEXT WINDOW, SETTING THE PYTHON PATH, A WORKING PYTHON EXAMPLE

Blender has a very powerful yet often overlooked feature. It exhibits an internal full fledged Python interpreter.

This allows any user to add functionalities by writing a Python script. Python is an interpreted, interactive, object-oriented programming language. It incorporates modules, exceptions, dynamic typing, very high level dynamic data types, and classes. Python combines remarkable power with very clear syntax. It was expressly designed to be usable as an extension language for applications that need a programmable interface, and this is why Blender uses it.

Of the two main ways of extending Blender, the other one being binary plugins, Python scripting is more powerful, versatile yet easier to comprehend and robust. It is generally preferred to use Python scripting than writing a plugin.

Actually Python scripting had somewhat limited functionalities up to Blender 2.25, the last of NaN releases. When Open Sourcing Blender many of the new developers gathered around the Foundations elected to work on it and, together with UI change, Python API is probably the single part of Blender which got the greater development. A full reorganization of what existed was carried out and many new modules added.

This evolution is still ongoing and even better integration is expected in forthcoming Blender versions.

Blender has a Text Window among its windows types accessible via the ▤ button of the Window Type menu or via **SHIFT F11**.

The newly opened Text window is grey and empty, with a very simple toolbar (fig. 1). From left to right there are the standard Window type selection button and the Window menu. Then the full screen button, followed by a toggle button which shows/ hides the line numbers for the text and the regular Menu Button.

The Menu Button (▤) allows to select which Text buffer is to be displayed, as well as allowing to create a new buffer or loading a text file.

PYTHON SCRIPTING.THE TEXT WINDOW

1 Text toolbar.

If you choose to load a file the Text Window temporarily becomes a File Selection Window, with the usual functions. Once a text buffer is in the Text window, this behaves as a very simple text editor. Typing on the keyboard produces text in the text buffer. As usual pressing **LMB** dragging and releasing **LMB** selects text. The following keyboard commands apply:

ALT-C or **CTRL-C**	- Copy the marked text into the text clipboard;
ALT-X or **CTRL-X**	- Cut out the marked text into the text clipboard;
ALT-V or **CTRL-V**	- Paste the text from the clipboard to the cursor in the Text Window;
ALT-S	- Saves the text as a text file, a File Selection Window appears;
ALT-O	- Loads a text, a File Selection Window appears;
ALT-F	- Pops up the Find toolbox;
SHIFT-ALT-F or **RMB**	- Pops up the File Menu for the Text Window;
ALT-J	- Pops up a Num Button where you can specify a linenumber the cursor will jump to;
ALT-P	- Executes the text as a Python script;
ALT-U	- Undo;
ALT-R	- Redo;
CTRL-R	- Reopen (reloads) the current buffer;
ALT-M	- Converts the content of the text window into 3D text (max 100 chars);

Blender's cut/copy/paste clipboard is *separate* from Window's clipboard. So normally you *cannot* cut/paste/copy out from/into Blender. To access your Windows clipboard use **SHIFT-CTRL-C SHIFT-CTRL-V**.

To delete a text buffer just press the 'X' button next to the buffer's name, just as you do for materials, etc.

The most notable keystroke is **ALT-P** which makes the content of the buffer being parsed by the internal Python interpreter built into Blender.

The next section will present an example of Python scripting. Before going on it is worth noticing that Blender comes with only the bare Python interpreter built in, and with a few Blender-specific modules.

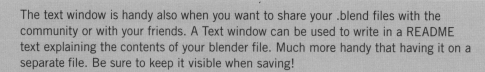

Other usages for the Text window

The text window is handy also when you want to share your .blend files with the community or with your friends. A Text window can be used to write in a README text explaining the contents of your blender file. Much more handy that having it on a separate file. Be sure to keep it visible when saving!

If you are sharing the file with the community and you want to share it under some licence you can write the licence in a text window.

To have access to the standard Python modules you need a complete working Python install. You can download this from http://www.python.org. Be sure to check on http://www.blender.org which is the *exact* Python version which was built into Blender to prevent compatibility issues.

Blender must also be made aware of *where* this full Python installation is. This is done by defining a PYTHONPATH environment variable.

Setting PYTHONPATH on Win95, 98, Me

Once you have installed Python in, say, C:\PYTHON22 you must open the file C:\AUTOEXEC.BAT with your favourite text editor, add a line:

```
SET PYTHONPATH=C:\PYTHON22;C:\PYTHON22\DLLS;C:\PYTHON22\LIB;C:\PYTHON22\LIB\LIB-TK
```

and reboot the system.

Setting PYTHONPATH on WinNT, 2000, XP

Once you have installed Python in, say, C:\PYTHON22 Go on the "My Computer" Icon on the desktop, **RMB** and select Properties. Select the Advanced tab and press the Environment Variables button.

Below the System Variables box, (the second box), hit New. If you are not an administrator you might be unable to do that. In this case hit New in the upper box.

Now, in the Variable Name box, type PYTHONPATH, in the Variable Value box, type:

```
C:\PYTHON22;C:\PYTHON22\DLLS;C:\PYTHON22\LIB;C:\PYTHON22\LIB\LIB-TK
```

Hit OK repeatedly to exit from all dialogs. You may or may not have to reboot, depending on the OS.

Setting PYTHONPATH on Linux and other UNIXes

Normally you will have Python already there. If not, install it. You will have to discover where it is. This is easy, just start a Python interactive shell by opening a shell and by typing `python` in there. Type the following commands:

```
>>> import sys
>>> print sys.path
```

and note down the output, it should look like

```
['', '/usr/local/lib/python2.2', '/usr/local/lib/python2.2 /plat-
linux2', '/usr/local/lib/python2.0/lib-tk', '/usr/local/lib/
python2.0/lib-dynload', '/usr/local/lib/python2.0/site-packages']
```

Add this to your favourite `rc` file as an environment variable setting. For example, add in your `.bashrc` the line

```
export PYTHONPATH=/usr/local/lib/python2.2:/usr/local/lib/
python2.2/plat-linux2:/usr/local/lib/python2.2/lib-tk:/usr/local/
lib/python2.2/lib-dynload:/usr/local/lib/python2.0/site-packages
```

all on a single line. Open a new login shell, or logoff and login again.

A working Python example

Now that you've seen that Blender is extensible via Python scripting and that you've got the basics of script handling and how to run a script, before smashing your brain with the full python API reference let's have a look to a quick working example.

We will present a tiny script to produce polygons. This indeed duplicates somewhat the **SPACE** `Add>>Mesh>>Circle` toolbox option, but will create 'filled' polygons, not just the outline.

To make the script simple yet complete it will exhibit a Graphical User Interface (GUI) completely written via Blender's API.

Headers, importing modules and globals

The first 32 lines of code are reported in code example 1.

```
001 ###################################################
002 #
003 # Demo Script for Blender 2.3 Guide
004 #
005 ###################################################S68
006 # This script generates polygons. It is quite useless
007 # since you can do polygons with ADD->Mesh->Circle
008 # but it is a nice complete script example, and the
009 # polygons are 'filled'
010 ###################################################
011
012 ###################################################
013 # Importing modules
014 ###################################################
015
016 import Blender
017 from Blender import NMesh
018 from Blender.BGL import *
019 from Blender.Draw import *
020
021 import math
022 from math import *
023
024 # Polygon Parameters
025 T_NumberOfSides = Create(3)
026 T_Radius        = Create(1.0)
027
028 # Events
029 EVENT_NOEVENT = 1
030 EVENT_DRAW    = 2
031 EVENT_EXIT    = 3
032
```

After the necessary comments with the description of what the script does there is the importing of Python modules (lines 016-022).

`Blender` is the main Blender Python API module. `NMesh` is the module providing access to Blender's meshes, while `BGL` and `Draw` give access to the OpenGL constants and functions and to Blender's windowing interface, respectively. The `math` module is Python's mathematical module, but since both the 'math' and the 'os' modules are built into Blender you don't need a full Python install for this!

The polygons are defined via the number of sides they have and their radius. These parameters have values which must be defined by the user via the GUI hence lines (025-026) creates two 'generic button' objects, with their default starting value.

Finally, the GUI objects works with, and generates, events. Events identifier are integers left to the coder to define. It is usually a good practice to define mnemonic names for events, as it is done here in lines (029-031).

Drawing the GUI

The code responsible for drawing the GUI should reside in a `draw` function (code example 2).

```
033 ##########################################################
034 # GUI drawing
035 ##########################################################
036 def draw():
037     global T_NumberOfSides
038     global T_Radius
039     global EVENT_NOEVENT,EVENT_DRAW,EVENT_EXIT
040
041     ########## Titles
042     glClear(GL_COLOR_BUFFER_BIT)
043     glRasterPos2d(8, 103)
044     Text("Demo Polygon Script")
045
046     ######### Parameters GUI Buttons
047     glRasterPos2d(8, 83)
048     Text("Parameters:")
049     T_NumberOfSides = Number("No. of sides: ", EVENT_NOEVENT,
                          10, 55, 210, 18,
050                       T_NumberOfSides.val, 3, 20, "Number of
                              sides of out polygon");
051     T_Radius        = Slider("Radius: ", EVENT_NOEVENT, 10,
                          35, 210, 18,
052                       T_Radius.val, 0.001, 20.0, 1, "Radius of
```

Code example 2: GUI drawing

```
                        the polygon");
053
054     ######### Draw and Exit Buttons
055     Button("Draw",EVENT_DRAW , 10, 10, 80, 18)
056     Button("Exit",EVENT_EXIT , 140, 10, 80, 18)
057
```

Lines (037-039) merely grant access to global data. The real interesting stuff starts from lines (042-044). The OpenGL window is initialised, and the current position set to x=8, y=103. The origin of this reference is the lower left corner of the script window. Then the title Demo Polygon Script is printed.

A further string is written (lines 047-048), then the input buttons for the parameters are created. The first (lines 049-050) is a Num Button, exactly alike those in the various Blender Button Windows. For the meaning of all the parameters please refer to the API reference. Basically there is the button label, the event generated by the button, its location (x,y) and its dimensions (width, height), its value, which is a data belonging to the Button object itself, the minimum and maximum allowable values and a text string which will appear as an help while hovering on the button, as a tooltip.

Lines (051-052) defines a Num Button with a slider, with a very similar syntax. Lines (055-056) finally creates a Draw button which will create the polygon and an Exit button.

Managing Events

The GUI is not drawn, and would not work, until a proper event handler is written and registered (code example 3).

**Code example 3:
Handling Events**

```
058 def event(evt, val):
059     if (evt == QKEY and not val):
060         Exit()
061
062 def bevent(evt):
063     global T_NumberOfSides
064     global T_Radius
065     global EVENT_NOEVENT,EVENT_DRAW,EVENT_EXIT
066
067     ######### Manages GUI events
068     if (evt == EVENT_EXIT):
```

```
069     Exit()
070 elif (evt== EVENT_DRAW):
071     Polygon(T_NumberOfSides.val, T_Radius.val)
072         Blender.Redraw()
073
074 Register(draw, event, bevent)
075
```

Lines (058-060) defines the keyboard event handler, here responding to the **QKEY** with a plain Exit() call.

More interesting are lines (062-072), in charge of managing the GUI events. Every time a GUI button is used this function is called, with the event number defined within the button as a parameter. The core of this function is hence a "select" structure executing different codes accordingly to the event number.

As a last call, the Register function is invoked. This effectively draws the GUI and starts the event capturing cycle.

Mesh handling

Finally, code example shows the main function, the one creating the polygon. It is a rather simple mesh editing, but shows many important points of the Blender's internal data structure.

```
076 ###################################################
077 # Main Body
078 ###################################################
079 def Polygon(NumberOfSides,Radius):
080
081 ######### Creates a new mesh
082 poly = NMesh.GetRaw()
083
084 #########Populates it of vertices
085 for i in range(0,NumberOfSides):
086     phi = 3.141592653589 * 2 * i / NumberOfSides
087     x = Radius * cos(phi)
088     y = Radius * sin(phi)
089     z = 0
090
091     v = NMesh.Vert(x,y,z)
```

Code example 4: Mesh handling

```
092      poly.verts.append(v)
093
094  #########Adds a new vertex to the center
095  v = NMesh.Vert(0.,0.,0.)
096  poly.verts.append(v)
097
098  #########Connects the vertices to form faces
099  for i in range(0,NumberOfSides):
100    f = NMesh.Face()
101    f.v.append(poly.verts[i])
102    f.v.append(poly.verts[(i+1)%NumberOfSides])
103    f.v.append(poly.verts[NumberOfSides])
104    poly.faces.append(f)
105
106  #########Creates a new Object with the new Mesh
107  polyObj = NMesh.PutRaw(poly)
108
109  Blender.Redraw()
```

The first important line here is number (082). Here a new mesh object, `poly` is created. The mesh object is constituted of a list of vertices and a list of faces, plus some other interesting stuff. For our purposes the vertices and faces lists are what we need.

Of course the newly created mesh is empty. The first cycle (lines 085-092) computes the x,y,z location of the `NumberOfSides` vertices needed to define the polygon. Being a flat figure it is z=0 for all.

Line (091) call the `NMesh` method `Vert` to create a new vertex object of co-ordinates (x,y,z). Such an object is then appended (line 096) in the `poly` Mesh `verts` list.

Finally (lines 095-096) a last vertex is added in the centre.

Lines (099-104) now connects these vertices to make faces. It is not required to create all vertices beforehand and then faces. You can safely create a new face as soon as all its vertices are there.

Line (100) creates a new face object. A face object has its own list of vertices `v` (up to 4) defining it. Lines (101-103) appends three vertices to the originally empty `f.v` list. The vertices are two subsequent vertices of the polygon and the central vertex. These vertices must be taken from the Mesh `verts` list. Finally line (104) appends the newly created face to the `faces` list of our `poly` mesh.

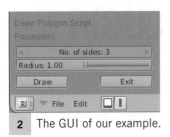

2 The GUI of our example.

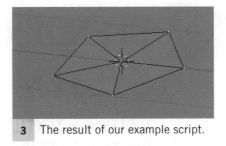

3 The result of our example script.

Conclusions

If you create a `polygon.py` file containing the above described code and load it into a Blender text window as you learned in the previous section and press **ALT-P** in that window to run it you will see the script disappearing and the window turn grey. In the lower left corner the GUI will be drawn (fig. 2).

By selecting, for example, 5 vertices and a radius 0.5, and by pressing the `Draw` button a pentagon will appear on the xy plane of the 3D window (fig. 3).

Python Reference

The Full Python Application Programmer Interface of Blender has a reference documentation which is a book by itself. For space reason it is not included here but rather on the CD-ROM.

Python Scripts

There are more than one hundred different scripts for Blender available on the net. As for plugins scripts are very dynamic, changing interface, functionalities and web location fairly quickly, so for an updated list and for a live link to them please refear to one of the two main blender sites, www.blender.org or www.elysiun.com.

CH. 21 BLENDER'S PLUGIN SYSTEM

WRITING A TEXTURE PLUGIN, WRITING A SEQUENCE PLUGIN

by Kent Mein

This section reports an in-depth reference for coding Blender's Texture and Sequence plugins.

Writing a Texture Plugin

In this Section we will write a basic texture plugin and then go through the steps to use a texture plugin. The basics behind a texture plugin is that you are given some inputs; position, and normal values as well as some other info. Then you return intensity, colour and/or normal information depending on the type of texture plugin.

All the files necessary to develop plugins as well as a few sample plugins can be found in the blender/plugins directory of your Blender installation. You can alternately get a bunch of plugins from http://www.cs.umn.edu/~mein/blender/plugins.

Plugins are supported (loaded/called) in Blender using the dlopen() family of calls. For those unfamiliar with the dlopen system it allows a program (Blender) to use a compiled object as if it were part of the program itself, similar to dynamically linked libraries, except the objects to load are determined at runtime.

The advantage of using the dlopen system for plugins is that it is very fast to access a function, and there is no overhead in interfacing to the plugin, which is critical when as (in the case of texture plugins) the plugin can be called several million times in a single render.

The disadvantage of the system is that the plugin code works just like it is part of Blender itself, if the plugin crashes, Blender crashes.

The include files found in the plugin/include/ subdirectory of the Blender installation document the Blender functionality provided to the plugins. This includes the Imbuf library functions for loading and working with images and image buffers, and noise and turbulence functions for consistent texturing.

BLENDER'S PLUGIN SYSTEM.WRITING A TEXTURE PLUGIN

Specification:

- *#include <plugin.h>*
  Every Blender plugin should include this header file, which contains all of the structures and defines needed to properly work with Blender.

- *char name[]="Tiles";*
  A character string containing the plugin name, this value will be displayed for the texture's title in the Texture Buttons window.

- *#define NR_TYPES 2 char stnames[NR_TYPES][16]= {"Square", "Deformed"};*
  Plugins are allowed to have separate subtypes for minor variations on algorithms - for example the default clouds texture in Blender has the "Default" and "Color" subtypes.

  NR_STYPES should be defined to the number of subtypes required by your plugin, and a name for each subtype should be given. Every plugin should have at least 1 subtype and a subtype name.

- *VarStruct varstr[]= {...};*
  The varstr contains all of the information Blender needs to display buttons for a plugin. Buttons for plugins can be numerical for input data, or text for comments and other information. Plugins are limited to a maximum of 32 variables.

  Each VarStruct entry consists of a type, name, range information, and a tool tip.

  The type defines the data type for each button entry, and the way to display the button. For number buttons this value should be a combination (ORed) of INT or FLO for the number format, and NUM, NUMSLI, or TOG, for the button type. Text buttons should have a type of LABEL.

  The name is what will be displayed on (or beside) the button. This is limited to 15 characters.

  The range information consists of three floats that define the default, minimum, and maximum values for the button. For TOG buttons the minimum is set in the pressed state, and the maximum is set in the depressed state.

  The tip is a string that will be displayed when the mouse is over this button (if the user has tool tips on). This has a limit of 80 characters, and should be set to the NULL string ("") if unused.

- *typedef struct Cast {...};*
  The cast structure is used in calling the doit function, and serves as a way to simply access each plugin's data values.

The cast should contain, in order, an integer or float for every button defined in the varstr, including text buttons. Typically these should have the same name as the button for simple reference.

- *float result[8];*
  The result array is used to pass information to and receive information from the plugin. The result values are mapped as follows:

Result Index	Significance	Range
result[0]	Intensity value	0.0 to 1.0
result[1]	Red color value	0.0 to 1.0
result[2]	Green color value	0.0 to 1.0
result[3]	Blue color value	0.0 to 1.0
result[4]	Alpha color value	0.0 to 1.0
result[5]	X normal displacement value	-1.0 to 1.0
result[6]	Y normal displacement value	-1.0 to 1.0
result[7]	Z normal displacement value	-1.0 to 1.0

The plugin should always return an intensity value. Returning RGB or a normal are optional, and should be indicated by the doit() return flag "1" (RGB) or "2" (Normal).

Before the plugin is called, Blender includes the current rendering-normal in result[5], result[6] and result[7].

- *float cfra*
  The cfra value is set by Blender to the current from before every render pass. This value is an the frame number +/- .5 depending on the field settings.

- *plugin_tex_doit prototype*
  The plugin_tex_doit function should be prototyped for use by the getinfo function. You do not need to change this line.

- *plugin_tex_getversion*
  This function must be in each plugin for it to be loaded correctly. You should not change this function.

- *plugin_but_changed*
  This function is used to pass information about what buttons the user changes in the interface. Most plugins should not need to use this function, only when the interface allows the user to alter some variable that forces the plugin to do recalculation (a random hash table for example).

BLENDER'S PLUGIN SYSTEM.WRITING A TEXTURE PLUGIN

- *plugin_init*
  If needed plugins may use this function to initialize internal data. NOTE: This init function can be called multiple times if the same plugin texture is copied. Do not init global data specific to a single instance of a plugin in this function.

- *plugin_getinfo*
  This function is used to communicate information to Blender. You should never need to change it.

- *plugin_tex_doit*
  The doit function is responsible for returning information about the requested pixel to Blender.

  The Arguments

  - *int stype*
    This is the number of the selected subtype, see the *NR_TYPES* and *char stypes* entries above.

  - *Cast *cast*
    The Cast structure which contains the plugin data, see the *Cast* entry above.

  - *float *texvec*
    This is a pointer to 3 floats, which are the texture coordinates for which a texture value is to be returned.

  - *float *dxt float *dyt*
    If these pointers are non-NULL they point to two vectors (two arrays of three floats) that define the size of the requested texture value in pixel space. They are only non-NULL when OSA is on, and are used to calculate proper anti aliasing.

The doit function should fill in the result array and return 0,1,2, or 3, depending on what values have been filled in. The doit function should *always* fill in an intensity value. If the function fills in a color value it should return 1, if it fills in a normal value it should return 2, if it fills in everything it should return 3.

Texture/Material Interaction

Blender is somewhat different from most 3D packages in the logical separation between textures and materials. In Blender textures are objects that return certain values, signal generators in fact. Materials control the mapping of textures onto objects, what is affected, how much, in what way, etc.Properly designed plugins should only include variables to affect the signal returned not the mapping of it. Buttons to control scale, range, axis, etc. are best only included when they make the texture easier to use (in the case of the size button in the Tiles plugin) or they speed up the calculation (the Intensity/Color/Bump subtypes in the Clouds2 plugin). Otherwise the Material Buttons make these buttons redundant, and the interface becomes needlessly complex.

Generic Texture Plugin:

```
#include "plugin.h"

/* Texture name */
char name[24]= "";

#define NR_TYPES 3
char stnames[NR_TYPES][16]= {"Intens","Color", "Bump"};
/* Structure for buttons,
 * butcode name default min max 0
 */

VarStruct varstr[]= {
    {NUM|FLO, "Const 1", 1.7, -1.0, 1.0, ""},
};


typedef struct Cast {
    float a;
} Cast;

float result[8];
float cfra;
int plugin_tex_doit(int, Cast*, float*, float*, float*);

/* Fixed Functions */
int plugin_tex_getversion(void) {
    return B_PLUGIN_VERSION;
}

void plugin_but_changed(int but) { }

void plugin_init(void) { }
```

```c
void plugin_getinfo(PluginInfo *info) {
    info->name= name;
    info->stypes= NR_TYPES;
    info->nvars= sizeof(varstr)/sizeof(VarStruct);

    info->snames= stnames[0];
    info->result= result;
    info->cfra= &cfra;
    info->varstr= varstr;

    info->init= plugin_init;
    info->tex_doit= (TexDoit) plugin_tex_doit;
    info->callback= plugin_but_changed;
}

int plugin_tex_doit(int stype, Cast *cast, float *texvec,
                    float *dxt, float *dyt) {
    if (stype == 1) {
        return 1;
    } if (stype == 2) {
        return 2;
    }
    return 0;
}
```

Our Modifications:

The first step is to come up with a game plan. What is this plugin going to do, how are the users going to interact with it. For this example we will create a simple texture that creates a simple brick/block pattern.

Now we'll copy our generic plugin to cube.c and will fill in the gaps.

Its always a good idea to add some comments. First off tell users what the plugin does, where they can get a copy, who they should contact for bugs/improvements, and any licensing restrictions on the code. When using comments make sure you use /* */ style comments. The plugins are in C and some C compilers do not accept // style comments.

```
/*
Description: This plugin is a sample texture plugin that creates
a simple brick/block pattern with it.

It takes two values a brick size, and a mortar size.
The brick size is the size of each brick.
the mortar size is the mortar size in between bricks.

Author: Kent Mein (mein@cs.umn.edu)
Website: http://www.cs.umn.edu/~mein/blender/plugins
Licensing: Public Domain
Last Modified: Tue Oct 21 05:57:13 CDT 2003
*/
```

Next we need to fill in the Name, you should really keep this the same as your .c file. preferably descriptive, less than 23 chars, no spaces, and all lowercase.

```
char name[24] = "cube.c";
```

We are going to keep this plugin simple, and only have one type that deals with intensity. So we need the following:

```
#define NR_TYPES         1
char stnames[NR_TYPES][16] = {"Default"};
```

For our user interface we are going to allow people to change; The size of the brick and mortar, as well as the intensity values returned for the brick and mortar. For that we need to edit the varstr and Cast. The Cast should have a variable for each entry in varstr.

```
/* Structure for buttons,
 *butcodename defaultminmaxTool tip
 */
VarStruct varstr[] = {
    {NUM|FLO, "Brick",.8,0.1, 1.0, "Size of Cell"},
    {NUM|FLO, "Mortar", .1,0.0, 0.4, "Size of boarder in cell"},
    {NUM|FLO, "Brick Int", 1,0.0, 1.0, "Color of Brick"},
    {NUM|FLO, "Mortar Int",0,0.0, 1.0, "Color of Mortar"},
};
```

```
typedef struct Cast {
    float brick,mortar, bricki, mortari;
} Cast;
```

Now we need to fill in plugin_tex_doit, we basically want to break down our texture into "cells" which will consist of a brick and the mortar along the bottom edges of that brick. Then determine if we are in the brick or the mortar. The following code should do that.

```
int plugin_tex_doit(int stype, Cast *cast, float *texvec,
                    float *dxt, float *dyt) {
    int c[3];
    float pos[3], cube;

    /* setup the size of our cell */
    cube = cast->brick + cast->mortar;

    /* we need to do is determine where we are inside of the
    current brick. */
    c[0] = (int)(texvec[0] / cube);
    c[1] = (int)(texvec[1] / cube);
    c[2] = (int)(texvec[2] / cube);

    pos[0] = ABS(texvec[0] - (c[0] * cube));
    pos[1] = ABS(texvec[1] - (c[1] * cube));
    pos[2] = ABS(texvec[2] - (c[2] * cube));

    /* Figure out if we are in a mortar position within the brick
       or not. */
    if ((pos[0] <= cast->mortar) || (pos[1] <= cast->mortar) ||
        (pos[2] <= cast->mortar)) {
      result[0] = cast->mortari;
    } else {
      result[0] = cast->bricki;
    }

    return 0;
}
```

One thing to note, the ABS function is defined in a header in plugins/include. There are some other common functions there as well be sure to take a look at what's there.

Compiling:

bmake is a simple utility (shell script) to aid in the compilation and development of plugins, and can be found in the plugins/ sub-directory of the Blender installation directory. It is invoked by: bmake (plugin_name.c) and will attempt to link the proper libraries and compile the specified C file properly for your system. If you are trying to develop plugins on a windows machine bmake may not work for you in that case you should look into using lcc. You can use the following to compile a plugin with lcc: Assuming you have your plugins in c:\blender\plugins. Here is an example of how you would compile the texture plugin sinus.c Open a dos prompt and do the following:

```
cd c:\blender\plugins\texture\sinus
lcc -Ic:\blender\plugins\include sinus.c
lcclnk -DLL sinus.obj c:\blender\plugins\include\tex.def
implib sinus.dll
```

 (Note: You'll want to make sure the lcc\bin directory is in your path)

Writing a Sequence Plugin

In this Section we will write a basic sequence plugin and then go through the steps use a sequence plugin. The basics behind a sequence plugin are you are given some inputs; 1-3 input image buffers as well as some other information and you output a resulting image buffer.

All the files necessary to develop plugins as well as a few sample plugins can be found in the blender/plugins directory. You can alternately get a bunch of plugins from http://www.cs.umn.edu/~mein/blender/plugins

Specification:

*   *#include <plugin.h>*
    Every Blender plugin should include this header file, which contains all of the structures and defines needed to properly work with Blender.

*   *char name[]="Blur";*
    A character string containing the plugin name, this value will be displayed for the texture's title in the Texture Buttons window.

- *VarStruct varstr[]= {...};*
  The varstr contains all of the information Blender needs to display buttons for a plugin. Buttons for plugins can be numerical for input data, or text for comments and other information. Plugins are limited to a maximum of 32 variables.

  Each VarStruct entry consists of a type, name, range information, and a tool tip.

  The type defines the data type for each button entry, and the way to display the button. For number buttons this value should be a combination (ORed) of INT or FLO for the number format, and NUM, NUMSLI, or TOG, for the button type. Text buttons should have a type of LABEL.

  The name is what will be displayed on (or beside) the button. This is limited to 15 characters.

  The range information consists of three floats that define the default, minimum, and maximum values for the button. For TOG buttons the minimum is set in the pressed state, and the maximum is set in the depressed state.

  The tip is a string that will be displayed when the mouse is over this button (if the user has tool tips on). This has a limit of 80 characters, and should be set to the NULL string ("") if unused.

- *typedef struct Cast {...};*
  The cast structure is used in calling the doit function, and serves as a way to simply access each plugin's data values.

  The cast should contain, in order, an integer or float for every button defined in the varstr, including text buttons. Typically these should have the same name as the button for simple reference.

- *float cfra*
  The cfra value is set by Blender to the current from before every render pass. This value is an the frame number +/- .5 depending on the field settings.

- *plugin_seq_doit prototype*
  The plugin_seq_doit function should be prototyped for use by the getinfo function. You do not need to change this line.

- *plugin_seq_getversion*
  This function must be in each plugin for it to be loaded correctly. You should not change this function.

- *plugin_but_changed*
  This function is used to pass information about what buttons the user changes in the interface. Most plugins should not need to use this function, only when the interface allows the user to alter some variable that forces the plugin to do recalculation (a random hash table for example).

- *plugin_init*
  If needed plugins may use this function to initialize internal data. NOTE: This init function can be called multiple times if the same plugin texture is copied. Do not init global data specific to a single instance of a plugin in this function.

- *plugin_getinfo*
  This function is used to communicate information to Blender. You should never need to change it.

- *plugin_seq_doit*
  The sequence doit function is responsible for applying the plugin's effect and copying the final data into the out buffer.

  The Arguments

  - *Cast *cast*
    The Cast structure which contains the plugin data, see the *Cast* entry above.

  - *float facf0*
    The value of the plugin's IPO curve for the first field offset. If the user hasn't made an IPO curve this ranges between 0 and 1 for the duration of the plugin.

  - *float facf1*
    The value of the plugin's IPO curve for the second field offset. If the user hasn't made an IPO curve this ranges between 0 and 1 for the duration of the plugin.

  - *int x int y*
    The width and height of the image buffers, respectively.

  - *Imbuf *ibuf1*
    A pointer to the first image buffer the plugin is linked to. This will always be a valid image buffer.

  - *Imbuf *ibuf2*
    A pointer to the second image buffer the plugin is linked to. Plugins using this buffer should check for a NULL buffer, as the user may not have attached the plugin to two buffers.

- *Imbuf *out*
  The image buffer for the plugin's output.

- *Imbuf *use*
  A pointer to the third image buffer the plugin is linked to. Plugins using this buffer should check for a NULL buffer, as the user may not have attached the plugin to three buffers.

ImBuf image structure

The ImBuf structure always contains 32 bits ABGR pixel data.

ImBuf structs are always equal in size, indicated by the passed *x* and *y* value.

User Interaction

There is no way for Blender to know how many inputs a plugin expects, so it is possible for a user to attach only one input to a plugin that expects two. For this reason it is important to always check the buffers your plugin uses to make sure they are all valid. Sequence plugins should also include a text label describing the number of inputs required in the buttons interface.

```
#include "plugin.h"
char name[24]= "";

/* structure for buttons,
 * butcode name default min max 0
 */

VarStruct varstr[]= {
    { LABEL, "In: X strips", 0.0, 0.0, 0.0, ""},
};


/* The cast struct is for input in the main doit function
   Varstr and Cast must have the same variables in the same order
*/

typedef struct Cast {
    int dummy; /* because of the 'label' button */
} Cast;

/* cfra: the current frame */
```

Generic Sequence Plugin:

```
float cfra;

void plugin_seq_doit(Cast *, float, float, int, int,
                     ImBuf *, ImBuf *, ImBuf *, ImBuf *);

int plugin_seq_getversion(void) {
   return B_PLUGIN_VERSION;
}

void plugin_but_changed(int but) {
}

void plugin_init() {
}

void plugin_getinfo(PluginInfo *info) {
   info->name= name;
   info->nvars= sizeof(varstr)/sizeof(VarStruct);
   info->cfra= &cfra;

   info->varstr= varstr;

   info->init= plugin_init;
   info->seq_doit= (SeqDoit) plugin_seq_doit;
   info->callback= plugin_but_changed;
}

void plugin_seq_doit(Cast *cast, float facf0, float facf1,
                     int xo, int yo, ImBuf *ibuf1, ImBuf *ibuf2,
                     ImBuf *outbuf, ImBuf *use) {
   char *in1= (char *)ibuf1->rect;
   char *out=(char *)outbuf->rect;

}
```

Our Modifications:

The first step is to come up with a game plan. What is this plugin going to do, how are the users going to interact with it. For this example we will create a simple filter that will have a slider for intensity from 0-255. If any of the R,G, or B components of a pixel in the source image are less then our chosen intensity, it will return black and alpha, otherwise it will return whatever is in the image. Now we'll copy our generic plugin to simpfilt.c and will fill in the gaps.

Its always a good idea to add some comments. First off tell users what the plugin does, where they can get a copy, who they should contact for bugs/improvments, and any licensing restrictions on the code. When using comments make sure you use /* */ style comments. The plugins are in c and some c compilers do not accept // style comments.

```
/*
 Description: This plugin is a sample sequence plugin that
 filters out lower intensity pixels.It works on one strip as
 input.
 Author: Kent Mein (mein@cs.umn.edu)
 Website: http://www.cs.umn.edu/~mein/blender/plugins
 Licensing: Public Domain
 Last Modified: Sun Sep7 23:41:35 CDT 2003
*/
```

Next we need to fill in the Name, you should really keep this the same as your .c file. preferably descriptive, less than 23 chars, no spaces, and all lowercase.

```
char name[24]= "simpfilt.c";
```

The Cast and varstr need to be in sync.We want one silder so we'll do the folowing:

```
varStruct varstr[]= {
    { LABEL, "In: 1 strips", 0.0, 0.0, 0.0, ""},
    { NUM|INT, "Intensity", 10.0, 0.0, 255.0, "Our threshold
      value"},
};

typedef struct Cast {
    int dummy;       /* because of the 'label' button */
    int intensity;
} Cast;
```

Now we need to fill in plugin_seq_doit. We basically want to loop through each pixel and if RGB are all less than intensity set the output pixel to: 0,0,0,255 else set it to the input values for that position.

```
int x,y;

for(y=0;y cast->intensity) &&
    (in1[1] > cast->intensity) &&
        (in1[2] > cast->intensity)) {
            out[0] = out[1] = out[2] = 0;
            out[3] = 255;
        } else {
            out[0] = in1[0];
            out[1] = in1[1];
            out[2] = in1[2];
            out[3] = in1[3];
        }
    }
}
```

So we wind up with simpfilt.c

Compiling:

bmake is a simple utility (shell script) to aid in the compilation and development of plugins, and can be found in the plugins/ sub-directory of the Blender installation directory. It is invoked by: bmake (plugin_name.c) and will attempt to link the proper libraries and compile the specified C file properly for your system. If you are trying to develop plugins on a windows machine bmake may not work for you in that case you should look into using lcc. You can use the following to compile a plugin with lcc: Assuming you have your plugins in c:\blender\plugins. Here is an example of how you would compile the sequence plugin sweep.c Open a dos prompt and do the following: (Note: You'll want to make sure the lcc\bin directory is in your path)

```
cd c:\blender\plugins\sequence\sweep
lcc -Ic:\blender\plugins\include sweep.c
lcclnk -DLL sweep.obj c:\blender\plugins\include\seq.def
implib sweep.dll
```

YABLE

YAFRAY

PART VII

BEYOND BLENDER

Being Blender extensible a series of scripts to export models to other rendering engine has been written by entusiastic users.

Here we will focus only on one of them, Yable, and on one of such external rendering engines: YafRay. YafRay has been chosen among the others because it is new, it is very promising, and very actively developed by a bunch of 'historical' Blender users.

Furthermore YafRay is Open Source and the last trend is toward a very tight integration of Blender and YafRay, as you will see in the latest news in Part IX.

CH. 22 FROM BLENDER TO YAFRAY USING YABLE

by Manuel Bastioni

What is Yable?

Yable is a Python script, originally devised by Andrea Carbone, allowing to export the Blender scene in the XML format of YafRay, so to be able to exploit that engine for highly photorealistic renderings. However, Yable is not a mere "format converter", but is a truly scene processing lab that allow to assign and change the lights, materials and enviromental settings taking full advantage of YafRay features. From another point of view we could consider Yable script as a GUI, able to visualize and manage with great simplicity the large quantity of parameters used by YafRay.

Which Yable?

The first versions of Yable (end of 2002) have been realised entirely by Andrea and, afterwards, as a result of the success of the script among the users, many different versions of the script have been issued, to correct bugs and add new features. It is important to point out the contribution of Alejandro Conty Estèvez, Alfredo "Eeshlo" de Greef, Christoffer Green, Leope, Johnny "guitargeek" Matthews, Jean-Michel "jms" Soler.

After the official release of Yable 0.30 many non-official patches has been issued, generically called YableX, and published on the Yable forum on www.Kino3d.com. For the purpose of this Chapter we have examined all those versions to come up with a new "official" version and decided to base it on the latest YableX release that, thanks to modifications carry out by Jms, works with the last release of Blender.

Where to get YableX?

The two main Blender sites, which you should know by now, has links to it, anyway the last version has been realized by Jms and can be downloaded from his site Zoo-Blender (http://www.zoo-logique.org/3D.Blender/index.htm). I recommend, however, to give a look at the official YafRay forum, in the exporters section: http://www.YafRay.org

Installing the script

Yable is a script, that is a simple text file that can be loaded in Blender, hence we cannot talk properly of an installation. As a matter of facts is sufficient to load it in Blender's Text Window and press **ALT-P** to launch it. Before doing so we must anyway pay attention to two fundamental points:

* You need a full Python installation (the right one for your Blender version), downloadable at www.python.org;

* You must edit line 81 of the Yable script.

The first is a necessary condition so that the script could find the required Python modules, while the second is needed to set up the directory in which the settings and the XML generated from Yable will be saved. Setting, for example, line 81 to:

```
YABLEROOT = "C:/"
```

Implies that every time that you export a scene from a file foo.blend, a new folder called foo will be created in C:/ containing all the elements of the scene. In this way, even if you close Blender, and then you reopen the file and restart the script, Yable will be able to retrieve the settings, since it search them in a folder that it has the same name of the current .blend file.

This automatic naming is very handy, but unfortunately implies also that if we want to save the .blend file with a different name, you must re-export it from Yable at least once, so that the settings will be written again. Otherwise you can copy the contents of the old folder into the new one.

If you want, you can also set up an external viewer that start automatically in order to show the result of the rendering: If you so desire you must edit line 90, setting the VIEWERAPP variable the path to the chosen application.

As said before, all the data will be saved in the directory defined as YABLEROOT, all *except* the textures. Is important that all the images used for the scene are in the same directory, and that such directory will be indicated correctly to Yable, but this is done at run time in the pertinent Text Button appearing as soon as the script is launched (fig. 1). The *full* path to the textures is required.

The Interface

The functions of Yable have been divided in three main screens, accessible by pressing the three upper buttons that you can see in figure 2.

Workflow philosophy

Once we have created a Blender scene, with objects, materials and lights, we can load and start the script, possibly splitting the main 3D Viewport in two, and turning one of the two halves into a Text Window. This way we will be able to see at the same time the scene and Yable GUI.

The Yable Workflow is as follows:

1. Select an object of the scene;

2. Go to the Material or Light part of the interface, depending on what you are defining, and press the Get Selected button. This way Yable retrieves the settings for the object (if any);

3. Edit the attributes. These are completely independent from Blender ones!

4. Press the Assign button to assign the parameters you entered to the object. Don't forget this step! A button Assign All can be used to assign the data to all selected objects.

Global Settings

This part of the GUI allows to access the functions of general scene settings (fig. 3).

Texture path

(fig. 3 #5) - The path of the texture could be redifined anytime.

FROM BLENDER TO YAFRAY.**GLOBAL SETTINGS**

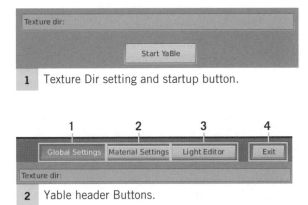

1 Texture Dir setting and startup button.

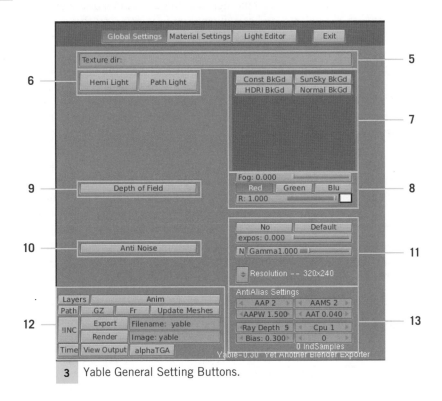

2 Yable header Buttons.

3 Yable General Setting Buttons.

Global Illumination

(fig. 3 #6) - Adds to the scene the global illumination, that is the simulation of the diffused light, originated in nature as an effect of the infinite mutual reflections and diffusions between the objects. Its effect is added to that any possible direct lights.

Path light and Hemi light are finalized to yield of the same effect, but using different algorithms that have advantages and disadvantages, for the description of which we send back to the specific YafRay Chapter.

Figure 4 shows the various options for Hemi or Path light. In the former case we can set up the colour using the Red, Green and Blue NumButton, or take the color from the background with the button Use Background color. It is possible to use this last feature when we use backgrounds based on images, even if the Use Background Button disappears by setting all the three RGB slider to 0.

In the Path Light case, on the other hand, the background image is used by default. Another difference between hemi and path light is the Depth parameter, that is referred to the number of bounces to be considered in the calculation of the exchange of reflections between the objects. To get a minimum of radiosity effect it is necessary to have at least two light interchanges.

Since the Path Light computation is rather complex a Cache option is provided, allowing to optimize and diminish the rendering times. It basically acts as a pre-process used to determine the zones of the image that need more samplings; As an example on a great flat surface we can presume that the diffuse lighting is quite uniform, and therefore we can carry out less calculations.

Parameters shared by both the global lights are the Power, the QMC, and the Samples. The Power indicates the power of the luminous emission, while the Samples indicates the accuracy of the sampling during the rendering: high values improve the clearness of the light (the hemi light have the tendency to become grainy) but this increase vary much the times required for calculation. QMC refers to the use of the Quasi Monte Carlo method for the determination of the zones to compute: it is based on sequences of quasi random numbers, and accelerates the rendering, even if, sometimes, it generate granular pattern of the image.

Background

(fig. 3 #7) - There are four options. Depending on the choice made some additional buttons appear, almost all are of immediate understanding (fig. 5).

The Const BkGd, is the easier to use (figure 5 top left): it is an homogenous colour defined by its RGB values.

The Normal BkGd (figure 5 bottom right) allows to use an image (the last version of YafRay supports JPG and TGA); the only parameter is the Power, that indicates the brilliance of the image.

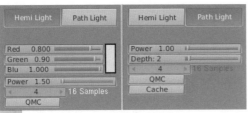

4 Yable Global Illumination settings.

5 Background settings.

The `HDRI BkGd` (figure 5 bottom left) is, perhaps, the one allowing for the maximum realism. The HDR (High Dynamic Range) Images, by storing pixel colours as floating point numbers contain many more data than other formats. Moreover, they are usually available as *probes*, that is as full 360° horizontal, 180° vertical backgrounds. After the we have obtained the appropriate images, is necessary to put them in the same folder of the textures, to write the name in the `Probe Name` button, and to set up the exposure that we want to use (positive means brighter).

Finally the `SunSky BkGd` (figure 5 top right) uses a sophisticated algorithm for the simulation of the conditions of Sun light. The position of the sun can be set by selecting an object in the Blender scene (usually an empty) and pressing the `Set Sun Pos` buttonand confirming. It is important to note that the dimension of the sun will depend also from the distance between the chosen object and the camera. A particularly important parameter for the construction of the scene is `Turbid`, that allows to regulate the value of the density of the atmospheric layers that envelop the planet: dense layers let to go through only determined wavelengths of the solar light, hence it changes both the color and the power of the light. The other buttons control the halo and the spread of the beams. The SunSky background, if used with Path Light or Hemi Light, is able to emit light in extremely realistic ways. In the case in which we don't want to use Global Illumination we can press the Sun button and Yable will add a Sun type light in the exported scene, that will simulate, more roughly but faster, the effect of the solar light.

Fog

(fig. 3 #8) - With the Fog slider we choose the amount of fog present in the scene (zero by default), while the color is chosen by selecting one of the three `Red`, `Green` and`Blue` button and by using the single Num Button below them (fig. 6).

Depht of field

(fig. 3 #9) - Is needed in order to mimic a real camera focal blur. This is a feature that YafRay will render in much shorter times than other rendering engines, because it is done as post-processing, this has some shortcomings in imprecise accounting of reflections.

The regulation is made by selecting an object whichever in the scene of Blender and pressing the button `Set Focus` (fig. 7). The point chosen in this way will be perfectly sharp. With the others two Num Buttons we can regulate the amplitude of the field depth: `Near Blur` influences on how much will the objects that are between the camera and the point of focus be blurred, while `Far Blur` affects the objects further than the focus from the camera.

Anti-noise Filter

(fig. 3 #10) - This too is a filter applied as post processing. It works in an iterative manner by taking some points within of a circular area and assign the same color if their colours differ more than a given threshold.

The amplitude of the circular area is determined by the `Radius` parameter (fig. 8), while the threshold is given by `Max Delta`. This is a very useful filter, but to use with care, because it has also a blurring effect that might compromise the quality of the result. Higher values of the delta tend to unify all.

Gamma correction, exposure, resolution

(fig. 3 #11) - A simple group of buttons that allows to set the brightness and the gamma of the complete rendering. The `No` Buttons exclude completely both post-processes. The `Default` Button that bring back the `expos` Num Button to the default value. The `Gamma` Num Button allows the regulation of the gamma (fig. 9).

The resolution Menu Button allows to choose the dimension of the rendered image. Pressing it, we can choose between the most common formats: 320x240, 480x320, 640x480, 640x512, 768x470, 1024x576, 1024x768 and 1280x960. Choosing the `Custom` option, two new buttons are visualized, that allow to set up any resolution.

FROM BLENDER TO YAFRAY.RENDERING SETTINGS

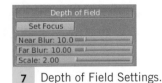

6 Fog settings.

7 Depth of Field Settings.

8 Anti Noise Filter Settings.

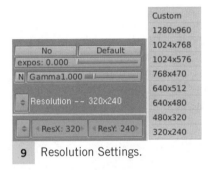

9 Resolution Settings.

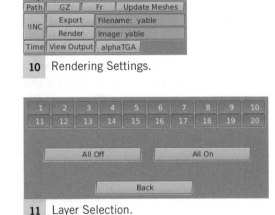

10 Rendering Settings.

11 Layer Selection.

Rendering settings

(fig. 3 #12) - This group of buttons allows to set details of the exported file and let to launch YafRay directly from Blender (fig. 10).

The fundamental keys are `Export`, `Render`, `Filename` and `Image`. The last two are needed in order to choose the name that will have the XML file and the rendered image. `Export` produces only, within the `YABLEROOT` directory all the necessary XML files while, if used with `Render`, will also execute YafRay and will produce the final image;finally, if the button View Output is also selected, at the end of the rendering Yable will launch also the application specified in `VIEWERAPP`, in order to see the result. Note that you must have YafRay in your path to be able to launch it within Blender.

The Layers button open a new panel for the choice of the layer to export (fig. 11).

The `Path` button forces the description of the scene to be exported using separate files (one main file, and sub-files to be saved in suitable folders, subdivided by materials and meshes). The location of such files will be indicated to YafRay by with the use of a full path.

To the contrary, the !INC Button will force Yable to produce a "monolithic" file. If at the moment of the export neither Path or !INC are used, Yable will use automatically the Path option.

Rendering Problems

Sometimes, by using different files, Yable incurs in some problems and may mix the objects created in previous rendering. In such case it's worthwhile to use the single file, that is surely overwritten every time, or to delete the old XMLs.

The Anim Button forces a different XML file to be exported for *each* frame of the Blender scene. Once the frames are rendered you can compose them into an animation by using Blender's Sequence Editor. The Anim button imply that the Fr (frame) button is also pressed, this adds to the chosen name for XML and images also a suffix that indicates the renderized frame. All the XMLs are saved in a separate subdirectory named as the blender file with the _MOVIE suffix.

An example

Suppose our YABLEROOT is C:/bar/ and we am working with the file robot.blend, when we press Export Yable will create, fist of all, a folder C:/bar/robot/; then, if I have used the Path option, inside of this directory will be created an XML main file, called robot.xml and two folders: Materials and Meshes, from which YafRay, reading the paths in robot.xml, will draw the datas of the materials and objects.

In the case in which we choose to use the !INC button, no folders will be created within C:/bar/robot/, but only a single file robot.xml, that contains all data.

Finally, if the Anim button has been utilized, another folder will be created, C:/bar/robot/robot_MOVIE/ containing as many XML robot.001.xml, robot.002.xml, robot.003.xml,... as there are frames in the animation.

Note that if the files of the animation are obtained with the Path option, it will be necessary to copy the Meshes and Materials folders in the robot_MOVIE folder. If the animation does not include transformations of morphing (as an example RVK), is safe to leave de-activated the button Update Mesh. Otherwise for every exported frame every mesh of the scene will be exported too.

The last three buttonsare GZ, Time, and alphaTGA: the first enable the creation of gzipped files, the second let the time employed for the rendering appear on the YafRay console and the third modifies the XML so that YafRay saves TGA images with the alpha channel.

FROM BLENDER TO YAFRAY.MATERIAL SETTINGS

Antialiasing settings

(fig. 3 #13) - AAP Num Button indicates the number of passes of antialiasing; putting it equal to zero indicates no antialias. AAMS adjust the number of samplings to use for every AA pass. AAPW adjust the pixel width parameter, that is the overlap of pixels; the range vary between 0 and 2, and using high values, we can obtains a better smoothness, even if sometimes too much accentuate. AAT establishes the value of threshold (AA_threshold) beyond which the pixel will be processed from the antialiasing: the value can vary between 0 (all points will be processed) and 1 (no pixel are processed). CPU indicates, if multiple CPU are present, how many should be usedfor rendering.

Material Settings

The second GUI panel contains the Material Setting. Here it is possible to assign to every object the material that will be used in the YafRay rendering. The Materials assigned with Yable and Blender materials are two different things: the script draws from the scene only some values, like the UV coordinates and the diffuse color. This latter only upon request of the user. The rest is all independent; from this point of view Yable is a sort of laboratory: it not only exports passively the scene, but it allows us to study and to apply new materials.

Once an object is selected we must press the Get Selected Button: new buttons will appear; containing YafRay settings if the Object already has them, or empty otherwise (fig. 12).

Shader Type

(fig. 12 #14) - This button allows to choose the Type of Material Shader to apply.

The Constant shader is the simplest, characterized only from the Red, Green and Blu Num Buttons. Crafter is a distinct case: it is an interface used to loading the Crafter shader, that is a stand alone program for the visual composition of materials. Generic is the more versatile material, and includes also the characteristics of the others, hence we will describe it deeply, using it like a paradigm for the general understanding.

Object Attributes

(fig. 12 #15) - Pressing this button some new buttons appear (fig. 12 on the right). They are very important characteristics, which are linked to the *Object* and not to the *Material* itself. The Cast Shadow toggles if the object projects shadows or not.

The Caustic IOR button enables the calculation of the caustics for the light beams that will pass through the object; these will be deflected according to the value of the refractive index indicated from CausIOR NumButton. High IOR values produce more sharp caustics (think, as an idea, to the lens that concentrates the solar beams in a point). The Receive Radio and the Emit Radio buttons, if pressed, will force the object to participate to the calculation of the global illumination, receiving and re-emitting energy. The Caustic Tcolor Num Buttons allows to specify the transmit-ted colour, that is the colour assumed from the light passing through the Object. The Caustic Rcolor Num Buttons, on the other hand, refers to the light reflected by the Object.

Note that even if we set correctly a material, it will participate to the effects of caustics and radiosity only if it is illuminated with appropriate lights, like the Path Light, or the Photon Light.

Diffuse and Specular Colors

(fig. 12 #16) - Is the basic color, and corresponds to the Diffuse Color in Blender ma-terials. The Bl button on the side is used take RGB values directly from the Blender Material. Pressing the button Add Specular Color new buttons appear similar to those just seen, used to set the specular color. Also in this case the meaning of this Colour is the same to that of Blender.

Reflection and Transmission Colours

(fig. 12 #17 and #18) - It is possible to set the Reflected and Transparency colors of the material. Note that also the transparency is set using the RGB Num Buttons to define a Colour, not just a plain "alpha" value.

The Transmit parameter does not decide the degree of transparency, but only which color of the light pass through (or is blocked by) the material. To make some example, using the black colour we impose that no color passes through the material, using the red one, we would mean that the object is transparent only for the red component of the light, using the white we let all the light to pass. Pressing also the buttons Refl2 and Transm2 which appears we can (and new RGB Num Buttons are created) define a different behaviour of the material at grazing light incidence.

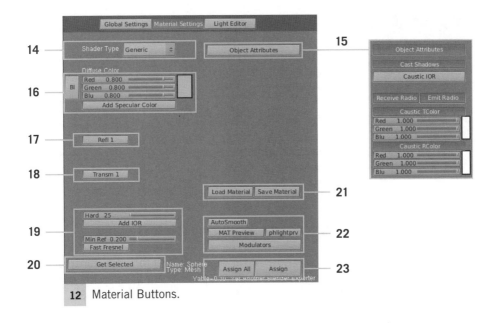

12 Material Buttons.

Hardness, Index of Refraction

(fig. 12 #19) - The `hard` parameter governs the sharpness of specular highlights exactly as in Blender. The refractive index `IOR` is fundamental in transparent objects, and is used in order to calculate the deviation of the light beams that crosses the material. As a result of this effect, the bodies immersed in a transparent medium appears to us distorted (think to a paddle immersed in the limpid water). The following table shows some IORs of common materials:

Material	IOR
Void	1.0
Air	1.00029
Ice	1.31
Water (at 20°C)	1.33
Ethylic Alcohol	1.36
Glycerin	1.473
Glass	1.52
Sapphire	1.77
Diamond	2.417

Get Selected

(fig.12 #20) - The Get Selected, to be pressed every time *after* you have selected the object and *before* starting tomodify the material.

Get Selected, Loading and saving the materials

(fig. 12 #21) - The Load Material and Save Material buttons allows to save material settings and to quickly call them back. A name can be given to each material.

Preview of the material, autosmooth and modulators

(fig. 12 #22) - The AutoSmooth Button is used to regulate the appearance of the surfaces. Pressing it an additional Num Button appears that regulated the angle under which the corner of the two facesis considered smooth, exactly as in Blender.

The Mat preview Button creates a preview of the material using a sample scene. The tga is saved in the current directory (for example, under Windows, it is saved in the folder in which the Blender executable resides.) The button phlightprv indicate "Photon Light Preview" and it is used to put a photonic light during the materials preview.

The Modulators Button allows to access a separate panel for the composition of advanced shaders formed by overlying layers. Every layer can be an image or a procedural texture. Obviously is possible to set the modality with which the layers must be mixed and also the percentage of transparency.

The panel at the beginning refers to the default modulators, that is used automatically if the Object has UV coordinates and is mapped with an image in Blender. Unfortunately, because of a bug, these formulations are not maintained by Yable, that continues to use the default settings. However all the successive layers of modulators that are added work correctly. In order to add a new component is sufficient to click on the Others button, and to choose the kind of modulator that we want. In figure 13 we see (starting from the top left, clockwise) the main panel, the panel adding new members, the menu Others, before and after the addiction of a new member:

It is possible to add an Image layer, a Clouds layer and a Marble one. The first thing is to assign a name at the modulator created, to do this it will be sufficient to write something of meaningful in place of GIVE_ME_A_NAME.

If the Modulator is an image it is necessary to insert the name of the image itself: only the name and extension, without path, which has been defined once for all before!

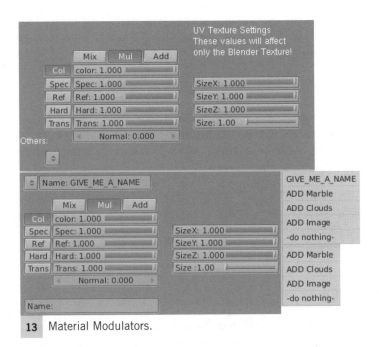

13 Material Modulators.

The parameters refers, by default, to bump mapping, that is to the relief effect that will be given to the object: using positive values rises clearer zones and lowers darker. The various size refer to the scaling of the UV coordinates (the three X, Y, Z axis may be scaled independently, or all together) while the various buttons Col, Spec, Ref, Hard and Trans have the usual meanings and indicates which characteristic, and by how much, is modified. At the end of the settings, press the Ok! button, to return to the main Material panel. At the end of the procedure the new added modulator will be in the Menu and can be selected and cancelled anytime, using the button Del that appear next to the Ok!, Canc and Back buttons.

The only type of mapping supported up to now is the UV type. It follow that the object must possess these coordinates, for which we sends back to the relevant Section of this Guide. If all is correctly executed, Yable will export automatically (without the adding of an image type modulator) both the UV coordinates and the used image. About this image we must pay attention to this: Yable does not use the image loaded in the texture of Blender's materials, but the one loaded in the Image Window (that is the one on which calculations for the positioning of the UV are made). Obviously, the images must all be in the usual folder specified at the start of the script.

Clouds and Marble Modulators insertion is similar to that for the Images, except that these panels have few additional, self explanatory, specific parameters for these two types of procedural texture.

Assign

(fig. 12 #23) - The `Assign` button finalizes the material and assigns it to the object. Don't forget this! The button Selected All allows to assign the settings to more than one selected objects.

 Saving a material and Assigning a material are two separate actions. If you assign it the Object acquires that material, if you save it, it will be available later on.

Light Settings

The lights setting in Yable is made with the same modality of the materials assignation: a light is selected in Blender, `Get Selected` is pressed andthe characteristics that we want to to export in YafRay are chosen and assigned definitively with `Assign`.

The type of light used in the scene of Blender *do not* have any relationship with the type of light that will be exported: the only parameters that will be surely conserved are the coordinates of the position of the lamp;all the rest, included the pointing direction can be assigned independently with Yable. In figure 14 we have represented a point light with the buttons Diffuse and Caustic activated, so to have an example that include the greater part of the available options.

Light Types

(fig. 14 #24) - The Menu let us choose between various types of direct light: `Point Light`, `Spot Ligth`, `Soft light`, `Area Light` and `Photon Light`. Accordingly to the light type the options immediately beneath varies. Figure 15 shows them all.

The Point lights a point source that emits light in all the directions. The power of the lamp is chosen with the `Power` Num Button, while its colour is set via RGB Num Buttons and is possible to choose if it must project or not a shadow with the `Cast Shadow` Button.

The Spot light is very similar to the Blender spot: the parameters `Blend` and `Falloff` have the same meaning, while `Width` represents the angular width of the light cone.

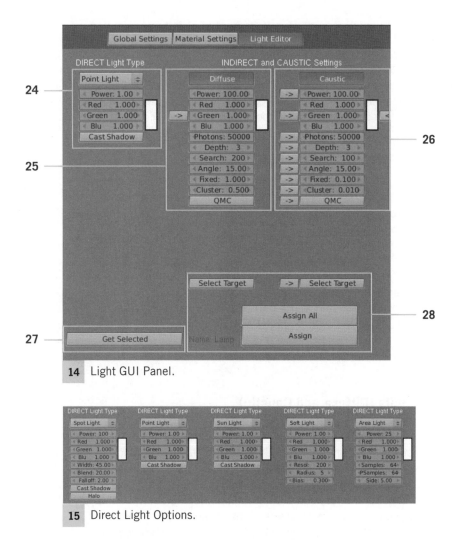

14 Light GUI Panel.

15 Direct Light Options.

Halo indicates the presence of the halo (volumetric light), by pressing it we add some new buttons: three Num Buttons for the Halo colour, Res = resolution of the shadow map, Density = quantity of fog contained in the halo, Blur = blur applied to shadow map, Samples = number of samplings used in the rendering.

The direction of the Spot is given via a target. We must press the Select Target button, select an Object to be the target of the spot in the Blender scene and finally press the Confirm Button to complete the operation.

Both the Point and the Spot light decreases following the physical law of the inverse square of the distance.

The Soft light is similar to the Pointlight, with the difference that it produces soft shadows. The shadows too much clean are one of the disadvantages of the raytrace engines, but this type of light, using a shadow map, safely resolves the problem. Besides the usual parameters, the `Radius` parameter, defines the width of the transition between shadow and light. The `Bias` parameter controls the proximity of the shadow to the object that produces it, while the `Resol` parameter controls the resolution of the shadow map: the higher is this parameter the better is the accuracy of the shadow.

The Sun light simulates the characteristic of the solar light, it seems not to decay with increasing of the distance (it is an impression due to the enormous power of the Sun). It is, therefore, a much simple light, in which we can only set up the color, and whose intensity remains constant.

The Area light is an extended luminous source. While all those already seen emit light from a point (in reality it corresponds, as an example, to the small filament of a light bulb), the area light is produced from a whole surface. YafRay admit also quadrilateral surfaces but Yable is limited to use only squares. The specific parameters are `Samples`, `Psamples` and `Side`, they are the number of general samplings, the number of samplings in the penumbra zone, and the length of the side of the light casting square.

Photon Lights (Diffuse and Caustic)

(fig. 14 #25 and #26) - Photonlight is a very peculiar kind of lamp: it behave in a more realistic way, referring itself to the theory of the light composed by a bundle of photons. These photons must literally be "shoot" towards the Objects, so as to calculate their behaviour when they travel through transparent bodies or are diffused by opaque ones. It is a very complex calculation, for which is not always desirable that it will be executed on all the elements of the scene;therefore we can specify it on a material to material and object by object basys via the parameters Receive and Emit.

Diffuse light: Enabling this button a Photon Light of Diffuse type will be add to the exported scene, overlapping the corresponding Direct light. The photons of this light have the capability to be reflected on diffusive surfaces. In this way calculations of the radiosity 'colour leakage' will be added in the rendering, to realize a realistic effect of Global Illumination. This can be done also via Path Light, but a carefully tuned Photon Light is much faster.

Caustic light: Caustic are concentrations of light caused from the refraction of the transparent objects. The Photon Light of Caustic type allows to account for this phenomenon correctly. Before going ahead, it is necessary to say that if targeted to objects with inadequate material, this light does not generate any effect. In fact the

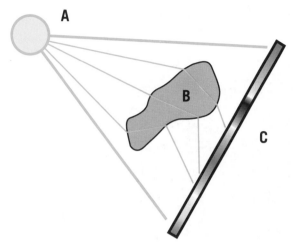

16 Caustics setup.

scene, to have caustics, must containa source light A, an opaque object C *receiving* the caustics and a transparent object B placed between these two *generating* the caustics (fig. 16).

- A must be a caustic photonlight;

- B must have a Material able to produce Caustics (exhibiting *at least* assigning at least Caustic IOR and Caustic Tcolor);

- C must have a Material able to receive the radiosity effects (for this the default material could be good, because this material export a simple shader that, without specify the received and emitted values of radiosity leave the choice to YafRay, that usually hold this values activated. If, indeed, a generic material is used, we must remember to activate the `Reiceve Radio` Toggle Button).

The Photon Light of Caustic and Diffuse type have the same parameters. The arrows button is used to impose the same value to more than one variables (for example the same color).

The `Photons` button set the number of photons that will be shot from the lamp, in common scene a few thousands of photons is enough but, to obtain a better results in terms of quality is recommended to set 50000 photons or more. The `Depth` button defines the number of bounces/transmissions the photons can do before YafRay ray tracing stops to handle it, and it is a particularly important data, mostly in the calculation of the Global illumination. 3 is a good value for acceptable results. `Search` indicates the numbers of photons that can be used to illuminate a single point of the

17 Mini modeled in Blender and rendered with YafRay.

Object surface, higher values is used to take in consideration also zones that receive few photons, with a shaded effect of illumination, while low value is used to give light only to the points really hit by photons completely, with more definite and "hard" boundaries. `Angle` is the angle of the projection cone with which the photon are shot: high values are used to cover a wide area, but with power fading when we depart from the center. `Fixed` is the abbreviation of fixedradius, and represent the radius in which the number of photons defined by `Search` must fall in order to consider the point of the surface illuminated. `cluster` is the smallest portion of lit surface able to contain a photon. The higher is this number the larger is the width of the cluster and, consequently, the less defined is the illumination effect. `QMC` is, again, the quasi-MonteCarlo method.

Yable Juicy example

What you see in (fig. 17) is a completely CG image realized by Xavier 'richie' Ligey, modelled with Blender and rendered with YafRay. The export has been made with Yable. There is no light at all in the scene, only a Hemi Light with an HDRI background. Xavier has been so kind as to give us the screenshots of the settings he has used in Yable.

Figure 18 shows the car paint, figure 19 shows the chrome material and figure 20 shows the glass material.

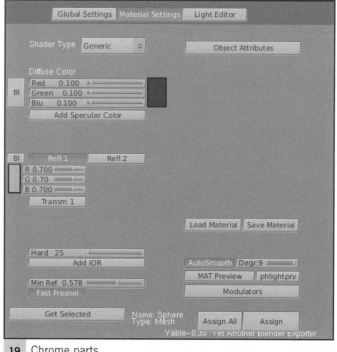

18 Car paint.

19 Chrome parts.

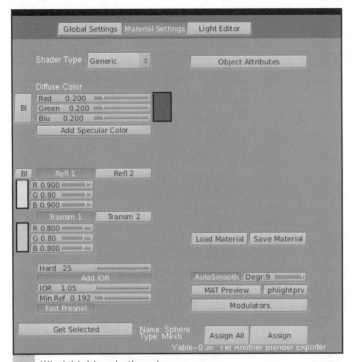

20 Windshield and other glasses.

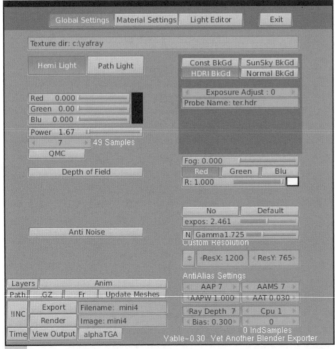

21 Scene global settings.

FROM BLENDER TO YAFRAY.THE JUICY EXAMPLE

A special thank to Alessandro Braccili, who helped me in Yable/YafRay understanding, and in the writing of this chapter.

CH. 23 YAFRAY

INSTALLATION, OVERVIEW, SHADERS, RENDERABLE OBJECTS, BACKGROUND, FILTERS

by Alejandro Conty Estevez, Chris Williamson, Johnny Matthews

By the time I started working with YafRay, I was checking out some blender exporters like BMRT and Lightflow. While I was writing some exporting and shading code, I began to be interested in how a raytracer could be written. So when the exams season was in full swing, I became bored (as weird as it may sound) and began to write the main program structure. Once I got a few test renders, I put it off for a year, till the next summer. Then, I wrote the XML loader and YafRay, called "noname" by that moment, began to be an usable program.

Alfredo joined the development almost at the same time. That was of great help. A month later a lot of necessary stuff, like acceleration, were finished and Alfredo ported a lot of his code to YafRay. As the famous hemilight.

Then Luis Fernando Ruiz, a friend of mine and classmate joined to give us a good web site. So we said good bye to that boring plain text web site. We also had the chance to see YafRay rendering on several computers concurrently when Luciano Campal wrote his hack to make YafRay able to work in a distributed way thanks to mosix. It was very exciting when we got access to a 20 computers room for testing. Things started to look very promising when Andrea came with Yable. An experimental export script for an experimental renderer that resulted in a very long thread of cool images at elYsiun. We saw the first nice images done with blender and rendered with YafRay thanks to him.

We didn't expect that boom. Neither Alfredo nor me. Of course it was the cool export script what was catching people, exporting easily from blender to a raytracer. We got very excited with all that support from the community. I still get impressed by what people can do with a simple tool like this.

Now more people are getting involved and helping. We begin to have a good documentation section and resources, most of which have been written by Chris Williamson. Basically, it's what you'll see in this chapter. But he is not the only one. YafRay is also getting very easy to use from blender thanks to Johnny Matthews. I think he spends almost every minute writting Extractor: a new export script for blender. It makes the exporting much more easy by getting all the data directly from blender with nearly no user interaction.

The current power of Extractor and its fast development point out that this could be the future official export scheme for exporting from blender. Anyway, efforts are being made to write a built-in exporter in blender. Alfredo contributed with a lot of shading compatibility code and did some experiments. So it seems we will be able to compare both python and built-in solutions at some point.

YafRay started as an experiment and still is. It's not finished and lacks a lot of features if you compare it with other render engines. I always think is not good enough and that it is hard to imagine what do people see in it. Since people like it for some reason, we now want to really convert it into a full rendering engine that deserves to be called "renderer". This will take some time to have fun coding. We want to add what YafRay lacks (particles, effects, etc...) and to improve global illumination. But only Alfredo De Greef and me are coding YafRay right not, so in order to keep the development up to an acceptable rate, we should get more people to code, more developers. I hope this happens sooner or later.

Finally, I want to thank all the blender community that supported this project. All those beautiful pictures are what really bring people to YafRay. Likewise, thanks to all the people who give ideas and thoughts on the forums to improve YafRay, and to Juan David G. Cobas for his very appreciated math support.

Installation

YafRay is available for Linux, Windows and Mac OSX. Download the package suitable for your OS at www.yafray.org.

YafRay for Windows

Run the installer program. It will create a directory called "yafray" on your c:\ drive. This directory contains the yafray.exe executable and the grammar file which are used by the loader. Also the installer copies three dll's into your Windows system directory. This dll's are for cygwin support. Finally, a batch file (yafray.bat) is copied into the Windows directory (we need this file in the PATH).

To run YafRay is easy. Just open a MS-DOS window, go to you working directory and type "yafray file.xml" or "yafray file.xml.gz". For example, if you want to work in `e:\raytracing\work` on an XML file which resides in `C:\Docs\xmls` named `test.xml`, you open a MS-DOS windows and:

```
c:\windows\>
c:\windows\> e:
e:> cd e:\raytracing\work
e:\raytracing\work> yafray c:\Docs\xmls\test.xml
```

One or more targa file, the output of the render, will be created in the `e:\raytracing\work` directory.

YafRay for Mac OSX

Expand the tarball. (stuffIt expander can expand tarball also). Double click on the expanded package to run installer. YafRay must be installed on the Root device (the one on which it has been installed MacOSX), *you cannot choose any other disk*

Installed files and location are: `/usr/sbin/yafray /usr/etc/gram.yafray`

YafRay utilization does not differ noticeably from the three OS, so you can refear to the previous section.

YafRay has just 2 files ' /usr/sbin/yafray ' and ' /usr/etc/gram.yafray' . But common user cannot acccess those directory via Mac OSX GUI usually, so the *OS X Package Manager* (OSXPM) can help you to uninstall packages from your disk.

YafRay on Linux

Expand the tarball.
`tar xvzf yafray-#.#.#.tar.gz`

Go into the newly created directory and configure it for your machine.
`./configure`

Make sure that zlib and jpeg support is enabled. If not, you need install devel pakages for libjpeg and libgz (check your distribution for it).

Build it!
`make`

If this fails you can try

```
cd src
make yafray
```

The executable is `yafray` and is a command Line program, whose usage is analogous to the what described In the "Windows" section.

Scene Description Language Overview

A YafRay Scene description file is an XML file complying to the definitions of this section. The renderer parses the XML from top to bottom. So if Block1 is referenced before Block2, it must be defined before Block2 (it must be above it in the XML)

```
<scene>

<shader type = "generic" name = "Default">;
   <attributes>
      <color r="0.750000" g="0.750000" b="0.800000" />
      <specular r="0.000000" g="0.000000" b="0.000000" />
      <reflected r="0.000000" g="0.000000" b="0.000000" />
      <transmitted r="0.000000" g="0.000000" b="0.000000" />
   </attributes>
</shader>

<transform
m00 = "8.532125" m01 = "0.000000" m02 = "0.000000" m03 = "0.000000"
m10 = "0.000000" m11 = "8.532125" m12 = "0.000000" m13 = "0.000000"
m20 = "0.000000" m21 = "0.000000" m22 = "8.532125" m23 = "0.000000"
m30 = "0.000000" m31 = "0.000000" m32 = "0.000000" m33 = "1.000000"
>
<object name = "Plane" shader_name = "Default" >
   <attributes>
   </attributes>
      <mesh>
      <include file = ".\Meshes\Plane.xml" />
      </mesh>
</object>
</transform>
```

```
<light type="pathlight" name="path" power= "1.000000" depth "2"
samples = "16" use_QMC = "on" cache"on"  cache_size="0.008000"
angle_threshold="0.200000"  shadow_threshold="0.200000" >
</light>
<camera name="Camera" resx="1024" resy="576" focal="1.015937" >
   <from x="0.323759" y="-7.701275" z="2.818493" />
   <to x="0.318982" y="-6.717273" z="2.640400" />
   <up x="0.323330" y="-7.523182" z="3.802506" />
</camera>

<filter type="dof" name="dof" focus = "7.97854234329" near_blur
"10.000000" far_blur "10.000000" scale "2.000000">
</filter>

<filter type"antinoise" name"Anti Noise" radius = "1.000000"
max_delta = "0.100000">
</filter>

<background type = "HDRI" name = "envhdri" exposure_adjust = "1">
   <filename value = "Filename.HDR" />
</background>

<render camera_name = "Camera" AA_passes = "2" AA_minsamples =
"2" AA_pixelwidth = "1.500000" AA_threshold = "0.040000"
   raydepth = "5" bias = "0.300000" indirect_samples = "1" gamma =
   "1.000000" exposure = "0.000000" background_name"envhdri" >
   <outfile value="butterfly2.tga"/>
   <save_alpha value="on"/>
</render>
</scene>
```

Dont worry! Its not as complex as it looks. Concentrate on the bold highlited tags.

The Tags work similar to HTML tags (also like brackets) each tag must have an opposite closing tag. Two tags together, with settings inside, is one block. A block can tell the renderer how to shade something, how big to render the image, what the shape of an object looks like, where it is etc etc.

In the example above, first a shader is defined, then an object (which is wrapped in its Transform Matrix), then a light is added then a camera, a filter, a background and finally the render settings (notice the closing </scene> tag)

Shaders

Base Shaders

These shader blocks determine the BiDirectional Reflectivity Function (BDRF) or Illumination Model that the object is shaded with. Each different base shader type has various inputs that can receive the outputs from other shader blocks, altering the surface characteristics .

Constant
A uniformly constant shader

```
<shader type = "constant" name = "Sphere.mat">
   <attributes>
      <color r="15.000000" g="15.000000" b="15.000000" />
   </attributes>
</shader>
```

Generic
The most versatile shader

```
<shader type = "generic" name = "Sphere.mat">
   <attributes>
      <color r="0.800000" g="0.800000" b="0.800000" />
      <specular r="1.000000" g="1.000000" b="1.000000" />
      <reflected r="0.000000" g="0.000000" b="0.000000" />
      <reflected2 r="1.000000" g="1.000000" b="1.000000" />
      <transmitted r="0.197183" g="0.197183" b="0.225352" />
      <transmitted2 r="1.000000" g="1.000000" b="1.000000" />
      <hard value = "25.000000"/>
      <IOR value = "1.592105"/>
      <min_refle value = "0.200000"/>
      <fast_fresnel value = "off"/>
   </attributes>
</shader>
```

Phong
Classic Phong shader

```
<shader type="phong" name="phongshader">
   <attributes>
      <environment value="fresnel"/>
```

```
    <<color value="rgb"/>
  </attributes>
</shader>
```

Procedural

These Shading blocks create various procedural patterns with inline values. No inputs are needed.

Marble

```
<shader type="marble" name="Marble" size="4.00" depth="4"
hard="off" turbulence="5" sharpness="5.00">
  <attributes>
  </attributes>
</shader>
```

- `size` : size of the marble effect, lower numbers = less veins, higher numbers = more veins
- `depth` : controls the number of iterations (number of noise frequencies added to the swirl)
- `hard` : controls the noise type, when set to "off" the noise varies smoothly while setting it to "on" will show more abrupt changes in color
- `turbulence` : controls the amount of noise turbulence
- `sharpness` : controls the sharpness of color 1 compared to color 2, the higher this value, the thinner the color band of color1. This effect is similar to the soft/sharp/sharper switches of the Blender marble texture, the difference is that it is more controlable here. The value must be at least 1 or higher.

Wood

```
<shader type="wood" name="Wood" size="5.00" depth="5" hard="off"
turbulence="40">
  <attributes>
  <ringscale_x value="5" />
  <ringscale_y value="5" />
  </attributes>
</shader>
```

1 Marble Shader.

2 Wood Shader.

3 Clouds Shader.

- `size`: size of the wood effect, lower numbers = less wood grain, higher numbers = more wood grain
- `depth` : controls the number of iterations (number of noise frequencies added to the swirl)
- `hard` : controls the noise type, when set to "off" the noise varies smoothly while setting it to "on" will show more abrupt changes in color
- `turbulence` : controls the amount of noise turbulence
- `ringscale_x` : controls the width of the wood rings in the x axis
- `ringscale_y` : controls the width of the wood rings in the y axis

Clouds

```
<shader type="clouds" name="Clouds" size="5.000" depth="3">
   <attributes>
   </attributes>
</shader>
```

- `size` : size of the cloud effect
- `depth` : controls the number of iterations (number of noise frequencies added to the swirl)

Meta Shaders

These allows the modification of other shader and the building of "chains" of simple shader to build a comlex shader

Color2float shading block
Takes a color as input & outputs a float

```
<shader type="color2float" name="c2f" input="input" >
    <attributes>
    </attributes>
</shader>
```

- `input` : input (color) to convert to float

Colorband shading block
Builds a color from a value input and a gradient. An unlimited number of modulators add nodes to the gradient. The shader interpolates the color values of the nodes at the given input value. In the below example, an input value of 0.12 would generate a colour between the first and second node, which are black and orange. So a dark orange would be the result.

```
<shader type="colorband" name="Colorband" >
    <attributes>
        <input value="Wood" />
    </attributes>
    <modulator value="0.00"><color r="0.00" g="0.00" b="0.00" />
    </modulator>
    <modulator value="0.26"><color r="1.00" g="0.36" b="0.00" />
    </modulator>
    <modulator value="0.66"><color r="1.00" g="1.00" b="0.00" />
    </modulator>
    <modulator value="1.00"><color r="1.00" g="1.00" b="1.00" />
    </modulator>
</shader>
```

Conetrace block
It can be used to get reflections or transmited color from environment. But it could be used also to get blurry ones.

```
<shader type="conetrace" name="env1" reflect="on/off"
angle="number"
samples="number" IOR="number">
    <attributes>
        <color ... />
    </attributes>
</shader>
```

YAFRAY.SHADERS

4 Spheres with varying levels of blurry reflections & refractions & a HDRI background.

5 Clouds shader & coords shader (z) into multiply shader.

- `reflect` : on will reflect the ray, off will refract the ray. angle: angle of the cone (around the ray) to be sampled, 0 for a simple sharp reflection/refraction
- `samples`: number of samples to take inside the cone IOR: index of refraction color: color to filter the incoming light

Coords shading block
Outputs a float based on object coords

```
<shader type="coords" name="PosY" coord="Y" >
   <attributes>
   </attributes>
</shader>
```

- `coord` : coordinate to use, either X, Y or Z

Float2color shading block
Takes a float as input & outputs a color

```
<shader type="float2color" name="f2c" input="input" >
   <attributes>
   </attributes>
</shader>
```

- `input` : input (float) to convert to color

6 Mixing fresnel & conetrace blocks.

Fresnel shading block
Can be used to get realistic reflections/refractions based on the angle of incidence

```
<shader type="fresnel" name="fresnel1" reflected="..."
transmitted="..."
   IOR="number" min_refle="number">
   <attributes>
   </attributes>
</shader>
```

- `reflected`: the input to use as reflected color (usually the conetrace output)
  transmitted: the input to use as transmitted color (usually another conetrace out put)
- `IOR`: index of refraction min_refle: minimal reflection amount.

HSV shading block
Builds a color from either any inputs or inline values for HSV components.

```
<shader type="HSV" inputhue="..."  inputsaturation="..."
inputvalue="..."
   hue="number" saturation="number" value="number" >
</shader>
```

As in the RGB color, if the inputs are omited, inline hue/saturation/value values are used.

YAFRAY.SHADERS

Image shading block
Assigns a bitmap image to the object according to its UV co-ordinates (outputs Color)

```
<shader type = "image" name = "bitmap">
<attributes>
   <filename value = "c:\filename.tga" />
</attributes>
</shader>
```

- `filename` : Path & name of bitmap to apply

Mix shading block
Mixes 2 inputs in different ways, depending on the mode used

```
<shader type="mix" name="mixMode" input1="Colorband0"
input2="Colorband" mode="add">
   <attributes>
   </attributes>
</shader>
```

- `input1` : First input to mix
- `input2` : Second input to mix
- `mode` : Possible mix modes (note, some modes output different results depending on the order of the imputs)

These are: Add, Average, Color Burn, Color Dodge, Darken, Difference, Exclusion, Freeze, Hard Light, Lighten, Multiply, Negation, Overlay, Reflect, Screen, Soft light, Stamp, Subtractive,

Multiply shading block
Multiplies (float) input values or input value and const value, outputs a float

```
<shader type="mul" name="Multiply" input1="input" input2="null"
value="5.30">
   <attributes>
   </attributes>
</shader>
```

7 Multiply shader with wood & marble as input.

8 Wood shader is input for sin, which in turn is an input for the Hue channel of an HSV shader - the color value of a phong shader.

- `input1` : First input to multiply
- `input2` : Second input to multiply (if null, input1 is multiplied with the inline 'value' setting)
- `value` : Value to multiply if input2 is null

RGB shading block
Builds a color from either any inputs or inline values for RGB components.

```
<shader type="RGB" inputred="..." inputgreen="..." inputblue="..." >
  <color ...>
</shader>
```

If one of the inputs is omited, then the default color given by "color" tag is used for that input.

Sin shading block
Generates float values based on sine wave and input.

```
<shader type="sin" name="Sin" input="input" >
  <attributes>
  </attributes>
</shader>
```

Wood shader is input for sin, which in turn is an input for the Hue channel of an HSV shader - the color value of a phong shader

Renderable Objects

yafray currently supports only Mesh Objects. An example of a simple tringular planar plate is:

```
<transform
m00 = "0.997525" m01 = "0.070303" m02 = "0.001329" m03 = "0.115816"
m10 = "-0.018745" m11 = "0.284097" m12 = "-0.958612" m13 = "1.522439"
m20 = "-0.067771" m21 = "0.956215" m22 = "0.284711" m23 = "3.272361"
m30 = "0.000000" m31 = "0.000000" m32 = "0.000000" m33 = "1.000000"
>

<object name = "Plane.002" shader_name = "Plane.002.mat" caus_IOR
= "1.500000" recv_rad = "on" emit_rad "on" shadow = "on">
   <attributes>
      <caus_tcolor r = "1.000000" g = "1.000000" b = "1.000000"/>
      <caus_rcolor r = "1.000000" g = "1.000000" b = "1.000000" />
   </attributes>
      <mesh autosmooth = "30.0" >
<points>
   <p x"4.403727"  y="-4.403728"  z="0.000000" />
   <p x="-4.403727"  y="-4.403727"  z="0.000000" />
   <p x="-4.403725"  y="4.403728"  z="0.000000" />
</points>
<faces>
   <f a="0" b="2" c="1" />
            </faces>
      </mesh>
</object>
</transform>
```

Transform tag

The Transform tag defines the transform matrix for the enclosed object (position, scale and rotation from the world origin point)

Object tag

The object tag defines the object geometry, it has a series of parameters:

- `caus_IOR`: Index of Refraction for Caustic Photons
- `recv_rad`: whether to receive radiosity (bounced light generated from Photon Lights)(on or off)
- `emit_rad`: whether to emit radiosity (on or off)
- `shadow`: whether or not to cast a shadow (on or off)
- `caus_tcolor`: the colour to tint transmitted photons (colours the refractive caustics)
- `caus_rcolor`: the colour to tint reflected photons (colours the reflective caustics)

The Mesh tag:

The key tag within an object definition is the Mesh tag, which define its geometry:

- `autosmooth`: threshold angle for the smoothing algorhythm (omit to get 'faceted' objects)

Within the mesh tag a <points> block defines the vertices of the mesh, while a <faces> block defines triangular faces by the indices of their three vertices.

Lights

yafray provides several kind of lights:

Spot Light

This is fairly similar to Blender's Spot Light

```
<light type="spotlight" name="spot" power="30.0" size="80"
blend="10"
beam_falloff="2" halo="on" res="512" blur="0.0" fog_density="0.20">
   <from x="-0.140436" y="4.175604" z="8.336139" />
   <to x="-0.140436" y="4.175604" z="0" />
   <color r="1" g="1" b="1" />
   <fog   r="1" g="1" b="1" />
</light>
```

YAFRAY.LIGHTS

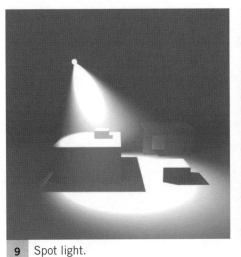

9 Spot light.

10 Point light.

- `size`: angle of the cone (half of blender's one!)
- `blend` and `beam_falloff`: same as in blender
- `halo`: Whenever to cast volumetic light and shadows or not
- `res`: Resolution of the shadowmap (only for volumetric shadows by now)
- `blur`: Blur applied to the volumetric shadows range from 0.0 to 1.0
- `fog_density`: Amount of fog in the halo
- `samples`: Number of samples to use for halo rendering. By default the same as res. The more samples, the less noise
- `from`: position of the light
- `to`: target of the light
- `color`: color of the light
- `fog`: color of volumetric light

Point Light

This is fairly similar to Blender's Lamp... but it casts shadows!

```
<light type = "pointlight" name= "omniLight" power= "1.000000"
cast_shadows= "on" >
    <from x="6.372691" y="3.340035" z="2.815973" />
    <color r="1.000000" g="1.000000" b="0.000000" />
</light>
```

- `power:` light intensity
- `cast_shadows` whether or not to cast (raytraced) shadows ('on' or 'off')
- `from:` position of the light
- `color:` rgb color of the light

Sun Light

This is again similar to Blender's Sun... but it casts shadows!

```
<light type ="sunlight" name="Lamp.001" power="1.000000" cast_
shadows="on">
    <from x="0.026929" y="-0.071142" z="3.552329" />
    <color r="1.000000" g="1.000000" b="1.000000" />
</light>
```

- `power:` intensity of the sunlight
- `cast_shadows:` whether or not to cast shadows (on or off)
- `from:` position of the light (direction is automatically towards the origin!)
- `color:` color of the light

Soft Light

```
<light type= "softlight" name="softomni" power="1.000000"
res="512" radius="5.000000" bias="0.300000" >
    <from x="0.026929" y="-0.071142" z="3.552329" />
    <color r="1.000000" g="1.000000" b="1.000000" />
</light>
```

- `power:` intensity of the light
- `res:` resolution of the shadowmap
- `radius:` radius of the blur (between shadowed & non-shadowed areas, creates the 'soft' look)
- `bias:` bias of the shadow map. 'Closeness' of the shadow to the object, if you have shadow that 'leaks' into areas it shouldn't, try decreasing the shadow bias.

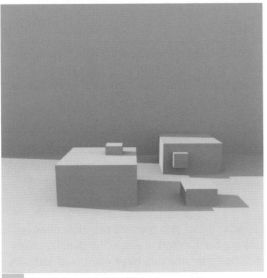

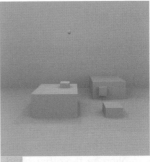

12 A soft light (dot represents light position).

13 Arealight, with Hemilight (white dot represents light position).

11 Sunlight, with hemilight to provide some diffuse shading.

Area Light

This is a light shed uniformly by a quadrilateral

```
<light type "arealight" name"Lamp.001" power="25.000000" samples="64.000000"
psamples="64.000000">
    <d  x = "-2.800729"  y = "-0.566380"  z = "3.235599" />
    <c  x = "-0.686398"  y = "-1.759042"  z = "3.833231" />
    <b  x = "0.541875"  y = "0.418420"  z = "3.833231" />
    <a  x = "-1.572455"  y = "1.611082"  z = "3.235599" />
    <color r="1.000000" g="1.000000" b="1.000000" />
</light>
```

- power: Intensity of the light
- samples: samples across area light surface
- psamples: penumbra predictionn (quality of blurred shadow edges)
- a,b,c & d: positions of the 4 corners of the rectangle that makes up the area light (Beware of orientation!)

Path Light

This indirect lighting system performs 'global illumination' by taking light from background and diffuse objects. It uses either a Monte Carlo raytracing algorythm (MC), or a Quasi Monte Carlo raytracing algorhythm (QMC). The results from either system can be rendered using an Irradiance Cache.

Since MC uses random sampling the results can be quite noisy. The more samples you take the less noise you'll see. Of course this results in longer render time. QMC sampling on the other hand produces less noise, but sometimes can result in descernable patterns in the shading of objects. Both noise and patterns can be reduced with yafray builtin Anti Noise Filter.

Path Light will produce nice radiosity effects. It can also produce caustics, however, as the photons that produce the caustics are not focused in a specific direction like the photon light, the caustic patterns will be softer unless a huge number of samples are taken.

```
<light type = "pathlight" name = "path" power = "1.000000" depth
= "2" caus_depth = "4" samples = "16" use_QMC = "on" cache =
"on" cache_size = "0.008000" angle_threshold = "0.200000" shadow_
threshold = "0.200000">
</light>
```

- power: intensity of the light
- samples: Number of samples to take per pixel to get a quick and dirty preview of your render, you can set this number low, then raise it to get the final render.
- depth: Number of ray bounces for each sample, at least 2 to get indirect lighting.
- caus_depth: Number of ray bounces when passing through caustic objects
- use_QMC: Whenever this is set 'on' will use quasi montecarlo sampling.
- cache: When this is set to on, Yafray will perform a prepass render to generate an irradiance cache
- cache_size: the size of the grid in the irradiance cache. smaller values will mean a higher resolution irradiance cache (& longer prepass times)
- angle_threshold: the angle between surface normals that determine whether the caching algorhythm considers the surface 'flat', if the surface normal variation is higher than this,the caching algorhytm takes more samples
- shadow_threshold: the minimum distance from the sample point an object can be before the caching algorhytm takes more samples

Using the Cached Pathlight

Using the Irradiance Cache feature can be tricky, the results are well worth it, as you can usually get the same quality image in a fraction of the render time.

The cache size is the size of a grid that the scene is divided up into. As the rays are shot into the scene, they intersect objects, the point at which the ray intersects the object will therefore fall into one of the boxes formed by the cache grid. At the time the ray hits this point the renderer first asks:

1. "Are there any other sample points within this box?" if the answer is no, a sample is taken, if there are other samples in the box it moves on to the next question:

2. "Are the surface normals of the other samples different to my current point?" (the angle of difference is defined by "angle_threshold") if the answer is yes, a sample is taken, if the surface normals are all the same it moves on to the next question:

3. "Is the Intersection Point close to any other object?" (the distance threshold is defined by "shadow_threshold" & the distance between the intersection point & the existing sample points plays a part) if the answer is yes, more samples are taken, if no, the sample point is skipped & the renderer moves on to the next intersection point.

By doing this, the renderer finds areas of the image that need more samples (areas of high detail), & areas that need less samples (Areas that have low detail, such as flat walls). Taking samples is the time consuming part of Global Illumination, by only taking samples where they are neccesary the cached pathlight can produce fantastic images in a comparatively short time.

It does rely on some manual tweaking to find the 'sweet spot' for the settings for any given scene. If the cache size is too small, practically every sample point will be taken anyway, as the the answer to question 1 will almost alway be 'no'. On the other hand if the cache size is too big, the distance in between sample points (which plays a part in determining whether another object is considered 'close') will be such that the answer to question 3 will almost always be 'yes'. Both of these situations will result in more samples being taken & the render taking longer.

Hemi Light

This indirect lighting system performs what is commonly called an 'Occlusion pass'. This produces a fast diffuse light in the scene by ignoring objects surface properties (colour) & just determining whether the point in question is in shadow or not. Because

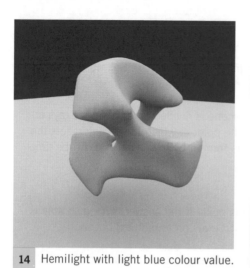

14 Hemilight with light blue colour value.

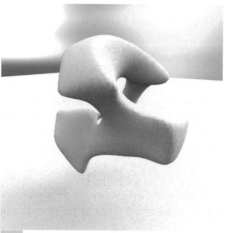

15 Hemilight with an HDRI image.

of this, the Hemilight will not produce colour bleeding between objects (unlike the pathlight). It uses either a Monte Carlo raytracing algorythm (MC), or a Quasi Monte Carlo raytracing algorhythm (QMC). Since MC uses random sampling the results can be quite noisy. The more samples you take the less noise you'll see, of course this results in longer render time. QMC sampling on the other hand produces less noise, but sometimes can result in descernable patterns in the shading of objects. Both noise and patterns can be reduced with yafray builtin Anti Noise Filter.

The Hemilight will assume that the scene is evenly lit, as if a huge sphere surounded the scene, lighting it with the color you specify in the 'color' tag. If you omit the color tag altogether, the hemilight will sample the render background if available (you can use this with HDRI backgrounds to get fast & realistic lighting simulations for compositing into a real scene).

```
<light type="hemilight" name="sky" power= "0.500000" samples =
"20" use_QMC = "on">
   <color r ="0.800000" g ="0.900000" b ="1.000000" />
</light>
```

- power: intensity of the light
- samples: Number of samples to take. Higher samples will mean a smoother result, but longer render times
- use_QMC: Whenever this is set 'on' will use quasi montecarlo sampling
- color: color of the diffuse light

Photon light

This is a focused light to produce radiosity and caustics effects.

```
<light type= "photonlight" name="Lamp.002caus" power =
"100.000000" photons = "50000" depth = "3" search = "100" angle =
"15.000000"
    mode = "caustic" fixedradius = "0.100000" cluster = "0.010000"
    use_QMC = "off" >
    <from x="6.372691" y="3.340035" z="2.815973" />
    <to x="0.285646" y="0.149627" z="1.397566" />
    <color r="1.000000" g="1.000000" b="1.000000" />
</light>
```

- `name`: Photonlight name
- `power` Scales the effect of the photon light, whether it be caustic or diffuse
- `mode`: sets the photon light to either diffuse, or caustic as detailed below
- `photons` number of photons to trace, the more photons, the more information to generate the photonmap from. Generally speaking, you should need less photons for diffuse photonlights
- `depth`: amount of reflections (bounces) or refractions the photons will perform
- `search`: Number of photons to gather while shading. higher values will soften the effect (when increasing the search, you should also increase the fixedradius)
- `fixedradius`: search radius when looking for photons (number of photons looked for is defined by 'search'
- `cluster`: this defines the smallest unit in the photonmap created. The smaller the number, the finer the photonmap
- `use_QMC`: Whenever this is set 'on' will use quasi monte carlo raytracing[1].
- `from`: position of the light
- `to`: target of the light
- `angle`: similar to size value for the spotlight, angle of the photon 'beam'
- `color`: color of the light

Photon lights have two modes, "caustic" and "diffuse". In the first mode the light will draw reflected and transmited photons, causing light to form caustic patterns of light that travel through transparent objects (ie objects that have the appropriate settings in their *Object* tag. In "diffuse" mode photons are reflected by diffuse surfaces in random directions to perform "radiosity" or "Global Illumination". In both modes only indirect light is stored (photons which have bounced at least once), so direct lighting still has to be done with a normal light.

Why not to work in both modes? You usually put different photon values for caustics than for radiosity. The needs change so is better to have two different lights for each task.

---

[1] http://www.coala.uniovi.es/wiki/index.php/YafrayGlossaryQMC

Tuning Photonlights

Photons

Choose a good value depending on the task, For radiosity you'll need few photons. For the caustics it depends on what resolution you want in the shapes.

Search, fixed radius & cluster

These settings are closely linked, you need to get the combination of all three settings right to acheive good looking results. The search setting defines how many photons to look for from a point, the fixed radius defines how far from that point to look for the photons. Once the photons have been gathered, the fixed radius area is gridded up into small 'clusters', the size of which is defined by the cluster setting. Any photons within the same cluster are averaged into one result (equivilent to 1 pixel in the photonmap).

If your diffuse or caustic effects look fractured into geometric shapes, the algorhythm is not finding the required number of photons (search) within the defined radius (fixed_radius). To fix this you need to make sure there are enough photons within the search radius to reach the search amount. To acheive this, you could either increase the total amount of photons (photons), increase the search radius (fixed_radius), or decrease the amount of photons searched for (search). Increasing the number of photons will slow down the first pass, you will probably have to add a *lot* more photons to see much change . Increasing the search radius will show results quickly but is also reliant on there being enough photons in the scene initially. large differences between the fixed_radius & cluster settings (eg high fixed radius & low cluster) will greatly increase rendering time (which makes sense, as each sample (which will be large due to the high fixed_radius) is being split into a lot of tiny clusters (because of the small cluster size). A good rule of thumb is:

fixed_radius/cluster = sqrt(search)

this means that if you are trying for 100 photons (search = 100) then fixed_radius divided by cluster should equal 10 (sqrt(100)=10) so if we set a cluster size of .01 then fixed_radius should be around .1 ((10*.01 = .1) = (.1/.01 = 10)).

Background

Adds a background image (environment map), colour or sky to your render.

Pathlight and Hemilight can sample the background colour and intensity to simulate real world lighting.

YAFRAY.BACKGROUND

Normal Image Background

```
<background type="image" name="envnorm" power="1.000000">
    <filename value="C:\directory\image.jpg"/>
</background>
```

- `type` - `image`: Allows you to use a bitmap image of one of the supported texture formats as a background. The image is mapped around the scene as a sphere, so the image should be in lattitude/longitude format (ratio 2:1)
- `name`: Background Name
- `Power`: Level of brightness of the bitmap. 1.0 is default, greater numbers will increase brightness, lower numbers will decrease brightness
- `filename`: full path & filename of the image, including the file extension

HDRI Background

```
<background type = "HDRI" name = "envhdri" exposure_adjust = "0">
    <filename value = "C:\directory\image.hdr" />
</background>
```

- `type` - `HDRI`: allows you to use a HDR image as a background. The HDRI is mapped around the scene as an angular map, not latitude longitude like the normal image background
- `name`: Background Name
- `exposure_adjust`: Similar to 'power' for a normal image background. 0 is default, increasing this will brighten the HDR, decreasing will darken (equivilent to adjusting the f-stop on a physical camera)
- `filename`: full path & filename of the HDRI, including the file extension

Constant Background

```
<background type="constant" name = "constbackg">
    <color r="1.000000" g="1.000000" b="1.000000"/>
</background>
```

- `type` - `constant`: lets you assign a single colour as the background
- `name`: Background Name
- `color`: r - red value of color (0.000000 - 1.000000) g - green value of color (0.000000 - 1.000000) g - green value of color (0.000000 - 1.000000). 1/1/1 is white, 0/0/0 is black

Sun/Sky Background

```
<background type="sunsky" name ="Sun1" turbidity ="4.000000"
add_sun="on" sun_power="1.000000"
    a_var="1.000000" b_var="1.000000" c_var="1.000000"
    d_var="1.000000" e_var="1.000000" >
    <from x="-0.007401" y="8.589217" z="3.737965"/>
</background>
```

- `type - sunsky`: lets you assign a realistic sky background with optional sun
- `turbidity`: Atmosphere density (eg mist/fog) the lower the number, the less visible the sky is. A value of 4 is a clear sky.

Camera

```
<camera name="Camera" resx="1024" resy="576" focal="1.015937">
    <from x="0.323759" y="-7.701275" z="2.818493"/>
    <to x="0.318982" y="-6.717273" z="2.640400"/>
    <up x="0.323330" y="-7.523182" z="3.802506"/>
</camera>
```

- `Name`: Name of the camera
- `resx`: Horizontal resolution (rendered image width in pixels)
- `resy`: Vertical Resolution (rendered image height in pixels)
- `res`: Resolution of the shadowmap (only for volumetric shadows by now)
- `focal`: Field of View. Equivilent to lens length in real world camera - 1.093 is roughly 35mm, 6.25 is roughly 200mm
- `from`: Position of the camera
- `to`: Target of the camera
- `up`: Cameras "Up Vector" - defines what is considered the 'up' direction of the camera

Render

Outputs an image file, based on the input from a 'Camera' block

You can have as many camera blocks and/or render blocks within the same XML, to save out the same view, with different output settings, or several different views (cameras) at various resolutions, with different backgrounds

Multiple View

YAFRAY.CAMERA

```
<render camera_name = "Camera" AA_passes = "2" AA_minsamples =
"2" AA_pixelwidth = "1.500000" AA_threshold = "0.040000"
   raydepth = "5" bias = "0.300000" gamma = "1.000000" exposure =
   "0.000000" background_name="background>
   <outfile value="C:\yablex\texture sample\texture sample.tga"/>
   <save_alpha value="on" />
</render>
```

- `AA_passes` : Sets the number of anti-alias passes to perform. A value of 0 means no anti-aliasing is done.
- `AA_minsamples` : Sets the number of samples per pass.

There are several ways to use these two parameters. You can set 'AA_minsamples' to a certain number, and set 'AA_passes' to 1, then after a first render pass all pixels which need it will be anti-aliased using the full number of samples set with 'AA_minsamples'. The old method is equivalent to setting 'AA_minsamples' to 1 and 'AA_passes' to the number of samples, then all pixels will be continually checked if they still need extra samples, this is in fact slower for normal raytracing pictures, but can be faster when rendering with hemi- or path-light. However, due to internal limitations this doesn't work well with high sample settings. You can also combine both methods, check pixels every pass and take more samples per pass at the same time, for instance for 16 samples total, you could try setting both AA_passes and AA_minsamples to 4 (4 x 4 = 16).

- `AA_pixelwidth` : Sets the amount of overlap of pixels used for AA.

The range is 1 to 2 (common choices are 1.5 or 2.0), the higher, the better and smoother the AA, but depending on your preference you might find the image to look a bit blurred. A value of 1.0 is equivalent to the old method.

- `AA_threshold` : Sets the threshold value at which point a pixel is considered for anti-aliasing.

The range is from 0.0 (anti-alias every pixel) to 1.0 (no anti-aliasing).

Since QMC is used, settings with low sample settings like in the example above can produce quite good results nevertheless.

Anti-aliasing is also done on the alpha channel.

- `save_alpha` : To save a rendered targa image with the alpha channel set value="on"

Filters

Anti Noise Filter

```
<filter type="antinoise" name="Anti Noise" radius = "1.000000"
max_delta = "0.100000">
</filter>
```

- `type-antinoise`: Post processes the rendered image, reducing noise resulting from too few pathlight, hemilight, or conetraced samples
- `name`: Name of the filter
- `radius`: Amount of blur to apply to the areas considered to have noise
- `max_delta`: Tolerance setting for noise. With higher values, more of the image will be considered 'noise' & will have the blur applied to them.

Depth of Field Filter

```
<filter type="dof" name="dof" focus = "12.5" near_blur
="10.000000" far_blur ="10.000000" scale ="2.000000">
</filter>
```

- `type-dof`: Post processes the rendered image, using depth information to apply an out of focus effect
- `name`: Name of the filter
- `focus`: Distance from the camera that is in focus (objects further away & closer than this point will be out of focus)
- `near_blur`: Amount to blur objects in front of the focus point.
- `far_blur`: Amount to blur objects behind the focus point.
- `scale`: Scales the area that is in focus. Higher values will decrease the effect of depth of field as the out of focus areas are pushed away from the focus area.

The Depth of Field filter is a 2D filter, ie a post processing technique, & as such, has advantages & disadvantages. It uses the rendered image, plus a Z Buffer (which tells the filter how far away each pixel is from the camera) to figure out which pixels are blurred or not blurred.

because its a 2D effect it has the advantage of being extremely quick. However there are a few disadvantages:

Reflections are not blurred correctly, if you look at a reflection, you'll notice that the reflection's blur is based on the distance from the camera of the *reflection plane*, not the *object in the reflection*

Because the DOF is done on a 2D image, rather than a 3D scene, the blur cannot know what is behind any given object, therefore often the edges of an extremely blurred object in the foreground will look smudgy or dirty.

If you keep these limitations in mind, the Depth of Field filter can produce great looking Depth of Field effects very quickly.

PART VIII

REFERENCE

This Part holds a detailed reference of all buttons, commands and windows.

CH. 24 BLENDER WINDOWS

GENERAL INTRODUCTION

This Chapter describes the general functions of the mouse and keyboard, both of which work uniformly throughout the Blender interface. Each Blender window also offers a number of specific options. These options are described in the following Chapters.

The Mouse

Each time you place the mouse cursor over the edge of a Blender window, the mouse cursor changes shape. When this happens, the following mouse keys are activated:

LMB (hold-move)

Drag the window edge horizontally or vertically. The window edge always moves in increments of 4 pixels, making it relatively easy to move two window edges so that they are precisely adjacent to each other, thus joining them.

MMB or RMB

A PopupMenu (fig. 1) prompts for Split Area, Join Areas or No Header.

Choosing Split Area, Blender allows you to indicate the exact split point or to cancel split by pressing **ESC**. Split divides the window into two windows, creating an exact copy of the original window.

Choosing Join Areas, Windows with a shared edge are joined if possible. The active Window remains.

If there is no Header in the Window, the Popup Menu contains also the item Add Header.

BLENDER WINDOWS.GENERAL INTRODUCTION

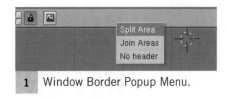

1 Window Border Popup Menu.

2 The Window Header.

3 Window Header Popup Menu.

The Window Header

Blender window headers (fig. 2), or toolbar, offer the following extra options in combination with mouse keys:

LMB on the header

The entire Blender window pops to the foreground.

CTRL LMB on the header

The entire Blender window pops to the background.

MMB (hold-move) on the header

If the Blender window is not wide enough to display the entire header, the **MMB** key can be used to horizontally pan the header.

RMB on the header

A PopupMenu (fig. 3) appears asking for Top, Bottom or No Header. That way the header can be moved to the top or the bottom of the Blender window or can be hidden.

You can add a header to a Window by pressing the middle Mouse over an edge of a headerless Window.

CH. 25 HOTKEYS IN-DEPTH REFERENCE

WINDOW, UNIVERSAL, OBJECTMODE, (MESH- CURVE- SURFACE- METABALL- AND FONT-) EDITMODE, ARMATURE, VERTEXPAINT AND FACESELECT HOTKEYS

Window HotKeys

Certain window managers also use the following hotkeys. So **ALT-CTRL** can be substituted for **CTRL** to perform the functions described below if a conflict arises.

CTRL-LEFTARROW

Go to the previous Screen.

CTRL-RIGHTARROW

Go to the next Screen.

CTRL-UPARROW or **CTRL-DOWNARROW**

Maximise the window or return to the previous window display size.

SHIFT-F4

Change the window to a Data View.

SHIFT-F5

Change the window to a 3D Window.

SHIFT-F6

Change the window to an IPO Window.

SHIFT-F7

Change the window to a Buttons Window.

SHIFT-F8

Change the window to a Sequence Window.

SHIFT-F9

Change the window to an Oops Window.

SHIFT-F10

Change the window to an Image Window.

SHIFT-F11

Change the window to a Text Window.

SHIFT-F12

Change the window to an Action Window.

Universal HotKeys

The following HotKeys work uniformly in all Blender Windows, if the Context allows:

ESC

This key always cancels Blender functions without changes.
or: FileWindow, DataView and ImageSelect: back to the previous window type.
or: the RenderWindow is *pushed* to the background (or closed, that depends on the operating system).

SPACE

Open the Toolbox.

TAB

Start or quit EditMode.

F1

Loads a Blender file. Changes the window to a FileWindow.

SHIFT-F1

Appends parts from other files, or loads as Library-data. Changes the window to a FileWindow, making Blender files accessible as a directory.

F2

Writes a Blender file. Change the window to a FileWindow.

SHIFT-F2

Exports the scene as a DXF file.

CTRL-F2

Exports the scene as a VRML1 file.

F3

Writes a picture (if a picture has been rendered). The file format is as indicated in the DisplayButtons. The window becomes a File Select Window.

CTRL-F3 (ALT-CTRL-F3 on MacOSX)

Saves a screendump of the active window. The file format is as indicated in the DisplayButtons. The window becomes a FileWindow.

SHIFT-CTRL-F3

Saves a screendump of the whole Blender screen. The fileformat is as indicated in the DisplayButtons. The window becomes a FileWindow.

F4

Displays the Logic Context (if a ButtonsWindow is available).

F5

Displays the Shading Context (if a Buttons Window is available), Light, Material or World Sub-contextes depends on active object.

F6

Displays the Shading Context and Texture Sub-context (if a ButtonsWindow is available).

F7

Displays the Object Context (if a ButtonsWindow is available).

F8

Displays the Shading Context and World Sub-context (if a ButtonsWindow is available).

HOTKEYS IN-DEPTH REFERENCE.UNIVERSAL

F9

Displays the Editing Context (if a ButtonsWindow is available).

F10

Displays the Scene Context (if a ButtonsWindow is available).

F11

Hides or shows the render window.

F12

Starts the rendering from the active camera.

LEFTARROW

Go to the previous frame.

SHIFT-LEFTARROW

Go to the first frame.

RIGHTARROW

Go to the next frame.

SHIFT-LEFTARROW

Go to the last frame.

UPARROW

Go forward 10 frames.

DOWNARROW

Go back 10 frames.

ALT-A

Change the current Blender window to Animation Playback mode. The cursor changes to a counter.

ALT-SHIFT-A

The current window, *plus* all 3DWindows go into Animation Playback mode.

IKEY

Insert Key menu. This menu differs from window to window.

JKEY

Toggle the render buffers. Blender allows you to retain two different rendered pictures in memory.

CTRL-O

Opens the last saved file.

QKEY

OK? Quit Blender. This key closes Blender. Blender quit is displayed in the console if Blender is properly closed.

ALT-CTRL-T

TimerMenu. This menu offers access to information about drawing speed. The results are displayed in a pop-up.

CTRL-U

OK, Save User defaults. The current project (windows, objects, etc.), including UserMenu settings are written to the default file that will be loaded every time you start Blender or set it to defaults by pressing **CTRL-X**.

CTRL-W

Write file. This key combination allows you to write the Blender file without opening a FileWindow.

ALT-W

Write Videoscape file. Changes the window to a FileWindow.

CTRL-X

Erase All. Everything (except the render buffer) is erased and released. The default scene is reloaded.

HOTKEYS IN-DEPTH REFERENCE.**OBJECTMODE**

Object Mode HotKeys

These hotkeys are mainly bound to the 3D Viewport Window, but many woks on Objects in most other windows, like IPOs and so on, hence they are summarized here.

HOME

All Objects in the visible layer are displayed completely, centered in the window.

PAGEUP

Select the next Object Key. If more than one Object Key is selected, the selection is shifted up cyclically. Only works if the AnimButtons->DrawKey is ON for the Object.

SHIFT-PAGEUP

Adds to selection the next Object Key.

PAGEDOWN

Select the previous Object Key. If more than one Object Key is selected, the selection is shifted up cyclically. Only works if the AnimButtons->DrawKey is ON for the Object.

SHIFT-PAGEDOWN

Adds to selection the previous Object Key.

ACCENT

(To the left of the **1KEY** on the US keyboard) Select all layers.

SHIFT-ACCENT

Revert to the previous layer setting.

TAB

Start/stop EditMode. Alternative hotkey: **ALT-E**.

AKEY

Selects/deselects all.

CTRL-A

Apply size and rotation. The rotation and dimensions of the Object are assigned to the ObData (Mesh, Curve, etc.). At first glance, it appears as if nothing has changed, but this can have considerable consequences for animations or texture mapping. This is best illustrated by also having the axis of a Mesh Object be drawn (EditButtons->Axis). Rotate the Object and activate Apply. The rotation and dimensions of the Object are 'erased'.

SHIFT-CTRL-A

If the active Object is automatically duplicated (see AnimButtons->DupliFrames or AnimButtons->Dupliverts), a menu asks `Make dupli's real?`. This option *actually* creates the Objects. If the active Mesh Object is deformed by a Lattice, a menu asks `Apply Lattice deform?`. Now the deformation of the Lattice is assigned to the vertices of the Mesh.

SHIFT-A

This is the AddMenu. In fact, it is the ToolBox that starts with the 'ADD' option. When Objects are added, Blender starts EditMode immediately if possible.

BKEY

Border Select. Draw a rectangle with the LeftMouse; all Objects within this area are *selected*, but *not* made active. Draw a rectangle with the RightMouse to *deselect* Objects. In orthonormal ViewMode, the dimensions of the rectangle are displayed, expressed as global coordinates, as an extra feature in the lower left corner. In Camera ViewMode, the dimensions that are to be rendered according to the DisplayButtons are displayed in *pixel* units.

SHIFT-B

Render Border. This only works in Camera ViewMode. Draw a rectangle to render a smaller cut-out of the standard window frame. If the option DisplayButtons->Border is ON, a box is drawn with red and black lines.

CKEY

Centre View. The position of the 3DCursor becomes the new centre of the 3DWindow.

ALT-C

Convert Menu. Depending on the *active* Object, a PopupMenu is displayed. This enables you to convert certain types of ObData. It only converts in one direction, everything ultimately degrades to a Mesh! The options are:

- Font -> Curve
- MetaBall -> Mesh The original MetaBall remains unchanged.
- Curve -> Mesh
- Surface -> Mesh

CTRL-C

Copy Menu. This menu copies information from the *active* Object to (other) *selected* Objects.

Fixed components are:

- Copy Loc: the X,Y,Z location of the Object. If a Child is involved, this location is the relative position in relation to the Parent.
- Copy Rot: the X,Y,Z rotation of the Object.
- Copy Size: the X,Y,Z dimension of the Object.
- DrawType: copies Object Drawtype.
- TimeOffs: copies Object time offset.
- Dupli: all Duplicator data (Dupliframes, Dupliverts and so on)
- Mass: Real time stuff.
- Damping: Real time stuff.
- Properties: Real time stuff.
- Logic Bricks: Real time stuff.
- Constraints: copies Object constraints.

If applicable:

- Copy TexSpace: The texture space.
- Copy Particle Settings: the complete particle system from the AnimButtons.

For Curve Objects:

- Copy Bevel Settings: all beveling data from the EditButtons.

Font Objects:

- Copy Font Settings: font type, dimensions, spacing.
- Copy Bevel Settings: all beveling data from the EditButtons.

Camera Objects:

- Copy Lens: the lens value.

SHIFT-C

CentreZero View. The 3DCursor is set to zero (0,0,0) and the *view* is changed so that all Objects, including the 3Dcursor, can be displayed. This is an alternative for **HOME**.

DKEY

Draw mode menu. Allows to select draw modes exactly as the corresponding menu in the 3D viewport header does.

SHIFT-D

Add Duplicate. The selected Objects are duplicated. Grab mode starts immediately thereafter.

ALT-D

Add Linked Duplicate. Of the selected Objects linked duplicates are created. Grab mode starts immediately thereafter.

CTRL-D

Draw the (texture) Image as wire. This option has a limited function. It can only be used for 2D compositing.

ALT-E

Start/stop EditMode. Alternative hotkey: **TAB**.

FKEY

If selected Object is a mesh Toggles Face selectMode on and off.

CTRL-F

Sort Faces. The *faces* of the *active* Mesh Object are sorted, based on the current view in the 3DWindow. The leftmost *face* first, the rightmost last. The sequence of *faces* is important for the Build Effect (AnimButtons).

GKEY

Grab Mode. Or: the *translation* mode. This works on selected Objects and *vertices*. Blender calculates the quantity and direction of the translation, so that they correspond *exactly* with the mouse movements, regardless of the ViewMode or view direction of the 3DWindow. Alternatives for starting this mode:

- **LMB** to draw a straight line.

The following options are available in *translation* mode:

Limitors:

- **CTRL**: in increments of 1 grid unit.
- **SHIFT**: fine movements.
- **SHIFT-CTRL**: in increments of 0.1 grid unit.

MMB toggles:
A short *click* restricts the current translation to the X,Y or Z axis. Blender calculates which axis to use, depending on the already initiated mouse movement. Click MiddleMouse again to return to unlimited translation.

- **XKEY, YKEY, ZKEY** constraints movement to X,Y,Z axis of the *global* reference.
- a *second* **XKEY, YKEY, ZKEY** constraints movement to X,Y,Z axis of the *local* reference.
- a *third* **XKEY, YKEY, ZKEY** removes constraints.
- **NKEY** enters numerical input, as well as any numeric key directly. **TAB** will switch between values, **ENTER** finalizes, **ESC** exits.
- **ARROWS**:These keys can be used to move the mouse cursor exactly 1 pixel.

Grabber can be terminated with:

- **LMB**, **SPACE** or **ENTER**: move to a new position.
- **RMB** or **ESC**: everything goes back to the old position.

Switching mode:

- **GKEY**: starts Grab mode again.
- **SKEY**: switches to Size (Scale) mode.
- **RKEY**: switches to Rotate mode.

ALT-G

Clear translations, given in Grab mode. The X,Y,Z locations of selected Objects are set to zero.

SHIFT-G

Group Selection

- Children: Selects all selected Object's Children.
- Immediate Children: Selects all selected Object's first level Children.
- Parent: Selects selected Object's Parent.
- Shared Layers: Selects all Object on the same Layer of active Object

IKEY

Insert Object Key. A *keyposition* is inserted in the current frame of all *selected* Objects. A PopupMenu asks what key position(s) must be added to the IpoCurves.

- Loc: The XYZ location of the Object.
- Rot: The XYZ rotation of the Object.
- Size: The XYZ dimensions of the Object
- LocRot: The XYZ location and XYZ rotation of the Object.

- LocRotSize: The XYZ location, XYZ rotation and XYZ dimensions of the Object.
- Layer: The layer of the Object.
- Avail: A position is only added to all the current IpoCurves, that is curves which already exists.
- Mesh, Lattice, Curve or Surface: depending on the type of Object, a VertexKey can be added.

CTRL-J

Join Objects. All *selected* Objects of the same type are added to the *active* Object. What actually happens here is that the *ObData* blocks are combined and all the selected Objects (except for the *active* one) are deleted. This is a rather complex operation, which can lead to confusing results, particularly when working with a lot of linked data, animation curves and hierarchies.

KKEY

Show Keys. The DrawKey option is turned ON for all selected Objects. If all of them were already ON, they are all turned OFF.

SHIFT-K

A PopupMenu asks: OK? Show and select all keys. The DrawKey option is turned ON for all selected Objects, and all Object-keys are selected. This function is used to enable *transformation* of the entire animation system.

LKEY

Makes selected Object local. Makes library linked objects local for the current scene.

CTRL-L

Link selected. Links some of the Active Object data to all selected Objects, the following menu entry appears only if applicable.

- To Scene: Creates a link of the Object to a scene.
- Object IPOs: Links Active Object IPOs to selected ones.
- Mesh Data: Links Active Object Mesh data selected ones.
- Lamp Data: Links Active Object Lamp data to selected ones.
- Curve Data: Links Active Object Curve data selected ones.
- Surf Data: Links Active Object Surf data selected ones.
- Material: Links Active Object Material to selected ones.

HOTKEYS IN-DEPTH REFERENCE.OBJECTMODE

1 Move Object(s) to layer Popup.

2 Numeric input panel

SHIFT-L

Select Linked. Selects all Objects somehow linked to active Object.

- `Object IPO`: Selects all Object(s) sharing active Object's IPOs.
- `Object Data`: Selects all Object(s) sharing active Object's ObData.
- `Current Material`: Selects all Object(s) sharing active Object's current Material.
- `Current Texture`: Selects all Object(s) sharing active Object's current Texture.

MKEY

Moves selected Object(s) to another layer, a pop-up appers (fig. 1). Use **LMB** to move, use **SHIFT-LMB** to make the object belong to multiple layers. If the selected Objects have different layers, this is 'OR'ed in the menu display. Use **ESC** to exit the menu. Press the "OK" button or **ENTER** to change the layer seting. The hotkeys (**ALT-**)(**1KEY, 2KEY**, ... - **OKEY**) work here as well (see 3DHeader).

NKEY

Number Panel (fig. 2). The location, rotation and scaling of the active Object are displayed and can be modified.

ALT-O

Clear Origin. The 'Origin' is erased for all Child Objects, which causes the Child Objects to move to the exact location of the Parent Objects.

SHIFT-O

If the selected Object is a Mesh toggles SubSurf onn/off. **CTRL-1** to **CTRL-4** switches to the relative SubSurf level for display purpouses. Rendering SUbSurf level has no HotKey.

CTRL-P

Make selected Object(s) the child(ren) of the active Object. If the Parent is a Curve then a popup offers two coiches:

* `Normal Parent`: Make a normal parent, the curve can be made a path later on.
* `Follow Path`: Automatically creates a Follow Path constraint with the curve as target.

If the Parent is an Armature, a popup offers three options:

* `Use Bone`: One of the Bones becomes the parent. The Object will not be deformed. A popup permits to select the bone. This is the option if you are modeling a robot or machinery
* `Use Armature`: The whole armature is used as parent for deformations. This is the choiche for organic beings.
* `Use Object`: Standard parenting.

In the second case further options asks if Vertex groups should not be created, should be created empty or created and populated.

ALT-P

Clears Parent relation, user is asked if he wishes to keep or clear parent-induced transforms.

* `Clear Parent`: the selected Child Objects are unlinked from the Parent. Since the transformation of the Parent disappears, this can appear as if the former Children themselves are transformed.
* `... and keep transform`: the Child Objects are unlinked from the Parent, and an attempt is made to assign the current transformation, which was determined in part by the Parent, to the (former Child) Objects.
* `Clear Parent inverse`: The inverse matrix of the Parent of the selected Objects is erased. The Child Objects remain linked to the Objects. This gives the user complete control over the hierarchy.

RKEY

Rotate mode. Works on selected Object(s). In Blender, a rotation is by default a rotation perpendicular to the screen, regardless of the view direction or ViewMode. The degree of rotation is *exactly* linked to the mouse movement. Try moving around the   rotation midpoint with the mouse. The rotation pivot point is determined by the state of the 3DWiewport Header buttons. Alternatives for starting this mode:

* **LMB** to draw a C-shaped curve.

The following options are available in rotation mode:

HOTKEYS IN-DEPTH REFERENCE.OBJECTMODE

Limitors:

- **CTRL**: in increments of 5 degrees.
- **SHIFT**: fine movements.
- **SHIFT-CTRL**: in increments of 1 degree.

MMB toggles:
A short *click* restricts the current rotation to the horizontal or vertical view axis.

- **XKEY, YKEY, ZKEY** constraints rotation to X,Y,Z axis of the *global* reference.
- a *second* **XKEY, YKEY, ZKEY** constraints rotation to X,Y,Z axis of the *local* reference.
- a *third* **XKEY, YKEY, ZKEY** removes constraints.
- **NKEY** enters numerical input, as well as any numeric key directly. **ENTER** finalizes, **ESC** exits.
- **ARROWS**:These keys can be used to move the mouse cursor exactly 1 pixel.

Rotation can be terminated with:

- **LMB**, **SPACE** or **ENTER**: move to a new rotation.
- **RMB** or **ESC**: everything goes back to the old rotation.

Switching mode:

- **GKEY**: switches to Grab.
- **SKEY**: switches to Size (Scale) mode.
- **RKEY**: starts Rotate mode again.

ALT-R

Clears Rotation. The X,Y,Z rotations of selected Objects are set to zero.

SKEY

Size mode or *scaling* mode. Works on selected Object(s). The degree of *scaling* is *exactly* linked to the mouse movement. Try to move from the (rotation) midpoint with the mouse. The pivot point is determined by the settings of the 3D Viewport header pivot Menu. Alternatives for starting scaling mode:

- **LMB** to draw a V-shaped line.

The following options are available in *scaling* mode:

Limitors:

- **CTRL**: in increments of 0.1.
- **SHIFT-CTRL**: in increments of 0.01.

MMB toggles:
A short *click* restricts the scaling to X, Y or Z axis. Blender calculates the appropriate axis based on the already initiated mouse movement. Click **MMB** again to return to free scaling.

- **XKEY, YKEY, ZKEY** constraints scaling to X,Y,Z axis of the *local* reference.
- a *second* **XKEY, YKEY, ZKEY** removes constraints.
- **NKEY** enters numerical input, as well as any numeric keydirectly. **ENTER** finalizes, **ESC** exits.
- **ARROWS**:These keys can be used to move the mouse cursor exactly 1 pixel.

Scaling can be terminated with:

- **LMB, SPACE** or **ENTER**: fixes the new dimension.
- **RMB** or **ESC**: everything goes back to the old dimension.

Switching mode:

- **GKEY**: switches to Grab.
- **SKEY**: starts Size mode again.
- **RKEY**: switches to Rotation.

ALT-S

Clears Size. The X,Y,Z dimensions of selected Objects are set to 1.0.

SHIFT-S

SnapMenu:

- `Sel->Grid`: Moves Object to nearest grid point.
- `Sel->Curs`: Moves Object to cursor.
- `Curs->Grid`: Moves cursor to nearest grid point.
- `Curs->Sel`: Moves cursor to selected Object(s).
- `Sel->Center`: Moves Objects to their barycentrum.

TKEY

Texture space mode. The position and dimensions of the texture space for the selected Objects can be changed in the same manner as described above for Grab and Size mode. To make this visible, the *drawing flag* EditButtons->TexSpace is set ON. A PopupMenu asks you to select: "Grabber" or "Size".

CTRL-T

Makes selected Object(s) track the Active Object. Old track method was Blender default tracking before version 2.30. The new method is the Constraint Track, this creates a fully editable constraint on the selected object targeting the active Object.

HOTKEYS IN-DEPTH REFERENCE.OBJECTMODE

ALT-T

Clears old style Track. Constraint track is removed as all constrains are.

UKEY

Makes Object Single User, the inverse operation of Link (**CTRL-L**) a pop-up appears with choices.

- `Object`: if other Scenes also have a link to this Object, the link is deleted and the Object is copied. The Object now only exists in the current Scene. The links *from* the Object remain unchanged.
- `Object & ObData`: Similar to the previous command, but now the ObData blocks with multiple links are copied as well. All selected Objects are now present in the current Scene only, and each has a unique ObData (Mesh, Curve, etc.).
- `Object & ObData & Materials+Tex`: Similar to the previous command, but now Materials and Textures with multiple links are also copied. All selected Objects are now unique. They have unique ObData and each has a unique Material and Texture block.
- `Materials+Tex`: Only the Materials and Textures with multiple links are copied.

VKEY

Switches in/out of Vertex Paint Mode.

ALT-V

Object-Image Aspect. This hotkey sets the X and Y dimensions of the selected Objects in relation to the dimensions of the Image Texture they have. Use this hotkey when making 2D Image compositions and multi-plane designs to quickly place the Objects in the appropriate relationship with one another.

WKEY

Opens Object Booleans Menu.

XKEY

`Erase Selected?` Deletes selected objects.

ZKEY

Toggles Solid Mode on/off.

SHIFT-Z

Toggles Shaded Mode on/off.

ALT-Z

Toggles Textured Mode on/off.

Edit Mode HotKeys - General

Again, Most of these hotkeys are usefull in the 3D Viewport when in Edit Mode, but many works on other Blender Objects, so they are summarized here.

Many Object Mode keys works in Edit mode too, but on the selected vertices or control points; among these Grab, Rotate, Scale and so on. These hotkeys are not repeated here.

TAB or ALT-E

This button starts and stops Edit Mode.

AKEY

Select/Unselect all.

BKEY-BKEY

Circle Select. If you press **BKEY** a second time after starting Border Select, Circle Select is invoked. It works as described above. Use **NUM+** or **NUM-** or **MW** to adjust the circle size. Leave Circle Select with **RMB** or **ESC**.

NKEY

Number Panel. Simpler than the Object Mode one, in Edit Mode works for Mesh, Curve, Surface: The location of the active vertex is displayed.

OKEY

Switch in/out of Proportional Editing.

SHIFT-O

Toggles between Smooth and Sharp Proportional Editing.

PKEY

SeParate. You can choose to make a new object with all selected vertices, edges, faces and curves or create a new object from each *separate* group of interconnected vertices from a popup. Note that for curves you cannot separate connected control vertices. This operation is the opposite of Join (**CTRL-J**).

CTRL-P

`Make Vertex Parent`. If one object (or more than one) is/are selected and the active Object is in Edit Mode with 1 or 3 vertices selected then the Object in Edit Mode becomes the Vertex Parent of the selected Object(s). If only 1 vertex is selected, only the *location* of this vertex determines the Parent transformation; the rotation and dimensions of the Parent do not play a role here. If three vertices are selected, it is a 'normal' Parent relationship in which the 3 vertices determine the rotation and location of the Child *together*. This method produces interesting effects with Vertex Keys. In EditMode, other Objects can be selected with **CTRL+RMB**.

CTRL-S

Shear. In EditMode this operation enables you to make selected forms 'slant'. This always works via the horizontal screen axis.

UKEY

Undo. When starting Edit Mode, the original ObData block is saved and can be returned to via **UKEY**. Mesh Objects have better Undo, see next section.

WKEY

Specials PopupMenu. A number of *tools* are included in this PopupMenu as an alternative to the Edit Buttons. This makes the buttons accessible as *shortcuts*, e.g. EditButtons->Subdivide is also '**WKEY, 1KEY**'.

SHIFT-W

Warp. Selected vertices can be bent into curves with this option. It can be used to convert a plane into a tube or even a sphere. The centre of the circle is the 3DCursor. The mid-line of the circle is determined by the horizontal dimensions of the selected vertices. When you start, everything is already bent 90 degrees. Moving the mouse up or down increases or decreases the extent to which *warping* is done. By zooming in/out of the 3Dwindow, you can specify the maximum degree of *warping*. The **CTRL** limitor increments warping in steps of 5 degrees.

EditMode Mesh Hotkeys

This section and the following higlights peculiar EditMode Hotkeys.

ALT-CTRL-RMB

Edge select.

EKEY

Extrude Selected. "Extrude" in EditMode transforms all the selected *edges* to *faces*. If possible, the selected faces are also duplicated. Grab mode is started directly after this command is executed.

FKEY

Make Edge/Face. If 2 vertices are selected, an *edge* is created. If 3 or 4 vertices are selected, a *face* is created.

SHIFT-F

Fill selected. All selected vertices that are bound by *edges* and form a closed polygon are filled with triangular *faces*. Holes are automatically taken into account. This operation is 2D; various layers of polygons must be filled in succession.

ALT-F

Beauty Fill. The edges of all the selected triangular faces are switched in such a way that equally sized faces are formed. This operation is 2D; various layers of polygons must be filled in succession. The Beauty Fill can be performed immediately after a Fill.

HKEY

Hide selected. All selected vertices and faces are temporarily hidden.

SHIFT-H

Hide Not Selected: All *non*-selected vertices and faces are temporarily hidden.

ALT-H

Reveal. All temporarily hidden vertices and faces are drawn again.

KKEY

Knife Tool Menu.

* `Face Loop Select:` (**SHIFT-R**) Face loops are higlighted starting from edge under mouse pointer. **LMB** finalizes, **ESC** exits.
* `Face Loop Cut:` (**CTRL-R**) Face loops are higlighted starting from edge under mouse pointer. **LMB** finalizes, **ESC** exits.
* `Knife (exact):` (**SHIFT-K**) Mouse starts draw mode. Selected Edges are cut at intersections with mouse line. **ENTER** or **RMB** finalizes, **ESC** exits.
* `Knife (midpoints):` (**SHIFT-K**) Mouse starts draw mode. Selected Edges intersecting with mouse line are cut in middle regardless of true intersection point. **ENTER** or **RMB** finalizes, **ESC** exits.

LKEY

Select Linked. If you start with an *unselected* vertex near the mouse cursor, this vertex is selected, together with all vertices that share an edge with it.

SHIFT-L

Deselect Linked. If you start with a *selected* vertex, this vertex is deselected, together with all vertices that share an edge with it.

CTRL-L

Select Linked Selected. Starting with *all* selected vertices, all vertices connected to them are selected too.

MKEY

Mirror. Opens a popup asking for the axis to mirror. 3 possible axis group are available, each of which contains three axes, for a total of nine choices. Axes can be Global (Blender Global Reference); Local (Current Object Local Reference) or View (Current View reference). Remember that mirroring, like scaling, happens with respect to the current pivot point.

ALT-M

Merges selected vertices at barycentrum or at cursorm depending on selection made on pop-up.

CTRL-N

Calculate Normals Outside. All normals from selected faces are recalcultated and consistently set in the same direction. An attempt is made to direct all normals 'outward'.

SHIFT-CTRL-N

Calculate Normals Inside. All normals from selected faces are recalculated and consistently set in the same direction. An attempt is made to direct all normals 'inward'.

ALT-S

Whereas **SKEY** scales in Edit Mode as it does in Object Mode, for Edit Mode a further option exists, **ALT-S** moves each vertex in the direction of its local normal, hence effectively shrinking/fattening the mesh.

CTRL-T

Make Triangles. All selected faces are converted to triangles.

UKEY

Undo. When starting Edit Mode, the original ObData block is saved and all subsequent changes are saved on a stack. This option enables you to restore the previous situation, one after the other.

SHIFT-U

Redo. This let you re-apply any undone changes up to the moment in which Edit Mode was entered.

ALT-U

Undo Menu. This let you choose the exact point to which you want to undo changes.

XKEY

Erase selected. A PopupMenu offers the following options:

- Vertices: all vertices are deleted. This includes the edges and faces they form.
- Edges: all edges with both vertices selected are deleted. If this 'releases' certain vertices, they are deleted as well. Faces that can no longer exist as a result of this action are also deleted.
- Faces: all faces with all their vertices selected are deleted. If any vertices are 'released' as a result of this action, they are deleted.
- All: everything is deleted.
- Edges and Faces: all selected edges and faces are deleted, but the vertices remain.
- Only Faces: all selected faces are deleted, but the edges and vertices remain.

YKEY

Split. This command 'splits' the selected part of a Mesh without deleting faces. The split parts are no longer bound by *edges*. Use this command to control *smoothing*. Since the split parts have vertices at the same position, selection with LKEY is recommended.

EditMode Curve Hotkeys

CKEY

Set the selected curves to cyclic or turn cyclic off. An individual curve is selected if at least one of the vertices is selected.

HOTKEYS IN-DEPTH REFERENCE.EDITMODE CURVE

EKEY

Extrude Curve. A vertex is added to the selected end of the curve. Grab mode is started immediately after this command is executed.

FKEY

Add segment. A segment is added between two selected vertices at the end of two curves. These two curves are combined into 1 curve.

HKEY

Toggle Handle *align/free*. Toggles the selected Bezier *handles* between *free* or *aligned*.

SHIFT-H

Set Handle *auto*. The selected Bezier *handles* are converted to *auto* type.

CTRL-H

Calculate Handles. The selected Bezier curves are calculated and all *handles* are assigned a type.

LKEY

Select Linked. If you start with an *non*-selected vertex near the mouse cursor, this vertex is selected together with all the vertices of the same curve.

SHIFT-L

Deselect Linked. If you start with a *selected* vertex, it is deselected together with all the vertices of the same curve.

MKEY

Mirror. Mirror selected control points exactly as for vertices in a Mesh.

TKEY

Tilt mode. Specify an extra axis rotation, i.e. the *tilt*, for each vertex in a 3D curve.

ALT-T

Clear Tilt. Set all axis rotations of the selected vertices to zero.

VKEY

Vector Handle. The selected Bezier *handles* are converted to *vector* type.

WKEY

The special menu for curves appears:

- `Subdivide`. Subdivide the selected vertices
- `Switch direction`. The direction of the selected curves is reversed. This is mainly for Curves that are used as *paths*!
- `Mirror`. Mirrors the selected vertices

XKEY

Erase Selected. A PopupMenu offers the following options:

- `Selected`: all selected vertices are deleted.
- `Segment`: a curve segment is deleted. This only works for single segments. Curves can be split in two using this option. Or use this option to specify the cyclic position within a cyclic curve.
- `All`: delete everything.

EditMode Surface Hotkeys

CKEY

Toggle Cyclic menu. A PopupMenu asks if selected surfaces in the 'U' or the 'V' direction must be cyclic. If they were already cyclic, this mode is turned off.

EKEY

Extrude Selected. This makes *surfaces* of all the selected *curves*, if possible. Only the edges of surfaces or loose curves are candidates for this operation. Grab mode is started immediately after this command is completed.

FKEY

Add segment. A segment is added between two selected vertices at the ends of two curves. These two curves are combined into 1 curve.

LKEY

Select Linked. If you start with an *non*-selected vertex near the mouse cursor, this vertex is selected together with all the vertices of the same curve or surface.

SHIFT-L

Deselect Linked. If you start with a *selected* vertex, this vertex is deselected together with all vertices of the same curve or surface.

MKEY

Mirror. Mirror selected control points exactly as for vertices in a Mesh.

SHIFT-R

Select Row. Starting with the last selected vertex, a complete row of vertices is selected in the 'U' or 'V' direction. Selecting `Select Row` a second time with the same vertex switches the 'U' or 'V' selection.

WKEY

The special menu for surfaces appears:

* `Subdivide`. Subdivide the selected vertices
* `Switch direction`. This will switch the normals of the selected parts.

XKEY

Erase Selected. A PopupMenu offers the following choices:

* `Selected`: all selected vertices are deleted.
* `All`: delete everything.

EditMode Metaball Hotkeys

MKEY

Mirror. Mirror selected control points exactly as for vertices in a Mesh.

EditMode Font Hotkeys

In Text Edit Mode most hotkeys are disabled, to allow text entering.

RIGHTARROW

Move text cursor 1 position forward.

SHIFT-RIGHTARROW

Move text cursor to the end of the line.

LEFTARROW

Move text cursor 1 position backwards.

SHIFT-LEFTARROW

Move text cursor to the start of the line.

DOWNARROW

Move text cursor 1 line forward.

SHIFT-DOWNARROW

Move text cursor to the end of the text.

UPARROW

Move text cursor 1 line back.

SHIFT-UPARROW

Move text cursor to the beginning of the text.

ALT-U

`Reload Original Data` (undo). When EditMode is started, the original text is saved. You can restore this original text with this option.

ALT-V

Paste text. The text file `/tmp/.cutbuffer` is inserted at the cursor location.

Armature Hotkeys

CTRL-TAB

Toggles Pose Mode on/off.

EKEY

Extrude Armature. An extra Bone is added to the selected Bone. Grab mode is started immediately thereafter.

LKEY

Select linked bones in a chain.

VertexPaint Hotkeys

SHIFT-K
All vertex colours are erased; they are changed to the current drawing colour.

UKEY
Undo. This undo is 'real'. Pressing Undo twice redoes the undone.

WKEY
Shared Vertexcol: The colours of all faces that share vertices are blended.

FaceSelect Hotkeys

TAB
Switches to EditMode, selections made here will show up when switching back to FaceSelectMode with **TAB**.

RKEY
Calls a menu allowing to rotate the UV coordinates or the VertexCol.

UKEY
Calls the UV Calculation menu. The following modes can the applied to the selected faces:

- Cube: Cubical mapping, a number button asks for the cubemap size
- Cylinder: Cylindrical mapping, calculated from the center of the selected faces
- Sphere: Spherical mapping, calculated from the center of the selected faces
- Bounds to x: UV coordinates are calculated from the actual view, then scaled to a boundbox of 64 or 128 pixels in square
- Standard x: Each face gets default square UV coordinates
- From Window: The UV coordinates are calculated using the projection as displayed in the 3DWindow

CH. 26 WINDOWS REFERENCE

INFO WINDOW, FILE WINDOW, 3D WINDOW, IPO-
WINDOW, SEQUENCE WINDOW, OOPS WINDOW,
ACTION WINDOW, NLA WINDOW, TEXTURE
WINDOW, SOUND WINDOW, IMAGE WINDOW,
IMAGE SELECT WINDOW, ANIMATION PLAYBACK-
WINDOW

The InfoWindow

Info Toolbar

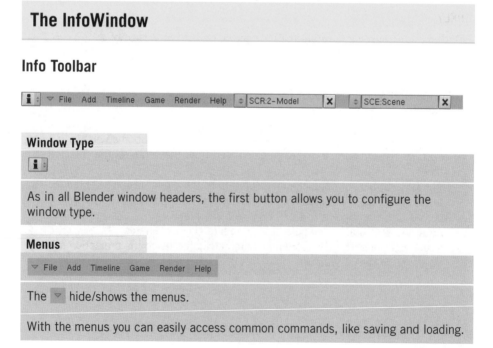

Window Type

As in all Blender window headers, the first button allows you to configure the
window type.

Menus

The ▽ hide/shows the menus.

With the menus you can easily access common commands, like saving and loading.

The menu entries are very common and doing the things they are labeled. They generally exibit "Blender wide" functions.

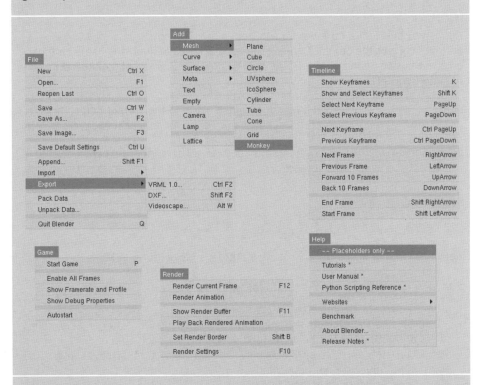

The pack items in the `File` Menu deserves some more explanations:

With *Pack Data* you can pack Images, Fonts and Sounds into the Blend-file, allowing to distribute easily your files as a single file. As a sign that your file is packed, a little icon of a parcel appears in the menu-bar.

Unpack Data unpacks packed data within the file into the current directory on your harddisk. It creates directories for textures, sounds and fonts there. It opens a popup whose entries should be self-explanatory.

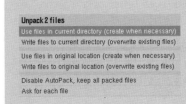

Screen Menu

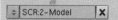

Allows you to select a different Screen from a list. The option Add New creates an exact copy of the current Screen. The copy is 'invisble': only the name on the adjacent button changes. HotKey for next or previous Screen: **ALT-ARROWLEFT** or **ALT-ARROWRIGHT**.

SCR:	Assign a new and unique name to the current Screen and then adds the new name to the list in alphabetical order.
Delete Screen	Delete Current Screen? The current Screen is deleted and released.

Scene Menu

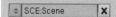

Select a different scene from a list. This button is blocked in EditMode.

Add New displays a PopupMenu with four options:

* "Empty": create a completely empty scene.
* "Link Objects": all Objects are linked to the new scene. The *layer* and *selection flags* of the Objects can be configured differently for each Scene.
* "Link ObData": duplicates Objects only. ObData linked to the Objects, e.g. Mesh and Curve, are not duplicated.
* "Full Copy": everything is duplicated.

SCE:	Assigns a new and unique name to the current Scene and places the new name in the list in alphabetical order.
Delete Screen	"OK? Delete Current Scene". This button deletes and releases the current Scene without deleting Objects. Objects without users are not written to a file.

The information text

www.blender.org 231 Ve:1347–1347 | Fa:1307–1316 | Mem:3.42M Cube

The standard text is:

* www.blender.org: the location at which the software can be obtained.
* 2.30: the version of Blender. This book is applicable to the V2.x series only.
* Ve: 4 Fa: 1: the number of *vertices* and *faces* in the current 3DWindow. If in doubt, use **NUM9** to count the *vertices* and *faces* again.

WINDOWS REFERENCE.INFO WINDOW

- Ob: 2-1: the number of *total* Objects and of *selected* Objects in the current 3DWindow.
- La: 0: the number of lamps in the current 3Dwindow.
- Mem: 2.03M: the amount of memory in use in Megabytes, not including fragmented memory.
- Cube (or similar): the name of the *active* Object.

Changes in EditMode

- Ve: 0-4 Fa: 0-1: The first numeric value is the number of *selected* vertices, the second is the *total* number of vertices. The numeric values for the second variable apply to *faces* and have the same significance.
- Plane (or similar): the name of the *active* Object.

During and after rendering

The values for the totals are changed to reflect the rendered picture. These values may be different from the totals displayed in the 3DWindow.

- Time: 00.01.56 (00:44): the pure rendering time for the last picture rendered in minutes/seconds/hundredths of a second and the actual extra rendering time in seconds/hundredths of a second. Excessive swap time or poor file accessibility can cause high 'extra rendering time'.

The Maximize button

Clicking the Maximize button will switch blenter in/out of full screen mode.

The Info Buttons

The Info Window allows you to configure personal settings. These settings are automatically loaded from the file $HOME/.B.blend each time Blender is started. Personal settings cannot be written to a file other than .B.blend. The HotKey **CTRL-U** can be used to overwrite the file .B.blend.

The bottom line of buttons selects the various settings:

View and Controls

Display:		Snap to grid:			Menu Buttons:		Toolbox Thresh.:	View rotation:	Middle mouse button:		Mousewheel:	
ToolTips	Object Info	Grab	Rotate		Auto Open		LMB: 5	Trackball	Rotate View	Pan View		Scroll Lines: 3
	Global Scene	Size			ThresA: 5	ThresB: 2	RMB: 5	Turntable		Emulate 3 Buttons		Invert Wheel Zoom
View & Controls		Edit Methods			Language & Font		Themes		Auto Save		System & OpenGL	File Paths

- `ToolTips` - Switch Tooltips on and off.
- `ObjectInfo` - Shows Object name and frame in 3D viewport.
- `Grab,Rotate,Size` - Makes relevant action take place in steps, as if **CTRL** were pressed.
- `Global Scene` - Forces the current scene to be displayed in all windows.
- `Auto Open, ThresA:, ThresB:` - Forces the menus to open even without a click, it the mouse stays still on them more than `ThresA:` tenth of seconds. Submenus are opened after `ThresB:` tenth of seconds.
- `LMB:, RMB:` - Time, in 1/10 of seconds in which a **LMB** or **RMB** pressed on 3D Viewport opens the Toolbox.
- `Trackball, Turnable` - Sets the behaviour of 3D window rotation method
- `Rotate View, Pan View`- Sets **MMB** functionality.
- `Emulate 3D buttons` - Makes **ALT LMB** equivalent to **MMB**
- `Scroll Lines:` - Controls wheel mouse scrolling
- `Invert Wheel Zoom` - toggles the Wheel directio to zoom in-zoom out

By default, the following *limitors* apply to *grabbing*, *rotating* and *scaling* (press the keys after click and hold with the mouse):

- (no key): fluid change
- **SHIFT**: finer control
- **CTRL**: large grid steps
- `SHIFT-CTRL`: small grid steps

The following alternatives can also be used (when the corresponding toggle button is ON):

- (no key): large grid steps
- **SHIFT**: small grid steps
- **CTRL**: fluid change
- **SHIFT-CTRL**: finer control

Edit Methods

Material linked to:		Mesh Undo		Auto keyframe on:		Duplicate with object:				
ObData	Object	Steps:32		Action	Object	Mesh	Surface	Curve	Text	Metaball
						Armature	Lamp	Material	Texture	Ipo
View & Controls		Edit Methods		Language & Font		Themes		Auto Save	System & OpenGL	File Paths

- `ObData, Object` - Toggles where Material data is linked to.

- Steps: - Sets the number of Undo steps to be stored.
- Action, Object - Toggles auto key framing for objects and actions.
- Duplicate with object: - This series of button specifies which data is really duplicated, and which is merely linked, when a object is duplicated (**SHIFT D**).

Blender allows you to reuse (i.e. link) data blocks to construct compact and efficient structures.

When one of these buttons is pressed, the indicated DataBlock is duplicated instead of linked when using **SHIFT-D**. The **ALT-D** command always makes a copy of the selected Objects with all other data linked.

The most commonly use of *links* is when activating the *Duplicate* commands: **ALT-D** create a copy of the selected Objects, reusing (i.e. linking to) all other data, including Meshes and Materials. **SHIFT-D** create a copy of the selected Objects, using these button settings to determine whether links to other data are created or duplicates of other data are created.

Language and Fonts

- International Fonts - Toggles the usage of international, antialiased, fonts.
- Select font - Allows for font customization.
- Font size: - Sets UI font size.
- Language: - Sets the language.
- Tooltips, Buttons, Toolbox - Sets which part of the UI is to be translated.

Themes:

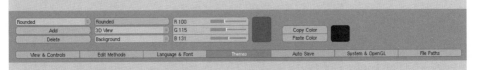

- Theme menu- Selects the Theme to applyto the interface.
- Add - Creates a new Theme.
- Delete - Delete current Theme.

When a theme is selected two menu buttons allow to select one UI context (3D View, UI and buttons and so on) and an UI item in that context (Background, Text, Grid and so on).

The neighbouring R, G, B sliders allows color definition for current item. Some items (Vertex Size, for example) are not defined by colors but by appropriate Num Buttons.

A copy/paste pair of buttons allow to set the same color to more items easily.

Auto Save:

Blender can save 'temp' files at regular intervals as a temporary backup or as extra protection against disasters. The files are identical to Blender files saved in the normal manner. If Blender is in EditMode when this function is used, only the original Data are saved, without saving the Data with which you are working. Blender saves 'temp' files in the specified 'temp' directory with the name "<process-id>.blend". This results in unique names for all 'temp' files, allowing multiple Blenders to simultaneously write 'temp' files on the same computer. When Blender is closed down, the file is renamed "quit.blend", making it easy to retrieve work in progress if the user inadvertently quits Blender.Blender writes files very quickly, which means that waiting time is kept to a minimum, allowing the user to continue working within a split second after saving files of 1-2 Mb.

- Auto Save Temp Files - Enable saving temporary .blend files.
- Minutes: - Time in minutes between auto saving.
- Open recent - Opens last saved temporary file.
- Versions - Sets how many .blend# files are to be kept as history every time a regular save is performed.

  If 'Versions' has a value of '2' and the file 'rt.blend' is being written:

  - rt.blend2 is deleted
  - rt.blend1 is renamed to rt.blend2
  - rt.blend is renamed to rt.blend1
  - rt.blend is rewritten.

WINDOWS REFERENCE.FILE WINDOW

System and OpenGL:

- `Light#` Menu - Selects one of the three possible OpenGL lights for solid view.
- `On,Vec,Col,Spe` - Sets the Light selected in the aforementioned menu on or off (Light1 cannot be off) and define the context (Position, Color and Specular color) of the three Num Buttons below.
- `X,Y,Z` - Sets the three components of the vector pointing to the OpenGL light.
- `R,G,B` - Sets the three components of the OpenGL light color.
- `sR,sG,sB` - Sets the three components of the OpenGL light color for specular highlights.
- `Enable all Codecs` - Enables all available codecs for rendering.
- `Mxing buffer:` - Sets the dimension of the Audio mixing buffer.
- `Emulate Numpad` - Forces regular 0 to 9 keys to act as NumPad 0-9 keys (if you are on a laptop...)
- `Disable Caps Lock` - Disables caps lock when entering Text.
- `Disable Sound` - Disables sound from being played.
- `File Filter Extensions` - Makes only file with extension to appear in image select windows.
- `Mipmaps` - Turns OpenGL MipMapping ON/OFF.
- `VertexArrays` - Turns OpenGL vertex arrays to ON/OFF.

File Path:

Defines all the directory where items are to be looked for/ saved by default, their name is self-explanatory.

The FileWindow

FileToolbar

LOAD FILE   Free: 9675.000 Mb Files: (0) 30   (0.000) 10.770 Mb

Window Type

As with every window header, the first button left enables you to set the window type.

Full Window

The second button expands the window to full screen or returns to the previous window display size; returns to the original screen setting (**CTRL-UPARROW**).

Sort Alpha

Files are sorted alphabetically. Directories are always sorted first.

Sort Time

Files are sorted by creation date.

Sort Size

Files are sorted by size.

Action type

Indicates what type of FileWindow this is. It is extremely important to continually verify that the correct Open or Save option is selected.

File list format

Indicates whether the file names are displayed in long or short format.

Hide dot-files

The ghost button hides dot-files (filenames with a leading dot).

Info

The header provides extra information about the status of the selected directory.

- Free: 81.106 Mb: the free disk space available.
- Files: (0) 72: the number of selected files between parentheses, followed by the total number of files.
- (0.000) 8.600 Mb: the total number of bytes in the selected files between parentheses, followed by the total for the entire directory.

FileWindow

The File Window is generally called up to read and write files. However, you can also use it to manage the entire file system. It also provides a handy overview of the internal structure of a Blender file, since it is the window used to browse a .blend file content when an append action **SHIFT-F1** is called for.

There are 4 'modes' for the FileWindow.

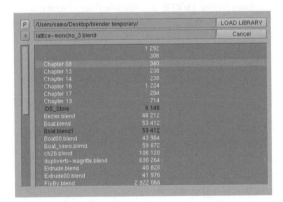

- FileManager: the standard mode.
- FileSelect: the FileHeader shows the action to be performed (Load, Save, etc.).
- DataSelect: display the Blender data system as files.
- DataBrowse: like DataSelect, but now as an alternative to a PopupMenu.

The FileWindow is optimised for reuse. The second and subsequent times the same directory is called up, the file system is not re-read. This saves considerable time, but can sometimes cause confusion if other processes have written files to the directory (the directory is always read again after Blender writes to it). If you have any doubts about the validity of the current display, press **DOTKEY**.

P button

Displays the parent directory. You can also use: **PKEY**.

Directory Name

The text right to the shows the current directory. You can also create a new directory. When you leave the text line (with **LMB** or **ENTER**), you will be asked: "OK? Make dir".

Preset Directories

The file $HOME/.Bfs contains a number of presets that are displayed in this menu. If a file is read or written, the directory involved is temporarily added to the menu.

File Name

The file name can be entered here. This text line can also be used to select files using *wildcards*. Example: enter '*.tga', then press **ENTER**. All files with the extension '.tga' are selected.

FileSelect

Blender commands such as F1 (read file) and F2 (write file) invoke a FileWindow in FileSelect mode. This mode is used to indicate a single file, i.e. the file in the FileName button. Press **ENTER** to initiate the action, e.g. read a Blender file. Use **ESC** to cancel the action. The FileManager functions also work in FileSelect mode. These only work on *selected* files. Standard functions in this window:

LMB

Indicates the *active* file. Its name is placed in the FileName button.

MMB

Indicates the *active* file and closes the FileWindow with the message OK.

RMB

Select files. For functional reasons, a **RMB** select here does not indicate the *active* file!

ENTER

Closes the FileWindow performing the desired action, returns with an OK message.

ESC

Closes the FileWindow with no further action.

PAGEDN

Scrolls down one page.

PAGEUP

Scrolls up one page.

HOME

Scrolls to the first file.

END

Scrolls to the last file.

NUM+

Automatic file-number increase. If there is a number in the active file name (such as rt01.tga), this number is incremented by one. This is quite handy when reading or writing sequential files.

NUM-

Automatic file number decrease (see previous description).

SLASH

Make the current directory the root directory: "/"

PERIOD

Re-read the current directory.

EKEY

For the *active* file: start the Unix editor defined in environment variable $WINEDITOR. For viewing text files.

IKEY

For the *active* file: start the Unix image viewer definde in environment variable $IMAGEEDITOR . For viewing or Editing images.

Read Libraries

Blender allows you to read in, append, or *link* (parts of) other files. If 'Load Library' is selected by invoking the File Whindow with **SHIFT-F1** the FileSelect appears in a special mode. Blender files are now highlighted as directories. They are accessible as a directory as well; they then display a situation in much the same way as DataView displays the internal Blender structure. Now you can select any number of blocks you wish using **RMB** and append them to the current structure with a simple **ENTER**. The complete 'underlying' structure is included: thus, if an Object is selected, the associated Ipo, ObData, Materials and Textures are included as well. If a Scene is selected, the entire Scene is appended to the current structure, Objects and all.

You can specify how you want this to be appended in the FileSelect Header:

Append

External blocks become a normal part of the current structure, and thus of the file as well, if the file is saved. Appending a second time causes the entire selection to be added again in its entirety. Since block names must be unique, the name of the appended blocks will differ slightly from the existing name (only the number in the name).

Link

This is the 'normal' use of Libraries. The specified blocks are added to the current structure here as well, but Blender remembers the fact that they are Library blocks. When the file is saved, only the name of the Library block and the name of the file from which the blocks were copied are saved, thus keeping the original file compact. When you read the file again, Blender reads the original file and then reads all the Library blocks from the other file(s). The names of the files and the blocks must not be changed, however. Blender keeps track of what Library blocks have already been read. Appending the same blocks twice has no consequences.

This enables more animators working on a project. Therefore a linked Object cannot be changed from the scene it is imported in.

FileManager

The FileManager function only works with selected files. The active file does not play a role here. Most of these commands do expect two FileWindows to be open. Commands such as **RKEY** (remove) and **TKEY** (touch) also work with a single Window. Note: when we say *files* here, we also mean directories.

WINDOWS REFERENCE.FILE WINDOW

AKEY
Select/deselect all files.

BKEY
Backup files to the other FileWindow. This allows files to be copied without changing the file date.

CKEY
Copy files to the other FileWindow. (Unix: cp -r) read.

LKEY
Link files to the other FileWindow. (Unix: ln)

MKEY
Move files to the other FileWindow. (Unix: mv)

RKEY
Remove files. For safety's sake: only empty directories. (Unix rm -f)

SHIFT-R
Remove files recursively. This deletes the entire contents of directories. (Unix: rm -rf)

TKEY
Update modification times of files. (Unix: touch)

DataView and DataBrowse

The DataView window can be invoked with **SHIFT-F4**. It allows you to view the entire internal Blender structure as a file system. Each DataBlock is listed as a file name. They are sorted by type in directories.

Currently, the functions are limited to:

- Select Objects by name. Click RightMouse on the file name. A LeftMouse click on a name makes the Object *active*. Note that an activated Object can also reside in a hidden *layer.*

- Setting and deleting Fake Users. (Press FKEY). A Fake User ensures that a DataBlock is always saved in a file, even if it has no users.

- Link Materials (**CTRL-L**). The links to *selected* Materials are all replaced by a link   to the *active* Material (LeftMouse, in the FileName button). This link option will   be expanded to other DataBlock types.

PopupMenus that contain more than 24 items and are thus unmanageably large, are replaced by the DataBrowse windows. Standard functions in this window:

LMB

Display the *active* DataBlock. This is placed in the FileName button.

MMB

Display the *active* DataBlock and close the DataBrowse with an OK message.

ENTER

Close the DataBrowse, return with an OK message.

ESC

Close the DataBrowse with no further action.

PAGEDN

Scroll down one page.

PAGEUP

Scroll up one page.

The 3DWindow

3D Toolbar

WindowType

As with every window header, the first button left allows you to set the window type.

Menus

The triangular button expand/collapses menus. Menus provide a self-explicative way to access to all Blender functions which can be performed in the 3D Window. They are context sensitive and will change depending on the selected Object and current Mode.

Windows with menus, as the 3D Viewport, does not have the standard "Full Window" and "Home" header buttons, actions which have moved to the View Menu.

Menu items are in general self-explanatory and the relative functionality has been explained in the Chapter 25 except for the **View** Menu, which is described here.

View Properties	Opens a floating panel allowing to set the properties (Grid Spacing, ClipStart and Clip End) of the 3D Viewport (Fig. 01)
Background Pic	Opens a floating panel allowing to load a picture to be used as a background in the 3D window. The image can be resized and its opacity determined in the panel. (Fig. 02)

01 View Properties

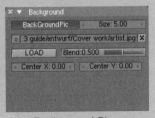

02 Background Pic

View

Next entry group, taking most of the menu and self explanatory, sets the Viewport viewing point, duplicating The Numeric Keypad functions and the **CKEY** and **HOME** Keys.

Those deserving an explanation are:

- Camera View, hotkey **NUM0**
- Top View, hotkey **NUM7**
- Front View, hotkey **NUM1**
- Right View, hotkey **NUM3**

All these views can be 'seen' from the other direction by using **SHIFT** modifier. Views can be Orthographic, Perspective. Blender offers this method from every view, not just from the X, Y or Z axes. Perspective is a more realistic view of the 3D scene, but the Ortographic one is more handy for editing (toggle with **NUM5**).

Local View/Global View allows the user to continue working with complex Scenes. The currently selected Objects are taken separately, centered and displayed completely. The use of 3DWindow layers is temporarily disabled. Reactivating this option restores the display of the 3DWindow in its original form. If a picture is rendered from a LocalView, only the Objects present are rendered *plus* the visible lamps, according to the layers that have been set. Activating a new Camera in LocalView does not change the Camera used by the Scene. These are toggled with the hotkey **NUM/**.

Orthographic, Perspective and Camera view. Blender offers this method from every view, not just from the X, Y or Z axes. Perspective is a more realistic view of the 3D scene, but the Ortographic one is more handy for editing (toggle with **NUM5**). Camera viewis the view as will be rendered (**NUM0**).

Viewport Navigation submenu contains menu entries for rotating and zooming the view.

Play back animation Plays back animation (**ALT-A**).

Mode

Allows to switch Mode among the allowed ones for active Object:

- `Object Mode` Mode (all) **TAB** toggles.
- `Object Edit` Mode (all) **TAB** toggles.
- `UV Face select` (Mesh) **FKEY** toggles.
- `Vertex Paint` (Mesh) **VKEY** toggles.
- `Texture Paint` (Mesh).
- `Pose Mode` (Armature) **CTRL-TAB**.

Draw Mode

This menu sets the drawing method. Respectively:

- BoundBox. The quickest method, for animation previews, for example.
- WireFrame.
- Solid. Zbuffered with the standard OpenGL lighting. **ZKEY** toggles between Wire Frame and Solid.
- Shaded. This is as good an approach as is possible to the manner in which Blender renders - with Gouraud shading. It displays the situation from a single frame of the Camera. **SHIFT-Z** toggles, use **CTRL-Z** to force a ecalculation.
- Textured.

Objects can have their own Draw Type, independent of the window setting (see EditButtons>>DrawType). The rule is that the minimum (more economic) Draw Mode is displayed.

Pivot Point

- Individual Object Centers
- 3D Cursor
- Median Point
- Bounding Box Center

This menudetermine the manner in which the Objects (or vertices) are *rotated* or *scaled* or *mirrored*.

Bounding Box Center The midpoint of the *boundbox* is the center of rotation or scaling. Hotkey: **COMMA**.

Median Point The median of all Objects or vertices is the center of rotation or scaling.

3D Cursor	The 3DCursor is the midpoint of rotation or scaling. Hotkey: **DOT**.
Individual Objects Center	All Objects rotate or scale around their own midpoints. In EditMode: all vertices rotate or scale around the Object midpoint.

Layers buttons

These 20 buttons show the available layers. In fact, a layer is nothing more than a *visibility flag*. This is an extremely efficient method for testing Object visibility. This allows the user to divide the work functionally.

For example: Cameras in layer 1, temporary Objects in layer 20, lamps in layers 1, 2, 3, 4 and 5, etc. All hotkey commands and tools in Blender take the layers into account. Objects in 'hidden' layers are treated as *unselected*.

Use **LMB** for selecting, **SHIFT-LMB** for adding/removing to/from the group of selected layers.

Hotkeys: **1KEY, 2KEY**, etc. **OKEY** for layers 1,2,3,4, etc. Use **ALT-1, ALT-2**, (... **ALT-O**) for layers 11, 12, ... 20. Here, as well, use **SHIFT** + Hotkey for adding/removing to/from the group of selected layers.

Lock

Every 3DWindow has it's own layer setting and active Camera. This is also true for a Scene: here it determines what layers - and what camera - are used to render a picture. The *lock* option links the layers and Camera of the 3DWindow to the Scene and vice versa: the layers and Camera of the Scene are linked to the 3DWindow. This method passes a layer change directly to the Scene and to all other 3DWindows with the "Lock" option ON. Turn the "Lock" OFF to set a layer or Camera *exclusively* for the current 3DWindow. All settings are immediately restored by turning the button back ON.

3D Window

The standard 3DWindow has:

* A grid. The dimensions (distance between the gridlines) and resolution (number of lines) can be set with the 3D Viewport floating Panel (View Menu. This grid is drawn as infinite in the presets of *ortho* ViewMode (Top, Front, Right view). In the other *views*, there is an finite 'floor'. Many Blender commands are adjusted to the *dimension* of the grid, to function as a standard

unit. Blender works best if the total 'world' in which the user operates continually falls more or less within the total grid floor (whether it is a space war or a logo animation).

- Axes in colour codes. The reddish line is the X axis, the green line is the Y axis, the blue line is the Z axis. In the Blender universe, the 'floor' is normally formed by the X and Y axes. The height and 'depth' run along the Z axis.
- A 3D cursor. This is drawn as a black cross with a red/white striped circle. A Left Mouse click moves the 3DCursor. Use the SnapMenu (**SHIFT-S**) to give the 3Dcursor a specific location. New Objects are placed at the 3D cursor location.
- Layers (visible in the header buttons). Objects in 'hidden' layers are not displayed. All hotkey commands and tools in Blender take the layers into account: Objects in the 'hidden' layers are treated as *not* selected. See the following paragraph as well.
- ViewButtons. Separate variables can be set for each 3Dwindow, e.g for the *grid* or the *lens*. Use the View Menu entries.

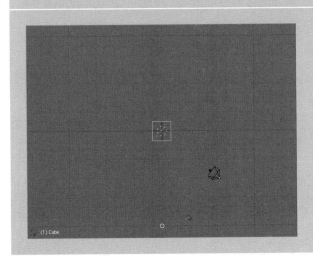

The Mouse

The mouse provides the most direct access to the 3DWindow. Below is a complete overview:

LMB

Position the 3DCursor.

CTRL-LMB

In EditMode: create a new vertex.

Press LMB and drag

These are the Gestures. Blender's gesture recognition works in three ways:

- Draw a straight line: start *translation* mode (Grabber)
- Draw a curved line: start *rotation* mode.
- Draw a V-shaped line: start *scaling* mode.

MMB

Rotate the direction of view of the 3DWindow. This can be done in two ways (can be set in the UserMenu):

- the *trackball* method. In this case, where in the window you start the mouse movement is important. The rotation can be compared to rotating a ball, as if the mouse grasps and moves a tiny miniscule point on a ball and moves it. If the movement starts in the middle of the window, the *view* rotates along the horizontal and vertical window axes. If the movement begins at the edge of the window, the *view* rotates along the axis perpendicular to the window.
- the *turntable* method. A horizontal mouse movement always results in a rotation around the global Z axis. Vertical mouse movements are corrected for the view direction, and result in a combination of (global) X and Y axis rotations.

SHIFT-MMB

Translate the 3DWindow. Mouse movements are always corrected for the view direction.

CTRL-MMB

Zoom in/out on the 3DWindow.

RMB

Select Objects or (in EditMode) vertices. The last one selected is also the *active* one. This method guarantees that a maximum of 1 Object and 1 vertex are always selected. This selection is based on graphics (the wireframe).

SHIFT-RMB

Adds/removes from selection Objects or (in EditMode) vertices. The last one selected is also the *active* one. Multiple Objects or *vertices* may also be selected. This selection is based on graphics too (the wireframe).

CTRL-RMB

Select Objects on the Object-centers. Here the wireframe drawing is not taken into account. Use this method to select a number of identical Objects in succession, or to make them active.

SHIFT-CTRL-RMB

Adds/removes from selection Objects. The last Object selected is also the *active* one. Multiple Objects can be selected.

ALT-CTRL-RMB

In Edit Mode: edge select.

SHIFT-ALT-CTRL-RMB

In Edit Mode: add/removes edges from selection.

Press RMB and drag

Select and start *translation* mode, the Grabber. This works with all the selection methods mentioned.

NumPad

The numeric keypad on the keyboard is reserved for *view* related hotkeys. Below is a description of all the keys with a brief explanation.

NUM/

LocalView. The Objects selected when this command is invoked are taken separately and displayed completely, centered in the window. See the description of 3DHeader>>LocalView.

NUM*

Copy the rotation of the *active* Object to the current 3DWindow. Works as if this Object is the camera, without including the translation.

NUM-, NUM+

Zoom in, zoom out. This also works for Camera ViewMode.

NUM.

Center and zoom in on the selected Objects. The *view* is changed in a way that can be compared to the LocalView option.

NUM5

Toggle between *perspective* and *orthonormal* mode.

NUM9

Force a complete recalculation (of the animation systems) and draw again.

NUM0

View from the current *camera*, or from the Object that is functioning as the *camera*.

CTRL-NUM0

Make the *active* Object the *camera*. Any Object can be used as the camera. Generally, a Camera Object is used. It can also be handy to let a spotlight function temporarily as a camera when directing and adjusting it. **ALT-NUM0** Revert to the previous *camera*. Only Camera Objects are candidates for 'previous camera'.

NUM-1

Front View. (along the positive Y axis, Z up)

CTRL-NUM1

Back View. (along the negative Y axis, Z up)

NUM3

Right View. (along the negative X axis, Z up)

CTRL-NUM3

Left View. (along the positive X axis, Z up)

NUM-7

Top View. (along the negative Z axis, Y up)

CTRL-NUM-7

Bottom view. (along the positive Z axis, Y up)

NUM2 NUM8

Rotate using the *turntable* method. Depending on the view, this is a rotation around the X and Y axis.

NUM4 NUM6

Rotate using the *turntable* method. This is a rotation around the Z axis.

SHIFT-NUM2 SHIFT-NUM8

Translate up or down; corrected for the view.

SHIFT-NUM4 SHIFT-NUM6

Translate up or down; correct for the view.

Hotkeys

The 3D Viewport hotkeys are hundreds and varyes if Blender is In Object or Edit Modes and on the basys of which object is active. The previous Chapter 25 contains them all, hence they are not repeated here.

Hotkeys

Fly Mode is invoked by **SHIFT-F**. Works only in Camera ViewMode. The mouse cursor jumps to the middle of the window. It works as follows:

- Mouse cursor movement indicates the view direction.
- **LMB** (repeated): Fly faster.
- **MMB** (repeated): Fly slower.
- **LMB** and **MMB** toghether: Set speed to zero.
- **CTRL**: translation downwards (negative Z).
- **ALT**: translation upwards (positive Z).
- **ESC**: Camera back to its starting position, terminate Fly Mode.
- **SPACE**: Leave the Camera in current position, terminate Fly Mode.

(Be careful when looking straight up or down. This causes confusing turbulence.)

The IPO Window

IPO Header

WindowType

As with every window header, the first button left allows you to set the window type.

Menus

The triangular button expand/collapses menus. Menus provide a self-explicative way to access all Blender functions which can be performed in the IPO Window. They are context sensitive and will change depending on the selected Object and current Mode.

Windows with menus, as the IPO Window, does not have the standard "Full Window" and "Home" header buttons, actions which have moved to the `View` Menu.

Menu items are in general self-explanatory and the relative functionality will be explained later on in the hotkeys section. The actions which do not have an hotkey are the Extrapolation settings:

Extend mode Constant
The end of selected IPO Curves are horizontally extrapolated.

Extend mode Direction
The ends of selected IPO Curves continue extending in the direction in which they end.

Extend mode Cyclic
The full length of the IPO Curve is repeated cyclically.

Extend mode Cyclic Extrapolation
The full length of the IPO Curve is extrapolated cyclic.

IPOType

Depending on the *active* Object, the various IPOsystems can be specified with these Menu button. These are (note they will not be all present at once):

*   `Object`
    Settings, such as the location and rotation, are animated for the *active* Object. All Objects in Blender can have this IPOblock.

- Material
  Settings of the *active* Material are animated for the *active* Object. A NumBut appears as an extra feature immediately to the right when this button is selected. This button indicates the number of the active Texture *channel*. Eight Textures, each with its own mapping, can be assigned per Material. Thus, per Material-IPO, 8 curves in the row OfsX, OfsY, ...Var are available.

- World
  Used to animate a number of settings for the WorldButtons. World too has several texture channels.

- VertexKey
  If the *active* Object has a VertexKey, the keys (Absolute or Relative) are drawn as horizontal lines. Only one IPO curve is available to interpolate between the Absolute keys, or as many curves as Keys are allowed for Relative Keys.

- Constrain
  If the *active* Object has a *constrain* its influence value can ba animated via an IPO. Each constrain has its own IPO used to display the speed-IPO.

- Sequence
  The active Sequence Effect can have an IPO Curve.

- Curve IPO
  If the *active* Object is a *path* Curve, this button can be used to display the speed (time) IPO.

- Camera IPO
  The active camera IPO curves are shown.

- Lamp IPO
  If the *active* Object is a Lamp, this button can be used to animate light settings, comprehensive of textures.

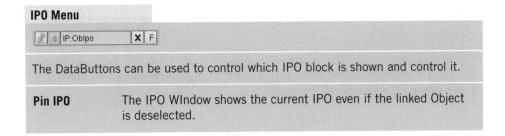

IPO Menu

The DataButtons can be used to control which IPO block is shown and control it.

| **Pin IPO** | The IPO WIndow shows the current IPO even if the linked Object is deselected. |

IPO Menu	Choose another IPOfrom the list of available IPOs. The option Add New makes a complete copy of the current IPO . This is not visible; only the name in the adjacent button will change. Only IPOs of the same type are displayed in the menu list.
IP:	Give the current IPOa new and unique name. After the new name is entered, it appears in the list, sorted alphabetically.
Users	If this button is displayed, there is more than one user for the IPO block. Use the button to make the IPO "Single User".
Unlink IPO	The current IPO is unlinked.
Fake User	The IPO block is saved eve in unused.

Copy to Buffer

All selected IPO Curves are copied to a temporary buffer.

Copy to Buffer

All selected *channels* in the IPO Window are assigned an IPO Curve from the temporary buffer. The rule is: the sequence in which they are copied to the buffer is the sequence in which they are pasted. A check is made to see if the number of IPO Curves is the same.

View Border

Draw a rectangle to indicate what part of the IPO Window should be displayed in the full window.

Lock

This button locks the update of the 3DWindow while editing in the IPO Window, so you can see changes maked to the IPO in realtime inthe 3DWindow. This option works extremely well with relative vertex keys.

IPO Window

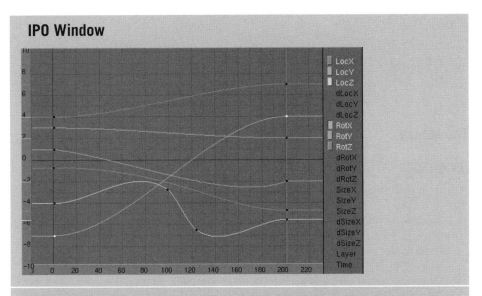

The IPO Window shows the contents of the IPO Block. Which one depends on the IPO Type specified in the header. The standard IPO Window has a grid with the time expressed horizontally in frames and vertical values that depend on the *channel*. There are 2 sliders at the edge of the IPO Window. How far the IPO Window is zoomed in can be seen on the sliders, which can also be used to move the *view*. The right-hand part of the window shows the available *channels*.

To make it easier to work with rotation-IPO Curves, they are displayed in degrees (instead of in radiants). The vertical scale relation is: 1.0 'Blender unit' = 10 degrees.

In addition to the IPO Curves, the VertexKeys are also drawn here. These are horizontal blue lines; the yellow line visualises the *reference* Key.

Each *channel* can be operated with two buttons:

IPO Curve Select

This button is only displayed if the *channel* has an IPO Curve. The button is the same colour as the IPO Curve. Use the button to select IPO Curves. Multiple buttons can be (de)selected using **SHIFT-LMB**.

Channel Select

A *channel* can be selected whether there is an IPO Curve or not. Only IPO Curves of selected channels are drawn. Multiple *channels* can be (de)selected using **SHIFT-LMB**.

The Mouse

CTRL-LMB

Create a new vertex. These are the rules:

- There is no IPOblock (in this window) *and* one *channel* is selected: a new IPO Block is created along with the first IPO Curve with one vertex.
- There is already an IPOblock, and a *channel* is selected without an IPO Curve: a new IPO Curve with one vertex is added.
- Otherwise a new vertex is simply added to the selected IPO Curve.
- This is *not* possible if multiple IPO Curves are selected or if you are in EditMode.

MMB

- On the *channels*; if the window is not high enough to display them completely, the visible part can be shifted vertically.
- On the sliders; these can be moved. This only works if you are zoomed in.
- The rest of the window; the *view* is translated.

CTRL-MMB

Zoom in/out on the IPO Window. You can zoom horizonally or vertically using horizontal and vertical mouse movements.

RMB

Selection works the same here as in the 3DWindow: normally one item is selected. Use **SHIFT** to add/remove from the selection.

- If the IPO Window is in IPO Key mode, the IPO Keys can be selected.
- If at least 1 of the IPO Curves is in EditMode, only its vertices can be selected.
- VertexKeys can be selected if they are drawn (horizontal lines).
- The IPO Curves can be selected.

RMB and drag

Select and start *translation* mode, i.e. the Grabber. The selection can be made using any of the four selection methods discussed above.

SHIFT-RMB

Adds/removes from the selection.

The HotKeys

NUM-, NUM+

Zoom in, zoom out.

PAGEUP

Select the next IPO Key. If more than one IPO Key is selected, the selection is shifted cyclically.

SHIFT-PAGEUP

Add the next IPO Key to the selection.

PAGEDOWN

Select the previous IPOKey. If more than one Object Key is selected, the selection is shifted cyclically.

SHIFT-PAGEUP

Add the previous IPOKey to the selection.

HOME

All visible curves are displayed completely, centered in the window.

TAB

All selected IPO Curves go into or out of EditMode. This mode allows you to transform individual vertices.

AKEY

Select All / deselect All. If any item is selected, first everything is deselected. Placing the mouse cursor above the *channels*, (de)selects all channels where there is a curve.

BKEY

Border select. Draw a rectangle with the LeftMouse; all items that fall within this rectangle are *selected*. Draw a rectangle with the RightMouse to *deselect*.

CKEY

If one vertex or one IPO Key is selected, the current *frame* number is set to this position.

SHIFT-D

Duplicate IPO. All selected vertices or IPO Keys are copied. Then *translation* mode is started automatically.

GKEY

Translation mode (the Grabber). This works on selected curves, keys or vertices. Alternatives for starting this mode:

* **RMB** and drag.

The following options are available in translation mode:

Limitors:

* **CTRL** increments of 1 frame or vertical unit.
* **SHIFT-CTRL** increments of 0.1 frame or vertical unit.
* **MMB** restricts the current translation to the X or Y axis. Blender calculates which axis to use, based on the already initiated mouse movement. Click MiddleMouse again to restore unlimited translation.
* **ARROWS**: With these keys the mouse cursor can be moved exactly 1 pixel.

Grabber can be terminated with:

* **LMB** or **SPACE** or **ENTER**: move to the new position.
* **RMB** or **ESC**: everything returns to the old position.

HKEY

Toggle Handle *align / free*.

SHIFT-H

Set Handle *auto*. The selected Bezier *handles* are converted to *auto* type.

IKEY

Insert Key. Vertices can be added to the visible curves in the IPO Window. A Popup-Menu asks you to make a choice:

* "Current Frame"; all visible curves get a vertex on the current frame.
* "Selected Keys"; (only in IPO Key mode) all selected IPO Keys get vertices for each visible curve, including IPO Curves that are not part of the IPOKey.

JKEY

Join vertices. Selected vertices or IPO Keys can be joined. A PopupMenu asks you to make a choice:

- "All Selected"; all selected vertices are replaced by a new one.
- "Selected doubles": all selected vertices that are closer to each other than 0.9 *frame* are joined.

KKEY

IPO Key mode ON/OFF. If the IPOblock is Object IPOtype, the Objects are redrawn with the option DrawKey ON (see the explanation under IPO Header).

RKEY

Recording mode. The X and Y movements of the mouse are linked to the height of the IPO Curve. Thus, this works with a maximum of two selected *channels* or IPO Curves. The old curve is completely deleted; the new one becomes a 'linear' type. You cannot change parts of curves with *recording*. The scale at which this happens is determined by the *view* of the IPO Window. A PopupMenu asks you to make a choice:

- "Still"; the current frame is used as the starting point.
- "Play anim"; the animation starts, allowing you to see the correlation with other animation systems.

During *recording* mode, the **CTRL** must be held down to actually start recording. Press **SPACEKEY** or **ENTER** or LeftMouse to stop *recording*. Use **ESCKEY** to undo changes.

SKEY

Scaling mode. This works on selected IPO Curves and vertices. The degree of *scaling* is *precisely* linked to the mouse movement. Try to move from the (rotation) midpoint with the mouse. In IPO Key mode, you can only *scale* horizontally.

Scaling mode. This works on selected IPO Curves and vertices. The degree of *scaling* is *precisely* linked to the mouse movement. Try to move from the (rotation) midpoint with the mouse. In IPO Key mode, you can only *scale* horizontally.

Limitors:

- **CTRL**: in increments of 0.1.
- **SHIFT-CTRL**: in increments of 0.01.
- **MMB** limits *scaling* to the X or Y axis. Blender calculates which axis to use based on the already initiated mouse movement. Click MiddleMouse again to return to free *scaling*.

- **ARROWS** These keys allow you to move the mouse cursor exactly 1 pixel.
- **XKEY** Make the horizontal *scaling* negative, the X-flip.
- **YKEY** Make the vertical *scaling* negative, the Y-flip.

Terminate size mode with:

- **LMB**, **SPACE** or **ENTER**: to finalize scaling.
- **RMB** or **ESC**: everything returns to its previous state.

SHIFT-S

Snap Menu.

- "Horizontal": The selected Bezier handles are set to horizontal.
- "To next": The selected handle or vertex is set to the same (Y) value as the next one.
- "To frame": The selected handles or vertices are set to the exact frame values.
- "To current frame": The selected handle or vertex is moved to the current frame.

TKEY

If an IPO Curve is selected: "IPOType". The type of selected IPO Curves can be changed. A PopupMenu asks you to make a choice:

- "Constant": after each vertex of the curve, this value remains constant, and is not interpolated.
- "Linear": linear interpolation occurs between the vertices.
- "Bezier": the vertices get a *handle* (i.e. two extra vertices) with which you can indicate the curvature of the interpolation curve.

If a Key is selected: "Key Type". The type of selected Keys can be changed.

- "Linear": linear interpolation occurs between the Keys. The Key line is displayed as a broken line.
- "Cardinal": fluent interpolation occurs between the Keys; this is the default.
- "BSpline": extra fluent interpolation occurs between the Keys, four Keys are now involved in the interpolation calculation. Now the positions *themselves* cannot be displayed precisely, however. The Key line is shown as a broken line.

VKEY

Vector Handle. The selected Bezier *handles* are converted to *vector* type.

XKEY

Erase selected. The selected vertices, IPO Keys or IPO Curves are deleted. If there are selected VertexKeys, they are also deleted.

The Sequence Window

Sequence Toolbar

WindowType

As with every window header, the first button left allows you to set the window type.

Menus

The triangular button expand/collapses menus. Menus provide a self-explicative way to access to all Blender functions which can be performed in the Sequence Window. They are context sensitive and will change depending on the selected Object.

Windows with menus, as the Sequence Window, does not have the standard "Full Window" and "Home" header buttons, actions which have moved to the View Menu.

Menu items are in general self-explanatory and the relative functionality will be explained later on in the hotkeys section.

DisplayImage

The window shows the result of the Sequences, i.e. a picture.

View Zoom

Move the mouse to zoom into or out of the SequenceWindow. This is an alternative for **CTRL-MMB** and **MW**. View Border Draw a rectangle to indicate what part of the SequenceWindow should be displayed in the full window.

Clear

| Clear |

Force a clear of all buffered images in memory.

SequenceWindow

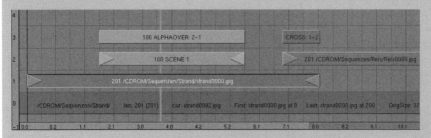

In the SequenceWindow you arrange your scenes, external pictures or movie files for the postproduction of your animation. The Strip in row 1 is a sequence of numbered jpeg-pictures. It will play for a few seconds and then SCENE 1 in row 2 will be superimposed with the ALPHAOVER effect in row 3. The ALPHAOVER generates some shadows, which can be seen in the film-strip below. In SCENE 1 (which is a normal Blender-scene) the titeling is done with the usual animation features from Blender, which makes that system a very flexible titler.

In the end a transition of strip in row 1 and the folowing in row 2 is done with the CROSS effect. The numbers 1-2 are representing the row numbers the effect applies to. The result is a smooth fade between the two strips in row one and two.

The mouse

LMB

The position of the mouse cursor becomes the current frame. If DisplayImage is ON, the Sequences at this position are read or calculated at this position.

MMB and drag

Depending on the position within the window:

- On the sliders; this can be moved.
- The rest of the window; the *view* is translated.

CTRL-MMB and drag

Zoom in/out on the IpoWindow. For ease of use, you can only zoom horizontally. Use the HeaderButton if you must zoom vertically as well.

RMB

Selection works the same way here as in the 3DWindow: normally a maximum of one Sequence strip is selected. Use **SHIFT** to extend or reduce the selection (*extend select*).

RMB and drag

Selects something and immediately starts *translation* mode, i.e. the Grabber.

SHIFT-RMB

Extend selection.

The Hotkeys

NUM+, NUM-

Zoom in, zoom out.

SHIFT-NUM+

Insert gap. One second is inserted at the current frame position. This only applies to strips that are totally to the right of the current frame.

ALT-NUM+

Insert gap. As above, but now 10 seconds are inserted.

SHIFT-NUM-

Remove gaps. All strips that are completely to the right of the current frame and do *not* start past the last frame are repositioned so that there is no longer an empty space.

NUM.

The last selected strip is displayed completely.

HOME

All visible Sequences are displayed completely, centered in the window.

AKEY

Select All / deselect All. If any strip is selected, everything is first deselected.

SHIFT-A

Add sequence. A PopupMenu asks you to make a choice. The first three are possible sources:

- "Images"; Specify with FileSelect (with **RMB** select!), what pictures will form a trip. If only 1 picture is selected, the strip is lengthened to 50 frames. Directories can also be specified; each directory then becomes a separate strip in the SequenceWindow.
- "Movie"; Specify with FileSelect (with **LMB** or **RMB**!) what movie will comprise a strip.
- "Audio"; Specify with FileSelect (with **LMB** or **RMB**!) what WAV file will comprise a strip.
- "Scene"; A PopupMenu asks you to specify the Scene that is to be inserted as a strip. The Scene is then rendered according to its own settings and processed in the Sequence system.

The following menu options are effects that work on pictures; two strips must be selected for this. The order of selection determines how the effects are applied.

- "Plugin"; a File Window let you choose a sequence plugin.
- "Cross"; a fluent transition from strip 1 to strip 2.
- "GammaCross"; This is a gamma-corrected cross. It provides a more 'natural' transition in which lighter parts are inserted before darker parts.
- "Add"; two strips are added together.
- "Sub"; the second strip is subtracted from the first.
- "Mul"; the strips are multiplied.
- "AlphaOver"; the second strip, with its *alpha*, is placed over the first. Pictures with *alpha* are normally 32 bits.
- "AlphaUnder"; the first strip is placed behind the second, with the *alpha* of the second strip.
- "AlphaOverDrop"; like "AlphaOver", but now with a drop shadow.

BKEY

Border select. Draw a rectangle with the LeftMouse; all strips that fall within this rectangle are *selected*. Draw a rectangle with the RightMouse to *deselect*.

CKEY

If one of the ends of a strip is selected (the triangles), the current frame is moved to this end. In all other cases, the Change menu is invoked. This menu allows you to change specific characteristics of the *active* strip.

If this is an Image strip:

- "Change Images". The FileSelect appears and new pictures can be specified.

If this is an Effect strip:

- "Switch a-b"; change the sequence of the effect.
- "Recalculate"; force a recalculation of the effect.
- "Cross, Gammacross, Add, ..."; change the type of effect.

If this is a Scene strip:

- "Update Start and End"; the start and end frame of the Scene is processed in the strip again.

ALT-D

Add Duplicate. All selected strips are copied. Immediately thereafter, *translation* mode is started. The images in an Image strip are reused; they take up no extra memory.

FKEY

"Set Filter". An extra Y filter can only be activated in Movie strips. This filter is for a stable video display with no flickering.

GKEY

Translation mode (the Grabber). This works on selected strips or the (triangular) ends of selected strips. Alternative for starting this mode: **RMB** and drag;. The following options are available in *translation* mode:

- Limitors: **SHIFT** with finer translation.
- **MMB** limits the current translation to the X or Y axis. Blender calculates which axis to use based on the already initiated mouse movement. Click MiddleMouse again to return to unlimited translation.
- **ARROWS**: These keys can be used to move the mouse cursor exactly 1 pixel.

Grabber can be terminated with:

- **LMB SPACE** or **ENTER**: move to the new position.
- **RMB** or **ESC**: everything returns to the old position.

MKEY

Make Meta. The selected strips are combined into a Meta strip. This only occurs if no unselected strips are linked to the selection by effects. Use **TAB** to view the contents of a Meta or to leave the Meta. Metas can be inside other Metas, and behave exactly like a normal Sequence strip. When Metas are duplicated, their contents are *not* linked!

ALT-M

Un-Meta. The selected Meta is 'unpacked' again.

NKEY

Opens the NKEY Panel. If the selected strip is a Movie strip it allows to set/unset the Y filter and the Mul factor.

If the selected strip is an Audio Strip it opens the relevant Panel, with Gain, Pan and Mute options.

SKEY

Snap menu. The PopupMenu offers you a choice:"Sequence to frame"; the selected strips are placed with their starting point on the current frame.

XKEY

Delete Sequence. The selected strips are deleted.

The OopsWindow

Oops Toolbar

WindowType

As with every window header, the first button allows you to set the window type.

WINDOWS REFERENCE.OOPS WINDOW

Full Window

□

Maximise the window, or return to the previous window display size; return to the previous screen setting (**CTRL-UPARROW**).

Home

All visible blocks are displayed completely, centered in the window (**HOME**).

View Zoom

±

Move the mouse to zoom in or out of the OopsWindow. This is an alternative to **CTRL-MMB**.

View Border

⊞

Draw a frame to indicate what part of the OopsWindow should be displayed in the full window.

Visible Select

- Lay: the *layer* setting of the Scene determines what Objects are drawn.
- Scene: all Scenes present are displayed.
- Object: all Objects of all visible Scenes are displayed, possibly limited by the "Lay" option.
- Mesh
- Curve: this is also for Surface and Font blocks.
- MetaBall
- Lattice
- Lamp
- Material
- Texture
- Ipo
- Library

OopsWindow

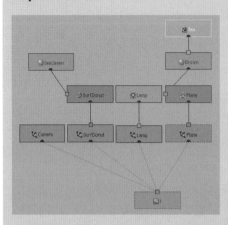

The OopsWindow gives a schematic overview of the current structure. Blender is based on an Object-Oriented Programming System (OOPS!). The building blocks are universal DataBlocks that are assigned relationships using *links*. The different DataBlocks in the OopsWindow can be recognised by an icon and the colour. The DataBlocks have a clearly visible 'entrance' and 'exit' between which *link* lines are drawn. The current Scene and the *active* Object have a frame with a dashed line.

The functionality of the OopsWindow is limited to visualisation. Links are created using the available HotKeys (**CTRL-L** in the 3DWindow) and with the DataButtons in the Headers. Selected Objects are also selected in the OopsWindow, and vice versa.

In the accompanying example, we see the Scene at the bottom, with four linked Object blocks. The Object blocks have links to the specific ObData; such as Mesh, Surface, Lamp. The Materials ("Brown" and "SeaGreen") are linked to the ObData and the Texture is linked to a Material.

The mouse

LMB and drag

These are the Gestures. Blender's gesture recognition works in two ways here:

- Draw a straight line: start *translation* mode.
- Draw a V-shaped line: start *scaling* mode.

MMB and drag

The *view* is translated.

CTRL-MMB and drag

Zoom in or out of the OopsWindow..

RMB

Select works here in the normal fashion: normally a maximum of one DataBlock is selected. Use **SHIFT** to enlarge or reduce the selection (*extend* select).

RMB and drag

Select and start *translation* mode, the Grabber.

SHIFT-RMB

Add/remove from selection.

CTRL-RMB

This selects and *activates* a DataBlock. This only works for Scenes and Objects.

The HotKeys

NUM+ NUM-

Zoom in, zoom out.

HOME

All visible blocks are displayed completely, centred in the window.

1KEY, 2KEY...0KEY

The visible *layers* of the current Scene can be set. Press **SHIFT** for *extend* select.

AKEY

Select All / deselect All. If one block is selected, everything is first eselected.

BKEY

Border select. Draw a rectangle with the **LMB**; all blocks that fall within this rectangle are *selected*. Draw a rectangle with the **RMB** to *deselect* the blocks.

GKEY

Translation mode (the Grabber). This works on selected blocks. Alternatives for starting this mode:

- **RMB** and drag
- **LMB** and drag to draw a straight line.

The following options are available in translation mode:

- **MMB** restricts the current translation to the X or Y axis. Blender calculates which axis to use based on the already initiated mouse movement. Click **MMB** again to restore unlimited translation.
- **ARROWS**: The mouse cursor can be moved exactly 1 pixel with these keys.

Grabber terminates with:

- **LMB SPACE ENTER**: move to a new position.
- **RMB** or **ESC**: everything returns to the old position.

LKEY

Select Linked Forward. All DataBlocks that are linked by a selected DataBlock are also selected. In this way, the entire underlying structure can be selected, starting with a selected Scene block.

SHIFT-L

Select Linked Backward. All *users* of selected DataBlocks are selected. This allows you to visualise what Objects the Material uses, starting with a selected Material block.

SKEY

Select Linked Backward. All *users* of selected DataBlocks are selected. This allows you to visualise what Objects the Material uses, starting with a selected Material block.

- **MMB** restricts the *scaling* to the X or Y axis. Blender calculates which axis to use based on the already initiated mouse movement. Click **MMB** again to return to free *scaling*.
- **ARROWS**: These keys move the mouse cursor exactly 1 pixel.

Exit size mode with:

- **LMB, SPACE** or **ENTER**: to finalize scaling.

SHIFT-S

Shuffle Oops. An attempt is made to minimise the length of the *link* lines for selected DataBlocks using parsed toggling.

ALT-S

Shrink Oops. The length of the *link* lines for the selected DataBlocks is shortened without causing the blocks to overlap.

The Action Window

Action Toolbar

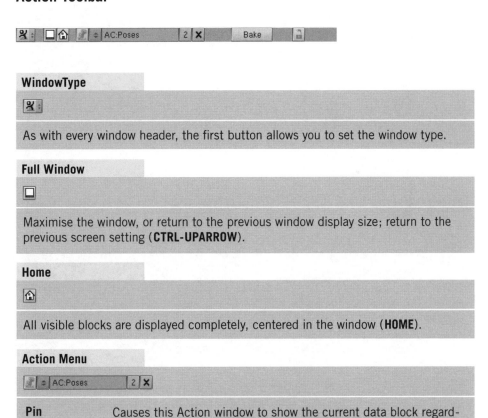

WindowType

As with every window header, the first button allows you to set the window type.

Full Window

Maximise the window, or return to the previous window display size; return to the previous screen setting (**CTRL-UPARROW**).

Home

All visible blocks are displayed completely, centered in the window (**HOME**).

Action Menu

Pin   Causes this Action window to show the current data block regardless of what object is selected or active.

Action Menu	Choose another Action from the list of available Actions. The option "Add New" makes a complete copy of the current Action. This is not visible; only the name in the adjacent button will change.
AC:	Give the current Action a new and unique name. After the new name is entered, it appears in the list, sorted alphabetically.
Users	If this button is displayed, there is more than one user for the Action block. Use the button to make the Action "Single User".
Unlink Action	The current Action is unlinked.

Bake

Generate an action based of the current action where the constraints effects are converted into IPO Keys.

Lock

This button locks the update of the 3DWindow while editing in the ActionWindow, so you can see changes maked to the Action in realtime in the 3DWindow.

ActionWindow

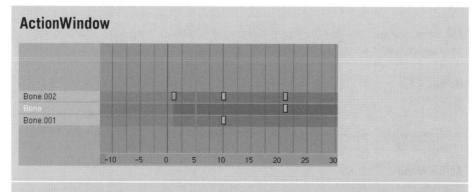

The ActionWindow gives an overview of the current Armature Keys and Relative Vertex Keys of the Object. It presents the time, in frames, on an horizontal axis and, vertically, as many stripes are there are bones in the armature or Relative Vertex Keys.

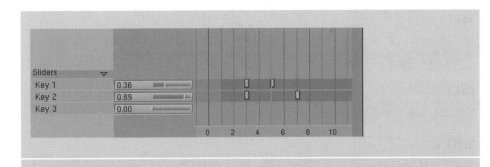

If the object is an armature bone Keys are represented as grey rectangle at the pertinent frame, yellow if selected. If it is a Mesh, Rectangles are present where a Key is assigned a given value. This can be assigned via IPO or via the sliders in the ActionWindow.

The mouse

LMB

Sets current frame.

MMB and drag

The *view* is translated.

CTRL-MMB and drag

Zoom in or out of the ActioWindow, this happens only horizontally.

RMB

Select a strip (if clicked on strip name) or a Key if clicked on a Key. Use **SHIFT** to enlarge or reduce the selection (*extend* select).

SHIFT-RMB

Add/remove from selection.

The HotKeys

HOME

All visible blocks are displayed completely, centred in the window.

AKEY

Select All / deselect All. If one block is selected, everything is first eselected.

BKEY

Border select. Draw a rectangle with the **LMB**; all blocks that fall within this rectangle are *selected*. Draw a rectangle with the **RMB** to *deselect* the blocks.

CKEY

Centers view at current frame.

SHIFT-D

Duplicates the selected Keys. Duplicates are automatically in Grab mode.

GKEY

Translation mode (the Grabber). This works on selected blocks and only horizontally, to change frame. The following options are available in *translation* mode:

- **ARROWS**: The mouse cursor can be moved exactly 1 pixel with these keys.
- **CTRL**: The Keys are displaced by 1 frame steps.
- **SHIFT-CTRL**: The Keys are displaced by 0.1 frame steps.

Grabber terminates with:

- **LMB, SPACE ENTER**: move to a new position.
- **RMB** or **ESC**: everything returns to the old position.

TKEY

Allows to define the type of interpolation for the selected strips:

- "Constant" is picewise constant (abrupt changes).
- "Linear"is linear interpolation (abrupt changes in derivative).
- "Bezier"is default fluid interpolation.

XKEY

Delete selected Keys.

The Non Linear Animation Window

NLA Toolbar

WINDOWS REFERENCE.NLA WINDOW

WindowType

As with every window header, the first button allows you to set the window type.

Full Window

Maximise the window, or return to the previous window display size; return to the previous screen setting (**CTRL-UPARROW**).

Home

All visible blocks are displayed completely, centered in the window (**HOME**).

Lock

This button locks the update of the 3DWindow while editing in the ActionWindow, so you can see changes maked to the Action in realtime in the 3DWindow.

NLAWindow

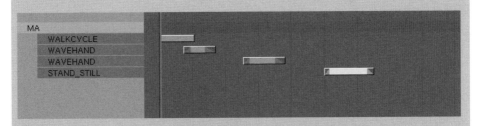

The NLAWindow gives an full overview of all the Armature Objects and allows a very fine and flexible control of each armature action, effectively allowing for action blending somewhat akin to how Relative Vertex Keys work on meshes.

The NLA window presents the time, in frames, on the horizontal axis and one strip for each armature, each armature strip can have as many action substrips as desired. It is important to have unlinked any normal Action from the armature when working with NLA because normal actions take precedence over NLA controls.

The Mouse

LMB

Sets current frame.

MMB and drag

The *view* is translated.

CTRL-MMB and drag

Zoom in or out of the NLAWindow, this happens only horizontally.

RMB

Select an Armature Strip (if clicked on strip name) or an Action Strip if clicked on it. Use SHIFT to enlarge or reduce the selection (*extend* select).

SHIFT-RMB

Add/remove from selection.

The HotKeys

HOME

All visible blocks are displayed completely, centred in the window.

AKEY

Select All / deselect All. If one block is selected, everything is first eselected. It behaves differently depending if the cursor is on the left (selects all armatures) or on the right (selects all actions) of the NLAWindow.

BKEY

Border select. Draw a rectangle with the **LMB**; all blocks that fall within this rectangle are *selected*. Draw a rectangle with the **RMB** to *deselect* the blocks.

SHIFT-D

Duplicates the selected Action(s). Duplicates are automatically in Grab mode and are assigned to new sub-strips.

GKEY

Translation mode (the Grabber). This works on selected Actions and only horizontally, to change frame. The following options are available in *translation* mode:

WINDOWS REFERENCE.

- **ARROWS**: The mouse cursor can be moved exactly 1 pixel with these keys.
- **CTRL**: The Keys are displaced by 1 frame steps.
- **SHIFT-CTRL**: The Keys are displaced by 0.1 frame steps.

Grabber terminates with:

- **LMB, SPACE ENTER**: move to a new position.
- **RMB** or **ESC**: everything returns to the old position.

NKEY

Brings up the "Numerical" window settings for the selected Action.

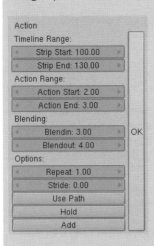

- "Strip Start" and "Strip End" defines the Action Strip placement. If the interval is greater than the actual Action duration the Action is performed slower to match the required duration, otherwise faster.
- "Action Start" and "Action End" defines the Action timeline "Windowing". The Actions are defined in their normal way and their duration is, by default, fa "Window" of frames going from first to last key. With this sliders it is possible to vary the Action "Windowing".
- "BlendIn" and "BlendOut" defines a number of frames at the begginning and at the end of the strip of "Reduced influence" of the Action. By care fully setting these and by letting action stripls slightly overlap you can blend fluidly different actions.
- "Repeat" Makes the strip contain as many copies of the action as desired. Great for Walkcycles.
- "Stride" in Walkcycles defines the length (in Blender Units) of a stride.
- "Use Path" Makes Blender use the Path to which the armature is parented, and its length, to make the Armature move according to Stride definition.
- "Hold" Makes the last pose to be held forever, instead than reverting to original state.
- "Add" Makes Blending addictive.

XKEY

Delete selected Keys.

The Text Window

Text Toolbar

WindowType

As with every window header, the first button allows you to set the window type.

Menu

The triangular button expand/collapses menus. Menus provide a self-explicative way to access to all Blender functions which can be performed in the Text Window. They are context sensitive and will change depending on the context.

Full Window

Maximise the window, or return to the previous window display size; return to the previous screen setting (**CTRL-UPARROW**).

Line Numbers

This button toggles showing of the line numbers on and off.

Text Menu

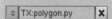

Choose another Text from the list of available Buffers. The option "Add New" opens a new empty buffer. The option "Open New" turns the Text Window into a File Selection Window an allows to load a Text Buffer from the disk.

As for Blender 2.30 two buffer exists by default, one named "KEYLIST" holding an hotkeys quick reference, the other named "LAYERS" ready to hold written layer descriptions.

TX: Give the current Text buffer a new and unique name. After the new name is entered, it appears in the list, sorted alphabetically.

Unlink Text The current Text Buffer is unlinked.

Font size

```
Screen 12   ⬍
```

Allows to switch from 12 to 15 point size for text.

TextWindow

The TextWindow is a simple but useful Texteditor, fully integrated into Blender. The main purpose of it is to write Python scripts, but it is also very useful to write comments in the Blendfile or to instruct other users the purpose of the scene.

```
1  ###################################################
2  #
3  # Demo Script for Blender 2.3 Guide
4  #
5  ###################################################S68
6  # This script generates polygons. It is quite useless
7  # since you can do polygons with ADD->Mesh->Circle
8  # but it is a nice complete script example, and the
9  # polygons are 'filled'
10 ###################################################
11
12 ###################################################
13 # Importing modules
14 ###################################################
15
16 import Blender
17 from Blender import NMesh
18 from Blender.BGL import *
19 from Blender.Draw import *
20
21 import math
22 from math import *
23
24 # Polygon Parameters
25 T_NumberOfSides = Create(3)
26 T_Radius        = Create(1.0)
27
28 # Events
29 EVENT_NOEVENT = 1
30 EVENT_DRAW    = 2
31 EVENT_EXIT    = 3
32
33 ###################################################
34 # GUI drawing
35 ###################################################
36 def draw():
37     global T_NumberOfSides
38     global T_Radius
39     global EVENT_NOEVENT,EVENT_DRAW,EVENT_EXIT
40
41     ########## Titles
```

The mouse

LMB

Sets the cursor position, defines a selection.

SHIFT-LMB

Adds/remove from selection.

MMB

Pan / translates window.

RMB

Opens a menu:

- "New" - Creates a new empty buffer.
- "Open" - Turns window in File Selection Window for loading a text buffer from disk.
- "Save" - Save text buffer to disc.
- "Save As" - Turns window in File Selection Window for saving the current text buffer to disc.

The HotKeys

ALT-C or CTRL-C

Copy the marked text into a temporary buffer.

SHIFT-ALT-F

Opens the same menu as **RMB**

ALT-J

Asks for a line number and makes the cursor jump to it.

ALT-M

Converts the text in the buffer into a 3D text object (Max 1000 chars).

ALT-O

Opens a Text buffer.

ALT-P

Executes the Text as a Python script.

ALT-R

Redo.

ALT-S

Saves the Text buffer.

ALT-U

Undo.

ALT-V or CTRL-V

Paste the marked text from the temporary buffer.

ALT-X or CTRL-X

Cut the marked text into a temporary buffer.

Windows

Blender's temporary buffer is separated from Window's clipboard. To access Window's clipboard use **SHIFT-CTRL-C**, **SHIFT-CTRL-V**, **SHIFT-CTRL-X**.

The Audio Timeline Window

The SoundWindow is currently most useful for the realtime part of Blender, which is not covered by this manual.

It is used to load and visualize sounds. You can grab and zoom the window like every other window in Blender.

SoundHeader

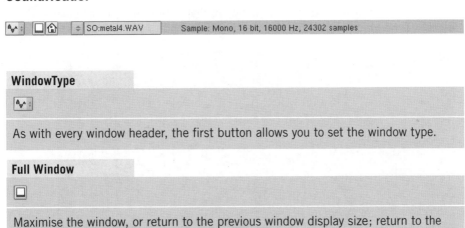

WindowType

As with every window header, the first button allows you to set the window type.

Full Window

Maximise the window, or return to the previous window display size; return to the previous screen setting (**CTRL-UPARROW**).

Home

All visible Sequences are completely displayed, centered in the window (**HOME**).

Sound Menu

Choose another Audio Stream from the list of available ones. The option "Add New" opend a File selection window to open a new Audio file.

SO: Give the current Audio Stream a new and unique name. After the new name is entered, it appears in the list, sorted alphabetically.

InfoText

Sample: Mono, 16 bit, 16000 Hz, 24302 samples

Provides some info about the currently activeAudio Stream.

InfoText

Sample: Mono, 16 bit, 16000 Hz, 24302 samples

Provides some info about the currently activeAudio Stream.

The Audio Window

The sound Audio Window represents the wave shape. Differently by all other Blender Time windows the time scale is here in seconds, not frames.

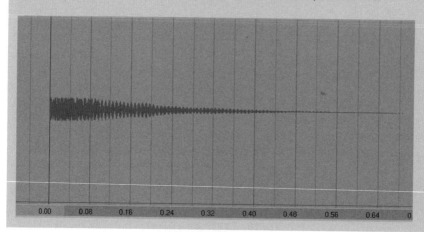

The ImageWindow

ImageHeader

Images in Blender are also DataBlocks. The ImageWindow is used for visualisation and UV-texturing.

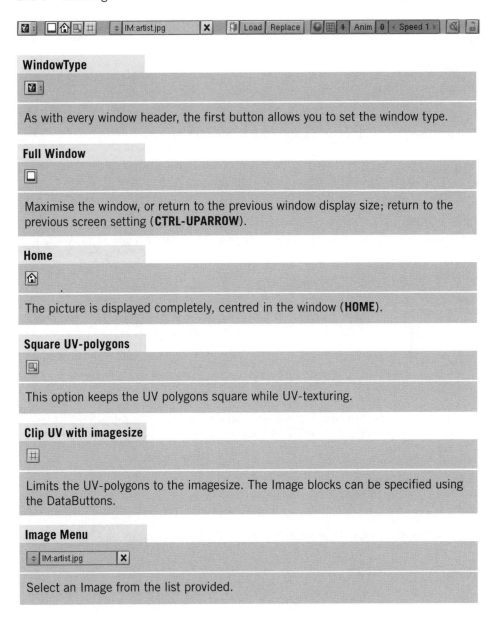

WindowType

As with every window header, the first button allows you to set the window type.

Full Window

Maximise the window, or return to the previous window display size; return to the previous screen setting (**CTRL-UPARROW**).

Home

The picture is displayed completely, centred in the window (**HOME**).

Square UV-polygons

This option keeps the UV polygons square while UV-texturing.

Clip UV with imagesize

Limits the UV-polygons to the imagesize. The Image blocks can be specified using the DataButtons.

Image Menu

Select an Image from the list provided.

IM:	Give the current Image a new and unique name. After the new name is entered, it is displayed in the list alphabetically.
Unlink	Unlinks the current image.

Pack

Packs the current image within the .blend file.

Load

Load a new Image. A Image Select Windows appears. The labelless button nearby let you specify the imagevia a standard File Select Window.

Replace

Replaces the current image wit a new one. A Image Select Windows appears. The labelless button nearby let you specify the imagevia a standard File Select Window.

RefMap

Uses the current image as a Reflection Map, ignoring UV coordinates.

Tile

Sets the image to tile mode. This way you can make a repeating pattern with a small part of an image. With **SHIFT-LMB** you indicate which part of the image should be used.

PartsX and PartsY

Defines the dimension of the tile mode.

Anim

Enables the texture-animation.

Animation start and end

Controls the start and end of the texture-animation.

Speed

Sets the speed of the animation, in frames per second.

Texture Paint

Enables Texture Paint mode.

Lock

When activated, changes made in the ImageWindow are shown in realtime in the 3DWindows.

ImageWindow

Images in Blender are also DataBlocks. The ImageWindow is used for visualisation and UV-texturing.

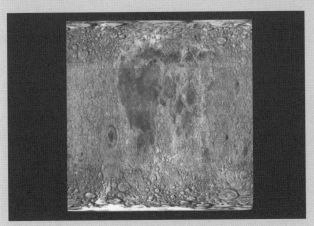

The use of the mouse and HotKeys is:

MMB

Translate the *view*.

NUM+, NUM-, MW

Zoom in, zoom out.

HOME

The picture is displayed completely, centred in the window.

CTRL-N

Replace Image Names. A menu asks you to enter an old and a new file name. All file names for Images with the old name or a name which starts with corresponding characters are replaced by the new name. This utility is especially useful for changing directories. Example: "old" = /data/, "new" = /pics/textures/. The file name "/data/marble.tga" is replaced by "/pics/textures/marble.tga".

The ImageSelectWindow

ImageSelectHeader

WindowType

As with every window header, the first button allows you to set the window type.

Full Window

Maximise the window, or return to the previous window display size; return to the previous screen setting (**CTRL-UPARROW**).

Remove

Delete the ".Bpib" help file in the current directory. A new ".Bpib" is only created once the directory is read again.

Dirview

Indicates whether the left part, where the directories are displayed, is shown.

Info

Indicates whether the lower part, where information about the active picture is displayed, is shown.

Images

Obsolete.

Magnify

The active picture is displayed twice as large.

ImageSelectWindow

In parts of the Blender interface where pictures can be loaded, you generally have the option of using a FileSelect window or the ImageSelect window. For the most part, the functionality is the same. The ImageSelect window reads the directory and examines each file to see if it is a recognisable image. After the entire directory is scanned, the images are loaded and displayed as a thumbnail and saved in the ".Bpib" file. If a ".Bpib" file already exists, it is first read in and compared to the contents of the directory.

P

Displays the parent directory (**PKEY**).

DirName:

This text box displays the current directory.

Preset Directories

The file $HOME/.Bfs contains a number of pre-sets that are shown in this menu. While a file is being read or written, the directory involved is temporarily added to the menu.

FileName:

The file name can be entered here.

Status Icons.

The different phases of ImageSelect:

- Was a ".Bpib" file found?
- Was the directory scanned completely?
- Have all the pictures been read in?

The mouse and HotKeys

LMB

Activate a file. The file name is placed in the FileName button.

MMB

Activate a file and return to the previous window type.

RMB

Select a file.

ENTER

Close the ImageSelectWindow; return with a OK message.

ESC

Close the ImageSelectWindow; no action is performed.

PAGEDN

Scroll down one page.

PAGEUP

Scroll up one page.

PKEY

Go to the parent directory.

The Animation Playback Window

To allow you to view sequences of rendered frames or AVIs, Blender has a simple, but efficient animation playback option. This playback is invoked with the "PLAY" button in the DisplayButtons. This button plays all of the numbered frames specified in the DisplayButtons->pics TextBut.

An alternative for starting the animation window is to type -a in the command line: blender -a . Blender first reads all the files in memory and then displays them as a flip book. Check in advance to make sure sufficient memory is available; you can see this with the FileWindow. Use **ESC** to stop the reading process.

The commands available in the playback window are:

ESC

Close the window.

ENTER

Start playback.

LEFTARROW, DOWNARROW

Stops the playback; if playback is already stopped, moves 1 frame back.

RIGHTARROW, UPARROW

Stops the playback; if playback is already stopped, moves 1 frame forward.

NUM0

Sets the playback at the first frame and switches 'cyclical' playback off. Pressing this key again turns cyclical playback on again and starts the playback at the beginning.

PAD1 to PAD9

The playback speed. 60, 50, 30, 25, 20, 15, 12, 10 and 6 frames per second, respectively.

LMB

Move the mouse horizontally through the playback window to scroll through the frames.

CH. 27 BUTTONS REFERENCE

BUTTONS WINDOW, LOGIC CONTEXT, SCRIPT CONTEXT, SHADING CONTEXT, OBJECT CONTEXT, EDITING CONTEXT, SCENE CONTEXT, OTHER PANELS

The Buttons Window

Buttons Header

The Buttons Window is so peculiar and presents so many characteristics that it deserves a treatment of its own.

Window Type	As with every window header, the first button enables you to set the window type.
Full Window	Maximise the window, or return to the previous window display size; return to the old screen setting (**CTRL-UPARROW**).
Home	The optimal *view* settings for the current window are restored (**HOME**).

Context Buttons

The following six buttons define the Context of the Button window. Depending on which of these buttons is pressed a second group of buttons may appear further right, defining a Sub-context.

Logic	Logic Context (**F4**). No Sub-contexts.
Script	Script Context. No Sub-contexts.
Shading	Shading Context (**F5**). Sub-contexts are Lamp Buttons, Material Buttons, Texture Buttons (**F6**), Radiosity Buttons and World Buttons (**F8**). Blender selects Sub-context smartly. If you are in Shading context with a Mesh Object selected and Material Sub-context, by selecting a Lamp you automatically switch to Lamp Sub-context and vice-versa. Selecting the camera switches to World Sub-context.
Object	Object Context (**F7**). No Sub-contexts.
Editing	Editing Context (**F9**). No Sub-contexts.
Scene	Scene Context (**F10**). Sub-contexts: Rendering; Animation/Playback and Sound Buttons.
Current Frame	The current frame number is displayed as a Num Button in the header.

Buttons Window

A Buttons Window is filled with Panels containing Buttons. Panels can be merged together and, if this is the case, the Panel presents multiple Tabs to select the buttons. Of course Tabs can be carried out of the panel to form new independent Panels. **LMB** and drag Panel/Tab header to achieve this. Drop the header out of a panel to explode, onto another's Panel header to collapse.

Panels can be arranged horizontally or vertically or freely, they can be collapsed to optimize space.

The Buttons Window global facilities are (Mouse clicks in the Buttons Windows but outside of any Panel):

MMB or MW	Panels contained in the Buttons Window are moved altogether. If they are placed horizontally in an horizontal window they are panned left-right, if they are placed vertically in a vertical window they are scrolled top-bottom.
CTRL-MMB	Within certain limits, a Buttons Window Panels can be zoomed in/out.
RMB	Panels Menu. You can select: Free, Horizontal and Vertical alignment for panels.
NUM+	Zoom in.
NUM−	Zoom out.
HOMEKEY	The optimal *view* settings for the current window are restored. If there is only one 3Dwindow in the current Screen, the NumPad commands for the 3DWindow also work in the Buttons Window.

Logic Context

The Logic Context is meant for making interactive 3D-animations in Blender. Blender acts then as a complete development tool for interactive worlds including a Game Engine to play the worlds. All is done without compiling the game or interactive world. Just press **PKEY** and it runs in realtime. This Book does not cover the realtime part of Blender, because it is a complex process which has the full attention of a separate Book. Furthermore going Open Source Blender had to discard some of its libraries which were closed sourced by third parties, hence Open Source Blender does not have a full Game Engine (yet!). However we like to give you a overview what can be done with Blender. Visit our website www.blender.org to see the latest developments of the Game Engine and find tutorials giving you a start in interactive 3D-graphics.

The Logic Context buttons are the only one not yet divided into Panels, mainly because they are mostly unused in 2.30. They can be logical separated in two parts. The left part contains global settings for elements of the game.

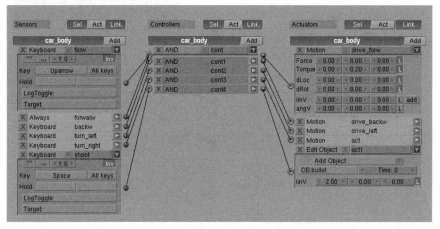

This includes settings for general physics, like the damping or mass. Here you also define if an object should be calculated with the build in physic or should be handled static or forming a level. Here you can also define properties of game objects, these properties can carry values which describe attributes of the object like variables in a programming language.

The right part of the Realtime Buttons is the command centre to add game logic to your objects and worlds. It consists of the sensors, controllers and actuators.

Sensors are like the senses of a life form, the react on key presses, collisions, contact with materials, timer events or values of properties.

The controllers are collecting events from the sensors and are able to calculate them to a result. Simple actuators are just doing a AND for example to test if a key is pressed and a certain time is over. There are also OR actuators and you also can use python-scripting to do more complex stuff.

The actuator then actually do things on the objects. This can be applying forces to objects to move or rotate them, playing predefined animations (via IPOs) or adding new objects.

The logic is connected (wired) with the mouse amongst the sensors, controllers and actuators. After that you are immediately able to play the game! If you discover something in the game you don't like, just stop, edit and restart. This way you get fantastic turnaround times in your development.

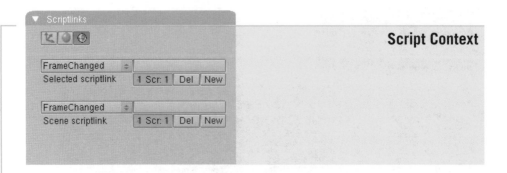

Script Context

Script Links - Linking scripts to Blender

Python scripts can be attached to Data Blocks with the Script Buttons window, and assigned events that define when they should be called. Just one Panel, `Script-links` is present.

Script Links can be added for the following Data Blocks

- Objects - Available when an Object is active;
- Cameras - Available when the active Object is a Camera;
- Lamps - Available when the active Object is a Lamp;
- Materials - Available when the active Object has a Material;
- Worlds - Available when the current scene contains a World;

These can be selected with the top row of Toggle Buttons in the Panel. Please note that only the Buttons which are applicable are present.

Selecting one of the Toggle Buttons brings up the `Selected Scriptlink` Buttons group in the middle of the Panel.

Data Blocks can have an arbitrary number of Script Links attached to them - additional links can be added and deleted with the `New` and `Del` buttons, similar to Material Indices. Scripts are executed in order, beginning with the script linked at index one.

When you have at least one Script Link the Event type Menu and link buttons are displayed. The link button should be filled in with the name of the Text Object containing the script to be executed.

The Event type indicates at what point the script will be triggered:

FrameChanged	This event is executed every time the user changes frame, and during rendering and animation playback. To provide more user interaction this script is also executed continuously during editing for Objects.
Redraw	This event is executed every time Blender redraws its Windows.

Scripts that are executed because of events being triggered receive additional input by objects in the Blender module.

*   The **Blender.bylink** object is set to True to indicate that the script has been called by a Script Link (as opposed to the user pressing **ALT-P** in the Text window).
*   The **Blender.link** object is set to contain the Data Block which referenced the script, this may be a Material, Lamp, Object, etc.
*   The **Blender.event** object is set to the name of the event which triggered the Script Link execution. This allows one script to be used to process different event types.

Scene Script Links

The Script Link buttons for Scenes are always available at the bottom of the Scriptlink Panel, and function exactly in the manner described above, but on a scene wide context. Events available for Scene Script Links are:

FrameChanged	This event is executed every time the user changes frame, and during rendering and animation playback.
OnLoad	This event is executed whenever the Scene is loaded, ie. when the file is initially loaded, or when the user switches to the current scene.
Redraw	This event is executed every time Blender redraws its Windows.

Shading Context

The Shading context is among the most complex, exhibiting five Sub-contexts and several Panels. Many of these Panels are condensed into a single Panel with Tabs in the default Blender settings.

Lamp Sub-context

The settings in these Sub-context visualise the Lamp Data Block. The Lamp Buttons are only displayed if the *active* Object is a Lamp.

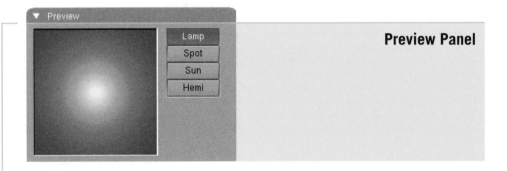

Preview Panel

As for all these Sub-contexts, except Radiosity, the first Panel contains a preview square window. Right of the Panel a column of four Toggle Buttons allows to select the Lamp Type:

Lamp	The standard lamp, a point light source.
Spot	The lamp is restricted to a conical space. The 3DWindow shows the form of the spotlight with a broken line.
Sun	The light shines from a constant direction; the distance has no effect. The position of the Lamp Object is thus unimportant, except for the rotation.
Hemi	Like Sun, but now light is shed in the form of half a sphere, a *hemisphere*. This method is also called *directional ambient*. It can be used to suggest cloudy daylight.

Lamp Panel

The top button row presents:

Lamp Data Block

Lamp Menu	Choose another Lamp Block from the list provided.
LA:	Shows the current Lamp name. **SHIFT-LMB** to edit it into a new and unique name.
Users	If the Lamp Block is used by more than one Object, this button shows the total number of Objects. Press the button to make the Lamp "Single User". This duplicates the Lamp Block.
Dist	For the lamp types Lamp and Spot, the distance affects the intensity of the light according to an inverse linear progression. With the option Quad, this can be changed.

Left button column presents

Quad	The distance from the Lamp is in inverse quadratic proportion to the intensity of the light. An inverse linear progression is standard (see the buttons Dist, Quad1 and Quad2).
Sphere	The Lamp only sheds light within a spherical area around itself. The radius of the sphere is determined by the Dist button.

Layer	Only Objects in the same layer(s) as the Lamp Object are illuminated. This enables you to use selective lighting, to give objects an extra accent or to restrict the effects of the lamp to a particular space. It also allows to you keep rendering times under control.
Negative	A lamp casts "negative" light.
No Diffuse	The lamp does not interact with the "Diffuse" shader of the objects.
No Specular	The lamp does not interact with the "Specular" shader of the object.

Right button column presents:

Energy	The intensity of the light. The standard settings in Blender assume that a minimum of two lamps are used.
R, G, B	The red, green and blue components of the light.
Quad1, Quad2	Coefficients for the light intensity formula of a Quad Lamp (Light intensity = D / (D + (quad1 * r) + (quad2 * r * r)) with D = Dist button. r = distance to the lamp.) The values of quad1 and quad2 at 1.0 produces the strongest quadratic progression. The values of quad1 and quad2 at 0.0 creates a special Quad lamp that is insensitive to distance.

Spot Panel

BUTTONS REFERENCE.SHADING CONTEXT

In the case of a Spot Lamp a full separate Panel is needed for additional settings. The left column contains:

Shadows	The Lamp can produce shadows. Shadow calculations are only possible with the Spot Lamps. The render option `Shadows` must also be turned ON in the Display Buttons to enable Shadows at a global level.
OnlyShadow	For spot Lamps (with `Shadow` ON), only the shadow is rendered. Light calculations are not performed and where there are shadows, the value of `Energy` is reduced.
Square	Spot Lamps can have square Spot boundaries with this option. For a better control over shadows and for slide projector effects.
Halo	The Lamp has a Halo. The intensity of the halo is calculated using a conic section. With the option `Halo step:` it also uses the shadow buffer (volumetric rendering). The scope of the spot halo is determined by the value of `Dist`.

The right column contains:

SpotSi	The angle of the beam measured in degrees. Use for shadow lamp beams of less than 160 degrees.
SpotBl	The softness of the spot edge.
HaloInt	The intensity of the spot halo. The scope of the spot halo is determined by `Dist`.
Shadow Buffer	Blender uses a *shadow buffer* algorithm. From the spotlight, a picture is rendered for which the distance from the spotlight is saved for each pixel. The shadow buffers are compressed, a buffer of 1024x1024 pixels requires, on average, only 1.5 Mb of memory. This method works quite quickly, but must be adjusted carefully. There are two possible side effects:

Aliasing. The shadow edge has a block-like progression. Make the spot beam smaller, enlarge the buffer or increase the number of `Samples` in the buffer.

Biasing. Faces that are in full light show *banding* with a block-like pattern. Set the `Bias` as high as possible and reduce the distance between `ClipSta` and `ClipEnd`.

ClipSta, ClipEnd	Seen from the Spot Lamp: everything closer than `ClipSta` always has light; everything farther away than `ClipEnd` always has shadow. Within these limits, shadows are calculated. The smaller the shadow area, the clearer the distinction the lamp buffer can make between small distances, and the fewer side effects you will have. It is particularly important to set the value of `ClipSta` as high as possible.
Samples	The shadow buffer is "sampled"; within a square area a test is made for shadow 3*3, 4*4 or 5*5 times. This reduces the *aliasing*.
Halo step	A value other than zero in the button `Halo step` causes the use of the shadow detection (volumetric rendering) for Halos. Low values cause better results and longer rendering times. A value of eight works fine in most cases.
Bias	The bias used for sampling the shadow buffer.
Soft	The size of the sample area. A large `Soft` value produces broader shadow edges.

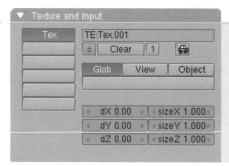

Texture and Input Panel

BUTTONS REFERENCE.SHADING CONTEXT

This texture panel, and the following, are a simplified version of the Material texture panels.

Left column contains:

Texture Channels	A Lamp has six *channels* with which Textures can be linked. Each *channel* has its own *mapping*, i.e. the manner in which the texture works on the lamp. The settings are in the buttons described below and in the Map To Panel.

Right column contains:

Texture Data Block	
TE:	The name of the Texture block. The name can be changed with this button.
Texture Menu	Select an existing Texture from the list provided, or create a new Texture Block.
Clear	The link to the Texture is erased.
Users	If the Texture Block has multiple users, this button shows the total number of users.
Auto Name	Blender assigns a name to the Texture.
Texture Mapping Input	Each Texture has a 3D coordinate (the texture coordinate) as input. The starting point is always the global coordinate of the 3D point that is seen in the pixel to be rendered. A lamp has three options for this.
Glob	The global coordinate is passed on to the texture.
View	The *view* vector of the lamp; the vector of the global coordinate to the lamp, is passed on to the texture. If the lamp is a Spot, the *view* vector is normalised to the dimension of the spot beam, allowing use of a Spot to project a "slide".

Object	An Object is used as source of co-ordinates. The Object name must be entered in the Text Button below.
Texture Input Transform	Use these buttons to adjust the texture coordinate more finely.
dX, dY, dZ	The extra translation of the texture coordinate.
sizeX, sizeY, sizeZ	The extra scaling of the texture coordinate.

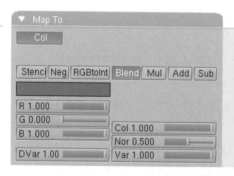

Map To Panel

Col	The texture affects the color of the lamp.
Stencil	Normally, textures are executed one after the other and placed over each other. A second Texture *channel* can completely replace the first. This option sets the *mapping* to *stencil* mode. No subsequent Texture can have an effect on the area the current Texture affects.
Neg	The inverse of the Texture is applied.
RGBtoInt	With this option, an RGB texture (affects color) is used as an Intensity texture (affects a value).
Blend	The Texture mixes the values.

Mul	The Texture multiplies the values.
Add	The Texture adds the values.
Sub	The Texture subtracts the values.
R, G, B	The color with which an Intensity texture blends with the current color.
DVar	The value with which the Intensity texture blends with the current value.
Col	The extent to which the texture affects the color.
Nor	The extent to which the texture affects the normal (not important here).
Var	The extent to which the texture affects the value (a variable, not important here).

Material Sub-context

The settings in this Buttons Window visualize the Material Data Block. The Material Panels and Buttons are only displayed if the *active* Object has a Material.

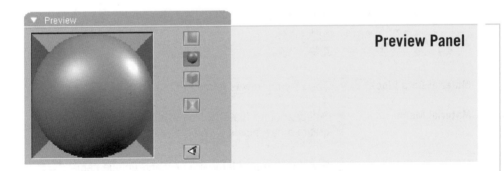

As for all these Sub-contexts, except Radiosity, the first Panel contains a preview square window. The top three buttons on the left governs the preview:

Plane	The preview plane only shows the X-Y coordinates.
Sphere	In the sphere-preview the Z axis is the vertical axis for the preview sphere; the X and Y axes revolve around this axis.
Cube	The cubic preview shows the material preview mapped on three sides of a cube, allowing to see the three possible mappings.

The further two buttons below are concerned with:

| **Background** | Use this button to select a light or a dark background. |
| **Refresh** | Use this button to refresh the material-preview. This ist mostly needed after changing frames while having a material-IPO. |

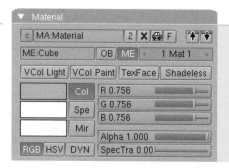

Material Panel

Material Data Block	The very top row is related to the Material Data Block.
Material Menu	Select another Material from the list provided, or create a new block.
MA:	Give the current Material a new and unique name.
Users	If the Material block is used by more than one Object, this button indicates the total number of users. Press the button to make the Material "Single User". An exact copy is created.

Remove Link	Delete the link to the material.
Auto Name	Blender assigns a name to the Material.
Fake User	Blender assigns a "Fake" user to the material, so that it is saved in the .blend file even if unlinked.
Copy to buffer	The complete settings for the Material and all the *mapping* are copied to a temporary buffer.
Copy from buffer	The temporary buffer is copied to the Material.

The row or buttons immediately below specify what the Material block is linked to, or must be linked to. By linking Materials directly to Objects, each Object is rendered in its own Material.

ME:	This Button indicates the block to which the Material is linked. This button can only be used to give the block another name. Possible blocks are:
	ME: Material is linked to a Mesh (ObData) block.
	CU: Material is linked to a Curve, Surface or Font (ObData) block.
	MB: Material is linked to a Meta Ball (ObData) block.
	OB: Material is linked to the Object itself.
OB	Use this button to link the current Material to the *Object*. Any link to the ObData block remains in effect. Links can be removed with the remove link button in top row.
1 Mat 1	An Object or ObData block may have more than one Material. This button can be used to specify which of the Materials must be displayed, i.e. which Material is *active*. The first digit indicates how many Materials there are; the second digit indicates the number of the *active* Material. Each face in a Mesh has a corresponding number: the "Material index". The number of *indices* can be specified with the Edit Buttons. Curves and Surfaces also have Material indices.

Third row of buttons governs:

VCol Light	If the Mesh vertices have colors (see Vertex Paint), they are added to the Material as extra *light*. The colors also remain visible without lamps. Use this option to render *radiosity*-like models.
VCol Paint	If the Mesh vertices have colors, this button replaces the basic color of the Material with these colors. Now light must shine on the Material before you can see it.
TexFace	A texture assigned with the UVEditor gives the color information for the faces.
Shadeless	This button makes the Material insensitive to light or shadow.

The block below defines at a time the three colors of the material and the behavior of the Object in Real Time simulations. This is selected with the bottom row of Toggle Buttons:

RGB	Most color sliders in Blender have two pre-set options: in this case, the color is created by mixing Red, Green, Blue.
HSV	The color sliders mix color with the Hue, Saturation, Value system. "Hue" determines the color, "Saturation" determines the amount of color in relation to gray and "Value" determines the light intensity of the color.
DYN	Adjust parameters for the dynamics options (not covered by this Book). The neighboring buttons changes completely.

For the Colors, whichever the mapping, above these Toggle Buttons there are three more Toggle Buttons on a column, with color preview on their left:

Color	The basic color of the Material (Diffuse Shader).
Spec	Specularity, the color of the sheen (Specular Shader).
Mir	The mirror color of the Material. This affects a environment or reflection map.

The color, selected by its Toggle Button, can be edited with the three Num Buttons on the right which, depending on color scheme, are:

R, G, B	These mix the color specified in RGB scheme (see RGB Button).
H, S, V	These mix the color specified in HSV scheme (see HSV Button). The last two Num Buttons are:

Third row of buttons governs:

Alpha	The degree of coverage, which can be used to make Materials transparent. Use the option ZTransp to specify that multiple transparent layers can exist. Without this option, only the Material itself is rendered, no matter what faces lie behind it. The transparent information is saved in an *alpha layer*, which can be saved as part of a picture.
SpecTra	This button makes areas of the Material with a sheen opaque. It can be used to give transparent Materials a "glass" effect.

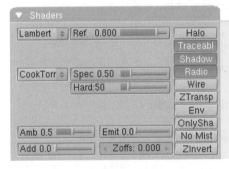

Shaders Panel

This Panel presents the Diffuse and Specular shader settings on the left and a column of Toggle Buttons on the right. On the left:

Diffuse Shader Menu	Three Diffuse Shaders are coded in Blender, depending on which is chosen the Num Buttons immediately on the right changes:
	Lambert - Blender default diffuse shader since ever.
Parameters:	Ref - Strength of reflectivity

Oren-Nayar - Blender new physical shader (v. 2.28).

Parameters:

> Ref - Strength of reflectivity

> Rough - Roughness of the surface

Toon - Blender new cartoon shader (v. 2.28).

Parameters:

> Ref - Strength of reflectivity

> Size - Angular width of lit region

> Smooth - Blurriness of light/shadow boundary

Specular Shader Menu

Four Specular Shaders are coded in Blender, depending on which is chosen the Num Buttons immediately on the right changes:

CookTorr - Blender default specular shader since ever.

Parameters:

> Spec - Strength of Specularity

> Hard - The hardness of the specularity. A large value gives a hard, concentrated sheen, like that of a billiard ball. A low value gives a metallic sheen.

Phong - Blender Phong shader (v. 2.28).

Parameters:

> Spec - Strength of Specularity

> Hard - The hardness of the specularity. A large value gives a hard, concentrated sheen, like that of a billiard ball. A low value gives a metallic sheen.

Blinn - Blender Physical shader (v. 2.28).

Parameters:

> Spec - Strength of Specularity

> Hard - The hardness of the specularity. A large value gives a hard, concentrated sheen, like that of a billiard ball. A low value gives a metallic sheen.

Parameters:

Refr - Refractive index to compute specularity. This does not include mirror-like reflections or glass-like refractions.

Toon - Blender new cartoon shader (v. 2.28).

Spec - Strength of Specularity

Size - Angular width of specular region

Smooth - Blurriness of specular/diffuse boundary

The bottom four Num Buttons are:

Amb	The degree to which the global Ambient color is applied, a simple form of environmental light. The global Ambient can be specified in the World Sub-context. Ambient is useful for giving the total rendering a softer, more colored atmosphere.
Emit	The Material "emits light", without shedding light on other faces of course, unless a Radiosity render is called for.
Add	This option adds some kind of glow to transparent objects, but only works with the Unified Renderer.
Zoffset	This button allows you to give the face to be rendered an artificial forward offset in Blender Zbuffer system. This only applies to Materials with the option ZTransp. This option is used to place cartoon figures on a 3D floor as images with alpha. To prevent the figures from "floating", the feet and the shadows drawn must be placed partially beneath the floor. The Zoffset option then ensures that the entire figure is displayed. This system offers numerous other applications for giving (flat) images of spatial objects the appropriate 3D placement.

The rightmost column of Toggle Buttons contains:

Halo	This buttons turns a regular material into a Halo material. both the **Material** and this Panel dramatically change. They are described below.

Traceable	This specifies whether or not shadow lamps can "see" the current Material. That is if object *cast* shadows.
Shadow	This button determines whether the Material can receive a shadow, that is if object *receive* casts shadows.
Radio	This button makes the Material to be taken into account in Radiosity calculations.
Wire	Only the *edges* of faces are rendered (normal rendering!). This results in an exterior that resembles a wire frame. This option can only be used for Meshes.
ZTransp	Transitional Zbuffers can only render opaque faces. Blender uses a modified method to Zbuffer transparent faces. This method requires more memory and calculation time than the normal Zbuffer, which is why the two systems are used alongside each other.
Env	Environment option. The Material is not rendered and the Zbuffer and render buffers are "erased" so that the pixel is delivered with Alpha = 0.0.
OnlyShadow	This option determines the alpha for transparent Materials based on the degree of shadow. Without a shadow the Material is not visible and the effect is that of a "floating" shadow.
NoMist	The Material is insensitive to "Mist" (see World Subcontext).
Zinvert	The Material is rendered with an inverse Zbuffer method; front and back are switched.

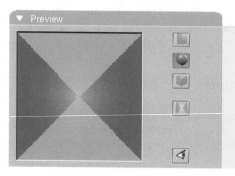

Preview Panel for Halo Materials

BUTTONS REFERENCE.SHADING CONTEXT

If a Material has the option `Halo` ON, a number of buttons change to specific halo settings. *Lens flares* can also be created here. Halos are rendered on the 3D location of the vertices. These are small, transparent round spots or pictures over which circles and lines can be drawn. They take Blender's Zbuffer into account; like any 3D element, they can simply disappear behind a face in the forefront.

Halos are placed over the currently rendered background as a separate layer, or they give information to the *alpha layer*, allowing halos to be processed as a post-process.

Only Meshes and Particle Effects can have halos. A Mesh with a halo is displayed differently in the 3DWindow; with small dots at the position of the vertices. Halos cannot be combined with "ordinary" faces within one Mesh.

As for all these Sub-contextes, except Radiosity, the first Panel contains a preview square window.

The preview now show the halo material, the top three buttons on the left loose functionality, the bottom two keep the functionalities they had for normal materials.

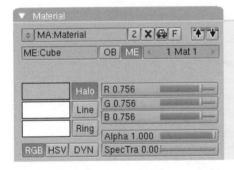

Material Panel for Halo Materials

The two top rows related to the Material Data Block maintains the meaning they had for normal Materials. The third line disappears and the bottom part of the Panel maintains the general functionality but colors now refer to:

Halo	The base color of the Halo.
Line	The base color of the Halo Lines, if any.
Ring	The base color of the Halo Rings, if any.

The color, selected by its Toggle Button, can be edited with the three Num Buttons on the right which, depending on color scheme, are:

R, G, B	These mix the color specified in RGB scheme.
H, S, V	These mix the color specified in HSV scheme.
Alpha	The degree of coverage, which can be used to make Halo more transparent.

Shaders Panel for Halo Materials

This Panel presents the Halo shader settings on the left and a column of Toggle Buttons on the right. On the left:

Halo Size	The Halo dimension, in Blender Units.
Hard	The hardness of the halo, a large value gives a strong, concentrated progression.
Add	Normally, the color of halos is calculated during rendering, giving a light emitting effect. Set the Add value to 0.0 to switch this off and make black or "solid" halos possible as well.
Rings	The number of rings rendered over the basic halo, if the corresponding toggle button on the right is enabled.
Lines	The number of sparkle-shaped lines rendered over the basic halo, if the corresponding toggle button on the right is enabled.

Star	The number of points on the star-shaped basic halo, if the corresponding toggle button on the right is enabled.
Seed	"Random" values are selected for the dimension of the *rings* and the location of the *lines* based on a fixed table. Seed determines an offset in the table.

If the Halo is of Flare type, selected with toggle Button on the right, five further Num Buttons appear:

FlareSize	The factor by which the post-process basic Flare is larger than the halo.
SubSize	The dimension of post-process sub Flares, multicolored dots and circles.
Boost	This gives the Flare extra strenght.
Fl.seed	The dimension and shape of the sub Flares is determined by a fixed table with "random" values. `Fl.seed` specifies an offset in the table.
Flares	The number of sub Flares.

The rightmost column of Toggle Buttons contains:

Halo	This buttons is on, if switched off turns back the Halo material to a regular one.
Flare	Each halo is now also rendered as a *lens flare*. This effect suggests the reflections that occur in a camera lens if a strong light source shines on it. A Flare consists of three layers:
	the ordinary halo, which has a 3D location, and can thus disappear behind a face.
	the basic Flare, which is the same halo, but possibly with other dimensions. This is placed over the entire rendering as a post-process.

the sub Flares, multi-colored dots and circles, that are also placed over the entire rendering as a post-process.

The `HaloSize` value not only determines the dimensions, but is also used to determine the visibility - and thus the strength - of the Flare rendered in the post-process. This way, a Flare that disappears slowly behind a face will decrease in size at a corresponding speed and gradually go out.

Rings	Determines whether rings are rendered over the basic halo.
Lines	Determines whether sparkle-shaped lines are rendered over the basic halo.
Star	Instead of being rendered as a circle, the basic halo is rendered in the shape of a star. The Num Button Star determines the number of points the star has.
HaloTex	Halos can be given textures in two ways:
	HaloTex OFF: the basic color of each halo is determined by the texture coordinate of the halo-vertex.
	HaloTex ON: each halo gets a complete texture area, in which, for example, an Image texture is displayed completely in each basic halo rendered.
HaloPuno	The vertex normal ("Puno" in Blender's turbo language) is used to help specify the dimension of the halo. Normals that point directly at the Camera are the largest; halos with a normal that point to the rear are not rendered. If there are no vertex normals in the Mesh (the Mesh only consists of vertices) the normalised local coordinate of the vertex is used as the normal.
XAlpha	Extreme Alpha. Halos can "emit light"; they can add color. This cannot be expressed with a normal alpha. Use this option to force a stronger progression in the alpha.
Shaded	Let the Halo receive light.

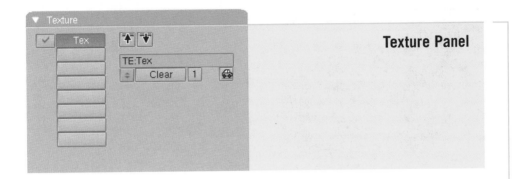

Texture Panel

Material textures are the most complex in Blender. There are three panels devoted to them. This first is concerned with texture channels, the second governs the input mapping, the last the output mapping.

Texture channels	A Material has eight *channels* to which Textures can be linked. Each *channel* has its own *mapping*, which is the effect the texture has on the material. Channels are grouped on a column on the left. For each active channel a Toggle button appears, allowing to switch off each single texture channel.
Copy to buffer	The up pointing arrow on the right of the Panel copies the complete *mapping* settings to a temporary buffer.
Copy from buffer	The down pointing arrow on the right of the Panel pastes the complete *mapping* settings from the temporary buffer.
Texture Data Block	
Texture Menu	Select an existing Texture from the list provided, or create a new Texture Block.
TE:	The name of the Texture block. The name can be changed with this button.
Clear	The link to the Texture is erased.
Users	If the Texture Block has multiple users, this button shows the total number of users.
Auto Name	Blender assigns a name to the Texture.

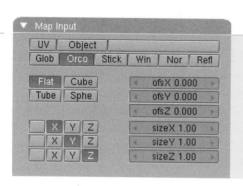

Map Input Panel

Each Texture has a 3D coordinate (the texture coordinate) as input. The starting point is generally the global coordinate of the 3D point that can be seen in the pixel to be rendered. A Material has the following Mapping options, given by the first two row of buttons:

UV	The U-V coordinates of a face or NURBS surface from an Object make up the texture coordinates. U-V is a commonly used term for specifying the mathematical space of a flat or curved surface.
Object	Every Object in Blender can be used as a source for texture coordinates. For this, the Object inverse trans-formation is applied to the global coordinate, which gives the *local* Object coordinate. This links the texture to the position, dimension and rotation of the Object. Generally, an Empty Object is used to specify the exact location of a Texture, e.g. to place a logo on the body of an airplane. Another commonly used approach is to have the "Texture Object" move to achieve an animated texture.
Object Name	The name of the Object used for the texture coordi-nates must be placed in this Text Button. If the Object does not exist, the button remains empty.
Glob	The global coordinate is passed on to the texture.
Orco	The standard setting. This is the *original coordinate* of the Mesh or another ObData block.

Stick	Sticky texture. Blender allows you to assign a texture coordinate to Meshes, which is derived from the manner in which the Camera view sees the Mesh. The screen coordinate (only X,Y) for each vertex is calculated and saved in the Mesh. This makes it appear as if the texture is projected from the Camera; the texture becomes "sticky" (see also Make `Sticky` in the Edit Buttons). Use `Sticky` to precisely match a 3D object with an Image Texture. Special *morphing* effects can also be achieved
Win	The screen coordinate (X,Y) is used as a texture coordinate. Use this method to achieve 2D *layering* of different Images.
Nor	The normal vector of the rendered face is used as a texture coordinate. Use this method to achieve *reflection mapping*, which is the suggestion of mirroring using a specially pre-calculated Image.
Refl	The reflection vector of the rendered face is used as a texture coordinate. This vector points in a direction that makes the face appear to be mirrored. Use this option to suggest a reflected surface with procedural textures such as "Marble" or "Clouds" and of course for the use with the EnvMap texture.
Mapping: 3D to 2D	For Image Textures only; the four buttons middle left in the Panel determines the manner is which the 3D coordinate is converted to 2D.
Flat	The X and Y coordinates are used directly.
Cube	Depending on the normal vector of the face, the X-Y or the X-Z or the Y-Z coordinates are selected. This option works well for stones, marbles and other regular textures,
Tube	This creates a tube-shaped mapping. The Z axis becomes the central axis, X and Y revolve around it.
Sphere	This causes a sphere-shaped mapping. The Z axis becomes the central axis, X and Y revolve around it.

Mapping: switch coordinates.	The three rows of buttons indicate the new X, Y and Z coordinates. Normally, the X is mapped to X, the Y to Y and Z to Z. You can act on the matrix to change this mapping. The first button, without label, of each row switches a coordinate completely off.
Mapping: coordinates linear transformation.	Use the right column of Num Buttons to finely adjust the texture coordinate.
ofsX, ofsY, ofsZ	The extra translation of the texture coordinate.
sizeX, sizeY, sizeZ	The extra scaling of the texture coordinate.

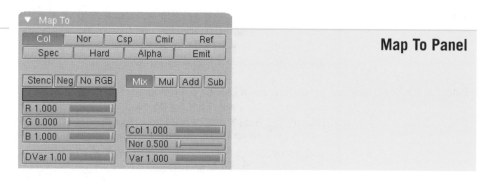

Map To Panel

The Map To Panel determines the effect of the Texture output for the current point.

Mapping: output to.	The top two rows of Buttons determines which property of the material is affected:
Col	The texture affects the basic, diffuse, color of the material.
Nor	The texture affects the rendered normal direction. It is a three state button, effects can be off, positive or negative. Only important for Image textures. The Stucci is the only procedural texture which effectively generate normal information (for now).
Csp	The texture affects the *specularity* color of the material.
Cmir	The texture affects the *mirror* color of the material.

Ref	The texture affects the value of the material *reflectivity*. This if a three state button: off, active and inverse.
Spec	The texture affects the value of specularity of the material. This if a three state button: off, active and inverse.
Hard	The texture affects the hardness value of the material. This if a three state button: off, active and inverse.
Alpha	The texture affects the alpha value of the material. This if a three state button: off, active and inverse.
Emit	The texture affects the Emit value of the material. This if a three state button: off, active and inverse.
Mapping: Texture additonal settings.	The group of buttons bottom left on the panel defines further settings on how the Texture output is handled.
Stencil	Normally, textures are executed one after the other and laid over one another. A second Texture *channel* can completely replace the first. With this option, the mapping goes into *stencil* mode. No subsequent Texture can have an effect on the area the current Texture affects.
Neg	The effect of the Texture is reversed.
No RGB	With this option, an RGB texture (affects color) is used as an Intensity texture (affects a value).
R, G, B (or H, S, V)	The color with which an Intensity-only texture blends with the current color.
DVar	The value with which the Intensity texture blends with the current value.
Mapping: output settings.	These buttons change the output of the Texture.
Mix	The Texture blends the values or color.
Mul	The Texture multiplies values or color.
Add	The Texture adds the values or color.

Sub	The Texture subtracts values or color.
Col	The extent to which the texture affects color.
Nor	The extent to which the texture affects the normal.
Var	The extent to which the texture affects a value.

Texture Sub-context

If there is an active Texture channel in a Material, Lamp or World Block, switching to Texture Sub-context (**F6**) populates the Buttons Window with Texture panels of the current Texture Block.

Each Texture has a 3D coordinate (the texture coordinate) as input, as described in the Material Sub-context. What happens in the Texture evaluation process is determined by the type of texture:

- Intensity textures: return one scalar value. The preview render in this window shows this as gray values.
- RGB textures: returns three, RGB, values; they always work on color.
- Bump textures: returns three values; they always work on the normal vector. Only the "Stucci" and "Image" texture can give normals.

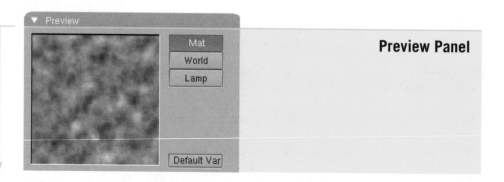

Preview Panel

BUTTONS REFERENCE.SHADING CONTEXT

As for all these Sub-contextes, except Radiosity, the first Panel contains a preview square window.

Right of the Window a column of three Toggle Buttons allows to select the Block of Textures, Blender automatically select the right one:

Mat	Material textures.
World	World textures.
Lamp	Lamp textures.
Default Var	This button brings all the texture values to the default.

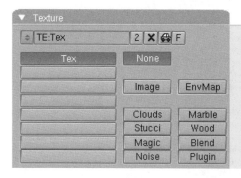

Texture Panel

Texture Data Block	The Texture Block in the top row indicate what Texture block is visualized.
Texture Menu	Select another Texture from the list provided, or create a new block.
TE:	Give the current Texture block a new and unique name.
Users	If the Texture block has more than one user, this button shows the total. Press the button to make the Texture "Single User". An exact copy is then created.
Remove Link	Delete the link to the Texture.

Auto Name	Blender assigns a name to the Texture.
Fake User	Blender assigns a "Fake" user to the texture, so that it is saved in the .blend file even if unlinked.

Below the Texture Block there are three columns of buttons, on the left:

Texture Channels	Eight or six buttons, depending if we are working on a Material, on a Lamp or on the World, showing the active Texture channes with their names.
	The two columns on the right select the type of texture. There are 11 types one of which, none, effectively is "no texture". Each of the other buttons select a particular kind of texture and opens at least a new, type-dependent, Panel. Texture types will be described in the relevant Panel description

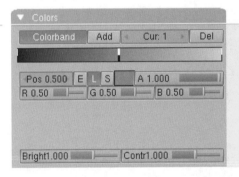

Colors Panel

This Panel allows to create a smooth color progression in place of an Intensity progression. Intensity textures are thus changed into an RGB texture. The use of Colorband with a sharp transition can cause *aliasing*.

Colorband	Switches the use of Colorband on or off.
Add	Adds a new color to the Colorband. This is by default placed at intensity 0.5 and is gray.
Cur:	The active color from the Colorband.

Del	Delete the active color.
Pos:	The position of the active color. Values range from 0.0 to 1.0. This can also be entered using **LMB** in the Colorband.
E, L, S	The interpolation type with which colors are mixed, i.e. "Ease", "Linear" and "Spline". The last gives the most fluid progression.
A, R, G, B	The Alpha and RGB value of the active color.
Bright	The "brightness" of the color or intensity of a texture. In fact, a fixed number is added or subtracted. This is not limited to Colorbands, but works for any texture.
Contr	The "contrast" of the color or intensity of a texture. This is actually a multiplication. This is not limited to Colorbands, but works for any texture.

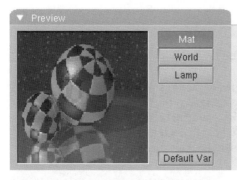

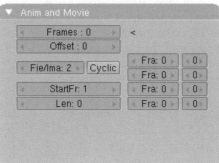

Image Texture Panel

Of the ten possible texture the Image one is the only requiring two additional Panels, this, and the `Crop` and `Anim` one.

The Image texture is the most frequently used and most advanced of Blender textures. The standard bump-mapping and perspective-corrected MipMapping, filtering and anti-aliasing built into the program guarantee outstanding image quality. Because pictures are two-dimensional, you must specify in the *mapping* buttons how the 3D texture coordinate is converted to 2D; *mapping* is a part of the Material Buttons. For best results UV mapping is required.

The first two row of Buttons in the Panel determines:

InterPol	This option interpolates the pixels of an Image. This becomes visible when you enlarge the picture. Turn this option OFF to keep the pixels visible - they are correctly anti-aliased. This last feature is useful for regular patterns, such as lines and tiles; they remain "sharp" even when enlarged considerably.
UseAlpha	Use the *alpha* layer of the Image.
CalcAlpha	Calculate an *alpha* based on the RGB values of the Image.
NegAlpha	Reverses the *alpha* value.
MipMap	Generates a series of pictures, each half the size of the former one. This optimizes the filtering process. When this option is OFF, you generally get a sharper image, but this can significantly increase calculation time if the filter dimension becomes large.
Fields	Video frames consist of two different images (fields) that are merged by horizontal line. This option makes it possible to work with field images. It ensures that when "Fields" are rendered the correct field of the Image is used in the correct field of the rendering. MipMapping cannot be combined with "Fields".
Rot90	Rotates the Image 90 degrees when rendered.

Movie	Movie files (AVIs supported by Blender, SGI-movies) and "anim5" files can also be used for an Image.
Anti	Graphic images such as cartoons and pictures that consist of only a few colors with a large surface filling can be *anti*-aliased as a built in pre-process.
St Field	Normally, the first field in a video frame begins on the first line. Some frame grabbers do this differently!

The following two lines presents the image Menu:

Image Data Block	
Image menu	You can select a previously created Image from the list provided. Image blocks can be reused without taking up extra memory.
File Name	Enter a file name here, after which a new Image block is created.
Users	Indicates the number of users for the Image. The "Single User" option cannot be activated here. It has no significance for Images.
Load Image	The (largest) adjacent window becomes an Image Select Window.
Pack	Indicates the packing of the image. Pressed means the image is packed into the Blendfile. Clicking on the Button packs or unpacks the image. If a unpack option is triggered the unpack-menu pops up.
Reload	Force the Image file to be read again.
Filter	The filter size used by the options `MipMap` and `Interpol`.

The following options determine what happens if the texture coordinate falls outside the Image.

Extend	Outside the Image the color of the edge is extended.
Clip	Outside the Image, an alpha value of 0.0 is returned. This allows you to "paste" a small logo on a large object.
ClipCube	The same as `Clip`, but now the "Z" coordinate is calculated as well. Outside a cubeshaped area around the Image, an *alpha* value of 0.0 is returned.
Repeat	The Image is repeated horizontally and vertically.

The following six Num Buttons allows for repetitions and offsetting:

Xrepeat	An (extra) number of repetitions in the X direction.
Yrepeat	An (extra) number of repetitions in the Y direction.
MinX, MinY, MaxX, MaxY	Use these to specify a *cropping*, the Image looks like becoming larger or smaller.

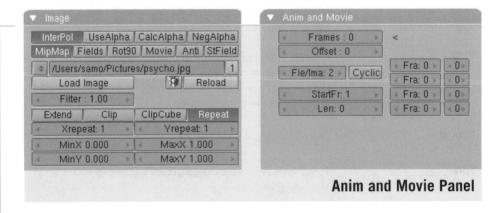

Anim and Movie Panel

This Panel is strictly related to the Image and is present only for Image type textures.

Frames	This activates the animation option; another image file (in the same Image block) will be read per rendered frame. Blender tries to find the other files by changing a number in the file name. Only the rightmost digit is interpreted for this. For example: 01.ima.099.tga + 1 becomes 01.ima.100.tga. The value of `Frames` indicates the total number of files to be used. If the option `Movie` is ON, this value must also be set. Now, however, a frame is continually taken from the same file.
Offset	The number of the first picture of the animation.
Fie/Ima	The number of fields per rendered frame. If no fields are rendered, even numbers must be entered here. (2 fields = 1 frame).
Cyclic	The animation Image is repeated *cyclically*.
StartFr:	The moment - in Blender frames - at which the animation Image must start.
Len	This button determines the length of the animation. By assigning Len a higher value than Frames, you can create a *still* at the end of the animation.
Fra	The `Fra` buttons allow you to create a simple montage within an animation Image. The left button, `Fra` indicates the frame number, the right-hand button indicates how long the frame must be displayed.

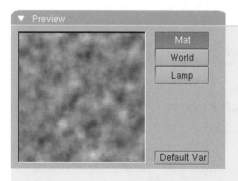

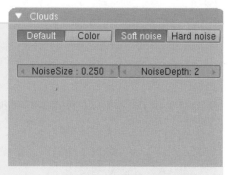

Clouds Texture Panel

Clouds is a *procedural texture*. This means that each 3D coordinate can be translated directly to a color or a value. In this case, a three-dimensional table with pseudo random values is used, from which a fluent interpolation value can be calculated with each 3D coordinate (thanks to Ken Perlin for his masterful article "An Image Synthesizer", fromthe SIGGRAPH proceedings 1985). This calculation method is also called *Perlin Noise*.

Default	The standard Noise, gives an Intensity.
Color	The Noise gives an RGB value.
Soft Noise, Hard Noise	There are two methods available for the Noise function.
NoiseSize	The dimension of the Noise table.
NoiseDepth	The depth of the Cloud calculation. A higher number results in a long calculation time, but also in finer details.

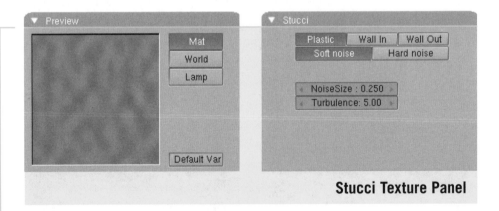

Stucci Texture Panel

Stucci is a 3D *procedural texture* generating Noise-based normals, rather than an Intensity or a Color.

Plastic	The standard Stucci.
Wall In, Wall out	This is where Stucci gets it name. This is a typical wall structure with holes or bumps.
Soft Noise, Hard Noise	There are two methods available for working with Noise.
NoiseSize	The dimension of the Noise table.
Turbulence	The depth of the Stucci calculations.

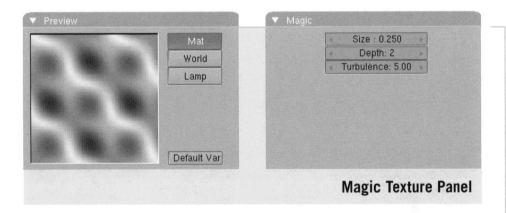

Magic Texture Panel

Magic is a *procedural texture*. The RGB components are generated independently with a sine formula.

Size	The dimensions of the pattern.
Depth	The depth of the calculation. A higher number results in a long calculation time, but also in finer details.
Turbulence	The strength of the pattern.

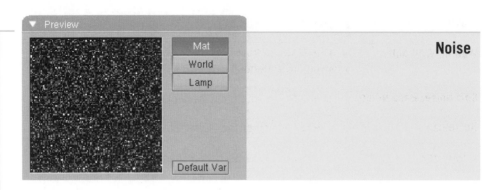

Noise

Although this looks great, it is not *Perlin Noise!* This is a true, randomly generated Noise. This gives a different result every time, for every frame, for every pixel.

It has no parameters and hence no Panel of its own.

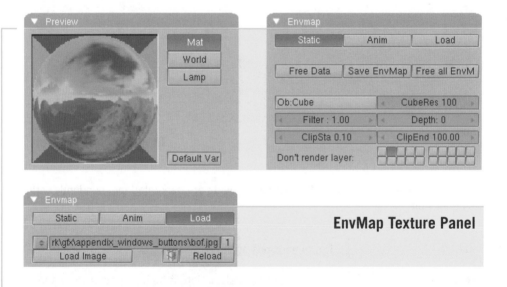

EnvMap Texture Panel

Blender uses cube-mapped environmental maps (EnvMaps) to fake reflections. This is a very peculiar texture computed at rendering time from the point of view of a given Object. Blender allows three types of EnvMaps:

Static	The EnvMap is only calculated once during an animation or after loading a file.

Dynamic	The EnvMap is calculated each time a rendering takes place. This means moving Objects are displayed correctly in mirroring surfaces.
Load	When saved as an image file, EnvMaps can be loaded from disk at a later time. This option allows the fastest rendering with pre-generated EnvMaps.
Free Data	This action releases all images associated with the EnvMap. This is how you force a recalculation when using a Static EnvMap.
Save EnvMap	You can save an EnvMap as an image file, in the format indicated in the Scene Context (**F10**).
Free all Env	This button does not only releases all images linked to the current EnvMap but also all other images linked to any other EnvMap in the whole scene.

If the EnvMap type is Load. The EnvMap image can be loaded via a regular Image block in the Blender structure:

Load Image	The (largest) adjacent window becomes an Image Select Window. Specify here what file to read in as EnvMap. If the loaded image is not a Blender EnvMap weird results can occur at rendering time.
Image Menu	You can select a previously loaded EnvMap from the list provided. EnvMap Images can be reused without taking up extra memory.
File Name	Enter an image file name here, to load as an EnvMap.
Users	Indicates the number of users for the Image.
Pack	Embeds the image in the .blend file.
Reload	Force the Image file to be read again.
Ob:	Fill in the name of an Object that defines the center and rotation of the EnvMap. This can be any Object in the current Scene.

CubeRes	The resolution in pixels of the EnvMap image.
Filter:	With this value you can adjust the sharpness or blurriness of the reflection.
Depth:	Forces the EnvMap to be computed this number of *additional* times. This is useful if several Objects are mirroring each one the other and multiple reflections occur.
ClipSta, ClipEnd	These values define the clipping boundaries when rendering the EnvMap images.
Don't render layer	Indicate with this option that faces that exist in a specific layer are *not* rendered in the environment map.

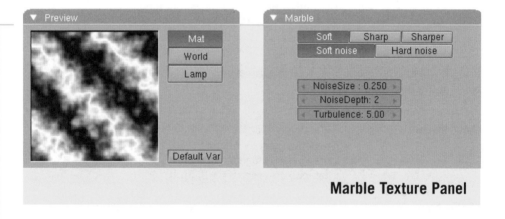

Marble Texture Panel

Marble is another *procedural texture*. In this case, bands are generated based on a sine formula and Noise turbulence. It returns an Intensity value only.

Soft, Sharp, Sharper	Three pre-sets for soft or more and more clearly defined Marble.
Soft Noise, Hard Noise	The Noise function works with two methods, as for other procedural textures.
NoiseSize	The dimensions of the Noise table.

NoiseDepth	The depth of the Marble calculation. A higher value results in greater calculation time, but also in finer details.
Turbulence	The turbulence of the sine bands.

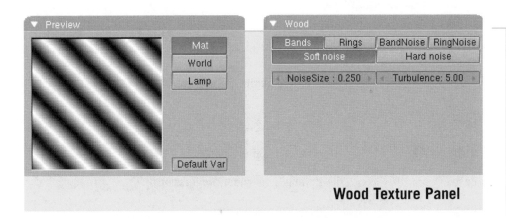

Wood Texture Panel

Wood is another *procedural texture*. In this case, bands are generated based on a sine formula. You can also add a degree of turbulence with the Noise formula. It returns an Intensity value only.

Bands	The standard Wood texture.
Rings	This suggests real wood rings.
BandNoise	Applying Noise gives the standard Wood texture a certain degree of turbulence.
RingNoise	Applying Noise gives the rings a certain degree of turbulence.
Soft Noise, Hard Noise	There are two methods available for the Noise function.
NoiseSize	The dimension of the Noise table.
Turbulence	The turbulence of the BandNoise and RingNoise types.

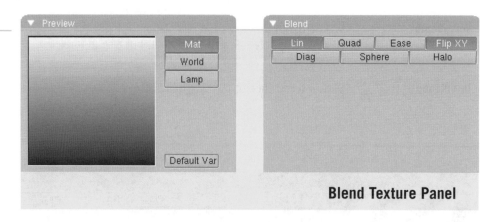

Blend Texture Panel

This is another procedural texture. It generates a progression in Intensity.

Lin	A linear progression.
Quad	A quadratic progression.
Ease	A flowing, non-linear progression.
Diag	A diagonal progression.
Sphere	A progression with the shape of a three-dimensional ball.
Halo	A quadratic progression with the shape of a three-dimensional ball.
Flip XY	The direction of the progression is flipped a quarter turn.

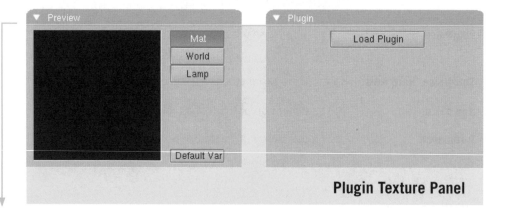

Plugin Texture Panel

Plugins are pieces of compiled C-code which can be loaded at runtime, to extend a programs features. After pressing `Load Plugin` you get a FileWindow which lets you choose a plugin. The plugins are platform specific, so be sure to load a plugin for your operating system.

Once the Plugin is loaded, the `Plugin` Panel is populated by the plugin specific buttons.

Radiosity Sub-context

Radiosity has been a modeling tool up to Blender 2.28, and is now both a modeling and a rendering tool. The Radiosity Sub-context reflects this duality.

By default it presents two Panels: Radio Render to set the parameters of Radiosity rendering and `Radio Tool` to set the parameters for the modeling Radio tool. In this latter case a new Panel, `Calculation` appears.

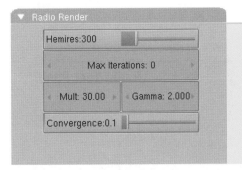

Radio Render Panel

This is presents parameters for Radiosity as a rendering tool, but its entries are also useful in Radiosity modeling. Radiosity Rendering takes into account only Objects whose Materials have the `Radio` Toggle Button enabled.

Hemires	The size of a hemicube; the color-coded images used to find the Elements that are visible from a "shoot Patch", and thus receive energy. Hemicubes are not stored, but are recalculated each time for every Patch that shoots energy. The `Hemires` value determines the Radiosity quality and adds significantly to the solving time.

Max iterations

When this button has a non-zero value, Radiosity solving stops after the indicated iteration step, *unless* the convergence criterion is met beforehand.

Mult, Gamma

The colorspace of the Radiosity solution is far more detailed than can be expressed with simple 24 bit RGB values. When Elements are converted to faces, their energy values are converted to an RGB color using the Mult and Gamma values. With the Mult value you can multiply the energy value, with Gamma you can change the contrast of the energy values.

Convergence

When the amount of unshot energy in an environment is lower than this value, the Radiosity solving stops. The initial unshot energy in an environment is multiplied by the area of the Patches. During each iteration, some of the energy is absorbed, or disappears when the environment is not a closed volume. In Blender standard coordinate system a typical emitter has a relative small area. The convergence value in is divided by a factor of 1000 before testing for that reason.

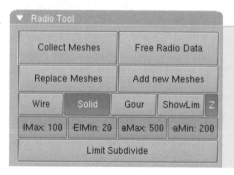

Radio Tool Panel

Collect Meshes

All selected and visible Meshes in the current Scene are converted to Patches. As a result some Buttons in the interface change color and a new Panel, Calculation, appears. Blender now has entered the Radiosity mode, and other editing functions are blocked until the button Free Radio Data is pressed. After the Meshes are collected, they are drawn in a pseudo lighting mode that clearly differs from the normal drawing.

Free Radio Data	All Patches, Elements and Faces are freed in memory. You always must perform this action after using Radiosity to be able to return to normal editing.
Replace Meshes	Once the Radiosity process has been performed, by clicking this button the faces of the current displayed Radiosity solution are converted to Mesh Objects with vertex colors. A new Material is added that allows immediate rendering. The input Meshes are lost.
Add New Meshes	As previous, but the input Meshes are kept.
Wire, Solid, Gour	Three drawmode options are included, independent of the indicated drawmode of a 3DWindow. Gouraud display, the smoothest, is only performed after the Radiosity process has started.
ShowLim, Z	This option visualizes the Patch and Element limits. By pressing the z option, the limits are drawn rotated differently. The white lines show the Patch limits, cyan lines show the Element limits.
ElMax, ElMin, PaMax, PaMin	The maximum and minimum size of a Element or Patch. These limits are used during all Radiosity phases. The unit is expressed in 0,0001 of the boundbox size of the entire environment.
Limit Subdivide	With respect to the values PaMax and PaMin, the Patches are subdivided. This subdivision is also automatically performed when a GO action has started.

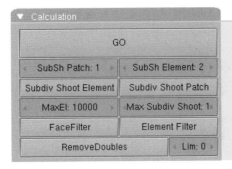

Calculation Panel

This Panel actually launches a Radiosity Modeling solution and handles its postprocessing.

GO	With this button you start the Radiosity simulation.
	The phases are:
1	Limit Subdivide. When Patches are too large, they are subdivided.
2	Subdiv Shoot Patch. The value of SubSh P defines the number of times the "Subdiv Shoot Patch" function is called. As a result, Patches are subdivided.
3	Subdiv Shoot Elem. The value of SubSh E defines the number of times the "Subdiv Shoot Element" function is called. As a result, Elements are subdivided.
4	Subdivide Elements. When Elements are still larger than the minimum size, they are subdivided. Now, the maximum amount of memory is usually allocated.
5	Solve. This is the actual "progressive refinement" method. The mousecursor displays the iteration step, the current total of Patches that shot their energy in the environment. This process continues until the unshot energy in the environment is lower than the Convergence or when the maximum number of iterations has been reached.
6	Convert to faces. The elements are converted to triangles or squares with "anchored" edges, to make sure a pleasant not-discontinue Gouraud display is possible.

This process can be terminated with **ESC** during any phase.

SubSh Patch	The number of times the environment is tested to detect Patches that need subdivision.
SubSh Element	The number of times the environment is tested to detect Elements that need subdivision.

Subdiv Shoot Patch	By shooting energy to the environment, errors can be detected that indicate a need for further subdivision of Patches. The subdivision is performed only once each time you call this function. The results are smaller Patches and a longer solving time, but a higher realismof the solution. This option can also be automatically performed when the GO action has started (see above).
Subdiv Shoot Element	By shooting energy to the environment, and detecting high energy changes (frequencies) inside a Patch, the Elements of this Patch are selected to be subdivided one extra level. The subdivision is performed only once each time you call this function. The results are smaller Elements and a longer solving time and probably more aliasing, but a higher level of detail. This option can also be automatically performed when the GO action has started (see above).
MaxEl	The maximum allowed number of Elements. Since Elements are subdivided automatically in Blender, the amount of used memory and the duration of the solving time can be controlled with this button. As a rule of thumb 20,000 elements take up 10 Mb memory.
Max Subdiv Shoot	The maximum number of shoot Patches that are evaluated for the "adaptive subdivision". If zero, all Patches with a non-zero Emit value are evaluated.
FaceFilter	After Radiosity calculation has occurred, Elements are converted to faces for display. A `FaceFilter` call forces an extra smoothing in the displayed result, without changing the Element values themselves.
Element Filter	After Radiosity calculation has occurred, this option filters Elements to remove aliasing artifacts, to smooth shadow boundaries, or to force equalized colors for the `RemoveDoubles` option.
RemoveDoubles	When two neighboring Elements have a displayed color that differs less than `Lim`, the Elements are joined.
Lim	This value is used by the previous button. The unit is expressed in a standard 8 bits resolution; a color range from 0 - 255.

World Sub-context

The settings in this Buttons Window visualize the World Data Block. It is linked to a Scene, and can therefore be reused by other Scenes. This block contains the settings for standard backgrounds, mist effects and the built-in star generator. The *ambient* color and *exposure* time can be set here as well.

Preview Panel

As for all these Sub-contextes, except Radiosity, the first Panel contains a preview square window.

Right of the Window a column of three Toggle Buttons allows to select the background type:

Blend	This option renders the background, the *sky*, with a natural progression. At the bottom of the image is the horizon color, at the top, the color of the zenith. The progression is not linear, but bent in the shape of a ball, depending on the *lens* value of the Camera.
Real	The option Real makes the position of the horizon real; the direction in which the camera is pointed determines whether the horizon or the zenith can be seen. This also influences the generated texture coordinates.
Paper	This option makes the Blend (if this is selected) or the texture coordinates completely flat, at Viewport level.

World Panel

World Data Block	The top row in this panel contains the World Data Block:
World Menu	Select another World from the list provided, or create a new block.
WO:	Give the current World block a new and unique name.
Users	If the World block has more than one user, this button shows the total number of users. Press the button to make the World "Single User". An exact copy is then created.
Remove Link	Delete the link to the World.
Fake User	Blender assigns a "Fake" user to the World, so that it is saved in the .blend file even if unlinked.
HoR, HoG, HoB	The color of the *horizon*.
ZeR, ZeG, ZeB	The color of the zenith. This is the point directly above an observer (on the earth!). The same color is also used for the *nadir* (the point directly below the observer).
AmbR, AmbG, AmbB	The color of the environmental light, the *ambient*. This is a rather primitive way to make the entire rendering lighter, or to change the color temperature.
Expos	The lighting time, *exposure*. In fact, this causes a global strengthening or reduction in all the lamps. Use this to give the rendering more contrast.

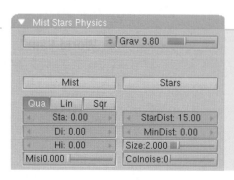

Myst, Stars, Physics Panel

The first row of this Panel is dedicated to the Realtime Physics engine (not covered in this Book):

Engine	This Menu allows to choose between different kind of engines:
	None
	Sumo
	ODE
	Dynamo
Grav	The value of gravity acceleration (9.8 m/s^2 on Earth).

The left buttons column handles Mist:

Mist	Activates the rendering of *mist*. All rendered faces and halos are given an extra *alpha* value, based on their distance from the camera. If a "sky" color is specified, this is filled in behind the *alpha*.
Qua, Lin, Sqr	Determines the progression of the mist. Quadratic, linear or inverse quadratic (square root), respectively. Sqr gives a thick "soupy" mist, as if the picture is rendered under water.
Sta	The start distance of the mist, measured from the Camera.

Di	The depth of the mist, with the distance measured from Sta.
Hi	With this option, the mist becomes thinner the higher it goes. This is measured from Z = 0.0. If the value of Hi is set to zero, this effect is turned off.
Misi	Mist intensity, the higher the thicker.

The right column of buttons handles stars:

Stars	Blender has an automatic star generator. These are standard halos that are only generated in the sky. With this option ON, stars are also drawn in the 3DWindow (as small points).
StarDist	The average distance between two stars. Do not allow this value to become too small, as this will generate an overflow.
MinDist	In reality, stars are light years apart. In the Blender universe, this distance is much smaller. To prevent stars from appearing too close to the Camera, you can set a MinDist value. Stars will never appear within this distance.
Size	The average screen dimensions of a star.
ColNoise	This value randomly selects star color.

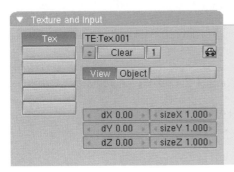

Texture and Input

This texture panel, and the following are a simplified version of the Material texture panels.

The left buttons column handles Mist:

Texture Channels	A World has six *channels* with which Textures can be linked. Each channel has its own *mapping*, i.e. the manner in which the texture works on the world. The settings are in the buttons described below and in the Map To Panel.
Texture Data Block	
Texture Menu	Select an existing Texture from the list provided, or create a new Texture Block.
TE:	The name of the Texture block. The name can be changed with this button.
Clear	The link to the Texture is erased.
Users	If the Texture Block has multiple users, this button shows the total number of users.
Auto Name	Blender assigns a name to the Texture.
Texture Mapping Input	Each Texture has a 3D coordinate (the texture coordinate) as input. The starting point is always the global coordinate of the 3D point that is seen in the pixel to be rendered. A world has only two options for this.
View	The *view* vector of the World; the vector of the global coordinate to the camera, is passed on to the texture.
Object	An Object is used as source of co-ordinates. The Object name must be entered in the Text Button below.
Texture Input Transform	Use these buttons to adjust the texture coordinate more finely.
dX, dY, dZ	The extra translation of the texture coordinate.
sizeX, sizeY, sizeZ	The extra scaling of the texture coordinate.

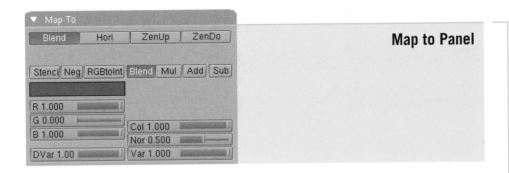

Map to Panel

The texture can only affect the color of the background. This can occur according to 4 schemes:

Blend	The texture works on the color progression in the sky.
Hori	The texture works on the color of the horizon.
ZenUp	The texture works on the color of the zenith above.
ZenDown	The texture works on the color of the zenith below.
Stencil	Normally, textures are executed one after the other and placed over each other. A second Texture *channel* can completely replace the first. This option sets the mapping to *stencil* mode. No subsequent Texture can have an effect on the area the current Texture affects.
Neg	The inverse of the Texture is applied.
RGBtoint	With this option, an RGB texture (affects color) is used as an Intensity texture (affects a value).
Blend	The Texture mixes the values.
Mul	The Texture multiplies the values.
Add	The Texture adds the values.
Sub	The Texture subtracts the values.
R, G, B	The color with which an Intensity texture blends with the current color.
DVar	The value with which the Intensity texture blends with the current value.

Col	The extent to which the texture affects the color.
Nor	The extent to which the texture affects the normal (not applicable here).
Var	The extent to which the texture affects the value (a variable, not applicable here).

Object Context

The Object Context shows the main Object Mode tools and is not divided into Subcontextes. It exhibits three Panels. A fourth is added if the selected Object is a Mesh.

Anim Settings Panel

Tracking Buttons	In Blender, Objects can be assigned a Track constraint (**CTRL-T**) in two way: an "Old Track" which is the Blender pre 2.30 way, and a true constraint. This latter is described in the `Constraints` Panel. THese buttons are applicable to:
	Objects Children of a Curve, following the Path, either the old pre-2.30 way (a normal parent and the curve set to "path") or the new way (a curve follow constraint) can follow the curve direction (`Follow` button).
	DupliVerted Objects, either on a Mesh or on a Particle system can give rotations to Objects (see `Effects` Panel). Because Objects have a rotation of their own, it is advisable to first erase this using **ALT-R**. If the Object is a Child, then erase the "Parent Inverse" as well using **ALT-P.**

Use these buttons to indicate how tracking must work:

Track X, Y, Z, -X, -Y, -Z	Specifies the direction axis; the axis that, for example, must point to the other Object.
UpX, UpY, UpZ	Specify what axis must point "up", in the direction of the (global) positive Z axis. If the "Track" axis is the same as the "Up" axis, this is turned off.
Draw Key	If Objects have an Object IPO, they can be drawn in the 3Dwindow as key positions. Key positions are drawn with this option ON and the IPO Keys ON (in the IPO Header). (**KKEY**).
DrawKeySel	Limits the drawing of *Object keys* to those selected.
PowerTrack	This option completely switches off the Object own rotation and that of its Parents. Only for Objects that "track" to another Object.
SlowPar	The value of `TimeOffset` is used to create a "delay" in the Parent relationship. This delay is cumulative and depends on the previous frame. When rendering anima- tions, the complete sequence must always be rendered, starting with the first frame.
DupliFrames	No matter how the Object moves, with its own Object IPOs or on a Curve path, a copy of the Object is made for every frame fromDupSta to DupEnd. The DupliFra- mes system is built for the specified frame interval.
DupliVerts	Child Objects are duplicated on all vertices of this Object (only with Mesh).
Rot	Dupliverted Object are rotated accordingly to the parent Mesh normals, and following what is stated by the Tracking Toggle Buttons.
No Speed	The DupliFrames are set to "still", regardless of the current frame.
DupSta, DupEnd	The start and end frame of the duplication.

DupOn, DupOff	Empty positions can be specified with the option DupliFrames. For example: DupOn =2, DupOff=8 sets two copies on every 10 frames. The duplicated Objects move over the animation system like a sort of train.
Offs Ob	The TimeOffset value works on its own Object IPO.
Offs Par	The TimeOffset value works on the Parent relationship of the Object.
Offs Particle	The TimeOffset value works on the Particle Effect.
TimeOffset	Depending on the previously mentioned pre-sets, the animation is shifted a number of frames. This does not work for VertexKeys.
Automatic Time	This generates automatic TimeOffset values for all *selected* Objects. The start value is the value of the TimeOffset button. A pop-up asks for the size of the interval. Blender looks at the Object's screen coordinates in the nearest 3DWindow and calculates the offset values from left to right.
PrSeed	The speed of the Object is printed.

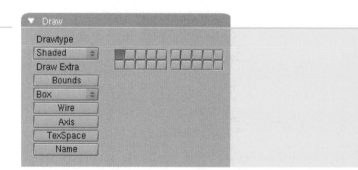

Draw Panel

The Draw Panel contains a layer set of buttons on the right, which is the equivalent of the **MKEY** Object Mode pop-up in the 3D Viewport, and moves the object to selected layer(s).

BUTTONS REFERENCE.OBJECT CONTEXT

Left column presents, top to bottom:

DrawType	Choose a preference for the standard display method in the 3D window from the list provided. The DrawType is compared with the DrawMode set in the 3D Window; the least complex method is the one actually used.
Bounds	A bounding object is displayed in the dimensions of the object. This is in addition to the Object drawing.
Boundary Display Menu	A bounding object is displayed in the dimensions of the object. This is in addition to the Object drawing.
Wire	A Wireframe is superimposed to the current Drawing method.
Axis	The axes are drawn with X, Y and Z indicated.
TexSpace	The texture space. This can be different from the BoundBox. It is displayed with broken lines.
Name	The name of the Object is printed at the Object centre.

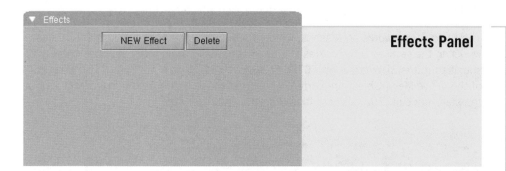

Effects Panel

The Effect Panel is so crowded of buttons that it is the only one bigger than the standard Panel dimension.

Three effects are currently built in: "Build", "Particles" and "Wave". Effects are a fixed part of the Object; they cannot have any links or multiple users.

If the Object has no Effects then just two buttons are present:

New Effect	Create a new Effect.
Delete	Delete the Effect.

Once an Effect has been added a Menu appears, allowing to choose Effect type. According to this type the buttons in the panel changes.

An Object might have multiple effects. A row of Radio Buttons without labels below the New Effect button toggle between them.

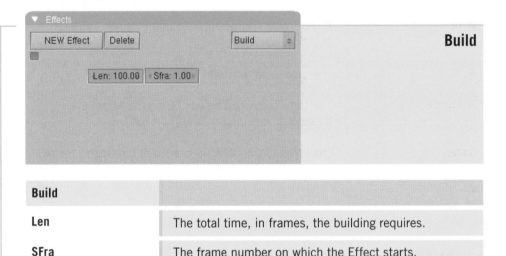

Build

Build	
Len	The total time, in frames, the building requires.
SFra	The frame number on which the Effect starts.

The Build Effect works on Meshes, which are built up face by face over time. It also works on the vertices in Halo Meshes. The sequence in which this happens can be specified in the 3DWindow with **CTRL-F**: Sort Faces (not in Edit Mode). The faces of the *active* Mesh Object are sorted. The current face in the 3DWindow is taken as the starting point. The leftmost face first, the rightmost face last.

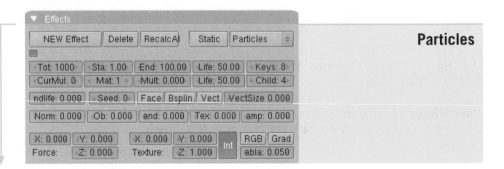

Particles

Particles are vertices with a default halo material (or Objects if the option "DupliVerts" is ON) that are generated more or less according to laws of physics. Use Particles for smoke, fire, explosions, a fountain, fireworks or a school of fish! With the Static option it is also possible to make fur or even plants.

A Particle system is pre-calculated as a pre-process (this can take some time). They can then be viewed in the 3DWindow in real time. Particles are a full-fledged part of Blender animation system. They can also controlled by Lattices. Only Meshes can have Particles.

Recalc All	Recalc the particle-system after changing the animation of the emitter mesh. This updates the particle-system.
Static	Making static particles. Particles now don't animate or move anymore, they follow the Object transformation. Static particles are generated one at each frame for the entire `Life` value. Use the `step` option to control this; `step`=2 means a particle every two frames.
Tot	The total number of Particles. Particles require quite a bit of memory (not in the file!) and rendering time, so specify this value carefully.
Sta, End	The start and end frame between which Particles are generated.
Life	The life span of each Particle.
Keys	Not all Particle locations are calculated and remembered for each frame for the entire particle system. This is only done for a fixed number of *key* positions between which interpolations are performed. A larger number of `Keys` gives a more fluid, detailed movement. This makes significant demands on the memory and time required to calculate the system.
CurMul	Particles can "multiply themselves" at the end of their lives. For each generation, certain particle settings are unique. This button determines which generation is displayed.
Mat	The Material used for the current generation of Particles.

Mult	This determines whether the particles multiply themselves. A value of 0.0 switches this off. A value of 1.0 means that each Particle multiplies itself. The particle system itself ensures that the *total* number of Particles is limited to the Tot value.
Life	The age of the Particles in the following generation.
Child	The number of children of a Particle that has multiplied itself.
RandLife	A factor that ascribes the age of Particles a (pseudo) random variation.
Seed	The offset in the random table.
Face	With this option particles are not only emitted from vertices, but also from the faces of the mesh.
Bspline	The Particles are interpolated from the keys using a B-spline formula. This give a much more fluid progression, but the particles no longer pass exactly through the key positions.
Vect	This gives particles a rotation direction. This can be seen in the Halo rendering. Particles that duplicate Objects now also give a rotation to these Objects.
Vect Size	The extent to which the speed of the Vect Particle works on the dimensions of the Halo.
Norm	The extent to which the vertex normal of the Mesh gives the Particle a starting speed. If the Mesh has no faces (and thus no vertex normals) the normalized *local* vertex coordinate is used as the starting speed.
Ob	The Extent to which the speed of the Object gives the Particle a starting speed. This makes a rotating cube become a sort of "sprinkler".
Rand	The extent to which a (pseudo) random value gives the Particle a starting speed.
Tex	The extent to which the Texture gives the Particle a starting speed. For this, only the last Texture of the Material is used, in channel number 8.

Damp	Use of damping reduces the speed, like a sort of friction.
Force X, Y, Z	A uniform force. This can simulate the effect of gravity or wind.
Texture X, Y, Z	A standard force that works on a Particle, determined by the texture. Textures can have an effect on the movement of Particles. The 3D coordinate of the Particle is passed to the texture per Particle key.
Int	The Intensity that is passed back from the texture is used as a factor for the standard texture force (previous three buttons).
RGB	The color of the texture has a direct effect on the speed of the Particle: Red on the X, Green on the Y and Blue on the Z component of the speed.
Grad	The gradient of the texture is calculated. This is the mathematical derivative. Four samples of the texture are combined to produce a speed vector. With *procedural* textures, such as Clouds, this method gives a very beautiful, turbulent effect. Set the number of "Keys" as high as possible to see the sometimes rather subtle twisting.
Nabla	The dimension of the area in which the *gradient* is calculated. This value must be carefully adjusted to the frequency of the texture.

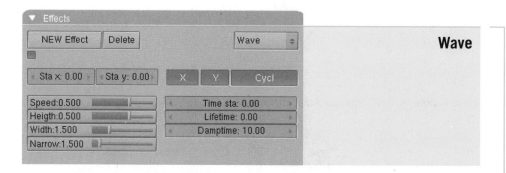

Wave

The Wave Effect adds a animated Wave to a Mesh. It is not limited to flat objects but can also be used to make a sphere "wobble".

Sta X, Sta Y	Starting Position of the Wave.
X, Y	Per default you have a XY Wave on your Object. With the Buttons X and Y you can enable or disable the wave generation for an axis.
Cycl	Makes wave generation cyclic in the animation.
Speed	Speed the Wave travels, can also be negative.
Height	Amplitude of the Wave.
Width	Width of the wave (wavelength)
Narrow	How narrow the next wave follows.
Time Sta	When (in frames of the animation) the wave generation should start.
Lifetime	How long (in frames) a wave exists
Damptime	How many frames the wave should attenuate.

Constraints Panel

The Constraint panel allowto add/remove Constraints on selected Objects. If no constraint is present then only the Add button is present. Otherwise a list of constraints is shown.

Add	Add menu, shows all available Constraints for given Object. These are:
	Copy Location - All Objects

`Copy Rotation` - All Objects	
`Track To` - All Objects	
`Lock Track` - All Objects	
`Follow Path` - All Objects	
`IK Solver` - Bones in Pose Mode	
`Action` - Bones in Pose Mode	
`Null` - All Objects	

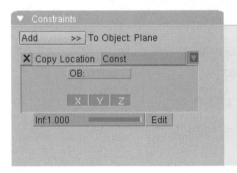

Constraints Item

Each Constraint item has some common controls:

Header	From left to right:
	A x button - deletes constraint;
	A label with constraint type;
	A text button with Constraint name
	A triangle button - collapses/expand constraint window.
Window	A window in the Panel with the various constraint settings.

Footer	From left to right.
	`Inf:` Influence of the constraint: 0=nothing; 1=full;
	`Edit` Opens an IPO Window allowing to edit the constraint influence in time.

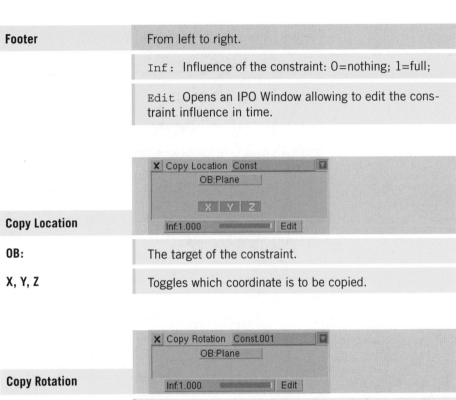

Copy Location	
OB:	The target of the constraint.
X, Y, Z	Toggles which coordinate is to be copied.

Copy Rotation	
OB:	The target of the constraint.

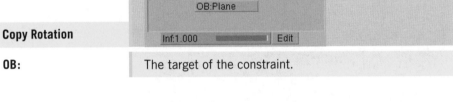

Track To	
OB:	The target of the constraint.
X, Y, Z, -X, -Y, -Z	The row of 6 Radio Buttons Toggles which axis should point to the target, and if it must be its positive or negative direction to point to the target.
X, Y, Z	The row of 3 Radio Buttons Toggles which axis should point up. If the same axis of the other Radio Group is chosen here an error occurs.

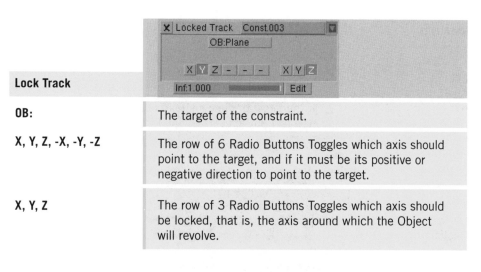

Lock Track

OB:	The target of the constraint.
X, Y, Z, -X, -Y, -Z	The row of 6 Radio Buttons Toggles which axis should point to the target, and if it must be its positive or negative direction to point to the target.
X, Y, Z	The row of 3 Radio Buttons Toggles which axis should be locked, that is, the axis around which the Object will revolve.

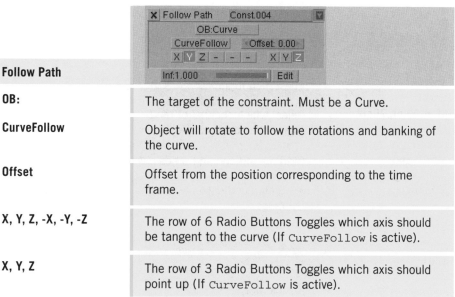

Follow Path

OB:	The target of the constraint. Must be a Curve.
CurveFollow	Object will rotate to follow the rotations and banking of the curve.
Offset	Offset from the position corresponding to the time frame.
X, Y, Z, -X, -Y, -Z	The row of 6 Radio Buttons Toggles which axis should be tangent to the curve (If CurveFollow is active).
X, Y, Z	The row of 3 Radio Buttons Toggles which axis should point up (If CurveFollow is active).

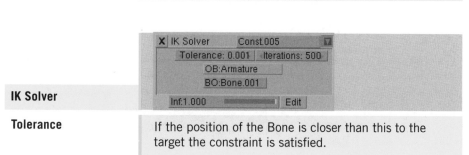

IK Solver

Tolerance	If the position of the Bone is closer than this to the target the constraint is satisfied.

Iterations	Maximum number of iterative steps performed trying to fulfil the constraint.
OB:	The target of the constraint.
BO:	If the target of the constraint is an Armature then a new text box appears asking for a specific Bone as a target.

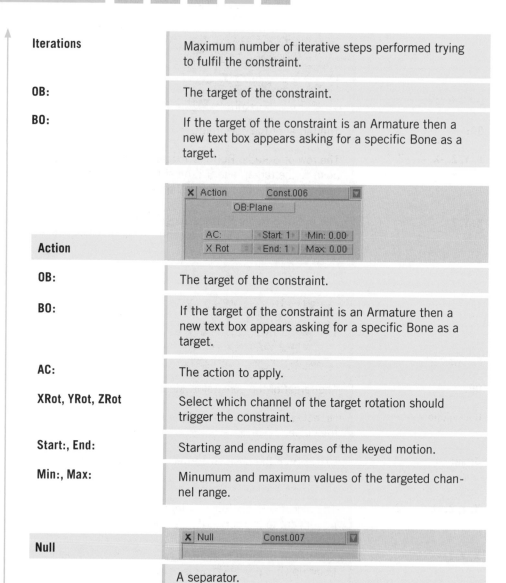

Action	
OB:	The target of the constraint.
BO:	If the target of the constraint is an Armature then a new text box appears asking for a specific Bone as a target.
AC:	The action to apply.
XRot, YRot, ZRot	Select which channel of the target rotation should trigger the constraint.
Start:, End:	Starting and ending frames of the keyed motion.
Min:, Max:	Minumum and maximum values of the targeted channel range.

Null	
	A separator.

Editing Context

The Editing Context shows the main Edit Mode tools and is not divided into Sub-contexts. It exhibits two Panels if the Object is not in Edit Mode. Further Panels are added if the Object is in Edit Mode, depending on the Object type.

The two Panels which are always present change their buttons according to the Object type anyway, so this reference is subdivided by Object type:

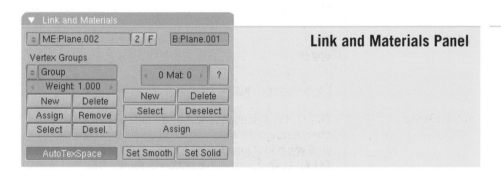

Link and Materials Panel

Mesh Data Block	On the first line:
Mesh Menu	Selects which Mesh Data Block is linked to this Object.
ME:	Shows Mesh Data Block name, allowing for changes.
Users	If the Mesh Block is used by more than one Object, this button shows the total number of Objects. Press the button to make the Mesh „Single User". This duplicates the Mesh Block.
F	Fake User button, to keep Mesh Data Block even if unlinked.
OB:	Shows Object name, allowing for changes.
Group Menu	Allow for selecting an existing vertex group.
Group Name	This Text Box shows the current vertex group name, allowing editing.
Weight	Sets the current vertex group bone deformation strength.

If the Mesh is in Edit Mode the following buttons also appear below:

New	A new group is created.
Delete	Current group is deleted.
Assign	Currently selected vertices are added to the current group.
Remove	Currently selected vertices are removed from the group.
Select	Vertices belonging to the group are added to current selection.
Desel.	Vertices belonging to the group are deselected.
AutoTexSpace	This option calculates the texture area automatically, after leaving Edit Mode. You can also specify a texture area yourself (Outside Edit Mode, in the 3D Window; **TKEY**), in which case this option is turned OFF.

On the right column:

1 Mat 1	This button can be used to specify which Material should be shown, i.e. which Material is *active*. The first digit indicates the amount of Materials, the second digit indicates the index number of the *active* Material. Each *face* in a Mesh has a corresponding number: the „Material index". The same is true of Curves and Surfaces.
?	In Edit Mode, this Button indicates what *index* number, and thus what Material, the selected faces have.
New	Make a new *index*. The current Material is assigned an extra link. If there was no Material, a new one is created.
Delete	Delete the current *index*. The current Material gets one less link. The already used index numbers are modified in the ObData.

Select	In Edit Mode, every vertex with the current *index* number is selected.
Deselect	In Edit Mode, every vertex with the current *index* number is deselected.
Assign	In Edit Mode, the current *index* number is assigned to the selected vertices.
Set Smooth	All selected faces are rendered with smoothly varying normals. Edges are not visible.
Set Solid	All selected faces are rendered with constant normals. Edges are visible.

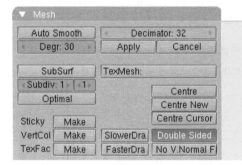

Mesh Panel

This panels owns two columns of buttons; on the left:

AutoSmooth	Automatic smooth rendering (not faceted) for meshes. The Button Set smooth must have been used on faces to make Auto Smooth work. The smoothing is not displayed in the 3D Window, only in renderings.
Degr:	Determines the degree in which faces can meet and still get smoothed by Auto Smooth.
SubSurf	This option turns a Mesh Object into a SubSurfed Mesh, meaning procedural smooth subdivision of Mesh objects.

Subdiv:	Number of subdivisions for SubSurfed Meshes in the 3D Viewport. The neighbouring labelless number sets the level of subdivision at rendering time. This allows fast editing on coarse SubSurfaced meshes and smooth rendering on fine SubSurfaced meshes.
Optimal	In Edit Mode the way of representing the original mesh changes, hiding edges and showing SubSurfed edges.
Sticky: Make/Delete	Blender allows you to assign a texture coordinate to Meshes that is derived from the way the Camera view sees the Mesh. The screen coordinates (only X,Y) are calculated from each vertex and these coordinates are stored in the Mesh. As if the texture is permanently projected and fixed on the Mesh as viewed fromthe Camera; it becomes "sticky". Use "sticky" to match a 3D object exactly with the Image Texture of a 3D picture. This option also allows you to create special *morphing* effects. If the image is already "sticky", the button allows you to remove this effect.
VertCol: Make/Delete	A color can be specified per vertex. This is required for the VertexPaint option. If the Object DrawType is "Shaded", these colors are copied to the vertex colors. This allows you to achieve a *Radiosity*-like effect (set `MaterialButtons>>VertCol` ON). If the Mesh is Double Sided, this is automatically turned off.
TexFac: Make/Delete	Assigns a texture per face. Will be automatically set when you use the UV-Editor to texture a realtime model.

For the right column:

Decimator	This is present only in Object Mode. It shows the total number of triangular faces of the Mesh (Quads are computed as two tris). You can reduce the number of faces with this Num Button. Faces are joined starting from the most "coplanar" ones. The result is shown in the 3D Window.
Apply, Cancel	If you are satisfied with mesh decimation you can make it permanent, otherwise you can revert to previous state.

TexMesh	Enter the name of another Mesh block here to be used as the source for the texture coordinates. *Morphing*-like effects can then be achieved by distorting the active Mesh. For example, a straight stream of water (as an animated texture) can be placed in a winding river.
Centre	Each ObData has its own local 3D space. The null point of this space is placed at the Object center. This option calculates a new, centered null point in the ObData. This may change texture coordinates.
Centre New	As above, but now the Object is placed in such a way that the ObData appears to remain in the same place.
Centre Cursor	The new null point of the object is the 3D-Cursor location.
SlowerDraw, FasterDraw	When leaving Edit Mode all edges are tested to determine whether they must be displayed as a wire frame. Edges that share two faces with the same normal are never displayed. This increases the recognisability of the Mesh and considerably speeds up drawing. With `SlowerDraw` and `FasterDraw`, you can specify that additional or fewer edges must be drawn when you are not in Edit Mode.
Double Sided	Only for display in the 3D Window; can be used to control whether double-sided faces are drawn. Turn this option OFF if the Object has a negative "size" value (for example an X-flip).
No V.Normal Flip	Because Blender normally renders double-sided, the direction of the normal (towards the front or the back) is automatically corrected during rendering. This option turns this automatic correction off, allowing "smooth" rendering with faces that have sharp angles (smaller than 100 degrees). Be sure the face normals are set consistently in the same direction (**CTRL-N** in Edit Mode).

Mesh Tools Panel

Left to right, and top to bottom:

Beauty	This is an option for the Subdivide command. It splits the faces into halves lengthwise, converting elongated faces to squares. If the face is smaller than the value of `Limit:`, it is not longer split in two.
Subdivide	Selected faces are divided into quarters; all edges are split in half.
Fract Subd	Fractal Subdivide. Like Subdivide, but now the new vertices are set with a random vector up or down. A pop-up asks you to specify the amount. Use this to generate landscapes or mountains.
Noise	Here Textures can be used to move the selected vertices up a specific amount. The local vertex coordinate is used as the texture coordinate. Every Texture type works with this option. For example, the Stucci produce a landscape effect. Or use Images to express this in relief.
Hash	This makes the sequence of vertices somewhat random.
Xsort	Sorts the vertices in the X direction. This creates interesting effects with VertexKeys or "Build Effects" for Halos.
To Sphere	All selected vertices are blown up into a spherical shape, with the 3DCursor as a midpoint. A requester asks you to specify the factor for this action.
Smooth	All edges with both vertices selected are shortened. This flattens sharp angles.

BUTTONS REFERENCE.EDITING CONTEXT

Flip Normals	Toggles the direction of the selected face(s) normals.
Rem Doubles	Remove Doubles. All selected vertices closer to one another than `Limit` are combined and redundant faces are removed.
Limit:	The value to be used in the `Rem Doubles` and other operations.
Extrude	Converts all selected *edges to faces*. If necessary, the selected faces are also duplicated. Grab mode starts immediately after this command is executed. If there are multiple 3DWindows, the mouse cursor changes to a question mark. Click at the 3D Window in which "Extrude" must be executed.
Screw	This tool starts a repetitive Spin with a screw-shaped revolution on the selected vertices. You can use this to create screws, springs or shell-shaped structures.
Spin	The Spin operation is a repetitively rotating Extrude. This can be used in every view of the 3D Window, the rotation axis is always through the 3D Cursor, perpendicular to the screen. Set the buttons Degr and Steps to the desired value. If there are multiple 3D Windows, the mouse cursor changes to a question mark. Click at the 3DWindow in which the Spin must occur.
Spin Dup	Like Spin, but instead of an "Extrude", there is duplication.
Degr	The number of degrees the Spin/SpinDup revolves.
Steps	The total number of Spin/SpinDup revolutions, or the number of steps of the Screw per revolution.
Turns	The number of revolutions the Screw turns.
Keep Original	This option saves the selected original for a Spin/SpinDup or Screw operation. This releases the new vertices and faces from the original piece.
Clockwise	The direction of the Screw or Spin/SpinDup, clockwise, or counterclockwise.

| Extrude Dup | This creates a repetitive Extrude along a straight line. This takes place perpendicular to the view of the 3D Window. |
| Offset | The distance between each step of the Extrude Dup. |

Mesh Tools 1 Panel

Top to bottom:

Centre	Moves the vertices altogether so that their barycentrum is set to the Object center.
Hide	All selected vertices are temporarily hidden (**HKEY**).
Reveal	This undoes the Hide option (**ALT-H**).
Select Swap	Toggle the selection status of all vertices.
NSize	The length of the face normals, if they are drawn.
Draw Normals	Indicates that the face normals must be drawn in Edit Mode.
Draw Faces	Indicates that the face must be drawn (as shaded blue/ purple) in Edit Mode.
Draw Edges	Indicates that the selected edges must be highlighted. Partially selected edges (one vertex only selected) have a color gradient.
All Edges	After leaving Edit Mode, all edges are drawn normally, without optimization.

Curve and Surface objects

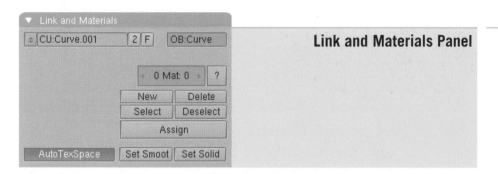

Link and Materials Panel

Curve/Surface Data Block	On the first line:
Curve Menu	Selects which Curve Data Block is linked to this Object.
CU:	Shows Curve Data Block name, allowing for changes.
Users	If the Curve/Surface Block is used by more than one Object, this button shows the total number of Objects. Press the button to make the Curve/Surface "Single User". This duplicates the Curve/Surface Block.
F	Fake User button, to keep Curve/Surface Data Block even if unlinked.
OB:	Shows Object name, allowing for changes.

Below, on the left:

AutoTexSpace	This option calculates the texture area automatically, after leaving Edit Mode. You can also specify a texture area yourself (Outside Edit Mode, in the 3D Window; **TKEY**), in which case this option is turned OFF.

On the right column there are the Material link buttons, whose behavior is identical than for a Mesh.

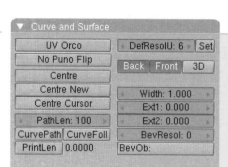

Curves and Surfaces Panel

This panels owns two columns of buttons for curves, just one for surfaces; on the left:

UV Orco	UV Orco makes Blender calculating an undeformed Curve/Surface to be used as reference for "Orco" texture coordinates.
No Puno Flip (Only Surfaces)	Blender renders by default double sided faces. That means you don't have to worry while modeling which directions normals point for faces. However, this can cause errors in calculating the vertex normals. This option forces Blender to calculate vertex normals without automatically flipping a face normal in the "right" direction while rendering. It is apparent with models with very irregular faces, which you still like to render Smooth using vertex normals.
Centre	Each ObData has its own local 3D space. The null point of this space is placed at the Object center. This option calculates a new, centered, null point in the ObData. This may change texture coordinates.
Centre New	As above, but now the Object is placed in such a way that the ObData appears to remain in the same place.
Centre Cursor	The new null point of the object is the 3D-Cursor location.

The following buttons are present only for Curve Objects:

PathLen	The length of the Curve path in frames, if there is no Speed IPO.

BUTTONS REFERENCE.EDITING CONTEXT

CurvePath	Specifies that the Curve becomes a *path*. Children of this Curve now move over the curve. All Curves can become a *path*, but a 5th order NURBS curve works best. It has no problems with movement and rotation discontinuity. This is an alternate to a Follow Path constraint.
CurveFollow	The Curve path passes a rotation to the Child Objects. The "Tracking" buttons determine which axis the path follows. In Edit Mode, horizontal lines are also drawn for a 3D curve. This determines the tilt, which is an extra axis rotation of the Child Objects. The *tilt* can be changed using the **TKEY**. Curve paths cannot give uniform perpendicular (aligned with the local Z axis) rotations. In that case, the "up" axis cannot be determined.
PrintLen	The length of the path is printed in Blender units.

On the second column, again present only for Curves:

DefResolU	The standard resolution in the U direction for curves.
Set	Assigns the value of DefResolU to all selected curves.
Back	Specifies that the back side of (extruded) 2D curves should be filled.
Front	Specifes that the front side of (extruded) 2D curves should be filled.
3D	The curve may now have vertices on each 3D coordinate; the front and back side are never rendered.
Width	The interpolated points of a curve can be moved farther apart or brought closer together.
Ext1	The depth of the extrude.
Ext2	The depth of the standard bevel.

| **BevResol** | The resolution of the standard bevel; the bevel eventually becomes a quarter circle. |
| **BevOb** | The "bevel" Object. Fill in the name of another Curve Object; this now forms the bevel. For each interpolated point on the curve, the "bevel Object" is, as it were, extruded and rotated. With this method, for example, you can create the rails of a roller coaster with a 3D curve as the base and two small squares as bevels. Set the values ResolU of both Curves carefully, given that this beveling can generate many faces. |

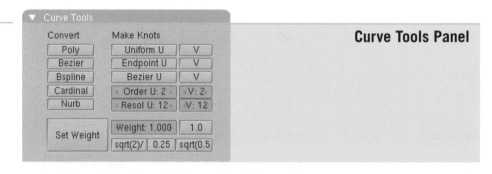

Curve Tools Panel

This Panel again shows Buttons which might or might not be there, according to the type of Object, curve or Surface.

Top to bottom, left to right:

Poly (**Bezier Curve only**)	A polygon only gives a linear interpolation of vertices.
Bezier (**Bezier Curve only**)	Vertices in a Bezier curve are grouped in threes; the *handles*. The most frequently used curve type for creating letters or logos.
Bspline	*future use*
Cardinal	*future use*
Nurb	*not used*. NURBS curves are separate Objects.

The right column handles quantities relative to NURBS:

Uniform U, V	Sets the *knots* so that the first and last handles are always included.
Bezier U, V	Sets the *knots* table in such a way that the NURBS behave like a Bezier.
Order U, V	The *order* is the "depth" of the curve calculation. Order one is a point, order two is linear, order three is quadratic, etc. Always use order five for Curve paths. Order five behaves fluently under all circumstances, without annoying discontinuity in the movement.
Reslol U, V	The resolution in which the interpolation occurs; the number of points that must be generated between two vertices in the curve.
Set Weight	NURBS curves have a "weight" per handle; the extent to which a handle participates in the interpolation. This button assigns the Weight value to all selected vertices.
Weight	The weight that is assigned with Set Weight.
1.0, sqrt(2)/4, 0.25, sqrt(0.5)	A number of pre-sets that can be used to create pure circles and spheres.

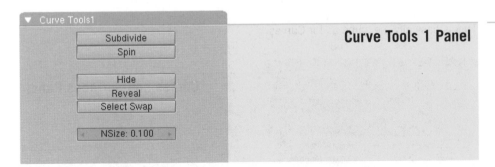

Curve Tools 1 Panel

This Panel again shows Buttons which might or might not be there, according to the type of Object, curve or Surface.

Top to bottom:

Subdivide	Create new handle in curves, between selected ones.
Spin (Curves of *Surface type* only)	Spins the Curve around the cursor to create a surface. A whole 360 degrees spin is performed.
Hide	All selected handles are temporarily hidden (**HKEY**).
Reveal	This undoes the hide option (**ALT-H**).
Select Swap	Toggle the selection status of all handles.
NSize	This determines the length of the "tilt" lines in 3D Curves.

Text objects

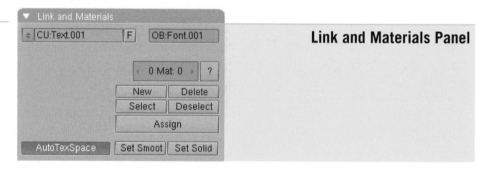

Link and Materials Panel

This is basically the same as for Curves.

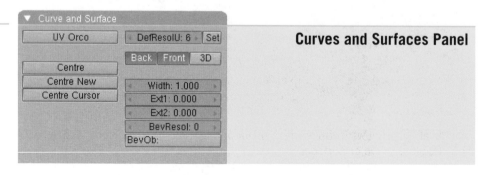

Curves and Surfaces Panel

This panels, again, shows the same items as for a (Bézier) Curve Object.

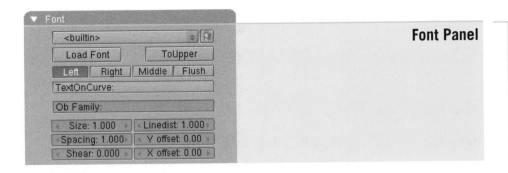

Font Panel

This Panel is Font specific, top to bottom:

Font Menu	Allows to choose between available (loaded) fonts.
Pack Button	Embeds/de-embeds the font into/from the current .blend file.
Load Font	Turns nearest largest window into a File Select Window and allows to select a True Type or PostScript font from the disk.
ToUpper	In Edit Mode, changes all letters into uppercase or, if there are no lowercase letters, changes all uppercase to lowercase letters.
Left, Right, Middle, Flush	All text is left, right, middle or flush-aligned.
TextOnCurve	Enter the name of a Curve Object here; this now forms the line along which the text is placed.
Ob Family	You can create fonts yourself within a Blender file. Each letter from this Font Object is then replaced by any Object you chose, and is automatically duplicated. This means that you can type with Objects! Objects to be considered as letters must belong to the same "family"; they must have a name that corresponds to the other letter Objects and with the name that must be entered in this button. Important: set the option DupliVerts ON in the Anim Panel. For example:
	"Ob Family" = Weird.
	The Objects that are to replace the letters a and b are called "Weirda" and "Weirdb", respectively.

Size	The letter size.
Linedist	The distance between two lines of text.
Spacing	The size of the space between two letters.
Shear	Changes the letters to italics.
Yoffset	This shifts the text up or down. For adjusting a `TextOnCurve`.
Xoffset	This moves the text left or right. For adjusting `TextOnCurve`.

Meta Objects

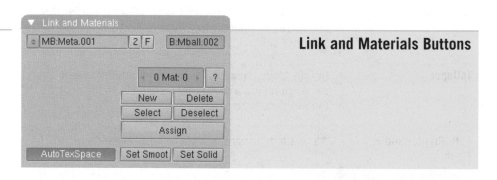

Link and Materials Buttons

Meta Data Block	On the first line:
Meta Menu	Selects which Meta Data Block is linked to this Object.
MB:	Shows Meta Data Block name, allowing for changes.
Users	If the Meta Block is used by more than one Object, this button shows the total number of Objects. Press the button to make the Meta "Single User". This duplicates the Meta Block.
F	Fake User button, to keep Meta Data Block even if unlinked.
OB:	Shows Object name, allowing for changes.

BUTTONS REFERENCE.EDITING CONTEXT

Below, on the left:

| AutoTexSpace | This option calculates the texture area automatically, after leaving Edit Mode. You can also specify a texture area yourself (Outside Edit Mode, in the 3D Window; **TKEY**), in which case this option is turned OFF. |

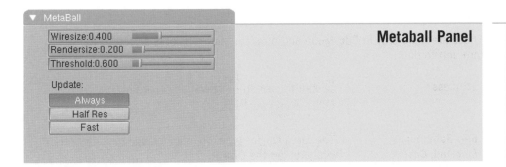

Metaball Panel

This panels is populated by buttons only if the base Meta Object is selected (The Meta Object with a name withou a trailing number). This because these settings apply to *all* Meta Object of the family.

Wiresize	The discretization step of the Meta Object in wireframe 3D Window, the larger the less accurate, but also the faster. Be careful with small values, as they use a lot of memory.
RenderSize	The resolution of the rendered Meta Ball.
Threshold	This value determines the global "stiffness" of the MetaBall.
Always, Half Res, Fast	In Edit Mode, the Meta Ball is completely recalculated during *transformations* (Always); or rather calculated in half resolution (Half Res); or is only recalculated after the *transformation* is complete (Fast).

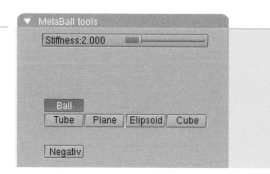

MetaBall Tools Panel

These are there only in Edit Mode and only if a Meta Object is selected. Top to bottom, left to right:

Stiffness	The stiffness can be specified separately on a per Meta Object basis.
Ball, Tube, Plane, Ellipsoid, Cube	The Meta Object type. You can change this after having created the Object.
Negative	The active "ball" has a negative effect on the other balls.

Empties

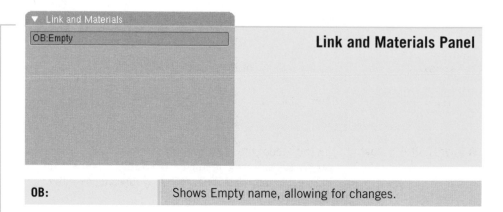

Link and Materials Panel

OB:	Shows Empty name, allowing for changes.

Camera Objects

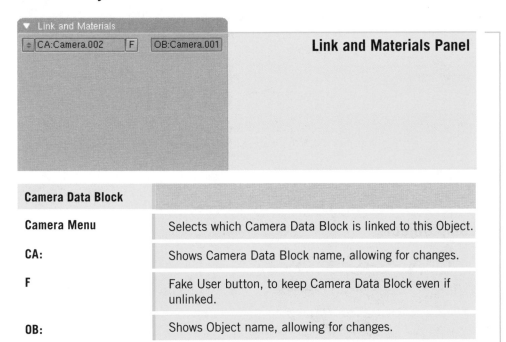

Link and Materials Panel

CA:Camera.002 F OB:Camera.001

Camera Data Block

Camera Menu	Selects which Camera Data Block is linked to this Object.
CA:	Shows Camera Data Block name, allowing for changes.
F	Fake User button, to keep Camera Data Block even if unlinked.
OB:	Shows Object name, allowing for changes.

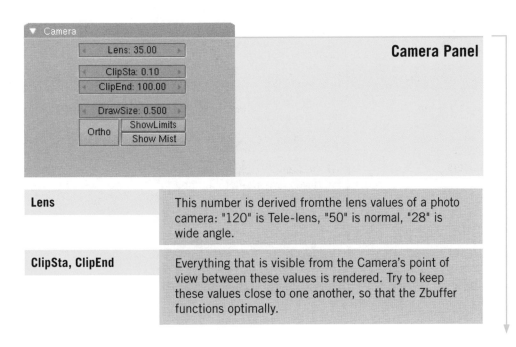

Camera Panel

Lens: 35.00
ClipSta: 0.10
ClipEnd: 100.00
DrawSize: 0.500
Ortho   ShowLimits
Show Mist

Lens	This number is derived fromthe lens values of a photo camera: "120" is Tele-lens, "50" is normal, "28" is wide angle.
ClipSta, ClipEnd	Everything that is visible from the Camera's point of view between these values is rendered. Try to keep these values close to one another, so that the Zbuffer functions optimally.

DrawSize	The size in which the Camera is drawn in the 3DWindow.
Ortho	A Camera can also render orthogonally. The distance from the Camera then has no effect on the size of the rendered objects.
ShowLimits	A line that indicates the values of ClipSta and ClipEnd is drawn in the 3D Window near the Camera.
ShowMist	A line that indicates the area of the "mist" (see World Buttons) is drawn near the Camera in the 3Dwindow.

Lamp Objects

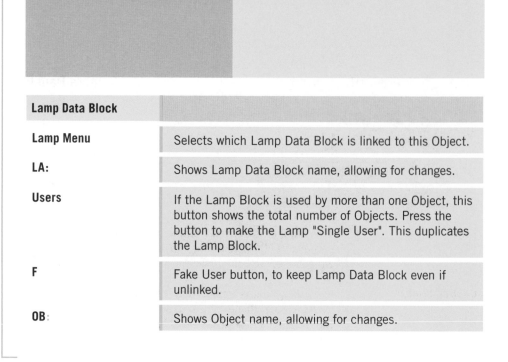

Link and Materials Panel

Lamp Data Block	
Lamp Menu	Selects which Lamp Data Block is linked to this Object.
LA:	Shows Lamp Data Block name, allowing for changes.
Users	If the Lamp Block is used by more than one Object, this button shows the total number of Objects. Press the button to make the Lamp "Single User". This duplicates the Lamp Block.
F	Fake User button, to keep Lamp Data Block even if unlinked.
OB:	Shows Object name, allowing for changes.

Armature Objects

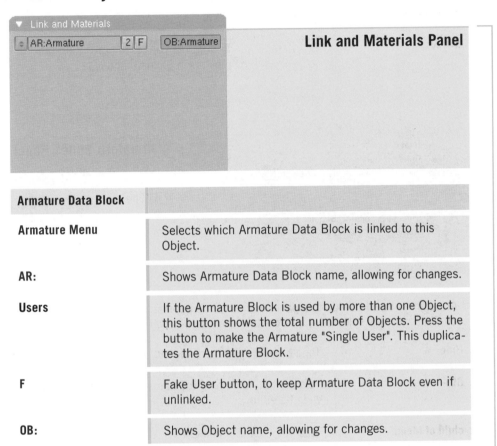

Link and Materials Panel

Armature Data Block	
Armature Menu	Selects which Armature Data Block is linked to this Object.
AR:	Shows Armature Data Block name, allowing for changes.
Users	If the Armature Block is used by more than one Object, this button shows the total number of Objects. Press the button to make the Armature "Single User". This duplicates the Armature Block.
F	Fake User button, to keep Armature Data Block even if unlinked.
OB:	Shows Object name, allowing for changes.

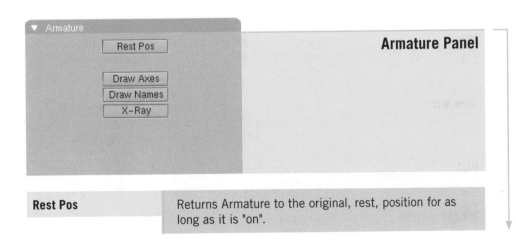

Armature Panel

Rest Pos	Returns Armature to the original, rest, position for as long as it is "on".

Draw Axes	Draw Axes for all bones.
Draw Names	Draw Names for all bones.
X-Ray	Draw armatures in front of objects, to prevent armatures to be hidden by meshes in Shaded mode.

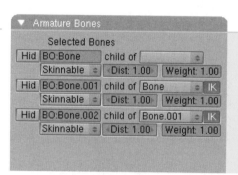

Armature Bones Panel

If Armature is in Edit Mode this panel appears, it is populated by a couple of lines for each Bone which is selected. Lines contain: tom, left to right:

Hide	Toggle visibility of the Bone out of Edit Mode.
BO:	Text Button containing the name of the bone, and allowing its editing.
child of Menu	This Menu Button allows to select any of the Bones in the armature which *can* be parent of current bone as parent. A Bone can be set orphan by selecting the empty menu entry.
IK	Toggles Inverse Kinematics calculation from this bone up to its Parent on or off. An IK chain always stays continuous.
Skin Menu	Sets bone to Skinnable or Unskinnable for Vertex Group creating purposes. All other entries in the menu are under development and do not work right now.
Dist	Bone deformation distance, for automatic skinning (deprecated).
Weight	Bone deformation weight, for automatic skinning (deprecated).

Lattice Objects

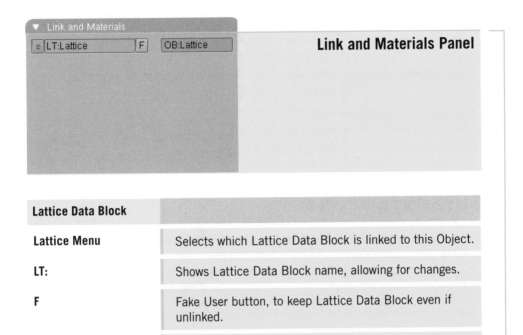

Link and Materials Panel

Lattice Data Block	
Lattice Menu	Selects which Lattice Data Block is linked to this Object.
LT:	Shows Lattice Data Block name, allowing for changes.
F	Fake User button, to keep Lattice Data Block even if unlinked.
OB:	Shows Object name, allowing for changes.

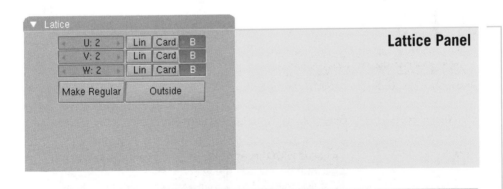

Lattice Panel

U, V, W	The three dimensions of the Lattice. If a new value is entered here, Lattice is placed in a regular, standard position.

Lin, Card, B	The manner in which the deformation is calculated can be specified separately for each dimension of the Lattice. The options are: `Linear Cardinal` spline and `B` spline. The last option gives the most fluid deformation.
Make Regular	This option sets the Lattice in a regular, standard position.
Outside	This type Lattice only displays vertices on the outside. The inner vertices are interpolated linearly. This makes working with large Lattices simpler.

Face Select and Paint Modes

If the Object, in Object Mode, has faces/vertices there are additional modes available. The Face Select mode allows for individual face selection, most useful in UV texturing, while Vertex Paint and Weight Paint Modes allows to handle vertex colors and weights of deformation groups. Texture Paint Mode allows to paint the Object Image Textures on the 3D Viewport rather than on the Image Window.

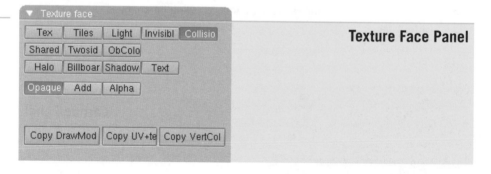

Texture Face Panel

This panel exists only in Face Select Mode. Left to right and top to bottom:

Tex	Faces with this attribute are rendered textured in the textured view and the realtime engine. If no texture is assigned to the face it will be rendered in a bright purple.
Tiles	Images can have a tile-mode assigned. In the Image-Window header you can indicate how many tiles an Image will be subdivided in. This button tells Blender to use this tile mode for the active face.

Light	The faces with this attribute are calculated with light in the realtime engine and the shaded views.
Invisible	This attribute makes faces invisible.
Collision	Faces with this attribute are taken into account for the real-time collision detection.
Shared	In Blender vertex colors are stored in each Face, thus allowing a different color for individual faces without having to add vertices. With this option, you can make sure that vertex colors are blended across faces if they share vertices.
Twoside	Faces with that attribute are rendered twosided.
ObColor	Each Object in Blender has an RGB color that can be animated with IPO-curves. With this option the realtime engine uses this ObColor instead of the vertex colors.
Halo	The faces are rendered as halos, which means the normals always pointing to the camera.
Billboard	Billboard with Z-axis constraint.
Shadow	Faces with this option set acting as shadow in the Real-time Engie. In fact the face "drops" on the floor. So you have to make sure the normal of the face points to the Z-axis. The face has to be located in the center of the Object (or slightly above). Best effect gives a texture with an alpha channel.
Text	Enable bitmap text on face
Opaque	The color of the textured face is normally rendered as color.
Add	This option makes the face being rendered transparent. The color of the face is added to what has already being drawn, thus achieving a bright "lightbeam"-like effect. Black areas in the texture are transparent, white is full bright.
Alpha	Depending on the alpha channel of the image texture, the polygon is rendered transparent.

To copy the Draw Modes from the active to the selected faces use the bottom line of Buttons.

Copy DrawMode	Copy the drawmode.
Copy UV+tex	Copy UV information and textures.
Copy VertCol	Copy the vertex colors.

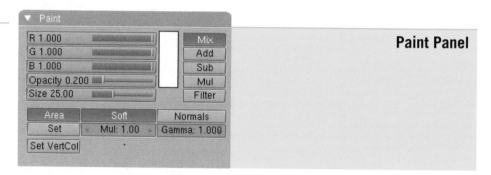

Paint Panel

This panel exists in all Paint Modes, with different meanings.

- In Vertex Paint Mode color is applied to vertices as a Vertex Color.
- In Weight Paint Mode no color is applied, rather a weight to the currently selected Vertex Group vertices for bone deformations. The amount of weight to be painted is specified in the Weight Num Button in the Link and Materials Panel.
- In Texture Paint Mode the Image Texture of the current object is painted, just as you can do on an Image Editor Window, but with the texture wrapped rather than planar.

Top to bottom and left to right:

R, G, B	The active color used for painting (Vertex Paint and Texture Paint only)
Opacity	The extent to which the vertex color changes while you are painting.
Size	The size of the brush, which is drawn as a circle during painting.

BUTTONS REFERENCE.EDITING CONTEXT

On the right column, after a box showing the color itself:

Mix	The manner in which the new color replaces the old when painting: the colors are mixed.
Add	The colors are added.
Sub	The paint color is subtracted from the vertex color.
Mul	The paint color is multiplied by the vertex color.
Filter	The colors of the vertices of the painted face are mixed together, with an "alpha" factor.
Area	In the back buffer, Blender creates an image of the painted Mesh, assigning each face a color number. This allows the software to quickly see what faces are being painted. Then, the software calculates how much of the face the brush covers, for the degree to which paint is being applied. You can set this calculation with the option `Area`.
Soft	This specifies that the extent to which the vertices lie within the brush also determine the brush effect.
Normals	The vertex normal (helps) determine the extent of painting. This causes an effect as if painting with light.
Set	The Mul and Gamma factors are applied to the vertex colors of the Mesh.
Mul	The number by which the vertex colors can be multiplied.
Gamma	The number by which the clarity of the vertex colors can be changed.
Set VertCol	Set vertex color of selection to current.

Scene Context

The Scene Context handles Global settings and is subdivided in three Sub-contextes:

Rendering Sub-context

This Sub-context handles rendering settings:

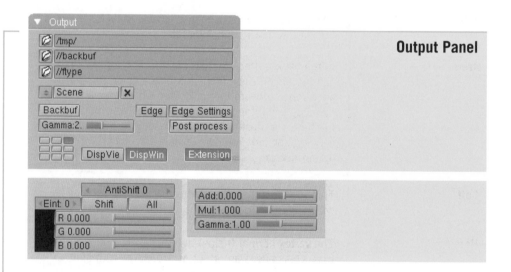

Output Panel

Top to bottom, and left to right:

/tmp/	Enter the name of the directory to which the rendered image must be written if the ANIM command is given and, when required, the first few letters of the file name. Blender automatically assigns files a number, frame 1 becoming 0001. In this example, pictures are written as the files /render/0001, /render/0002 etc. If you enter "/render/rt" in the button, the files will be called /render/rt0001, /render/rt0002... Blender creates the specified directories itself if they do not already exist. The small square button to the left of the Text Button is used to invoke a File Select. Use it to select the output directory, and possibly a file name, and press **ENTER** to assign this to the Text Button.

//Backbuf

Enter a name of a image file to be used as a background. Blender uses the rendered *alpha* to determine the extent to which this background is visible. A code can be processed into the file name, which allows an already rendered animation to be used as a background. Be sure that a "#" is placed at the end. This is replaced by the current (four-digit) frame number. For example: /render/work/rt.# becomes /render/work/rt.0101 at frame 101. The small button to the left of the Text Button invoke an Image Select Window. Specify the file and press **ENTER** to assign it to the Text Button.

//Ftype

Use an "Ftype" file, to indicate that this file serves as an example for the type of graphics format in which Blender must save images. This method allows you to process "color map" formats. The colormap data are read from the file and used to convert the available 24 or 32 bit graphics. If the option RGBA is specified, standard color number 0 is used as the transparent color. Blender reads and writes (Amiga) IFF, Targa, (SGI) Iris and CDi RLE colormap formats. Here, as well, the small button to the left of the Text Button can be used to invoke an Image Select Window.

Scene Link Menu

Each Scene can use another Scene as a "Set". This specifies that the two Scenes must be integrated when rendered. The current Lamps then have an effect on both Scenes. The render settings of the Set, such as the Camera, the *layers* and the World used, are replaced by those of the current Scene. Objects that are linked to both Scenes are only rendered once. A Set is displayed with light gray lines in the 3DWindow. Objects from a Set cannot be selected here.

BackBuf

Activate the use of a background picture.

Edge

In a post-render process an outline will be added to the objects in the rendering. Together with special prepared materials, this causes a cartoon-like picture.

Edge Settings

Opens a small dialog allowing for Edge settings:

Antishift

With the Unified Renderer reduces by this amount the intensity of edges between faces sharing the same material

Eint	Sets the intensity for the edge-rendering. Too high values causes outlining of single polygons.
Shift	With the Unified Renderer the outlines are shifted a bit.
All	Also consider transparent faces for edge-rendering with the Unified Renderer
R, G, B	Edge color.
Gamma	This slider is present only if the `Unified Renderer` Toggle Button is on and tunes Gamma correction for blending Oversampled images (see).
Post Process	This Button is present only if the `Unified Renderer` Toggle Button is on and opens a a dialog with three sliders:
Add	Value to be added to colors
Mul	Value by which multiply colors
Gamma	Gamma color correction.
Window Location	This matrix of nine buttons visualize the standard position in which the Render Window appears on the screen.
DispView	The rendering can also be displayed in the 3Dwindow instead of in a separate window. This occurs, independent of the resolution, precisely within the render borders of Camera *view*. Use **F11** to remove or recall this image.
DispWin	The rendering occurs in a separate window. Use **F11** to move this window to the foreground or background.
Extensions	Filename extensions (*.xxx) will be added to the filename, needed mostly for Windows systems.

BUTTONS REFERENCE.SCENE CONTEXT

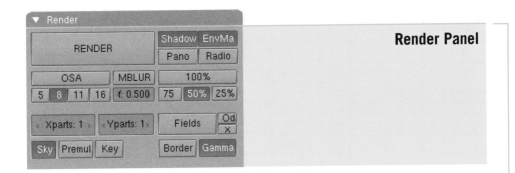

Render Panel

Main rendering settings. Top to bottom, and left to right:

RENDER	Start the rendering. This is a "blocking" process. A square mouse cursor indicates that Blender is busy (Hotkey: **F12**). Rendering can also take place in the "background". Use the command line for this.
Shadows	This turns shadow rendering on. Shadow can only be created by Spot Lamps.
EnvMap	Enables EnvMap calculations.
Pano	Blender can render panoramas. To do this, a number of pictures are rendered, where the number in question corresponds with the value of Xparts. For each "part", the Camera is rotated in such a way that a continuous panorama is created. For the width of the panorama of the Camera Lens, adjust the Xparts and the SizeX for the picture. The total width of the picture, in pixels becomes: Xparts * SizeX. These are the settings for a 360 degree panorama: Xparts = 8, SizeX = 720, lens = 38.6.
Radio	Perform a Radiosity calculation before rendering.
OSA	OverSampling. This option turns anti-aliasing on, to achieve "soft" *edges* and perfectly displayed Image textures. OSA rendering generally takes 1.5 to 2 times longer than normal rendering.

5, 8, 11, 16	Blender uses a Delta Accumulation rendering system with *jittered sampling*. These numbers are pre-sets that specify the number of *samples*; a higher value produces better *edges*, but slows down the rendering.
MBLUR	This option mimics a natural (or long) shutter time by accumulating multiple frames. The value of Osa (5,8,11,16) defines the number of accumulated images. Setting the OSA option makes each accumulated image having antialising.
Bf:	Defines the length of the shutter time, in frames.
100%, 75%, 50%, 25%	These pre-sets allow you to render smaller pictures. It also affects the size of "shadow buffers", hence Memory consumption and CPU times.
Xparts, Yparts	OSA rendering of large images, in particular, can take up a lot of memory. In addition to all the shadow buffers and texture maps and the faces themselves, this takes up 10 to 16 bytes per pixel. For a 2048x1024 picture, this requires a minimum of 32 Mb free memory. Use this option to subdivide the rendering into "parts". Each part is rendered independently and then the parts are combined. The Xparts are particularly important when rendering Ztransp faces.
Fields	Specifies that two separate *fields* are rendered. Each field is a complete picture. The two fields are merged together in such a way that a "video frame" is created.
Odd	This option indicates that the first field in a video frame begins on the first line.
x	With "Field" rendering, this switches the time difference between the two fields off (0.5 frame).
Sky	If a World has "sky", this is filled in in the background. The alpha is not altered, but the transparent colors "contaminate" the background colors, which makes the image less suitable for post-processing.

Premul

"Sky" is never filled in. The *alpha* in the picture is delivered as "Premul": a white pixel with alpha value 0.5 becomes: (RGBA bytes) 128, 128, 128, 128. The color values are thus multiplied by the alpha value in advance. Use "Premul" alpha for postprocessing such as filtering or *scaling*. Remember to select the RGBA option before saving. When Blender reads RGBA files, "Premul" is considered the standard.

Key

"Sky" is never filled in. The *alpha* and color values remain unchanged. A white pixel with an alpha value of 0.5 becomes: (RGBA bytes) 255, 255, 255, 128. What this means is especially clear when rendering Halos: the complete transparency information is in the (hidden) *alpha* layer. Many drawing programs work better with "Key" alpha.

Border

This allows you to render a small cut-out of the image. Specify a render "border" with **SHIFT-B** in the 3DWindow (in Camera *view* of course). A cut-out is always inserted in a complete picture, including any "Back-Buf" that may be present.

Gamma

Colors cannot be normally added together without consequences, for example when rendering anti-aliasing. This limitation is caused by the way light is displayed by the screen: the color value 0.4 does not appear half as strong as 0.8 (actually it is nearly 0.56!). This can be solved by assigning the display-hardware an extremely high gamma correction: gamma 2.3 or even higher. This gives a really pale image with "washed out" dark tints to which dithering must be applied. Blender renders everything internally already gamma-corrected. This produces a more stable anti-aliasing for the eye, i.e. anti-aliasing that does not "swim". To see this difference, render a "Shadeless" white plane *with* OSA - and with and without "Gamma". The only time this option should be set to OFF is when Blender is used for *image composition*.

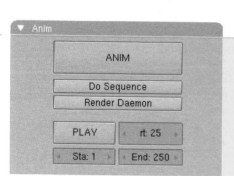

Anim Panel

Main rendering settings for animations. Top to bottom, and left to right:

ANIM	Start rendering a sequence. This is a "blocking" process. A square mouse cursor indicates that Blender is busy. Animations can also be rendered in the "background". Use the command line for this.
Do Sequence	Specifies that the current Sequence strips must be rendered. To prevent memory problems, the pictures of the complete Sequence system are released per rendering, except for the current frame.
Render Deamon	Currently not supported.
Play	This starts an animation playback window. All files from the "Pics" directory are read and played.
rt	For debugging purposes.
Sta, End	The start and end frame of an ANIM rendering.

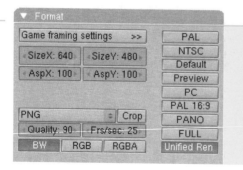

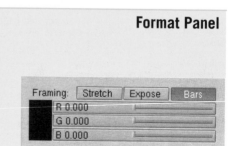

Format Panel

Image format and dimensions; on the left column, top to bottom and left to right:

Game Framing Settings	Opens a panel with realtime settings (not covered by this Book)
Stretch, Expose, Bars	Defines how to handle screens of sizes different than those foreseen in the realtime application.
R, G, B	Color of the fill-in (if any)
SizeX, SizeY	The size of the rendering in pixels. The actual value is also determined by the percentage buttons (100%, 75%, etc.).
AspX, AspY	The pixel relationship. The pixels in monitors and video cards are not usually exactly square. These numbers can be used to specify the relative dimension of a pixel.
Image type Menu	This Menu specify the graphics file format in which images are saved, either for stills and animations.
Crop	Specifies that the "Border" rendering must not be inserted in the total image. For Sequences, this switches the automatic picture *scaling off.* If the pictures are enlarged, the outside edges are cut off.
Quality	Specifies the quality of the JPEG compression. Also for Movies.
Set Codec	If an AVI Codec is selected the quality Num Button turns to a `Set Codec` Button opening the relevant dialog.
Frs/sec	Frame rate for the AVI formats.
BW	After rendering, the picture is converted to black & white. If possible, the results are saved in an 8 bit file.
RGB	The standard. This provides 24 bit graphics.
RGBA	If possible (not for JPEG), the *alpha* layer is also saved. This provides 32 bit graphics.

On the right column there are a set of rendering pre-sets:

PAL	The European video standard: 720 x 576 pixels, 54 x 51 aspect.
NTSC	The American video standard: 720 x 480 pixels, 10 x 11 aspect.
Default	Like PAL, but here the render settings are also set.
Preview	For preview rendering: 640 x 512 pixels at 50%.
PC	For standard PC graphics: 640 x 480 pixels.
PAL 16:9	Wide-screen PAL.
PANO	A standard Panorama setting.
FULL	For large screens: 1280 x 1024 pixels.
Unfied Renderer	Turns Unified rendering on.

Animation/Playback Sub-context

This Sub-context handles Animations at a "Global" level:

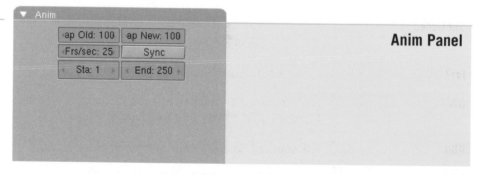

Anim Panel

Left to right, and top to bottom:

Map Old, Map New	This button can be used to modify the internal time calculation. Map Old gives the previous value in frames; Map New specifies the number of frames that must

	be rendered. Only the mutual relations between these values are important. Use this only to speed up or slow down the entire animation system. The absolute value "frame" now becomes relative, which can be quite confusing if the animation must still be modified.
Frs/sec	The The Frames per second ratio in the real time engine (not coverd by this book).
Sync	Enables "real time" audio when playing an animation, skipping frames if needed, to check for proper video/audio synchronization.
Sta, End	Duplicates the buttons in the Anim Panel of the Rendering Sub-context.

Sound Sub-context

This Sub-context handles the new Audio tools added in Blender 2.28:

Sound Panel

Left to right, and top to bottom:

Sound Menu	Selects which Sound Data Block is shown.
SO:	Shows Sound Data Block name, allowing for changes.
Copy Sound	Makes a duplicate of the current Sound Data Block.

Between this menu and the next some info about the Sound is shown.

File Menu	Selects a loaded WAV file.
File Text Box	Shows the current file name and allows for editing.
Single User	The neighboring Num Button shows the number of Sound Data Block linked to the file.
Pack	Packs the WAV file into the .blend file.
Load Sample	Allows loading of a new Sound WAV file.
Play	Plays current Sound.
Volume	Sets playback volume.
Pitch	Sets playback pitch.
Loop	Loops sound.
Ping Pong	If Sound is looped toggles between a normal looping (sound is played, then played again etc.) when OFF and a forward-and-back looping (sound is played beginning to end, then end to beginning in reverse, then beginning to end again etc.) when ON.

Listener Panel

Top to bottom, after a few info about the Game Mixrate there are few Realtime Engine-specific settings:

Volume	Sets the maximum overall volume of all sounds.
Doppler	Allows to vary the amount of Doppler effect in games.

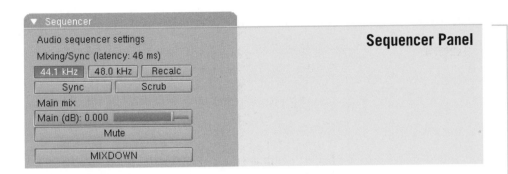

Sequencer Panel

This Panel handles the different settings for Audio strips in the Sequence Editor. Top to bottom and left to right, after some text declaring the mixing latency:

44.1kHz, 48.0kHz
Use this sampling rate, globally, in mixing. CDs and most applications use 44.1kHz. You can use the higher 48.0kHz rate if you want.

Recalc
Recalculates *all* audio sequences loaded in Blender to match the current sampling rate. This is done non-destructively (the original samples are retained). If you change the mixing rate you must perform a recalculation or the audio will go out of sync.

Sync
When activated, the global frame rate is synced to the sample clock. Frames get dropped when the video can't keep up with the audio. You can deactivate Sync if you want *every* frame to be calculated and displayed. This is most useful for the sequence editor, if you want to have Blender cache all images in a sequence. This duplicates the Sync button in the Anim Panel.

Scrub
When this button is activated, you will be able to hear a tiny part of the audio at the current frame whenever you change the frame number. This applies to moving the frame bar in IPO-, NLA-, Action- or Sequence editor windows, or using the cursor keys to change the current frame. Very useful for knowing "where you are".

Main (dB)
Set the master gain in dB. Use this slider for globally scaling the volume of your audio. You should set this slider lowenough to avoid clipping, but as high as possible to reduce noise.

The setting of this slider also applies to the MIXDOWN function (see below).

Mute	Mutes all audio (but still sync).
MIXDOWN	This is the audio counterpart of the ANIM button in the Render Sub-context buttons. When you press this button, Blender will write a .WAV file to the output directory, the same where any rendered animation will go (see the Output Panel of the Render Sub-context).
	The file will be named just like the animation AVI file, but with a different extension (0001_0250.wav for Sta frame 1 and End frame 250, and will contain the complete audio of the current scene as a single WAV file.
	This WAV file will contain any Audio Strip from the sequence editor and can then be mastered externally and merged into the final movie file.

Panels out of the Buttons Window

With the new interface Blender has Panels, most of which called via the **NKEY** apperaring in the 3D Window or other window and performing actions which were in the Buttons Window of previous Blender Versions

3D ViewPort

Floating panels in the 3D Viewport Window.

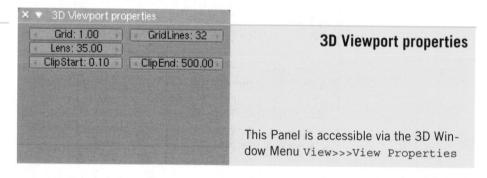

	3D Viewport properties
× ▼ 3D Viewport properties	
Grid: 1.00 GridLines: 32	
Lens: 35.00	
ClipStart: 0.10 ClipEnd: 500.00	This Panel is accessible via the 3D Window Menu View>>>View Properties

Left to right and top to bottom:

Grid	Sets the distance between grid lines (in Blender units, 1.0 by default)

GridLines	The number of grid lines to show in rotated 3D views.
Lens	A "zoom factor" similar to Camera Lens value. Has a meaning only in perspective view.
ClipSart, ClipEnd	Start and End of the clip region for the 3D Viewport Window, works like Camera ones.

Background

This Panel is accessible via the 3D Window Menu View>>>Background Image. Many of these buttons appear only if the context allow them.

Left to right and top to bottom:

BackGroundPic	This option displays/hides a picture in the background of the 3DWindow. Standard Image blocks are used; re-using an Image does not consume any additional memory. The Background Pic is only drawn in ortho and Camera view. It is always centered around the global nulpoint. In camera View, it is completely displayed in the viewport.
Size	The size in Blender units for the width of the Background Pic. Only of interest in *ortho*.
Image Menu	Select an existing Image from the list provided.
LOAD	The Window changes into an Image Select Window. Use this to specify the picture to be used as the Background Pic. The picture is added to the Blender structure as an Image block.
Blend	The factor with which the gray of the 3DWindow is blended with the background picture.

Center X, Center Y	Allows for an offset of the Background Pic, making it not centered in the origin any more.
TextureBrowse	Specify a Texture to be used as the Background Pic. This only works for Image Textures. The Texture Buttons have extensive options for an animated Image Texture, which allows you to achieve an animated Background Pic. Use this option for *rotoscoping*, for example. This is a technique in which video images are used as examples or as a basis for 3D animation.

NKEY Panel

This Panel is accessible via **NKEY** in the 3D Window.

Left to right and top to bottom:

OB:	The current Object name.
Par:	The Parent of the current Object, if any.

In Object Mode:

LocX, LocY, LocZ	The position of the Object center.
RotX, RotY, RotX	The position of the Object center.
SizX, SizY, SizX	The three scale factor of the Object

In Edit Mode:

Vertex X, Vertex Y, Vertex Z	The three coordinates of the selected vertex, or of the median point of the selected vertices, if any.

IPO Window

Floating panels in the IPO Window.

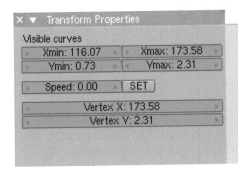

Transform Properties

This Panel is accessible via **NKEY**.

Left to right and top to bottom:

Xmin, Xmax, Ymin, Ymax	The numbers above these buttons specify the boundbox of all the visible curves in the IPO Window. Use the buttons to enter a new value.
Speed, Set	In certain cases, the exact speed of a translation caused by Object IPOs must be determined. Proceed as follows to do this:
	In the IPO Window, make only the LocX, LoxY, LocZ (or any other congruent set of 3) curves visible.
	Set the IPO Key option ON (**KKEY** in the IPOWindow).
	Select the keys that must be assigned a particular speed.
	Set the speed. Only keys that already have a speed and direction can be changed, this means that the handles of the IPO of the selected Key must not be horizontal. If the speed is 0.0, nothing happens.
	Press the Set Button.
Vertex X, Vertex Y	The two coordinates of the selected vertex, or of the median point of the selected vertices, if any.

CH. 28 COMMAND LINE ARGUMENTS

Blender can also be run from the command line. In the following I will assume you are in Blender's directory or that Blender executable is in your PATH. This second option is the preferred one. Please refer to your friendly OS manual to know what a PATH is and how to have Blender in it.

Plain `blender` runs the whole thing just as if you clicked the Blender icon.

Adding command line arguments can force different behaviours. The general syntax is.

```
blender [options] [file]
```

The basic option to remember is -h, that is the help option... once you remember this Blender will tell you all the others... a sort of magic word.

```
blender -h
```

Yields:

```
Blender V 2.28
Usage: blender [options ...] [file]

Render options:
  -b <file>              Render <file> in background
  -S <name>              Set scene <name>
  -f <frame>             Render frame <frame> and save it
  -s <frame>             Set start to frame <frame> (use with -a)
  -e <frame>             Set end to frame (use with -a)<frame>
  -a                     Render animation

Animation options:
  -a <file(s)>           Playback <file(s)>
  -p <sx> <sy>           Open with lower left corner at <sx>, <sy>
  -m                     Read from disk (Don't buffer)
```

```
Window options:
-w                          Force opening with borders
-W                          Force opening without borders
-p <sx> <sy> <w> <h>        Open with lower left corner at <sx>, <sy>
                            and width and height <w>, <h>


Game Engine specific options:
-g fixedtime                Run on 50 hertz without dropping frames
-g vertexarrays             Use Vertex Arrays for rendering (usually
                            faster)
-g noaudio                  No audio in Game Engine
-g nomipmap                 No Texture Mipmapping
-g linearmipmap             Linear Texture Mipmapping instead of Nea
                            rest (default)


Misc options:
-d                          Turn debugging on
-noaudio                    Disable audio on systems that support audio
-h                          Print this help text
-y                          Disable OnLoad scene scripts, use
-Y                          to find out why its y
-R                          Register .blend extension
```

Let's analyze these.

Render Options

The most important set of options. They allow you to do background rendering. This implies that you render an image without having to run the Blender GUI. This uses some less memory and, usually, much less CPU time.

It is important to note that there are very few parameters which can be passed via the command line. Image dimensions, file types etc. need to have been set before via the Blender GUI and saved in a .blend file.

To render a still image (assuming the still is in frame number 1):

```
blender -b yourfile.blend -f 1
```

To render an animation going from frame 1 to frame 100:

```
blender -b yourfile.blend -s 1 -e 100 -a
```

Animation Options

These allows to play back an animation:

```
blender -a yourfile.avi
```

Useful if you used Blender built in Jpeg Codec and don't know how to play back the AVI.

Window Options

These options forces Blender to open its window with specified dimensions.

-W forces the default full-screen opening.
-w forces a non-full screen opening.

If no other parameters are given the window occupies the entire screen, but it is not 'maximized'. if the -p switch is given the the position and dimension of the window can be specified.

```
blender -w -p 128 128 1024 768
```

Forces Blender to open as a 1024x768 window with its lower left corner in (128,128)

Other Options

The Game Engine options are not covered in this manual. The Miscellaneous Options turns on debugging features (-d), suppress audio (-noaudio), disable automatic running of 'On Load' scripts (-y) register '.blend' extension in the Operating System (-R) and provides the list of all options (-h).

BLENDER 2.32 RELEASE

PART IX

LAST NEWS

This Book was tailored on Blender 2.30 and 2.31. Blender 2.32 was released at the very final stages of production of this Book, yet the novelties were so relevant that we could not ignore the release and leave you with outdated material!

This Part contains a single chapter, but what a chapter! A complete, organized presentation of all new stuff in Blender 2.32.

CH. 29 BLENDER 2.32 RELEASE

With this release Blender has not only been extended with a lot of new options, such as ray tracing and displacement mapping, but also offers the beta-test of an integrated support for the famous Yafray renderer.

Below you will find the full release notes and additional documentation.

Blender 2.32 and Yafray are included in the book CDROM, or can be downloaded from from www.blender3d.org.

Rendering

Ray tracing

This is a revision of the old NeoGeo raytracer, dusted off, improved quite a lot, and nicely integrated in the rest of rendering pipeline. The choice to add the raytracer to Blender (again) was mainly based on the fact that previous considerations - far too slow to be usable - might have been acceptable in the early nineties, but not more than 10 years later! With even Renderman adopting it little over a year ago, we now can consider raytracing as viable alternative for animation rendering as well.

Nevertheless, the implementation remains quite basic and targeted at integration with the rest of Blender and artistic control. The new options will provide an artist with much more freedom to create 3d graphics, but for ultimate realism the external Yafray is a better choice. We believe that both together will move Blender out of the nineties and firmly put it in this new millennium!

- Set the **F10** (Render buttons) option "Ray" to enable ray tracing for rendering. In Blender this is an integrated method, still using zbuffer and scanline rendering for 'first hit' rendering.

BLENDER 2.32 RELEASE.RENDERING

1   Raytraced shadows.

2   Raytrace (mirror floor), plus environment mapping (sphere) and radiosity (soft shadow) can all be combined in a single render pass.

- New options are almost all found in the 'Shading context' buttons (**F5**), for Materials, Lamps and World. For Materials the settings for Mirror and Transparency have been joined together in a new buttons Panel.
- Blender uses an Octree to optimize ray intersections. The way it works now, it gives best speed when you keep the total environment as compact as possible. For example, exclude exterior objects, walls or floors from being added in the Octree by disabling their Material "Traceable" value.
- Environment maps are rendered before raytracing is initialized and enabled. This to make sure environment maps remain fast to use.
- known issue: the raytracing code doesn't calculate for each ray bounced/refracted the new correct filtering and oversampling values. This will make reflected/ refracted image textures somewhat more blurry than expected.

Raytraced shadows

- All lamp types in Blender can have a ray traced shadow. Only for spotlights still the extra choice exists to use shadowbuffers, which still is a useful feature in many situations.
- For Sun and Hemi the actual position of the lamp doesn't matter then, in this case it traces a ray in the constant Sun/Hemi direction.
- Set (**F10**) "OSA" on for correct over sampling. This will result in smooth antialiased, but sharp shadows.
- The (**F10**) option "Shadow" enables or disables both shadowbuffer and raytrace shadow calculation.

Soft shadows

- Since there are a lot of variables associated with soft shadow, for this release they only are available for Area lights. Allowing spot & normal lamp to have soft shadow is possible, but will require a reorganization of the Lamp buttons, and will need review of 3D drawing methods.
- Apart from 'area' size, you can individually set amount of samples in X and Y direction (for area lamp type 'Rect').
- Soft shadows have four options:
  - "Clip circle" : only uses a circular shape of samples, gives smoother results
  - "Dither" : use a 2x2 dither mask
  - "Jitter" : applys a pseudo-random offset to samples
  - "Umbra" : extra emphasis on area that's fully in shadow.--> New:

Area Lights

A new lamp type has been added: "Area". This uses the radiosity formula (Stoke) to calculate the amount of energy which is received from a plane. Result is very nice local light, which nicely spreads out.
Working with Area light requires more work to get the optimal lighting conditions, like with real lamps in a studio and a real camera. This is the main reason why a new exposure method was added (see below).

- Since area lights realistically are sensitive for distance (quadratic), the effect it has is quickly too much, or too less. For this the "Dist" value in Lamp has to be used. Set it at Dist=10 to have reasonable light on distance 10 Blender units (assumed you didnt scale lamp object). The default "Dist" value for lamps in Blender (20) will most typically give an overflow in standard Blender scenes!
- Area lamps have a 'gamma' option to control the light spread
- Area lamp builtin sizes: square, rect, cube & box. Only first 2 are implemented. Set a type, and define area size.
- Button area size won't affect the amount of energy. But scaling the lamp in 3d window will do. This is to cover the case when you scale an entire scene, the light then will remain identical If you just want to change area lamp size, use buttons when you dont want to make the scene too bright or too dark
- Plan is to extend area light with 3d dimensions, boxes and cubes.
- Note that area light is one-sided, towards negative Z.

Ray Transparency

- Enable it with setting "RayTransp" in the new "Transp and Mirror" Panel. Please note that alpha is default at 1.0 in Blender, giving fully opaque. Typically a quick nice result can be achieved with setting a Fresnel value, and leave the Alpha slider at 1.0.

- Set "IOR" for 'index of refraction'. Realistic values range from 1.1 (water) to 1.5 (glass).
- Set a correct "Depth" value to denote the maximum amount of recursions for a single ray to be refracted. A value of '5' typically is an acceptable minimum.
- For correct refraction calculus, 3D models MUST have normals pointing in the right direction (consistently pointing outside). That way, refraction can 'detect' the thickness of a transparent material, whether it enters or leaves it. So, model for realistic glass always both sides of a surface.
- When not rendering with ray tracing enabled, 'RayTransp' materials will render solid. This gives better previews, but also makes envmaps look better, since environment maps are rendered without ray tracing.
- 'Ray transp' rendering doesn't end with alpha information (alpha is 1.0).
- New Material option "ShadowTra" will invoke a ray to all "ray shadow" lamps, evaluating the alpha of all faces it encounters. The result will look like a transparent shadow.

This is a true shading option, and not an option for Lamps, nor for a transparent Object giving transparent shadows. Main reason is to be able to control rendering speed.

Ray Mirror

- You need to set both the Material option "Ray Mirror" as give the slider "RayMirr" a value larger than zero.
- Textures work on this value as well, with a new MapTo channel
- the RGB colors for "Mir" define the mirror-reflection color.
- Set a correct "Depth" value to denote the maximum amount of recursions for a single ray to be reflected. A value of '2' typically already gives acceptable results.

Fresnel effect

Both transparency as mirror reflection can be controlled with a Fresnel effect in Blender, meaning it is depending on the angle between the surface normal and the viewing direction. Typically, the larger the angle (on the outer side, the outline) the more reflection or the more opaque a Material becomes.

It took several testing releases before the optimal Fresnel code was found. What is released now is a hybrid version, allowing 'real' Fresnel, but also giving artistic freedom and control. This is provided with two settings:

- "Fresnel": the 'power' of the function, the higher the more strong the falloff is.
- "Fac": a controlling 'factor' to adjust how the blending happens
  Set the first value at 5.0, and the second at 1.25 for something that matches 'real' Fresnel.

Fresnel works for transparent mode "Ztransp" as well (not raytraced).

Exposure and brightness

Previously Blender clipped color straight with '1.0' (or 255) when it exceeds the possible RGB space. This causes ugly banding when light overflows.
Using an exponential correction formula, this now can be nicely corrected.

The World buttons (**F6**) have two new options for it:

- "Exp" the exponentional curvature, with 0.0 being linear, and 1.0 being curved
- "Range" sets the range of input colors to mapped to visible colors (0.0-1.0).

Better bump textures

Improved method to calculate normals for procedural textures such as Marble, wood, clouds. Instead of the old method it now derives the normal based sampling the texture additionally with three little offsets in x, y and z. This gives nice and correct results, superior to the old method (which just rotated a normal a bit).

Gaussian sampling

Normally, while rendering OSA, each sub-pixel sample in Blender counts equally, and together make up the pixel color.

With 'Gauss' option set (**F10** menu) each sub-pixel sample creates a small weighted mask with variable size, which (can) affect neighbouring pixels as well. The result is smoother edges, less sensitive for gamma, and well suited to reduce motion-aliasing (when things move extreme slow).

This is result of *long* period of research in NeoGeo days, and based on every scientific sampling/reconstructing theory we could find. Plus a little bit of our selves. :-)

Currently the Gauss option only works for edges of normal faces. It does not work for transparent rendering, not to solve high frequencies (aliasing) from ray trace render, nor for the Unified render. All topics to work on another time.

BLENDER 2.32 RELEASE.DISPLACEMENT MAPPING

Various

- Adjusted specular max to 511, The Blinn shader has again this incredible small spec size.
- New option "Translucency" (Shading panel) will enable shading when light shines on the backside as well. It only includes diffuse shading, not specular (of course!).

  Translucency is a "Map to" texture channel as well. Translucency works nice to give half-transparent Materials a light emitting effect. See for example in the image to the left the effect of the spotlight on the transparent faces.

Displacement mapping

Displacement mapping is a powerful technique that allows a texture input, either proceedural, or image, to manipulate the position of rendered faces. Unlike Normal or Bump mapping, where the normals are skewed to give an illusion of a bump, this creates real bumps. They cast shadows, occlude other objects, and do everything real geometry can do.

The shaders/shadowbuffers/raytracer can't tell that you didn't model it that way.

Displacement mapping is set up to behave as a texture chanel. With one very important difference.

In order to manipulate the positions of renderfaces smoothly, they have to be very small[1]. This eats memory and CPU time.

For distant/non-critical items, NOR mapping should still be used. Compared to NOR maps, displacement imposes very little additional CPU cost per renderface, but you can NOR map independantly of renderface count. Use of displacement quickly leads to million face scenes.

Use displacement when you need your scene to use more accurate geometry (note shadows on rightmost "cube").

Currently there are at most 2 renderfaces per mesh face (or equivilent on other object). If a quad face is not flat, it renders as two triangles.

To help get high renderface counts without bogging the machine down during editing, you can subsurf a mesh. The faces of the implicit surface (gray) are the faces that become renderfaces.

---

[1] I am working on an adaptive subdivide that will only divide the faces that really need it. ie; if far from camera, or texture changing slowly, the renderfaces would remain large to speed up rendering.

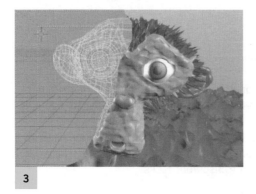

3

Setting an object's material to WIRE, and selecting ALL EDGES (in editmode) is a good way to visualize the displaced renderfaces.

To allow you to subdivide at rendertime without rounding off your edges, a new type of subsurf has been created - "Simple subsurf". By selecting "Simple Subdiv." as the subdivide type, the mesh will be subdivided at rendertime to the level shown in the render numbox, without changing it's overall shape.

To speed editing, it is best to keep the 3D view subdivide level low, and the render subdivide level high. But use caution. The amount of memory used for subsurf goes up tremendously at high values. It's not uncommon to lock up a computer for many many minutes this way.

Where to use Displacement

Displacement textures work for all 3D object types. However, because of need for fine renderfaces, not all objects are equally well suited for displacement mapping.

From best to worst, displacement works the following object types using the method listed to control the renderface size.

- Subsurf Meshes. Renderface size is controled with render subsurf level. Displacement really likes smooth normals.
- Simple Subsurf meshes. Control renderfaces with render subsurf level. There is a pitfall at sharp edges however if the texture there is not neutral gray.
- Manualy (editmode) subdivided meshes. Control renderfaces with number of subdivides. (This can be combined with the above methods.) Displaces exactly the same Simple Subsurf, but slows editing down because of the OpenGL overhead of drawing the extra faces. (You can't turn the edit subdivide level down this way).

BLENDER 2.32 RELEASE.DISPLACEMENT MAPPING

- Metaballs. Control renderfaces with render wiresize. Small wire == more faces. The following are available, but currently don't work well. It is recomended that you convert the following to meshes before applying displacement.
- Open Nurbs surfaces. Control renderfaces with U/V DefResolu. Higher numbers give more faces. (Note normal errors),
- Closed Nurbs Surfaces. Control with DefResolu control. (Note the normal errors, and how impicit seam shows).
- Curves and Text. Control with DefResolu control. Higher gives more renderfaces. (Note that the large flat surfaces have few renderfaces to displace).

How to use Displacement

Simply put, divide the surface into small renderfaces with the above methods, then use Displace like you would any texture.
However. . .

There are currently two modes in which displacement works in:

- Displace renderverts by intensity (verts move along vertex normals)
- Displace renderverts by texture normal (Verts move acording to texture's nor input)

The two modes are not exclusive. The amount of each type can be mixed using the sliders in the Material->MapTo panel. Not all textures provide both types of input though. Stucci, for example, only provides Normal, while Magic only provides intensity (derived from color). Cloud, Wood, and Marble provide both. Image provides both intensity and a derived Normal.

The intensity displacement is controled with the new *Disp* slider.

The Normal displacement is controlled by the *Nor* slider.

Intensity displacement, gives a smoother, more continuous surfce, since the vertexes are displaced only outward. Normal displace, gives a more agregated surface, since the verts are displaced in multiple directions.

The depth of the displacement is scaled with an object's scale, but not with the relative size of the data.

This means if you double the size of an object in object mode, the depth of the displacement is also doubled, so the relativedisplacement appears the same.
If you scale inside editmode, the displacement depth is not changed, and thus the relative depth appears smaller.

Neutral gray means 0 displacement.

For positive displacement, white is a peak, black is a valley.

For negative displacement it is reversed.

When making custom displace maps, start with a flood of 50% gray. Note how the edges of the cubes to the right remain sharp. If the background was not 50% gray, there would be a bevel or a lip there. Some adjustment can be done using the Texture->color panel's Brightness and Contrast sliders, but it is best to start off right.

Sharp lines in disp maps, can cause normal problems, since a renderface can be requested to move only one of it's verts a great distance relative to the other 2-3. You tend to get better results if a small gaussian blur is run on the image first.

Texture OSA is not currently working for images mapped to displacement. A suitable filter-size function needs to be located.

Blender 2.32: Yafray

Yafray is an open source, high quality photorealistic render system, as being developed on www.yafray.org. With the 2.32 Blender release, the two programs now will closely cooperate.

In the main Render buttons of Blender (**F10**), you now can choose for the Yafray renderer as well, using a dropdown menu in the "Render" Panel.

Yafray rendering currently works by exporting an intermediate xml file to a temporary directory. Yafray should be installed properly first. Windows users should be able to export immediately, other platforms first need to set the export directory in the Blender user-default section, Windows user can set this export directory too, but is not needed.

After rendering, the resulting image is loaded back into Blender. This means that for the user it is just press **F12** and wait for the result as if it were made by blender, this also works for animations.

Materials are exported using a new Blender shader which emulates most of Blender's material functionality, including texture mapping, some procedurals and raytracing settings. Some things need a bit of additional tweaking from the user, like bump mapping levels and raytracing settings.

BLENDER 2.32 RELEASE.YAFRAY

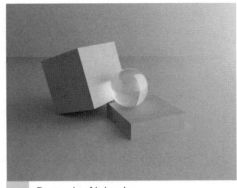

4 From yafray.org gallery, image by Pucks.

5 Demo, by Alejandro.

Light is yet another thing that needs tweaking. Light power levels work quite different in Yafray, so the user has to adjust it to get the desired lighting level in Yafray, Blender's 'sphere' mode probably needs the least amount of tweaking.

Spots and arealights (quad) are also used as emmiters for photons. But these are global photons, not old photonlight, so no (direct) caustics from point lights supported yet.

The pathlight ('Full' option in GI menu) does support caustics from GI (indirect illumination, lights reflecting of other objects), sky and arealights.

For global illumination there is a new panel where you can setup the usual skydome method (hemilight), full GI (pathlight) and also cache mode and photons (globalphotonlight).

While developing this there were a lot of path problems. Most of them are solved now, but some could possibly still experience some problems on win32 or OS X.

Please bear in mind this is still for beta test mostly, awaiting feedback for further improvements. Yafray now is offered as download from www.blender3d.org as well.

Blender 2.32, new features and fixes

New in Blender:

* Particle duplicators: when an Object has an Ipo, the timing for each duplicated Object is corrected for the lifetime of particle.

Remark: this won't work for object location (is at particle) or for particle type 'Vect' which gives a rotation already. But now you can (for example) scale an Object small, and let it grow over time.

- Blender Meshes now have a limit of 2 Billion faces (instead of 64k). This doesn't break backward or upward compatibility, but will cause .blend files to grow about 30% in size.
- UI: all Blender versions (OS's) now have identical cursors.
- 3D Window: new preferences for display of grid, axes and floor. You can find it in the 3D View Properties panel (access with pulldown menu).
- Mesh editmode: new tool "Bevel" (**WKEY**) will give all faces (non selected too) a beveling effect. Move mouse to control the amount, which is drawn as a preview. After confirm, a requestor allows to indicate a subdivision level.
  Remark: this is a first implementation, which is still slow for larger Meshes, or for higher subdivision levels.
- Mesh editmode; "Select non-manifold" option in "Select" pulldown menu, which select vertices to indicate which edges don't have exactly 2 faces.
- Mesh editmode: "Select more" and Select less, in pulldown menus and accessible with hotkeys **CTRL+PadPlus/Minus**. It selects vertices having an edge with other vertex selected.
- Mesh editmode: "Select Random", in pulldown menu. It selects a random percentage of vertices, the percentage can be set with a requester that pops up.
- Mesh editmode: new Loop Cut functionality:
- after choosing a loop to cut you go into a second mode that lets you choose where exactly on the edge you want to cut. The placement is in percentages, so 0% is one side of the edge, and 100% is the other side.
- holding **CTRL** snaps the placement to whole percentages. 1.00 instead of the standard 0.01 of a percentage.
- Pressing **S** while you place the cut turns on Smooth-subdivide for the cut (or as I like to call it: Loopcutsubdividesmooth :)
- the percentages and the ON/OFF for smooth cut can be seen in the view3D header.
- Mesh editmode: press numpad-dotkey to center view around selection
- FaceSelect mode (UV textures):
  Two new options to uv auto calculation added. "From window to sphere" and "From window to cylinder".

The differences to other sphere/cylinder mapping option is:

1. the "around" settings of the 3D view sets the projection center

2. the origin of the polar/spherical coordinate system always points out of the screen. so the rotation of the view affects mapping.

3. in the cylinder case the radius of the projection cylinder is read by a popup button.

BLENDER 2.32 RELEASE.PYTHON

Basically what you need to do is rotate the viewport until the cylinder/sphere is aligned with the depth (Z axis) of the view, as if you where looking through the mesh from one end to another (makes more sense in the case of a cylinder), and choose the new mapping option.

- Armature editmode: support for hide and unhide of Bones added. Accessible via menus and hotkeys **HKEY, shift-HKEY, alt-HKEY**.
- Armatures: "Delay Deform" option added.
  The button is under the X-ray bones button in the edit buttons. With this armature option selected, manipulations in pose mode will only deform children after the transformation is finished. While hardly an optimal solution, this gives about 4 times speed up.
- The main window header now displays the current file name.
- Delete key can be correctly used for text input in Blender now
- Blender now reads/writes BMP images.

Python

We began to ship some scripts with Blender itself, starting with a few import/export ones; these scripts can be accessed from Blender menus: File->Import, File->Export.

The new Scripts Window also has a menu where these plus 'Misc' can be accessed. More categories will be added later.

To be registered in Blender menus, scripts must have a special header and be either at the <user home or Blender installation dir>/.blender/scripts or the user defined Scripts dir (Info Window -> File Paths -> Scripts).

For more info, please check the top Announcement at the Python & Plugins forum at www.elysiun.com

Further new features:

- functions basename and splitext to Blender.sys;
- Blender.Registry module, for persistent data;
- Scripts Window, to substitute the Text Editor as the window to display script guis: now more than one running script can be accessed from the same window;

Known issue:

Blender still uses Python 2.2, and it doesn't include a Python library with all modules compiled in. This can cause some errors when people want to use external modules, but have Python 2.3 installed on their system. This will be addressed in the next release.

- Python 'make' system: Scons
  Work has been done for a very promising new cross platform code building system for Blender. Especially to replace 'autoconf', which has maintenance and compatibility problems here. Scons supports all platforms and OS's, an even nicely generates MSVC project files.

  The Scons files are in cvs now, but not approved yet to officially replace autoconf.

Bug fixes

- Weight Painting now works for all painting modes. It used not to with option "Area" set in Paint Panel.
- Pressing **F12** (or other keys) during render caused crashes, this because the event queue was evaluated without keeping track of a rendering already being in progress.
- Texture Paint mode didn't work in 2.31a, restored.
- MacOSX: calling up Quicktime dialog doesn't freeze anymore when you choose "options".
- MacOSX: texture plugins and sequence plugins now work (check directory plugins in distribution directory)
- Armatures: constraint targets inside other Armatures weren't transforming correctly (grab, rotate, scale).
- Armatures: update issues solved with Armatures being parent of Lattice.
- Armatures: general overhaul of Armature constraint/parenting code which resulted in faster drawing and less lag.
- Mesh editmode: Loop Cut tool now doesn't affect hidden vertices and faces.
- Add a new Scene, with option "Full Copy" now also create new Ipos.
- 3D Window: 'draw extra' axis for Lamp was on wrong location.
- 3D Window: in EditMode CTRL+RightMouse allows for selection of other Objects again. This is useful for assigning vertex parent.
- 3D Window: FaceSelect mode, the 'unwrap UV' pulldown menu option doesn't crash anymore
- Code that limited zooming in and zooming out for spaces like sequencer, audiotimeline, etc. was accidentally removed in 2.30, causing crashes in extreme zooms. This has been put back.
- Numerical input while 'transform': using it for scaling works correctly now. In previous release it reset other values to zero.
- Fixed B&W images saving (R G and B were not correctly converted, causing wrong brightness of colors).
  (During the past month a lot more bugs were fixed as reported using the tracker on projects.blender.org. It's just too much to mention all, thanks & keep reporting!)

BLENDER 2.32 RELEASE.BUG FIXES

Various fixes

- Pulldown menus added for Image, Sound, Action, Oops, NLA windows. This as part of ongoing UI project. In current version most buttons from headers have been moved to pulldowns now. For a next release we'll look at methods how to bring back pulldown options (user-defined) as icon buttons in headers again.
- 3D Window: **NKEY** menu now displays the 'w' value for Nurbs curves again
- translations: added simple first Chinese translation for UI, Czech translation file fixed, added Brazilian Portuguese
- laptop users: option 'no numpad' now accepts minuskey for numerical input while in transform mode.
- Decimator tool for Meshes: display-list is correctly updated now, and it frees deform weights (vertex groups) correctly
- All 'number' buttons in UI: pressing Enter key with mouse pointer over the button increases/decreases value again.
- Freetype fonts: when using it for 3D font object, it now corrects the character size for the linedist as set in Blender. This only shows for non-standard fonts.
- Context switching for 'Shading buttons' now happens when these buttons are invisible as well, causing the **F5** hotkey to always show the correct buttons.
- TextWindow: HOME and END keys work here now.

APPENDICES A B C D E F G

QUICK HOTKEYS LIST

SUPPORTED VIDEOCARDS

CHANGELOGS

THE BLENDER DEVELOPMENT

THE BLENDER DOCUMENTATION

LICENCES

GLOSSARY

PART X

APPENDICES

AP. A QUICK HOTKEYS LIST

Based on the original work by Joeri Kassenaar, rearranged by Bastian Salmela.

Symbols

WORKS IN
IPO Window
Sequence Window
Image Select Window
Text Edit Window
Object Mode
Edit Modes
Object or Edit Modes
Pose Mode
Object Oriented Window
Render Window

QUICK HOTKEYS LIST

WORKS IF

⊡	An Object is selected
△	Mesh Vertex/vertices is/are selected
⚊	IPO keys are selected
▪	Sequence Strip is selcted
☰	To be on a Button Window
▢	Data Selected
⌒	A Curve is selected
⚊	IPO Handles selected
▣	A Render Window exists
◌	An Armature is selected
▣	An Image Select Window Exists
⚒	In Object Mode

Causes

☐	A Menu to Appear
⊔	A Toolbox to Appear
⬭	A File Select dialog

USES

🖫	LMB
🖫	RMB

Tab

KEY	WORKS...		ACTION
TAB	IN ⊞ ⩘ ⚡		Object mode / Edit mode
	IF ▣		
TAB	IN ▩		Toggle Meta strip
	IF ◼		
TAB	IN ⊞ ◟ ⚡		Object / Edit (unposed)
	IF ◟		
CTRL – TAB	IN ⊞ ◟ ⚡		Object / Pose Mode
	IF ◟		
SHIFT – TAB	IN ☰		Tab in Text Mode

Numpad

KEY	WORKS...		ACTION
. DEL	IN ⊞ ⚡		Local view w / o moving
	IF ▣		
/	IN ⊞ ⚡		Local view & cursor / previous view
	IF ▣		
*	IN ⊞ ⚡		Rotate view to object orientation mode
	IF ▣		
+ / -	IN ⊞ ⚡		Zoom in/out
+ / -	IN ⊞ ▢		Increase PVE, (Grab/Rot./Scale)
	IF △		

QUICK HOTKEYS LIST

		Action
+ / -	≥ ⎰ 🎞 ⊞	Zoom in/out
0	≥ # ◻	Go to current camera view
CTRL – 0	≥ # 🐭	set Camera View
ALT – 0	≥ # 🐭	Restore last camera to view
1 3 7	≥ # 🐭	Font / Right / Top view
CTRL – 1 3 7	≥ # 🐭	Back / Left / Bottom view
2 4 6 8	≥ # 🐭	Rotate view
5	≥ # 🐭	Perspective / orthographic view
SHIFT – 7	≥ # ⊞	Zoom view to fit all objects
9	≥ # 🐭	Redraw

Numbers

KEY	WORKS...	ACTION
~	≥ # 🐭	Display all layers
SHIFT – ~	≥ # 🐭	Display all layers / previous layers
CTRL – ~	≥ # 🐭	Lock/Unlock layers & camera to scene
0-9	≥ # 🐭	Swap layers 1-10
SHIFT – 0-9	≥ # 🐭	Add/remove layers 1-10 to layer setting

	WORKS...	ACTION
ALT – 0-9	≅ ⊞ 🖰	Swap layers 11-20
SHIFT – ALT – 0-9	≅ ⊞ 🖰	Add/remove layers 11-20 to layer setting
-	≅ ⊞ 🖰	swap layer 11
SHIFT – -	≅ ⊞ 🖰	Add/remove layer 11 to layer setting
=	≅ ⊞ 🖰	Swap layer 12
SHIFT – =	≅ ⊞ 🖰	Add/remove layer 12 to layer setting
CTRL – 1-4	≅ ⊞ 🖰	If Object is SubSurfed sets Subsurf Level
	IF ⊡	

Specials

KEY	WORKS...	ACTION
,	≅ ⊞ 🖰	Rotation/scaling around bounding box
.	≅ ⊞ 🖰	Rotation/scaling around cursor

Arrow Keys

KEY	WORKS...	ACTION
UP/DOWN	≅ ⊞ 🖰	10 frames forward / backward
RIGHT/LEFT	≅ ⊞ 🖰	1 frame forward/backward
SHIFT – UP/RIGHT	≅ ⊞ 🖰	Jump to last frame

QUICK HOTKEYS LIST

		Action
SHIFT – DOWN/LEFT	IN ⊞ 🖱	Jump to first frame
CTRL – UP/DOWN	IN ⊞ 🖱	Active window full/small screen
CTRL – RIGHT/LEFT	IN ⊞ 🖱	Screen configuration forward/backward

•

Arrow Keys - Grab/Rotate/Scale behaviour

KEY	WORKS...	ACTION
Arrow	IN 〰 🎞 ⊟	Adjust arrow in direction
Arrow	IN ⊞ 🖱 IF ⊡ △	Adjust arrow in direction (Grab coarse adjust)
SHIFT – Arrow	IN ⊞ 🖱 IF ⊡ △	Adjust (grab fine adjust)
CTRL – Arrow	IN ⊞ 🖱 IF ⊡ △	Adjust (grab coarse grid snap center)
SHIFT – CTRL – Arrow	IN ⊞ 🖱 IF ⊡ △	Adjust (grab fine grid snap center)

Mouse

KEY	WORKS...	ACTION
LMB	IN ⊞	Place cursor/gesture/vertex paint
CTRL – LMB	IN ⊞ 〰 ☐ IF ☐	Add vertex

		ACTION
MMB	⌗	Trackball
MMB	⌗	Translate view
SHIFT – MMB	⌗	Translate view (see numpad CTRL – 2468)
CTRL – MMB	⌗	Zoom view (see number +/-)
RMB	⌗	Select •
SHIFT – RMB	⌗	Add to selection
CTRL – RMB	⌗	Select object by closest object center
SHIFT – CTRL – RMB	⌗	Add selection by closest object center
CTRL – RMB		Select object & affect active object
SHIFT – CTRL – RMB		Add to selection & affect active object

A

KEY	WORKS...	ACTION
A	⌗	Select / deselect All
A		Select / deselect All
SHIFT-A	⌗	Add menu
CTRL-A	⌗	Apply location and rotation
ALT-A	⌗	Play Animation

QUICK HOTKEYS LIST

SHIFT – CTRL – A	IN	Apply Latice / Make duplis real
	IF	
SHIFT – ALT – A	IN	Play Anim in current and all 3d windows

B

KEY	WORKS...	ACTION
B	IN	Border select / deselect
	IF	
B	IN	Border select / deselect
	IF	
BB	IN	Circle Border select / deselect
	IF	
SHIFT – B	IN	Define render Border
	IF	

C

KEY	WORKS...	ACTION
C	IN	Center windows around 3d cursor
C	IN	Snaps current frame to selected key
	IF	
C	IN	Change images
	IF	

SHIFT – C	IN	# ↙		Cursor on origin, window on home

CTRL – C	IN	# ↙		Copy menu
	IF	▢	◉	

ALT – C	IN	# ↙		Convert menu
	IF	▢	◉	

D

KEY		WORKS...			ACTION
D	IN	⤳	🖑		Duplicate
	IF	⤢			
SHIFT – D	IN	#	▦	🖑	Duplicate
	IF	■	◡	◉	
CTRL – D	IN	#	🖑		Display alpha of images as wire
	IF	◉			
ALT – D	IN	#	🖑		Add data-linked duplicate
	IF	◉			

E

KEY		WORKS...	ACTION
E	IN	# ▢	Extrude (by grabbing-G returns if Rot./Scale)
	IF	△	
E R	IN	# ▢	Extrude by Rotating
	IF	△	

QUICK HOTKEYS LIST

	WORKS...	ACTION
E S	IN ⊞ ▢	Extrude by Scaling
	IF △	

F

KEY	WORKS...	ACTION
F	IN ⊞ ▢	Make edge/face. / Connect curve
	IF △ ⚙	
F	IN ⊞ 🖿	Face select display on / off
	IF ▣	
CTRL – F	IN ⊞ ▢	Flip selected triangle edeges
CTRL – F	IN ⊞ 🖿	Sort faces
	IF ▣	
ALT – F	IN ⊞ ▢	Beauty fill
	IF ▢	
ALT – F	IN ⊞ 🖿	Make first base
	IF ▣	
SHIFT – ALT – F	IN ☰	Save and open text files menu
	IF ▢	

G

KEY	WORKS...	ACTION
G	IN ⊞ 🖿	Grabber
	IF △ ▣	

KEY	WORKS...		ACTION
G	IN		Grabber
	IF		
SHIFT – G	IN		Group Menu
	IF		
ALT – G	IN		Clear location
	IF		
ALT – G	IN		Clear location
	IF		

H

KEY	WORKS...		ACTION
H	IN		Handle type: align / free
	IF		
H	IN		Hide selected vertices
	IF		
SHIFT – H	IN		Hande type: auto (see also V)
	IF		
SHIFT – H	IN		Hide deselected vertices
	IF		
CTRL – H	IN		Automatic Handle calculation
	IF		
ALT – H	IN		Reveal hidden
	IF		

QUICK HOTKEYS LIST

I

KEY	WORKS...		ACTION
I	IN ⊞ ⋈ ↙		Insert Keyframe menu
	IF □ ⊡		

J

KEY	WORKS...		ACTION
J	IN ⊞ ⋈ ▦ ▨		swap render page of render window
	IF ↙ ⊡		
SHIFT – J	IN ⊞ □		Join selected triangles to quads
	IF △		
CTRL – J	IN ⊞ ↙		Join selected objects (see also P)
	IF ⊡		
CTRL – J	IN ⋈ ↙		join selected keys
	IF ⌐		

K

KEY	WORKS...		ACTION
K	IN ⊞ □		Knife Menu
K	IN ⊞ ↙		Draw/hide object keys
K	IN ⋈ ↙		Show Keys/Show Curves
K	IN □		Prints NURBS knot weights
	IF ⌒		

KEY	WORKS...		ACTION
SHIFT – K	IN	⊞ ☐	Knife Tool
	IF	△	
SHIFT – K	IN	⊞ ☐	Clear vertexpaint colors
SHIFT – K	IN	⩘ ⭳	Show and select all keys

L

KEY	WORKS...		ACTION
L	IN	⊞ ⭨	Make local menu (see also U)
	IF	▢ ⊙	
L	IN	⊞ ☐	Select vertices linked to cursor
L	IN	▦	Select linked objects
SHIFT – L	IN	⊞ ⭨	Select linked menu
	IF	▢ ⊙	
CTRL – L	IN	⊞ ⭨	Make link menu
	IF	▢ ⊙	
CTRL – L	IN	⊞ ☐	Select vertices linked to selected vertex
	IF	△	
ALT – L	IN	⊞ ⭨	Make local menu
	IF	▢ ⊙	

QUICK HOTKEYS LIST

M

KEY		WORKS...	ACTION
M	IN	⊞ ▢	Mirror
	IF	△ ⚚	
M	IN	⊞ ⬓ ↿	Move to layer(s)
	IF	▢ ⊡	
M	IN	▦ ↿	Make a meta strip
	IF	▧	

N

KEY		WORKS...	ACTION
N	IN	⊞ ⬓ ▦ ⬏	Number menu (numeric loc/rot/size entry)
	IF	▢ ▧ ⚚ ⟂ ⊡	
N	IN	▦	Rename
	IF	▢	
CTRL – N	IN	⊞ ▢	Recalculate normals outside
	IF	△	
CTRL – N	IN	⊞ ▢	Recalculate bone rolls
	IF	◁	
SHIFT – CTRL – N	IN	⊞ ▢	Recalculate normals inside
	IF	△	

O

KEY	WORKS...			ACTION
0	IN ⊞ ☐			Normal / Proportional vertex edit (PVE)
	IF ☐			
ALT – 0	IN ⊞ ⟋⟍ ⤸			Clear origin
	IF ⊡			
SHIFT – 0	IN ⊞ ☐			Sharp / Smooth falloff for PVE
	IF ☐			
SHIFT – 0	IN ⊞ ⟱			Toggle SubSurf
CTRL – 0	IN ⊞ ⟋⟍ ▦			Open file
	IF ⬙			

P

KEY	WORKS...			ACTION
P	IN ⊞ ☐			Separate vertices into objects (see also J)
	IF △ �⟍			
P	IN ⊞ ⤸			Starts realtime
CTRL – P	IN ⊞ ⤸			Make parent
	IF ⊡			
CTRL – P	IN ⊞ ⟱			Make vertex parent
	IF △ ⟍			
ALT – P	IN ⊞ ⤸			Clear Parent menu
	IF ☐ ⊡			

QUICK HOTKEYS LIST

ALT – P	IN	≣	Run a script in Text Edit window
SHIFT – CTRL – P	IN	⌗ ↰	Make parent without inverse
	IF	◉	

Q

KEY	WORKS...		ACTION
Q	IN		Quit Blender menu
	IF	☐	

R

KEY	WORKS...		ACTION
R	IN	⌗ ↺	Rotate
	IF	△ ◉	
SHIFT – R	IN	⌗ ☐	Faceloop select
	IF	△	
SHIFT – R	IN	⌗ ☐	Select Row of nurbs
	IF	⌐	
CTRL – R	IN	⌗ ☐	Faceloop Split
	IF	△	
ALT – R	IN	⌗ ↰	Clear rotation
	IF	◉	
ALT – R	IN	⌗ ◟	Clear rotation
	IF	◟	

S

KEY	WORKS...		ACTION
S	IN ⊞ ⌵ ⤴ ▦		Scale
	IF △ ◉		
SHIFT – S	IN ⊞ ⌵ ⤴		Snap-to menu
	IF ☐ ◉		
CTRL – S	IN ⊞ ☐		Shear
	IF ☐		
ALT – S	IN ⊞ ☐		Shrink/Fatten [rmb] function
	IF ☐		
ALT – S	IN ⊞ ✎		Clear Size
	IF ✎		
SHIFT – ALT – S	IN ☰		Select text menu.

T

KEY	WORKS...		ACTION
T	IN ⊞ ⤴		Texture space menu (grab&rotate textures)
	IF ☐ ◉		
T	IN ⊞ ☐		Tilt of 3d curve (see F9 & press 3D button)
	IF ⟋		
CTRL – T	IN ⊞ ☐		convert to Triangles
	IF △		
CTRL – T	IN ⊞ ⤴		Make Track-to
	IF ◉		

QUICK HOTKEYS LIST

ALT – T	IN	# ↰	Clear Track-to
	IF	⊙	
CTRL – ALT – T	IN	#	Blenchmark

U

KEY	WORKS...		ACTION
U	IN	# ↰	Single User menu
	IF	▢ ⊙	
U	IN	# ▢	Reload data buffer. (undo)
U	IN	# ▢	True mesh Undo
	IF	△	
SHIFT – U	IN	# ▢	True mesh Redo
	IF	△	
CTRL – U	IN	↰	Save current file as user default
	IF	⬭	
ALT – U	IN	# ▢	True mesh Undo Menu
	IF	△	

V

KEY	WORKS...		ACTION
V	IN	# ↰	VertexPaint on / off
V	IN	# ⩗ ▢	Vector handle (see also H)
	IF	⌐	

SHIFT – V	IN	# ☐	Align view to selected
	IF	△	
ALT – V	IN	# ↖	Object resize to materials-texture aspect
	IF	⊙	
SHIFT – ALT – V	IN	☰	View menu for positioning cursor
	IF	☐	

W

KEY		WORKS...	ACTION
W	IN	# ☐	Special edit menu
	IF	☐	
SHIFT – W	IN	# ☐	Warp selected vertices around cursor
	IF	◊	
CTRL – W	IN	⋈ ↖	Write file
	IF	⬭	
ALT – W	IN	↖	Write selected as videoscape format
	IF	⊙ ⬭	

X

KEY		WORKS...	ACTION
X	IN	# ⋈ ▦ ↖	Erase menu
	IF	☐ ◊ ⊙	

QUICK HOTKEYS LIST

X	IN ⊞ ▢	Local/global constrain (grab, rotate, scale)
	IF △	
CTRL – X	IN ⊞ ⋀ ▦ ↰	Delete all, reload default file (see also U)

Y

KEY	WORKS...	ACTION
Y	IN ⊞ ▢	Split selected from the rest
	IF △	
Y	IN ⊞ ▢	Local/global constrain (grab, rotate,scale)
	IF △	

Z

KEY	WORKS...	ACTION
Z	IN ⊞ ↰	Wire / Solid view
Z	IN ⊞ ▢	Local/global constrain (grab, rotate, scale)
	IF △	
Z	IN 🖼	Zoom/trans. render window (see F12 & F11)
	IF 🖼	
SHIFT – Z	IN ⊞ ↰	Wire / Shaded view
CTRL – Z	IN ⊞ ↰	Shaded calculation view
ALT – Z	IN ⊞ ↰	Solid / Textured (potato) view

AP. B   SUPPORTED VIDEOCARDS

GRAPHICS COMPATIBILITY, WINDOWS, LINUX, MACOS X, CARD MANUFACTURERS, CHIPSET MANUFACTURERS, CARD TYPES

Graphics Compatibility

Blender requires a 3D accelerated graphics card that supports OpenGL. We strongly recommend making sure you are using the latest version of the drivers for your graphics card before attempting to run Blender. See the Upgrading section below if you are unsure how to upgrade your graphics drivers.

Additionally here are some tips to try if you are having trouble running Blender, or if Blender is running with very low performance.

The foundation site www.blender.org hosts an on-line database of Graphic cards, Operating Systems, Drivers and Blender performances. You are strongly advised to check that. In the following there is an extract of the tests done so far. These are mailnly for Windows platforms.

Graphics cards are generally marketed and sold by a different company than the one that makes the actual chipset that handles the graphics functionality. For example, a Diamond Viper V550 actually uses an NVidia TNT2 chipset, and a Hercules Prophet 4000XT uses a PowerVR Kyro chipset. Often both the card manufacturer and the chipset maker will offer drivers for your card, however, we recommend always using the drivers from the chipset maker, these are often released more frequently and of a higher quality.

The easiest way of finding out what graphics chipset is used by your card is to consult the documentatioon (or the box) that came with your graphics card, often the chipset is listed somewhere (for example on the side of the box, or in the specifications page of the manual, or even in the title, ie. a "Leadtek WinFast GeForce 256"). Often the graphics card will also display its name/model and a small logo when you power on the computer. Once you know what graphics card you have, the next step is to determine what chipset is used by the card. One way of finding this out is to look up the

SUPPORTED VIDEOCARDS

manufacturer in the card manufacturers table and follow the link to the manufacturers website, once there find the product page for your card model; somewhere on this page it should list the chipset that the card is based on.

Most consumer graphics cards are optimized for 16-bit color mode (High Color, as opposed to True Color). So you might want to try this color depth if you experience problems. Renderings will anyway be true color!

Some cards many not be able to accelerate 3D at higher resolutions, try lowering your display resolution if you have problems. Some cards may also have problems accelerating 3D for multiple programs at a time - make sure Blender is the only 3D application running. If Blender runs but displays incorrectly, try lowering the hardware acceleration level, if posible.

Windows

On Windows the Display Properties dialog, selecting the Settings tab, shows, in the Display field, the names of your monitor and graphics card. This should tell you Card and Chipset. The Display Properties dialog also allows you to set color depth, resolution and acceleration level.

Display Properties

The display properties dialog has many usefull settings for changing the functioning of your graphics card. To open the display properties dialog, go to **Start Menu** -> **Settings** -> **Control Panel** and select the Display icon, or right-click on your desktop and select Properties.

Advanced display properties

The advanced display properties dialog has settings for controlling the function of your graphics driver, and often has additional settings for tweaking the 3D acceleration. To open the advanced display properties dialog open the Display Properties as described above, then open the Settings tab, and click on the Advanced button in the lower right corner.

If Blender performances are not good try to disable any OpenGL Anti-Aliasing feature of your video card.

Linux

On Linux, and most unices the graphical interface runs upon XFree86, http:
//www.xfree86.org/ hardware 3d accelleration is provided by the Direct Rendering
Infrastructure (DRI) subproject.

You can usually get both in one convenient package from your distribution, Linux distributions geared at beginning users even come with X installed by default.

Blender needs both X and OpenGL to be able to work, it can work without an accelle-
rated graphics card, but it will run faster with accelleration, of course.

If you are using a distribution (like Red Hat, Debian, Mandrake, SuSE) installing the
XFree86 (also called 'X11', or 'X' for short) package(s), you usually get enough to
run blender, and modern distributions will come with a version of X from the current
stable branch, 4.x. The most recent version at the time of writing is 4.3, with 4.4
around the corner. 4.0 and higher are fine, and x 3.x might even work, but almost no
one uses that nowadays.

In case your distribution doesn't come with X preinstalled, it shouldn't be hard to do it
yourself, for example, on Debian you do:

```
apt-get install x-window-system
```

Et voilá, you've got yourself a graphical system!

Supported hardware

For an overview of cards supported in the current version of XFree86,
see: http://www.xfree86.org/current/Status.html

The DRI project provides XFree86 with 3d hardware accelerated drivers: DRI homepa-
ge: http://dri.sourceforge.net/ http://dri.sourceforge.net/cgi-bin/moin.cgi/Status
For a detailed overview, broken down by chipset and supported features: http:
//dri.sourceforge.net/doc/dri_driver_features.phtml

Tables in the following will be more specific, for compatibilities, but it must be
stressed that there are Open Source drivers and Proprietary drivers:

For what concerns ATI, Mach64 (Rage Pro), Rage 128 (Standard, Pro, Mobility), as
well as Radeons up to 9200 Open Source drivers exists.

SUPPORTED VIDEOCARDS

On the Proprietary, Closed Source, drivers side: ATI has a linux section at http://www.ati.com/support/driver.html. Radeon 9800, 9700, 9600, 9500, 9200, 9100, 9000, 8500 are supported. Nvidia too has linux drivers available at: http://www.nvidia.com/object/linux.html. Some distributions might also provide these drivers themselves.

Blender should work without problems with all these drivers, but occassionaly a bug is exposed. In such a case the Blender and DRI developers work together to determine in what part the bug lies and fix it.

If you experience problems with DRI you can try to set

```
LIBGL_ALWAYS_INDIRECT=1
```

as an environment variable in your .bashrc or watever. This is a very drastic easure since it will disable hardware acceleration completely. http://dri.sourceforge.net/cgi-bin/moin.cgi/TestingAndDebugging has many tips on debugging.

MacOS X

Issues with Blender and Mac OSX are very unusual. The only tips which can be given are to make sure you have at least 8 Mb of video RAM, and to use the "thousands of colors" setting unless you have more than 16 Mb of video RAM.

Here, as in Windows, disabling graphic card AA can lead to better performances.

Graphics Compatibility Test Results

In the table herebelow good (or bad) performance refers community collected results and condensate several threads in the varoius Blender forums.

It is obviously incomplete, since no extensive tests have ever been carried out, and could be inaccurate, sice drivers could have been released, solving problems. It is nevertheless a precious starting point. Beware than this list is concerned with Modelling and Rendering, not with the real time engine, which is not covered by this Book. Good performances in modelling can becomepoor in realtime. Please refer to the Gamekit Book for a list relative to the game engine too.

'OK' means Blender roons smoothly; 'MG' means minor glitches; 'PP' works with poor performances; 'NO' means problems; 'NT' means not tested.

Card Manufacturers

Company	Commonly used chipset
3Dfx	3Dfx
AOpen	NVidia/Sis
Asus	NVidia
ATI	ATI
Creative	NVidia
Diamond Multimedia	NVidia/S3
Elsa	NVidia
Gainwand	NVidia/S3
Gigabyte	NVidia
Hercules	NVidia/PowerVR
Leadtek	3DLabs/NVidia
Matrox	Matrox
Videologic	PowerVR/S3

Chipset Manufacturers

Company	Chipsets
3Dfx	Banshee/Voodoo
URL	http://www.voodoofiles.com/type.asp?cat_id=0
3DLabs	Permedia
URL	http://www.3dlabs.com/support/drivers/index.htm
ATI	Rage/Radeon
URL	http://mirror.ati.com/support/driver.html

SUPPORTED VIDEOCARDS

Intel	i740/i810/i815
URL	http://developer.intel.com/design/software/drivers/platform/
Matrox	G200/G400/G450
URL	http://www.matrox.com/mga/support/drivers/home.cfm
NVidia	Vanta/Riva 128/Riva/TNT/GeForce
URL	
PowerVR	KYRO/KYRO II
URL	http://www.powervr.com/Downloads.asp
Rentition	Verite
URL	http://www.micron.com/content.jsp?path=Products/ITG
S3 Garphics	Savage
URL	http://www.s3graphics.com/DRVVIEW.HTM
SiS	300/305/315/6326
URL	http://www.sis.com/support/driver/index.htm
Trident Microsystems	Blade/CyberBlade
URL	http://www.tridentmicro.com/site/go.asp?dest=drivers

Card Types

Chip Manufacturer/Model	Win 98	Win 2000	Win XP	Linux	MacOS X
3Dfx					
Banshee	PP	NT	NT	NT	NT
Voodoo 3000	PP	PP	NT	NT	NT
Voodoo 5500	OK	NT	NT	NT	NT
3D Labs					
Wildcat	NT	OK	NT	NT	NT

Chip Manufacturer/Model	Win 98	Win 2000	Win XP	Linux	MacOS X
ATI					
All-In-Wonder 128	PP	NT	NT	NT	NT
Rage II 3D	PP	NT	NT	NT	NT
Rage Pro 3D	PP	NT	NT	NT	NT
Radeon DDR VIVO	OK	OK	NT	NT	NT
Radeon 7500	OK	NT	OK	NT	OK
Radeon 9000	NO	NT	NT	NO	NT
Radeon 9700	NT	NT	NT	NO	NT
128 Fury	NT	NT	NT	NO	NT
Radeon Mobility M7LW	NT	NT	NT	MG	NT
Radeon Mobility M6	NT	NT	OK	NT	NT
Radeon Mobility 7500	NT	NT	NT	OK	NT
Radeon Mobility 8500	NT	NT	NO	NT	NT
Radeon Mobility 9000	NT	NT	OK	NT	OK
Intel					
82845G/GL	NT	NT	NO	NT	NT
i810	NT	NT	NT	NO	NT
Matrox					
Millenium G200	PP	PP	NT	NT	NT
Millenium G400	PP	PP	NT	NT	NT
Millenium G450	PP	PP	NT	NT	NT
Parhelia	NT	NT	OK	NT	NT
NVidia					
TNT	OK	OK	NT	NT	NT
Vanta	OK	OK	NT	NT	NT

SUPPORTED VIDEOCARDS

TNT2	OK	OK	NO	NT	OK
GeForce DDR	OK	NT	NT	NT	NT
GeForce 2	OK	MG	OK	OK	NT
GeForce 2 MX400	NT	NT	OK	OK	NT
GeForce 2 GTS	NT	OK	OK	OK	NT
GeForce 4	NT	NT	OK	NT	NT
GeForce 4 MX	NT	NT	OK	OK	NT
PowerVR					
Kyro	MG	MG	NT	NT	NT
Rendition					
Radeon Mobility 7500	PP	NT	NT	NT	NT
S3					
Virge	OK	NT	NT	NT	NT
Trio 64	PP	NT	NT	NT	NT
Savage 4	NT	PP	NT	NT	NT
Super Savage	NT	NT	NO	NT	NT
Savage Pro	NO	NT	NT	NT	NT
SiS					
6326	PP	NT	NT	NT	NT
315	NT	NT	NO	NT	NT

AP. C BLENDER 2.31 CHANGELOG

The Blender 2.31 release was mainly a bug-fix release, based on user feedback on 2.30 and shortcomings we found while proofreading the manual text. This book has been fully verified with 2.31, and is the recommended release to be used for examples and tutorials.

Release notes Blender 2.31

Blender 2.30 -> 2.31 changelog

New features

- Added buttons drawing Theme 'Rounded'. This uses a new feature in button code that enables aligning buttons in groups together. Will be implemented for the default 'Shaded' theme later.
- New default startup file built in. Only shows when you delete .B.blend in your home directory. It has mainly been designed to match the 2.3 manual best. Most obvious change is not starting with a 4-split 3D Window anymore.
- Important note: all buttons to call an "Image Select Browser" have been removed from Blender. This is instable code, and caused far too many crashes. The functionality is still accessible though by holding **CTRL** while pressing a "Load" button for images. This as 'undocumented' feature for power users. :)
- Mesh Subdivision Surfaces: now supports 'hide' option as well (**HKEY**).

New features

- New module: Lattice
- New module: Texture (mostly done already, only missing access to IPO, EnvMap, ColorBand & Plugin)
- Bugfix: Object.makeParent
- NMesh: new vertex grouping methods: .renameVertGroup, .getVert GroupNames
- Doc updates

Bug Fixes

- Interface: removing a window edge (Join Areas) sometimes removed the wrong edge. Was a very old bug... but showed up in new standard default file.
- AntiAlias fonts: file paths longer than 64 characters caused crash. Is 256 now.
- Themes: switching main Theme didn't update button draw type for Theme buttons themselves.
- IPO Window: using the new Transform Properties Panel, some buttons caused the event being handled double, giving weird results.
- IPO Window: Sometimes the Transform Properties Panel was drawn with zero size. Added a more strict version check for this to prevent it.
- **F6** Texture Buttons: browsing a new texture for a Lamp only gave the Add New option.
- **F6** Texture Buttons: the `Default Vars` now resets the environment mapping settings as well.
- UV Image Editor: saving an image (after using Texture Paint) now is in same type as original image (was Targa only).
- 3D Window: when using a SpotLight in 'Textured Draw mode' (aka Potato mode) the 'Solid Draw mode' turned out black. (Bug since 2.0!)
- 3D Window: the **MKEY** 'movetolayer' option doesn't close anymore on numeric input. Somewhere before 2.25 this was changed... weird. Now you can set layers with numeric buttons, including using **ALT** for numbers larger than 10, and using SHIFT for extend-select buttons. Press OK or Enter to close the menu.
- 3D Window: **CTRL-1** (or 2,3,4) crashed when no Object as active. This hotkey is for setting subdivision level for Meshes.
- 2.30 error: clicking to select Objects at same location now correctly cycles through the available Objects again.
- 2.30 error: **CTRL-SHIFT-F3** allows screen capture of entire Blender window again. (For OSX: also press **ALT** for screen capture).
- 2.30 error: the `Emulate 2` button mouse option, allowing **ALT-LMB** for **MMB** now works again.
- Fixed in Unified render (now is actually usable!):
- alpha was wrong for halos with lines or rings
- halo rendering wrong combined with spothalo
- no antialiasing with sky when rendering spothalo
- cleaned some weird usage of gamma for spothalo and sky (when rendering sky + spothalo, sky got gamma corrected (Note: "Unified render" renders all in a single pass, whilst normally Blender renders in separate layers for opaque faces, transparent faces, halos and sky. The layers then are merged using alpha, which can cause several (depth) errors.)
- When rendering a 'square spot' it displayed rotated wrong in an Environment Map.
- When rendering Material with option "Wire", rendering in parts gave errors.
- When rendering a Mesh with multiple users (linked-duplicates) it caused a crash when it used UV faces.

- Rendering specular highlights for Sun light works correctly again.
- Pressing **ESC** during rendering now reacts immediately again. This was reported fixed before, but accidentally un-committed from the code.
- Rendering shadeless Material with UV "TexFace" option had a wrong gamma.
- Rendering started with mouse cursor in a 3D window now renders "Local View" or unlocked layer settings again.
- Rendering with Meshes using `Smooth` appearance always had `Auto smooth` set on. Was introduced for Radiosity render in 2.28c. Now it only uses `Auto smooth` when the radiosity render is actually used.
- Removed old hack from rendering, which enabled a Border render in a previously rendered image. It was badly implemented and crashed too often. Related to this, code was cleaned up which prevents errors as reported in rendering with Border and `Fields`.
- The default built-in font was not rendered when using background rendering (blender -b on commandline).
- Converting a 3D closed curve (Bezier or NURBS) to a Mesh (**ALT-C**) the result was a bunch of unconnected vertices.
- Constraints: Fixed the lag with Follow Path.
- Constraints: prevented creating endless loops.
- Mesh Vertex Keys: now can have up to 64k vertices, was 32k.
- Mesh Editmode: using Undo caused vertex colors and UV texture information to get lost.
- Mesh Editmode: using Undo caused 'hide' status of vertices being lost. Solved by storing this in the Mesh themselves, so the 'hide' status will be restored when leaving/entering EditMode.
- Mesh EditMode: the Knife Tool sometimes cut unselected edges as well
- Mesh Editmode: Fixed crash when try to faceloop-cut (**SHIFT-R**, **CTRL-R**) with a Mesh having an edge that didn't belong to any face. These tools now also update the vertex counter as displayed in 'Info header'.
- Mesh object: `Subdiv` level 0 and draw type `Optimal` caused Mesh not drawing in EditMode.
- Armatures/Meshes: using Parent `Armature>>Name` Groups puts the Mesh in a state that is ready for weight paint.
- MetaBalls: the displaylists were re-created for each redraw of 3d window, causing an enormous slowdown. Now it runs smooth again. (Old bug!)
- Blender didn't rename 'temp save' file to quit.blend at quit. Was reported on OSX and Linux.
- Materials: The stencil option only worked for one channel with normal-mapping. Now it works for all as it's supposed to be.
- OSX: using the F10 RenderButtons Play option now pops the window to the front. This also for starting blender from command line.
- OSX: the preferred AntiAlias font couldnt be written in .b.blend (unless you manually install the font in ~/.blender/)
- MS Windows, Blender Text editor: Using clipboard to copy/paste text (**CTRL+C** and **CTRL+V**) works with correct line endings.

Various fixes

- Interface: cleaned up aligning and positioning of buttons in most Panels (for manual)
- Added decorations to 'Minimal' buttons Theme to make it usable, also restored the 2.2x drawing style for buttons as 'OldSkool' Theme.
- 2.30 error: in 3D window selecting Objects wasn't updated correctly in all situations.
- 2.30 error: **CTRL-LMB** click allows selecting Objects in EditMode again.
- 2.30 error, the new toolbox and floating menus were closed when mouse left the menu immediately. Is now a safety of 40 pixels again.
- Action Window: zooming in increased with factor 5.
- Buttons Window: the Panel background color+alpha is part of Theme settings now.
- 3D window, when setting a render border in camera view (**SHIFT-B**) the associated render option is set as well.
- 3D Window: OpenGL render option is icon in window header again, and now uses Theme Color for background as well.
- 3D Window: a Constraint now draws a blue dashed line to its parent.
- 3D Window: Enter EditMode from FaceSelect mode correctly selects vertices again
- 3D Window: transform option (**SKEY**) allows typing in zero scaling value.
- 3D Window: Warp transform option (**SHIFT-W**) allows typing in values.
- 3D Window: the header didn't display 'Mesh' pulldown menu when VertexPaint mode and EditMode were both active.
- 3D Window: modes 'VertexPaint' and 'Weightpaint' and 'Texturepaint' allow draw mode wire-extra again.
- Image Window: the buttons in header were messed up in 2.30
- TextEditor window: the hotkeys **ALT-N** (new) and **ALT-O** (open) now also work when no 'text block' is active or available in Blender.
- File Browse window: text sometimes was drawn over outer border.
- Theme for TextWindow now allows color for text as well.
- **F5** MaterialButtons: when you set Halo, and Star, then disable Halo, the TexFace button was set. The fix also prevents RGB from being reaset to 1.0.
- **F5** MaterialButtons: OB and ME buttons in 2nd Panel didnt work properly. Also the 1 Mat 1 buttons didnt display in all situations.
- **F6** TextureButtons: Crop and Anim Panel had wrong name... now Anim and Movie. This Panel now draws buttons always, because it is for the 'anim option' (sequence of files) which is different from 'movie' option (single file).
- **F6** ObjectButtons: added to the Constraint Panel buttons indicating the 'Active Bone' or 'Active Object', like previously (2.2x) was drawn in constraint buttons header.
- **F6** TextureButtons: Colorband color sliders didnt update the colorband
- **F9** EditButtons: moved vertex group buttons to first Panel. These buttons should be available outside editmode as well.

- **F9** EditButtons: changed decimator slider into number-button, with only 1 vertex in Mesh the slider didn't display OK. The slider also provided insufficient space for the full text.
- Constraints: sometimes its data was not available (null) after reading file, causing a crash. Code has been secured.
- In render output window; using Pad-plus and minus zoom now always includes a zoom level 1.0 now.
- Mesh EditMode: Knife tool now has correct cursor, for all platforms.
- Mesh EditMode, Knife Tool: **ESC** for pop-up menu was not handled, and pressing ENTER at pop-up menu caused 'mouse trail' call to exit.
- OSX: is now compiled with optimizing, giving a speed gain of 10-20%.
- OSX: using the Apple Quicktime dialog when choosing a movie format (**F10** render buttons) still can cause a freeze when you choose the Options button. This has been verified by Apple as a system bug. We added a warning when you choose this option in Blender.

BLENDER CHANGELOG.VARIOUS FIXES

AP. D   THE BLENDER DOCUMENTATION PROJECT

About the Blender Documentation Project

The Blender Documentation Project is the branch of Blender Foundation specifically aimed at giving Blender a complete Open Content documentation.

The Documentation Board, moderated by Bart Veldhuizen and Stefano Selleri, manages the Open Content documentation. This is managed at the CVS server at cvs.blender.org in the BlenderManual repository.

Blender documentation is written in DocBook XML (www.docbook.org) according to few guidelines published on blender main site (www.blender.org).

How to contribute

First of all you must put up a full DockBook environment to test and translate your XML to HTML or PDF or whatever. Then you must set up a CVS client.

If you are working in a UNIX environment of any flavour, and Linux in particular, these tools are there by default or are anyway easily recoverable in your installation CD or in the net.

For Windows too there are free softwares to access a CVS server and handle DocBook XML, but these needs to be downloaded from the net. Once you have a full CVS and DocBook install you can download the compleded blender documentation XML and work on it!

THE BLENDER DOCUMENTATION PROJECT

If you would like to contribute changes, additions or correction to the Blender documentation, we prefer to receive themas *patches* to the DocBook/XML files. Assuming some basic knowledge about CVS usage, this is easy. Here's how you do it:

First of all, before you start working check out the latest CVS tree and work on those files directly. Changes are made to the CVS repository almost daily and you don't want to work on outdated files. Updates are fast as only the changes are downloaded to your workstation.

When you're ready, you issue the following command:

```
cvs diff -u -w BlenderManual.xml > BlenderManual.xml.diff
```

The differences between your local copy and the copy in the CVS repository will be stored in `BlenderManual.xml.diff`. If you want to submit multiple patches, please do a diff for each file separately and send them to the DocBoard mailing list.

AP. E   JOINING THE CODERS

Software development

We host our own *SourceForge* style projects space, at projects.blender.org . Here the official Blender Foundation release is hosted (bf-blender), but there's room for other Blender or 3D related projects as well. We're open for developers to create experimental Blender trees or even complete forks. The most renown example is the Tuhopuu project, which is a Blender source tree open for all experiments, which has given us a lot of useful new features in Blender the past year.

If you like to add a new project, just make an account at the projects site, a link for proposing projects can then be found at ‚My Page'. Please bear in mind that new projects should preferably consist out of multiple developers, for CVS and mailing lists to be of use.

The Blender source code is available in many different ways:

- online with ViewCVS (projects.blender.org)
- through connecting to the CVS server (see chapter 02)
- as a downloadable CVS checkout (www.blender3d.org)

We are still in the process of updating a lot of documentation, so please check on www.blender.org regular for updates. Also the ‚getting involved' link on the site will give up-to-date information on current projects and roadmaps.

If you like to join the team, or find out what currently goes on, best is to join our general developers mailing list, a link can be found on the projects.blender.org front page.

JOINING THE CODERS

Also on the forums of blender.org many discussions take place on development issues.

The irc.freenode.net #blendercoders is our central meeting point, here also the weekly meeting takes place, usually on sunday afternoon. Reports of the meeting are posted on the developers mailing list.

Bug Tracking

If you have found a bug in Blender, you can report it using the bug tracker, you can find it linked in the main menu at blender.org. Please read the instructions carefully and provide as much information as possible with your report. Most important for you to verify is:

- can it be reproduced, and how?
- does it give same errors with previous releases of Blender?
- does it give same errors on a different machine?

Every relevant detail you can provide helps. Including information such as the following:

- Operating system and version
- Blender version (or CVS date)
- Graphics card driver version
- Hardware configuration details

Before you submit your bug, please check the existing reports in the tracker to see if someone has already submitted the same. If the bug report already exists, please add your additional comments to the existing bug.

Another helpful thing to do is to look through the current bugs in the tracker, and try and confirm them. This can help determine if bugs are specific to a particular platform or configuration, and also saves a developers' time from having to verify that the bug actually exists first, before fixing it. If you have confirmed an existing bug, or if you can't reproduce it, please leave your comments on the bug's report in the tracker.

AP. F LICENSES

Blender itself is released under GNU General Public License. Blender Documentation is released under the Open Content license. Both these licenses are reported here below.

Blender Foundation has prepared a license of its own, modeled on the basis of Perl's Artistic License aimed at Blender artists wishing to distribute their blender files, Python scripts movies an images freely yet maintaining a more direct control on their creations.

These three licenses are reported here below.

Open Content License

This is the License for This Style Guide as well as for the whole Blender Core Documentation. You are kindly requested to produce any contribution to the Blender Documentation Project using this License. If your contribution is outside Core documentation (as a tutorial, demo .blend file, images or animation) and you wish to use a more restrictive License, you can use the *Blender Artistic License*.

The source of the Open Content License is http://opencontent.org/opl.shtml. It is repeated below for easier reference.

OpenContent License (OPL)
Version 1.0, July 14, 1998.

This document outlines the principles underlying the OpenContent (OC) movement and may be redistributed provided it remains unaltered. For legal purposes, this document is the license under which OpenContent is made available for use.

The original version of this document may be found at http://opencontent.org/opl.shtml.

LICENSES

Blender Artistic License

This is the License designed for Tutorials, .blend example files, still images and animations. It is more restrictive than the Blender Documentation License and is thought to protect more the intellectual rights of the artist producing the Tutorial/Blend File/Still/Animation. (Loosely adapted from Perl Artistic License) Authors can of course choose the less restrictive Blender Documentation License, but no material will be hosted on the Foundation Site unless it abides to one of these two licenses.

It is highly advisable to prepare a zipped package containing, besides the Tutorial etc. files, a file called LICENSE containing this license.

If you are distributing a .blend file alone it is still advisable to add a LICENSE file, otherwise you can add the license in a text buffer of Blender and make sure it shows up when opening the file.

If you are releasing binary files like printable tutorials and you don't want to include the whole license (why wouldn't you?) or are releasing single images or animations, you can also add, in the text, in a corner of the image or in the last frames the wording:

(C) *Year* *your name* - released under Blender Artistic License - www.blender.org

Herebelow, the License Itself:

The "Blender Artistic License"

Preamble:

The intent of this document is to state the conditions under which a Tutorial guide, a Blender file, a still image or an animation (in the following all four will be addressed as 'Item') may be copied, such that the Copyright Holder maintains some semblance of artistic control over the development of the Item, while giving the users of the package the right to use and distribute the Item in a more-or-less customary fashion, plus the right to make reasonable modifications.

Definitions:

"Item" refers to the collection of files distributed by the Copyright Holder, and derivatives of that collection of files created through textual modification, binary modification,
image processing, format translation and/or modifications using Blender.

"Standard Version" refers to such a Item if it has not been modified, or has been modified in accordance with the wishes of the Copyright Holder as specified below.

"Copyright Holder" is whoever is named in the copyright or copyrights for the Item.

"You" is you, if you're thinking about copying or distributing this Item.

"Reasonable copying fee" is whatever you can justify on the basis of media cost, duplication charges, time of people involved, and so on. (You will not be required to justify it to the Copyright Holder, but only to the computing community at large as a market that must bear the fee.)

"Freely Available" means that no fee is charged for the Item itself, though there may be fees involved in handling the Item. It also means that recipients of the Item may redistribute it under the same conditions they received it.

1. You may make and give away verbatim copies of the Standard Version of this Item without restriction, provided that you duplicate all of the original copyright notices and associated disclaimers.

2. You may apply any modification derived from the Public Domain or from the Copyright Holder. An Item modified in such a way shall still be considered the Standard Version.

3. You may otherwise modify your copy of this Item in any way, provided that you insert a prominent notice in each changed file - except images - stating how and when you changed that file, that you keep note in a separate text file of any change/deletion/addition of images, and provided that you do at least ONE of the following:

a) place your modifications in the Public Domain or otherwise make them Freely Available, such as by posting said modifications to Usenet or an equivalent medium, or placing the modifications on a major archive site such as Blender Foundation www.blender.org, or by allowing the Copyright Holder to include your modifications in the Standard Version of the Package.

b) use the modified Item only within your corporation or organization.

c) make other distribution arrangements with the Copyright Holder.

4. You may distribute this Item electronically, provided that you do at least ONE of the following:

a) distribute a Standard Version together with instructions (in a README file, in a text window of Blender) on where to get the Standard Version.

b) make other distribution arrangements with the Copyright Holder.

5. If this Item is a Tutorial documentation or a still image you can redistribute it as hard copy, provided that you do at least ONE of the following:

a) distribute a printout of Standard Version with at most mere typesetting changes, stating clearly who is the Copyright holder and where to get the Standard Version.

b) make other distribution arrangements with the Copyright Holder.

6. You may charge a reasonable copying fee for any distribution of this Item. You may not charge a fee for this Item itself. However, you may distribute this Item in aggregate with other (possibly commercial) programs as part of a larger (possibly commercial) software distribution provided that you do not advertise this Item as a product of your own.

7. If this Item is a Blender File the rendered output from it obtained via Blender does not automatically fall under the copyright of this Item, but belongs to whoever generated them, and may be sold commercially, and may be aggregated with this Item.

8. The name of the Copyright Holder may not be used to endorse or promote products derived from this Item without specific prior written permission.

9. THIS ITEM IS PROVIDED "AS IS" AND WITHOUT ANY EXPRESS OR IMPLIED WARRANTIES, INCLUDING, WITHOUT LIMITATION, THE IMPLIED WARRANTIES OF MERCHANTIBILITY AND FITNESS FOR A PARTICULAR PURPOSE.

GNU General Public License

The Blender source code is licensed under the GNU General Public License (the GPL). This license allows you to use, copy, modify, and distribute the program and the source code. The GPL only applies to the program itself, not to this manual nor to any works created by people using the program.

GNU General Public License
Version 2, June 1991

Copyright (C) 1989, 1991 Free Software Foundation, Inc., 59 Temple Place, Suite 330, Boston, MA 02111-1307 USA

Everyone is permitted to copy and distribute verbatim copies of this license document, but changing it is not allowed.

Preamble

The licenses for most software are designed to take away your freedom to share and change it. By contrast, the GNU General Public License is intended to guarantee your freedom to share and change free software--to make sure the software is free for all its users. This General Public License applies to most of the Free Software Foundation's software and to any other program whose authors commit to using it. (Some other Free Software Foundation software is covered by the GNU Library General Public License instead.) You can apply it to your programs, too.

When we speak of free software, we are referring to freedom, not price. Our General Public Licenses are designed to make sure that you have the freedom to distribute copies of free software (and charge for this service if you wish), that you receive source code or can get it if you want it, that you can change the software or use pieces of it in new free programs; and that you know you can do these things.

To protect your rights, we need to make restrictions that forbid anyone to deny you these rights or to ask you to surrender the rights. These restrictions translate to certain responsibilities for you if you distribute copies of the software, or if you modify it.

For example, if you distribute copies of such a program, whether gratis or for a fee, you must give the recipients all the rights that you have. You must make sure that they, too, receive or can get the source code. And you must show them these terms so they know their rights.

We protect your rights with two steps: (1) copyright the software, and (2) offer you this license which gives you legal permission to copy, distribute and/or modify the software.

Also, for each author's protection and ours, we want to make certain that everyone understands that there is no warranty for this free software. If the software is modified by someone else and passed on, we want its recipients to know that what they have is not the original, so that any problems introduced by others will not reflect on the original authors' reputations.

Finally, any free program is threatened constantly by software patents. We wish to avoid the danger that redistributors of a free program will individually obtain patent licenses, in effect making the program proprietary. To prevent this, we have made it clear that any patent must be licensed for everyone's free use or not licensed at all.

The precise terms and conditions for copying, distribution and modification follow.

LICENSES

3. You may copy and distribute the Program (or a work based on it, under Section 2) in object code or executable form under the terms of Sections 1 and 2 above provided that you also do one of the following:

a) Accompany it with the complete corresponding machine-readable source code, which must be distributed under the terms of Sections 1 and 2 above on a medium customarily used for software interchange; or,

b) Accompany it with a written offer, valid for at least three years, to give any third party, for a charge no more than your cost of physically performing source distribution, a complete machine-readable copy of the corresponding source code, to be distributed under the terms of Sections 1 and 2 above on a medium customarily used for software interchange; or,

c) Accompany it with the information you received as to the offer to distribute corresponding source code. (This alternative is allowed only for noncommercial distribution and only if you received the program in object code or executable form with such an offer, in accord with Subsection b above.)

The source code for a work means the preferred form of the work for making modifications to it. For an executable work, complete source code means all the source code for all modules it contains, plus any associated interface definition files, plus the scripts used to control compilation and installation of the executable. However, as a special exception, the source code distributed need not include anything that is normally distributed (in either source or binary form) with the major components (compiler, kernel, and so on) of the operating system on which the executable runs, unless that component itself accompanies the executable.

If distribution of executable or object code is made by offering access to copy from a designated place, then offering equivalent access to copy the source code from the same place counts as distribution of the source code, even though third parties are not compelled to copy the source along with the object code.

4. You may not copy, modify, sublicense, or distribute the Program except as expressly provided under this License. Any attempt otherwise to copy, modify, sublicense or distribute the Program is void, and will automatically terminate your rights under this License. However, parties who have received copies, or rights, from you under this License will not have their licenses terminated so long as such parties remain in full compliance.

5. You are not required to accept this License, since you have not signed it. However, nothing else grants you permission to modify or distribute the Program or its derivative works. These actions are prohibited by law if you do not accept this License. Therefore, by modifying or distributing the Program (or any work based on the Program), you indicate your acceptance of this License to do so, and all its terms and conditions for copying, distributing or modifying the Program or works based on it.

6. Each time you redistribute the Program (or any work based on the Program), the recipient automatically receives a license from the original licensor to copy, distribute or modify the Program subject to these terms and conditions. You may not impose any further restrictions on the recipients' exercise of the rights granted herein. You are not responsible for enforcing compliance by third parties to this License.

7. If, as a consequence of a court judgment or allegation of patent infringement or for any other reason (not limited to patent issues), conditions are imposed on you (whether by court order, agreement or otherwise) that contradict the conditions of this License, they do not excuse you from the conditions of this License. If you cannot distribute so as to satisfy simultaneously your obligations under this License and any other pertinent obligations, then as a consequence you may not distribute the Program at all. For example, if a patent license would not permit royalty-free redistribution of the Program by all those who receive copies directly or indirectly through you, then the only way you could satisfy both it and this License would be to refrain entirely from distribution of the Program.

If any portion of this section is held invalid or unenforceable under any particular circumstance, the balance of the section is intended to apply and the section as a whole is intended to apply in other circumstances.

It is not the purpose of this section to induce you to infringe any patents or other property right claims or to contest validity of any such claims; this section has the sole purpose of protecting the integrity of the free software distribution system, which is implemented by public license practices. Many people have made generous contributions to the wide range of software distributed through that system in reliance on consistent application of that system; it is up to the author/donor to decide if he or she is willing to distribute software through any other system and a licensee cannot impose that choice.

This section is intended to make thoroughly clear what is believed to be a consequence of the rest of this License.

8. If the distribution and/or use of the Program is restricted in certain countries either by patents or by copyrighted interfaces, the original copyright holder who places the Program under this License may add an explicit geographical distribution limitation excluding those countries, so that distribution is permitted only in or among countries not thus excluded. In such case, this License incorporates the limitation as if written in the body of this License.

9. The Free Software Foundation may publish revised and/or new versions of the General Public License from time to time. Such new versions will be similar in spirit to the present version, but may differ in detail to address new problems or concerns.

Each version is given a distinguishing version number. If the Program specifies a version number of this License which applies to it and "any later version", you have the option of following the terms and conditions either of that version or of any later version published by the Free Software Foundation. If the Program does not specify a version number of this License, you may choose any version ever published by the Free Software Foundation.

10. If you wish to incorporate parts of the Program into other free programs whose distribution conditions are different, write to the author to ask for permission. For software which is copyrighted by the Free Software Foundation, write to the Free Software Foundation; we sometimes make exceptions for this. Our decision will be guided by the two goals of preserving the free status of all derivatives of our free software and of promoting the sharing and reuse of software generally.

NO WARRANTY

11. BECAUSE THE PROGRAM IS LICENSED FREE OF CHARGE, THERE IS NO WARRANTY FOR THE PROGRAM, TO THE EXTENT PERMITTED BY APPLICABLE LAW. EXCEPT WHEN OTHERWISE STATED IN WRITING THE COPYRIGHT HOLDERS AND/OR OTHER PARTIES PROVIDE THE PROGRAM "AS IS" WITHOUT WARRANTY OF ANY KIND, EITHER EXPRESSED OR IMPLIED, INCLUDING, BUT NOT LIMITED TO, THE IMPLIED WARRANTIES OF MERCHANTABILITY AND FITNESS FOR A PARTICULAR PURPOSE. THE ENTIRE RISK AS TO THE QUALITY AND PERFORMANCE OF THE PROGRAM IS WITH YOU. SHOULD THE PROGRAM PROVE DEFECTIVE, YOU ASSUME THE COST OF ALL NECESSARY SERVICING, REPAIR OR CORRECTION.

12. IN NO EVENT UNLESS REQUIRED BY APPLICABLE LAW OR AGREED TO IN WRITING WILL ANY CO-PYRIGHT HOLDER, OR ANY OTHER PARTY WHO MAY MODIFY AND/OR REDISTRIBUTE THE PROGRAM AS PERMITTED ABOVE, BE LIABLE TO YOU FOR DAMAGES, INCLUDING ANY GENERAL, SPECIAL, INCIDENTAL OR CONSEQUENTIAL DAMAGES ARISING OUT OF THE USE OR INABILITY TO USE THE PROGRAM (INCLUDING BUT NOT LIMITED TO LOSS OF DATA OR DATA BEING RENDERED INACCURA-TE OR LOSSES SUSTAINED BY YOU OR THIRD PARTIES OR A FAILURE OF THE PROGRAM TO OPERATE WITH ANY OTHER PROGRAMS), EVEN IF SUCH HOLDER OR OTHER PARTY HAS BEEN ADVISED OF THE POSSIBILITY OF SUCH DAMAGES.

END OF TERMS AND CONDITIONS

How to Apply These Terms to Your New Programs

If you develop a new program, and you want it to be of the greatest possible use to the public, the best way to achieve this is to make it free software which everyone can redistribute and change under these terms.

To do so, attach the following notices to the program. It is safest to attach them to the start of each source file to most effectively convey the exclusion of warranty; and each file should have at least the "copyright" line and a pointer to where the full notice is found.

<one line to give the program's name and a brief idea of what it does.> Copyright (C) <year> <name of author>

This program is free software; you can redistribute it and/or modify it under the terms of the GNU General Public License as published by the Free Software Foundation; either version 2 of the License, or (at your option) any later version.

This program is distributed in the hope that it will be useful, but WITHOUT ANY WARRANTY; without even the implied warranty of MERCHANTABILITY or FITNESS FOR A PARTICULAR PURPOSE. See the GNU General Public License for more details.

You should have received a copy of the GNU General Public License along with this program; if not, write to the Free Software Foundation, Inc., 59 Temple Place, Suite 330, Boston, MA 02111-1307 USA

Also add information on how to contact you by electronic and paper mail.

If the program is interactive, make it output a short notice like this when it starts in an interactive mode:

Gnomovision version 69, Copyright (C) year name of author Gnomovision comes with ABSOLUTELY NO WARRANTY; for details type `show w'. This is free software, and you are welcome to redistribute it under certain conditions; type `show c' for details.

The hypothetical commands `show w' and `show c' should show the appropriate parts of the General Public License. Of course, the commands you use may be called something other than `show w' and `show c'; they could even be mouse-clicks or menu items--whatever suits your program.

You should also get your employer (if you work as a programmer) or your school, if any, to sign a "copyright disclaimer" for the program, if necessary. Here is a sample; alter the names:

Yoyodyne, Inc., hereby disclaims all copyright interest in the program 'Gnomovision' (which makes passes at compilers) written by James Hacker.

<signature of Ty Coon>, 1 April 1989
Ty Coon, President of Vice

This General Public License does not permit incorporating your program into proprietary programs. If your program is a subroutine library, you may consider it more useful to permit linking proprietary applications with the library. If this is what you want to do, use the GNU Library General Public License instead of this License.

LICENSES

AP. G GLOSSARY

A-Z

A

Active   *See also:* Selected.

Blender makes a distinction between *selected* and *active*. Only one Object or item can be *active* at any given time, for example to allow visualization of data in buttons.

An active object is one that is in EditMode, or is immediately switchable to EditMode (usually by **TAB**). No more than one object is active at any moment. Typically, the most recent selected object is active.

Actuator   *See also:* LogicBrick, Sensor, Controller.

A LogicBrick that acts like a muscle of a lifeform. It can move the object, or also make a sound.

Alpha

The alpha value in an image denotes opacity, used for blending and antialiasing.

Ambient light

Light that exists everywhere without any particular source. Ambient light does not cast shadows, but fills in the shadowed areas of a scene.

Anti-aliasing

An algorithm designed to reduce the stair-stepping artifacts that result from drawing graphic primitives on a raster grid.

GLOSSARY

AVI

"Audio Video Interleaved". A container format for video with synchronized audio. An AVI file can contain different compressed video and audio-streams.

B
Back-buffer

Blender uses two buffers in which it draws the interface. This double-buffering system allows one buffer to be displayed, while drawing occurs on the back-buffer. For some applications in Blender the back-buffer is used to store color-coded selection information.

Bevel

Beveling removes sharp edges from an extruded object by adding additional material around the surrounding faces. Bevels are particularly useful for flying logos, and animation in general, since they reflect additional light from the corners of an object as well as from the front and sides.

Bounding box

A six-sided box drawn on the screen that represents the maximum extent of an object.

Bump map

A grayscale image used to give a surface the illusion of ridges or bumps. In Blender bumpmaps are called Nor-maps.

C
Channel

Some DataBlocks can be linked to a series of other DataBlocks. For example, a Material has eight *channels* to link Textures to. Each IpoBlock has a fixed number of available *channels*. These have a name (LocX, SizeZ, enz.) which indicates how they can be applied. When you add an IpoCurve to a channel, animation starts up immediately.

Child   *See also:* Parent.

Objects can be linked to each other in hierarchical groups. The Parent Object in such groups passes its transformations through to the Child Objects.

Clipping

The removal, before drawing occurs, of vertices and faces which are outside the field of view.

Controller

A LogicBrick that acts like the brain of a lifeform. It makes decisions to activate muscles (Actuators), either using simple logic or complex Python scripts.

D

DataBlock (or "block")

The general name for an element in Blender's Object Oriented System.

Doppler effect

The Doppler effect is the change in pitch that occurs when a sound has a velocity relative to the listener. When a sound moves towards the listener the pitch will rise. when going away from the listener the pitch will drop. A well known example is the sound of an ambulance passing by.

Double-buffer

Blender uses two buffers (images) to draw the interface in. The content of one buffer is displayed, while drawing occurs on the other buffer. When drawing is complete, the buffers are switched.

E

EditMode   *See also:* ObjectMode, Vertex (pl. vertices).

The mode for making intra-object graphical changes. Blender has two modes for making changes graphically. EditMode allows intra-object changes (moving, scaling rotating, deleting, and other operations on selected vertices of the active object). By contrast, ObjectMode allows inter-object changes (operations on selected objects).

Switch between EditMode and ObjectMode with Hotkey: **TAB**

Extend select

Adds new selected items to the current selection (**SHIFT-RMB**)

Extrusion

The creation of a three-dimensional object by pushing out a two-dimensional outline and giving it height, like a cookie-cutter. It is often used to create 3D text.

F

Face

The triangle and square polygons that form the basis for Meshes or for rendering.

GLOSSARY

Field

Frames from videos in NTSC or PAL format are composed of two interlaced *fields*.

FaceSelectMode

Mode to select faces on an object. Most important for texturing objects. Hotkey: **FKEY**

Flag

A programming term for a variable that indicates a certain status.

Flat shading

A fast rendering algorithm that simply gives each facet of an object a single color. It yields a solid representation of objects without taking a long time to render. Pressing **ZKEY** switches to flat shading in Blender.

Fps

Frames per second. All animations, video, and movies are played at a certain rate. Above ca. 15fps the human eye cannot see the single frames and is tricked into seeing a fluid motion. In games this is used as an indicator of how fast a game runs.

Frame

A single picture taken from an animation or video.

G Gouraud shading

A rendering algorithm that provides more detail. It averages color information from adjacent faces to create colors. It is more realistic than flat shading, but less realistic than Phong shading or ray-tracing. The hotkey in Blender is **CTRL-Z**.

Graphical User Interface GUI   *See also:* OpenGL.

The whole part of an interactive application which requests input from the user (keyboard, mouse etc.) and displays this information to the user. Blenders GUI is designed for an efficient modeling process in an animation company where time equals money. Blenders whole GUI is done in OpenGL.

H Hierarchy

Objects can be linked to each other in hierarchical groups. The Parent Object in such groups passes its transformations through to the Child Objects.

Ipo

The main animation curve system. Ipo blocks can be used by Objects for movement, and also by Materials for animated colors.

I

IpoCurve

The Ipo animation curve.

Item

The general name for a selectable element, e.g. Objects, vertices or curves.

K

Keyframe

A frame in a sequence that specifies all of the attributes of an object. The object can then be changed in any way and a second keyframe defined. Blender automatically creates a series of transition frames between the two keyframes, a process called "tweening."

L

Lathe

A lathe object is created by rotating a two-dimensional shape around a central axis. It is convenient for creating 3D objects like glasses, vases, and bowls. In Blender this is called "spinning".

Layer

A visibility flag for Objects, Scenes and 3DWindows. This is a very efficient method for testing Object visibility.

Link

The reference from one DataBlock to another. It is a "pointer" in programming terminology.

Local

Each Object in Blender defines a *local* 3D space, bound by its location, rotation and size. Objects themselves reside in the *global* 3D space.

A DataBlock is *local*, when it is read from the current Blender file. Non-local blocks (library blocks) are linked parts from other Blender files.

GLOSSARY

LogicBrick

See also: Sensor, Controller, Actuator

A graphical representation of a functional unit in Blender's game logic. LogicBricks can be Sensors, Controllers or Actuators.

M

Mapping

The relationship between a Material and a Texture is called the 'mapping'. This relationship is two-sided. First, the information that is passed on to the Texture must be specified. Then the effect of the Texture on the Material is specified.

Mipmap

Process to filter and speed up the display of textures.

MPEG-I

Video compression standard by the "Motion Pictures Expert Group". Due to its small size and platform independence, it is ideal for distributing video files over the internet.

O

ObData block

The first and most important DataBlock linked by an Object. This block defines the Object *type*, e.g. Mesh or Curve or Lamp.

Object

The basic 3D information block. It contains a position, rotation, size and transformation matrices. It can be linked to other Objects for hierarchies or deformation. Objects can be "empty" (just an axis) or have a link to ObData, the actual 3D information: Mesh, Curve, Lattice, Lamp, etc.

ObjectMode

See also: EditMode

The mode for making inter-object graphical changes. Blender has two modes for making changes graphically. ObjectMode allows inter-object changes (moving, scaling rotating, deleting and other operations on selected objects). By contrast, EditMode allows intra-object changes (operations on selected vertices in the active object).

Switch between ObjectMode and EditMode with Hotkey: **TAB**.

OpenGL OGL

OpenGL is a programming interface mainly for 3D applications. It renders 3D objects to the screen, providing the same set of instructions on different computers and graphics adapters. Blenders whole interface and 3D output in the real-time and interactive 3D graphic is done by OpenGL.

Oversampling; OSA
See: Anti-aliasing

Overscan

Video images generally exceed the size of the physical screen. The edge of the picture may or may not be displayed, to allow variations in television sets. The extra area is called the overscan area. Video productions are planned so critical action only occurs in the center safe title area. Professional monitors are capable of displaying the entire video image including the overscan area.

P

Parent
See also: Child

An object that is linked to another object, the parent is linked to a child in a parent-child relationship. A parent object's coordinates become the center of the world for any of its child objects.

Perspective view

In a perspective view, the further an object is from the viewer, the smaller it appears. See orthographic view.

Pivot

A point that normally lies at an object's geometric center. An object's position and rotation are calculated in relation to its pivot-point. However, an object can be moved off its center point, allowing it to rotate around a point that lies outside the object.

Pixel

A single dot of light on the computer screen; the smallest unit of a computer graphic. Short for "picture element."

Plug-In

A piece of (C-)code loadable during runtime. This way it is possible to extend the functionality of Blender without a need for recompiling. The Blender plugin for showing 3D content in other applications is such a piece of code.

GLOSSARY

Python

The scripting language integrated into Blender. Python[1] is an interpreted, interactive, object-oriented programming language.

Quaternions

Instead of using a three-component Euler angle, quaternions use a four-component vector. It is generally difficult to describe the relationships of these quaternion channels to the resulting orientation, but it is often not necessary. It is best to generate quaternion keyframes by manipulating the bones directly, only editing the specific curves to adjust lead-in and lead-out transitions.

Render

To create a two-dimensional representation of an object based on its shape and surface properties (i.e. a picture for print or to display on the monitor).

Rigid Body

Option for dynamic objects in Blender which causes the game engine to take the shape of the body into account. This can be used to create rolling spheres for example.

Selected

Blender makes a distinction between *selected* and *active* objects. Any number of objects can be *selected* at once. Almost all key commands have an effect on *selected* objects. Selecting is done with the right mouse button.

Sensor   *See also:* LogicBrick, Controller, Actuator.

A LogicBrick that acts like a sense of a lifeform. It reacts to touch, vision, collision etc.

Single User

DataBlocks with only one user.

Smoothing

A rendering procedure that performs vertex-normal interpolation across a face before lighting calculations begin. The individual facets are then no longer visible.

---

[1] http://www.python.org/

T

Transform

Change a location, rotation, or size. Usually applied to Objects or vertices.

Transparency   *See also:* Alpha.

A surface property that determines how much light passes through an object without being altered.

U

User

When one DataBlock references another DataBlock, it has a user.

V

Vertex (pl. vertices)

The general name for a 3D or 2D point. Besides an X,Y,Z coordinate, a vertex can have color, a normal vector and a selection flag. Also used as controlling points or handles on curves.

Vertex array

A special and fast way to display 3D on the screen using the hardware graphic acceleration. However, some OpenGL drivers or hardware doesn't support this, so it can be switched off in the InfoWindow.

W

Wireframe

A representation of a three-dimensional object that only shows the lines of its contours, hence the name "wireframe."

X

X, Y, Z axes

The three axes of the world's three-dimensional coordinate system. In the FrontView, the X axis is an imaginary horizontal line running from left to right; the Z axis is a vertical line; and Y axis is a line that comes out of the screen toward you. In general, any movement parallel to one of these axes is said to be movement along that axis.

X, Y, and Z coordinates

The X coordinate of an object is measured by drawing a line that is perpendicular to the X axis, through its centerpoint. The distance from where that line intersects the X axis to the zero point of the X axis is the object's X coordinate. The Y and Z coordinates are measured in a similar manner.

GLOSSARY

Z-buffer

For a Z-buffer image, each pixel is associated with a Z-value, derived from the distance in 'eye space' from the Camera. Before each pixel of a polygon is drawn, the existing Z-buffer value is compared to the Z-value of the polygon at that point. It is a common and fast visible-surface algorithm.